OISHINBO

A la Carte

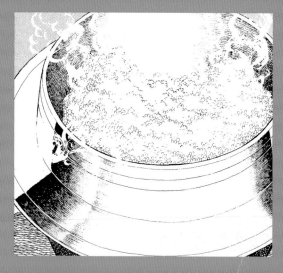

The Joy of Rice

Story by **Tetsu Kariya**
Art by **Akira Hanasaki**

OISHINBO
A la Carte

The Joy of Rice

The recipe on this and the following page is for the dish "Scallop Rice," which appears in the story "The Season for Oysters" on page 165.

Plain white rice, sometimes accompanied by side dishes, has been the staple of the Japanese diet for centuries—so much so that *gohan* and *meshi*, the main words for "cooked rice," have also come to mean "meal." But they also have a long tradition of dishes made from rice mixed together with other ingredients, most notably *takikomi gohan*, where ingredients are cooked together with the rice, and *maze gohan*, where the ingredients are mixed into previously cooked rice.

◆Ingredients

1/4 lbs. scallops
1/2 Tbsp. soy sauce
2 Tbsp. sake
2 cups rice

Scallop Rice

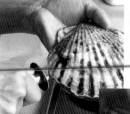

1

Hold the scallop shell by the flat side, slip a knife inside the shell and slice quickly to open it.

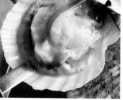

2

Once open, slide the knife between the shell and the meat and scoop out the meat.

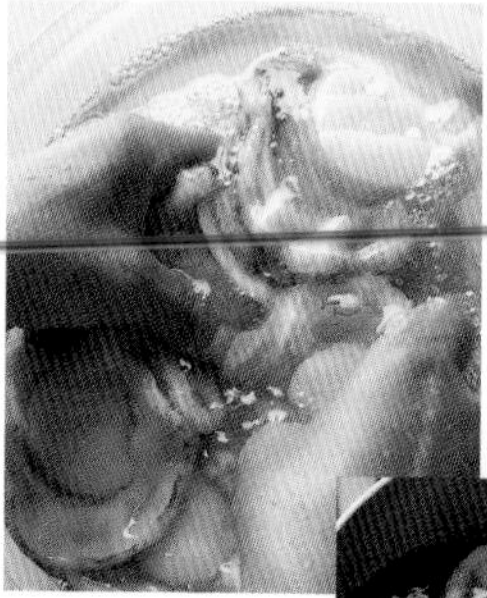

3

Gently rinse the meat in water about as salty as seawater and wash off any dirt or sand.

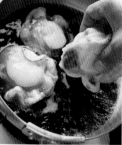

4

Mix the soy sauce and sake with 2 cups of water and bring to a light boil in a saucepan. Place the scallops in the pan and boil.

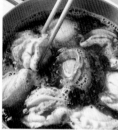

5

After it comes to a boil again, remove the scallops and pour the broth into a different bowl to cool down.

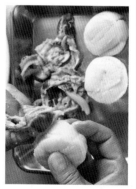

6

The midgut gland attached to the meat is not eaten. Leave the midgut gland on the scallop meat to simmer out the flavor. After boiling, remove the gland with your fingers and discard.

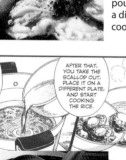

YOU MIX SOY SAUCE WITH SAKE AND BOIL IT, THEN PLACE THE SCALLOP IN IT AND COOK IT FOR ABOUT A MINUTE.
AFTER THAT, YOU TAKE THE SCALLOP OUT, PLACE IT ON A DIFFERENT PLATE, AND START COOKING THE RICE.
AND WHEN COOKING THE RICE, YOU POUR THE BROTH YOU USED TO COOK THE SCALLOP INTO THE RICE.

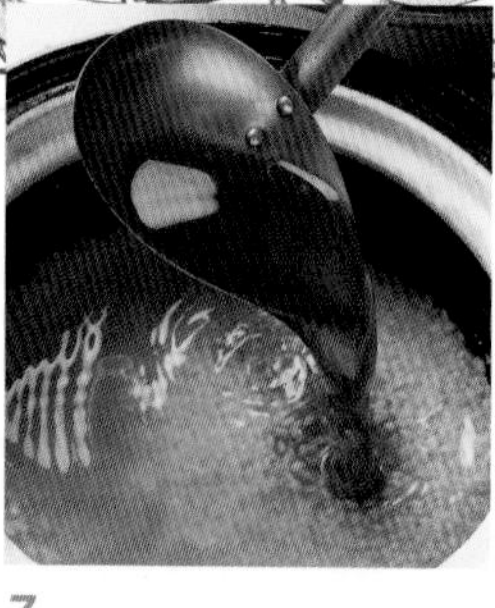

7

Mix the broth from step 5 with water in the rice cooker and cook as usual.

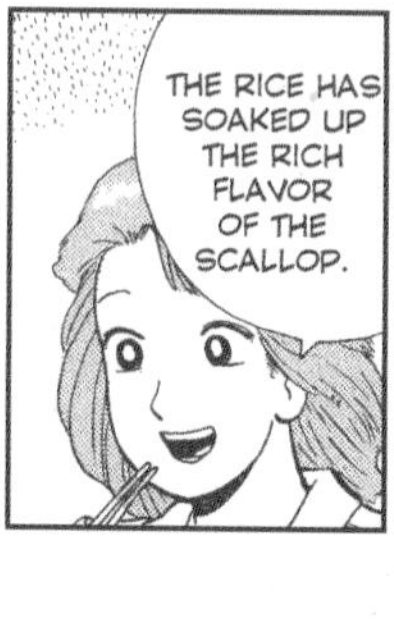

THE RICE HAS SOAKED UP THE RICH FLAVOR OF THE SCALLOP.

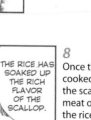

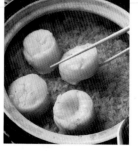

8

Once the rice is cooked, place the scallop meat on top of the rice. If the scallop meat is large, break it into smaller pieces. Put the lid back on the pot and let the meat steam well. Then break the scallop into bite-sized chunks and mix into the rice.

Contents

Characters and Story Summary

Yamaoka Shirō
The (anti-?)hero of the series, he's a journalist for the *Tōzai News* placed in charge of the Ultimate Menu project

Kaibara Yūzan
A prominent artist, as well as founder and director of The Gourmet Club, he's Yamaoka's father and rival

Kurita Yūko
Yamaoka's partner on the Ultimate Menu project and later his wife

Ōhara Daizō
Publisher of the *Tōzai News*

Koizumi Kyōichi
Executive editor of the *Tōzai News*

Tanimura Hideo
Director of *Tōzai's* Arts & Culture department

Tomii Tomio
Deputy director under Tanimura

Tōyama Tōjin
A famed ceramicist and gourmet

Kyōgoku Mantarō
A wealthy businessman and gourmet

Futaki Mariko
A coworker and now friend of Yamaoka and Kurita's at the paper

Okaboshi Seiichi
Chef/owner of Yamaoka's local hangout

Nakagawa Tokuo
Head chef at the Gourmet Club

As part of the celebrations for its 100th anniversary, the publishers of the *Tōzai News* have commissioned the creation of the "Ultimate Menu," a model meal embodying the pinnacle of Japanese cuisine. This all-important task has been entrusted to Yamaoka, an inveterate cynic who possesses zero initiative—but also an incredibly refined palate and an encyclopedic knowledge of food.

Yamaoka was trained from a young age by his father, Kaibara, a man widely revered for his sense of taste and feared for his ferocious temper. Father-son relations are strained, to say the least, and degenerate even further after Kaibara agrees to head the "Supreme Menu" project of the *Teito Times*, rival paper to the *Tōzai News*.

As Yamaoka and Kurita go about conducting the research for the Ultimate Menu, they're helped along by their boss, the avuncular Tanimura, and sometimes helped and sometimes stymied by the excitable Tomii. Kyōgoku and Tōyama, two stalwarts always up for a good meal, are frequent companions, as are coworkers Mitani and Tabata. And at the end of the day you can usually find them at Okaboshi's, planning the next step of their grand culinary adventure!

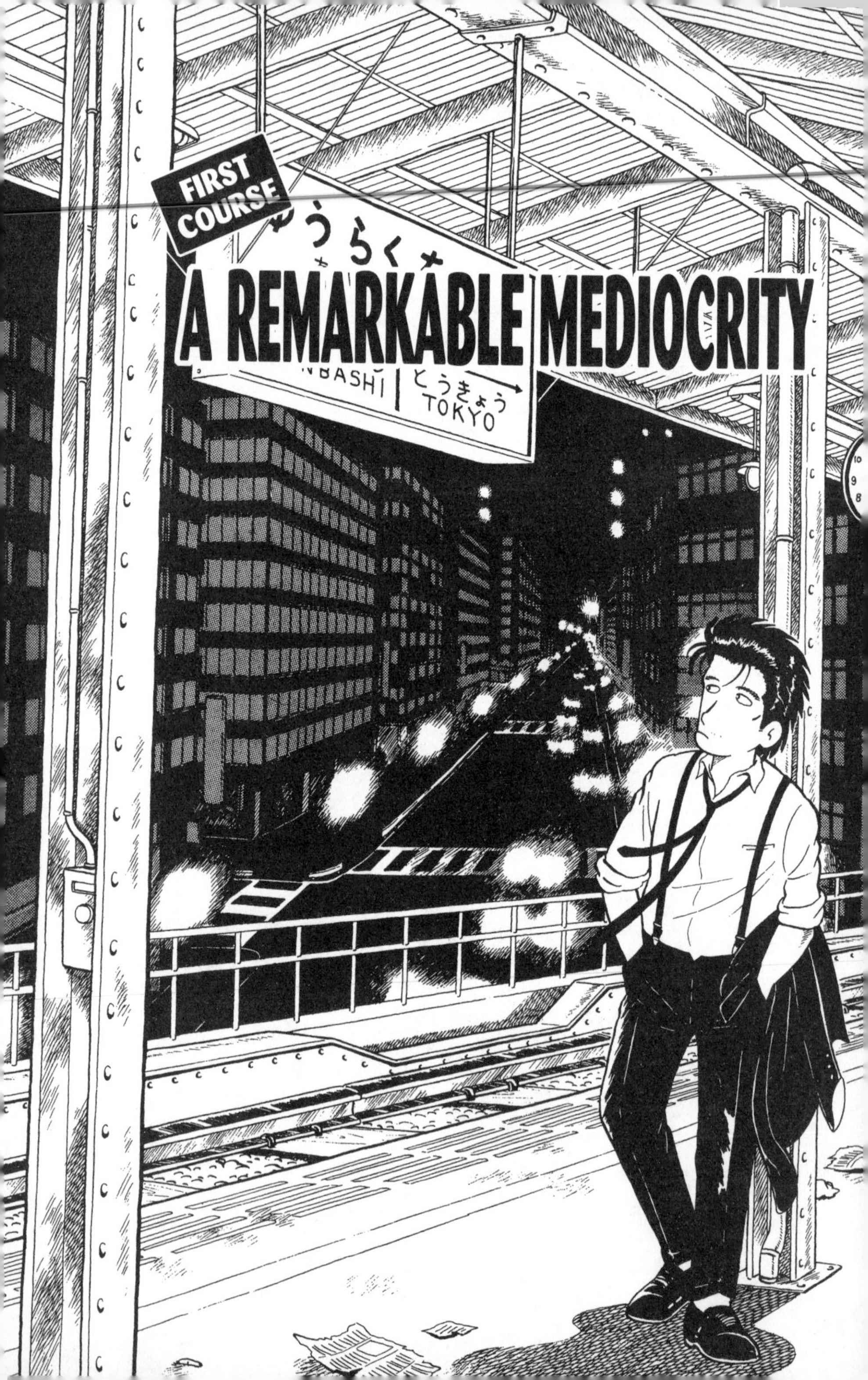
FIRST COURSE
A REMARKABLE MEDIOCRITY
うらく
NBASHI
とうきょう
TOKYO

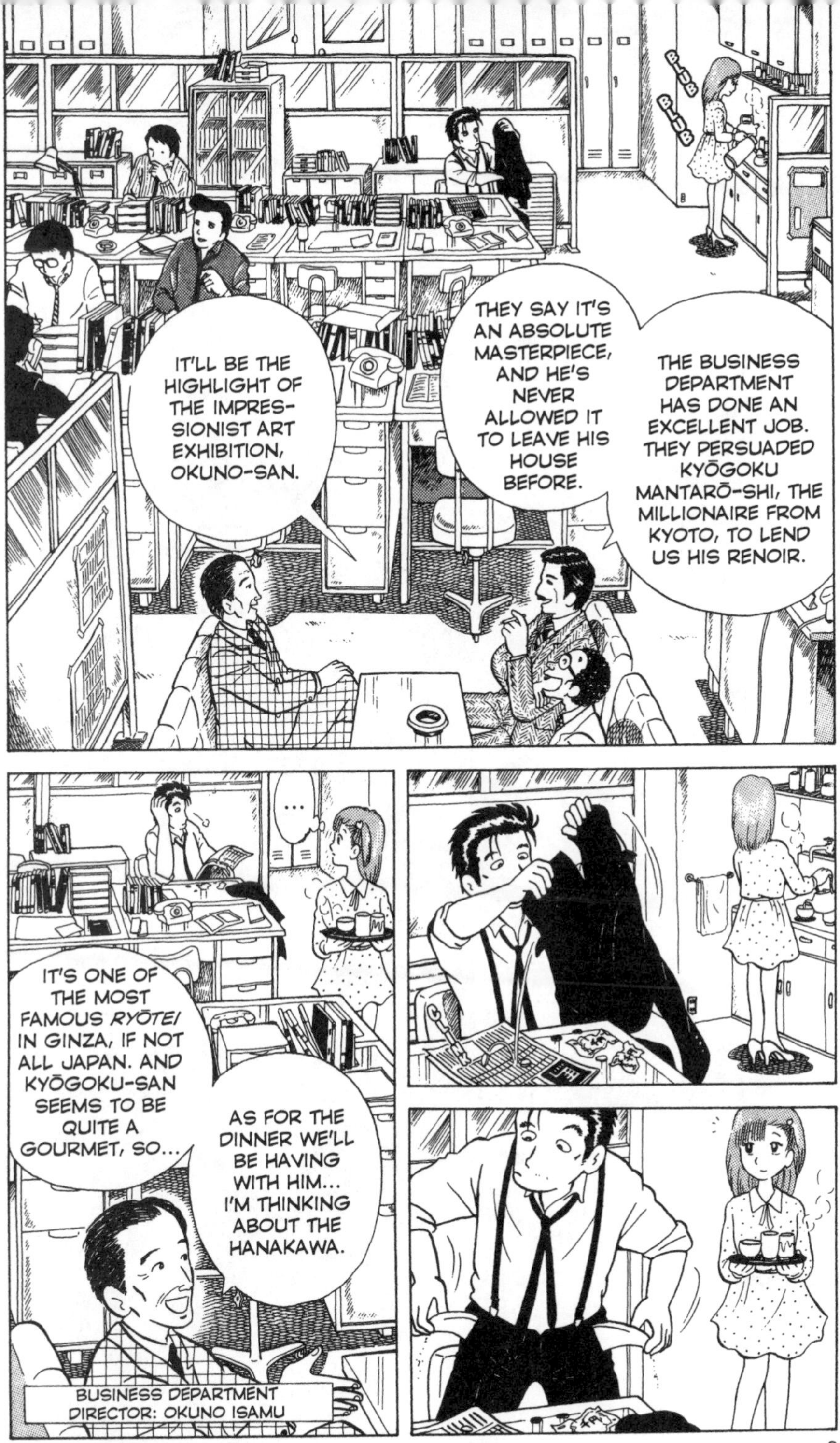
BLUB
BLUB
THE BUSINESS DEPARTMENT HAS DONE AN EXCELLENT JOB. THEY PERSUADED KYŌGOKU MANTARŌ-SHI, THE MILLIONAIRE FROM KYOTO, TO LEND US HIS RENOIR.
THEY SAY IT'S AN ABSOLUTE MASTERPIECE, AND HE'S NEVER ALLOWED IT TO LEAVE HIS HOUSE BEFORE.
IT'LL BE THE HIGHLIGHT OF THE IMPRESSIONIST ART EXHIBITION, OKUNO-SAN.
...
AS FOR THE DINNER WE'LL BE HAVING WITH HIM... I'M THINKING ABOUT THE HANAKAWA.
IT'S ONE OF THE MOST FAMOUS *RYŌTEI* IN GINZA, IF NOT ALL JAPAN. AND KYŌGOKU-SAN SEEMS TO BE QUITE A GOURMET, SO...
BUSINESS DEPARTMENT DIRECTOR: OKUNO ISAMU

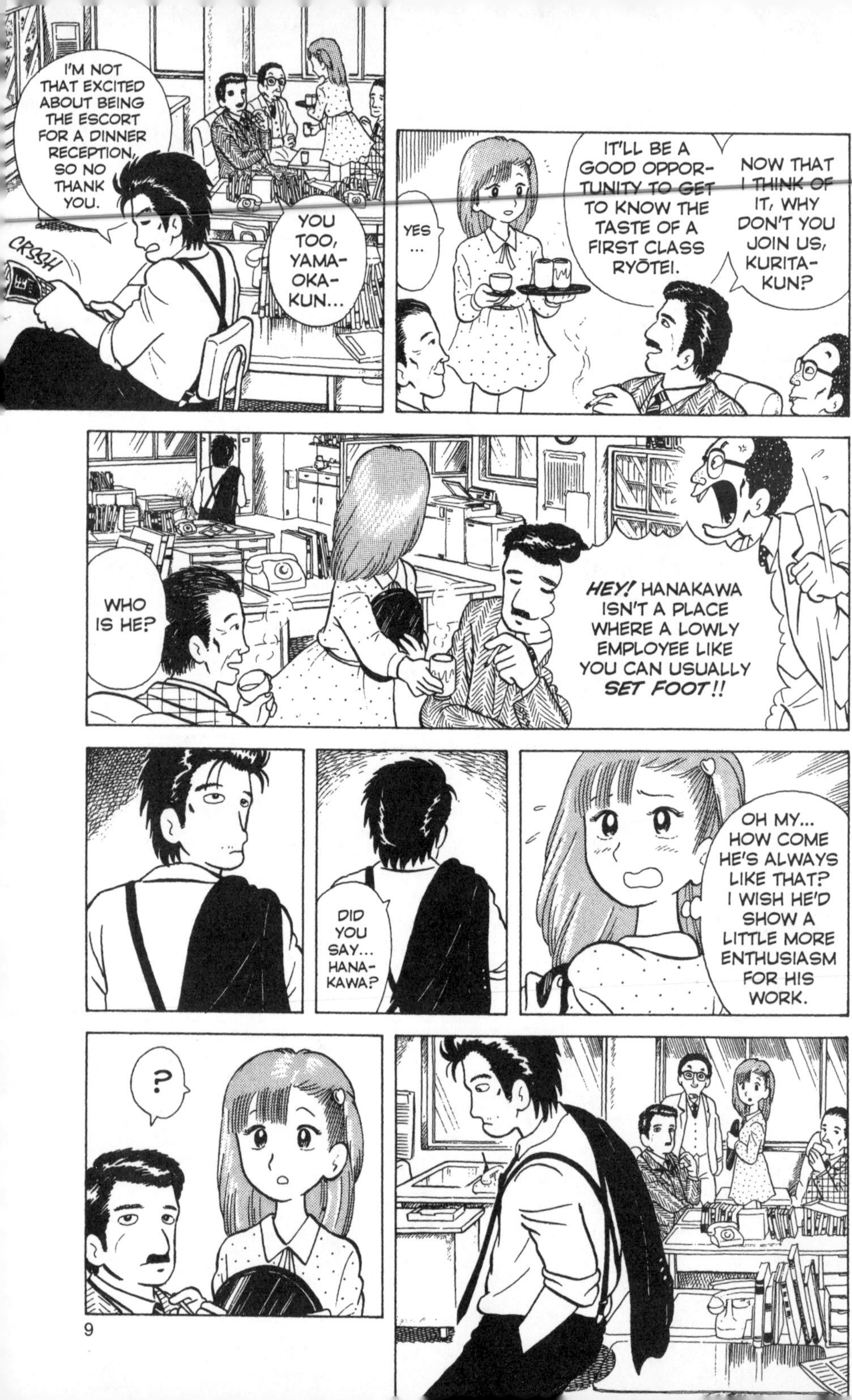
NOW THAT I THINK OF IT, WHY DON'T YOU JOIN US, KURITA-KUN?
IT'LL BE A GOOD OPPORTUNITY TO GET TO KNOW THE TASTE OF A FIRST CLASS RYŌTEI.
YES...
YOU TOO, YAMA-OKA-KUN...
I'M NOT THAT EXCITED ABOUT BEING THE ESCORT FOR A DINNER RECEPTION, SO NO THANK YOU.
CRSSH
HEY! HANAKAWA ISN'T A PLACE WHERE A LOWLY EMPLOYEE LIKE YOU CAN USUALLY SET FOOT!!
WHO IS HE?
OH MY... HOW COME HE'S ALWAYS LIKE THAT? I WISH HE'D SHOW A LITTLE MORE ENTHUSIASM FOR HIS WORK.
DID YOU SAY... HANA-KAWA?
?

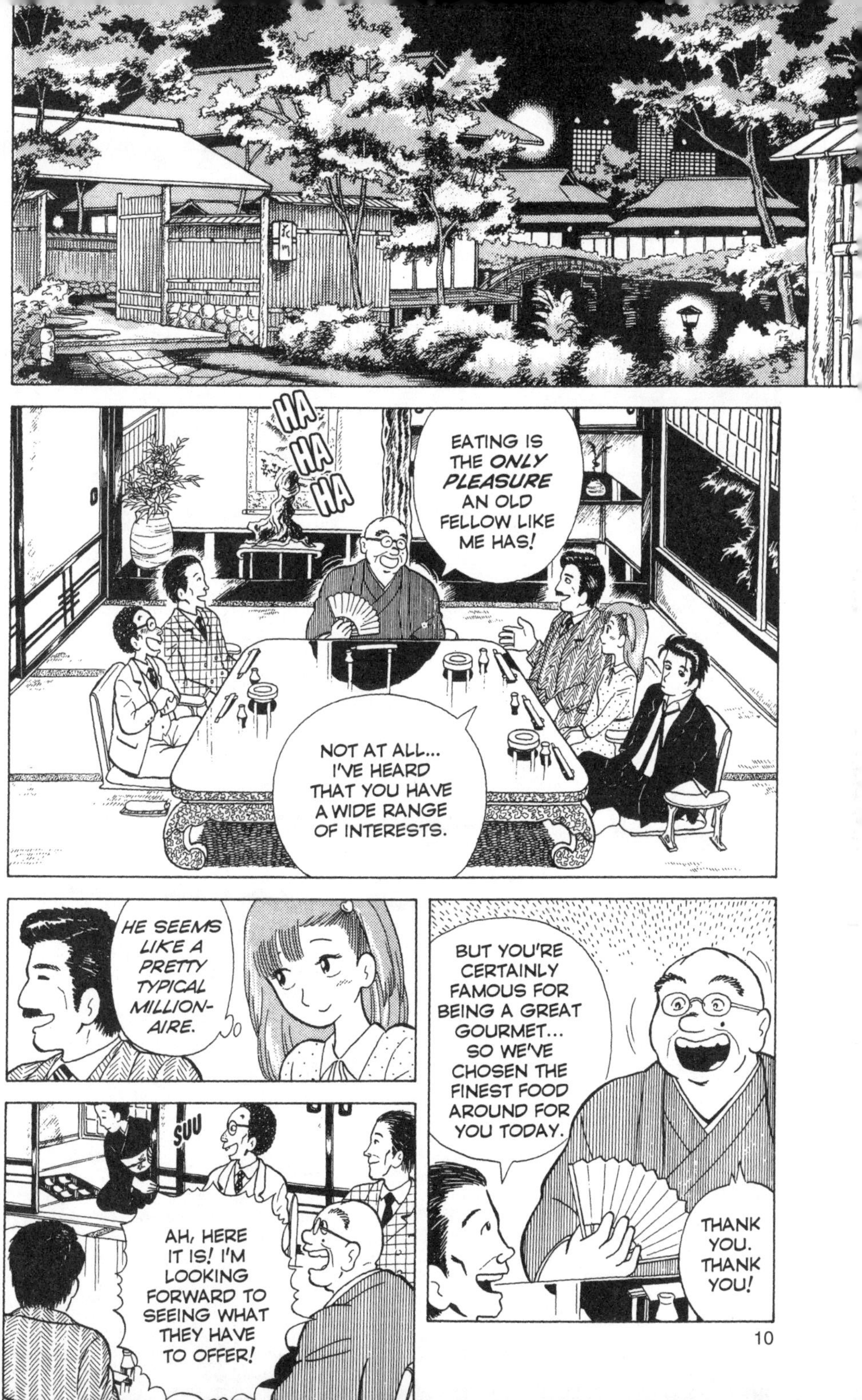
EATING IS THE *ONLY PLEASURE* AN OLD FELLOW LIKE ME HAS!
HA HA HA
NOT AT ALL... I'VE HEARD THAT YOU HAVE A WIDE RANGE OF INTERESTS.
BUT YOU'RE CERTAINLY FAMOUS FOR BEING A GREAT GOURMET... SO WE'VE CHOSEN THE FINEST FOOD AROUND FOR YOU TODAY.
THANK YOU. THANK YOU!
HE SEEMS LIKE A PRETTY TYPICAL MILLION-AIRE.
SUU
AH, HERE IT IS! I'M LOOKING FORWARD TO SEEING WHAT THEY HAVE TO OFFER!

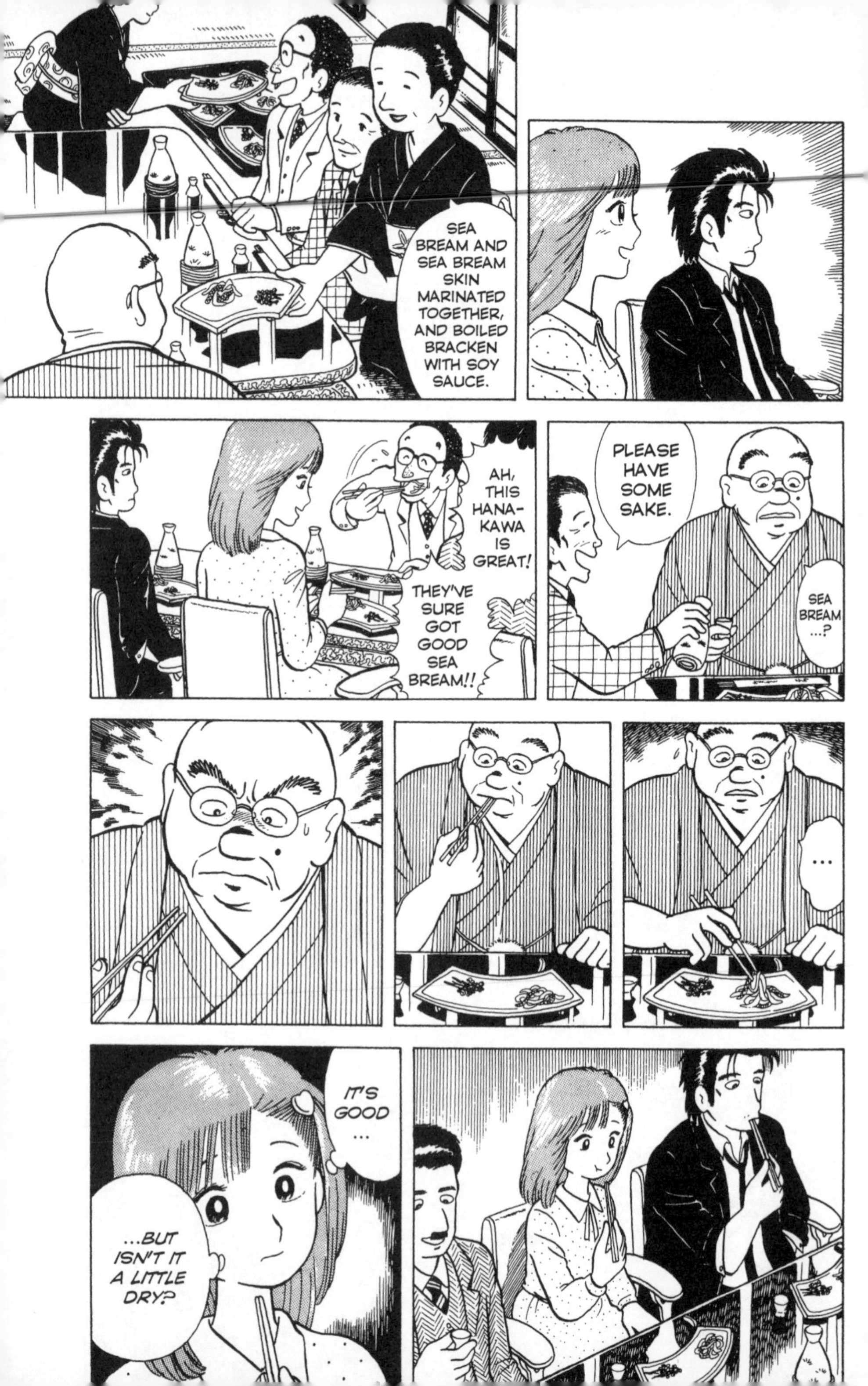
SEA BREAM AND SEA BREAM SKIN MARINATED TOGETHER, AND BOILED BRACKEN WITH SOY SAUCE.
PLEASE HAVE SOME SAKE.
SEA BREAM ...?
AH, THIS HANAKAWA IS GREAT!
THEY'VE SURE GOT GOOD SEA BREAM!!
...
IT'S GOOD ...
...BUT ISN'T IT A LITTLE DRY?

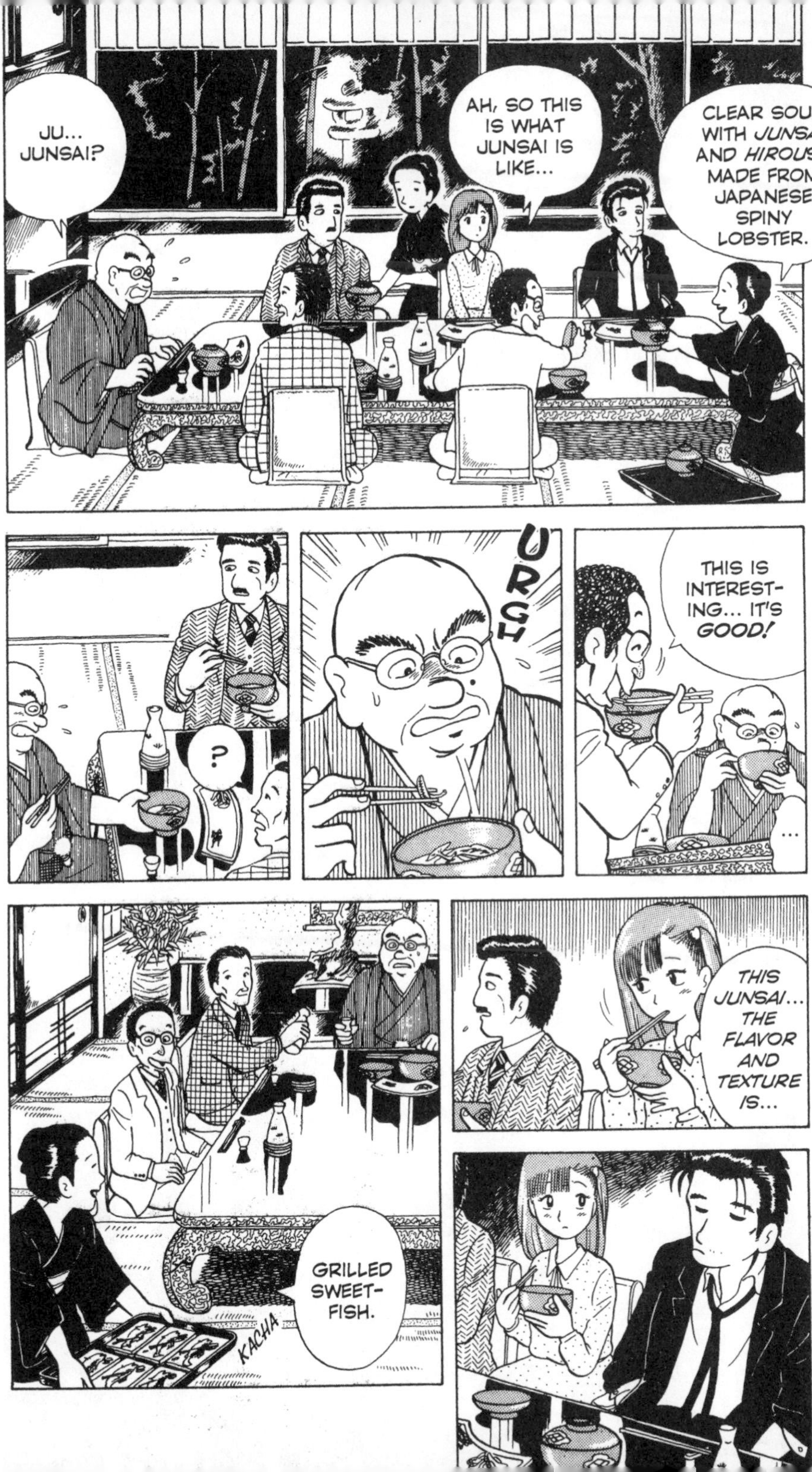
CLEAR SOUP WITH *JUNSAI* AND *HIROUSU* MADE FROM JAPANESE SPINY LOBSTER.
AH, SO THIS IS WHAT JUNSAI IS LIKE...
JU... JUNSAI?
THIS IS INTEREST-ING... IT'S *GOOD!*
...
URGH
?
THIS JUNSAI... THE FLAVOR AND TEXTURE IS...
GRILLED SWEET-FISH.
KACHA

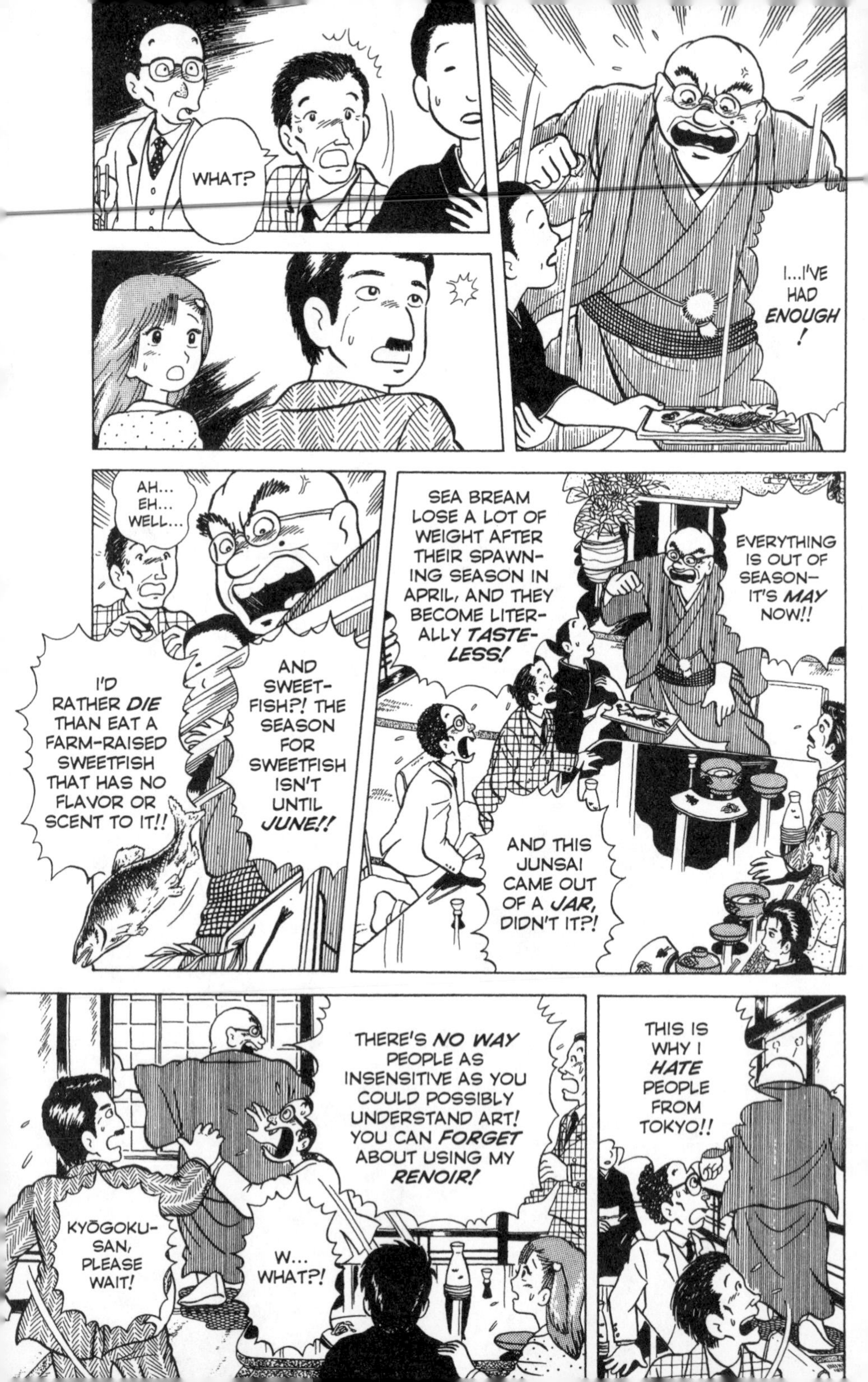
I...I'VE HAD *ENOUGH*!
WHAT?
EVERYTHING IS OUT OF SEASON—IT'S *MAY* NOW!!
SEA BREAM LOSE A LOT OF WEIGHT AFTER THEIR SPAWNING SEASON IN APRIL, AND THEY BECOME LITERALLY *TASTELESS!*
AND THIS JUNSAI CAME OUT OF A *JAR*, DIDN'T IT?!
AND SWEETFISH?! THE SEASON FOR SWEETFISH ISN'T UNTIL *JUNE!!*
I'D RATHER *DIE* THAN EAT A FARM-RAISED SWEETFISH THAT HAS NO FLAVOR OR SCENT TO IT!!
AH... EH... WELL...
THIS IS WHY I *HATE* PEOPLE FROM TOKYO!!
THERE'S *NO WAY* PEOPLE AS INSENSITIVE AS YOU COULD POSSIBLY UNDERSTAND ART! YOU CAN *FORGET* ABOUT USING MY *RENOIR!*
W... WHAT?!
KYŌGOKU-SAN, PLEASE WAIT!

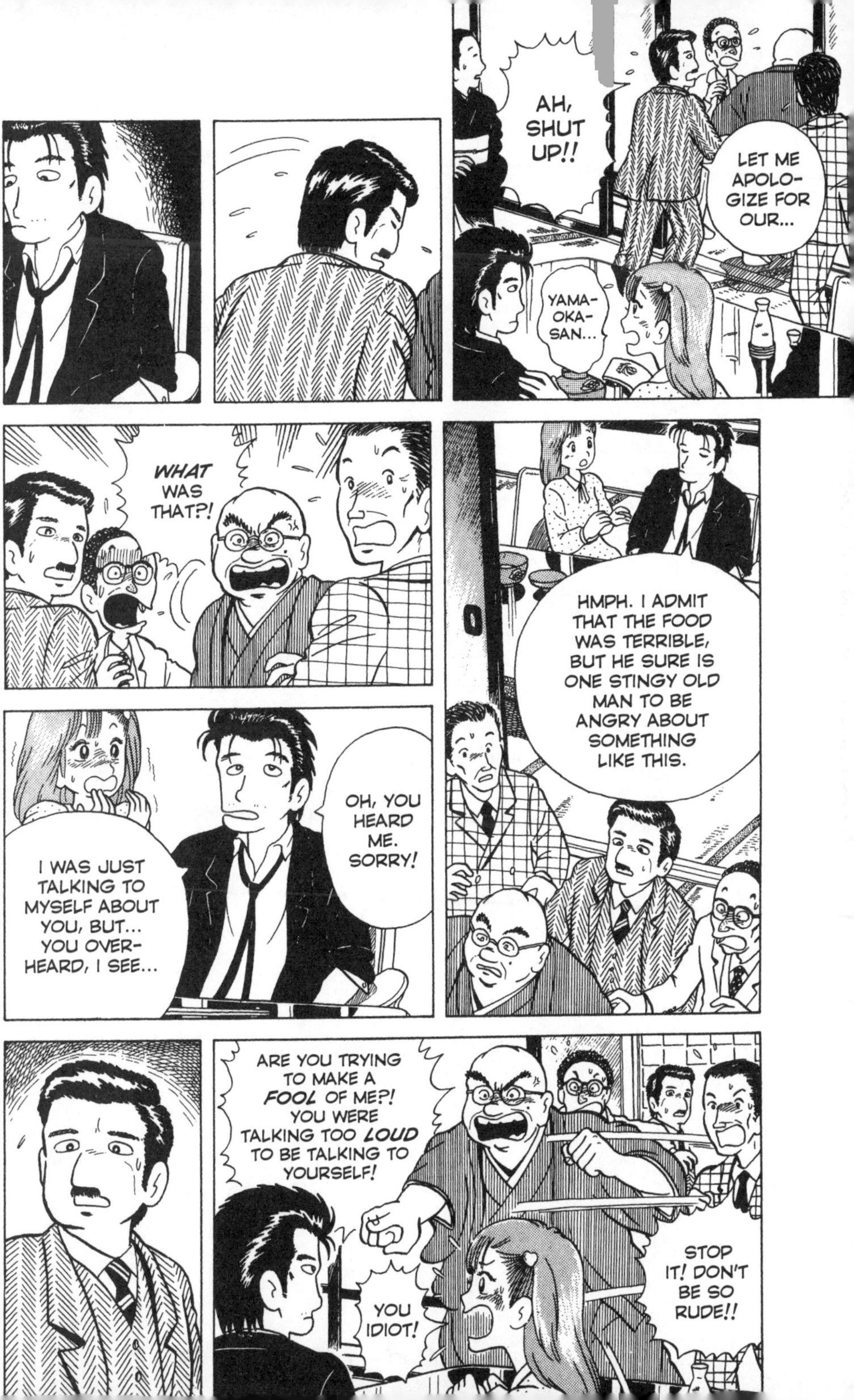
LET ME APOLOGIZE FOR OUR...
AH, SHUT UP!!
YAMA-OKA-SAN...
HMPH. I ADMIT THAT THE FOOD WAS TERRIBLE, BUT HE SURE IS ONE STINGY OLD MAN TO BE ANGRY ABOUT SOMETHING LIKE THIS.
WHAT WAS THAT?!
OH, YOU HEARD ME. SORRY!
I WAS JUST TALKING TO MYSELF ABOUT YOU, BUT... YOU OVER-HEARD, I SEE...
ARE YOU TRYING TO MAKE A FOOL OF ME?! YOU WERE TALKING TOO LOUD TO BE TALKING TO YOURSELF!
STOP IT! DON'T BE SO RUDE!!
YOU IDIOT!

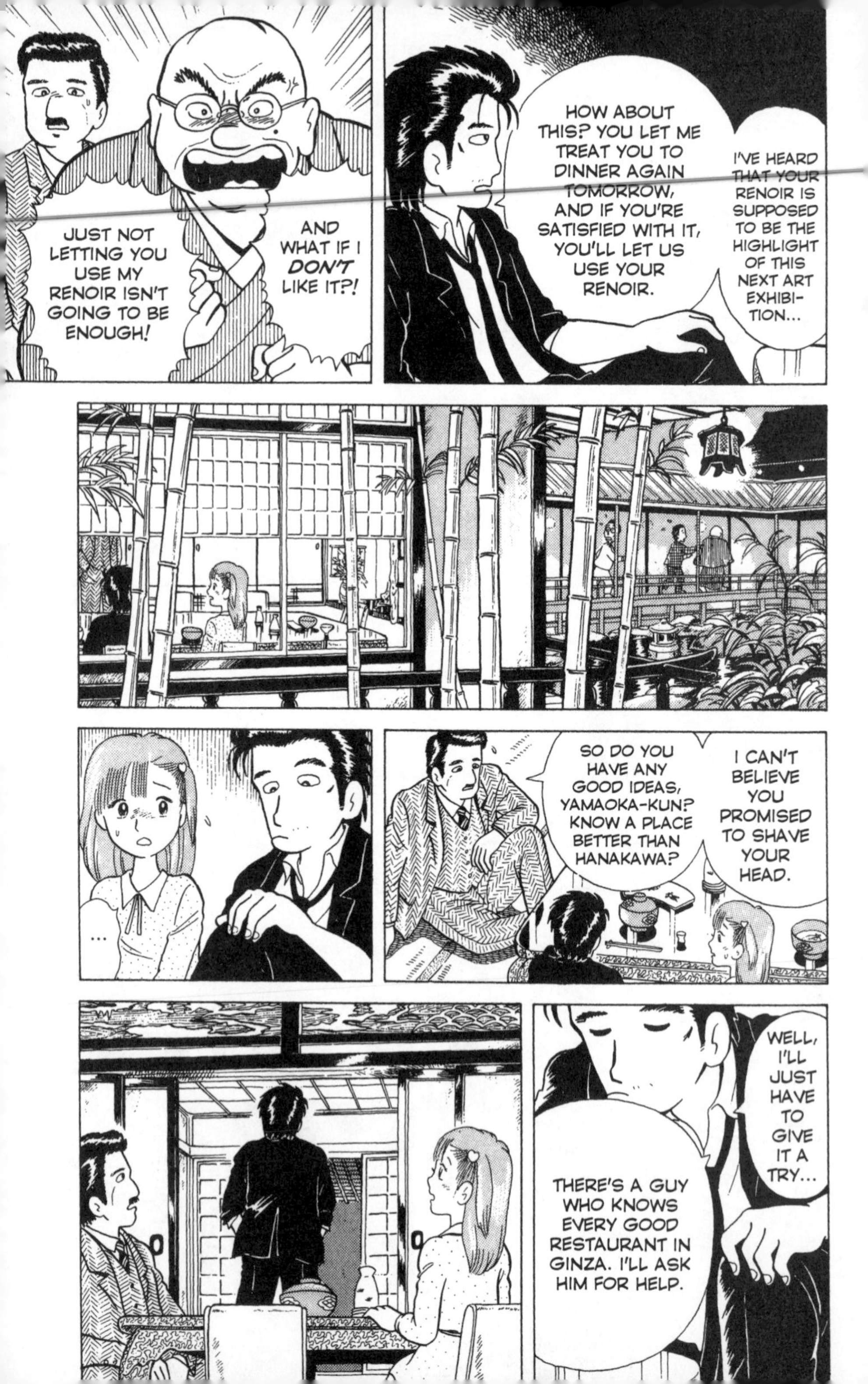
I'VE HEARD THAT YOUR RENOIR IS SUPPOSED TO BE THE HIGHLIGHT OF THIS NEXT ART EXHIBITION...
HOW ABOUT THIS? YOU LET ME TREAT YOU TO DINNER AGAIN TOMORROW, AND IF YOU'RE SATISFIED WITH IT, YOU'LL LET US USE YOUR RENOIR.
AND WHAT IF I *DON'T* LIKE IT?!
JUST NOT LETTING YOU USE MY RENOIR ISN'T GOING TO BE ENOUGH!
I CAN'T BELIEVE YOU PROMISED TO SHAVE YOUR HEAD.
SO DO YOU HAVE ANY GOOD IDEAS, YAMAOKA-KUN? KNOW A PLACE BETTER THAN HANAKAWA?
...
WELL, I'LL JUST HAVE TO GIVE IT A TRY...
THERE'S A GUY WHO KNOWS EVERY GOOD RESTAURANT IN GINZA. I'LL ASK HIM FOR HELP.

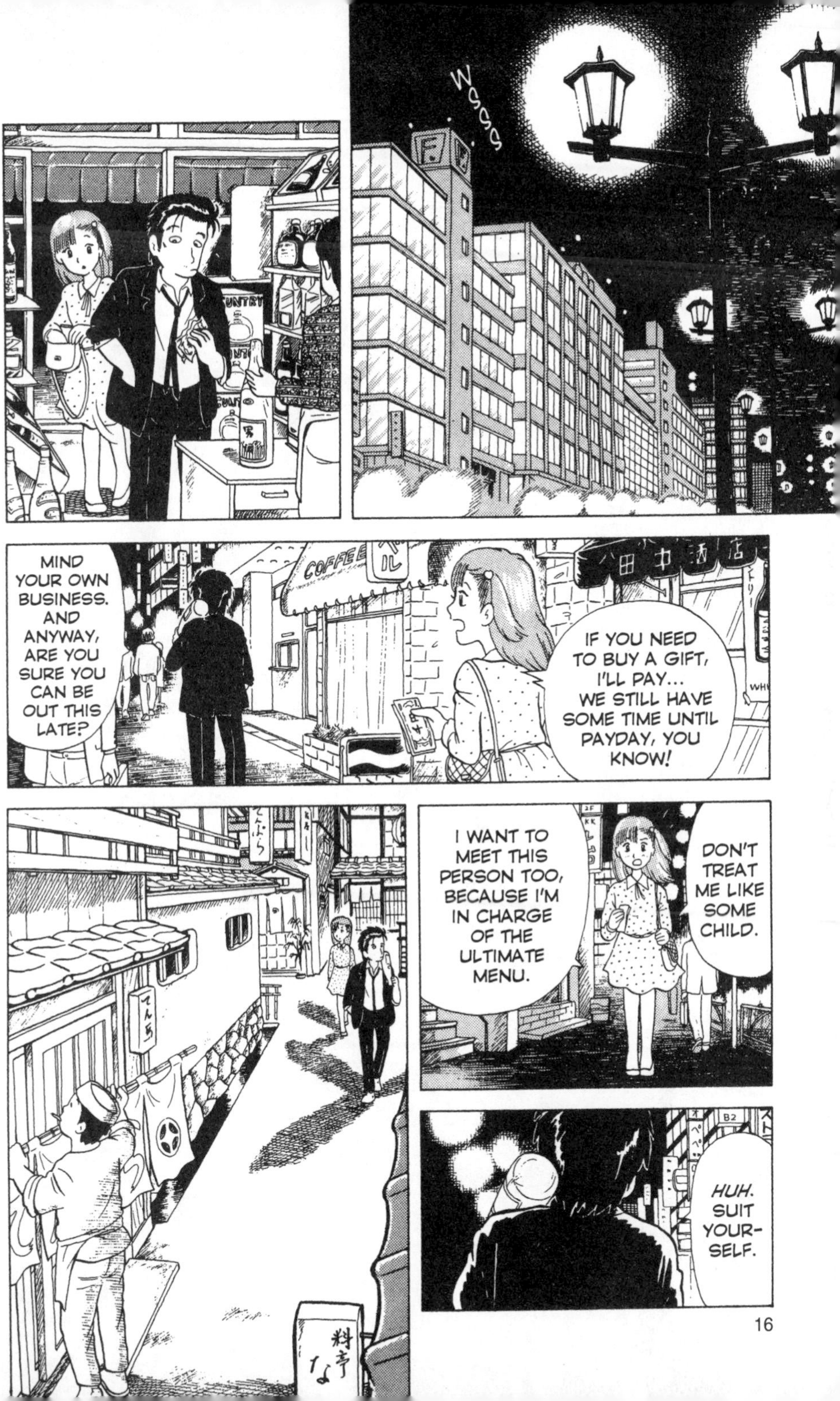
WSSSS
IF YOU NEED TO BUY A GIFT, I'LL PAY... WE STILL HAVE SOME TIME UNTIL PAYDAY, YOU KNOW!
MIND YOUR OWN BUSINESS. AND ANYWAY, ARE YOU SURE YOU CAN BE OUT THIS LATE?
DON'T TREAT ME LIKE SOME CHILD.
I WANT TO MEET THIS PERSON TOO, BECAUSE I'M IN CHARGE OF THE ULTIMATE MENU.
HUH. SUIT YOURSELF.

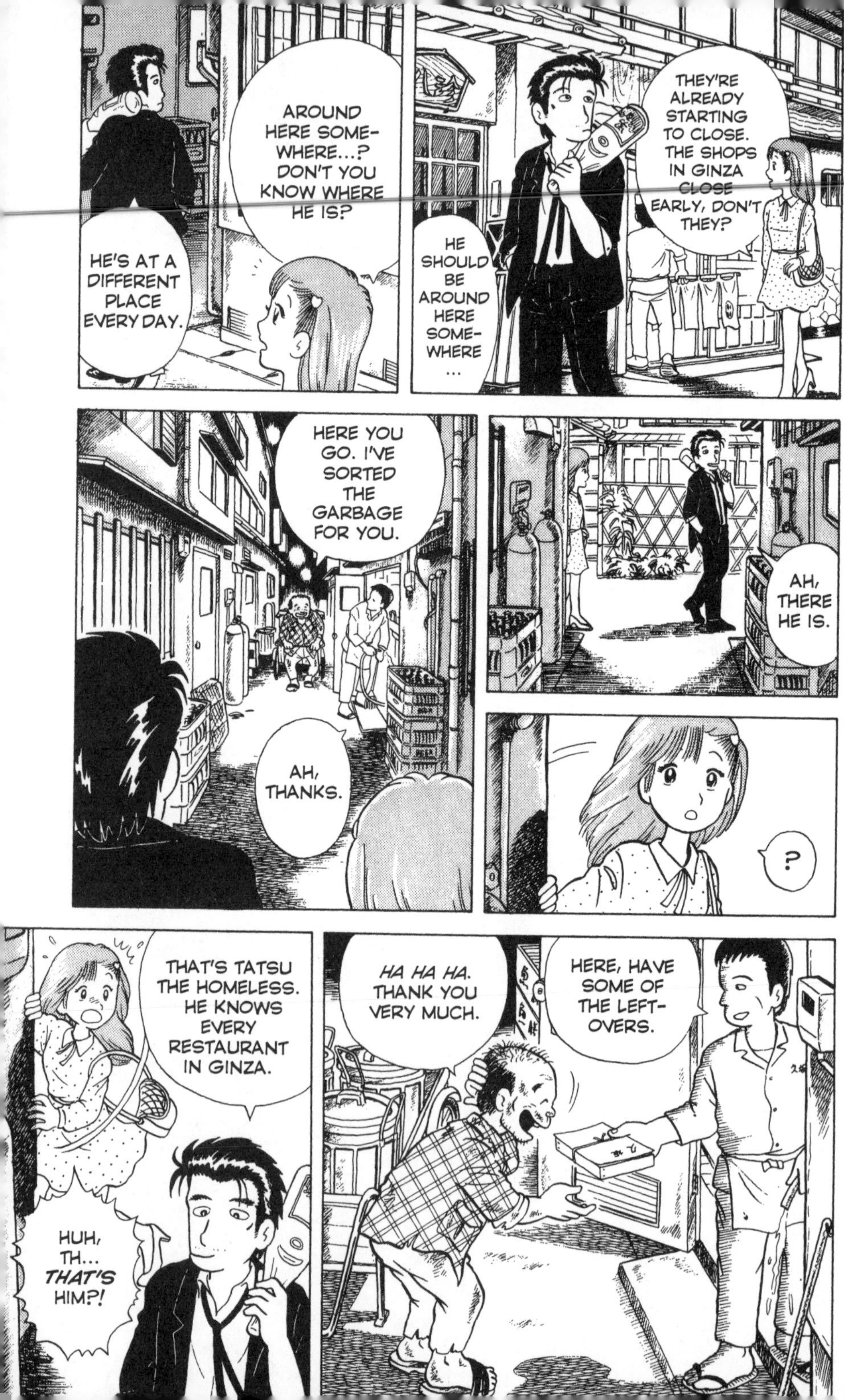
THEY'RE ALREADY STARTING TO CLOSE. THE SHOPS IN GINZA CLOSE EARLY, DON'T THEY?
HE SHOULD BE AROUND HERE SOME-WHERE ...
AROUND HERE SOME-WHERE...? DON'T YOU KNOW WHERE HE IS?
HE'S AT A DIFFERENT PLACE EVERY DAY.
AH, THERE HE IS.
?
HERE YOU GO. I'VE SORTED THE GARBAGE FOR YOU.
AH, THANKS.
HERE, HAVE SOME OF THE LEFT-OVERS.
HA HA HA. THANK YOU VERY MUCH.
THAT'S TATSU THE HOMELESS. HE KNOWS EVERY RESTAURANT IN GINZA.
HUH, TH... ***THAT'S*** HIM?!

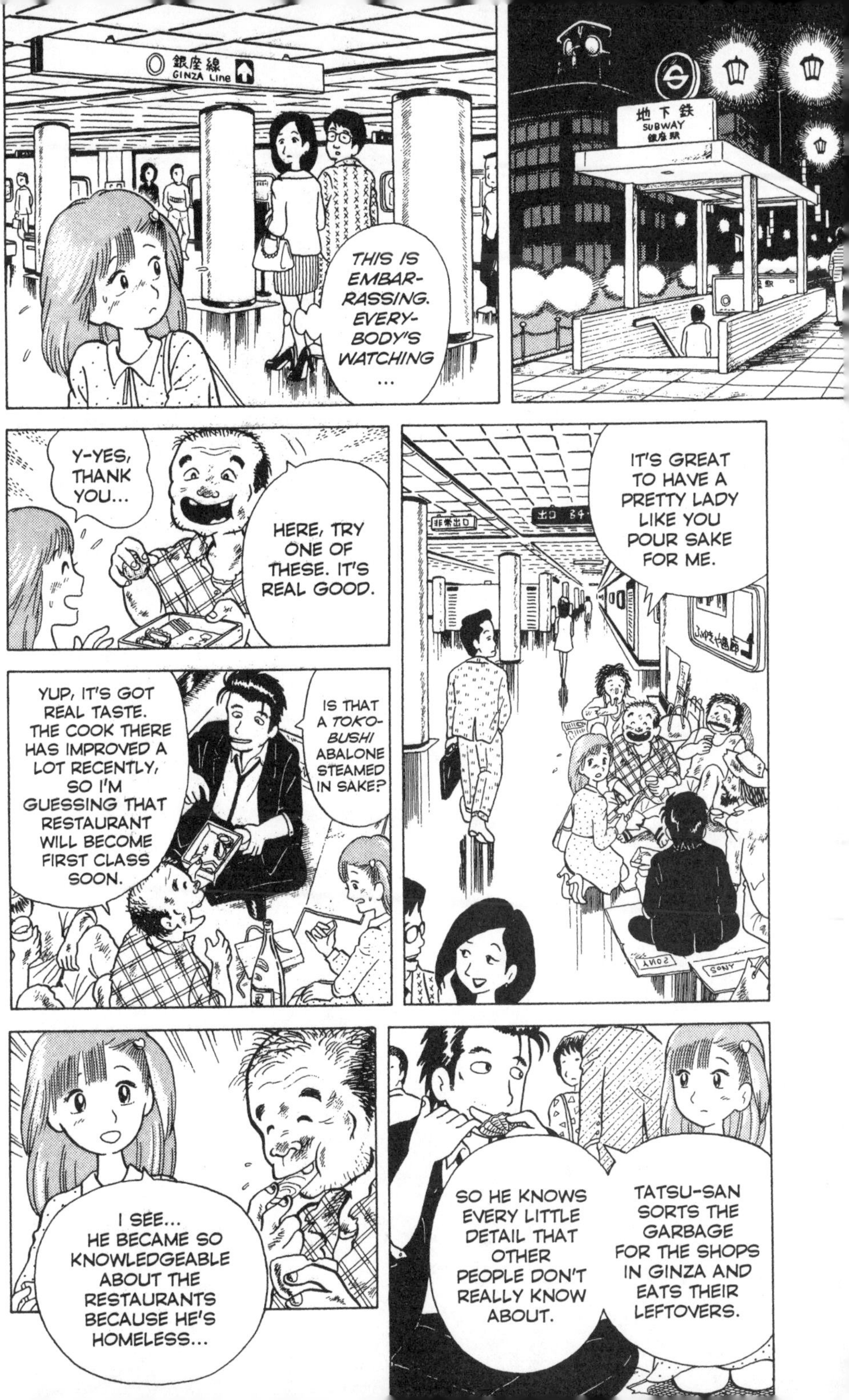

地下鉄
SUBWAY
銀座駅
銀座線
GINZA Line
THIS IS EMBARRASSING. EVERYBODY'S WATCHING...
IT'S GREAT TO HAVE A PRETTY LADY LIKE YOU POUR SAKE FOR ME.
HERE, TRY ONE OF THESE. IT'S REAL GOOD.
Y-YES, THANK YOU...
IS THAT A *TOKOBUSHI* ABALONE STEAMED IN SAKE?
YUP, IT'S GOT REAL TASTE. THE COOK THERE HAS IMPROVED A LOT RECENTLY, SO I'M GUESSING THAT RESTAURANT WILL BECOME FIRST CLASS SOON.
TATSU-SAN SORTS THE GARBAGE FOR THE SHOPS IN GINZA AND EATS THEIR LEFTOVERS.
SO HE KNOWS EVERY LITTLE DETAIL THAT OTHER PEOPLE DON'T REALLY KNOW ABOUT.
I SEE... HE BECAME SO KNOWLEDGEABLE ABOUT THE RESTAURANTS BECAUSE HE'S HOMELESS...

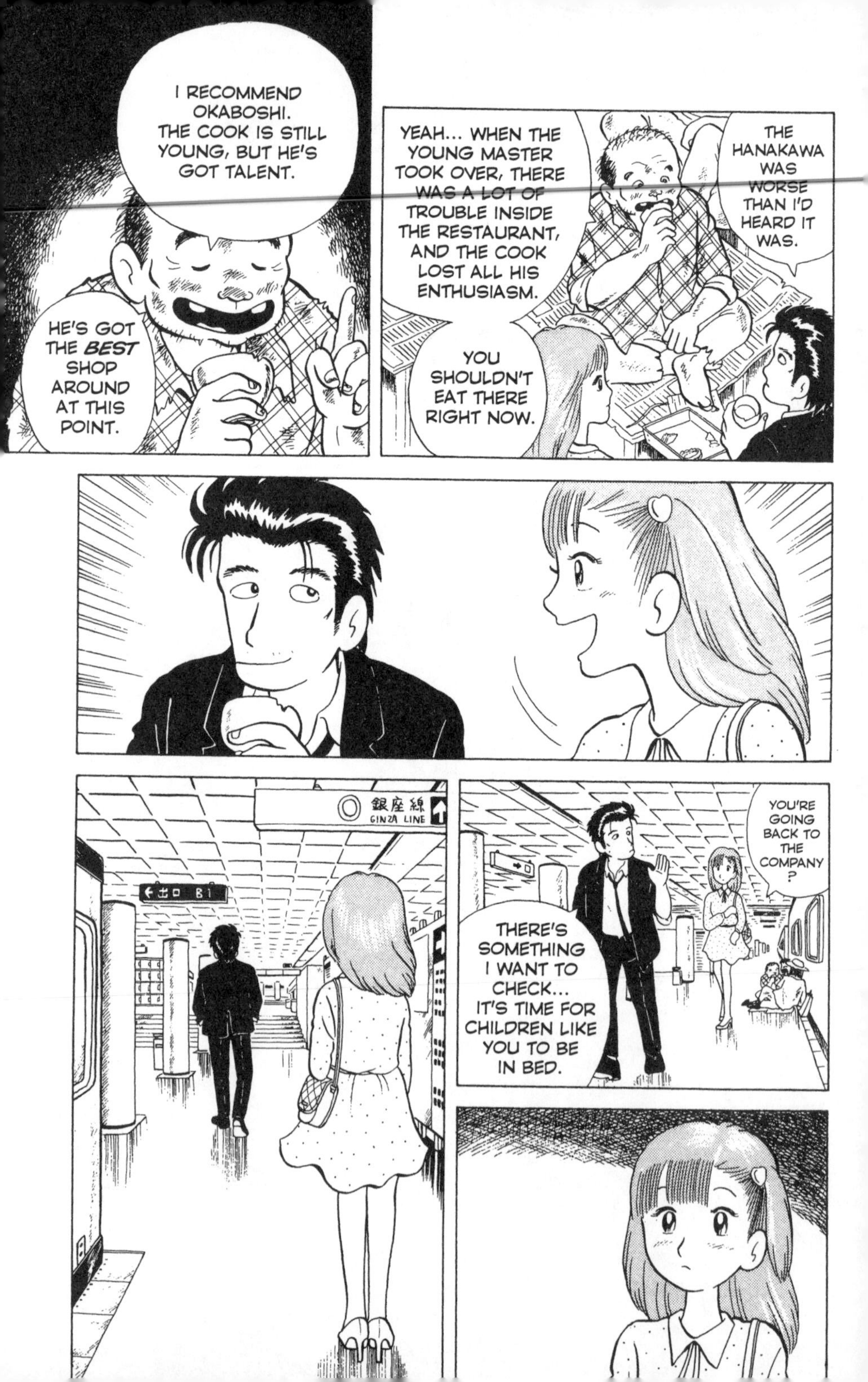
THE HANAKAWA WAS WORSE THAN I'D HEARD IT WAS.
YEAH... WHEN THE YOUNG MASTER TOOK OVER, THERE WAS A LOT OF TROUBLE INSIDE THE RESTAURANT, AND THE COOK LOST ALL HIS ENTHUSIASM.
YOU SHOULDN'T EAT THERE RIGHT NOW.
I RECOMMEND OKABOSHI. THE COOK IS STILL YOUNG, BUT HE'S GOT TALENT.
HE'S GOT THE *BEST* SHOP AROUND AT THIS POINT.
YOU'RE GOING BACK TO THE COMPANY?
THERE'S SOMETHING I WANT TO CHECK... IT'S TIME FOR CHILDREN LIKE YOU TO BE IN BED.
銀座線 GINZA LINE
←出口 B1

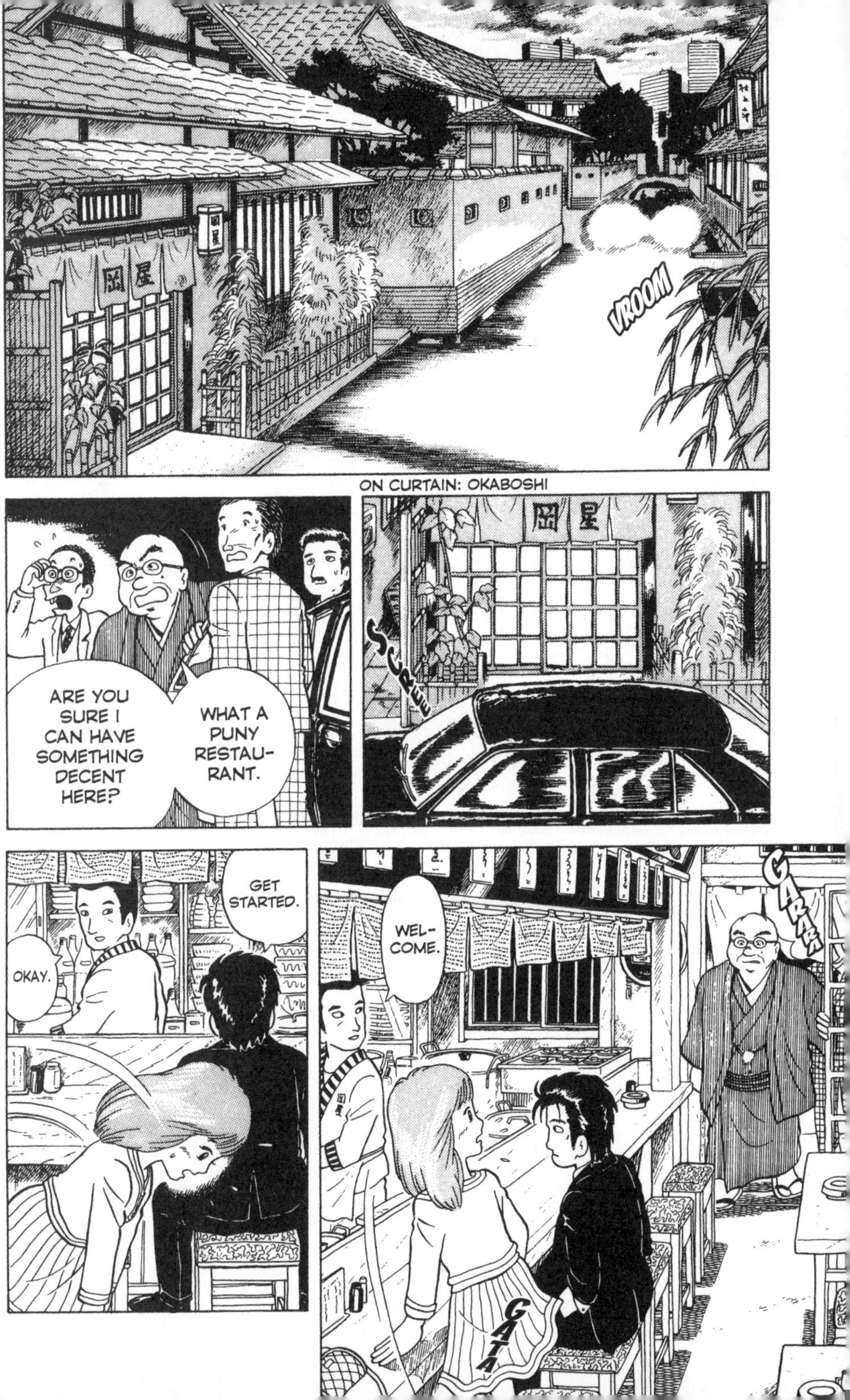
VROOM
ON CURTAIN: OKABOSHI
SCREEE
WHAT A PUNY RESTAURANT.
ARE YOU SURE I CAN HAVE SOMETHING DECENT HERE?
GARARA
WELCOME.
GATA
GET STARTED.
OKAY.

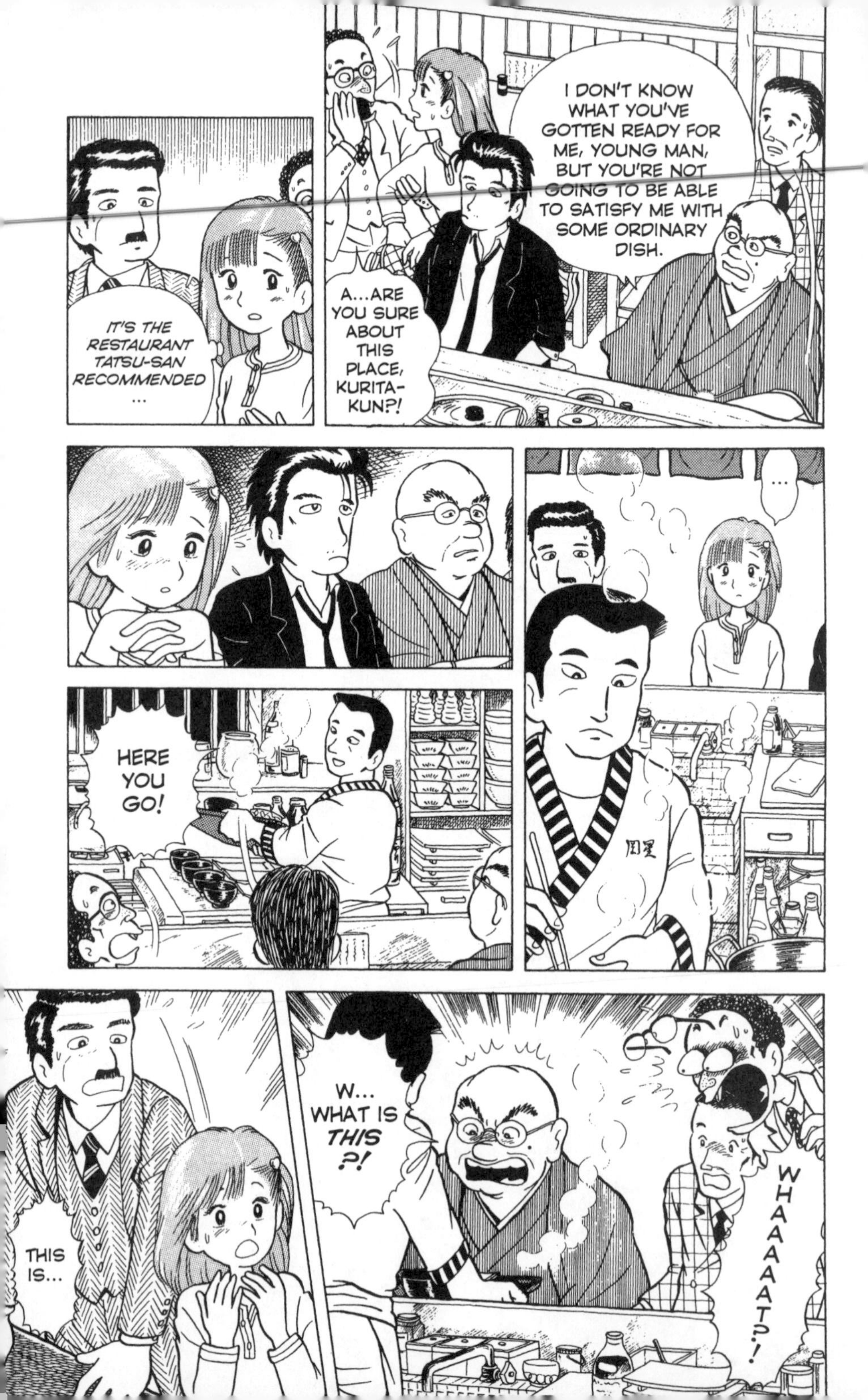
I DON'T KNOW WHAT YOU'VE GOTTEN READY FOR ME, YOUNG MAN, BUT YOU'RE NOT GOING TO BE ABLE TO SATISFY ME WITH SOME ORDINARY DISH.
A...ARE YOU SURE ABOUT THIS PLACE, KURITA-KUN?!
IT'S THE RESTAURANT TATSU-SAN RECOMMENDED ...
...
HERE YOU GO!
WHAAAAAT?!
W... WHAT IS THIS?!
THIS IS...

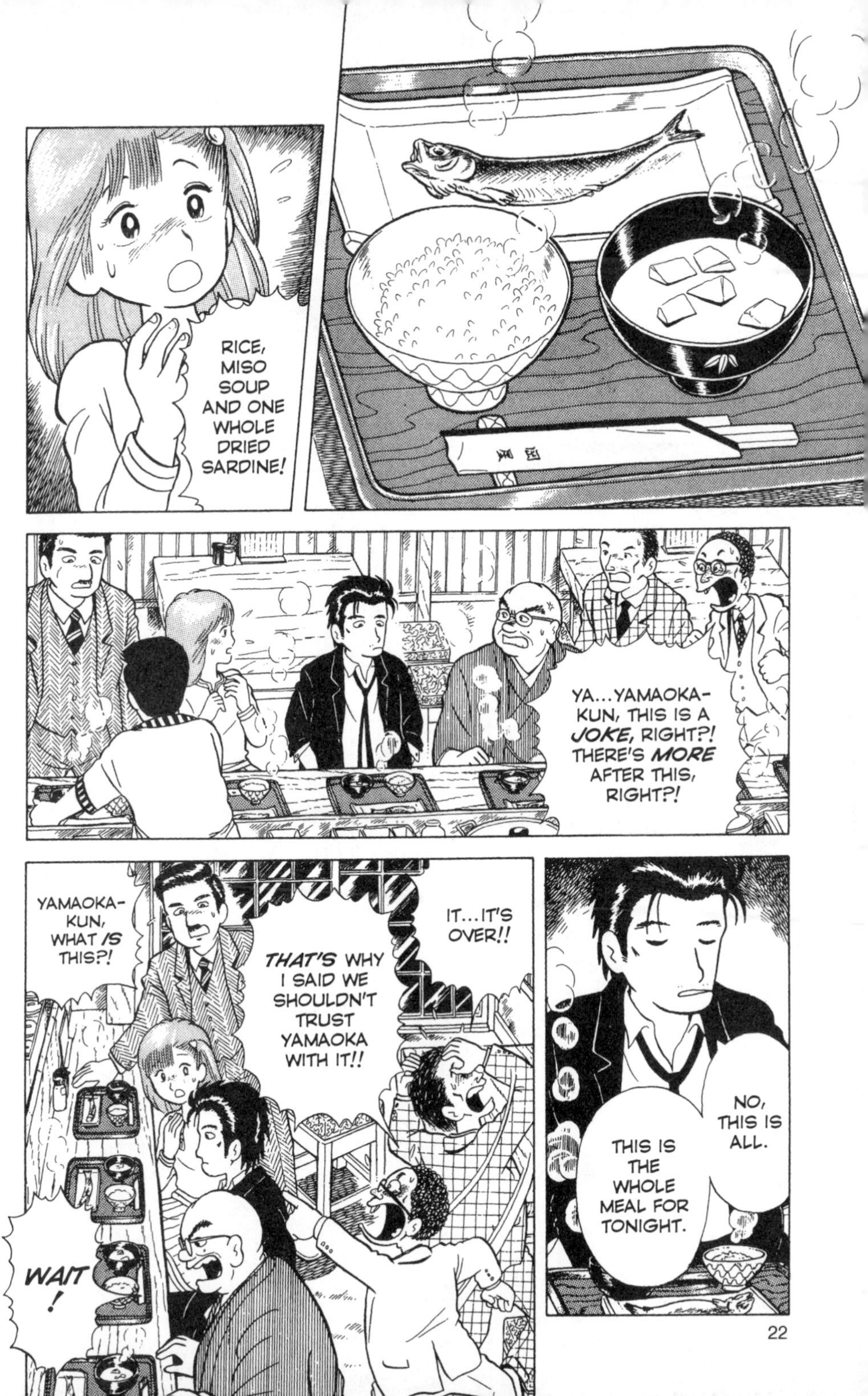

RICE, MISO SOUP AND ONE WHOLE DRIED SARDINE!
YA...YAMAOKA-KUN, THIS IS A ***JOKE***, RIGHT?! THERE'S ***MORE*** AFTER THIS, RIGHT?!
NO, THIS IS ALL.
THIS IS THE WHOLE MEAL FOR TONIGHT.
IT...IT'S OVER!!
THAT'S WHY I SAID WE SHOULDN'T TRUST YAMAOKA WITH IT!!
YAMAOKA-KUN, WHAT ***IS*** THIS?!
WAIT!

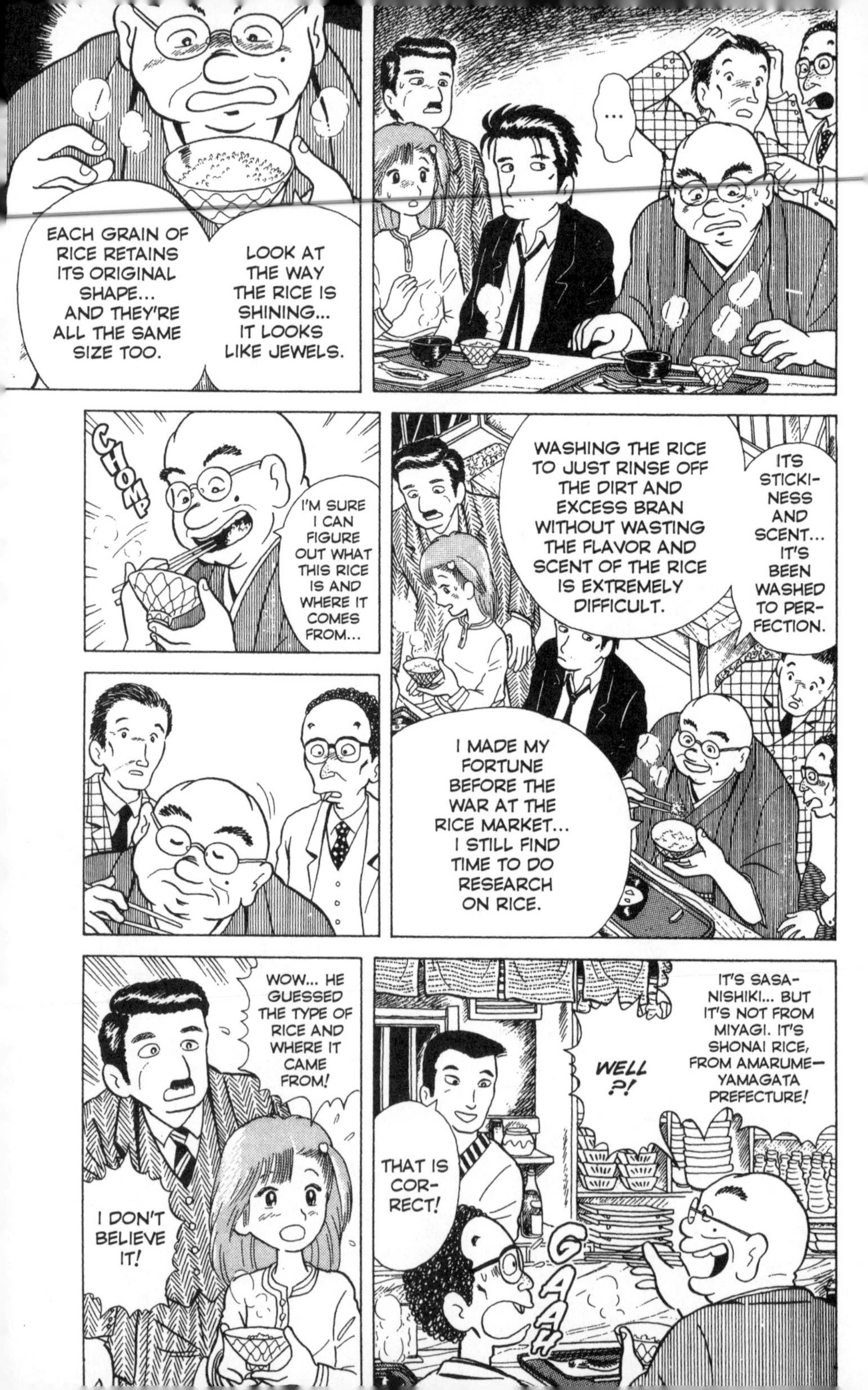
...
LOOK AT THE WAY THE RICE IS SHINING... IT LOOKS LIKE JEWELS.
EACH GRAIN OF RICE RETAINS ITS ORIGINAL SHAPE... AND THEY'RE ALL THE SAME SIZE TOO.
ITS STICKINESS AND SCENT... IT'S BEEN WASHED TO PERFECTION.
WASHING THE RICE TO JUST RINSE OFF THE DIRT AND EXCESS BRAN WITHOUT WASTING THE FLAVOR AND SCENT OF THE RICE IS EXTREMELY DIFFICULT.
I MADE MY FORTUNE BEFORE THE WAR AT THE RICE MARKET... I STILL FIND TIME TO DO RESEARCH ON RICE.
CHOMP
I'M SURE I CAN FIGURE OUT WHAT THIS RICE IS AND WHERE IT COMES FROM...
IT'S SASANISHIKI... BUT IT'S NOT FROM MIYAGI. IT'S SHONAI RICE, FROM AMARUME-YAMAGATA PREFECTURE!
WELL ?!
THAT IS CORRECT!
GAAAH
WOW... HE GUESSED THE TYPE OF RICE AND WHERE IT CAME FROM!
I DON'T BELIEVE IT!

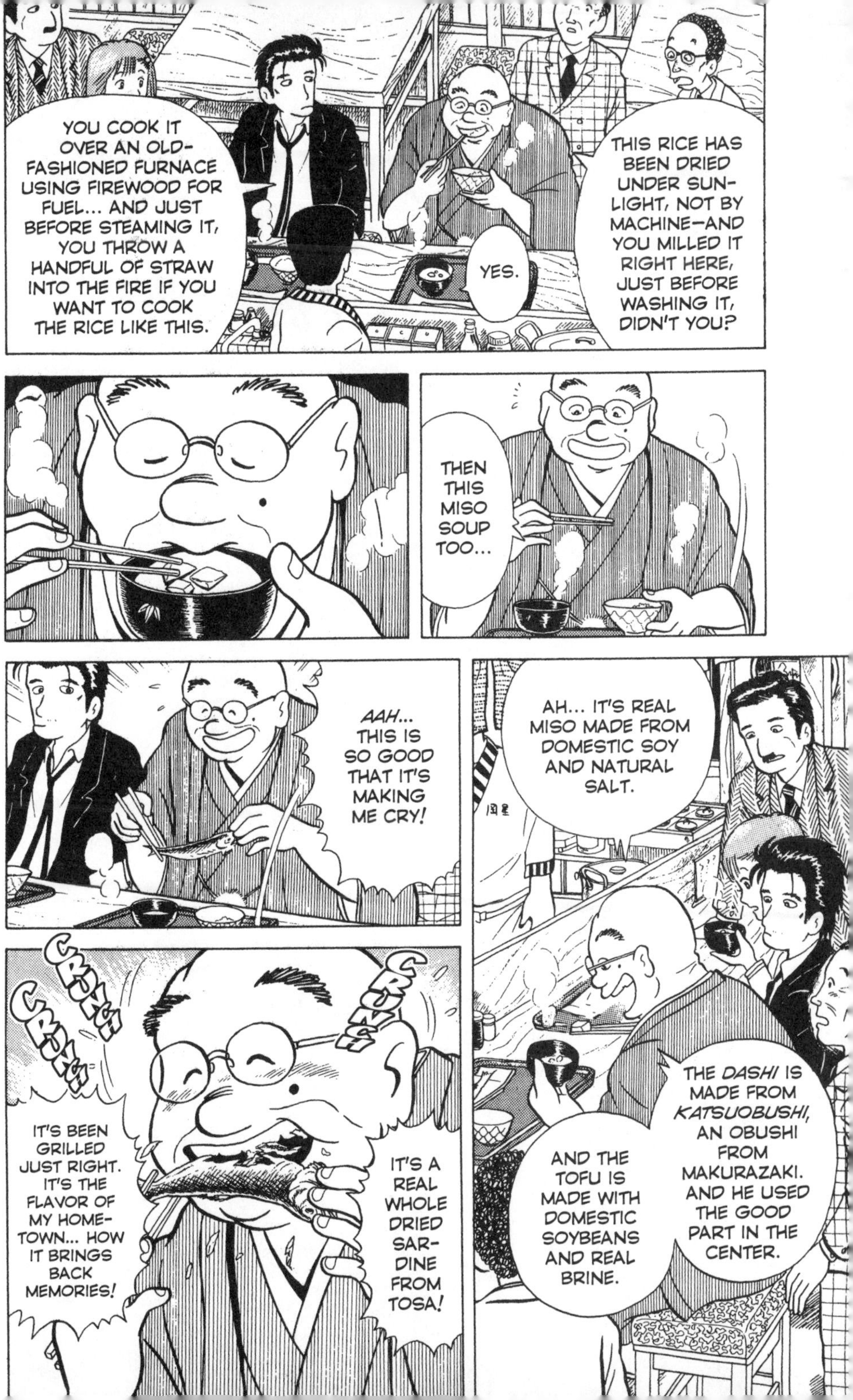
THIS RICE HAS BEEN DRIED UNDER SUN-LIGHT, NOT BY MACHINE—AND YOU MILLED IT RIGHT HERE, JUST BEFORE WASHING IT, DIDN'T YOU?
YES.
YOU COOK IT OVER AN OLD-FASHIONED FURNACE USING FIREWOOD FOR FUEL... AND JUST BEFORE STEAMING IT, YOU THROW A HANDFUL OF STRAW INTO THE FIRE IF YOU WANT TO COOK THE RICE LIKE THIS.
THEN THIS MISO SOUP TOO...
AH... IT'S REAL MISO MADE FROM DOMESTIC SOY AND NATURAL SALT.
THE *DASHI* IS MADE FROM *KATSUOBUSHI*, AN OBUSHI FROM MAKURAZAKI. AND HE USED THE GOOD PART IN THE CENTER.
AND THE TOFU IS MADE WITH DOMESTIC SOYBEANS AND REAL BRINE.
AAH... THIS IS SO GOOD THAT IT'S MAKING ME CRY!
CRUNCH
IT'S A REAL WHOLE DRIED SAR-DINE FROM TOSA!
CRUNCH
CRUNCH
IT'S BEEN GRILLED JUST RIGHT. IT'S THE FLAVOR OF MY HOME-TOWN... HOW IT BRINGS BACK MEMORIES!

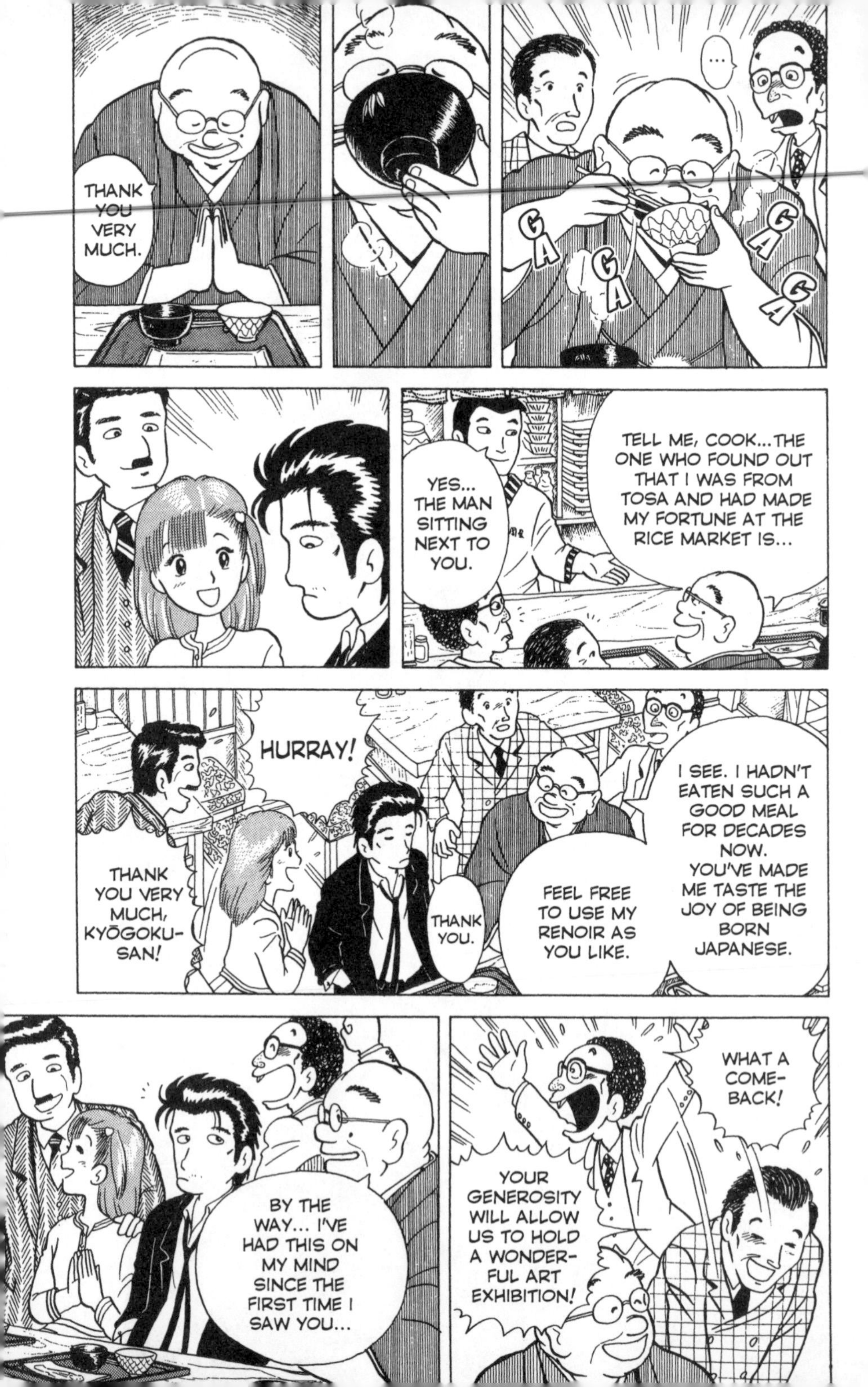
...
GA
GA
GA
GA
THANK YOU VERY MUCH.
TELL ME, COOK...THE ONE WHO FOUND OUT THAT I WAS FROM TOSA AND HAD MADE MY FORTUNE AT THE RICE MARKET IS...
YES... THE MAN SITTING NEXT TO YOU.
I SEE. I HADN'T EATEN SUCH A GOOD MEAL FOR DECADES NOW. YOU'VE MADE ME TASTE THE JOY OF BEING BORN JAPANESE.
FEEL FREE TO USE MY RENOIR AS YOU LIKE.
HURRAY!
THANK YOU.
THANK YOU VERY MUCH, KYŌGOKU-SAN!
WHAT A COME-BACK!
YOUR GENEROSITY WILL ALLOW US TO HOLD A WONDERFUL ART EXHIBITION!
BY THE WAY... I'VE HAD THIS ON MY MIND SINCE THE FIRST TIME I SAW YOU...

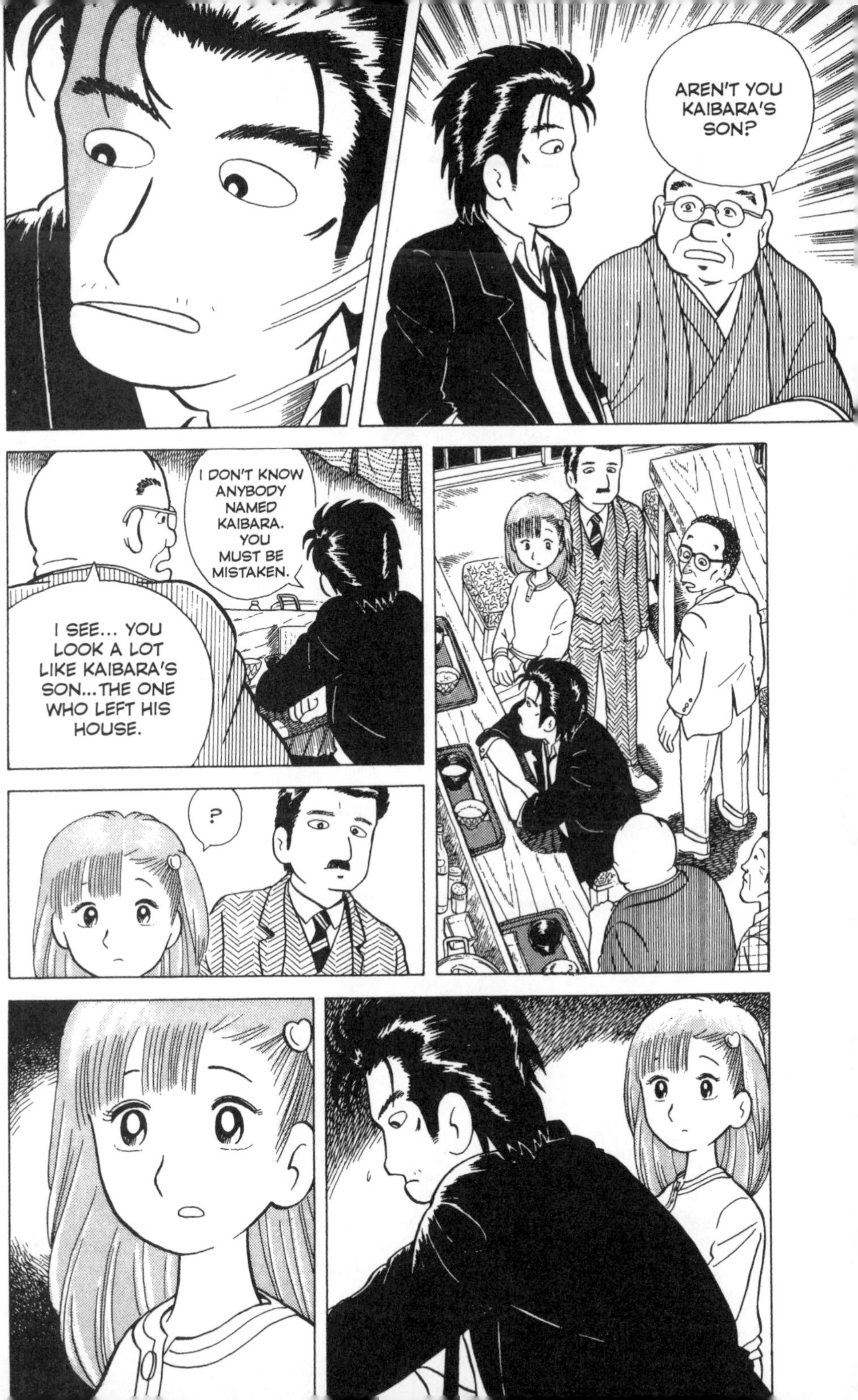
AREN'T YOU KAIBARA'S SON?
I DON'T KNOW ANYBODY NAMED KAIBARA. YOU MUST BE MISTAKEN.
I SEE... YOU LOOK A LOT LIKE KAIBARA'S SON...THE ONE WHO LEFT HIS HOUSE.
?

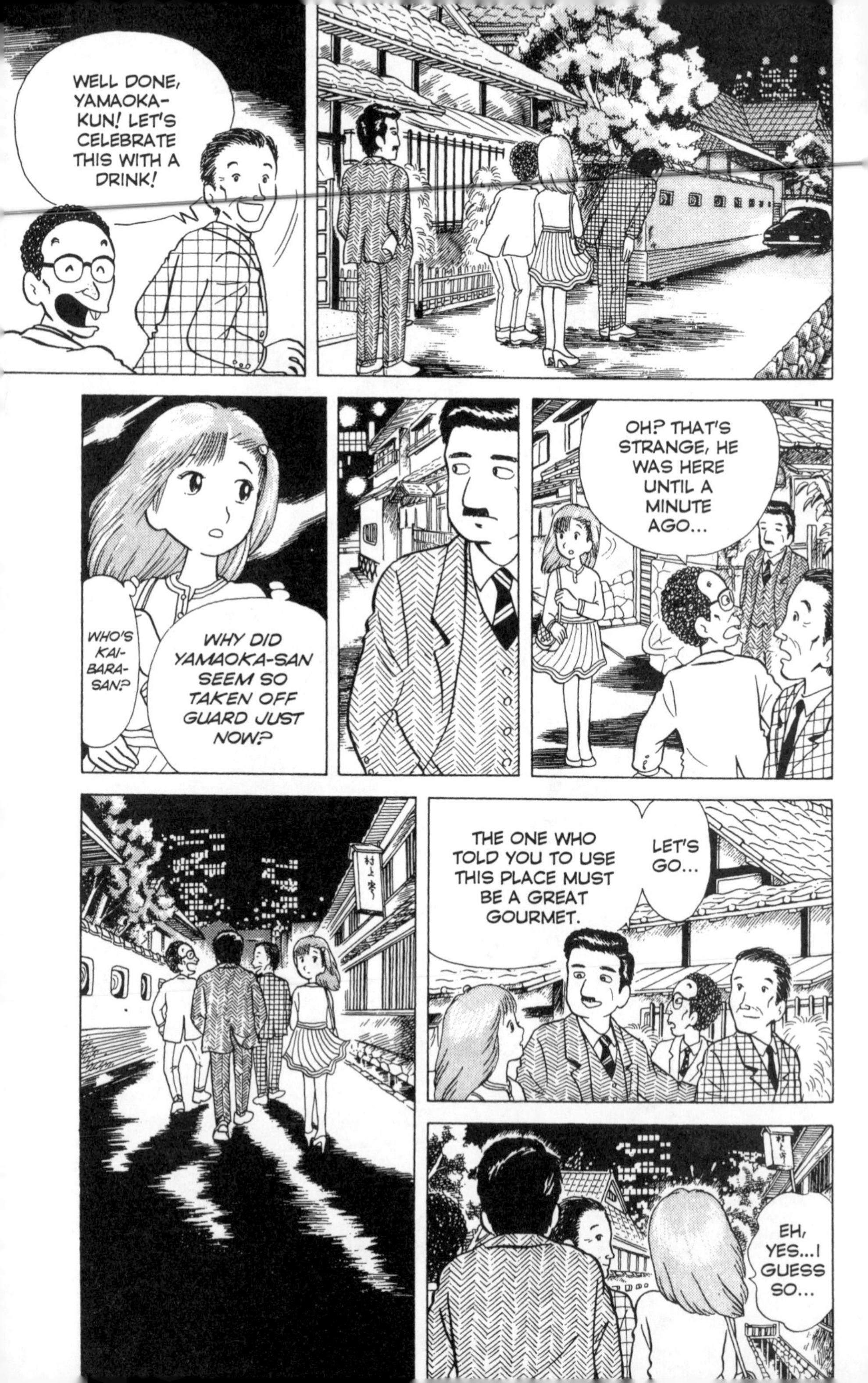
WELL DONE, YAMAOKA-KUN! LET'S CELEBRATE THIS WITH A DRINK!
OH? THAT'S STRANGE, HE WAS HERE UNTIL A MINUTE AGO...
WHY DID YAMAOKA-SAN SEEM SO TAKEN OFF GUARD JUST NOW?
WHO'S KAI-BARA-SAN?
LET'S GO...
THE ONE WHO TOLD YOU TO USE THIS PLACE MUST BE A GREAT GOURMET.
EH, YES...I GUESS SO...

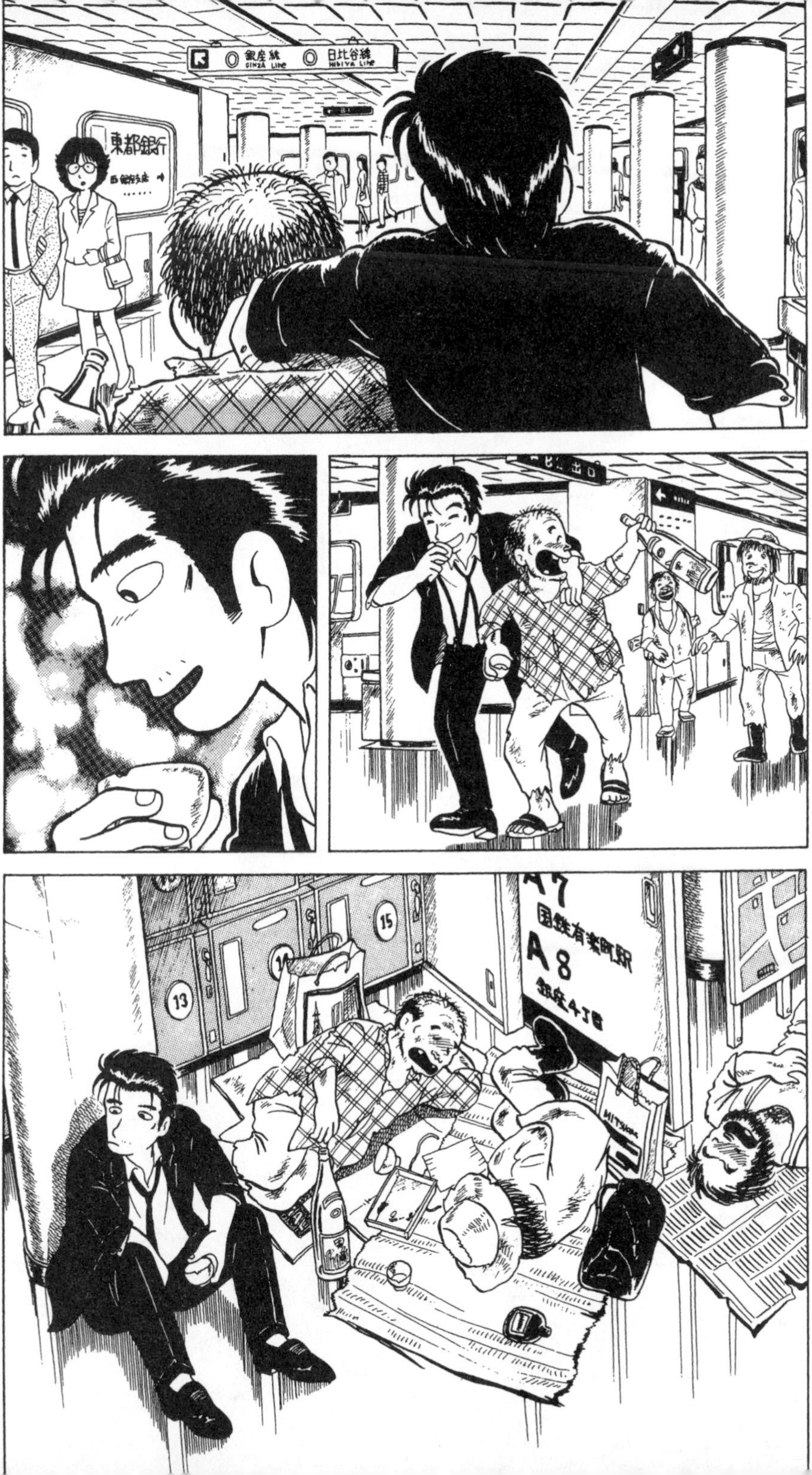
銀座線
GINZA Line
日比谷線
HIBIYA Line
東都銀行
A7
国鉄有楽町駅
A8
銀座4丁目

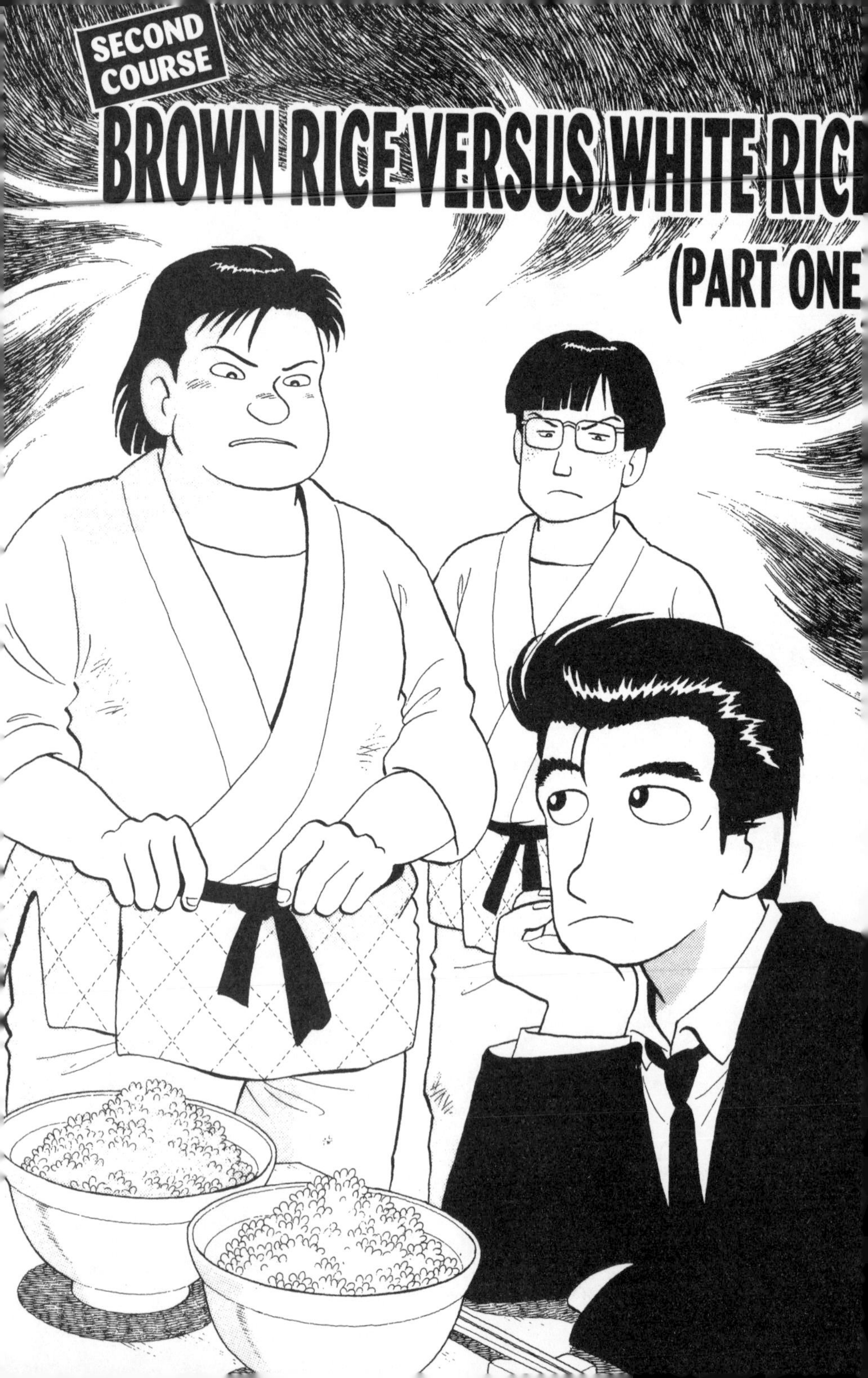
SECOND COURSE
BROWN RICE VERSUS WHITE RIC
(PART ONE

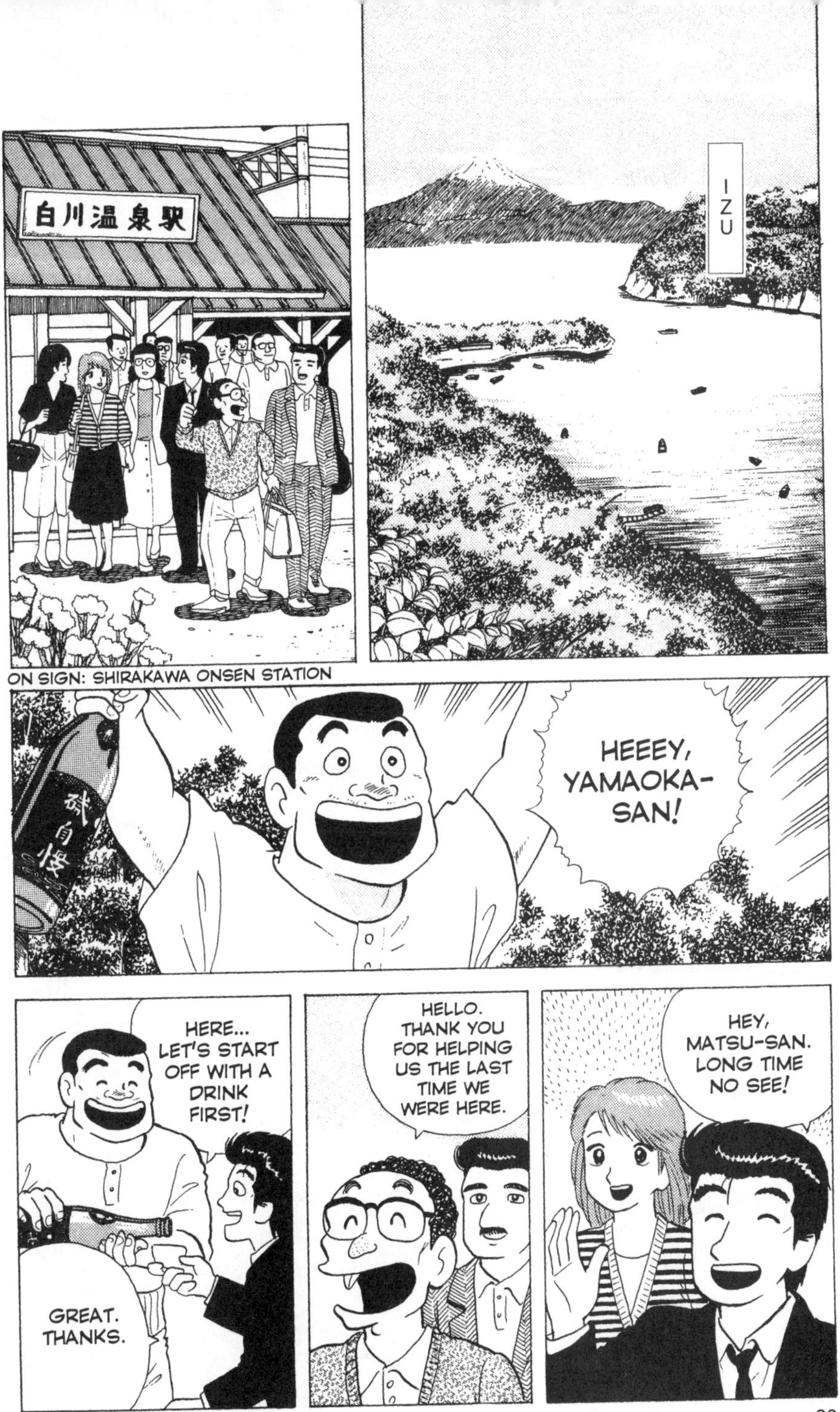
IZU
白川温泉駅
ON SIGN: SHIRAKAWA ONSEN STATION
HEEEY, YAMAOKA-SAN!
HEY, MATSU-SAN. LONG TIME NO SEE!
HELLO. THANK YOU FOR HELPING US THE LAST TIME WE WERE HERE.
HERE... LET'S START OFF WITH A DRINK FIRST!
GREAT. THANKS.

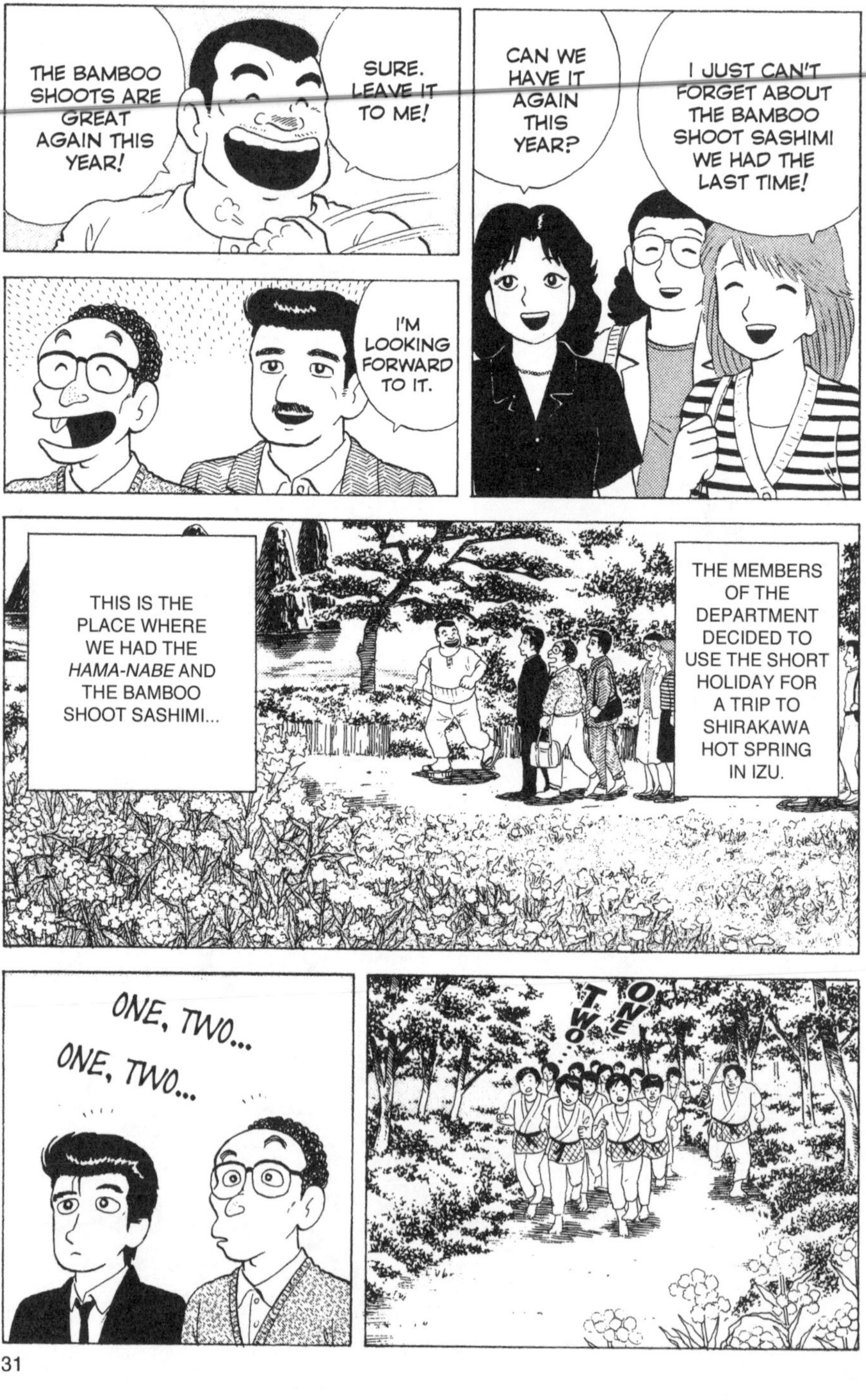
I JUST CAN'T FORGET ABOUT THE BAMBOO SHOOT SASHIMI WE HAD THE LAST TIME!
CAN WE HAVE IT AGAIN THIS YEAR?
SURE. LEAVE IT TO ME!
THE BAMBOO SHOOTS ARE GREAT AGAIN THIS YEAR!
I'M LOOKING FORWARD TO IT.
THE MEMBERS OF THE DEPARTMENT DECIDED TO USE THE SHORT HOLIDAY FOR A TRIP TO SHIRAKAWA HOT SPRING IN IZU.
THIS IS THE PLACE WHERE WE HAD THE *HAMA-NABE* AND THE BAMBOO SHOOT SASHIMI...
ONE
TWO
ONE, TWO...
ONE, TWO...

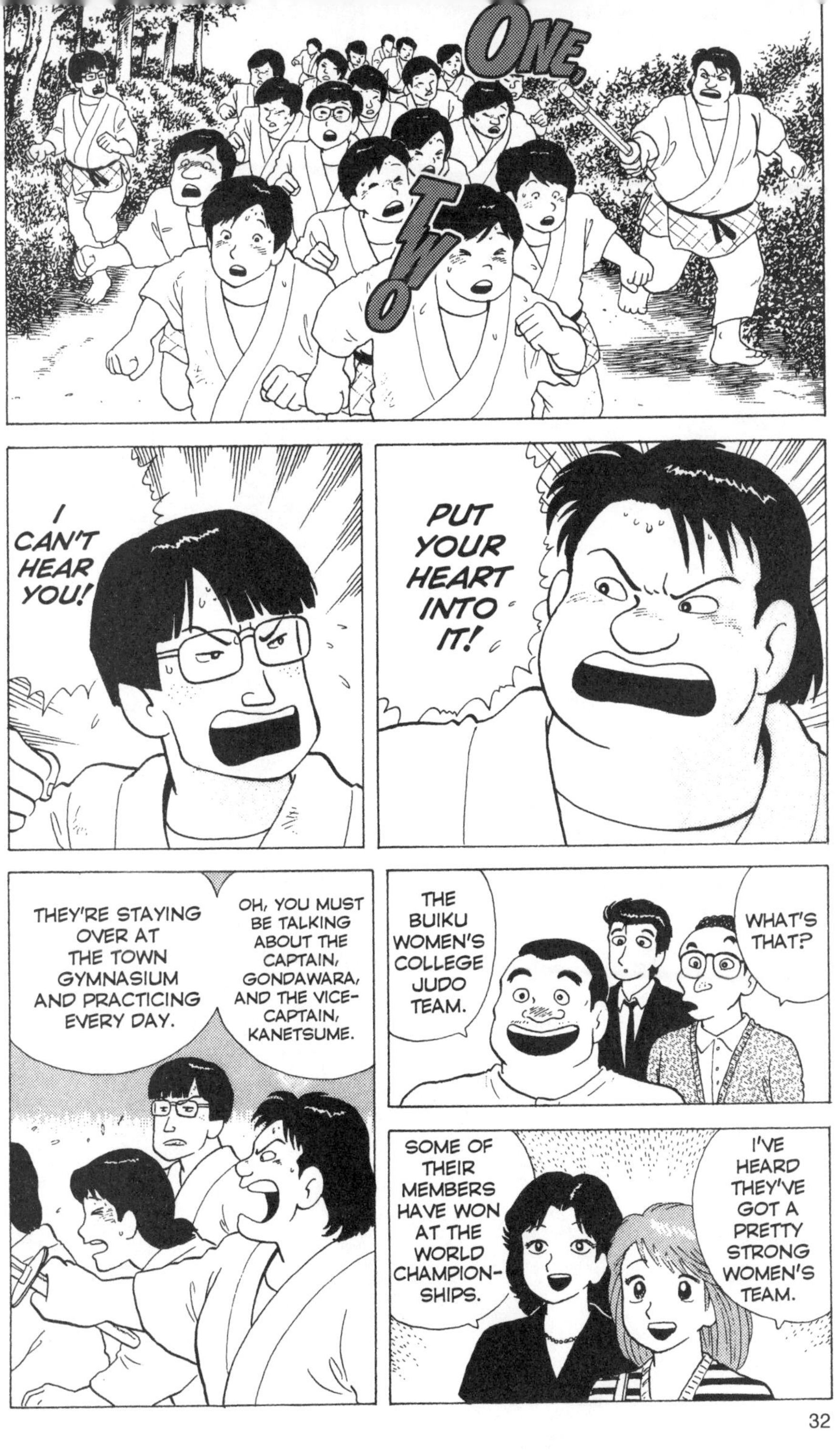
ONE,
TWO
PUT YOUR HEART INTO IT!
I CAN'T HEAR YOU!
WHAT'S THAT?
THE BUIKU WOMEN'S COLLEGE JUDO TEAM.
I'VE HEARD THEY'VE GOT A PRETTY STRONG WOMEN'S TEAM.
SOME OF THEIR MEMBERS HAVE WON AT THE WORLD CHAMPIONSHIPS.
OH, YOU MUST BE TALKING ABOUT THE CAPTAIN, GONDAWARA, AND THE VICE-CAPTAIN, KANETSUME.
THEY'RE STAYING OVER AT THE TOWN GYMNASIUM AND PRACTICING EVERY DAY.

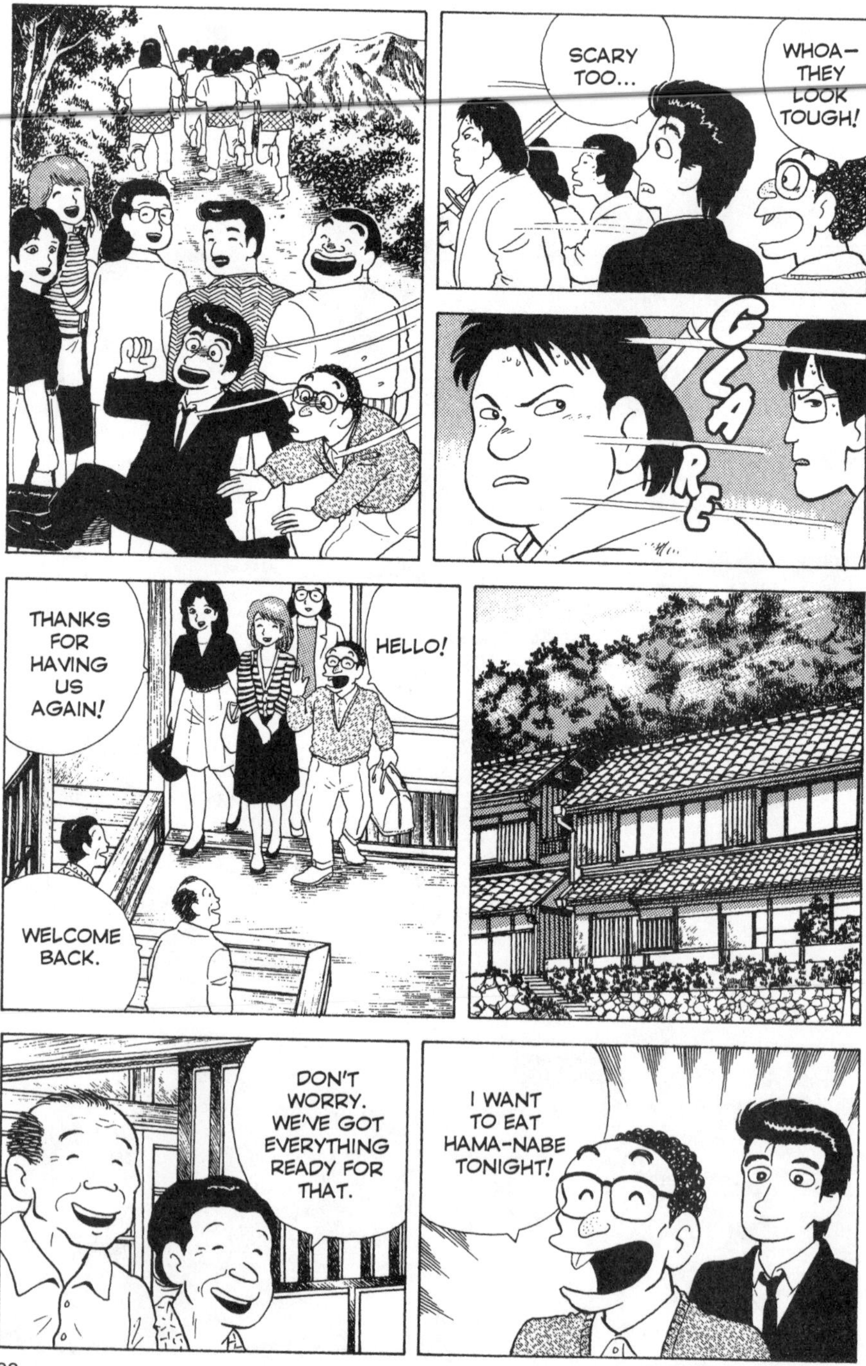
WHOA— THEY LOOK TOUGH!
SCARY TOO...
GLARE
HELLO!
THANKS FOR HAVING US AGAIN!
WELCOME BACK.
I WANT TO EAT HAMA-NABE TONIGHT!
DON'T WORRY. WE'VE GOT EVERYTHING READY FOR THAT.

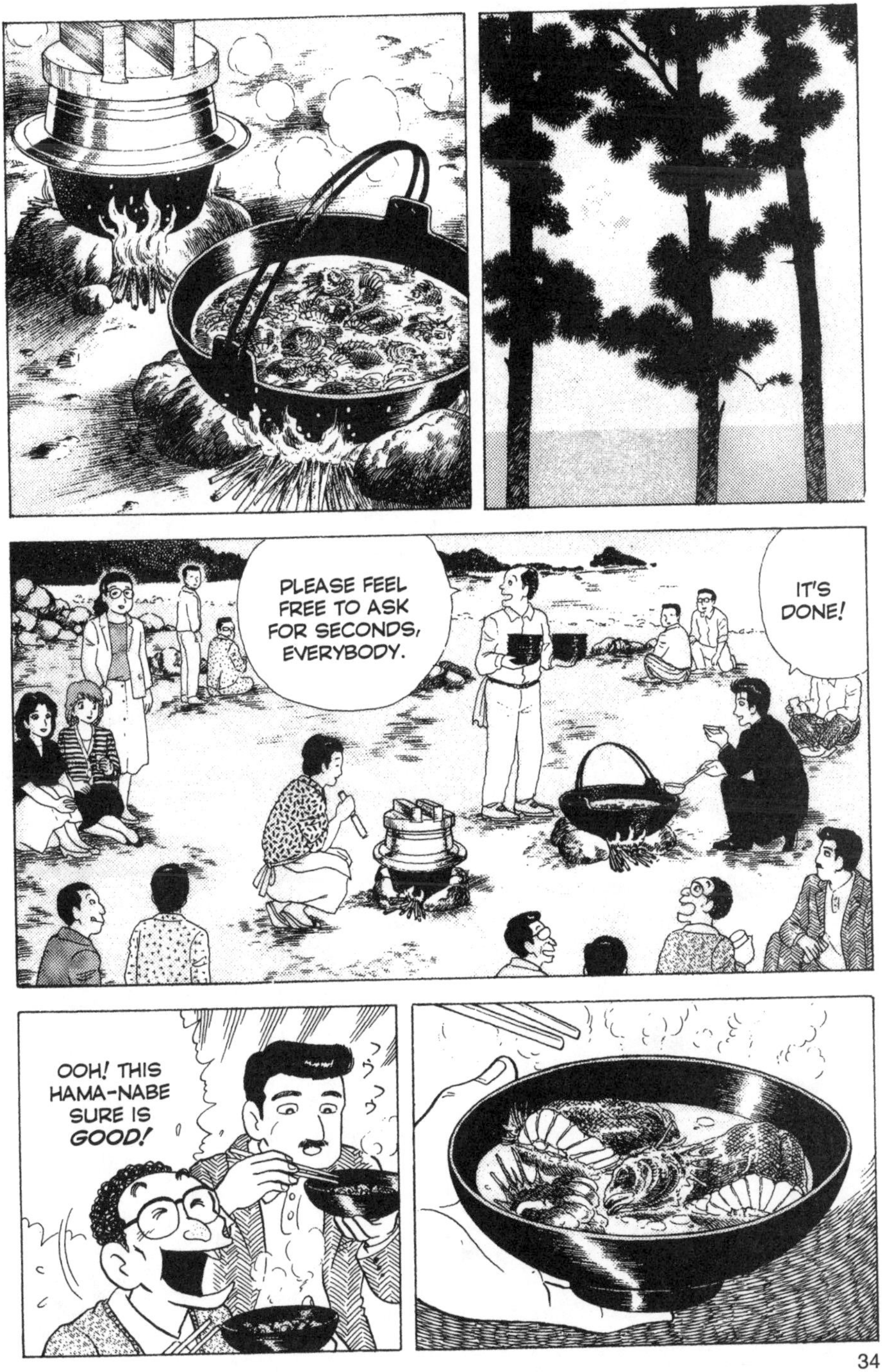
IT'S DONE!
PLEASE FEEL FREE TO ASK FOR SECONDS, EVERYBODY.
OOH! THIS HAMA-NABE SURE IS *GOOD!*

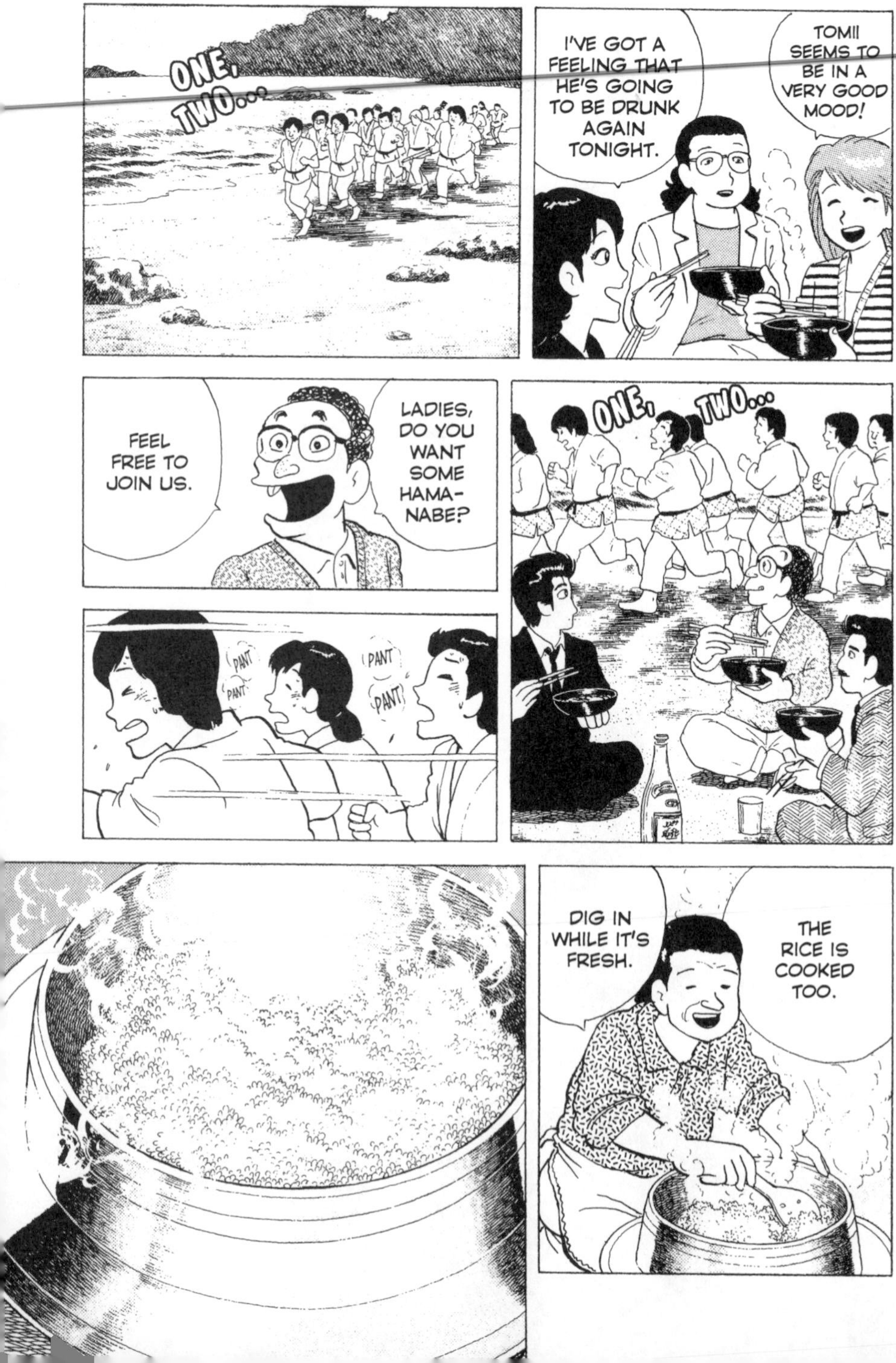

TOMII SEEMS TO BE IN A VERY GOOD MOOD!
I'VE GOT A FEELING THAT HE'S GOING TO BE DRUNK AGAIN TONIGHT.
ONE, TWO...
ONE, TWO...
LADIES, DO YOU WANT SOME HAMA-NABE?
FEEL FREE TO JOIN US.
PANT PANT
PANT PANT
PANT
THE RICE IS COOKED TOO.
DIG IN WHILE IT'S FRESH.

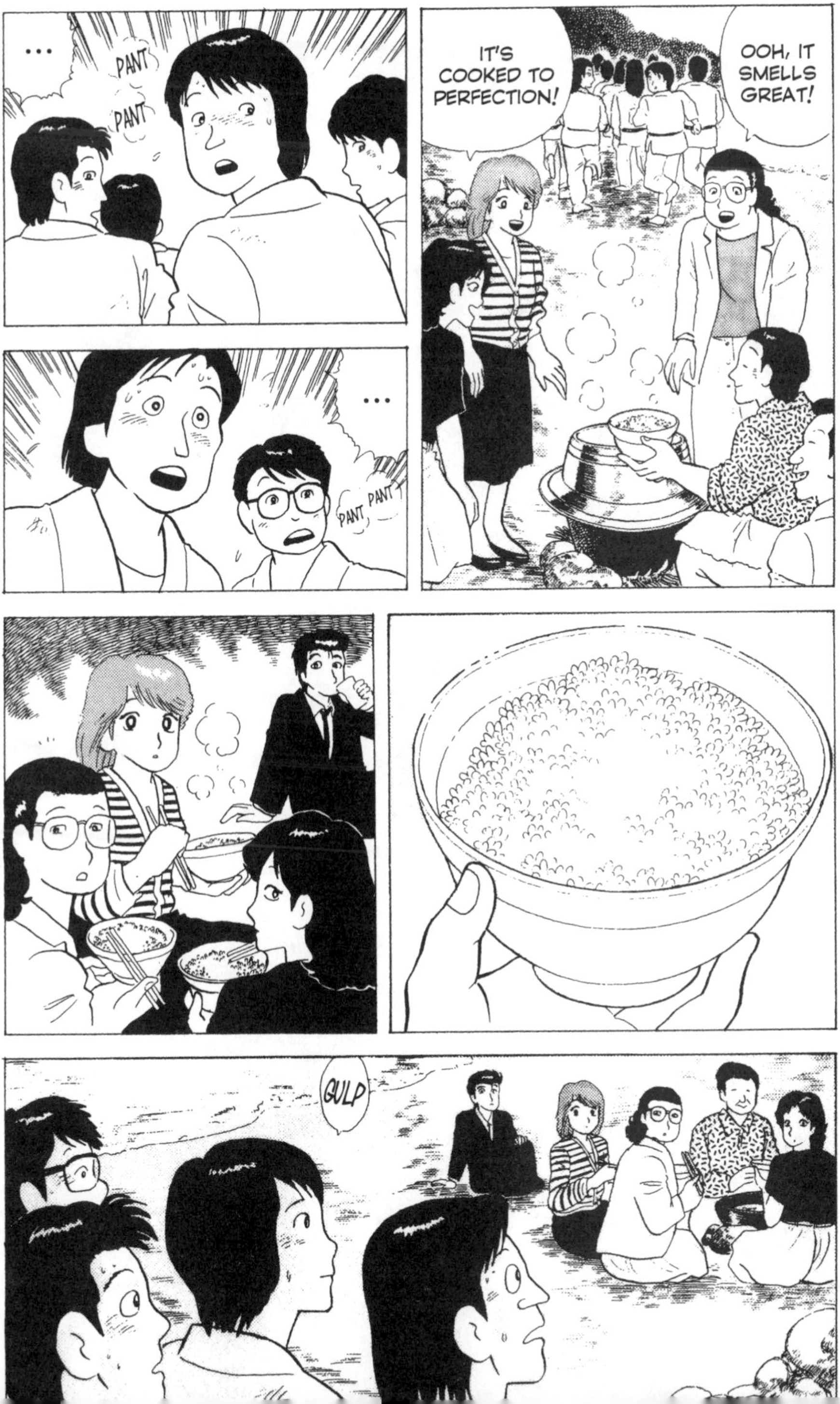
OOH, IT SMELLS GREAT!
IT'S COOKED TO PERFECTION!
...
PANT
PANT
...
PANT
PANT
GULP

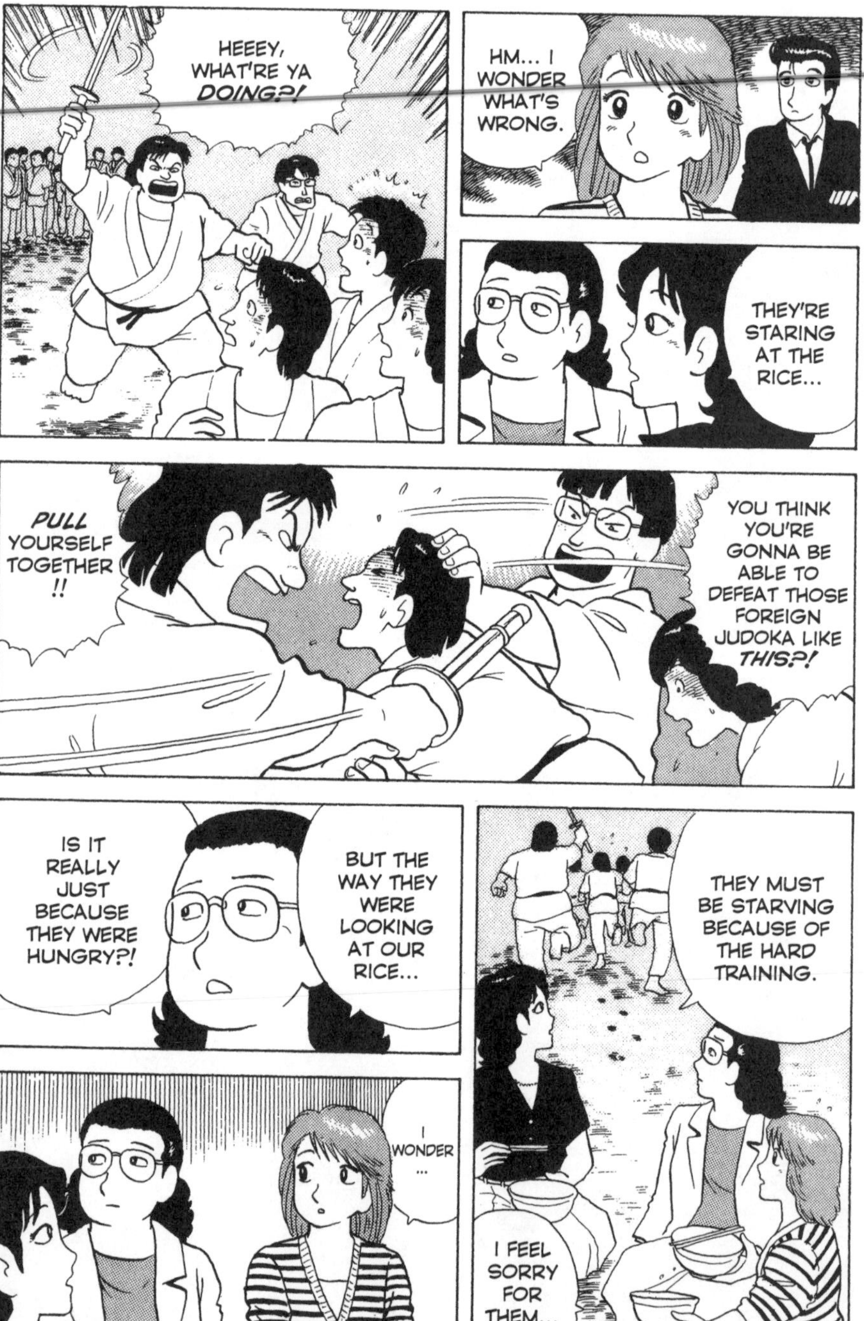
HM... I WONDER WHAT'S WRONG.
THEY'RE STARING AT THE RICE...
HEEEY, WHAT'RE YA *DOING?!*
YOU THINK YOU'RE GONNA BE ABLE TO DEFEAT THOSE FOREIGN JUDOKA LIKE *THIS?!*
PULL YOURSELF TOGETHER !!
THEY MUST BE STARVING BECAUSE OF THE HARD TRAINING.
I FEEL SORRY FOR THEM...
BUT THE WAY THEY WERE LOOKING AT OUR RICE...
IS IT REALLY JUST BECAUSE THEY WERE HUNGRY?!
I WONDER ...

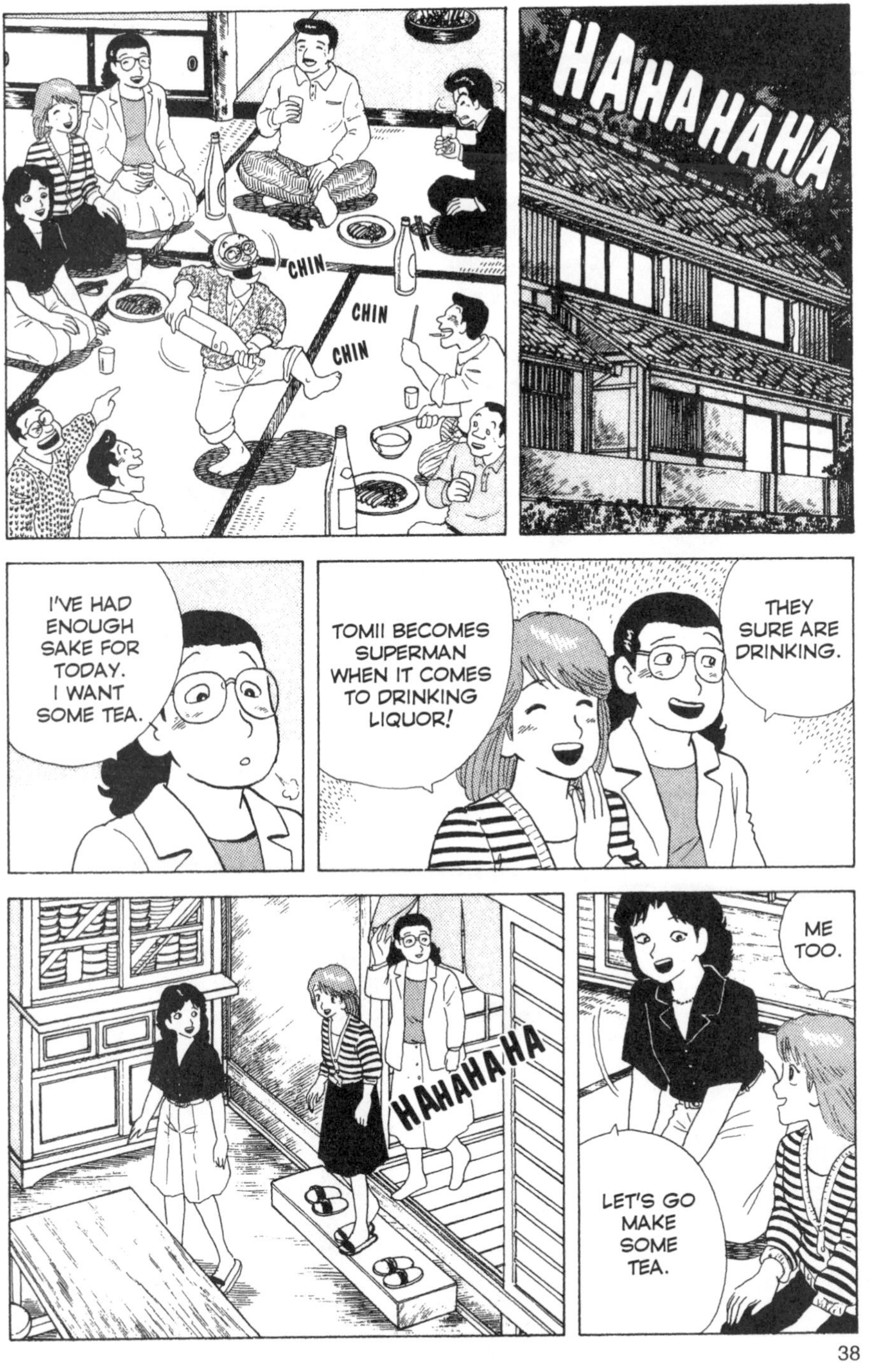
HAHAHAHAHA
CHIN
CHIN
CHIN
THEY SURE ARE DRINKING.
TOMII BECOMES SUPERMAN WHEN IT COMES TO DRINKING LIQUOR!
I'VE HAD ENOUGH SAKE FOR TODAY. I WANT SOME TEA.
ME TOO.
LET'S GO MAKE SOME TEA.
HAHAHAHA

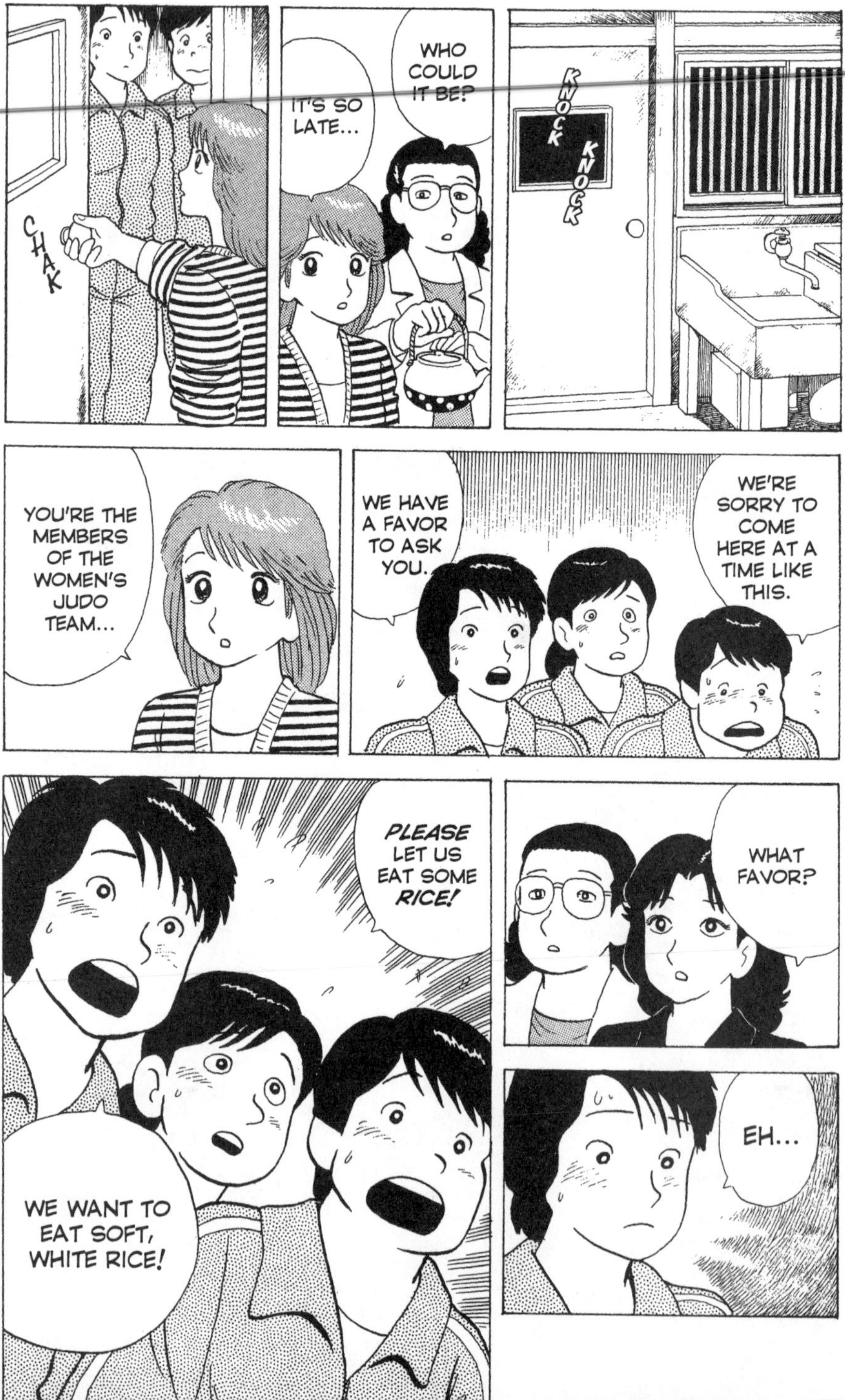
KNOCK
KNOCK
WHO COULD IT BE?
IT'S SO LATE...
CHAK
WE'RE SORRY TO COME HERE AT A TIME LIKE THIS.
WE HAVE A FAVOR TO ASK YOU.
YOU'RE THE MEMBERS OF THE WOMEN'S JUDO TEAM...
WHAT FAVOR?
EH...
PLEASE LET US EAT SOME *RICE!*
WE WANT TO EAT SOFT, WHITE RICE!

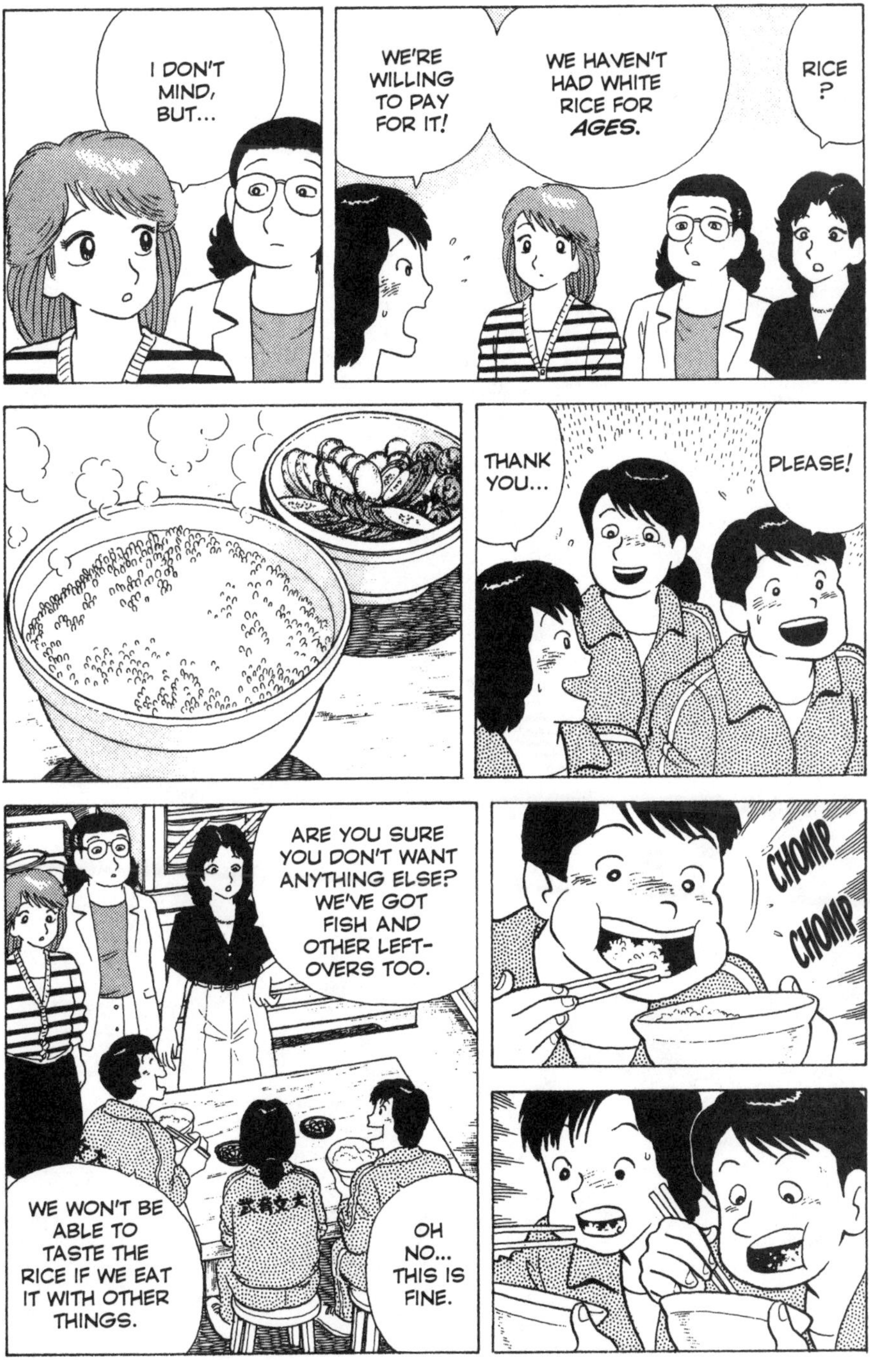
RICE ?
WE HAVEN'T HAD WHITE RICE FOR AGES.
WE'RE WILLING TO PAY FOR IT!
I DON'T MIND, BUT...
PLEASE!
THANK YOU...
CHOMP
CHOMP
ARE YOU SURE YOU DON'T WANT ANYTHING ELSE? WE'VE GOT FISH AND OTHER LEFT-OVERS TOO.
OH NO... THIS IS FINE.
WE WON'T BE ABLE TO TASTE THE RICE IF WE EAT IT WITH OTHER THINGS.

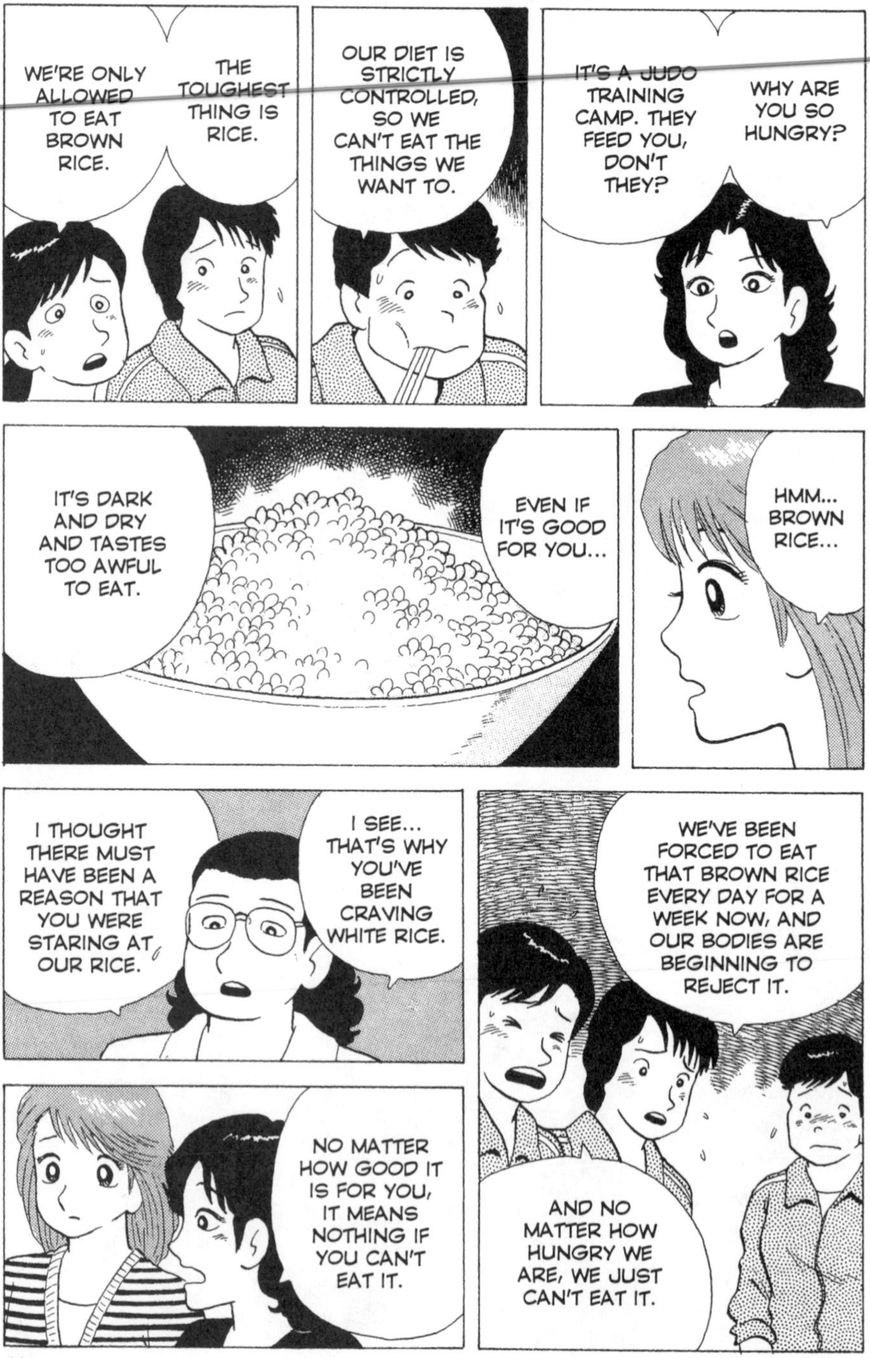
WHY ARE YOU SO HUNGRY?
IT'S A JUDO TRAINING CAMP. THEY FEED YOU, DON'T THEY?
OUR DIET IS STRICTLY CONTROLLED, SO WE CAN'T EAT THE THINGS WE WANT TO.
THE TOUGHEST THING IS RICE.
WE'RE ONLY ALLOWED TO EAT BROWN RICE.
HMM... BROWN RICE...
EVEN IF IT'S GOOD FOR YOU...
IT'S DARK AND DRY AND TASTES TOO AWFUL TO EAT.
WE'VE BEEN FORCED TO EAT THAT BROWN RICE EVERY DAY FOR A WEEK NOW, AND OUR BODIES ARE BEGINNING TO REJECT IT.
AND NO MATTER HOW HUNGRY WE ARE, WE JUST CAN'T EAT IT.
I SEE... THAT'S WHY YOU'VE BEEN CRAVING WHITE RICE.
I THOUGHT THERE MUST HAVE BEEN A REASON THAT YOU WERE STARING AT OUR RICE.
NO MATTER HOW GOOD IT IS FOR YOU, IT MEANS NOTHING IF YOU CAN'T EAT IT.

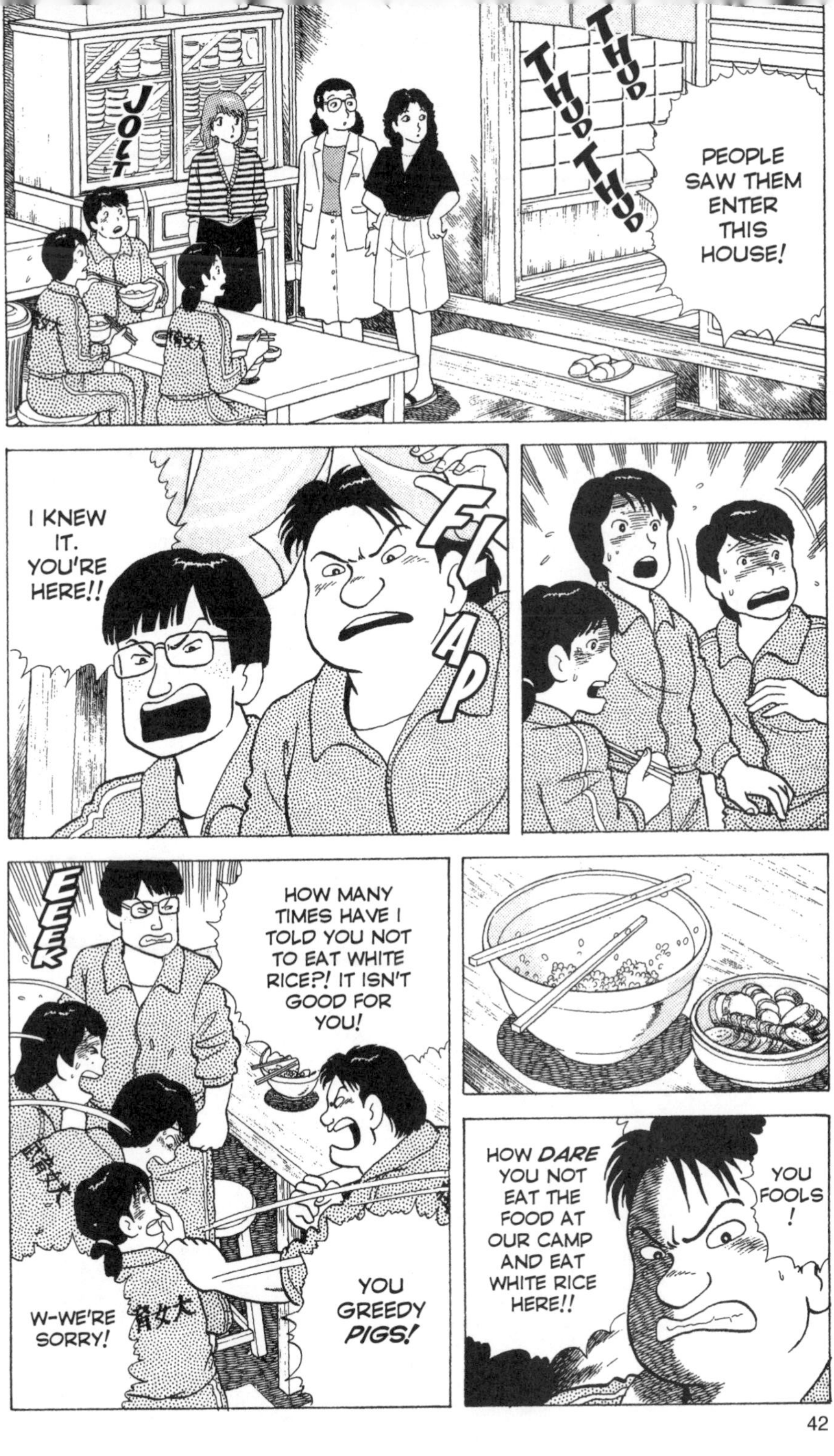

THUD
THUD
THUD
PEOPLE SAW THEM ENTER THIS HOUSE!
JOLT
FLAP
I KNEW IT. YOU'RE HERE!!
YOU FOOLS!
HOW *DARE* YOU NOT EAT THE FOOD AT OUR CAMP AND EAT WHITE RICE HERE!!
HOW MANY TIMES HAVE I TOLD YOU NOT TO EAT WHITE RICE?! IT ISN'T GOOD FOR YOU!
EEEK
YOU GREEDY *PIGS!*
W-WE'RE SORRY!

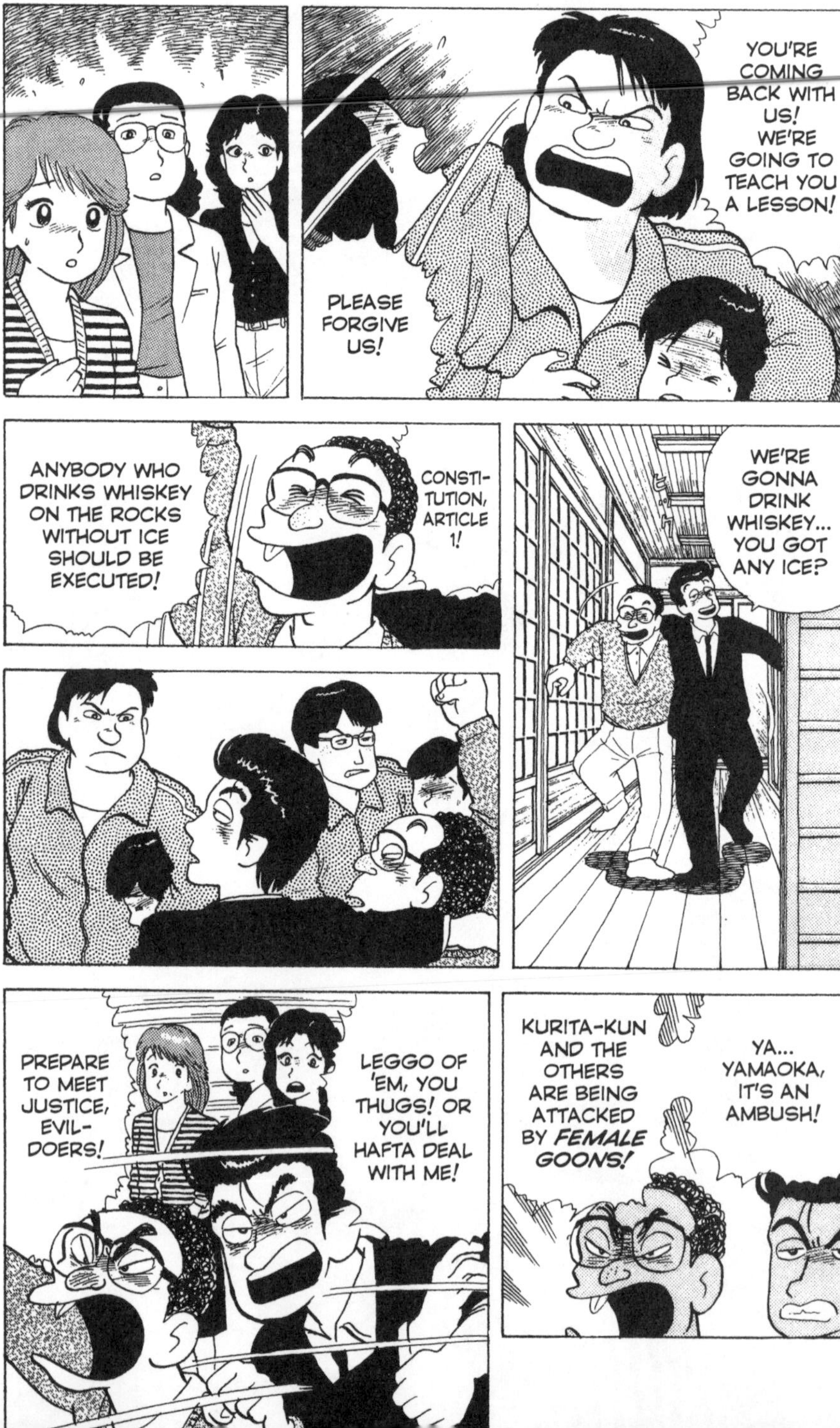
YOU'RE COMING BACK WITH US! WE'RE GOING TO TEACH YOU A LESSON!
PLEASE FORGIVE US!
WE'RE GONNA DRINK WHISKEY... YOU GOT ANY ICE?
CONSTI-TUTION, ARTICLE 1!
ANYBODY WHO DRINKS WHISKEY ON THE ROCKS WITHOUT ICE SHOULD BE EXECUTED!
YA... YAMAOKA, IT'S AN AMBUSH!
KURITA-KUN AND THE OTHERS ARE BEING ATTACKED BY *FEMALE GOONS!*
LEGGO OF 'EM, YOU THUGS! OR YOU'LL HAFTA DEAL WITH ME!
PREPARE TO MEET JUSTICE, EVIL-DOERS!

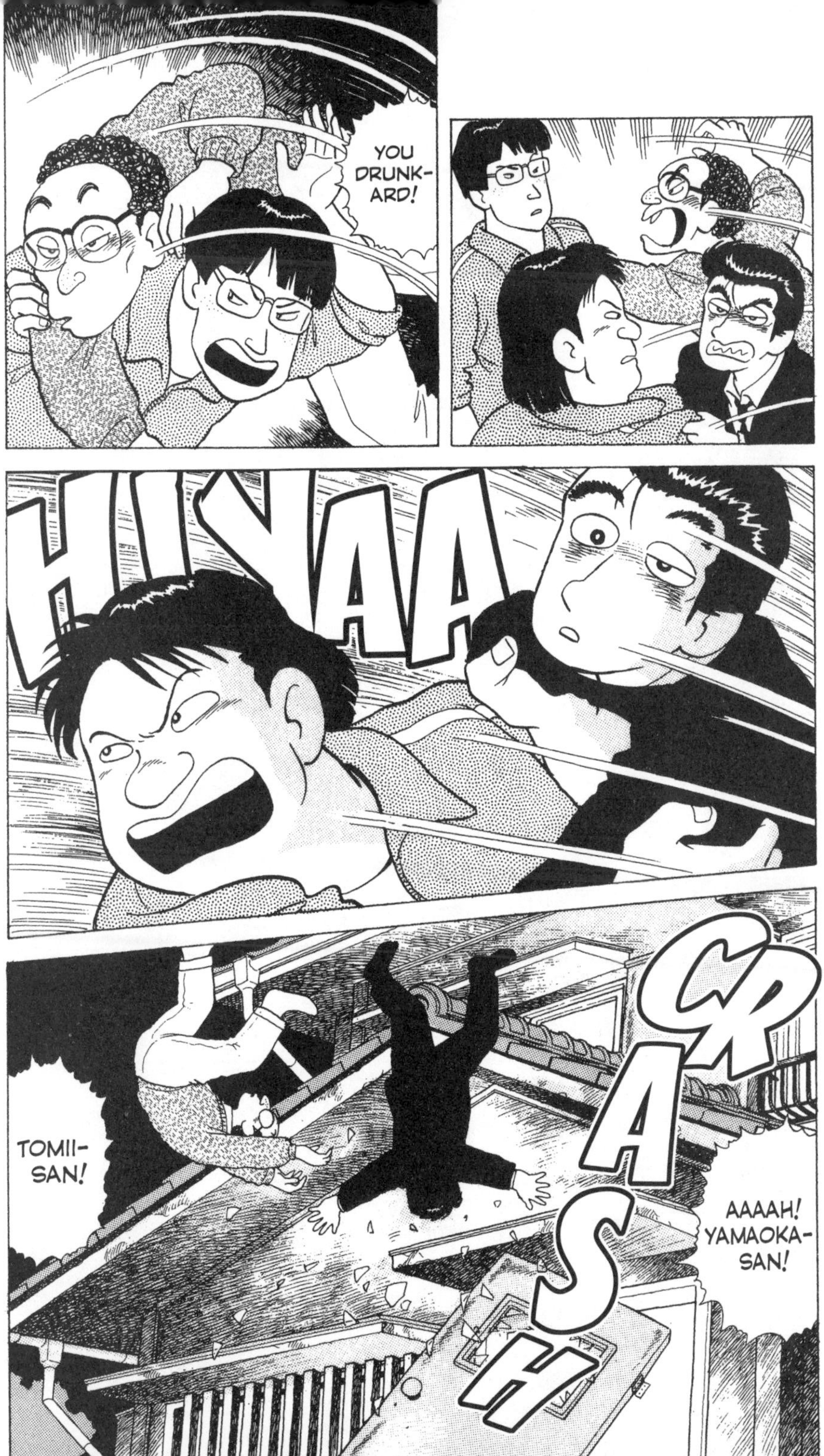
YOU DRUNK-ARD!
HIYAA
CRASH
AAAAH! YAMAOKA-SAN!
TOMII-SAN!

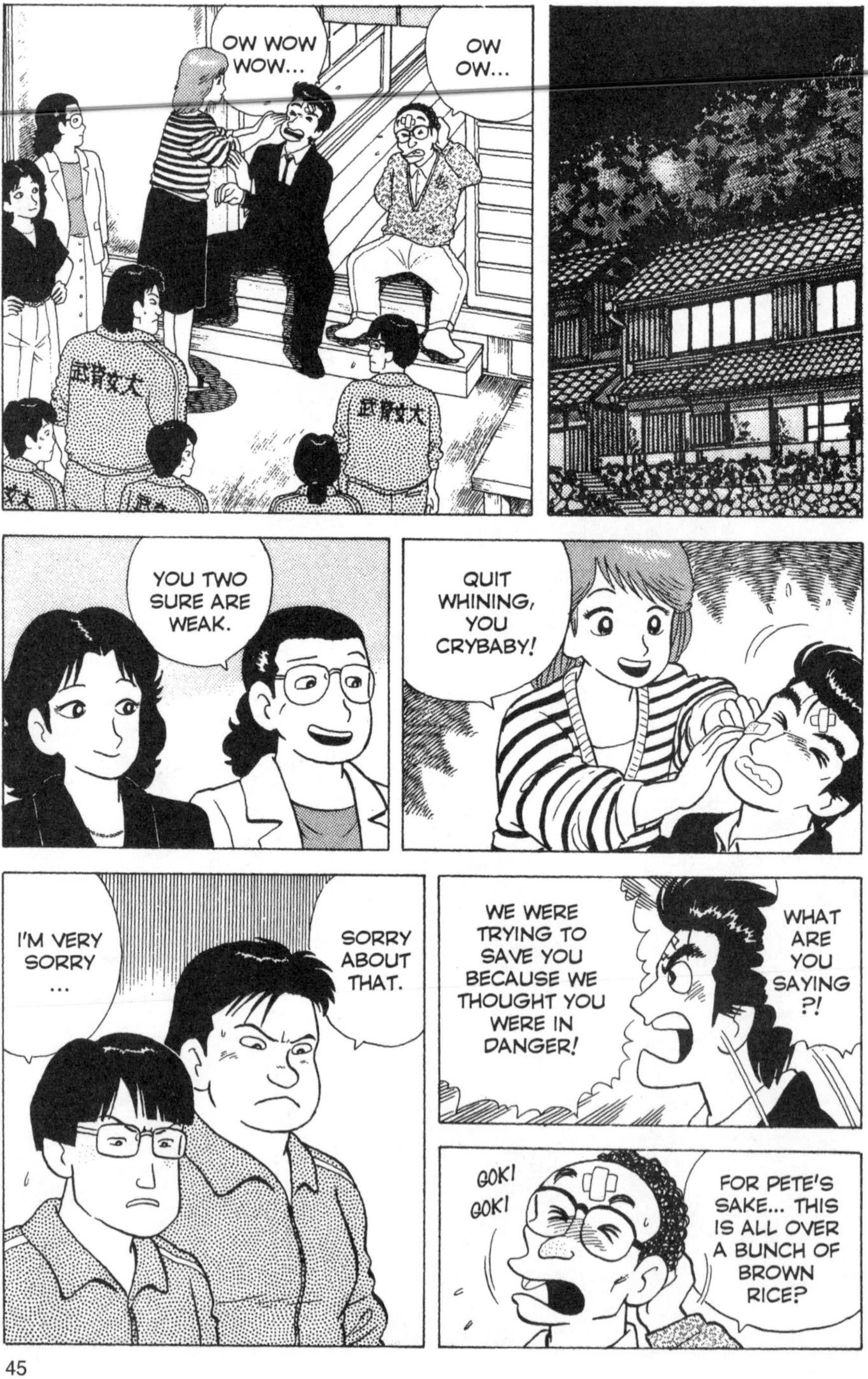
OW OW...
OW WOW WOW...
QUIT WHINING, YOU CRYBABY!
YOU TWO SURE ARE WEAK.
WHAT ARE YOU SAYING?!
WE WERE TRYING TO SAVE YOU BECAUSE WE THOUGHT YOU WERE IN DANGER!
FOR PETE'S SAKE... THIS IS ALL OVER A BUNCH OF BROWN RICE?
GOK! GOK!
SORRY ABOUT THAT.
I'M VERY SORRY ...

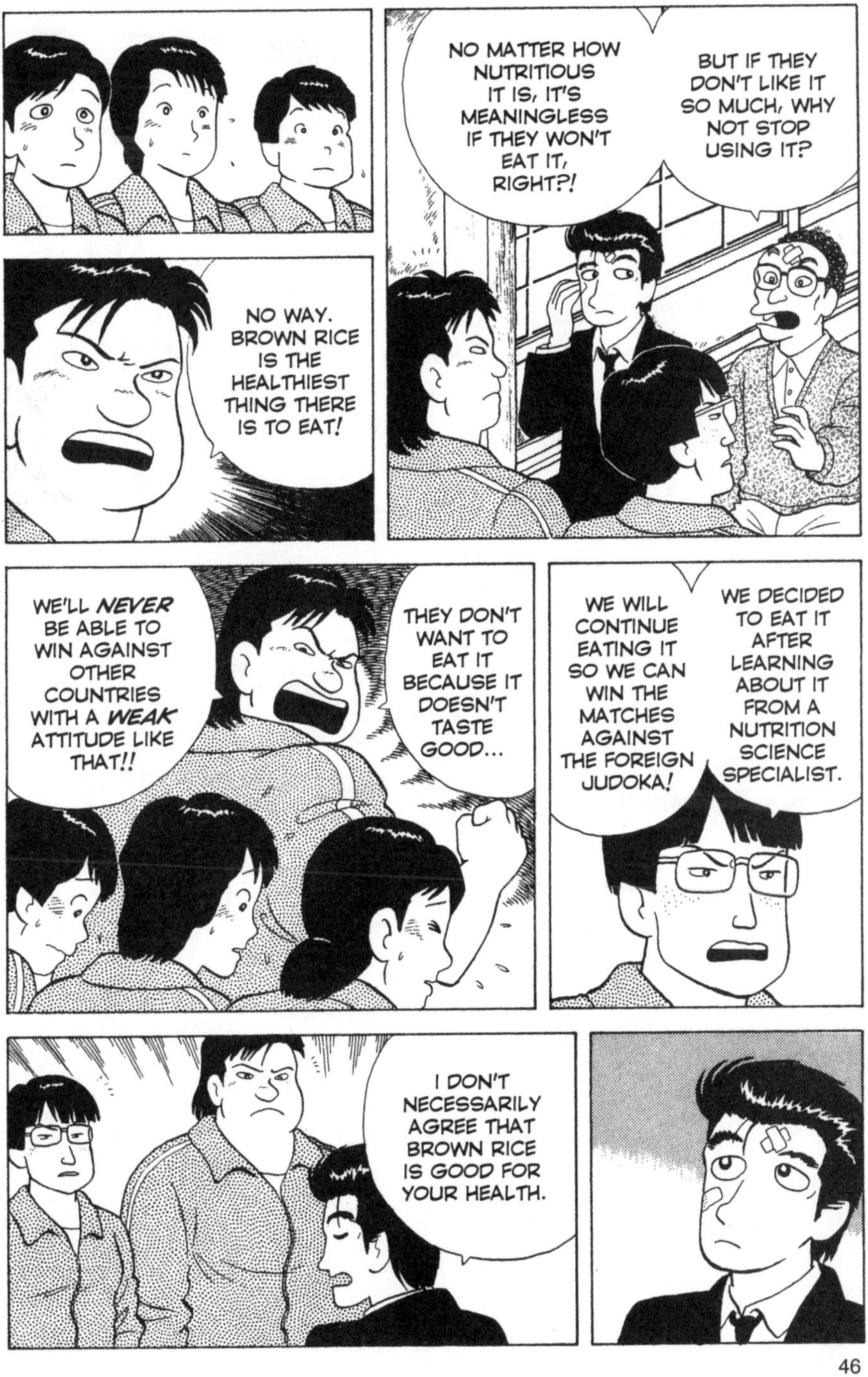
BUT IF THEY DON'T LIKE IT SO MUCH, WHY NOT STOP USING IT?
NO MATTER HOW NUTRITIOUS IT IS, IT'S MEANINGLESS IF THEY WON'T EAT IT, RIGHT?!
NO WAY. BROWN RICE IS THE HEALTHIEST THING THERE IS TO EAT!
WE DECIDED TO EAT IT AFTER LEARNING ABOUT IT FROM A NUTRITION SCIENCE SPECIALIST.
WE WILL CONTINUE EATING IT SO WE CAN WIN THE MATCHES AGAINST THE FOREIGN JUDOKA!
THEY DON'T WANT TO EAT IT BECAUSE IT DOESN'T TASTE GOOD...
WE'LL *NEVER* BE ABLE TO WIN AGAINST OTHER COUNTRIES WITH A *WEAK* ATTITUDE LIKE THAT!!
I DON'T NECESSARILY AGREE THAT BROWN RICE IS GOOD FOR YOUR HEALTH.

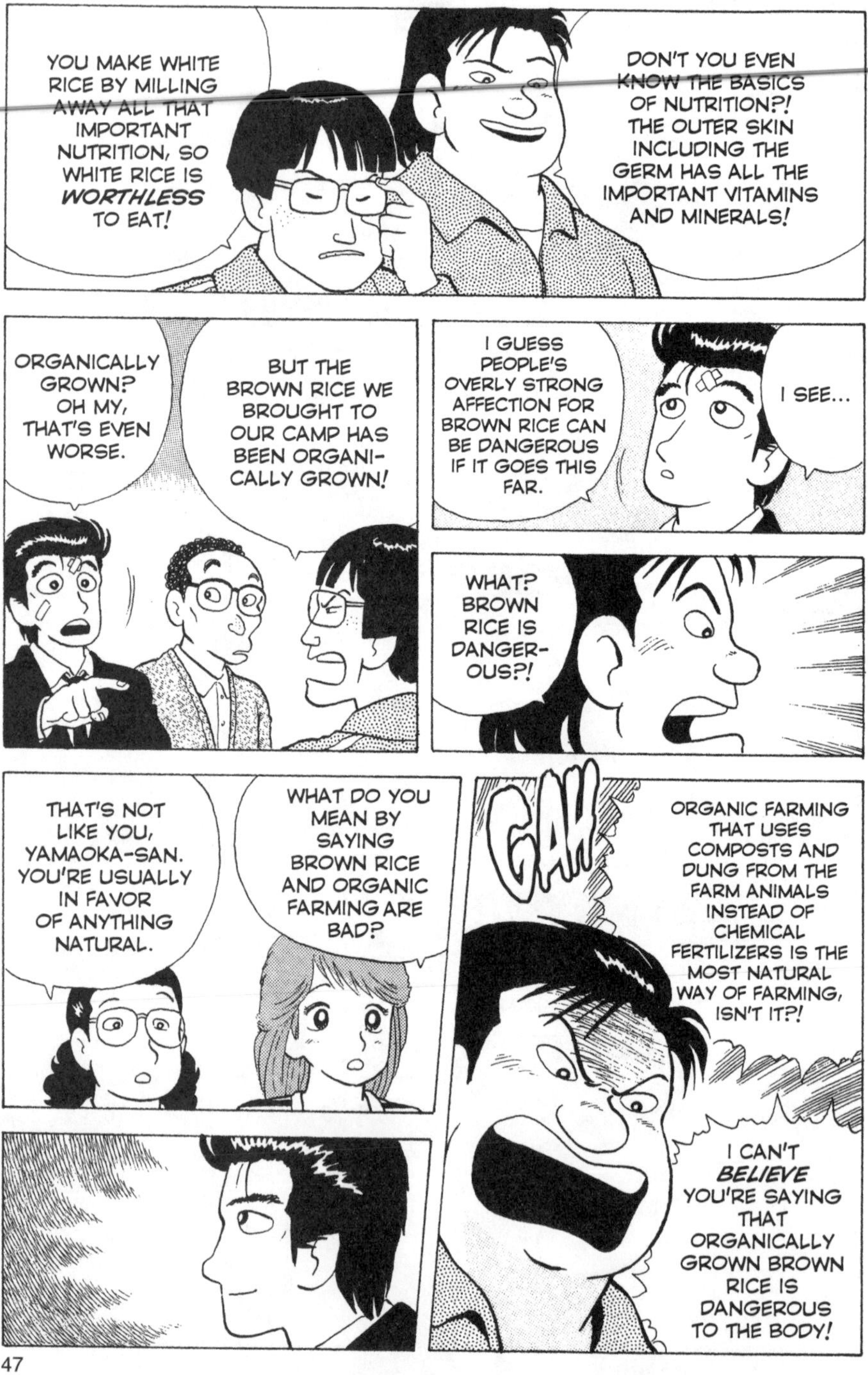
YOU MAKE WHITE RICE BY MILLING AWAY ALL THAT IMPORTANT NUTRITION, SO WHITE RICE IS *WORTHLESS* TO EAT!
DON'T YOU EVEN KNOW THE BASICS OF NUTRITION?! THE OUTER SKIN INCLUDING THE GERM HAS ALL THE IMPORTANT VITAMINS AND MINERALS!
BUT THE BROWN RICE WE BROUGHT TO OUR CAMP HAS BEEN ORGANICALLY GROWN!
ORGANICALLY GROWN? OH MY, THAT'S EVEN WORSE.
I GUESS PEOPLE'S OVERLY STRONG AFFECTION FOR BROWN RICE CAN BE DANGEROUS IF IT GOES THIS FAR.
I SEE...
WHAT? BROWN RICE IS DANGEROUS?!
THAT'S NOT LIKE YOU, YAMAOKA-SAN. YOU'RE USUALLY IN FAVOR OF ANYTHING NATURAL.
WHAT DO YOU MEAN BY SAYING BROWN RICE AND ORGANIC FARMING ARE BAD?
GAH
ORGANIC FARMING THAT USES COMPOSTS AND DUNG FROM THE FARM ANIMALS INSTEAD OF CHEMICAL FERTILIZERS IS THE MOST NATURAL WAY OF FARMING, ISN'T IT?!
I CAN'T *BELIEVE* YOU'RE SAYING THAT ORGANICALLY GROWN BROWN RICE IS DANGEROUS TO THE BODY!

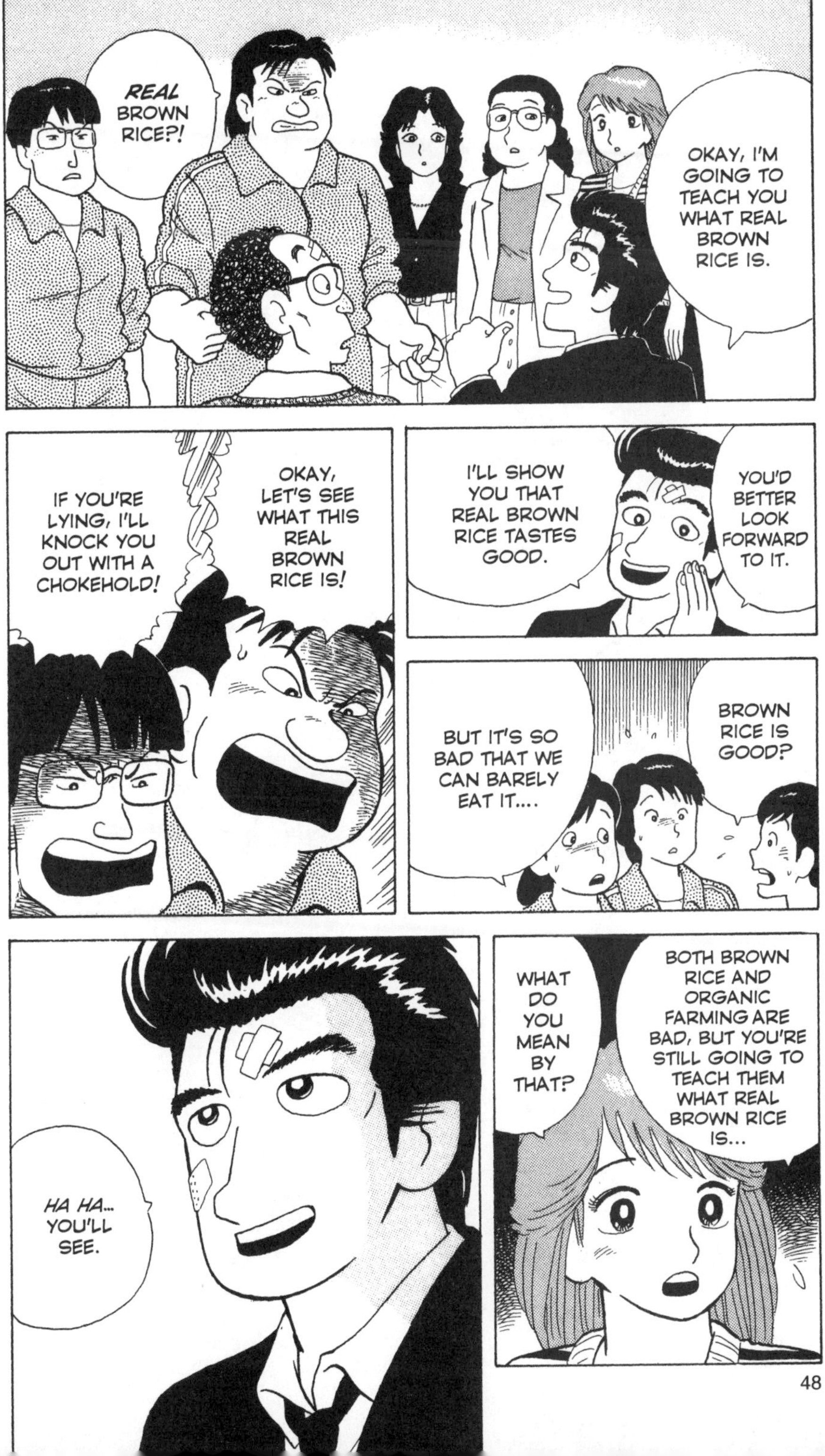
OKAY, I'M GOING TO TEACH YOU WHAT REAL BROWN RICE IS.
REAL BROWN RICE?!
YOU'D BETTER LOOK FORWARD TO IT.
I'LL SHOW YOU THAT REAL BROWN RICE TASTES GOOD.
BROWN RICE IS GOOD?
BUT IT'S SO BAD THAT WE CAN BARELY EAT IT....
OKAY, LET'S SEE WHAT THIS REAL BROWN RICE IS!
IF YOU'RE LYING, I'LL KNOCK YOU OUT WITH A CHOKEHOLD!
BOTH BROWN RICE AND ORGANIC FARMING ARE BAD, BUT YOU'RE STILL GOING TO TEACH THEM WHAT REAL BROWN RICE IS...
WHAT DO YOU MEAN BY THAT?
HA HA... YOU'LL SEE.

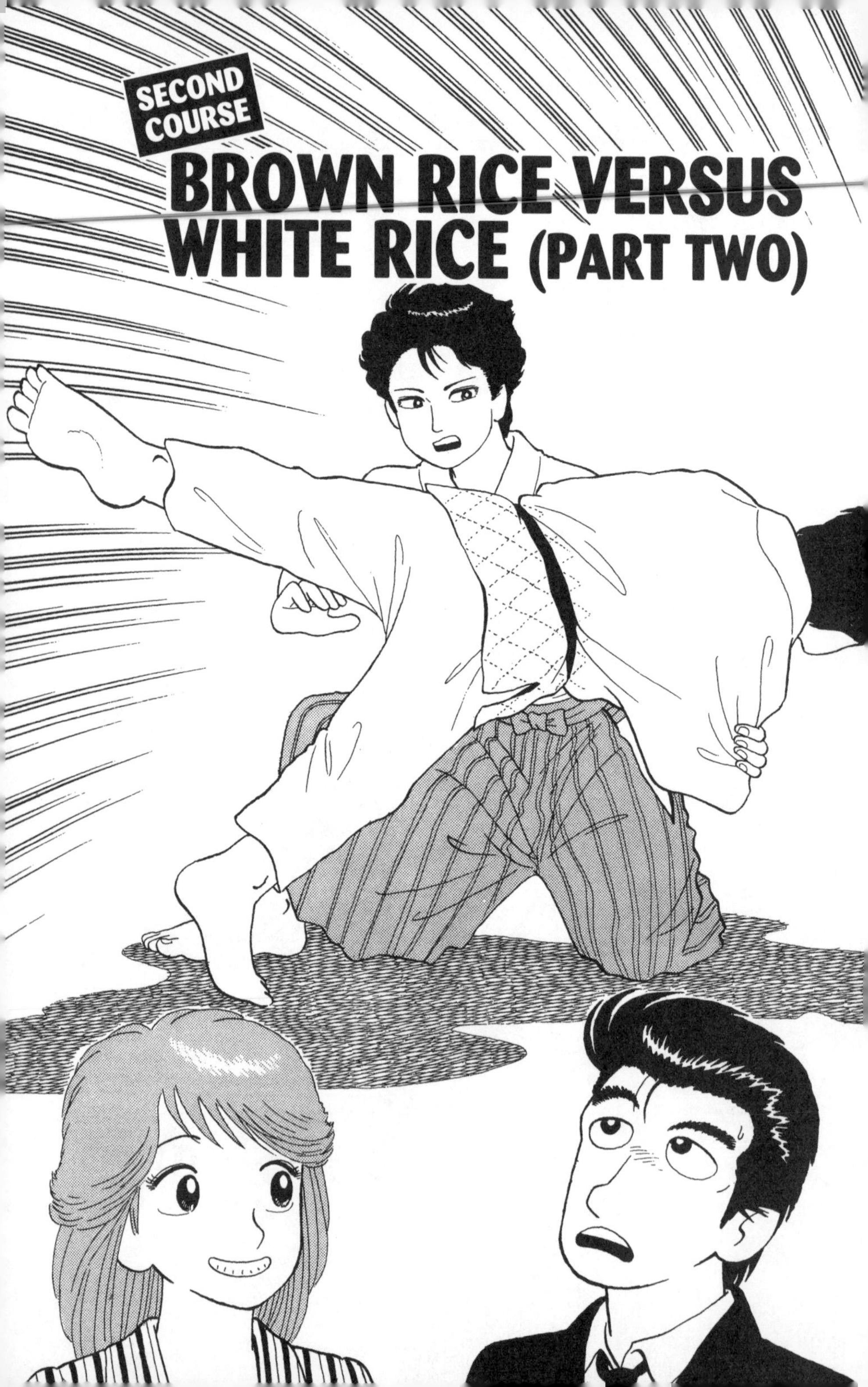
SECOND COURSE
BROWN RICE VERSUS WHITE RICE (PART TWO)

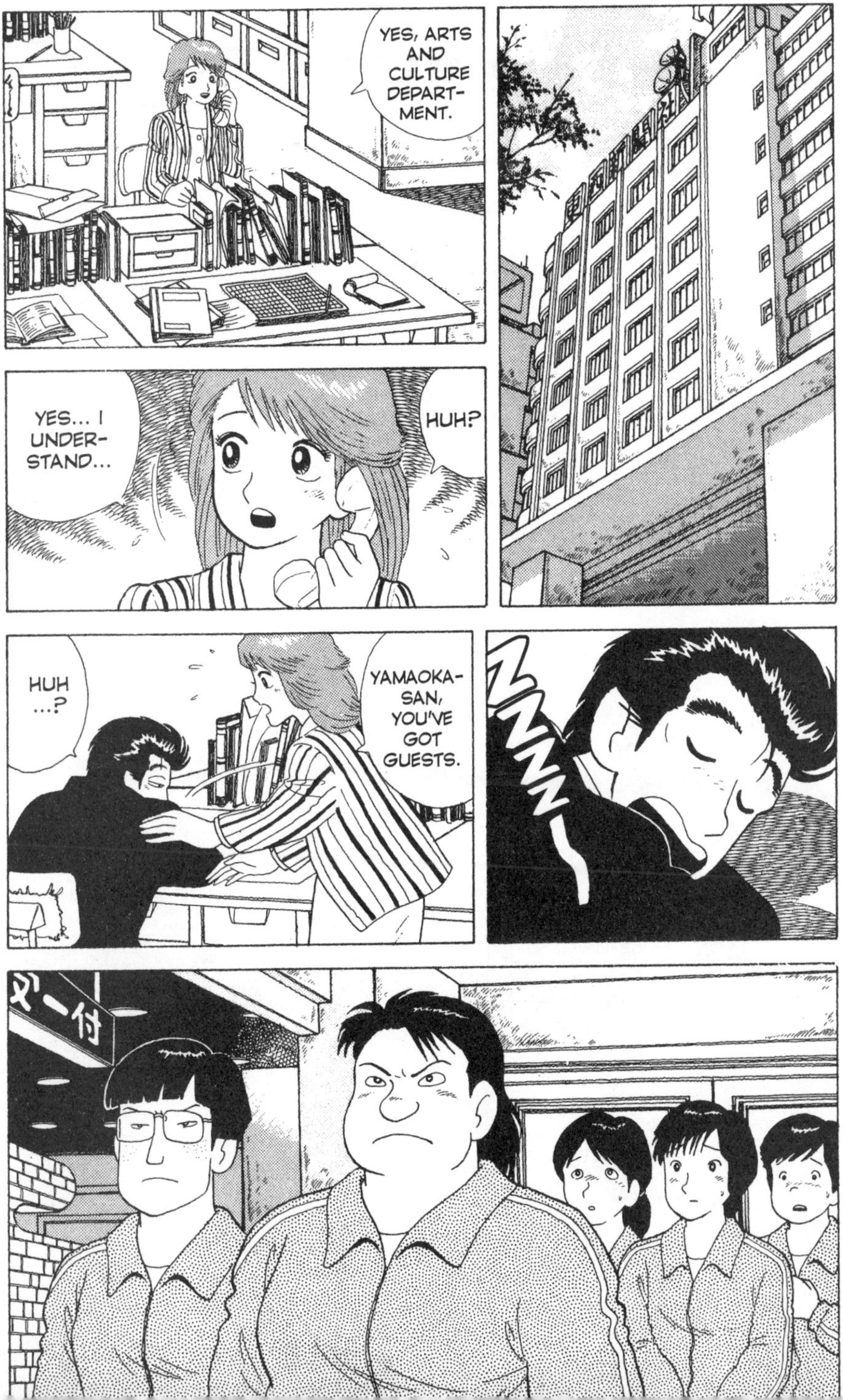
YES, ARTS AND CULTURE DEPART-MENT.
HUH?
YES... I UNDER-STAND...
NNNN—
YAMAOKA-SAN, YOU'VE GOT GUESTS.
HUH ...?

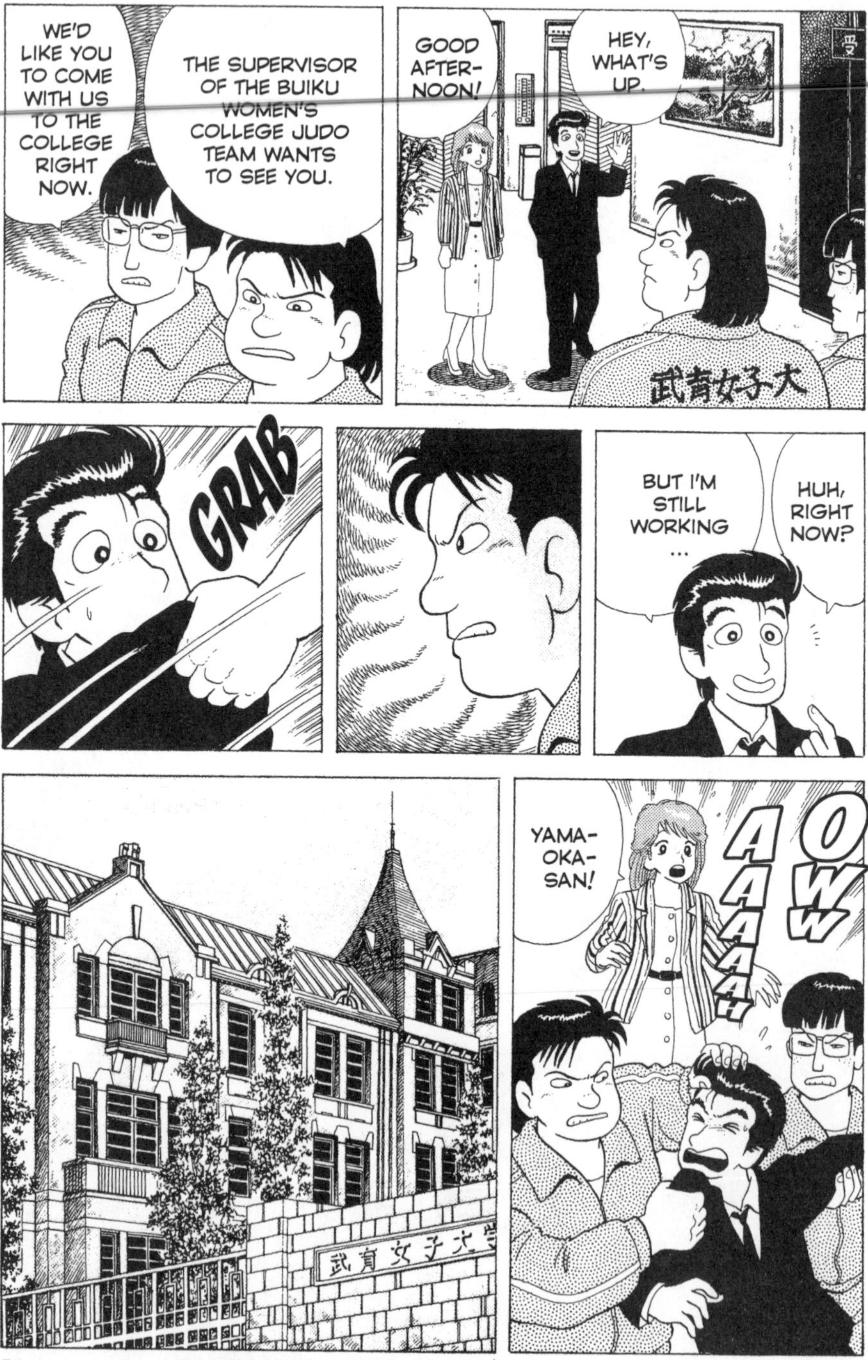
HEY, WHAT'S UP.
GOOD AFTERNOON!
武育女子大
THE SUPERVISOR OF THE BUIKU WOMEN'S COLLEGE JUDO TEAM WANTS TO SEE YOU.
WE'D LIKE YOU TO COME WITH US TO THE COLLEGE RIGHT NOW.
HUH, RIGHT NOW?
BUT I'M STILL WORKING ...
GRAB
OWW
AAAAAAH
YAMA-OKA-SAN!
武育女子大

ON SIGN: BUIKU WOMEN'S COLLEGE

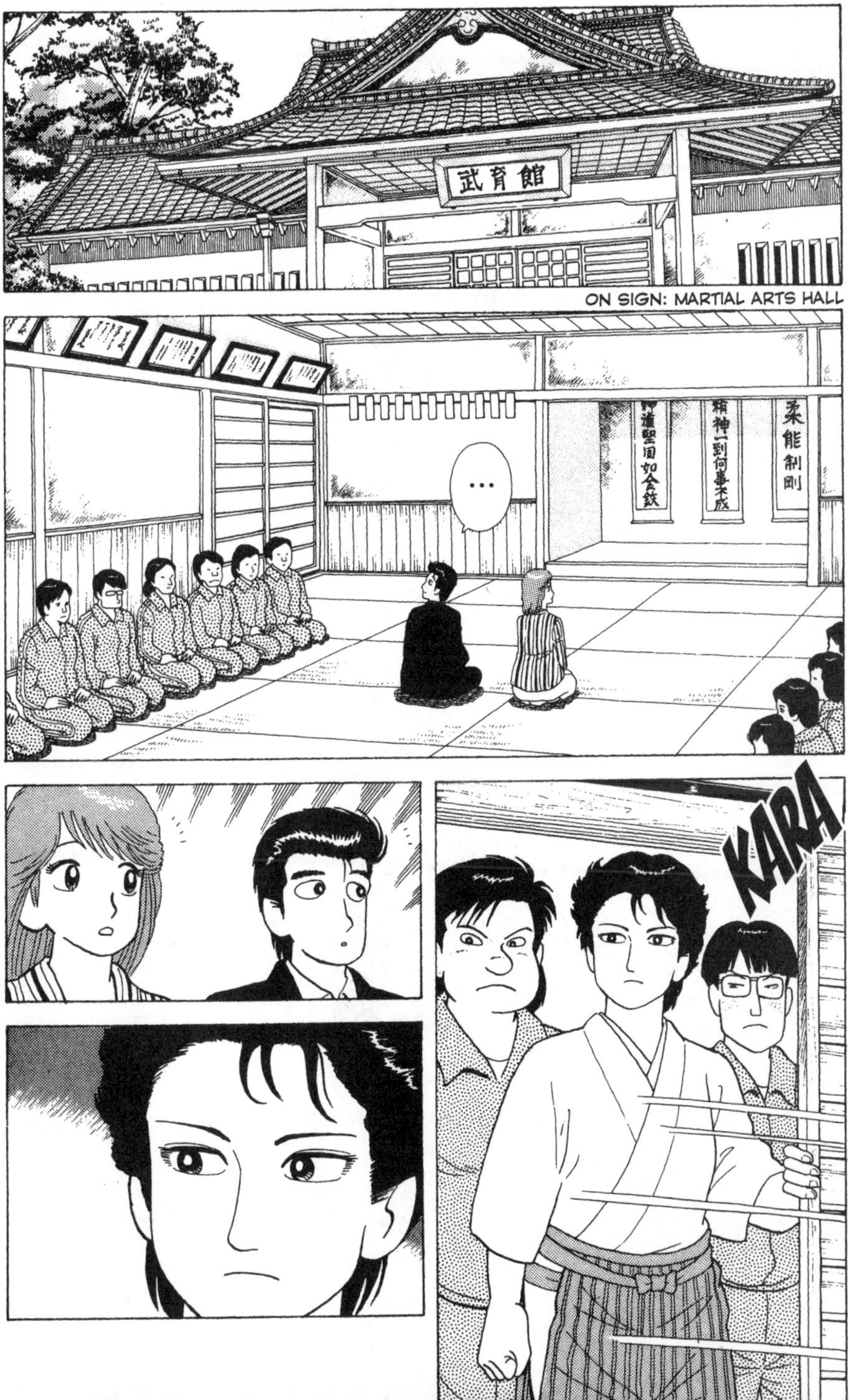
ON SIGN: MARTIAL ARTS HALL
...
KARA

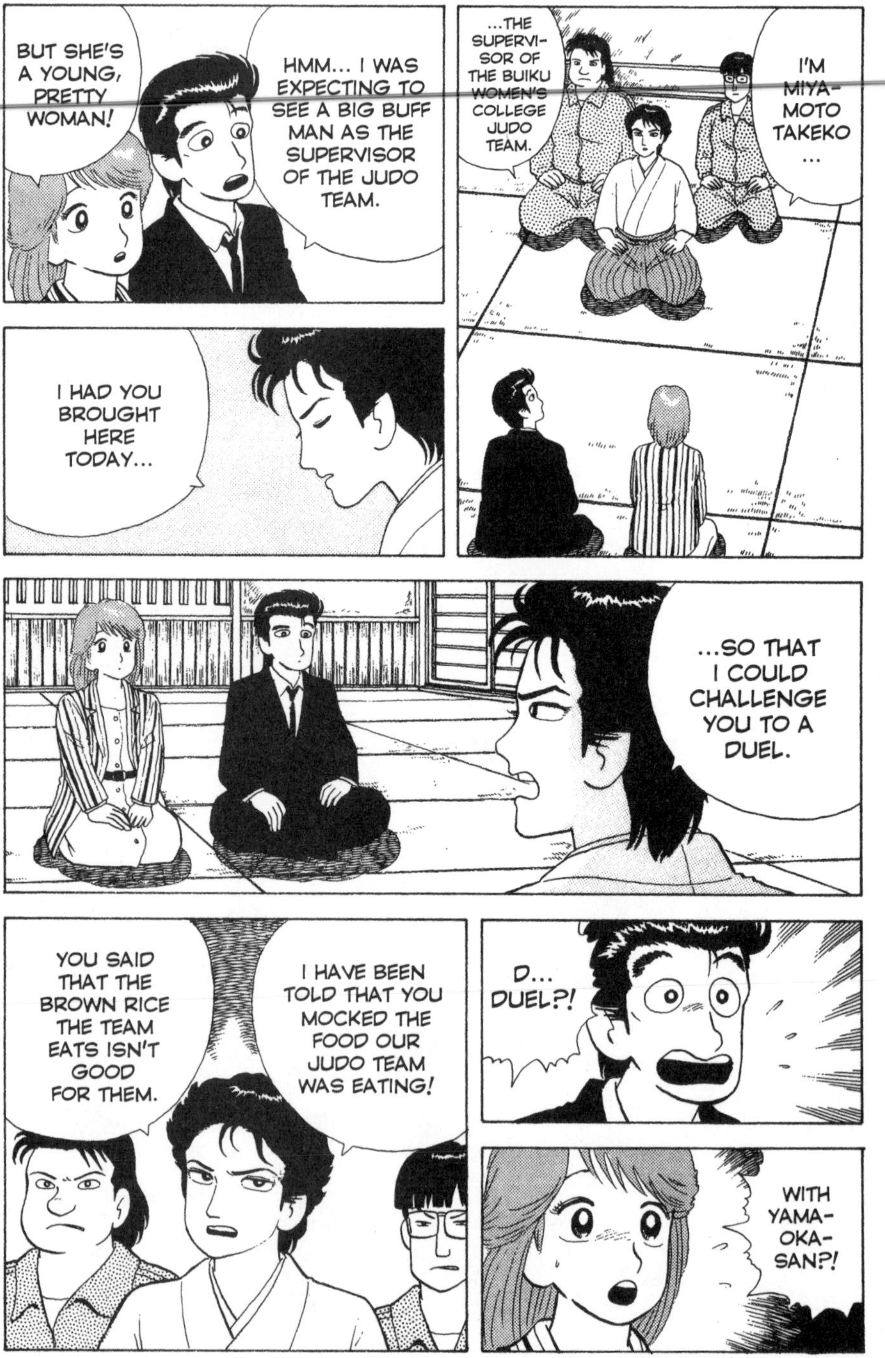
I'M MIYA-MOTO TAKEKO...
...THE SUPERVI-SOR OF THE BUIKU WOMEN'S COLLEGE JUDO TEAM.
HMM... I WAS EXPECTING TO SEE A BIG BUFF MAN AS THE SUPERVISOR OF THE JUDO TEAM.
BUT SHE'S A YOUNG, PRETTY WOMAN!
I HAD YOU BROUGHT HERE TODAY...
...SO THAT I COULD CHALLENGE YOU TO A DUEL.
D... DUEL?!
WITH YAMA-OKA-SAN?!
I HAVE BEEN TOLD THAT YOU MOCKED THE FOOD OUR JUDO TEAM WAS EATING!
YOU SAID THAT THE BROWN RICE THE TEAM EATS ISN'T GOOD FOR THEM.

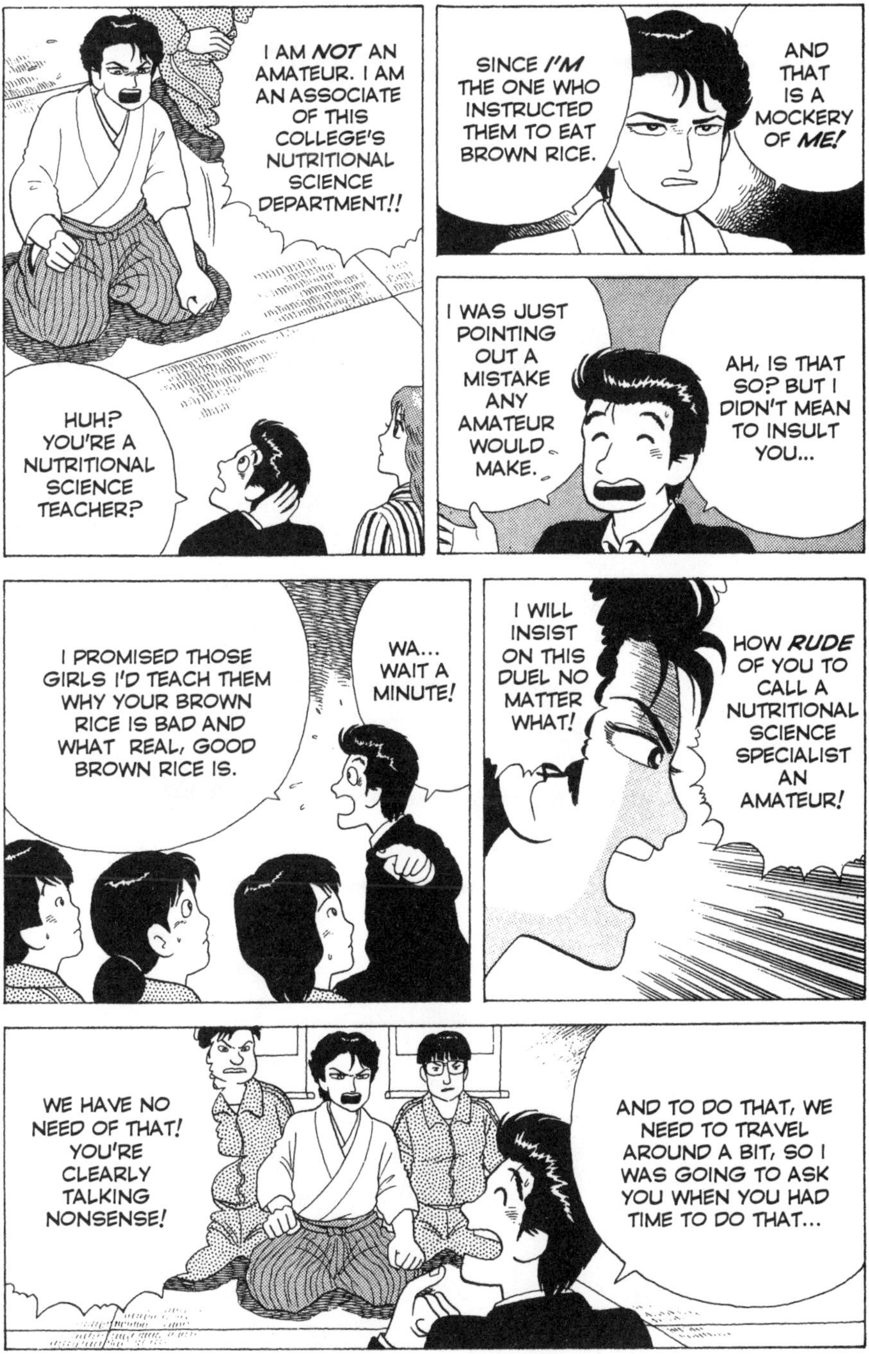
AND THAT IS A MOCKERY OF *ME!*
SINCE *I'M* THE ONE WHO INSTRUCTED THEM TO EAT BROWN RICE.
AH, IS THAT SO? BUT I DIDN'T MEAN TO INSULT YOU...
I WAS JUST POINTING OUT A MISTAKE ANY AMATEUR WOULD MAKE.
I AM ***NOT*** AN AMATEUR. I AM AN ASSOCIATE OF THIS COLLEGE'S NUTRITIONAL SCIENCE DEPARTMENT!!
HUH? YOU'RE A NUTRITIONAL SCIENCE TEACHER?
HOW ***RUDE*** OF YOU TO CALL A NUTRITIONAL SCIENCE SPECIALIST AN AMATEUR!
I WILL INSIST ON THIS DUEL NO MATTER WHAT!
WA... WAIT A MINUTE!
I PROMISED THOSE GIRLS I'D TEACH THEM WHY YOUR BROWN RICE IS BAD AND WHAT REAL, GOOD BROWN RICE IS.
AND TO DO THAT, WE NEED TO TRAVEL AROUND A BIT, SO I WAS GOING TO ASK YOU WHEN YOU HAD TIME TO DO THAT...
WE HAVE NO NEED OF THAT! YOU'RE CLEARLY TALKING NONSENSE!

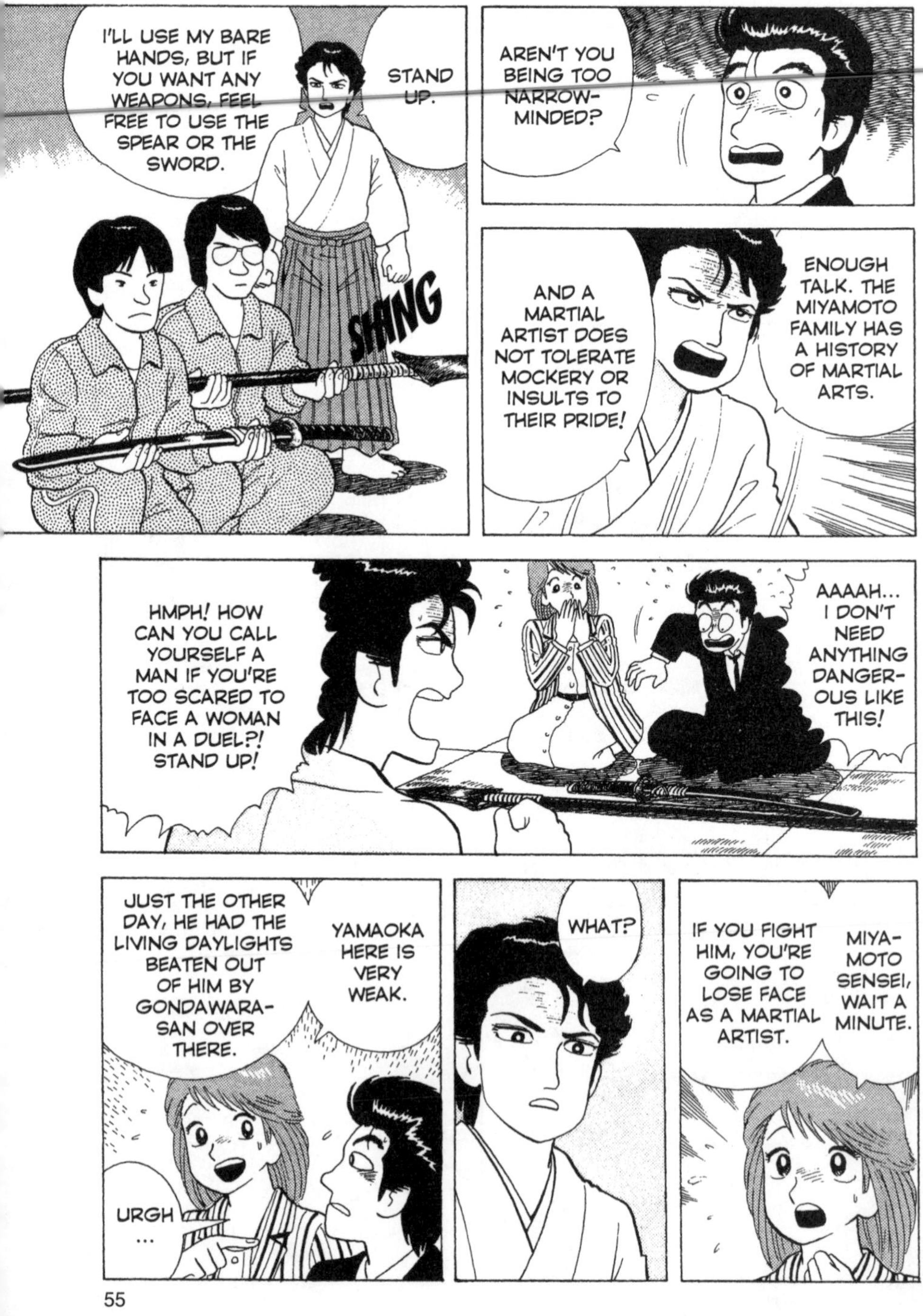
AREN'T YOU BEING TOO NARROW-MINDED?
ENOUGH TALK. THE MIYAMOTO FAMILY HAS A HISTORY OF MARTIAL ARTS.
AND A MARTIAL ARTIST DOES NOT TOLERATE MOCKERY OR INSULTS TO THEIR PRIDE!
STAND UP.
I'LL USE MY BARE HANDS, BUT IF YOU WANT ANY WEAPONS, FEEL FREE TO USE THE SPEAR OR THE SWORD.
SHING
AAAAH... I DON'T NEED ANYTHING DANGER-OUS LIKE THIS!
HMPH! HOW CAN YOU CALL YOURSELF A MAN IF YOU'RE TOO SCARED TO FACE A WOMAN IN A DUEL?! STAND UP!
MIYA-MOTO SENSEI, WAIT A MINUTE.
IF YOU FIGHT HIM, YOU'RE GOING TO LOSE FACE AS A MARTIAL ARTIST.
WHAT?
YAMAOKA HERE IS VERY WEAK.
JUST THE OTHER DAY, HE HAD THE LIVING DAYLIGHTS BEATEN OUT OF HIM BY GONDAWARA-SAN OVER THERE.
URGH ...

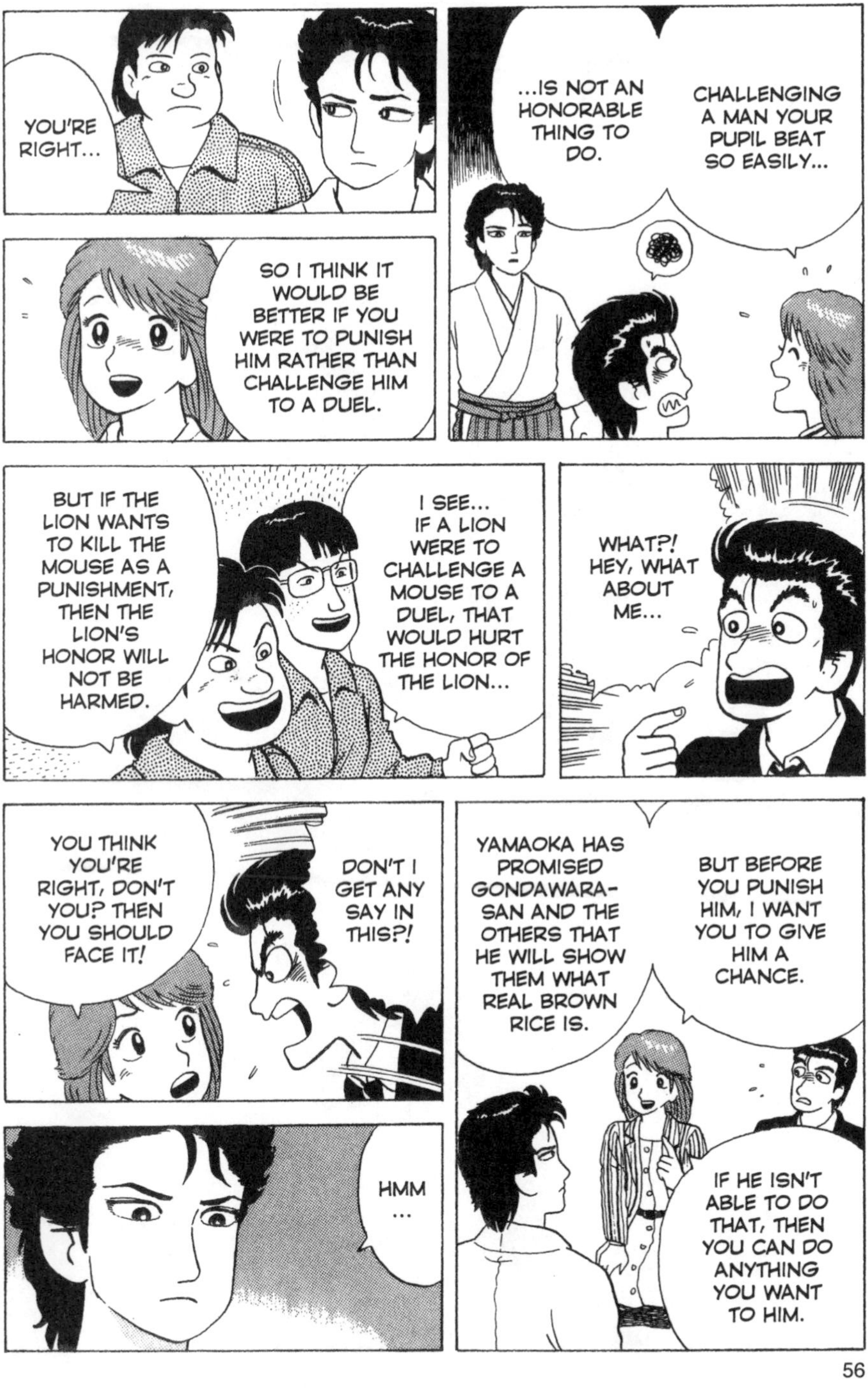
CHALLENGING A MAN YOUR PUPIL BEAT SO EASILY...
...IS NOT AN HONORABLE THING TO DO.
YOU'RE RIGHT...
SO I THINK IT WOULD BE BETTER IF YOU WERE TO PUNISH HIM RATHER THAN CHALLENGE HIM TO A DUEL.
WHAT?! HEY, WHAT ABOUT ME...
I SEE... IF A LION WERE TO CHALLENGE A MOUSE TO A DUEL, THAT WOULD HURT THE HONOR OF THE LION...
BUT IF THE LION WANTS TO KILL THE MOUSE AS A PUNISHMENT, THEN THE LION'S HONOR WILL NOT BE HARMED.
BUT BEFORE YOU PUNISH HIM, I WANT YOU TO GIVE HIM A CHANCE.
YAMAOKA HAS PROMISED GONDAWARA-SAN AND THE OTHERS THAT HE WILL SHOW THEM WHAT REAL BROWN RICE IS.
IF HE ISN'T ABLE TO DO THAT, THEN YOU CAN DO ANYTHING YOU WANT TO HIM.
DON'T I GET ANY SAY IN THIS?!
YOU THINK YOU'RE RIGHT, DON'T YOU? THEN YOU SHOULD FACE IT!
HMM ...

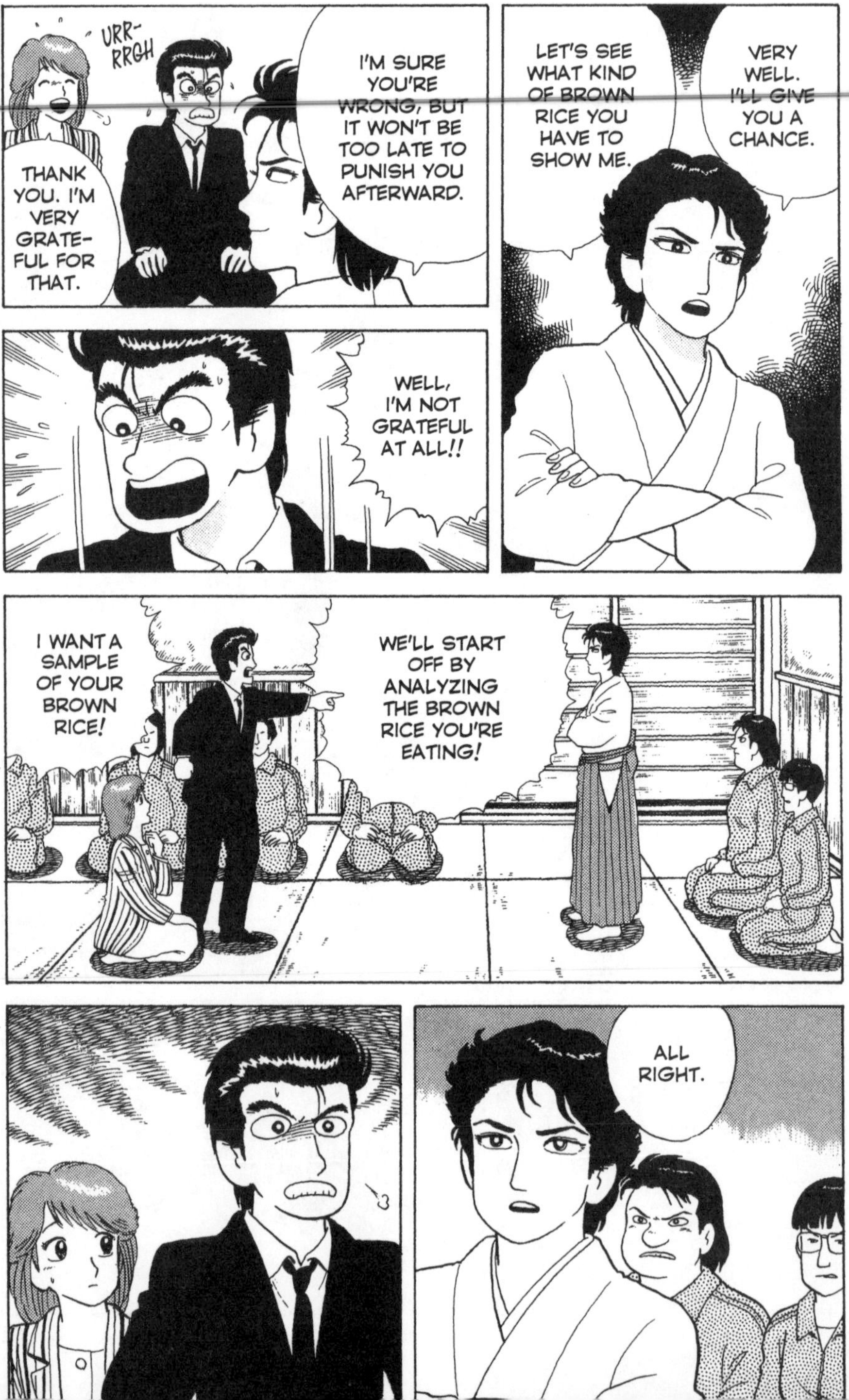
VERY WELL. I'LL GIVE YOU A CHANCE.
LET'S SEE WHAT KIND OF BROWN RICE YOU HAVE TO SHOW ME.
I'M SURE YOU'RE WRONG, BUT IT WON'T BE TOO LATE TO PUNISH YOU AFTERWARD.
URR-RRGH
THANK YOU. I'M VERY GRATE-FUL FOR THAT.
WELL, I'M NOT GRATEFUL AT ALL!!
WE'LL START OFF BY ANALYZING THE BROWN RICE YOU'RE EATING!
I WANT A SAMPLE OF YOUR BROWN RICE!
ALL RIGHT.

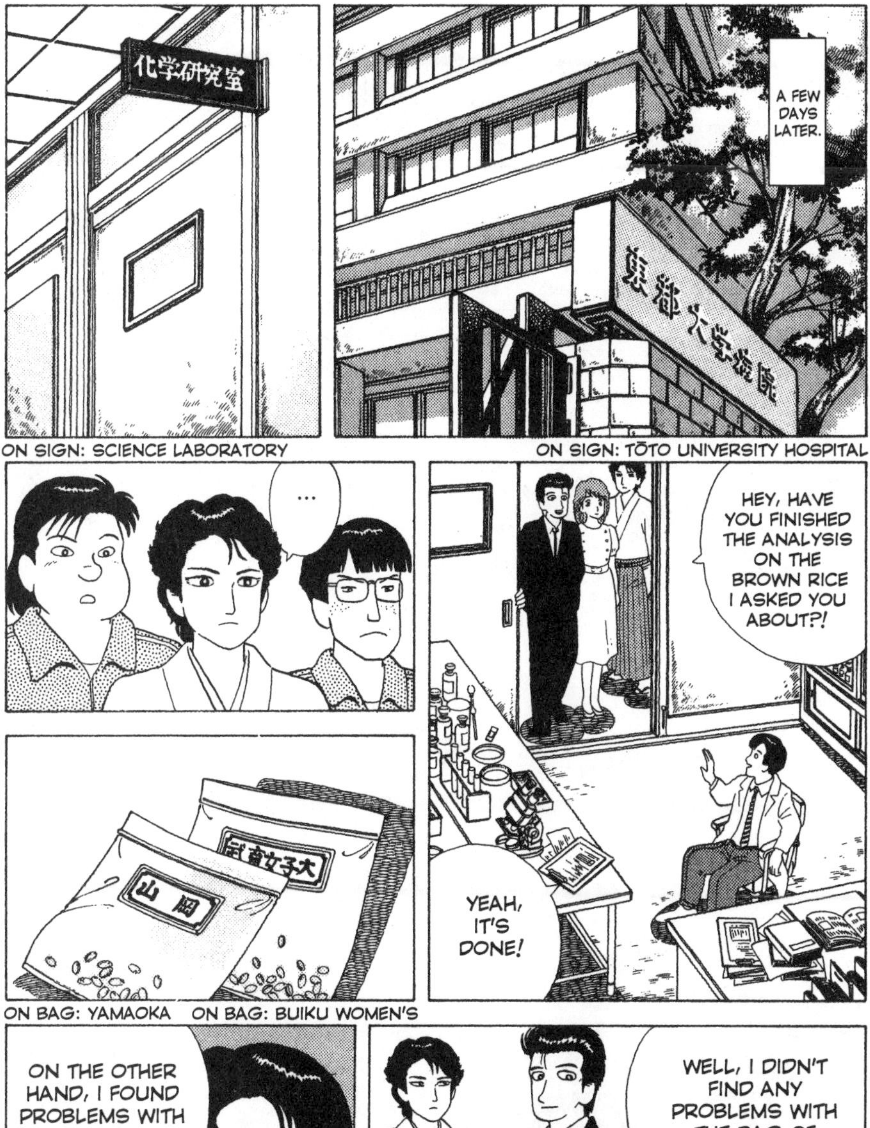
A FEW DAYS LATER.
ON SIGN: TŌTO UNIVERSITY HOSPITAL
ON SIGN: SCIENCE LABORATORY
HEY, HAVE YOU FINISHED THE ANALYSIS ON THE BROWN RICE I ASKED YOU ABOUT?!
YEAH, IT'S DONE!
...
ON BAG: YAMAOKA ON BAG: BUIKU WOMEN'S
WELL, I DIDN'T FIND ANY PROBLEMS WITH THE BAG OF BROWN RICE LABELED YAMAOKA.
THAT'S THE RICE I ALWAYS EAT.
ON THE OTHER HAND, I FOUND PROBLEMS WITH THE BROWN RICE LABELED BUIKU WOMEN'S.

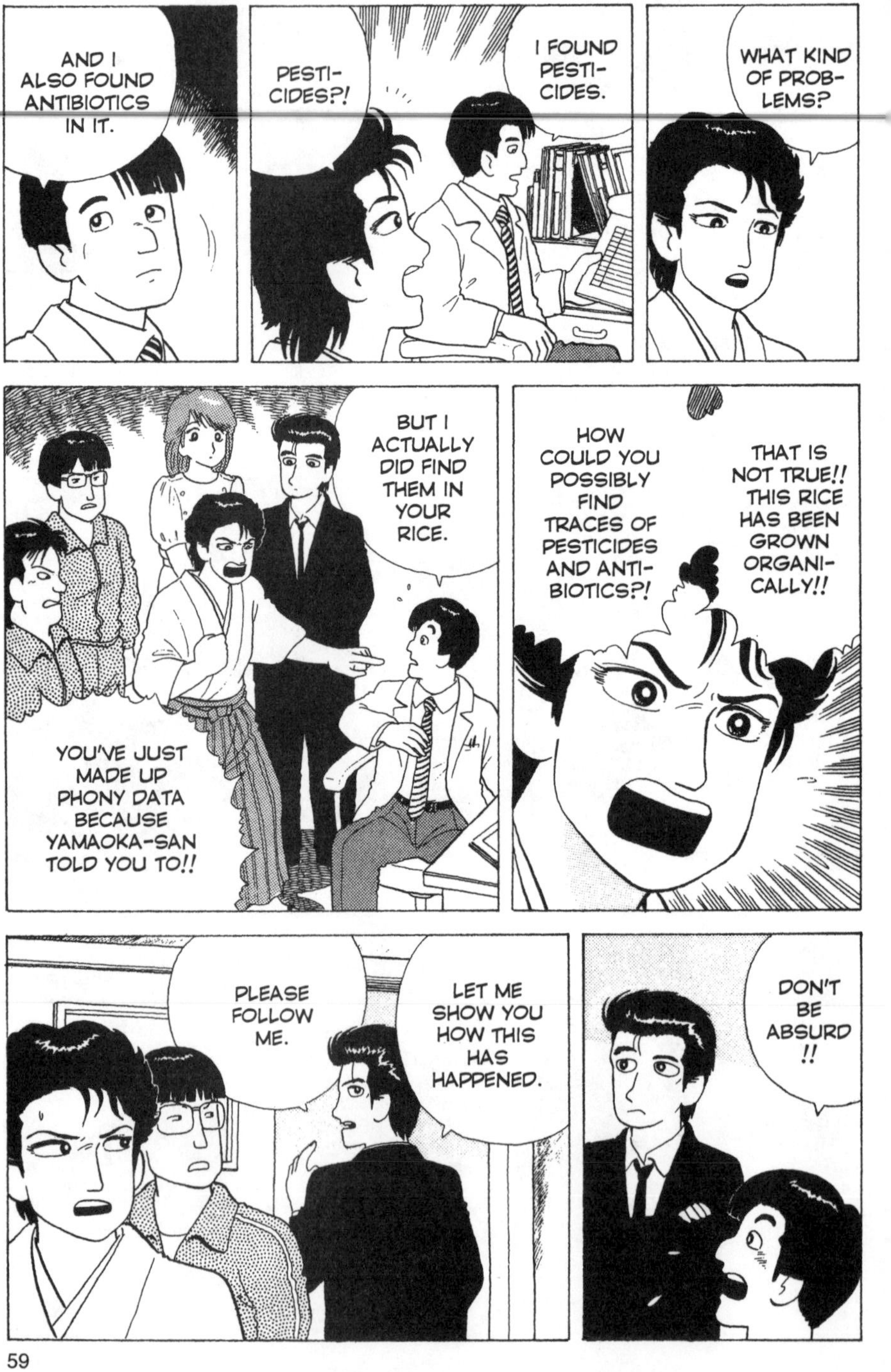
WHAT KIND OF PROBLEMS?
I FOUND PESTICIDES.
PESTICIDES?!
AND I ALSO FOUND ANTIBIOTICS IN IT.
THAT IS NOT TRUE!! THIS RICE HAS BEEN GROWN ORGANICALLY!!
HOW COULD YOU POSSIBLY FIND TRACES OF PESTICIDES AND ANTIBIOTICS?!
BUT I ACTUALLY DID FIND THEM IN YOUR RICE.
YOU'VE JUST MADE UP PHONY DATA BECAUSE YAMAOKA-SAN TOLD YOU TO!!
DON'T BE ABSURD !!
LET ME SHOW YOU HOW THIS HAS HAPPENED.
PLEASE FOLLOW ME.

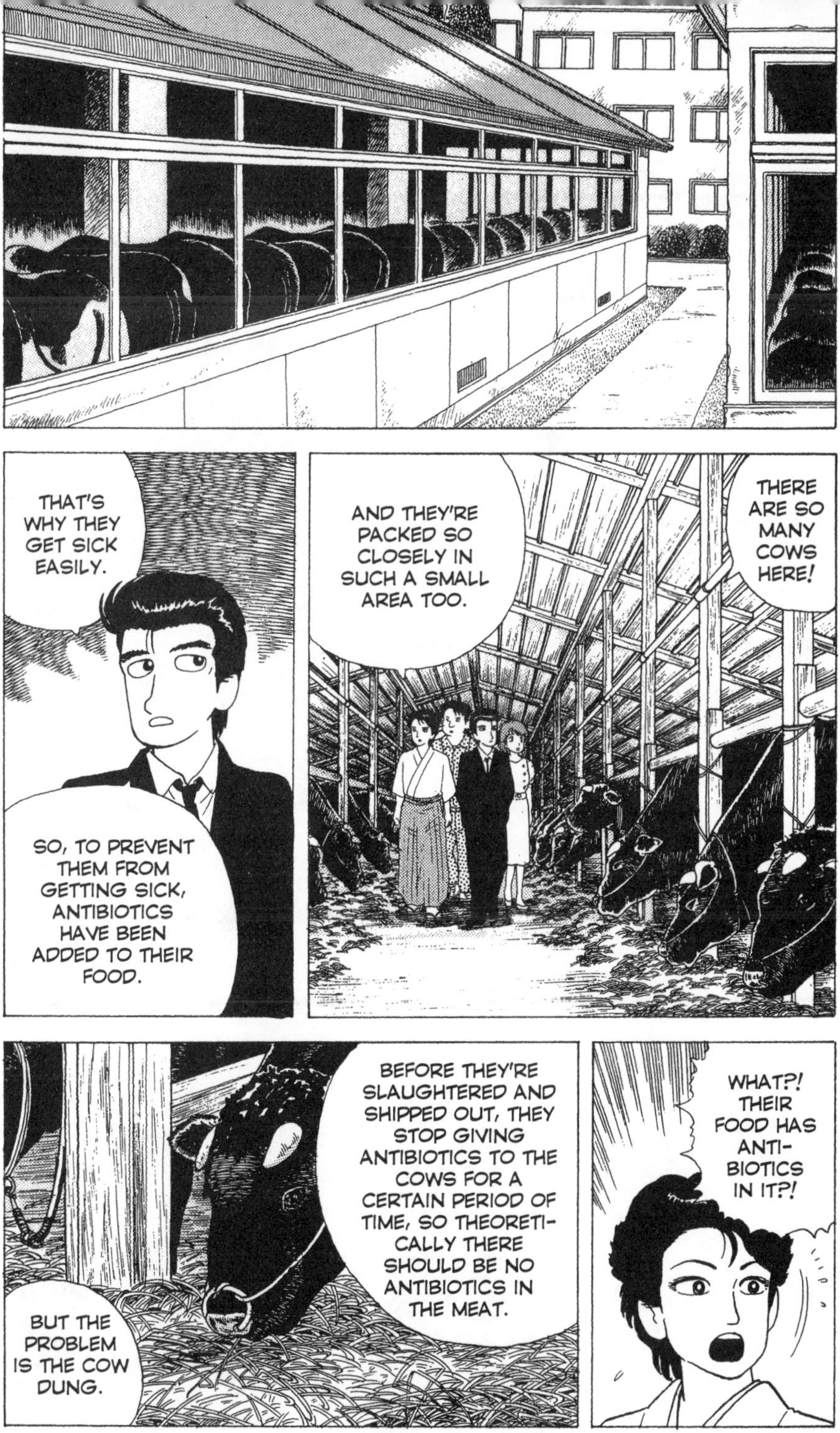
THERE ARE SO MANY COWS HERE!
AND THEY'RE PACKED SO CLOSELY IN SUCH A SMALL AREA TOO.
THAT'S WHY THEY GET SICK EASILY.
SO, TO PREVENT THEM FROM GETTING SICK, ANTIBIOTICS HAVE BEEN ADDED TO THEIR FOOD.
WHAT?! THEIR FOOD HAS ANTI-BIOTICS IN IT?!
BEFORE THEY'RE SLAUGHTERED AND SHIPPED OUT, THEY STOP GIVING ANTIBIOTICS TO THE COWS FOR A CERTAIN PERIOD OF TIME, SO THEORETI-CALLY THERE SHOULD BE NO ANTIBIOTICS IN THE MEAT.
BUT THE PROBLEM IS THE COW DUNG.

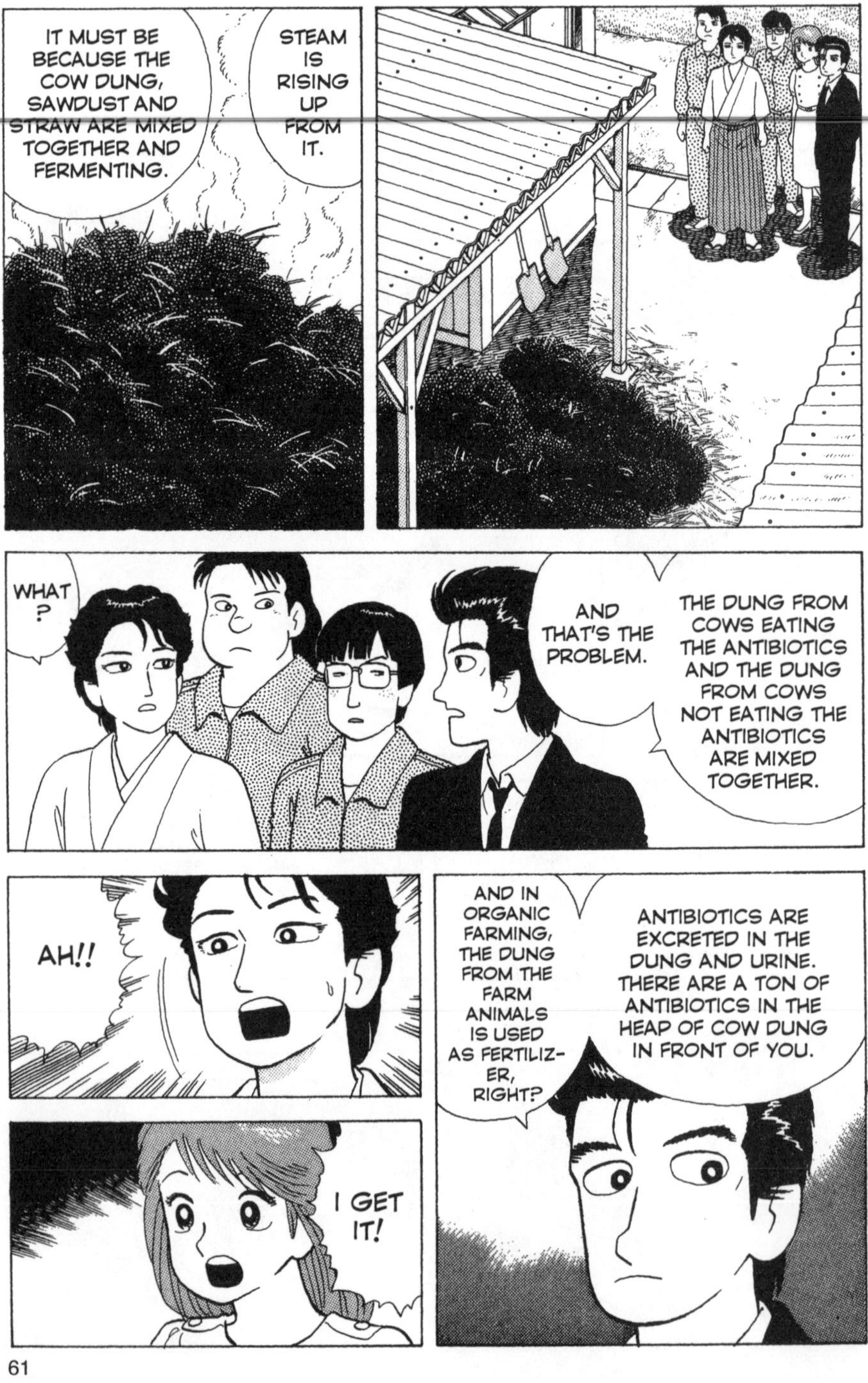
STEAM IS RISING UP FROM IT.
IT MUST BE BECAUSE THE COW DUNG, SAWDUST AND STRAW ARE MIXED TOGETHER AND FERMENTING.
THE DUNG FROM COWS EATING THE ANTIBIOTICS AND THE DUNG FROM COWS NOT EATING THE ANTIBIOTICS ARE MIXED TOGETHER.
AND THAT'S THE PROBLEM.
WHAT?
ANTIBIOTICS ARE EXCRETED IN THE DUNG AND URINE. THERE ARE A TON OF ANTIBIOTICS IN THE HEAP OF COW DUNG IN FRONT OF YOU.
AND IN ORGANIC FARMING, THE DUNG FROM THE FARM ANIMALS IS USED AS FERTILIZ- ER, RIGHT?
AH!!
I GET IT!

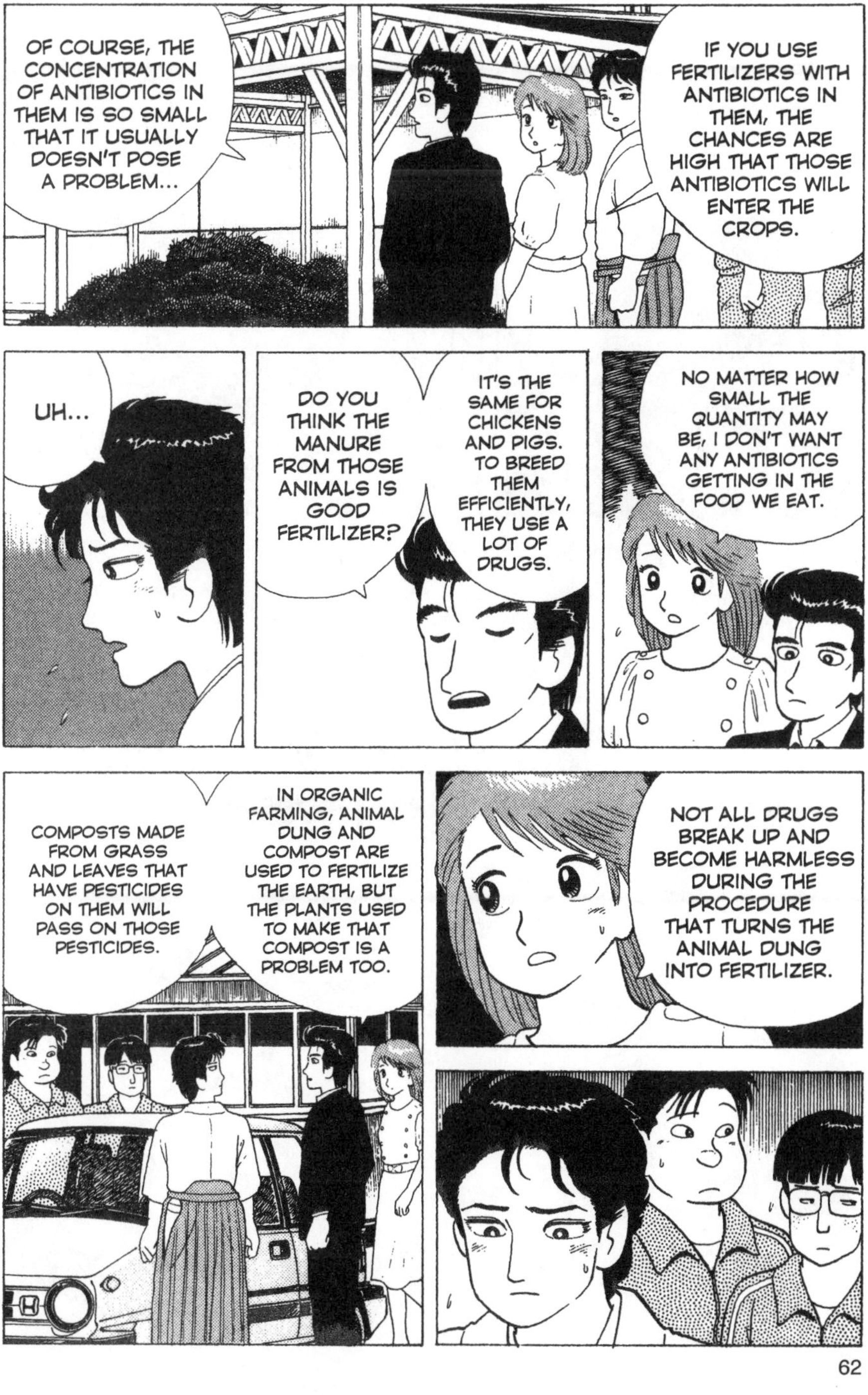
IF YOU USE FERTILIZERS WITH ANTIBIOTICS IN THEM, THE CHANCES ARE HIGH THAT THOSE ANTIBIOTICS WILL ENTER THE CROPS.
OF COURSE, THE CONCENTRATION OF ANTIBIOTICS IN THEM IS SO SMALL THAT IT USUALLY DOESN'T POSE A PROBLEM...
NO MATTER HOW SMALL THE QUANTITY MAY BE, I DON'T WANT ANY ANTIBIOTICS GETTING IN THE FOOD WE EAT.
IT'S THE SAME FOR CHICKENS AND PIGS. TO BREED THEM EFFICIENTLY, THEY USE A LOT OF DRUGS.
DO YOU THINK THE MANURE FROM THOSE ANIMALS IS GOOD FERTILIZER?
UH...
NOT ALL DRUGS BREAK UP AND BECOME HARMLESS DURING THE PROCEDURE THAT TURNS THE ANIMAL DUNG INTO FERTILIZER.
IN ORGANIC FARMING, ANIMAL DUNG AND COMPOST ARE USED TO FERTILIZE THE EARTH, BUT THE PLANTS USED TO MAKE THAT COMPOST IS A PROBLEM TOO.
COMPOSTS MADE FROM GRASS AND LEAVES THAT HAVE PESTICIDES ON THEM WILL PASS ON THOSE PESTICIDES.

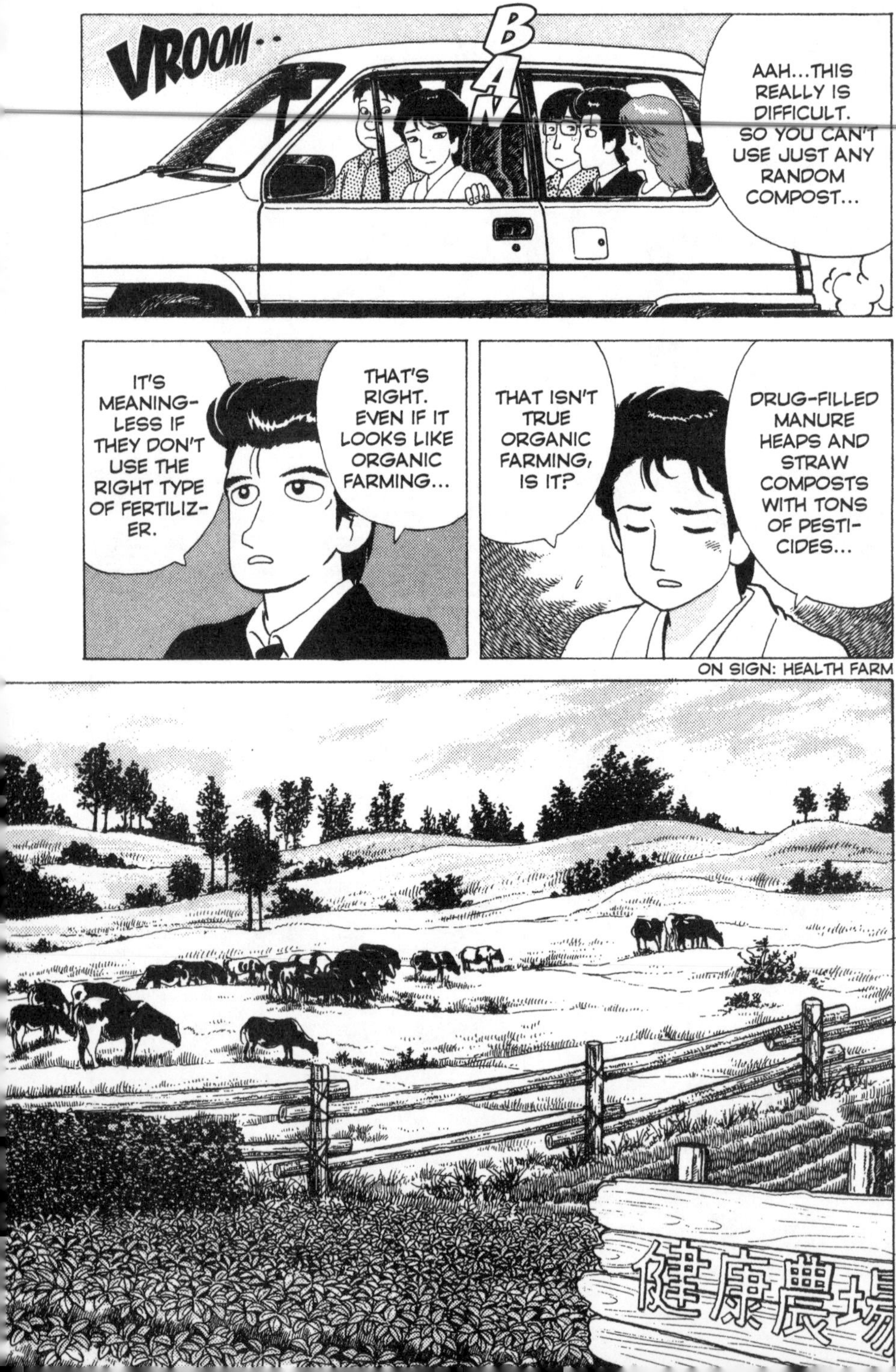
VROOM..
BAN
AAH...THIS REALLY IS DIFFICULT. SO YOU CAN'T USE JUST ANY RANDOM COMPOST...
DRUG-FILLED MANURE HEAPS AND STRAW COMPOSTS WITH TONS OF PESTI-CIDES...
THAT ISN'T TRUE ORGANIC FARMING, IS IT?
THAT'S RIGHT. EVEN IF IT LOOKS LIKE ORGANIC FARMING...
IT'S MEANING-LESS IF THEY DON'T USE THE RIGHT TYPE OF FERTILIZ-ER.
ON SIGN: HEALTH FARM
健康農場

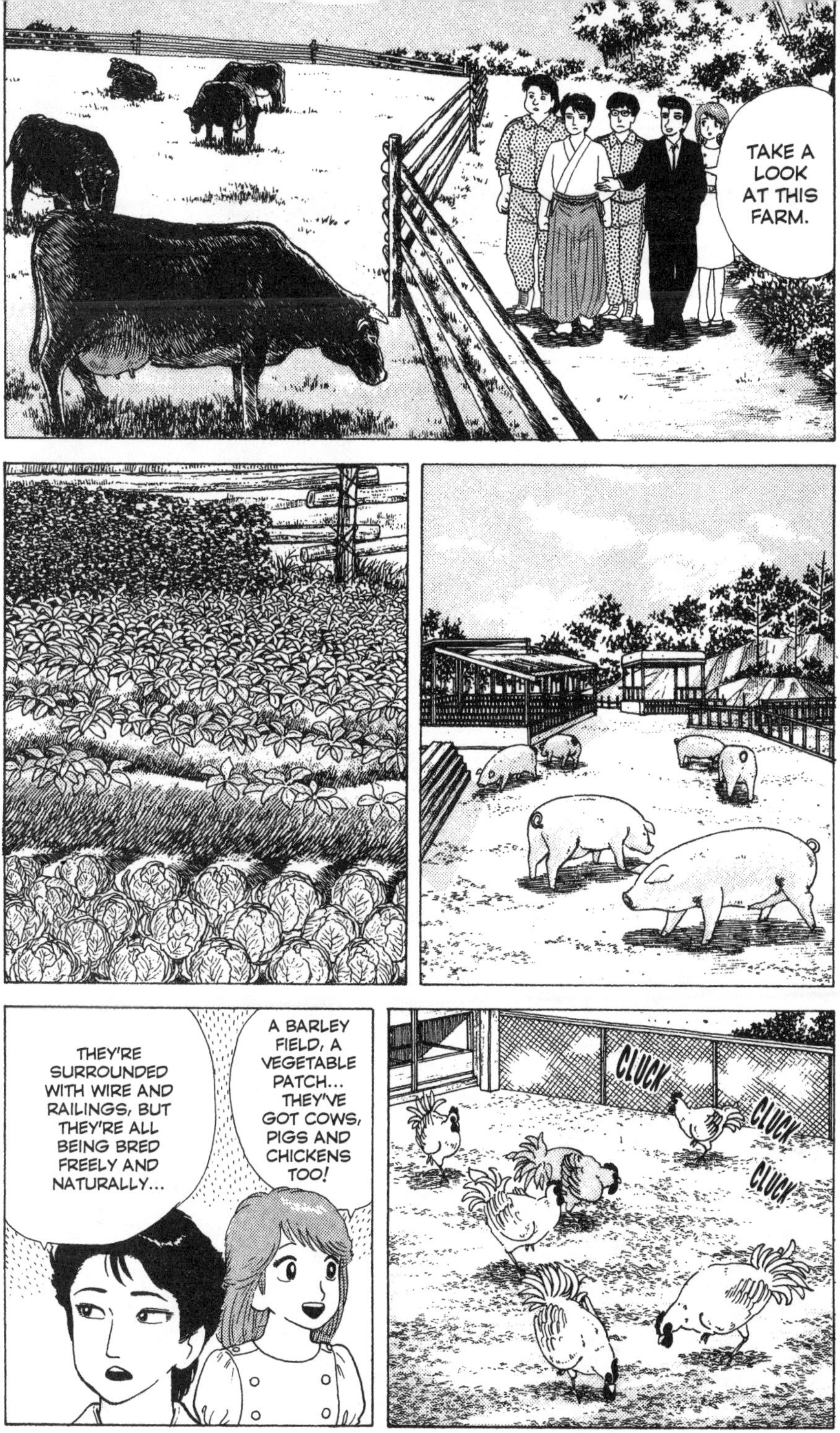
TAKE A LOOK AT THIS FARM.
CLUCK
CLUCK
CLUCK
A BARLEY FIELD, A VEGETABLE PATCH... THEY'VE GOT COWS, PIGS AND CHICKENS TOO!
THEY'RE SURROUNDED WITH WIRE AND RAILINGS, BUT THEY'RE ALL BEING BRED FREELY AND NATURALLY...

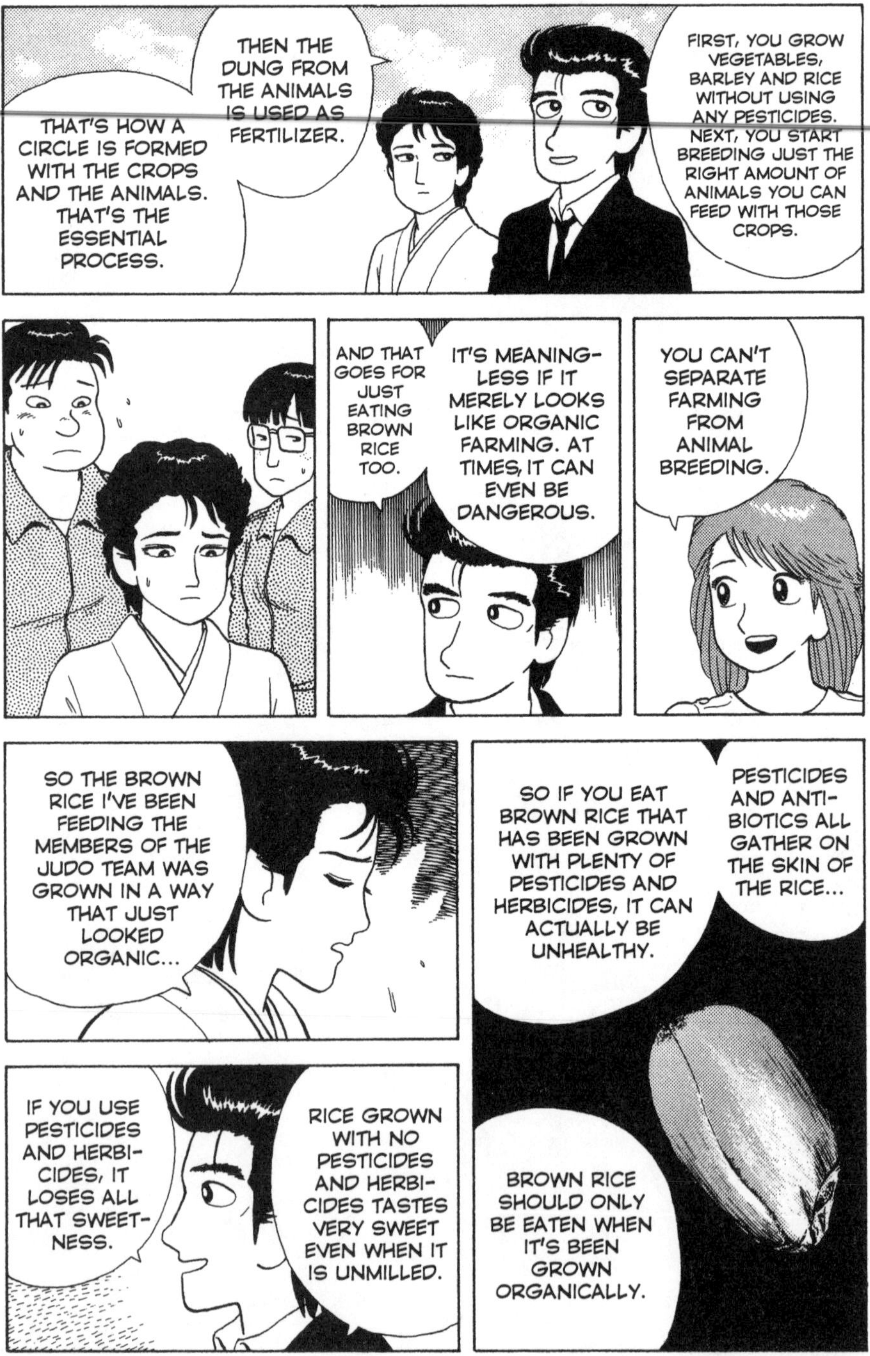
FIRST, YOU GROW VEGETABLES, BARLEY AND RICE WITHOUT USING ANY PESTICIDES. NEXT, YOU START BREEDING JUST THE RIGHT AMOUNT OF ANIMALS YOU CAN FEED WITH THOSE CROPS.
THEN THE DUNG FROM THE ANIMALS IS USED AS FERTILIZER.
THAT'S HOW A CIRCLE IS FORMED WITH THE CROPS AND THE ANIMALS. THAT'S THE ESSENTIAL PROCESS.
YOU CAN'T SEPARATE FARMING FROM ANIMAL BREEDING.
IT'S MEANING-LESS IF IT MERELY LOOKS LIKE ORGANIC FARMING. AT TIMES, IT CAN EVEN BE DANGEROUS.
AND THAT GOES FOR JUST EATING BROWN RICE TOO.
PESTICIDES AND ANTI-BIOTICS ALL GATHER ON THE SKIN OF THE RICE...
SO IF YOU EAT BROWN RICE THAT HAS BEEN GROWN WITH PLENTY OF PESTICIDES AND HERBICIDES, IT CAN ACTUALLY BE UNHEALTHY.
BROWN RICE SHOULD ONLY BE EATEN WHEN IT'S BEEN GROWN ORGANICALLY.
SO THE BROWN RICE I'VE BEEN FEEDING THE MEMBERS OF THE JUDO TEAM WAS GROWN IN A WAY THAT JUST LOOKED ORGANIC...
RICE GROWN WITH NO PESTICIDES AND HERBI-CIDES TASTES VERY SWEET EVEN WHEN IT IS UNMILLED.
IF YOU USE PESTICIDES AND HERBI-CIDES, IT LOSES ALL THAT SWEET-NESS.

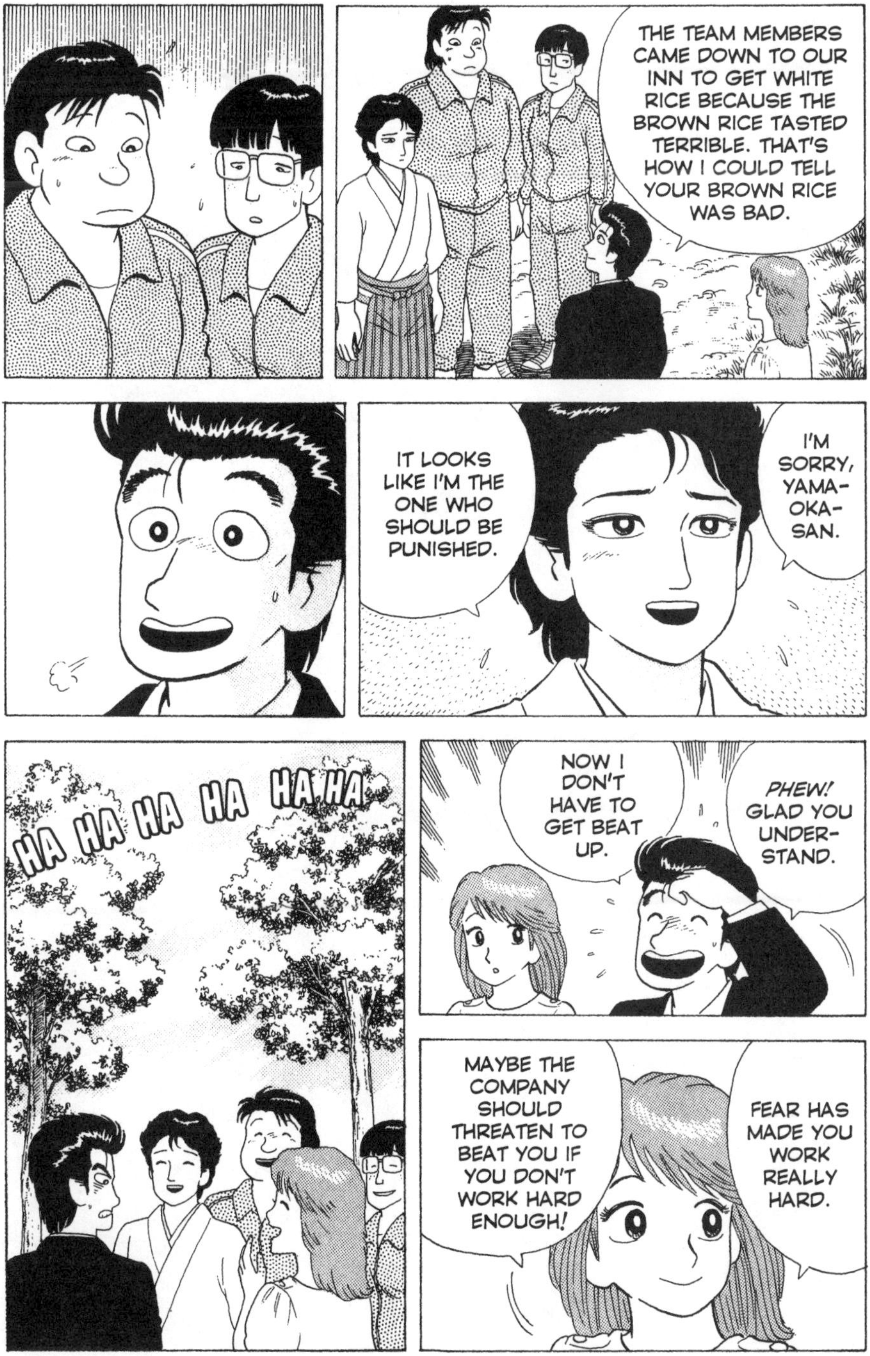
THE TEAM MEMBERS CAME DOWN TO OUR INN TO GET WHITE RICE BECAUSE THE BROWN RICE TASTED TERRIBLE. THAT'S HOW I COULD TELL YOUR BROWN RICE WAS BAD.
I'M SORRY, YAMA-OKA-SAN.
IT LOOKS LIKE I'M THE ONE WHO SHOULD BE PUNISHED.
PHEW! GLAD YOU UNDER-STAND.
NOW I DON'T HAVE TO GET BEAT UP.
FEAR HAS MADE YOU WORK REALLY HARD.
MAYBE THE COMPANY SHOULD THREATEN TO BEAT YOU IF YOU DON'T WORK HARD ENOUGH!
HA HA HA HA HA HA

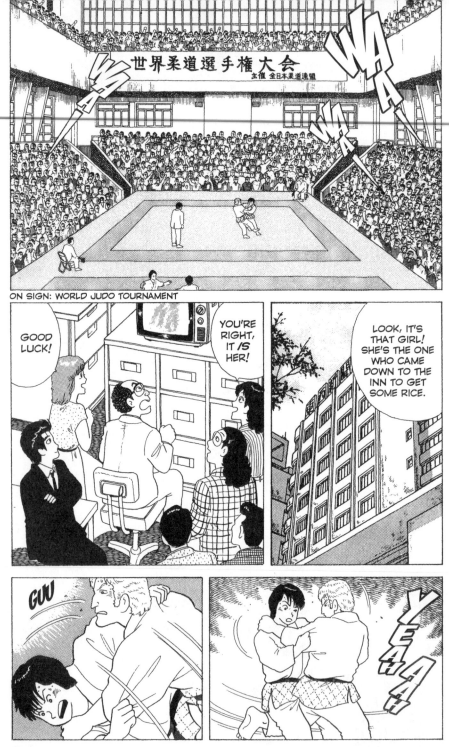

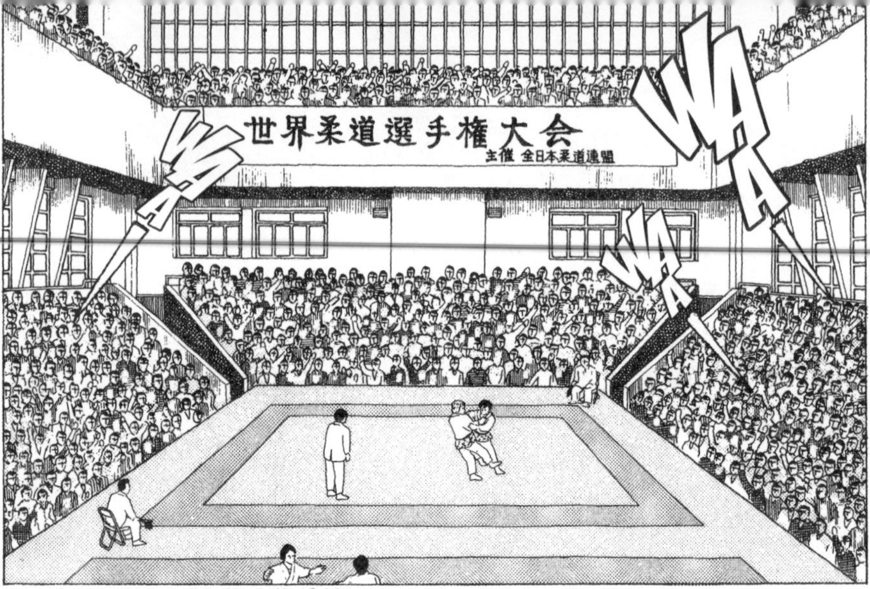
WAA
WAA
WAA
世界柔道選手権大会
主催 全日本柔道連盟
ON SIGN: WORLD JUDO TOURNAMENT

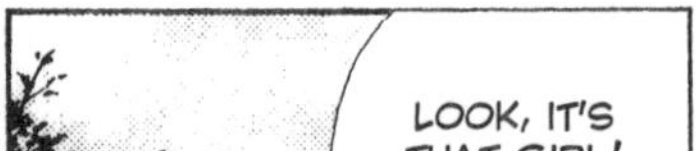
LOOK, IT'S THAT GIRL! SHE'S THE ONE WHO CAME DOWN TO THE INN TO GET SOME RICE.

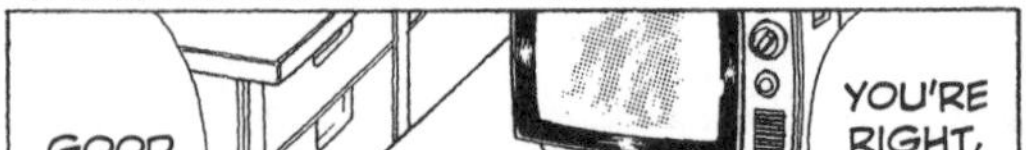
YOU'RE RIGHT, IT *IS* HER!
GOOD LUCK!

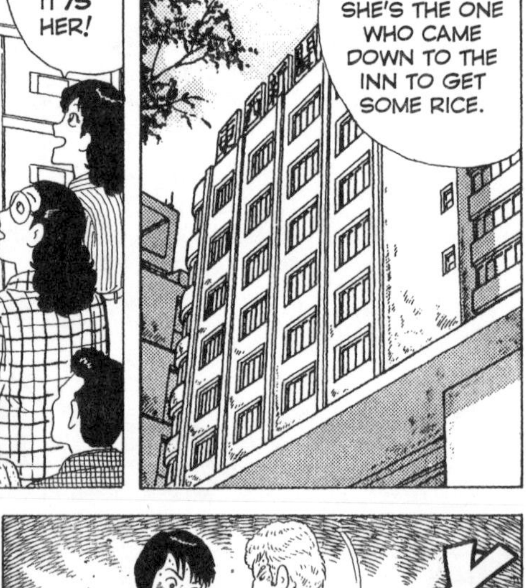
YEAAAAH

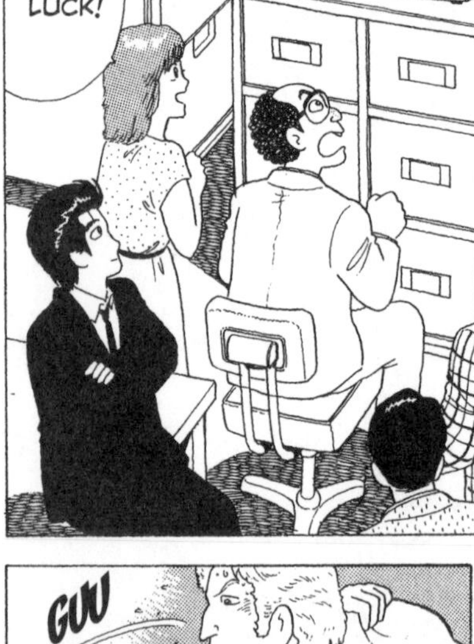
GUU

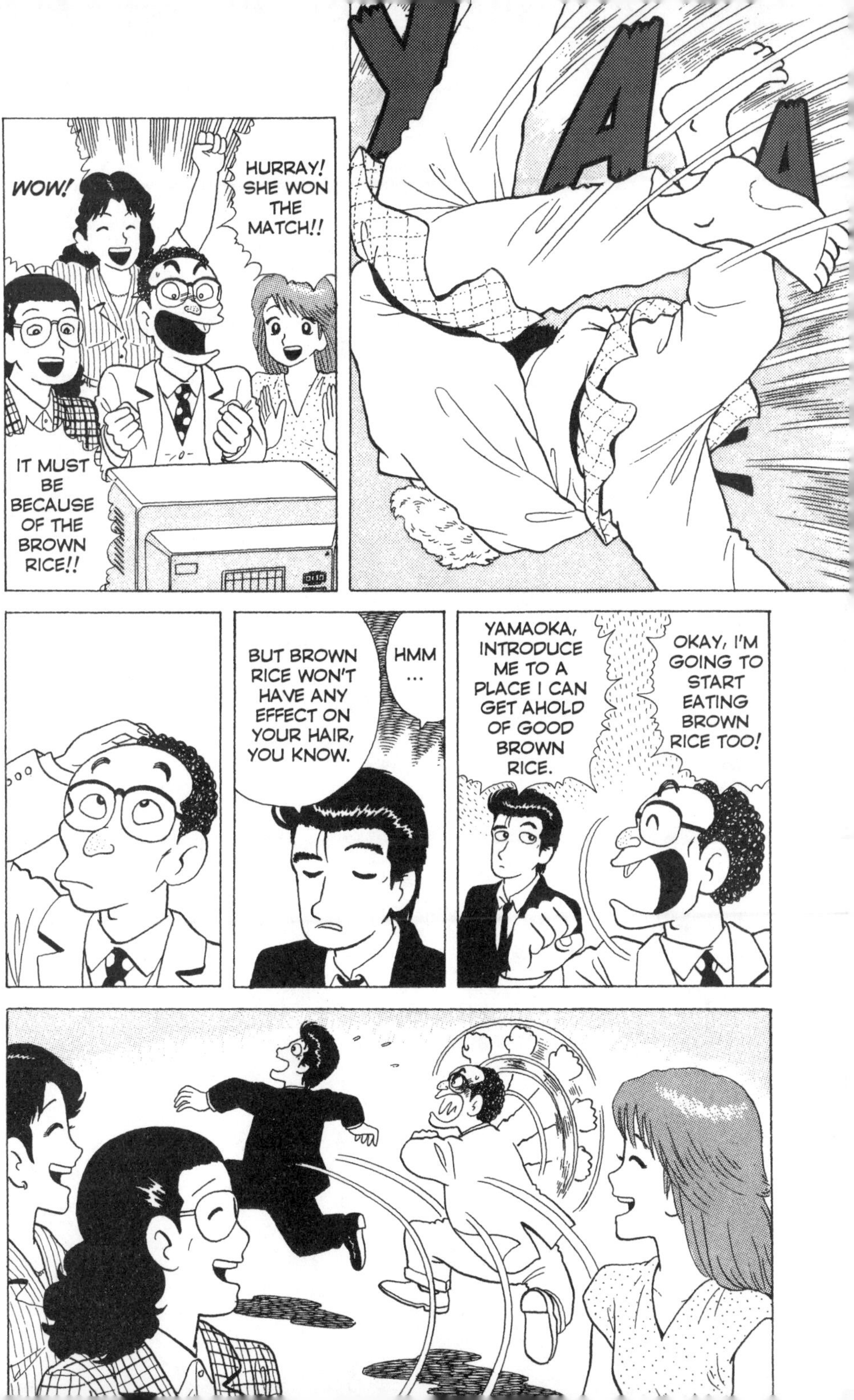
YAA
HURRAY! SHE WON THE MATCH!!
WOW!
IT MUST BE BECAUSE OF THE BROWN RICE!!
OKAY, I'M GOING TO START EATING BROWN RICE TOO!
YAMAOKA, INTRODUCE ME TO A PLACE I CAN GET AHOLD OF GOOD BROWN RICE.
HMM ...
BUT BROWN RICE WON'T HAVE ANY EFFECT ON YOUR HAIR, YOU KNOW.

ZZZZ

OISHINBO

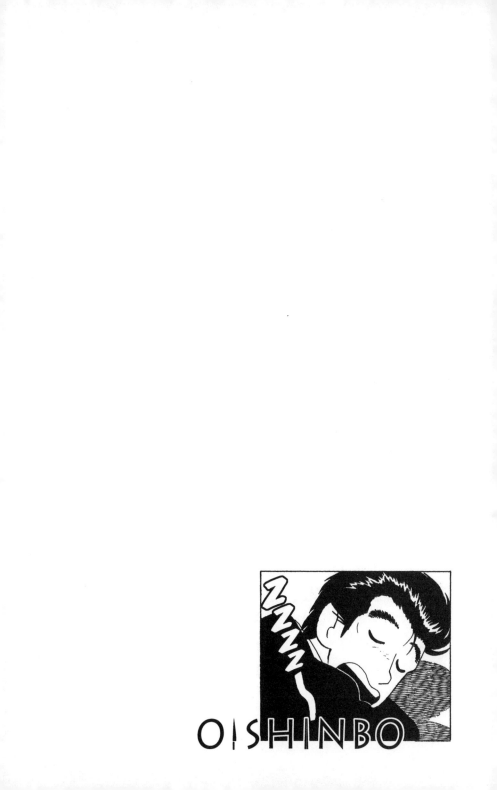

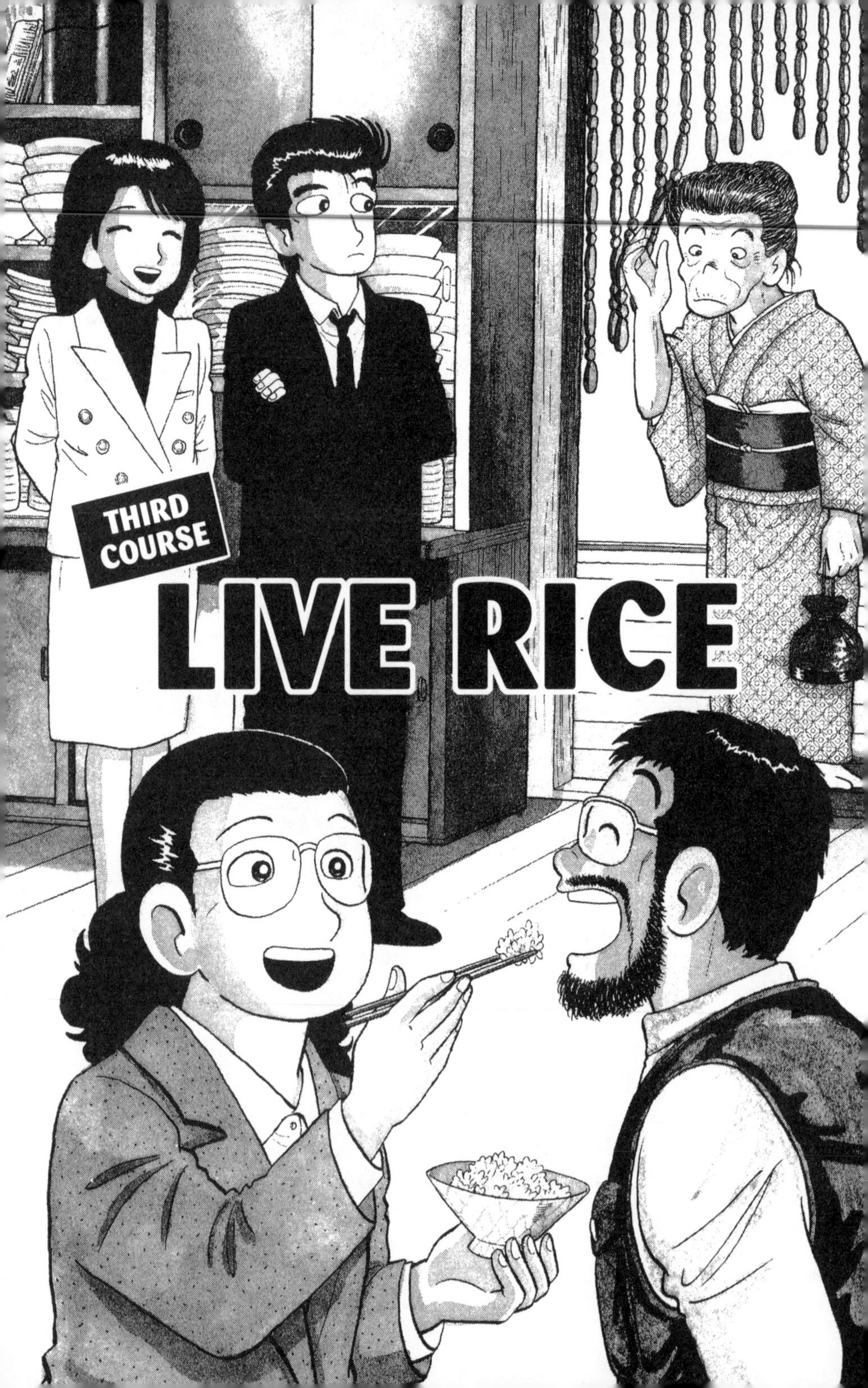
THIRD COURSE
LIVE RICE

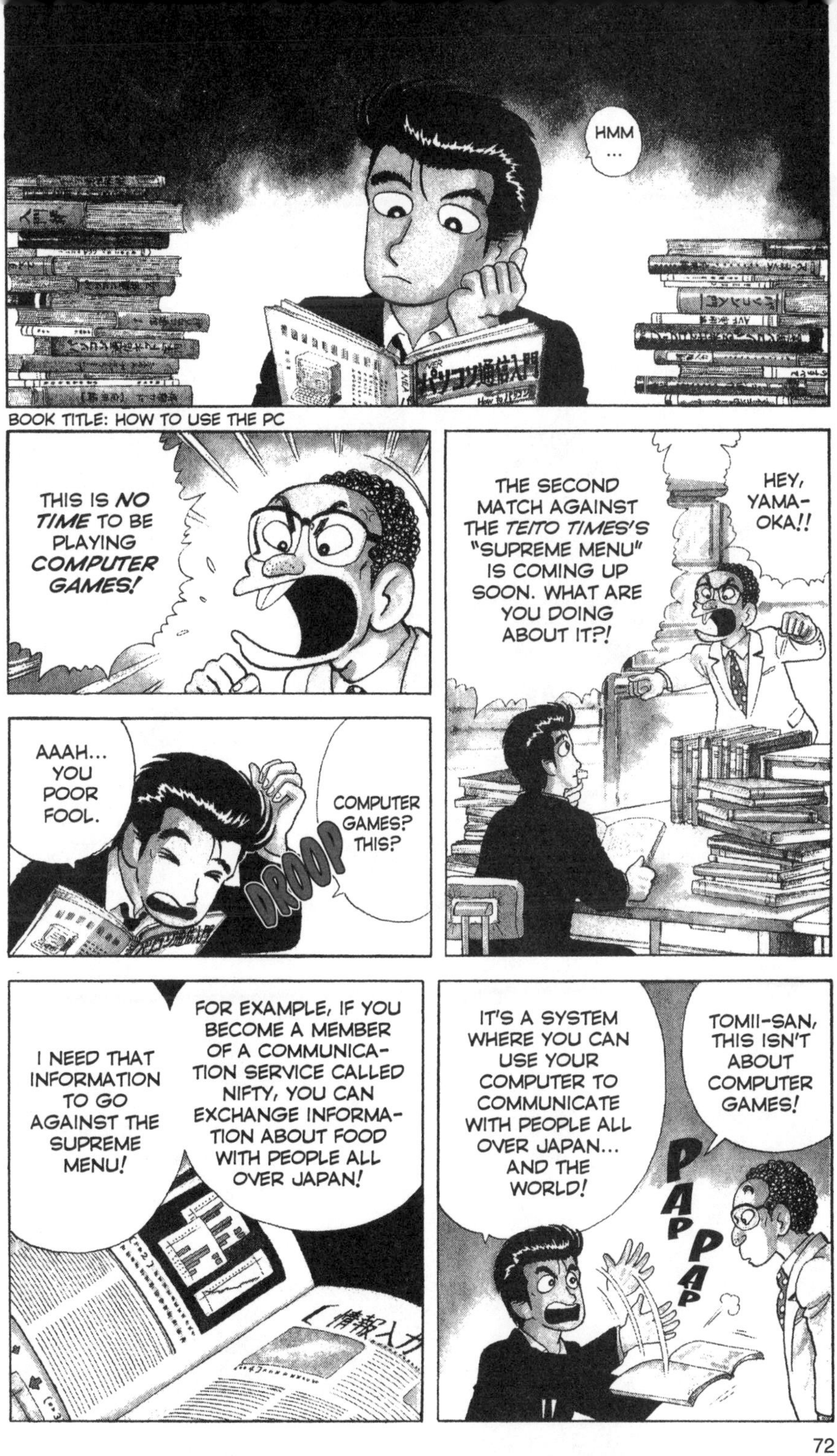
HMM ...
BOOK TITLE: HOW TO USE THE PC
HEY, YAMAOKA!!
THE SECOND MATCH AGAINST THE TEITO TIMES'S "SUPREME MENU" IS COMING UP SOON. WHAT ARE YOU DOING ABOUT IT?!
THIS IS NO TIME TO BE PLAYING COMPUTER GAMES!
COMPUTER GAMES? THIS?
AAAH... YOU POOR FOOL.
DROOP
TOMII-SAN, THIS ISN'T ABOUT COMPUTER GAMES!
IT'S A SYSTEM WHERE YOU CAN USE YOUR COMPUTER TO COMMUNICATE WITH PEOPLE ALL OVER JAPAN... AND THE WORLD!
PAP PAP PAP
FOR EXAMPLE, IF YOU BECOME A MEMBER OF A COMMUNICATION SERVICE CALLED NIFTY, YOU CAN EXCHANGE INFORMATION ABOUT FOOD WITH PEOPLE ALL OVER JAPAN!
I NEED THAT INFORMATION TO GO AGAINST THE SUPREME MENU!

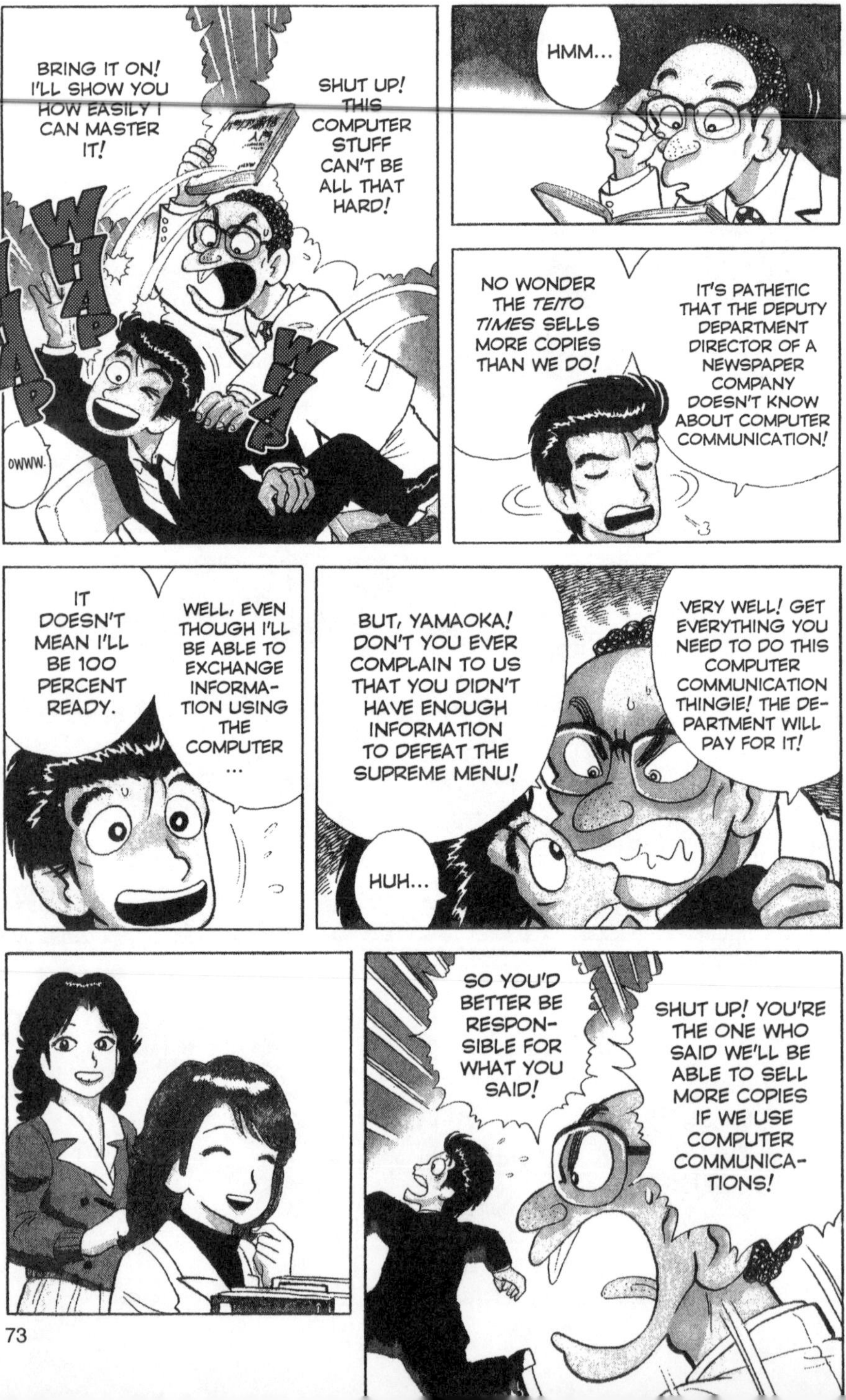
HMM...
IT'S PATHETIC THAT THE DEPUTY DEPARTMENT DIRECTOR OF A NEWSPAPER COMPANY DOESN'T KNOW ABOUT COMPUTER COMMUNICATION!
NO WONDER THE *TEITO TIMES* SELLS MORE COPIES THAN WE DO!
SHUT UP! THIS COMPUTER STUFF CAN'T BE ALL THAT HARD!
BRING IT ON! I'LL SHOW YOU HOW EASILY I CAN MASTER IT!
WHAP
WHAP
WHAP
OWWW.
VERY WELL! GET EVERYTHING YOU NEED TO DO THIS COMPUTER COMMUNICATION THINGIE! THE DE-PARTMENT WILL PAY FOR IT!
BUT, YAMAOKA! DON'T YOU EVER COMPLAIN TO US THAT YOU DIDN'T HAVE ENOUGH INFORMATION TO DEFEAT THE SUPREME MENU!
HUH...
WELL, EVEN THOUGH I'LL BE ABLE TO EXCHANGE INFORMA-TION USING THE COMPUTER ...
IT DOESN'T MEAN I'LL BE 100 PERCENT READY.
SHUT UP! YOU'RE THE ONE WHO SAID WE'LL BE ABLE TO SELL MORE COPIES IF WE USE COMPUTER COMMUNICA-TIONS!
SO YOU'D BETTER BE RESPON-SIBLE FOR WHAT YOU SAID!

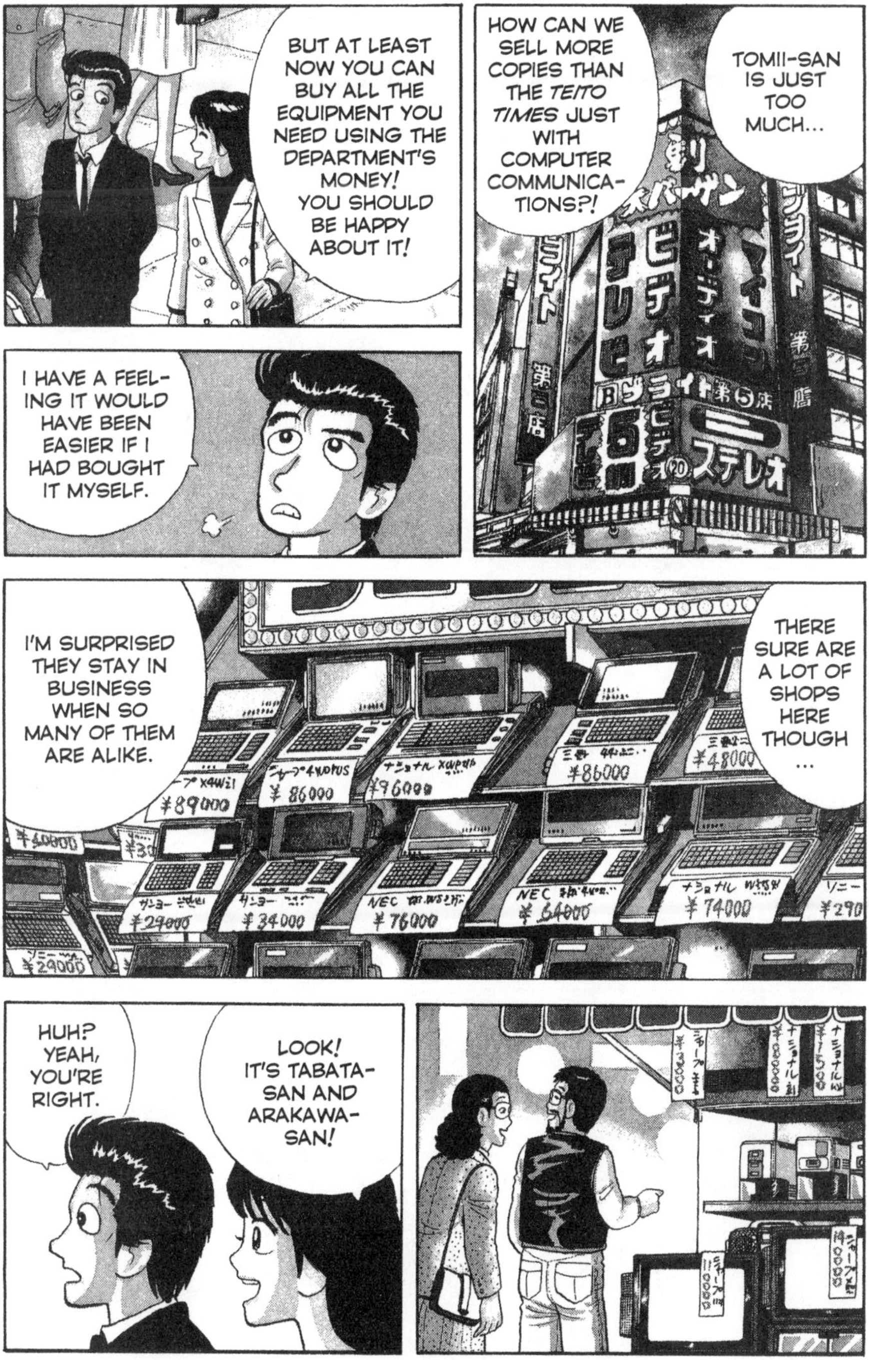
TOMII-SAN IS JUST TOO MUCH...
HOW CAN WE SELL MORE COPIES THAN THE *TEITO TIMES* JUST WITH COMPUTER COMMUNICATIONS?!
BUT AT LEAST NOW YOU CAN BUY ALL THE EQUIPMENT YOU NEED USING THE DEPARTMENT'S MONEY! YOU SHOULD BE HAPPY ABOUT IT!
I HAVE A FEELING IT WOULD HAVE BEEN EASIER IF I HAD BOUGHT IT MYSELF.
THERE SURE ARE A LOT OF SHOPS HERE THOUGH ...
I'M SURPRISED THEY STAY IN BUSINESS WHEN SO MANY OF THEM ARE ALIKE.
LOOK! IT'S TABATA-SAN AND ARAKAWA-SAN!
HUH? YEAH, YOU'RE RIGHT.

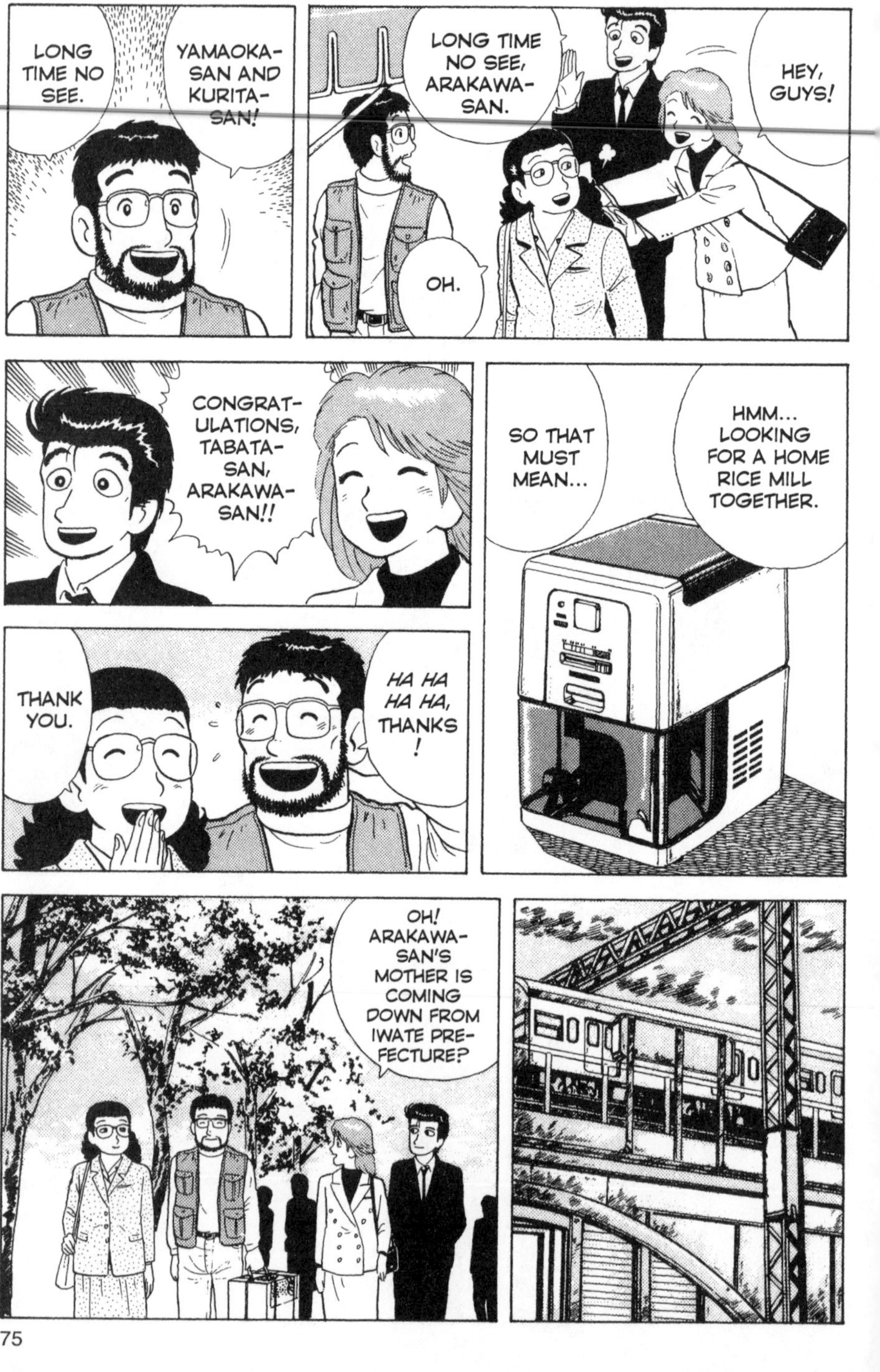
HEY, GUYS!
LONG TIME NO SEE, ARAKAWA-SAN.
OH.
YAMAOKA-SAN AND KURITA-SAN!
LONG TIME NO SEE.
HMM... LOOKING FOR A HOME RICE MILL TOGETHER.
SO THAT MUST MEAN...
CONGRATULATIONS, TABATA-SAN, ARAKAWA-SAN!!
HA HA HA HA, THANKS!
THANK YOU.
OH! ARAKAWA-SAN'S MOTHER IS COMING DOWN FROM IWATE PREFECTURE?

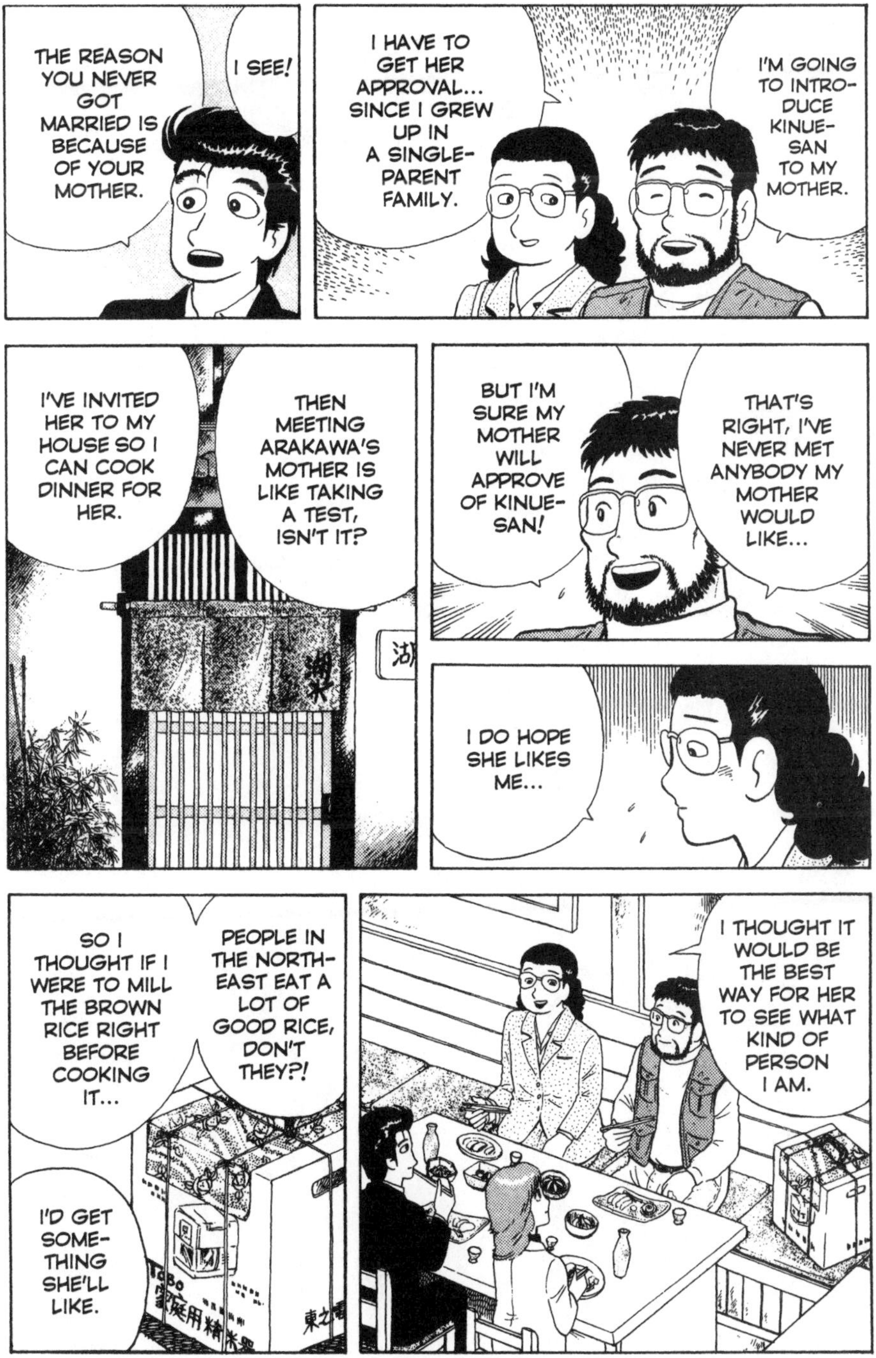
I'M GOING TO INTRODUCE KINUE-SAN TO MY MOTHER.
I HAVE TO GET HER APPROVAL... SINCE I GREW UP IN A SINGLE-PARENT FAMILY.
I SEE!
THE REASON YOU NEVER GOT MARRIED IS BECAUSE OF YOUR MOTHER.
THAT'S RIGHT, I'VE NEVER MET ANYBODY MY MOTHER WOULD LIKE...
BUT I'M SURE MY MOTHER WILL APPROVE OF KINUE-SAN!
I DO HOPE SHE LIKES ME...
THEN MEETING ARAKAWA'S MOTHER IS LIKE TAKING A TEST, ISN'T IT?
I'VE INVITED HER TO MY HOUSE SO I CAN COOK DINNER FOR HER.
I THOUGHT IT WOULD BE THE BEST WAY FOR HER TO SEE WHAT KIND OF PERSON I AM.
PEOPLE IN THE NORTHEAST EAT A LOT OF GOOD RICE, DON'T THEY?!
SO I THOUGHT IF I WERE TO MILL THE BROWN RICE RIGHT BEFORE COOKING IT...
I'D GET SOMETHING SHE'LL LIKE.

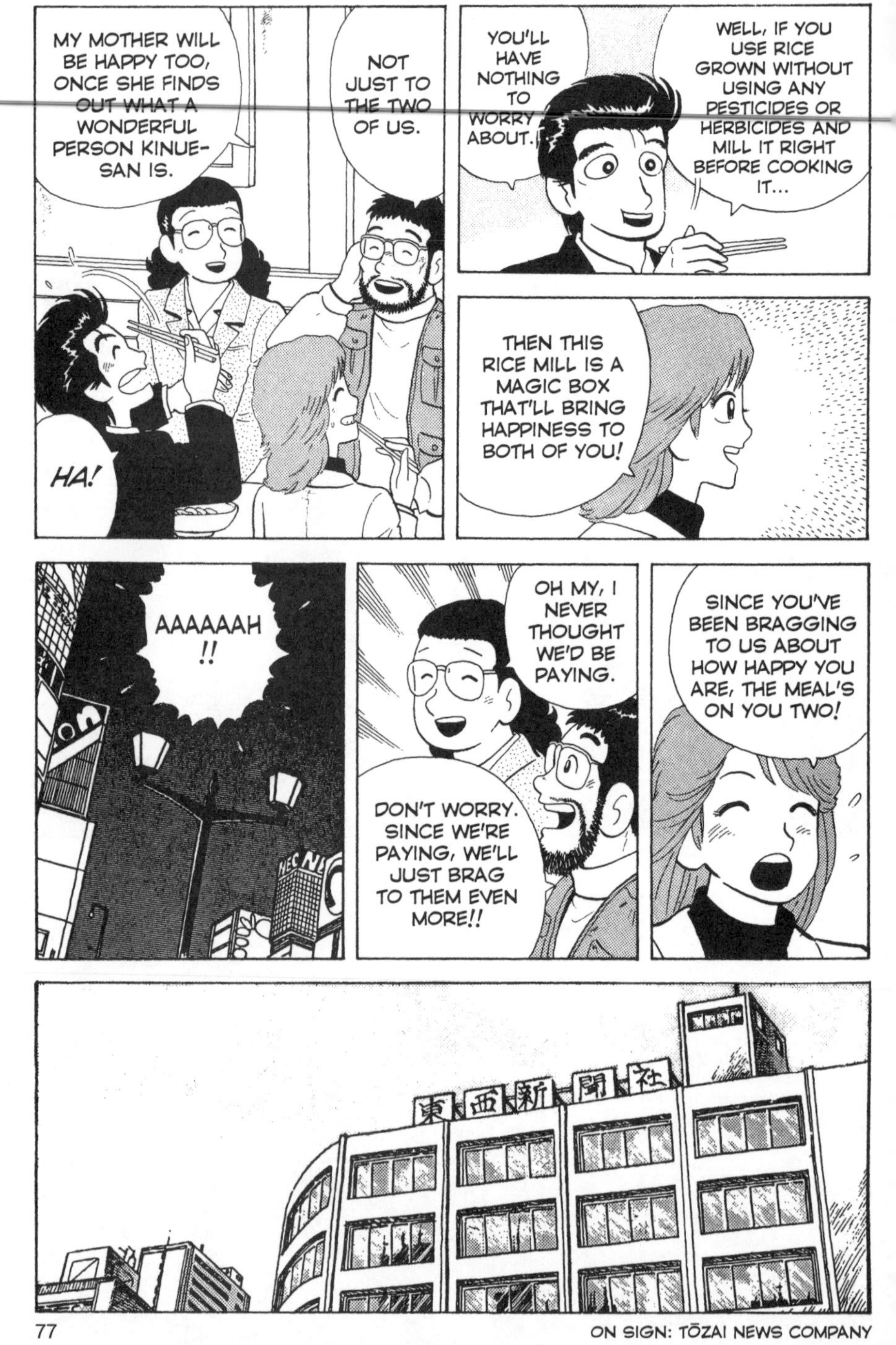
WELL, IF YOU USE RICE GROWN WITHOUT USING ANY PESTICIDES OR HERBICIDES AND MILL IT RIGHT BEFORE COOKING IT...
YOU'LL HAVE NOTHING TO WORRY ABOUT.
THEN THIS RICE MILL IS A MAGIC BOX THAT'LL BRING HAPPINESS TO BOTH OF YOU!
NOT JUST TO THE TWO OF US.
MY MOTHER WILL BE HAPPY TOO, ONCE SHE FINDS OUT WHAT A WONDERFUL PERSON KINUE-SAN IS.
HA!
SINCE YOU'VE BEEN BRAGGING TO US ABOUT HOW HAPPY YOU ARE, THE MEAL'S ON YOU TWO!
OH MY, I NEVER THOUGHT WE'D BE PAYING.
DON'T WORRY. SINCE WE'RE PAYING, WE'LL JUST BRAG TO THEM EVEN MORE!!
AAAAAAH!!
東西新聞社

ON SIGN: TŌZAI NEWS COMPANY

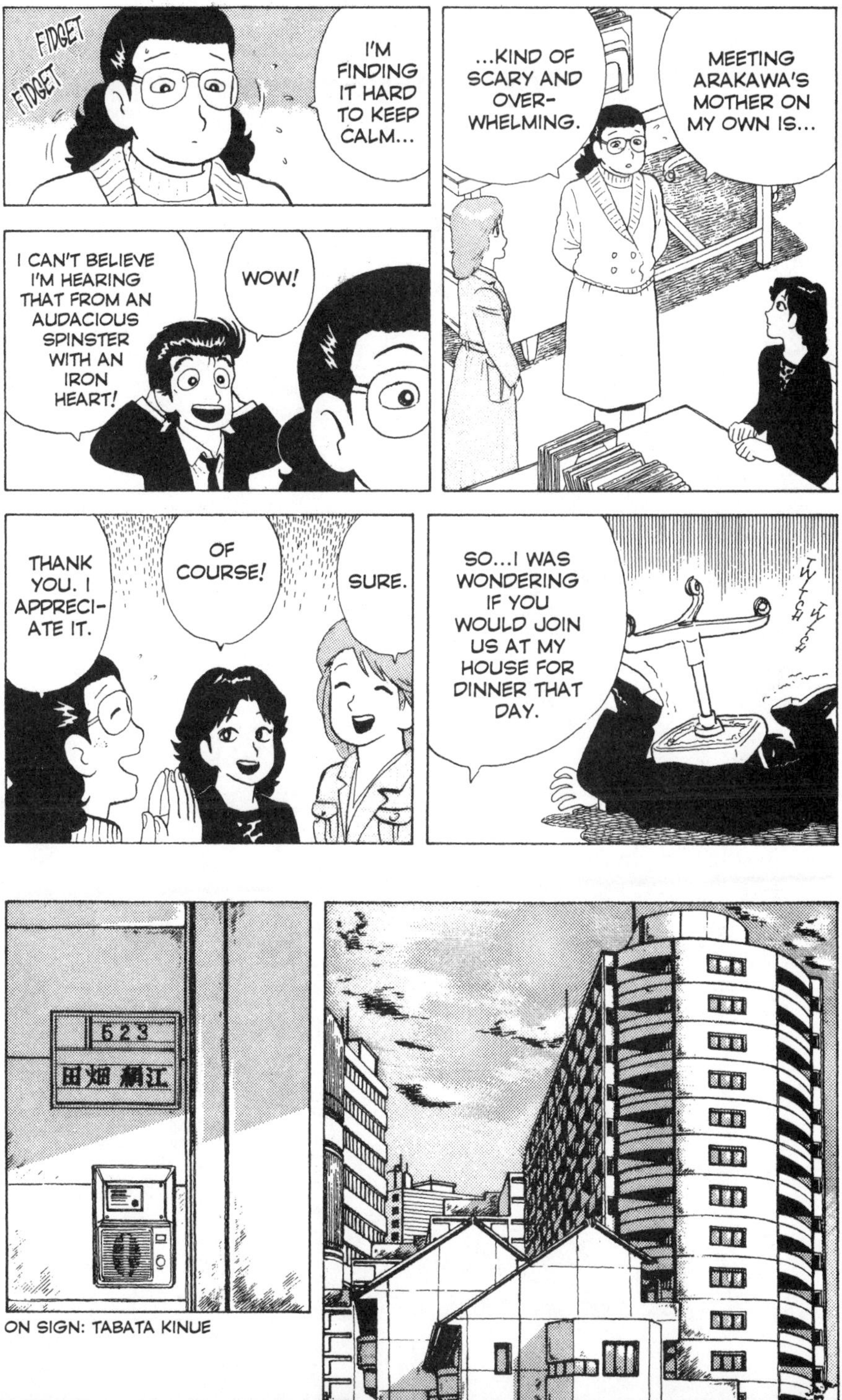
MEETING ARAKAWA'S MOTHER ON MY OWN IS...
...KIND OF SCARY AND OVER-WHELMING.
I'M FINDING IT HARD TO KEEP CALM...
FIDGET FIDGET
WOW!
I CAN'T BELIEVE I'M HEARING THAT FROM AN AUDACIOUS SPINSTER WITH AN IRON HEART!
SO...I WAS WONDERING IF YOU WOULD JOIN US AT MY HOUSE FOR DINNER THAT DAY.
TWITCH TWITCH
SURE.
OF COURSE!
THANK YOU. I APPRECI-ATE IT.
523
田畑 桐江
ON SIGN: TABATA KINUE

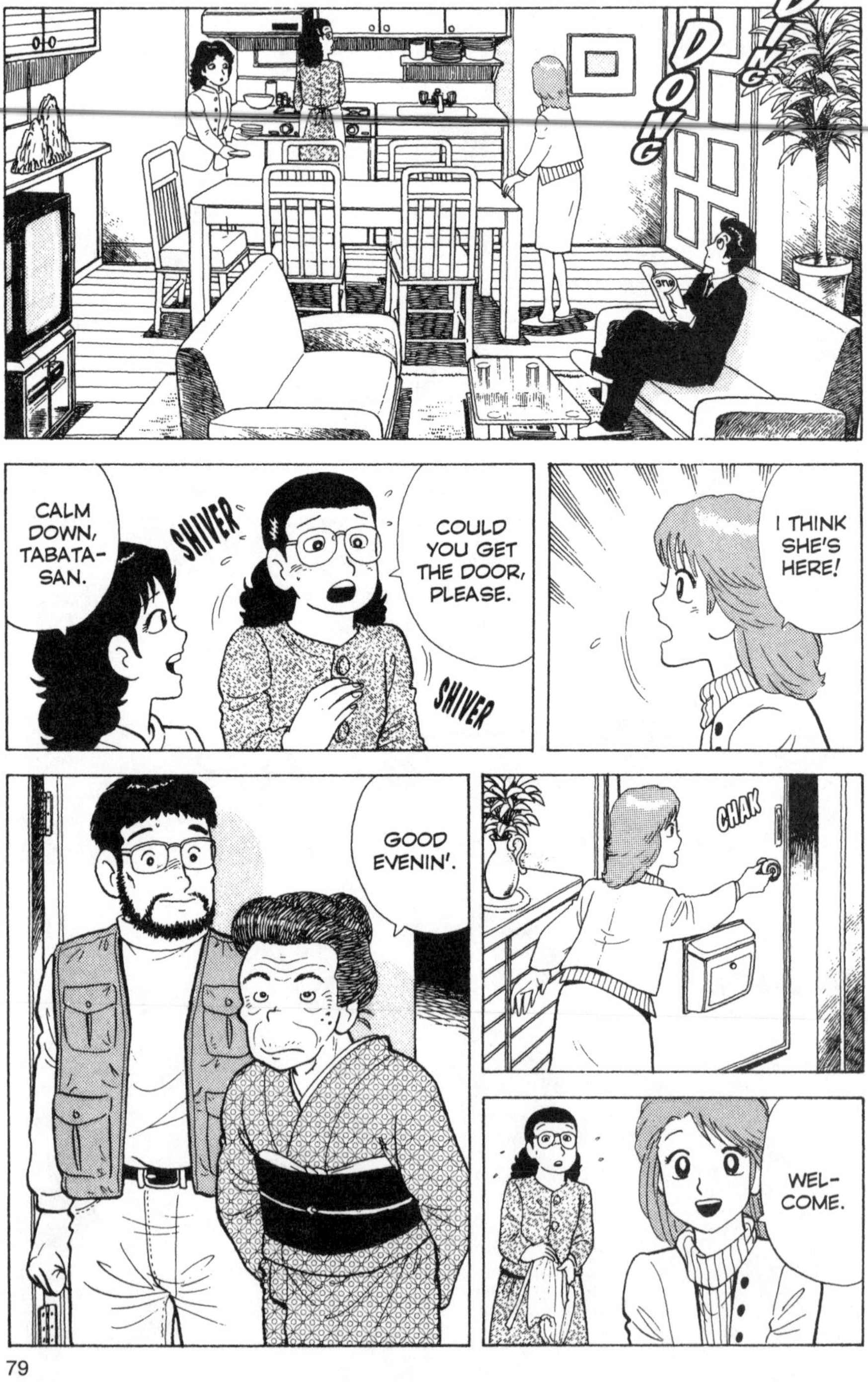
DING
DONG
I THINK SHE'S HERE!
COULD YOU GET THE DOOR, PLEASE.
SHIVER
CALM DOWN, TABATA-SAN.
SHIVER
CHAK
WEL-COME.
GOOD EVENIN'.

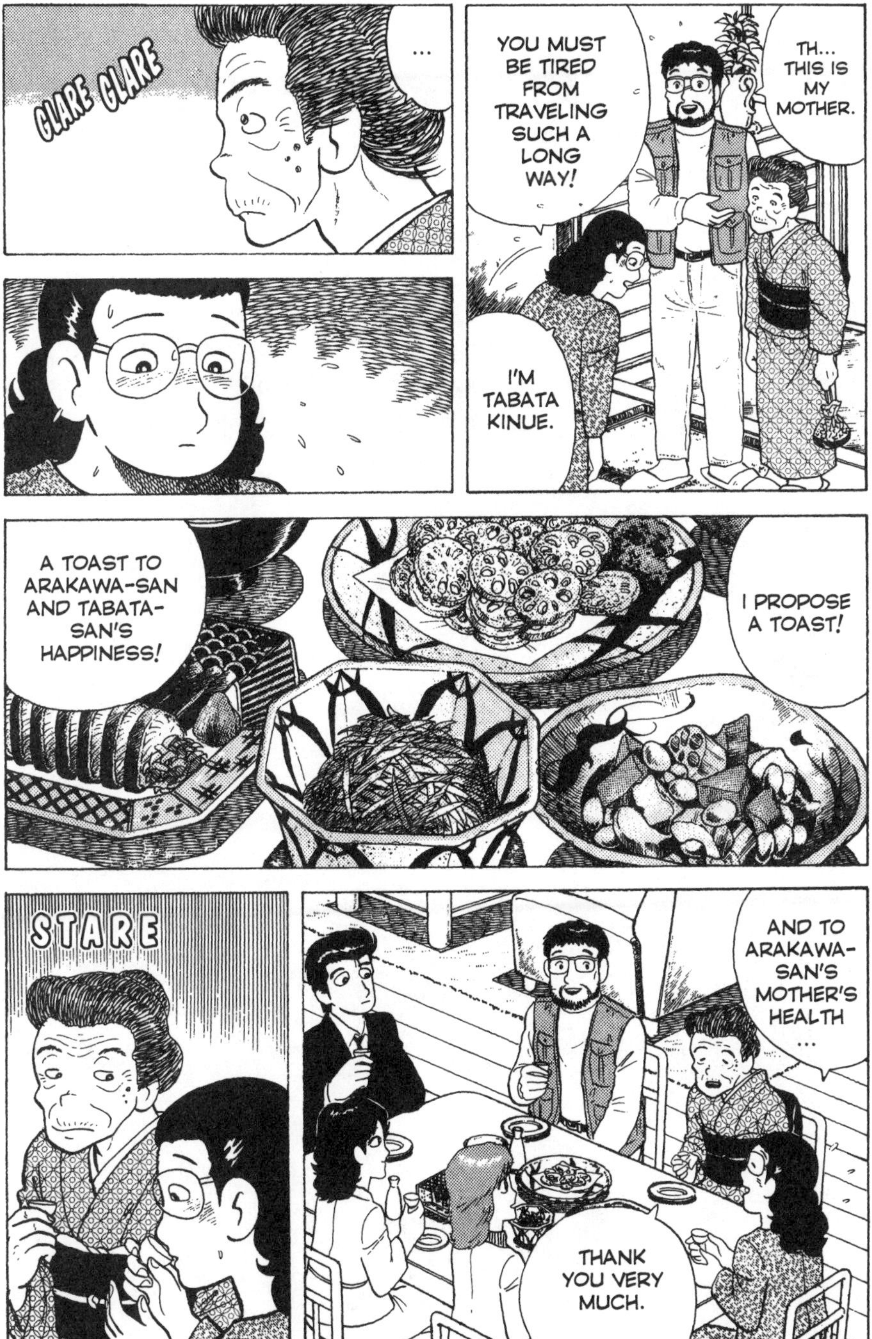
TH... THIS IS MY MOTHER.
YOU MUST BE TIRED FROM TRAVELING SUCH A LONG WAY!
I'M TABATA KINUE.
...
GLARE GLARE
I PROPOSE A TOAST!
A TOAST TO ARAKAWA-SAN AND TABATA-SAN'S HAPPINESS!
AND TO ARAKAWA-SAN'S MOTHER'S HEALTH ...
THANK YOU VERY MUCH.
STARE

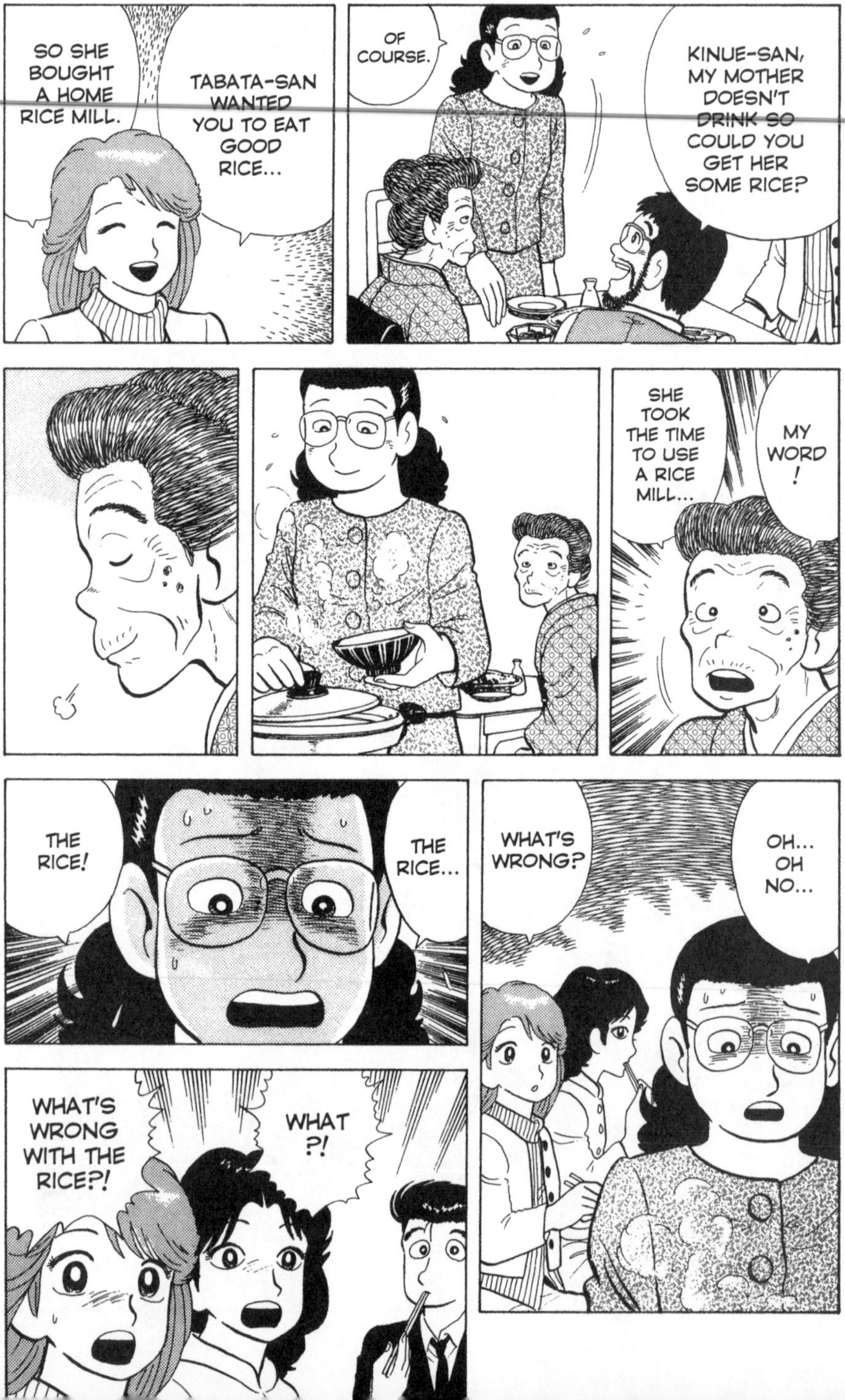
KINUE-SAN, MY MOTHER DOESN'T DRINK SO COULD YOU GET HER SOME RICE?
OF COURSE.
TABATA-SAN WANTED YOU TO EAT GOOD RICE...
SO SHE BOUGHT A HOME RICE MILL.
MY WORD!
SHE TOOK THE TIME TO USE A RICE MILL...
OH... OH NO...
WHAT'S WRONG?
THE RICE...
THE RICE!
WHAT ?!
WHAT'S WRONG WITH THE RICE?!

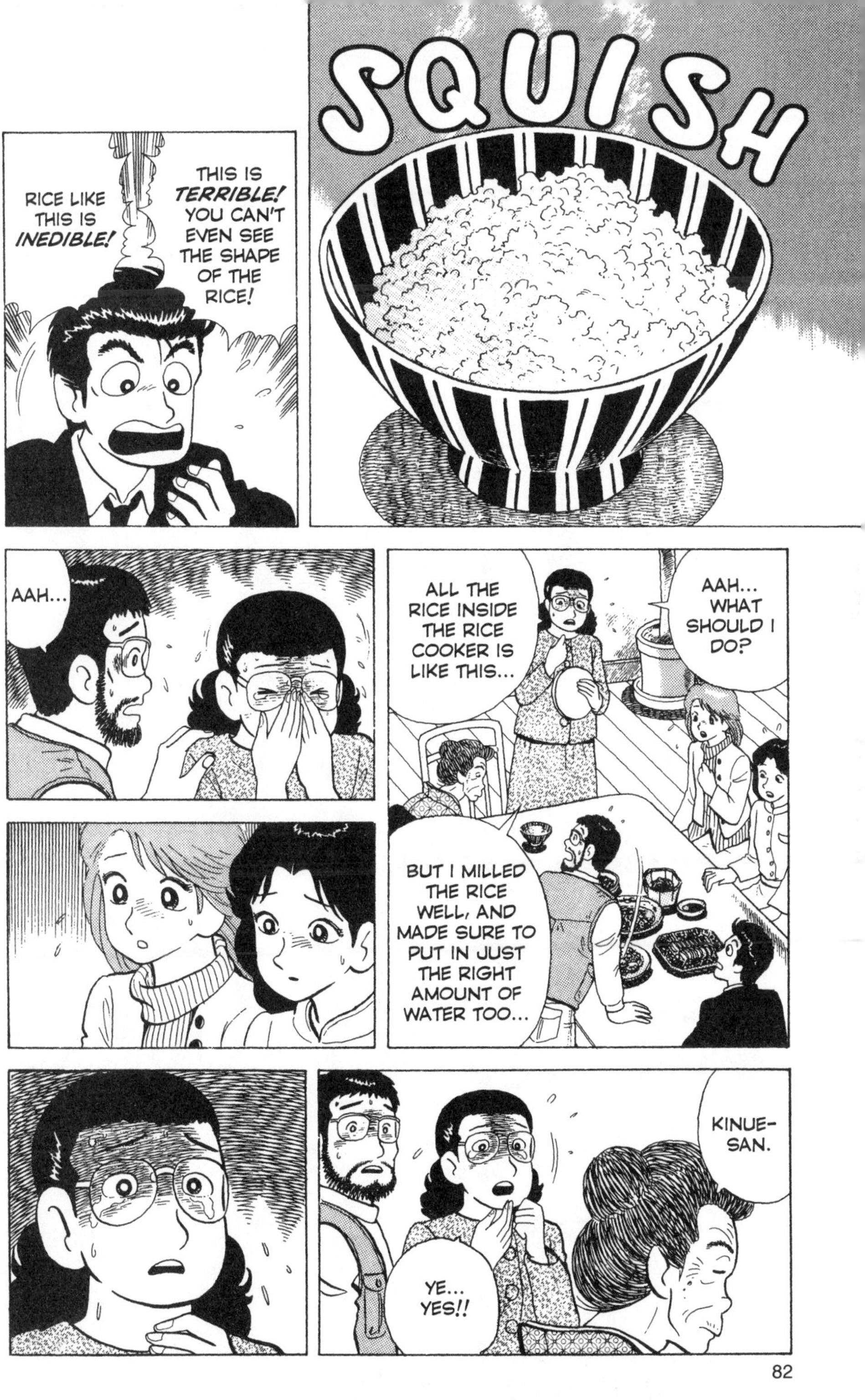
SQUISH
THIS IS *TERRIBLE!* YOU CAN'T EVEN SEE THE SHAPE OF THE RICE!
RICE LIKE THIS IS *INEDIBLE!*
AAH... WHAT SHOULD I DO?
ALL THE RICE INSIDE THE RICE COOKER IS LIKE THIS...
BUT I MILLED THE RICE WELL, AND MADE SURE TO PUT IN JUST THE RIGHT AMOUNT OF WATER TOO...
AAH...
KINUE-SAN.
YE... YES!!

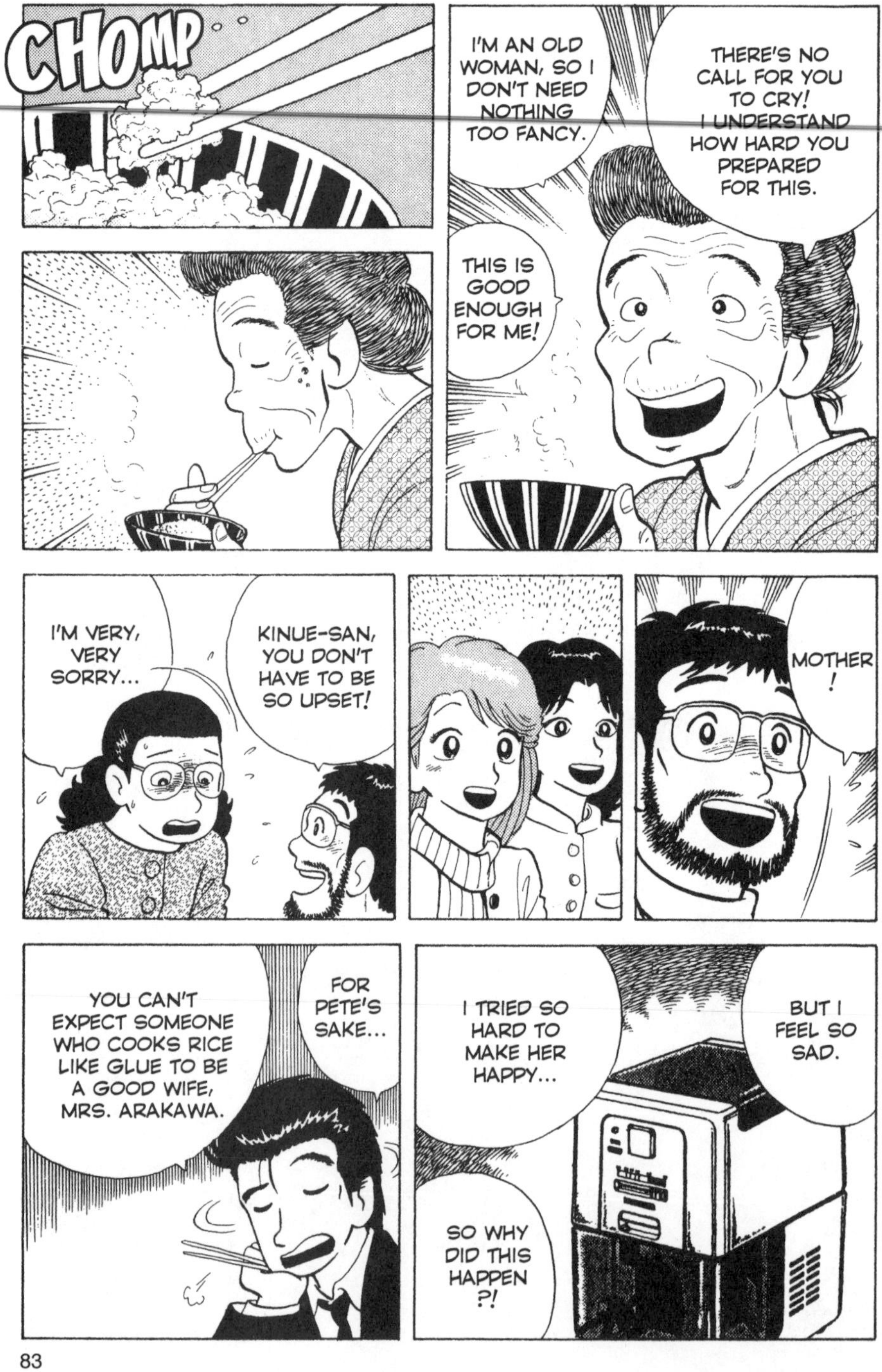
THERE'S NO CALL FOR YOU TO CRY! I UNDERSTAND HOW HARD YOU PREPARED FOR THIS.
I'M AN OLD WOMAN, SO I DON'T NEED NOTHING TOO FANCY.
THIS IS GOOD ENOUGH FOR ME!
CHOMP
MOTHER!
KINUE-SAN, YOU DON'T HAVE TO BE SO UPSET!
I'M VERY, VERY SORRY...
BUT I FEEL SO SAD.
I TRIED SO HARD TO MAKE HER HAPPY...
SO WHY DID THIS HAPPEN ?!
FOR PETE'S SAKE...
YOU CAN'T EXPECT SOMEONE WHO COOKS RICE LIKE GLUE TO BE A GOOD WIFE, MRS. ARAKAWA.

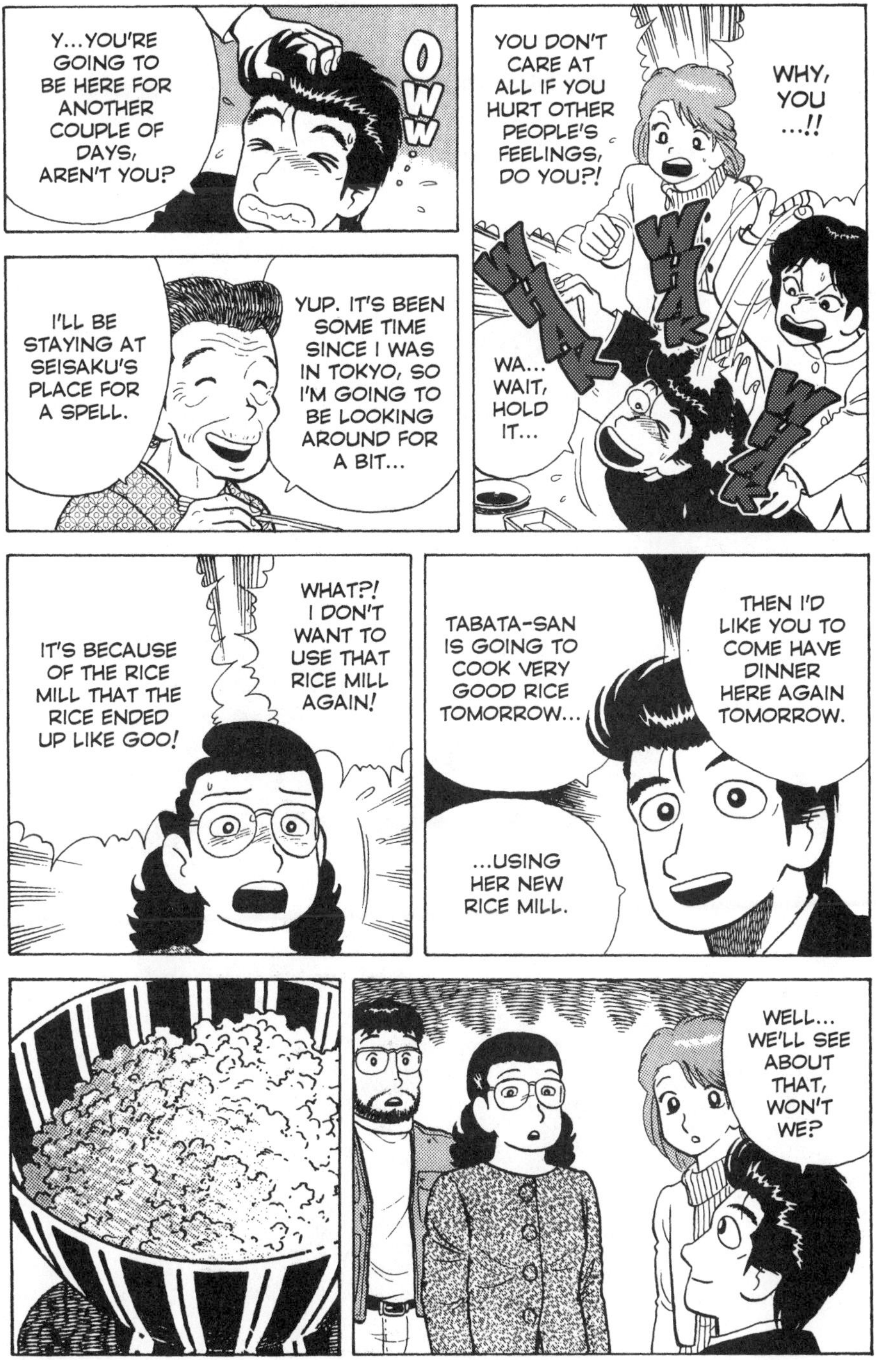
WHY, YOU ...!!
YOU DON'T CARE AT ALL IF YOU HURT OTHER PEOPLE'S FEELINGS, DO YOU?!
WHAK
WHAK
WHAK
WA... WAIT, HOLD IT...
OWW
Y...YOU'RE GOING TO BE HERE FOR ANOTHER COUPLE OF DAYS, AREN'T YOU?
YUP. IT'S BEEN SOME TIME SINCE I WAS IN TOKYO, SO I'M GOING TO BE LOOKING AROUND FOR A BIT...
I'LL BE STAYING AT SEISAKU'S PLACE FOR A SPELL.
THEN I'D LIKE YOU TO COME HAVE DINNER HERE AGAIN TOMORROW.
TABATA-SAN IS GOING TO COOK VERY GOOD RICE TOMORROW...
...USING HER NEW RICE MILL.
WHAT?! I DON'T WANT TO USE THAT RICE MILL AGAIN!
IT'S BECAUSE OF THE RICE MILL THAT THE RICE ENDED UP LIKE GOO!
WELL... WE'LL SEE ABOUT THAT, WON'T WE?

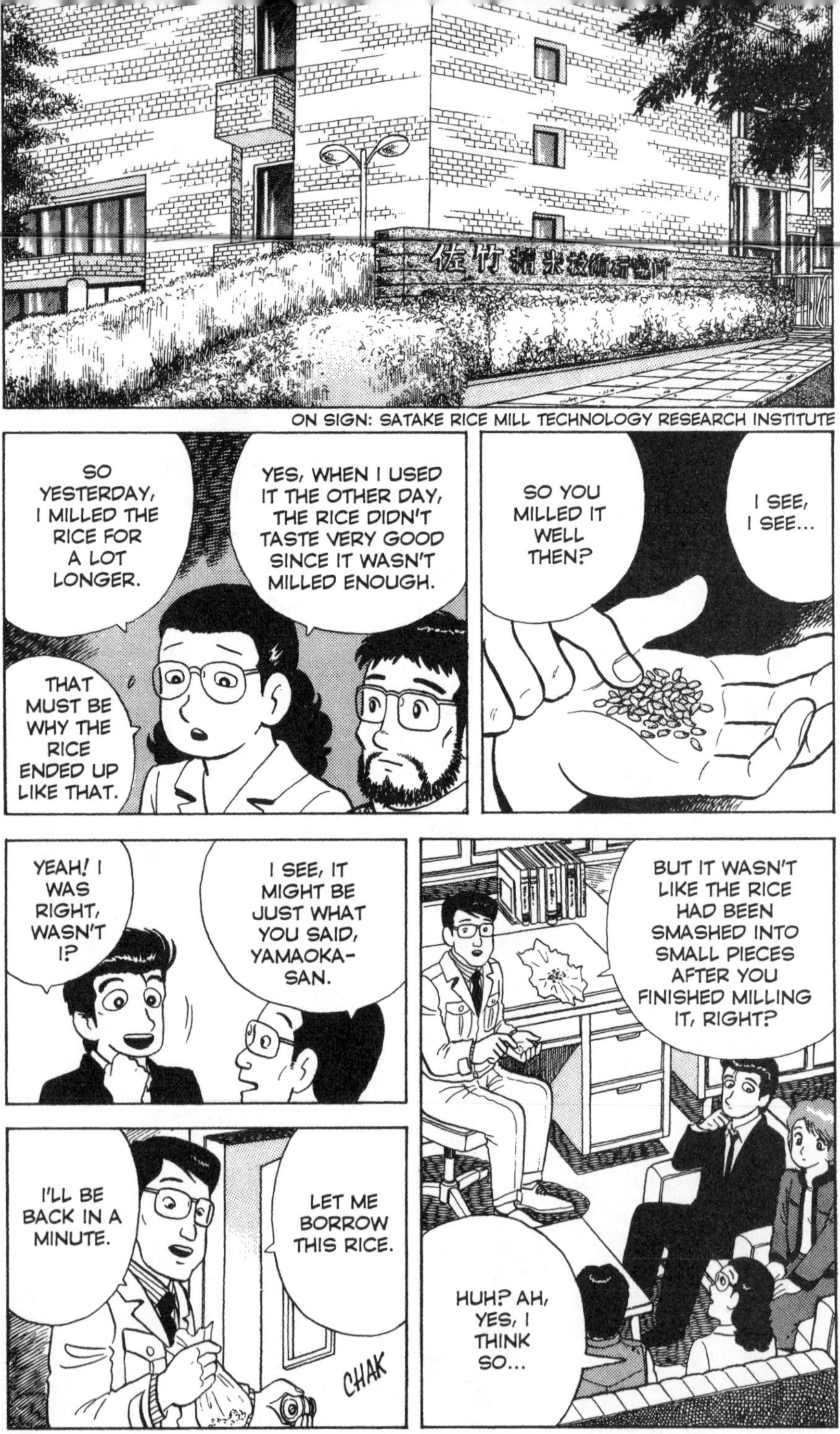
佐竹精米技術研究所
ON SIGN: SATAKE RICE MILL TECHNOLOGY RESEARCH INSTITUTE
I SEE, I SEE...
SO YOU MILLED IT WELL THEN?
YES, WHEN I USED IT THE OTHER DAY, THE RICE DIDN'T TASTE VERY GOOD SINCE IT WASN'T MILLED ENOUGH.
SO YESTERDAY, I MILLED THE RICE FOR A LOT LONGER.
THAT MUST BE WHY THE RICE ENDED UP LIKE THAT.
BUT IT WASN'T LIKE THE RICE HAD BEEN SMASHED INTO SMALL PIECES AFTER YOU FINISHED MILLING IT, RIGHT?
HUH? AH, YES, I THINK SO...
I SEE, IT MIGHT BE JUST WHAT YOU SAID, YAMAOKA-SAN.
YEAH! I WAS RIGHT, WASN'T I?
LET ME BORROW THIS RICE.
I'LL BE BACK IN A MINUTE.
CHAK

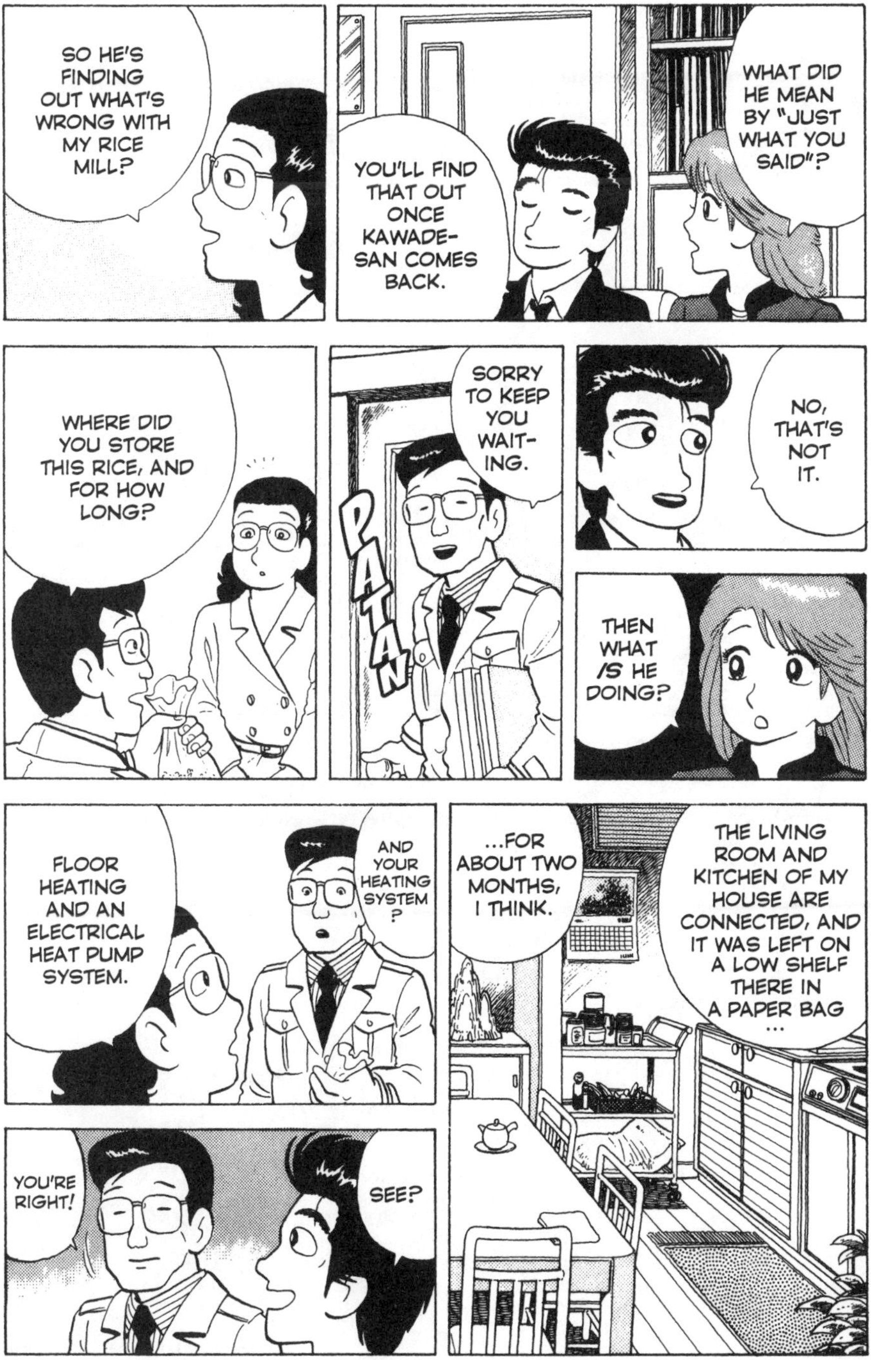
WHAT DID HE MEAN BY "JUST WHAT YOU SAID"?
YOU'LL FIND THAT OUT ONCE KAWADE-SAN COMES BACK.
SO HE'S FINDING OUT WHAT'S WRONG WITH MY RICE MILL?
NO, THAT'S NOT IT.
THEN WHAT IS HE DOING?
SORRY TO KEEP YOU WAITING.
PATAN
WHERE DID YOU STORE THIS RICE, AND FOR HOW LONG?
THE LIVING ROOM AND KITCHEN OF MY HOUSE ARE CONNECTED, AND IT WAS LEFT ON A LOW SHELF THERE IN A PAPER BAG ...
...FOR ABOUT TWO MONTHS, I THINK.
AND YOUR HEATING SYSTEM?
FLOOR HEATING AND AN ELECTRICAL HEAT PUMP SYSTEM.
SEE?
YOU'RE RIGHT!

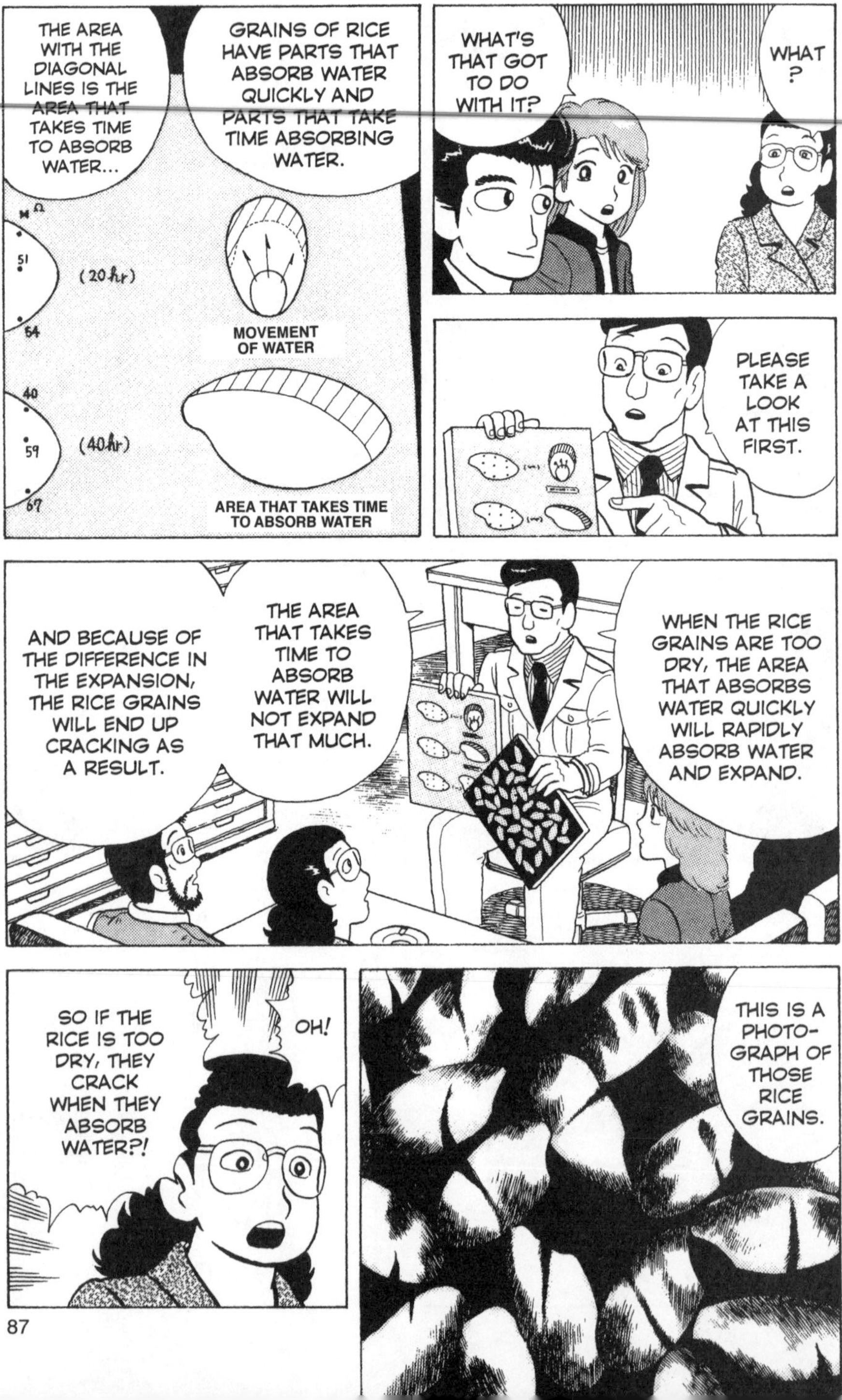
WHAT?
WHAT'S THAT GOT TO DO WITH IT?
PLEASE TAKE A LOOK AT THIS FIRST.
GRAINS OF RICE HAVE PARTS THAT ABSORB WATER QUICKLY AND PARTS THAT TAKE TIME ABSORBING WATER.
THE AREA WITH THE DIAGONAL LINES IS THE AREA THAT TAKES TIME TO ABSORB WATER...
51
(20 hr)
54
MOVEMENT OF WATER
40
59
(40 hr)
67
AREA THAT TAKES TIME TO ABSORB WATER
WHEN THE RICE GRAINS ARE TOO DRY, THE AREA THAT ABSORBS WATER QUICKLY WILL RAPIDLY ABSORB WATER AND EXPAND.
THE AREA THAT TAKES TIME TO ABSORB WATER WILL NOT EXPAND THAT MUCH.
AND BECAUSE OF THE DIFFERENCE IN THE EXPANSION, THE RICE GRAINS WILL END UP CRACKING AS A RESULT.
THIS IS A PHOTOGRAPH OF THOSE RICE GRAINS.
OH!
SO IF THE RICE IS TOO DRY, THEY CRACK WHEN THEY ABSORB WATER?!

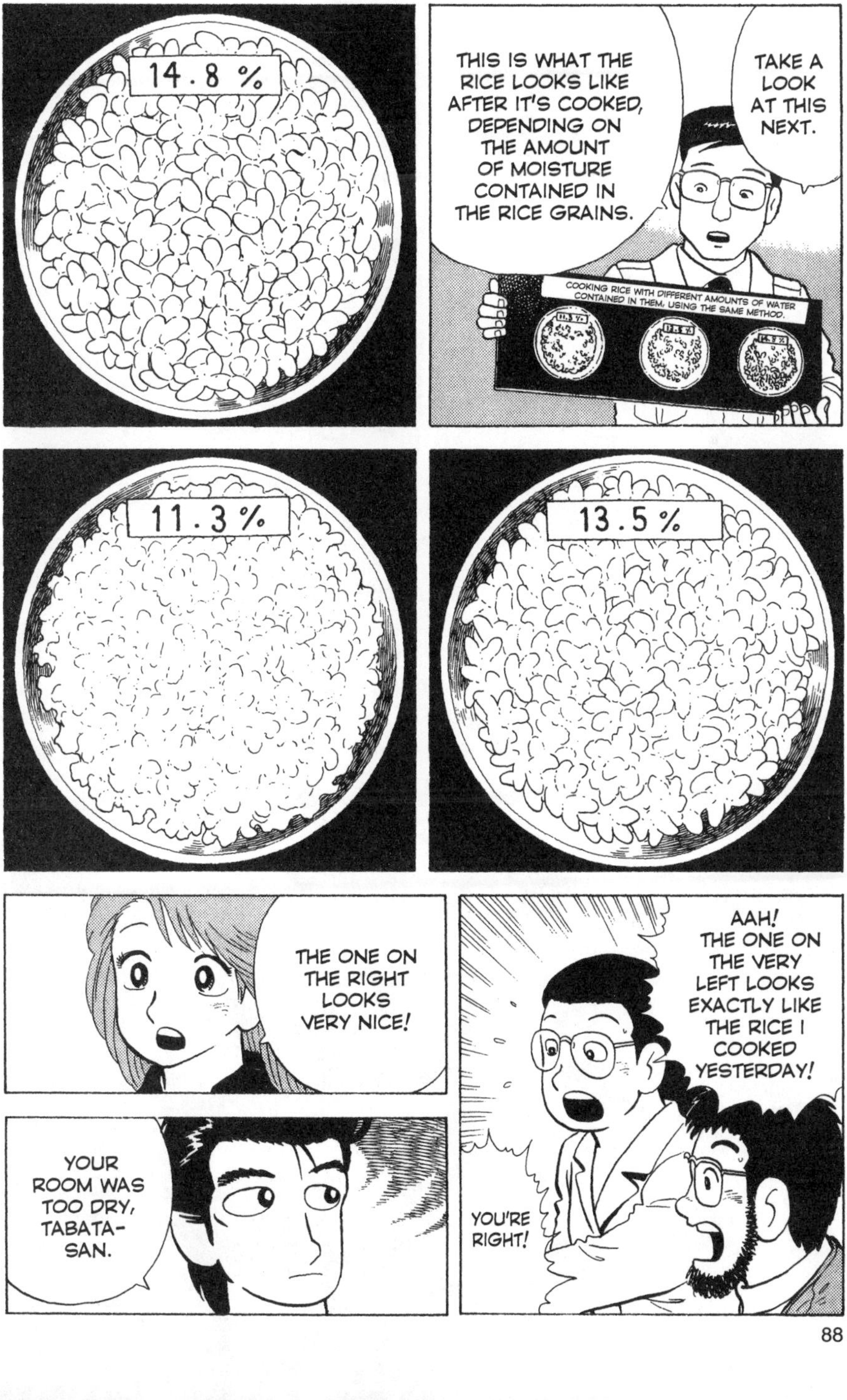
TAKE A LOOK AT THIS NEXT.
THIS IS WHAT THE RICE LOOKS LIKE AFTER IT'S COOKED, DEPENDING ON THE AMOUNT OF MOISTURE CONTAINED IN THE RICE GRAINS.
COOKING RICE WITH DIFFERENT AMOUNTS OF WATER CONTAINED IN THEM, USING THE SAME METHOD.
14.8 %
13.5 %
11.3 %
AAH! THE ONE ON THE VERY LEFT LOOKS EXACTLY LIKE THE RICE I COOKED YESTERDAY!
YOU'RE RIGHT!
THE ONE ON THE RIGHT LOOKS VERY NICE!
YOUR ROOM WAS TOO DRY, TABATA-SAN.

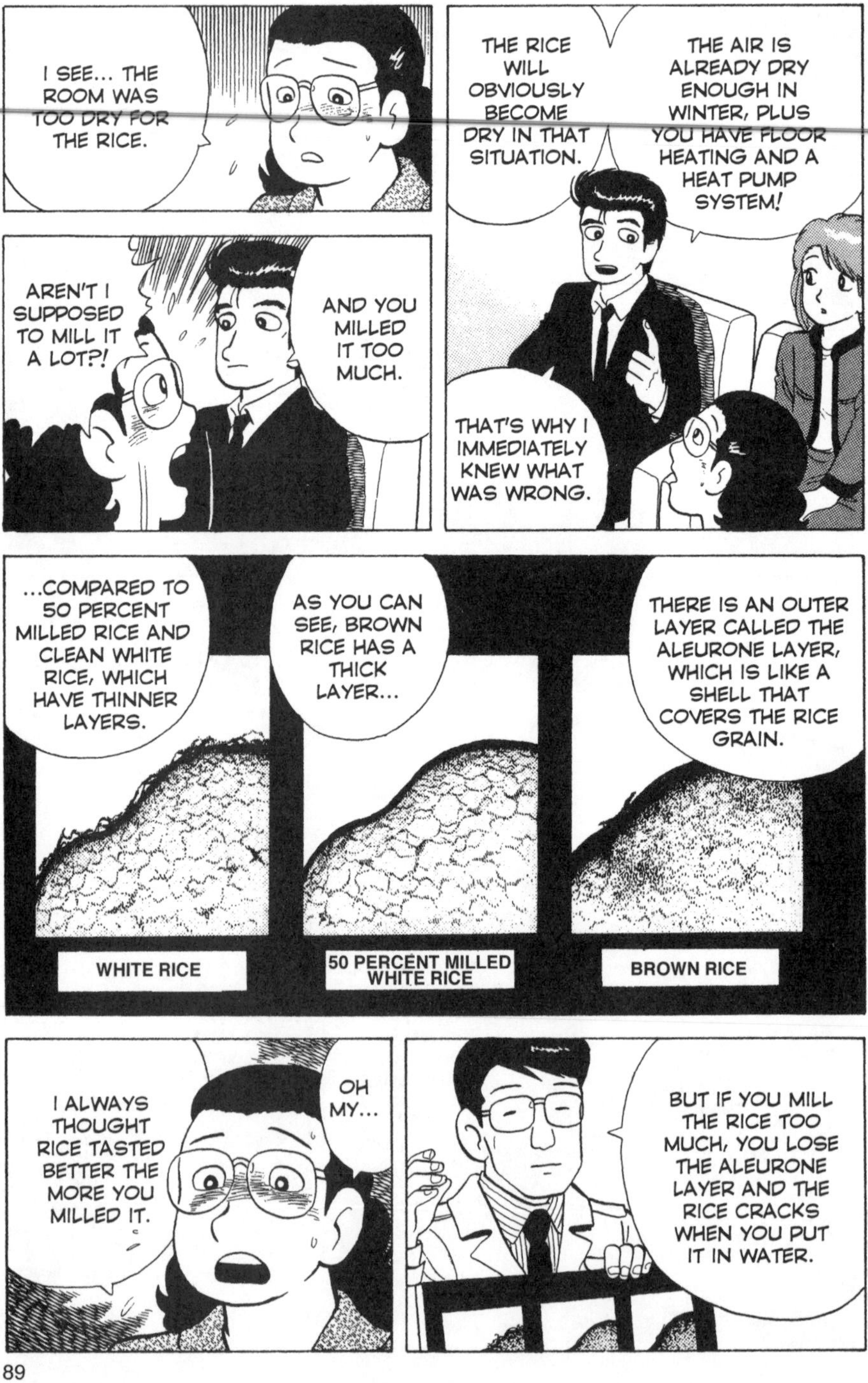
THE AIR IS ALREADY DRY ENOUGH IN WINTER, PLUS YOU HAVE FLOOR HEATING AND A HEAT PUMP SYSTEM!
THE RICE WILL OBVIOUSLY BECOME DRY IN THAT SITUATION.
THAT'S WHY I IMMEDIATELY KNEW WHAT WAS WRONG.
I SEE... THE ROOM WAS TOO DRY FOR THE RICE.
AND YOU MILLED IT TOO MUCH.
AREN'T I SUPPOSED TO MILL IT A LOT?!
THERE IS AN OUTER LAYER CALLED THE ALEURONE LAYER, WHICH IS LIKE A SHELL THAT COVERS THE RICE GRAIN.
BROWN RICE
AS YOU CAN SEE, BROWN RICE HAS A THICK LAYER...
50 PERCENT MILLED WHITE RICE
...COMPARED TO 50 PERCENT MILLED RICE AND CLEAN WHITE RICE, WHICH HAVE THINNER LAYERS.
WHITE RICE
BUT IF YOU MILL THE RICE TOO MUCH, YOU LOSE THE ALEURONE LAYER AND THE RICE CRACKS WHEN YOU PUT IT IN WATER.
OH MY...
I ALWAYS THOUGHT RICE TASTED BETTER THE MORE YOU MILLED IT.

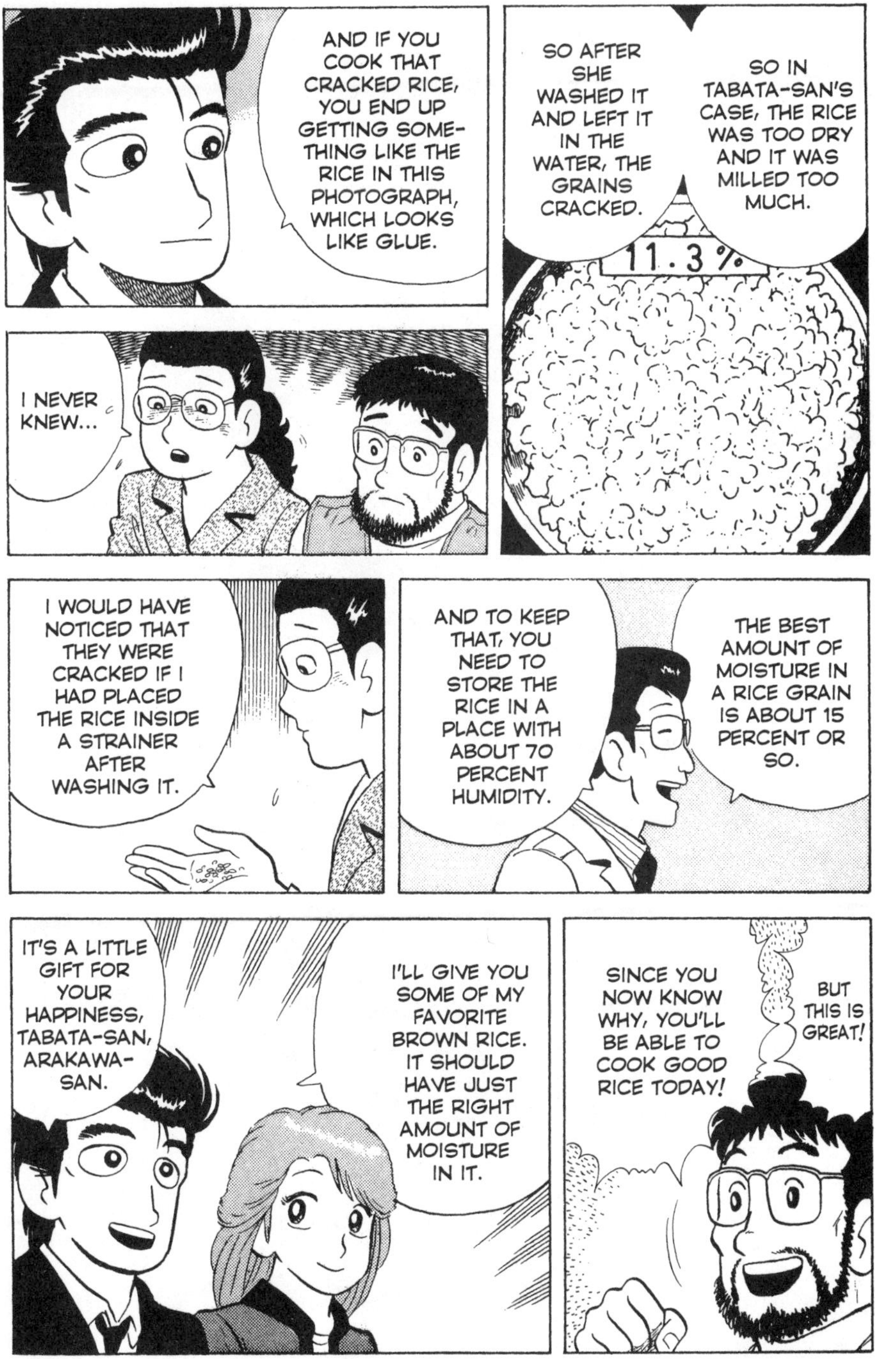
SO IN TABATA-SAN'S CASE, THE RICE WAS TOO DRY AND IT WAS MILLED TOO MUCH.
SO AFTER SHE WASHED IT AND LEFT IT IN THE WATER, THE GRAINS CRACKED.
11.3%
AND IF YOU COOK THAT CRACKED RICE, YOU END UP GETTING SOME-THING LIKE THE RICE IN THIS PHOTOGRAPH, WHICH LOOKS LIKE GLUE.
I NEVER KNEW...
THE BEST AMOUNT OF MOISTURE IN A RICE GRAIN IS ABOUT 15 PERCENT OR SO.
AND TO KEEP THAT, YOU NEED TO STORE THE RICE IN A PLACE WITH ABOUT 70 PERCENT HUMIDITY.
I WOULD HAVE NOTICED THAT THEY WERE CRACKED IF I HAD PLACED THE RICE INSIDE A STRAINER AFTER WASHING IT.
BUT THIS IS GREAT!
SINCE YOU NOW KNOW WHY, YOU'LL BE ABLE TO COOK GOOD RICE TODAY!
I'LL GIVE YOU SOME OF MY FAVORITE BROWN RICE. IT SHOULD HAVE JUST THE RIGHT AMOUNT OF MOISTURE IN IT.
IT'S A LITTLE GIFT FOR YOUR HAPPINESS, TABATA-SAN, ARAKAWA-SAN.

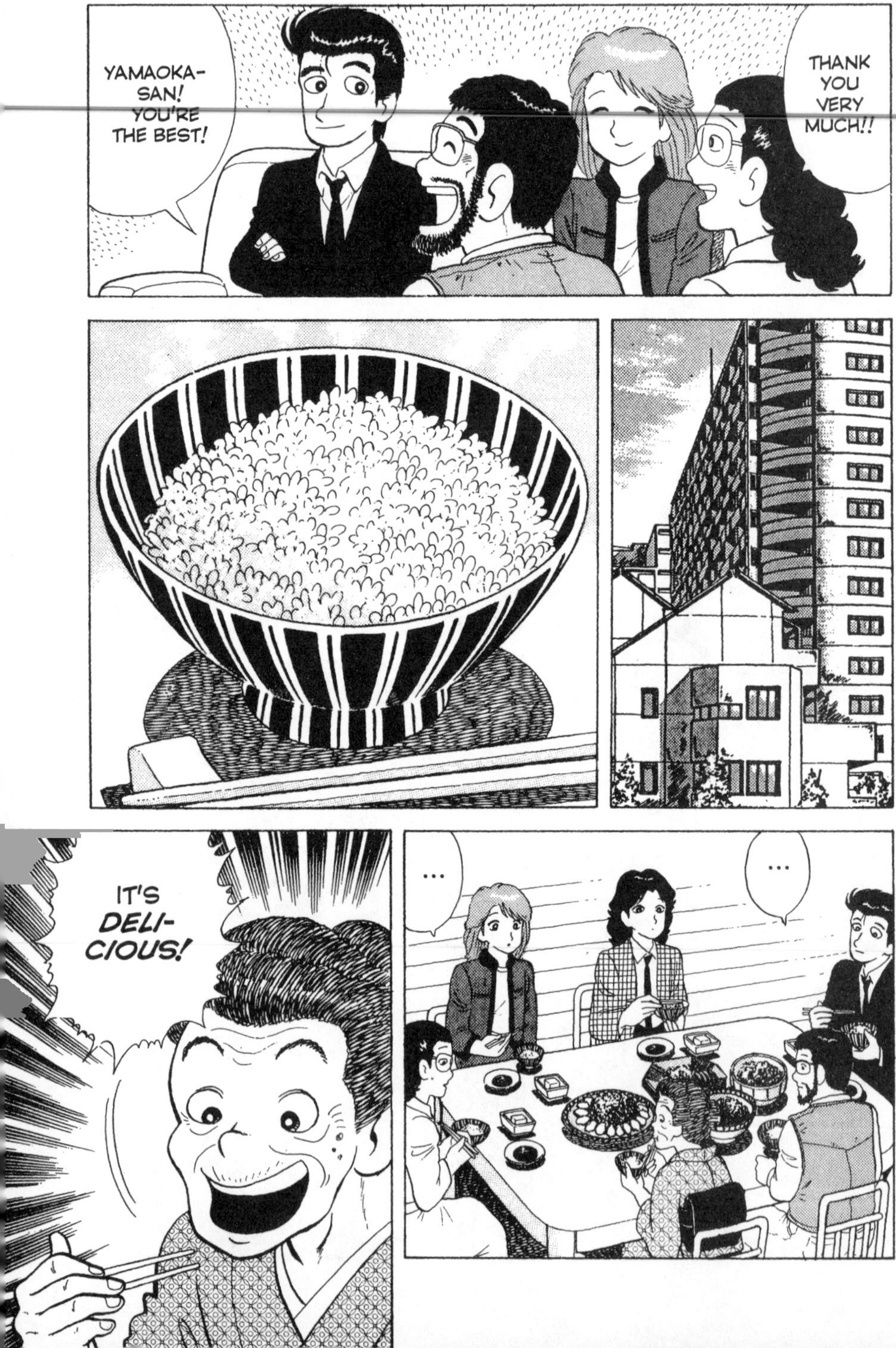
THANK YOU VERY MUCH!!
YAMAOKA-SAN! YOU'RE THE BEST!
...
...
IT'S DELICIOUS!

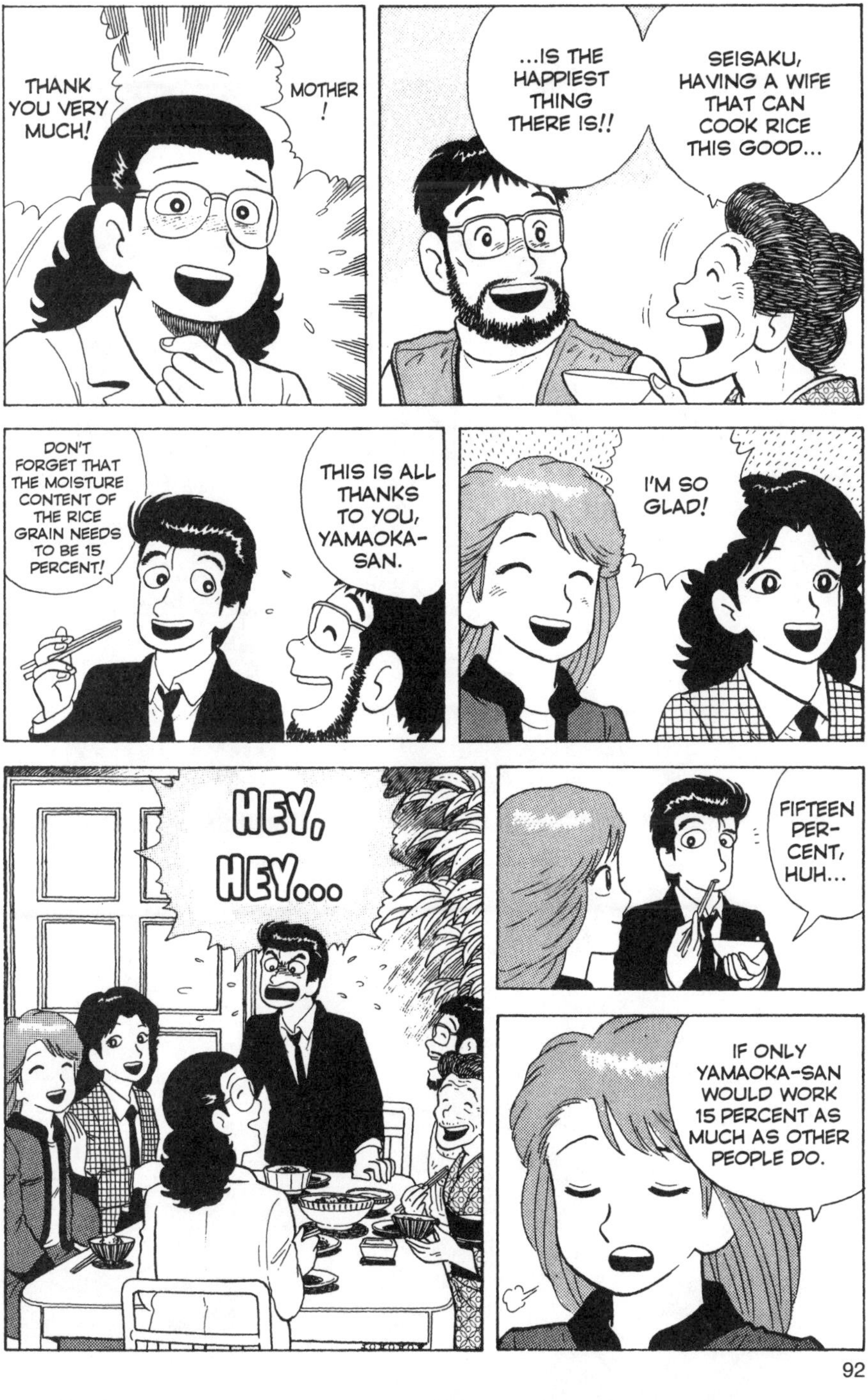
SEISAKU, HAVING A WIFE THAT CAN COOK RICE THIS GOOD...
...IS THE HAPPIEST THING THERE IS!!
MOTHER!
THANK YOU VERY MUCH!
I'M SO GLAD!
THIS IS ALL THANKS TO YOU, YAMAOKA-SAN.
DON'T FORGET THAT THE MOISTURE CONTENT OF THE RICE GRAIN NEEDS TO BE 15 PERCENT!
FIFTEEN PER-CENT, HUH...
IF ONLY YAMAOKA-SAN WOULD WORK 15 PERCENT AS MUCH AS OTHER PEOPLE DO.
HEY, HEY...

FOURTH COURSE COMPANIONS OF RICE

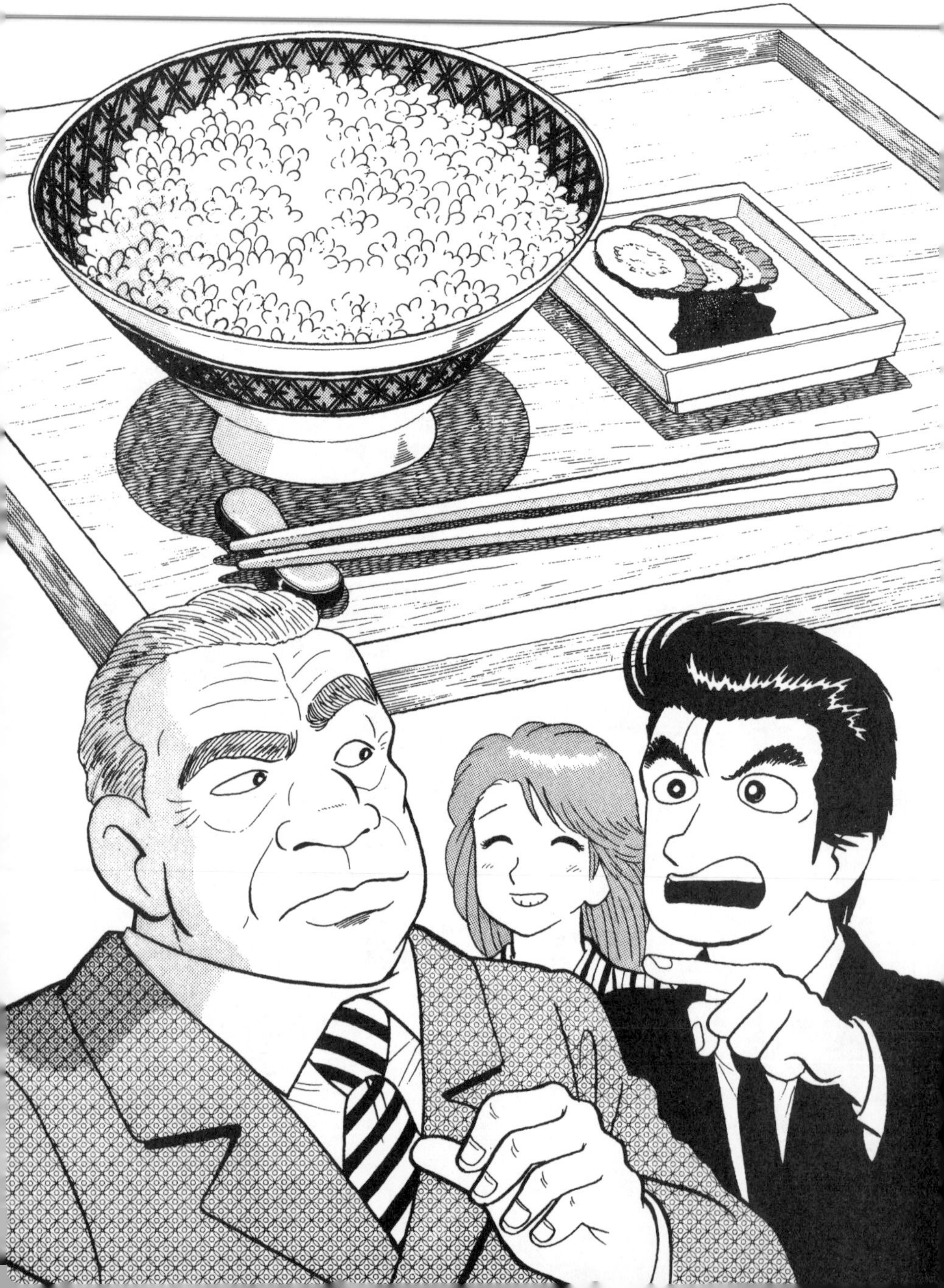

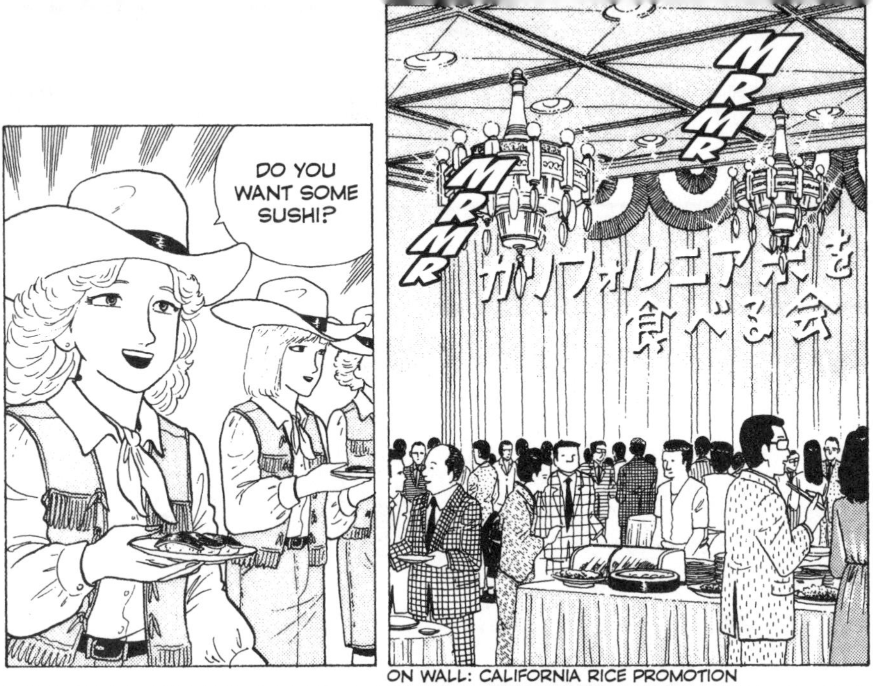
MRMRMR
MRMRMR
カリフォルニア米を食べる会
DO YOU WANT SOME SUSHI?

ON WALL: CALIFORNIA RICE PROMOTION

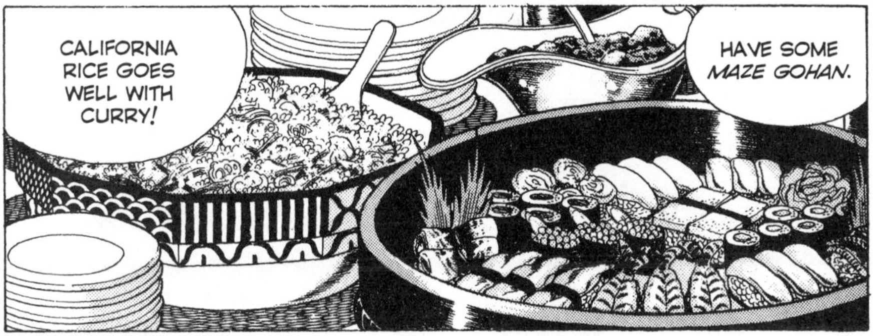
HAVE SOME *MAZE GOHAN*.
CALIFORNIA RICE GOES WELL WITH CURRY!

ON BELT: MISS CALIFORNIA

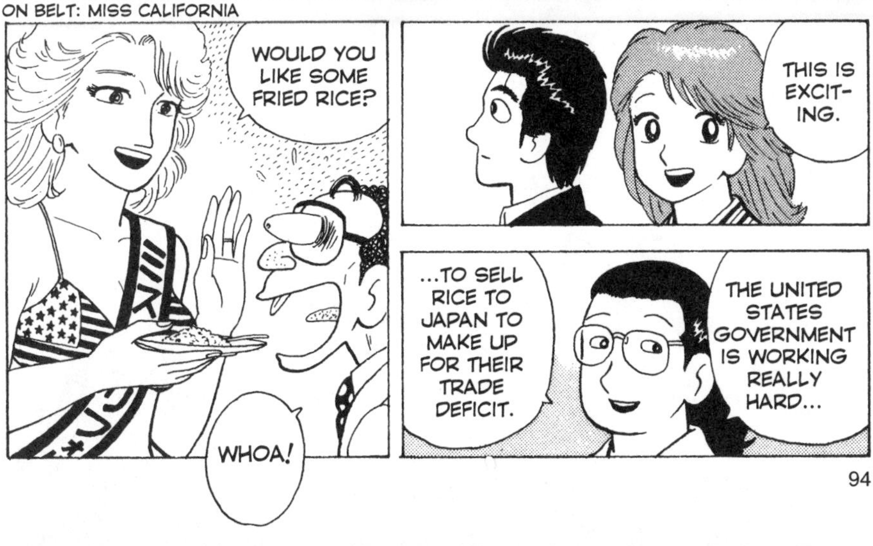
THIS IS EXCIT-ING.
THE UNITED STATES GOVERNMENT IS WORKING REALLY HARD...
...TO SELL RICE TO JAPAN TO MAKE UP FOR THEIR TRADE DEFICIT.
WOULD YOU LIKE SOME FRIED RICE?
WHOA!

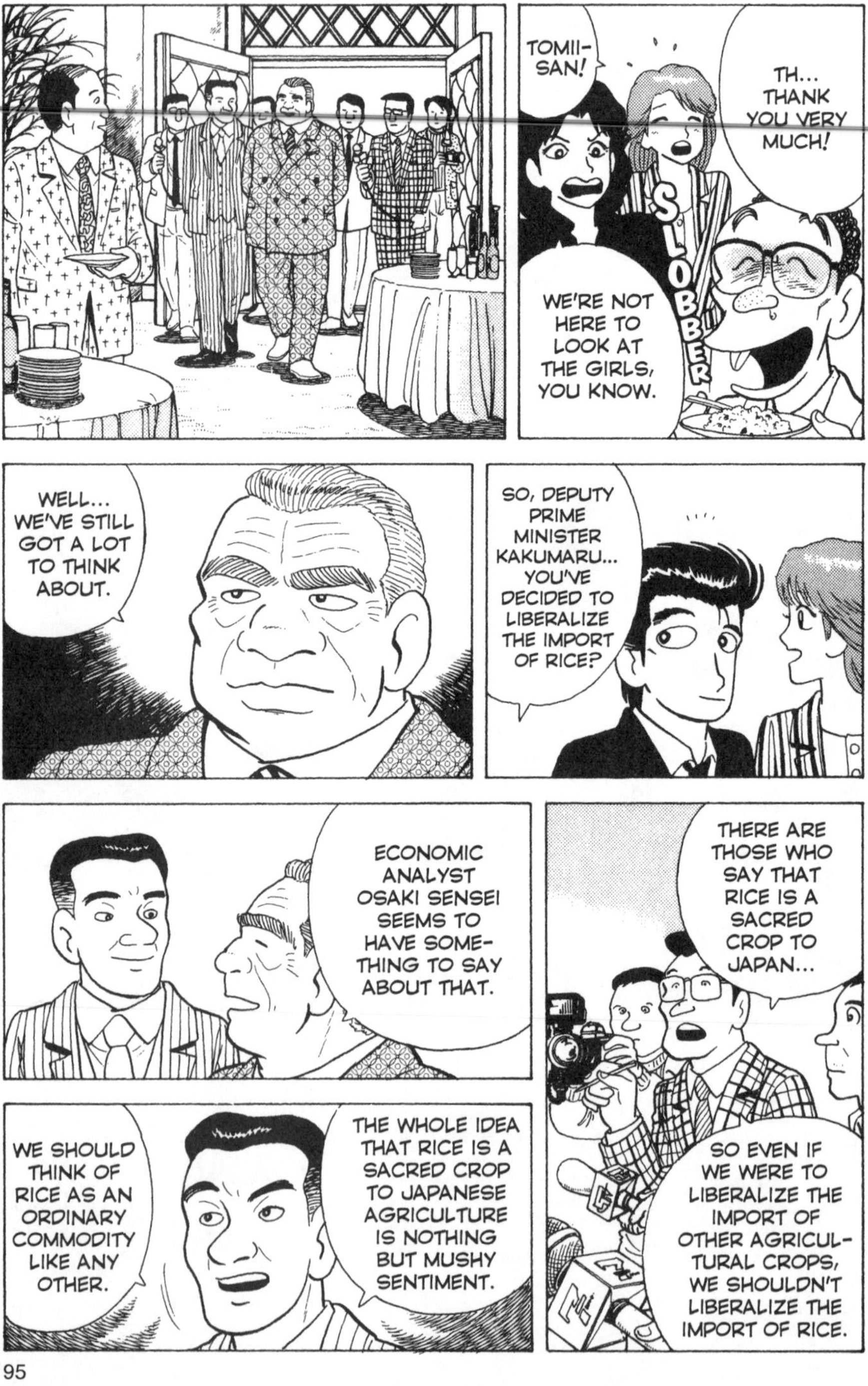
TH... THANK YOU VERY MUCH!
TOMII-SAN!
SLOBBER
WE'RE NOT HERE TO LOOK AT THE GIRLS, YOU KNOW.
SO, DEPUTY PRIME MINISTER KAKUMARU... YOU'VE DECIDED TO LIBERALIZE THE IMPORT OF RICE?
WELL... WE'VE STILL GOT A LOT TO THINK ABOUT.
THERE ARE THOSE WHO SAY THAT RICE IS A SACRED CROP TO JAPAN...
SO EVEN IF WE WERE TO LIBERALIZE THE IMPORT OF OTHER AGRICUL-TURAL CROPS, WE SHOULDN'T LIBERALIZE THE IMPORT OF RICE.
ECONOMIC ANALYST OSAKI SENSEI SEEMS TO HAVE SOME-THING TO SAY ABOUT THAT.
THE WHOLE IDEA THAT RICE IS A SACRED CROP TO JAPANESE AGRICULTURE IS NOTHING BUT MUSHY SENTIMENT.
WE SHOULD THINK OF RICE AS AN ORDINARY COMMODITY LIKE ANY OTHER.

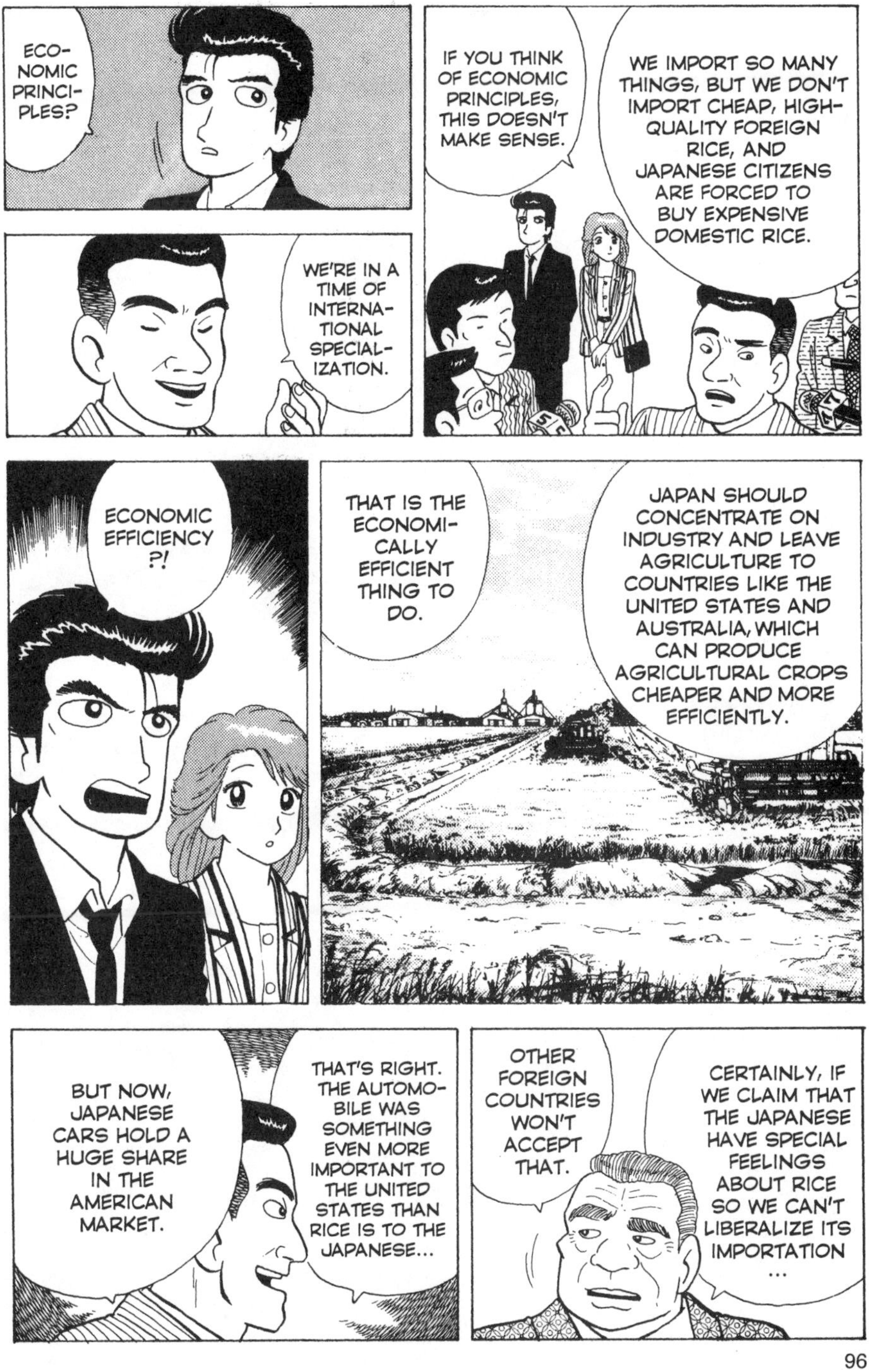
WE IMPORT SO MANY THINGS, BUT WE DON'T IMPORT CHEAP, HIGH-QUALITY FOREIGN RICE, AND JAPANESE CITIZENS ARE FORCED TO BUY EXPENSIVE DOMESTIC RICE.
IF YOU THINK OF ECONOMIC PRINCIPLES, THIS DOESN'T MAKE SENSE.
ECO-NOMIC PRINCI-PLES?
WE'RE IN A TIME OF INTERNA-TIONAL SPECIAL-IZATION.
JAPAN SHOULD CONCENTRATE ON INDUSTRY AND LEAVE AGRICULTURE TO COUNTRIES LIKE THE UNITED STATES AND AUSTRALIA, WHICH CAN PRODUCE AGRICULTURAL CROPS CHEAPER AND MORE EFFICIENTLY.
THAT IS THE ECONOMI-CALLY EFFICIENT THING TO DO.
ECONOMIC EFFICIENCY ?!
CERTAINLY, IF WE CLAIM THAT THE JAPANESE HAVE SPECIAL FEELINGS ABOUT RICE SO WE CAN'T LIBERALIZE ITS IMPORTATION ...
OTHER FOREIGN COUNTRIES WON'T ACCEPT THAT.
THAT'S RIGHT. THE AUTOMO-BILE WAS SOMETHING EVEN MORE IMPORTANT TO THE UNITED STATES THAN RICE IS TO THE JAPANESE...
BUT NOW, JAPANESE CARS HOLD A HUGE SHARE IN THE AMERICAN MARKET.

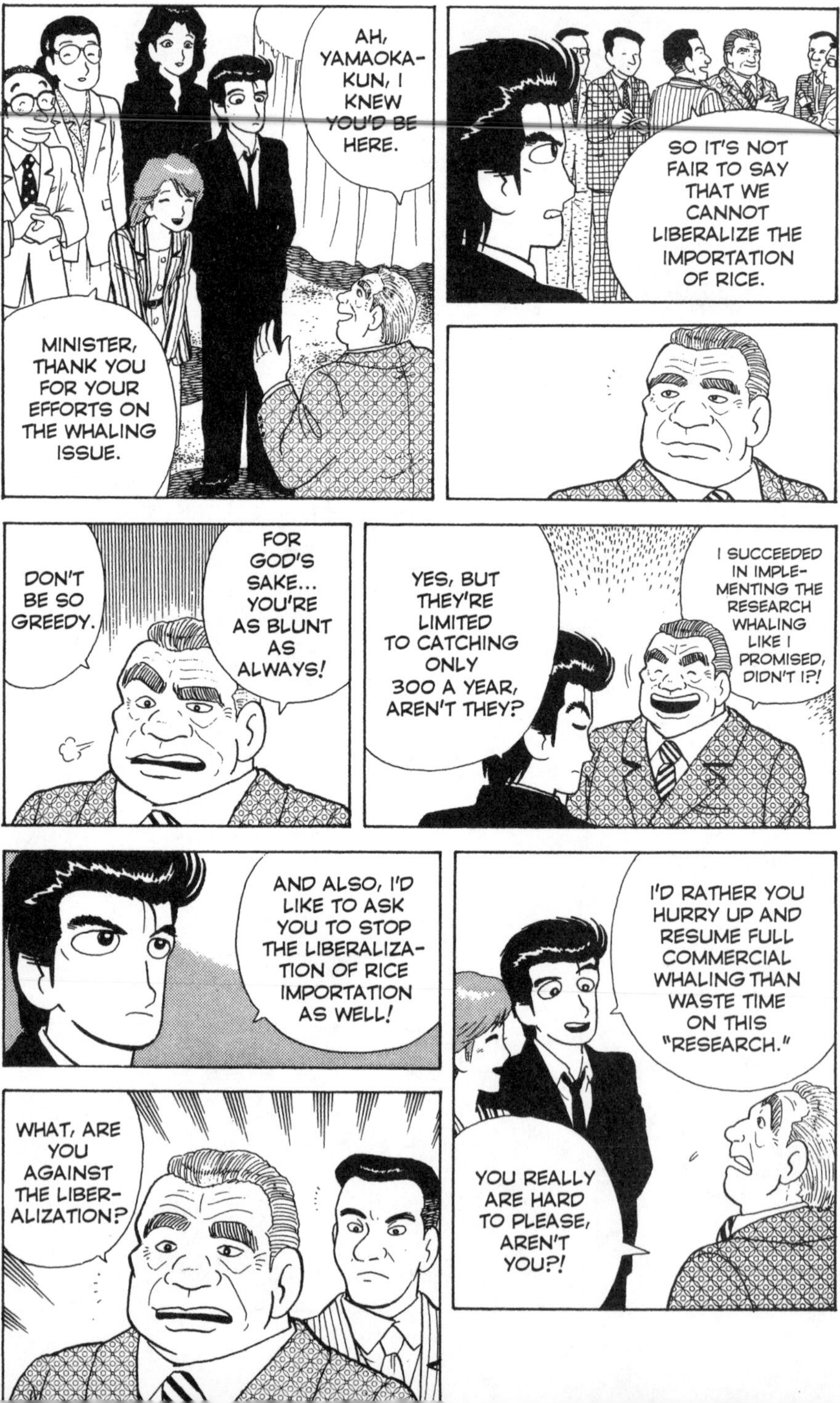
SO IT'S NOT FAIR TO SAY THAT WE CANNOT LIBERALIZE THE IMPORTATION OF RICE.
AH, YAMAOKA-KUN, I KNEW YOU'D BE HERE.
MINISTER, THANK YOU FOR YOUR EFFORTS ON THE WHALING ISSUE.
I SUCCEEDED IN IMPLEMENTING THE RESEARCH WHALING LIKE I PROMISED, DIDN'T I?!
YES, BUT THEY'RE LIMITED TO CATCHING ONLY 300 A YEAR, AREN'T THEY?
FOR GOD'S SAKE... YOU'RE AS BLUNT AS ALWAYS!
DON'T BE SO GREEDY.
I'D RATHER YOU HURRY UP AND RESUME FULL COMMERCIAL WHALING THAN WASTE TIME ON THIS "RESEARCH."
YOU REALLY ARE HARD TO PLEASE, AREN'T YOU?!
AND ALSO, I'D LIKE TO ASK YOU TO STOP THE LIBERALIZATION OF RICE IMPORTATION AS WELL!
WHAT, ARE YOU AGAINST THE LIBERALIZATION?

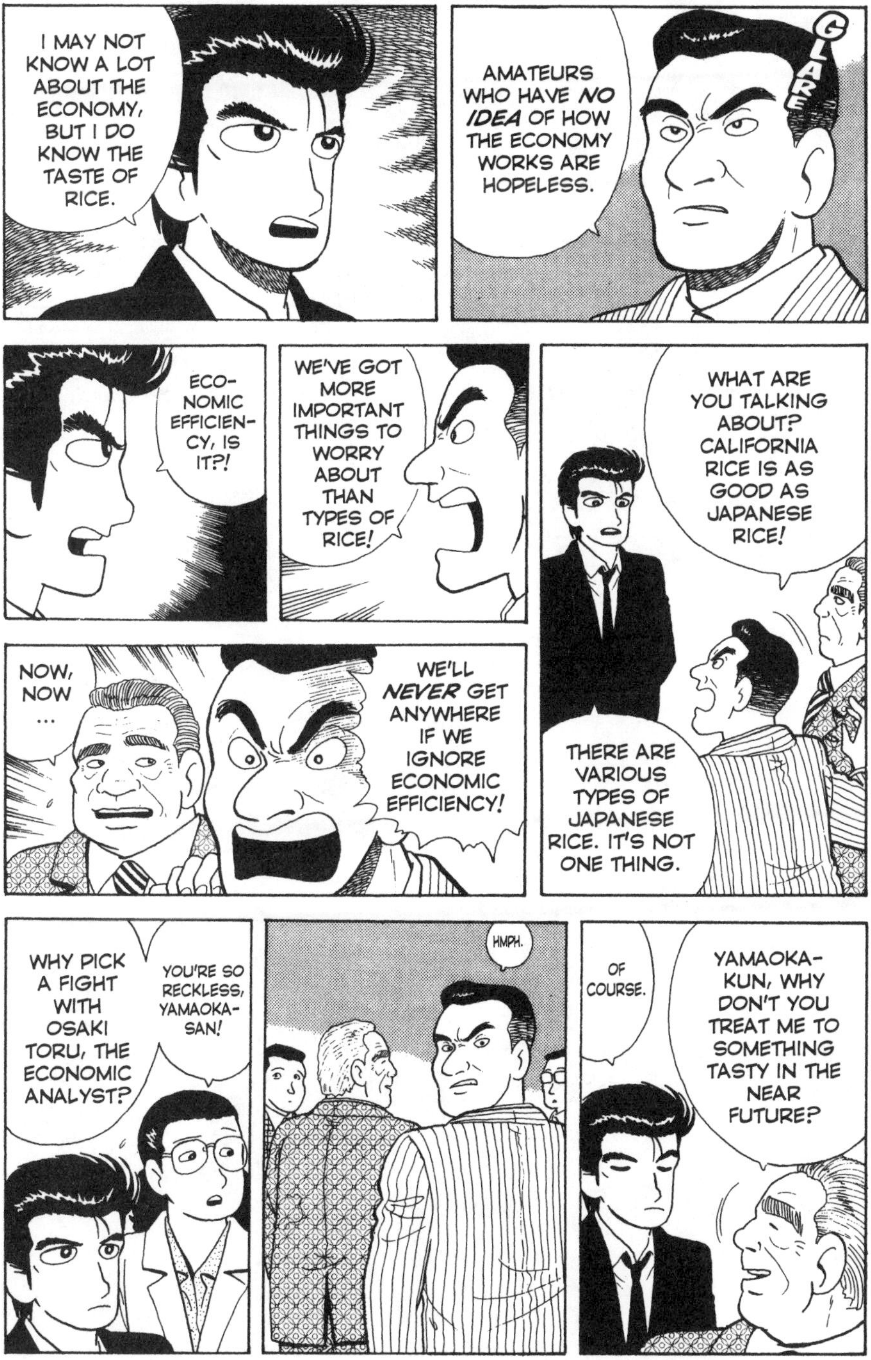
GLARE
AMATEURS WHO HAVE NO IDEA OF HOW THE ECONOMY WORKS ARE HOPELESS.
I MAY NOT KNOW A LOT ABOUT THE ECONOMY, BUT I DO KNOW THE TASTE OF RICE.
WHAT ARE YOU TALKING ABOUT? CALIFORNIA RICE IS AS GOOD AS JAPANESE RICE!
THERE ARE VARIOUS TYPES OF JAPANESE RICE. IT'S NOT ONE THING.
WE'VE GOT MORE IMPORTANT THINGS TO WORRY ABOUT THAN TYPES OF RICE!
ECO-NOMIC EFFICIEN-CY, IS IT?!
WE'LL NEVER GET ANYWHERE IF WE IGNORE ECONOMIC EFFICIENCY!
NOW, NOW ...
YAMAOKA-KUN, WHY DON'T YOU TREAT ME TO SOMETHING TASTY IN THE NEAR FUTURE?
OF COURSE.
HMPH.
YOU'RE SO RECKLESS, YAMAOKA-SAN!
WHY PICK A FIGHT WITH OSAKI TORU, THE ECONOMIC ANALYST?

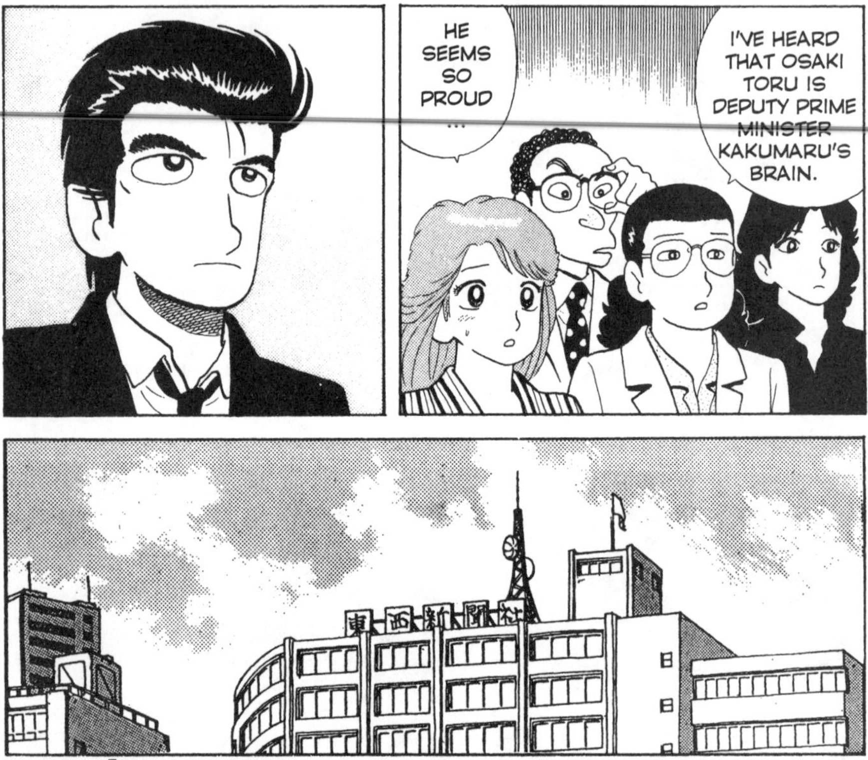
I'VE HEARD THAT OSAKI TORU IS DEPUTY PRIME MINISTER KAKUMARU'S BRAIN.
HE SEEMS SO PROUD ...

ON SIGN: TŌZAI NEWS COMPANY

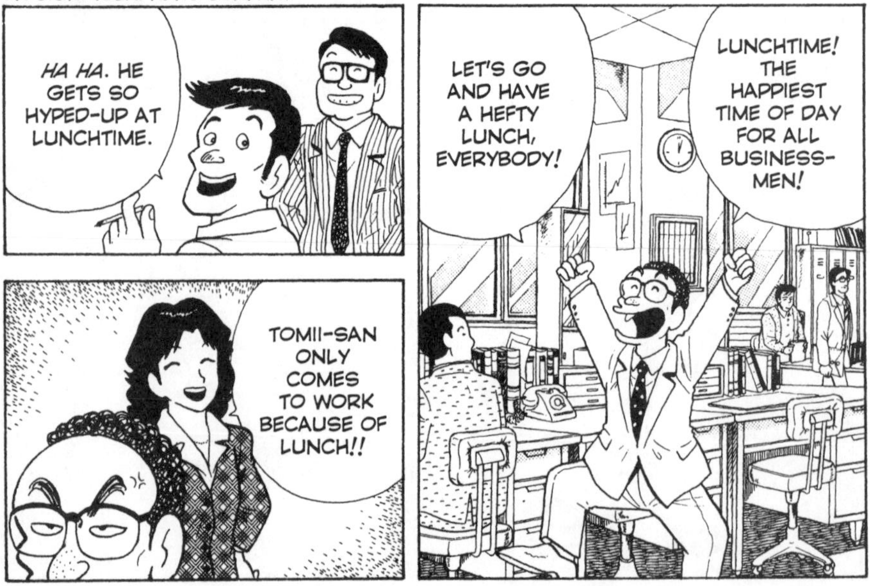
LUNCHTIME! THE HAPPIEST TIME OF DAY FOR ALL BUSINESS-MEN!
LET'S GO AND HAVE A HEFTY LUNCH, EVERYBODY!
HA HA. HE GETS SO HYPED-UP AT LUNCHTIME.
TOMII-SAN ONLY COMES TO WORK BECAUSE OF LUNCH!!

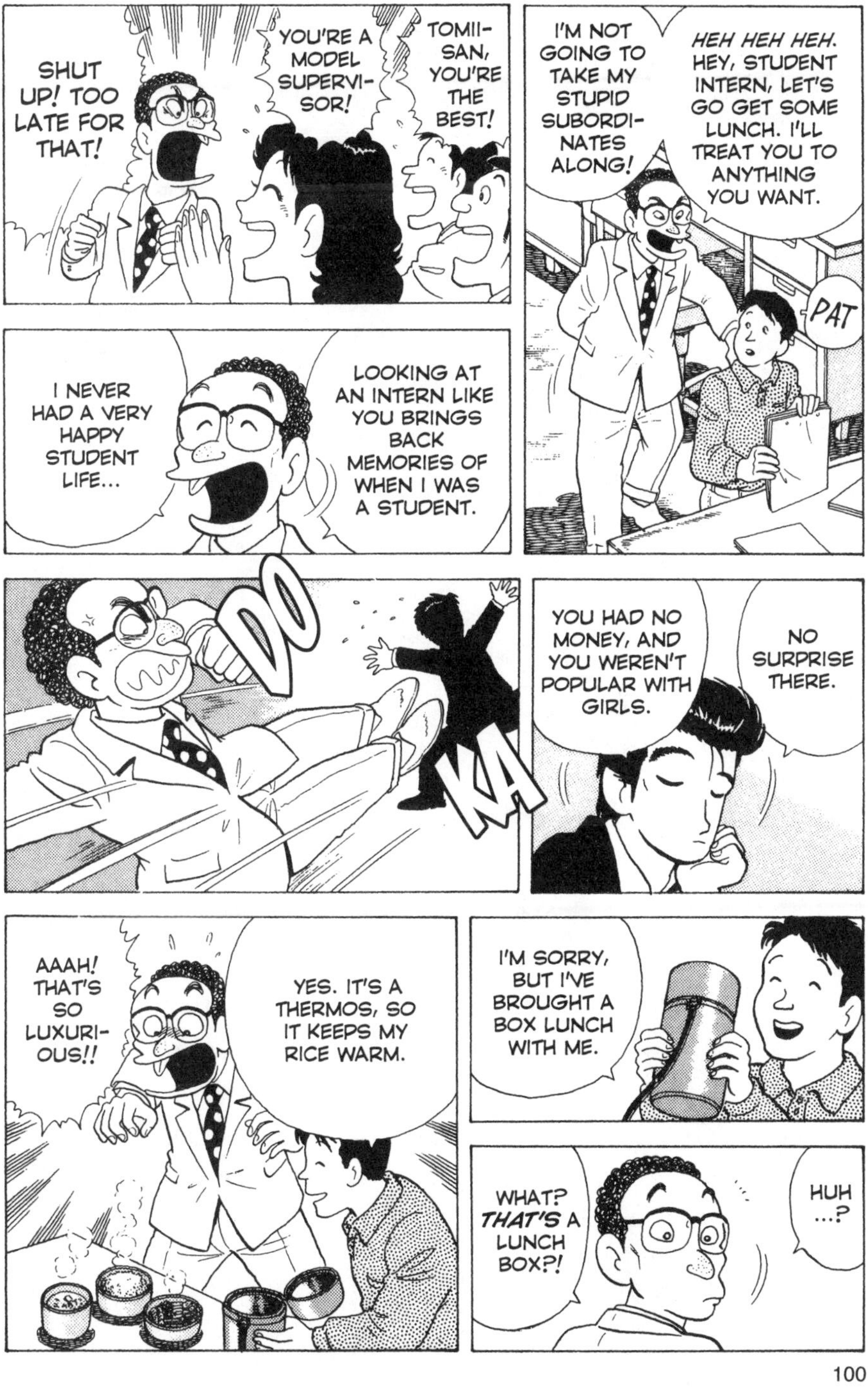
HEH HEH HEH. HEY, STUDENT INTERN, LET'S GO GET SOME LUNCH. I'LL TREAT YOU TO ANYTHING YOU WANT.
I'M NOT GOING TO TAKE MY STUPID SUBORDINATES ALONG!
PAT
TOMII-SAN, YOU'RE THE BEST!
YOU'RE A MODEL SUPERVISOR!
SHUT UP! TOO LATE FOR THAT!
LOOKING AT AN INTERN LIKE YOU BRINGS BACK MEMORIES OF WHEN I WAS A STUDENT.
I NEVER HAD A VERY HAPPY STUDENT LIFE...
NO SURPRISE THERE.
YOU HAD NO MONEY, AND YOU WEREN'T POPULAR WITH GIRLS.
DO
KA
I'M SORRY, BUT I'VE BROUGHT A BOX LUNCH WITH ME.
HUH ...?
WHAT? *THAT'S* A LUNCH BOX?!
YES. IT'S A THERMOS, SO IT KEEPS MY RICE WARM.
AAAH! THAT'S SO LUXURIOUS!!

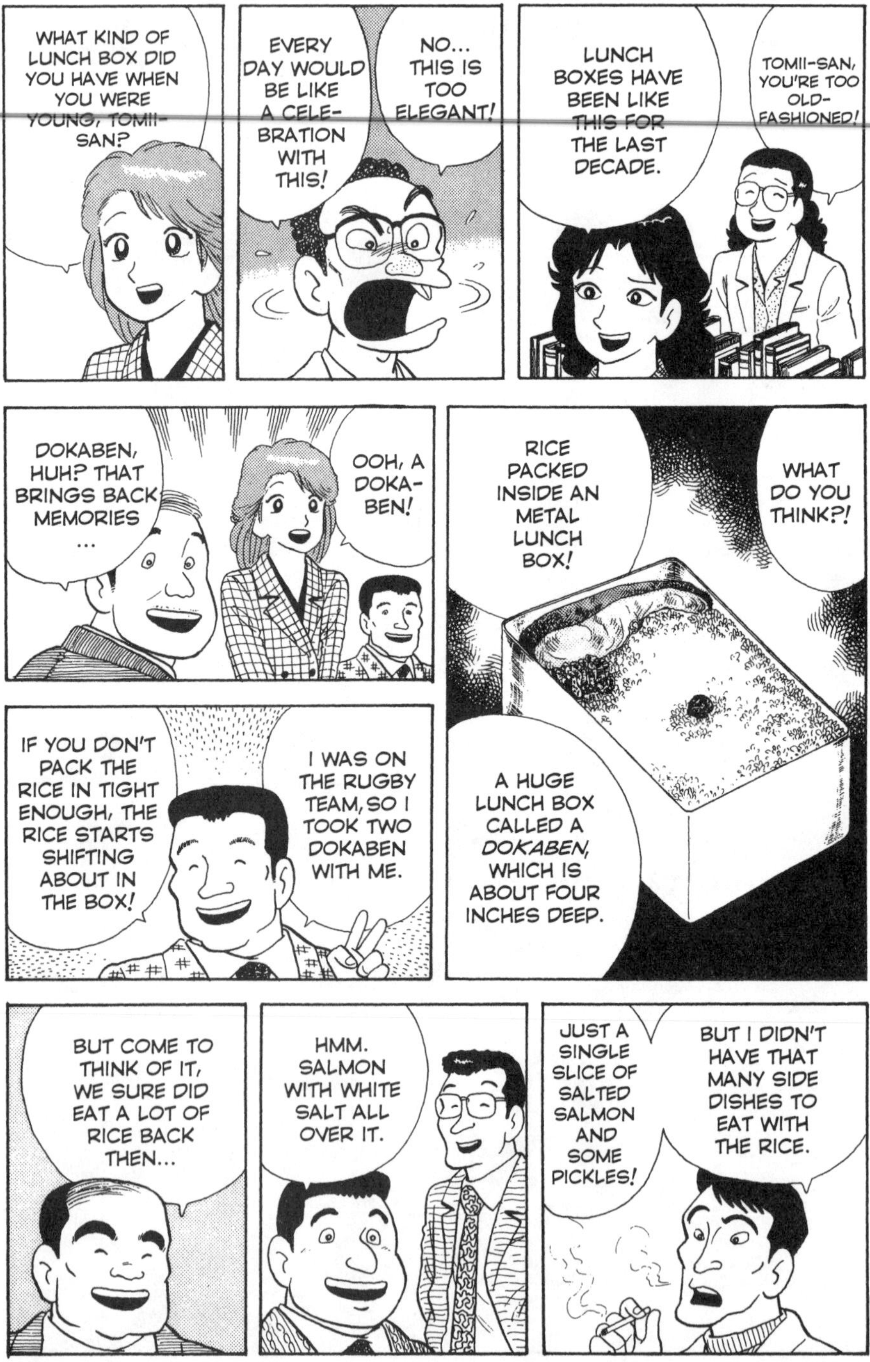

TOMII-SAN, YOU'RE TOO OLD-FASHIONED!
LUNCH BOXES HAVE BEEN LIKE THIS FOR THE LAST DECADE.
NO... THIS IS TOO ELEGANT!
EVERY DAY WOULD BE LIKE A CELE-BRATION WITH THIS!
WHAT KIND OF LUNCH BOX DID YOU HAVE WHEN YOU WERE YOUNG, TOMII-SAN?
WHAT DO YOU THINK?!
RICE PACKED INSIDE AN METAL LUNCH BOX!
A HUGE LUNCH BOX CALLED A *DOKABEN*, WHICH IS ABOUT FOUR INCHES DEEP.
OOH, A DOKA-BEN!
DOKABEN, HUH? THAT BRINGS BACK MEMORIES ...
I WAS ON THE RUGBY TEAM, SO I TOOK TWO DOKABEN WITH ME.
IF YOU DON'T PACK THE RICE IN TIGHT ENOUGH, THE RICE STARTS SHIFTING ABOUT IN THE BOX!
BUT I DIDN'T HAVE THAT MANY SIDE DISHES TO EAT WITH THE RICE.
JUST A SINGLE SLICE OF SALTED SALMON AND SOME PICKLES!
HMM. SALMON WITH WHITE SALT ALL OVER IT.
BUT COME TO THINK OF IT, WE SURE DID EAT A LOT OF RICE BACK THEN...

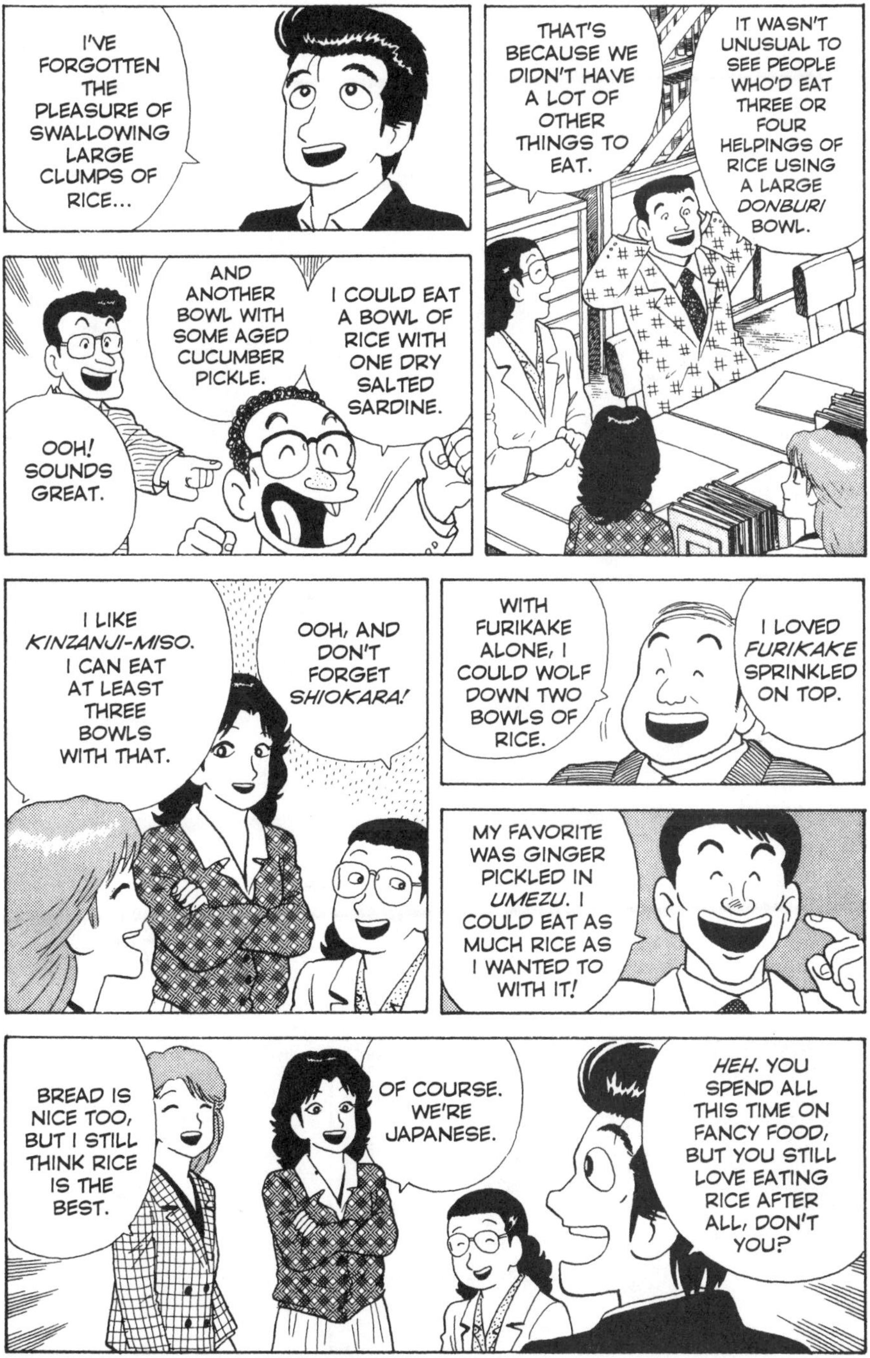
IT WASN'T UNUSUAL TO SEE PEOPLE WHO'D EAT THREE OR FOUR HELPINGS OF RICE USING A LARGE *DONBURI* BOWL.
THAT'S BECAUSE WE DIDN'T HAVE A LOT OF OTHER THINGS TO EAT.
I'VE FORGOTTEN THE PLEASURE OF SWALLOWING LARGE CLUMPS OF RICE...
I COULD EAT A BOWL OF RICE WITH ONE DRY SALTED SARDINE.
AND ANOTHER BOWL WITH SOME AGED CUCUMBER PICKLE.
OOH! SOUNDS GREAT.
I LOVED *FURIKAKE* SPRINKLED ON TOP.
WITH FURIKAKE ALONE, I COULD WOLF DOWN TWO BOWLS OF RICE.
MY FAVORITE WAS GINGER PICKLED IN *UMEZU*. I COULD EAT AS MUCH RICE AS I WANTED TO WITH IT!
OOH, AND DON'T FORGET *SHIOKARA!*
I LIKE *KINZANJI-MISO*. I CAN EAT AT LEAST THREE BOWLS WITH THAT.
HEH. YOU SPEND ALL THIS TIME ON FANCY FOOD, BUT YOU STILL LOVE EATING RICE AFTER ALL, DON'T YOU?
OF COURSE. WE'RE JAPANESE.
BREAD IS NICE TOO, BUT I STILL THINK RICE IS THE BEST.

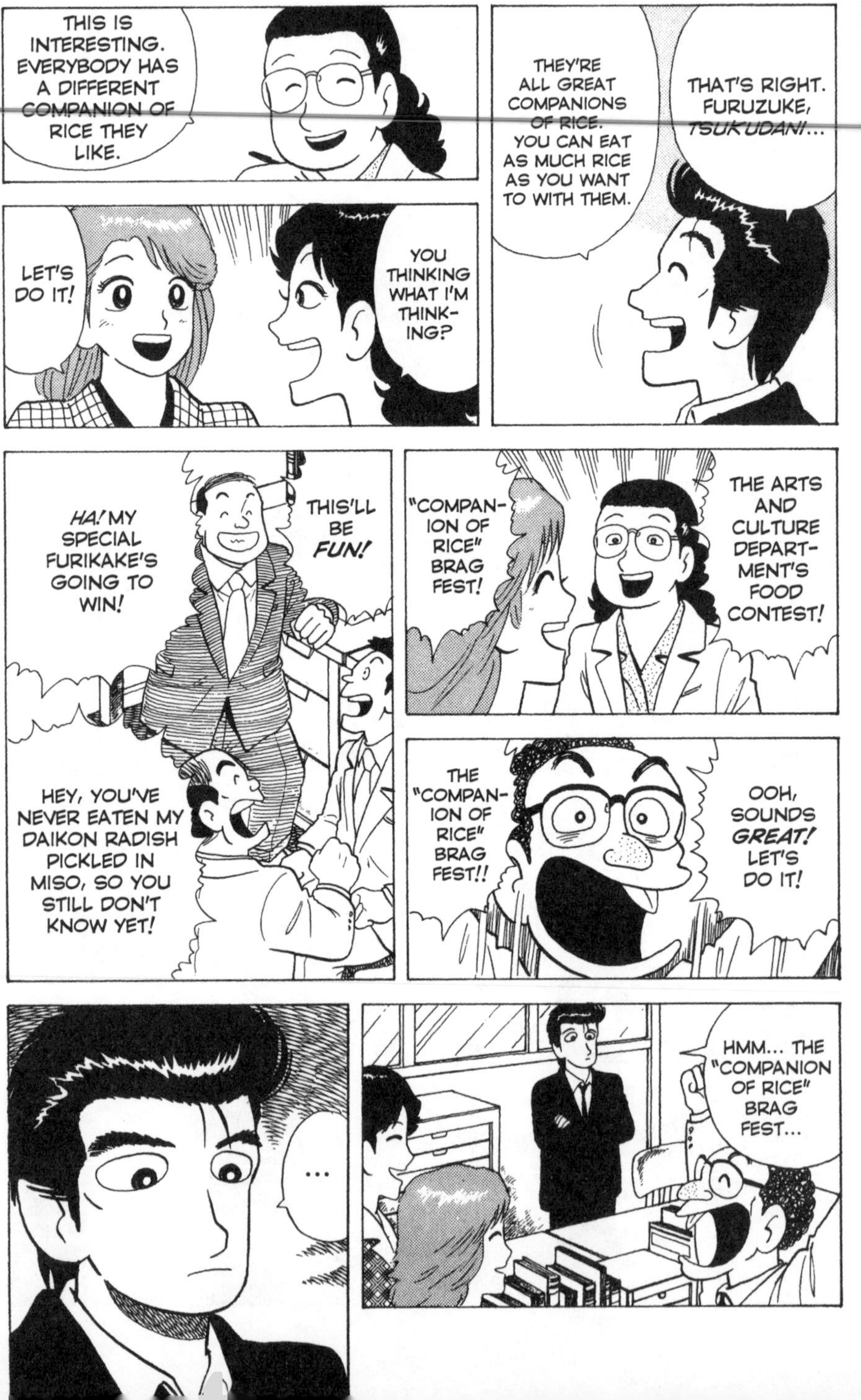
THAT'S RIGHT. FURUZUKE, *TSUKUDANI*...
THEY'RE ALL GREAT COMPANIONS OF RICE. YOU CAN EAT AS MUCH RICE AS YOU WANT TO WITH THEM.
THIS IS INTERESTING. EVERYBODY HAS A DIFFERENT COMPANION OF RICE THEY LIKE.
YOU THINKING WHAT I'M THINK-ING?
LET'S DO IT!
THE ARTS AND CULTURE DEPART-MENT'S FOOD CONTEST!
"COMPAN-ION OF RICE" BRAG FEST!
OOH, SOUNDS *GREAT!* LET'S DO IT!
THE "COMPAN-ION OF RICE" BRAG FEST!!
THIS'LL BE *FUN!*
HA! MY SPECIAL FURIKAKE'S GOING TO WIN!
HEY, YOU'VE NEVER EATEN MY DAIKON RADISH PICKLED IN MISO, SO YOU STILL DON'T KNOW YET!
HMM... THE "COMPANION OF RICE" BRAG FEST...
...

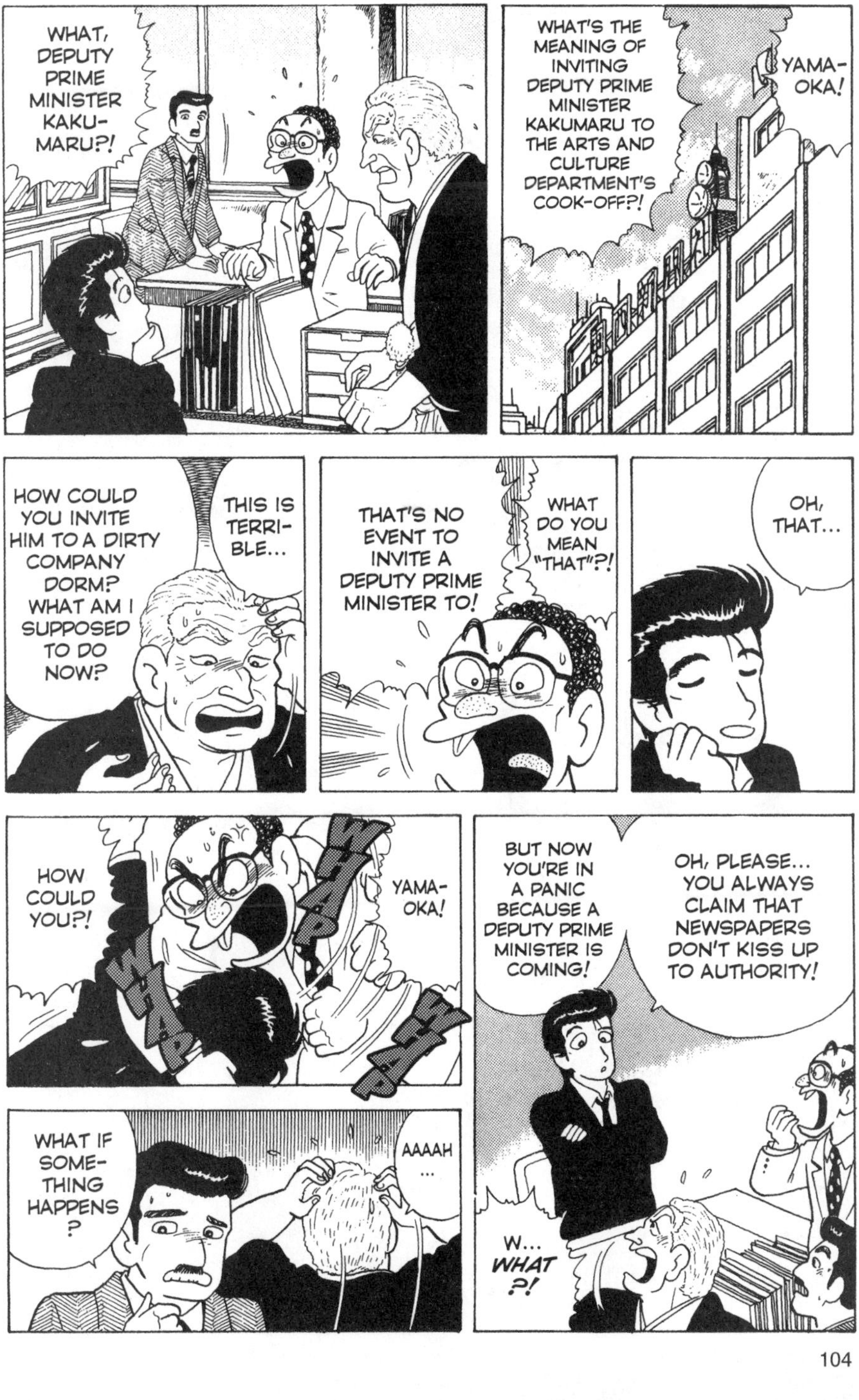
YAMA-OKA!
WHAT'S THE MEANING OF INVITING DEPUTY PRIME MINISTER KAKUMARU TO THE ARTS AND CULTURE DEPARTMENT'S COOK-OFF?!
WHAT, DEPUTY PRIME MINISTER KAKU-MARU?!
OH, THAT...
WHAT DO YOU MEAN "THAT"?!
THAT'S NO EVENT TO INVITE A DEPUTY PRIME MINISTER TO!
THIS IS TERRI-BLE...
HOW COULD YOU INVITE HIM TO A DIRTY COMPANY DORM? WHAT AM I SUPPOSED TO DO NOW?
OH, PLEASE... YOU ALWAYS CLAIM THAT NEWSPAPERS DON'T KISS UP TO AUTHORITY!
BUT NOW YOU'RE IN A PANIC BECAUSE A DEPUTY PRIME MINISTER IS COMING!
W... WHAT?!
YAMA-OKA!
HOW COULD YOU?!
WHAP
WHAP
WHAP
AAAAH ...
WHAT IF SOME-THING HAPPENS?

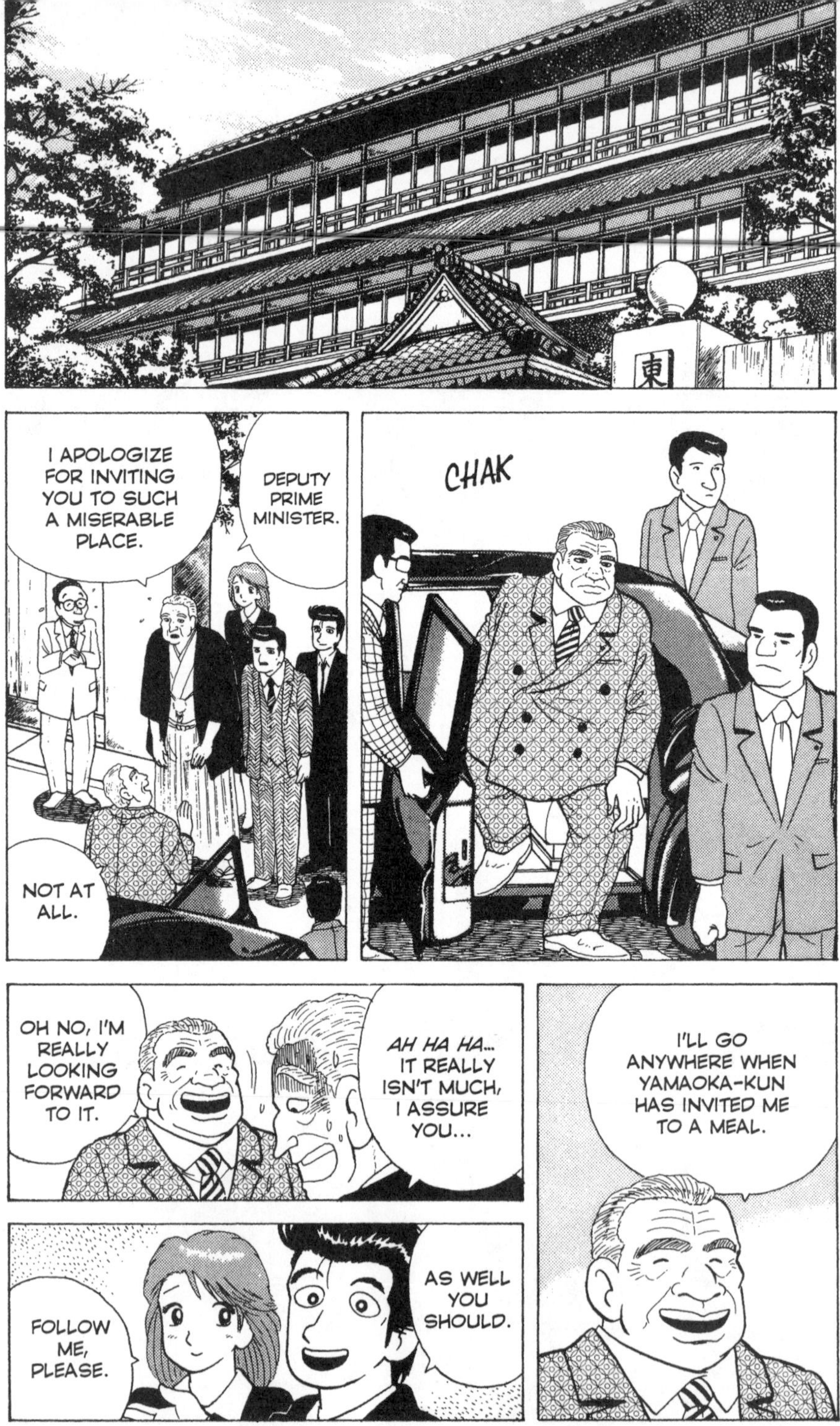
東
CHAK
DEPUTY PRIME MINISTER.
I APOLOGIZE FOR INVITING YOU TO SUCH A MISERABLE PLACE.
NOT AT ALL.
I'LL GO ANYWHERE WHEN YAMAOKA-KUN HAS INVITED ME TO A MEAL.
AH HA HA... IT REALLY ISN'T MUCH, I ASSURE YOU...
OH NO, I'M REALLY LOOKING FORWARD TO IT.
AS WELL YOU SHOULD.
FOLLOW ME, PLEASE.

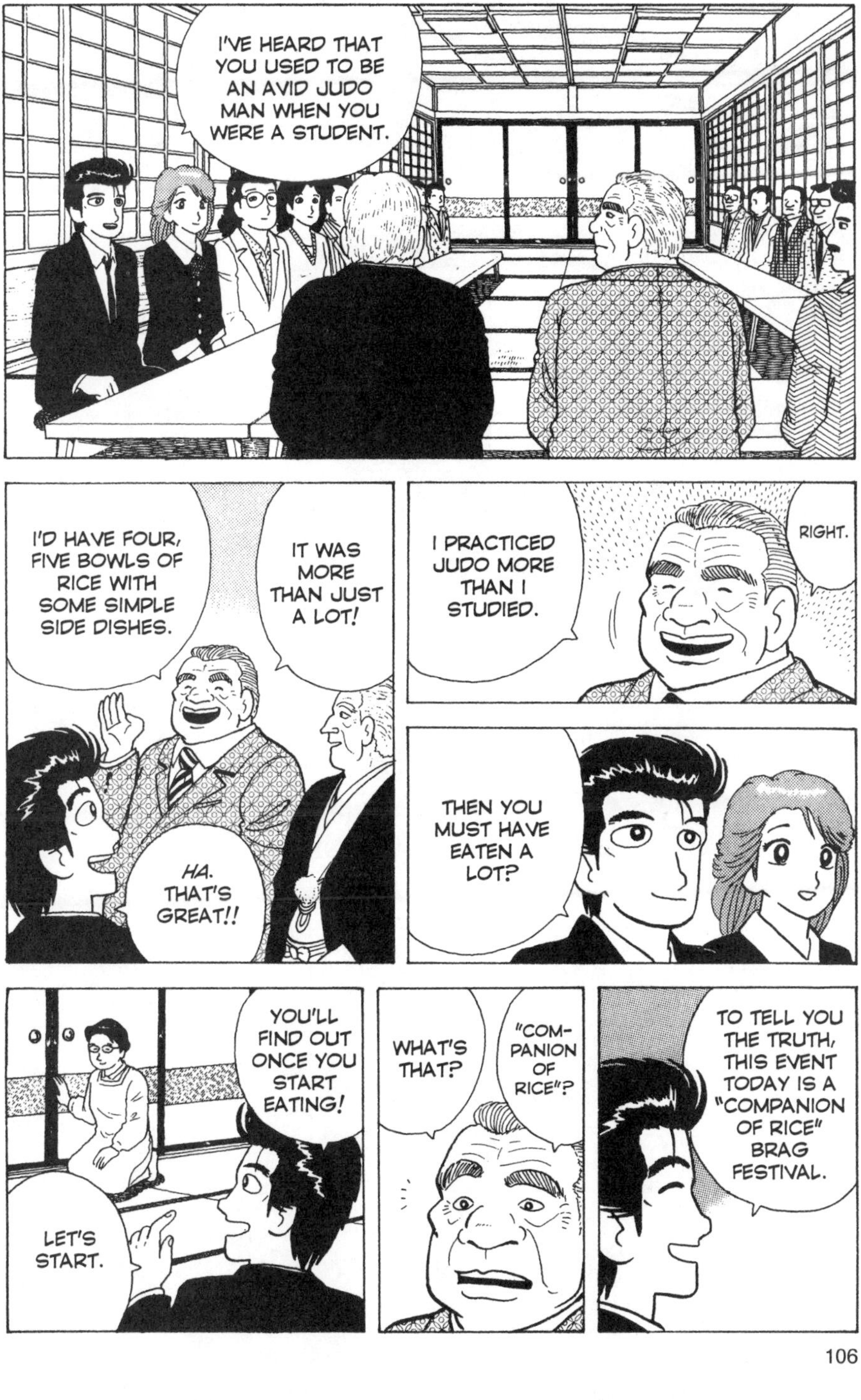
I'VE HEARD THAT YOU USED TO BE AN AVID JUDO MAN WHEN YOU WERE A STUDENT.
RIGHT.
I PRACTICED JUDO MORE THAN I STUDIED.
THEN YOU MUST HAVE EATEN A LOT?
IT WAS MORE THAN JUST A LOT!
I'D HAVE FOUR, FIVE BOWLS OF RICE WITH SOME SIMPLE SIDE DISHES.
HA. THAT'S GREAT!!
TO TELL YOU THE TRUTH, THIS EVENT TODAY IS A "COMPANION OF RICE" BRAG FESTIVAL.
"COMPANION OF RICE"?
WHAT'S THAT?
YOU'LL FIND OUT ONCE YOU START EATING!
LET'S START.

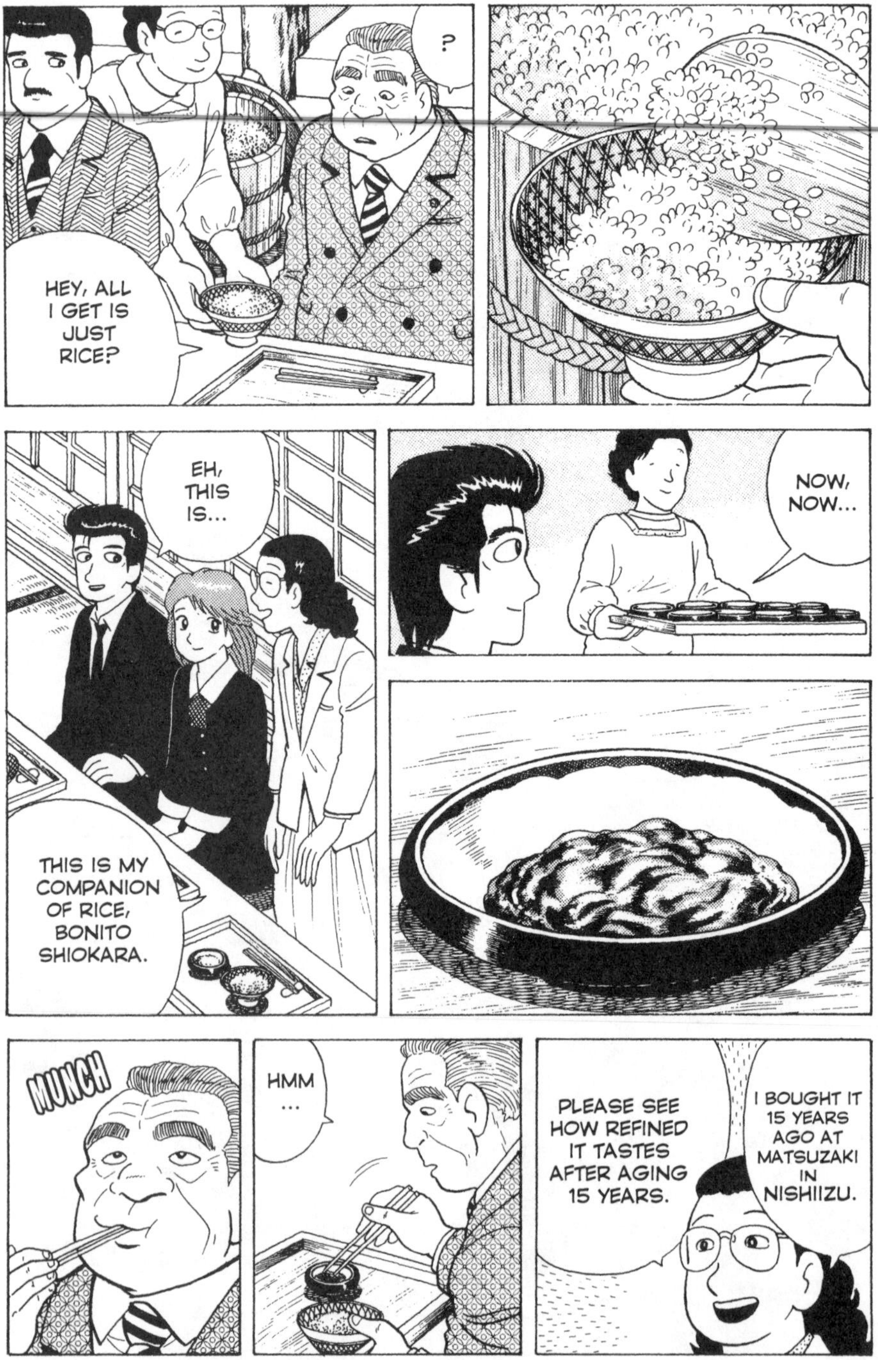
?
HEY, ALL I GET IS JUST RICE?
NOW, NOW...
EH, THIS IS...
THIS IS MY COMPANION OF RICE, BONITO SHIOKARA.
I BOUGHT IT 15 YEARS AGO AT MATSUZAKI IN NISHIIZU.
PLEASE SEE HOW REFINED IT TASTES AFTER AGING 15 YEARS.
HMM ...
MUNCH

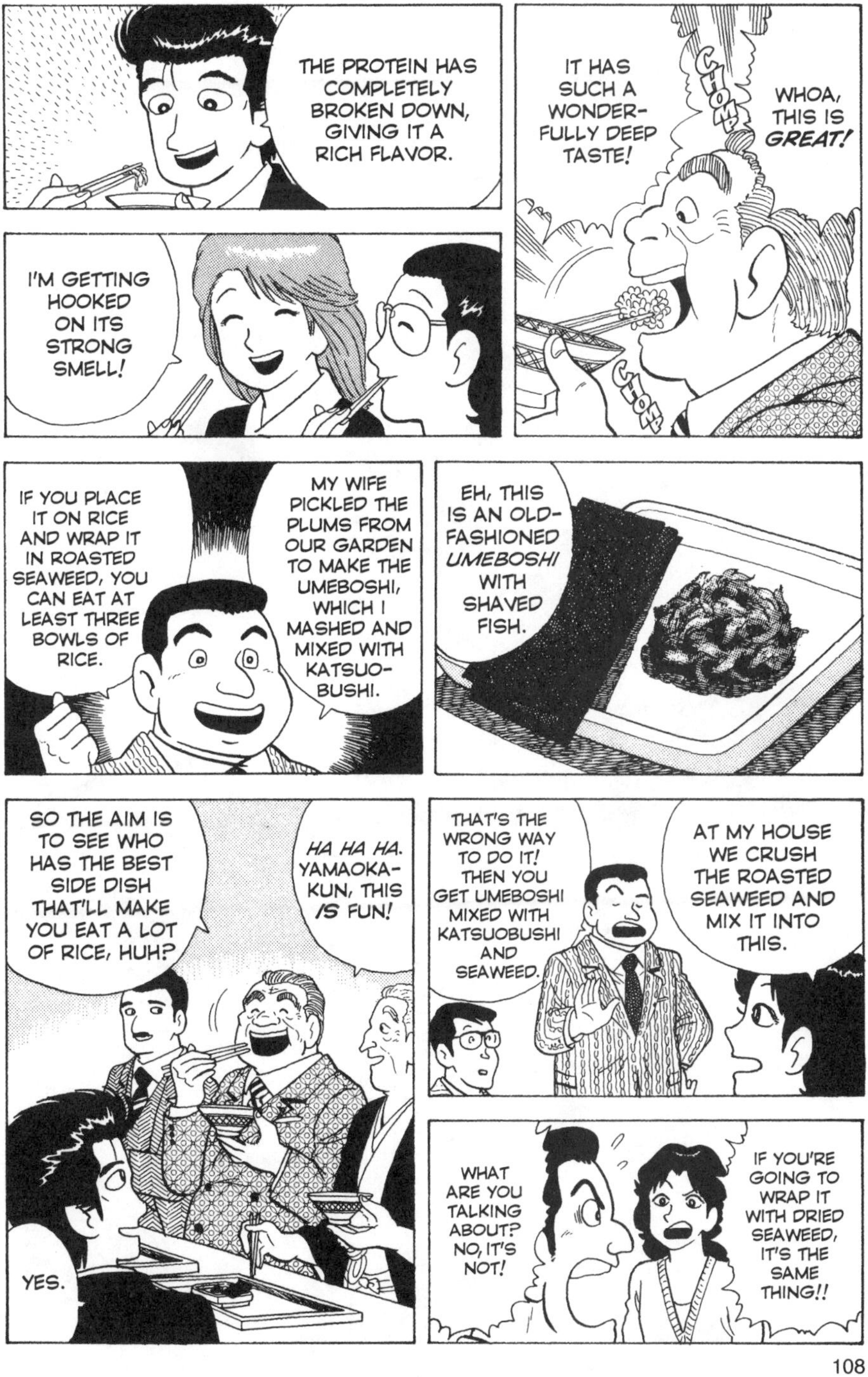
WHOA, THIS IS GREAT!
CHOMP
IT HAS SUCH A WONDERFULLY DEEP TASTE!
CHOMP
THE PROTEIN HAS COMPLETELY BROKEN DOWN, GIVING IT A RICH FLAVOR.
I'M GETTING HOOKED ON ITS STRONG SMELL!
EH, THIS IS AN OLD-FASHIONED UMEBOSHI WITH SHAVED FISH.
MY WIFE PICKLED THE PLUMS FROM OUR GARDEN TO MAKE THE UMEBOSHI, WHICH I MASHED AND MIXED WITH KATSUOBUSHI.
IF YOU PLACE IT ON RICE AND WRAP IT IN ROASTED SEAWEED, YOU CAN EAT AT LEAST THREE BOWLS OF RICE.
AT MY HOUSE WE CRUSH THE ROASTED SEAWEED AND MIX IT INTO THIS.
THAT'S THE WRONG WAY TO DO IT! THEN YOU GET UMEBOSHI MIXED WITH KATSUOBUSHI AND SEAWEED.
IF YOU'RE GOING TO WRAP IT WITH DRIED SEAWEED, IT'S THE SAME THING!!
WHAT ARE YOU TALKING ABOUT? NO, IT'S NOT!
HA HA HA. YAMAOKA-KUN, THIS IS FUN!
SO THE AIM IS TO SEE WHO HAS THE BEST SIDE DISH THAT'LL MAKE YOU EAT A LOT OF RICE, HUH?
YES.

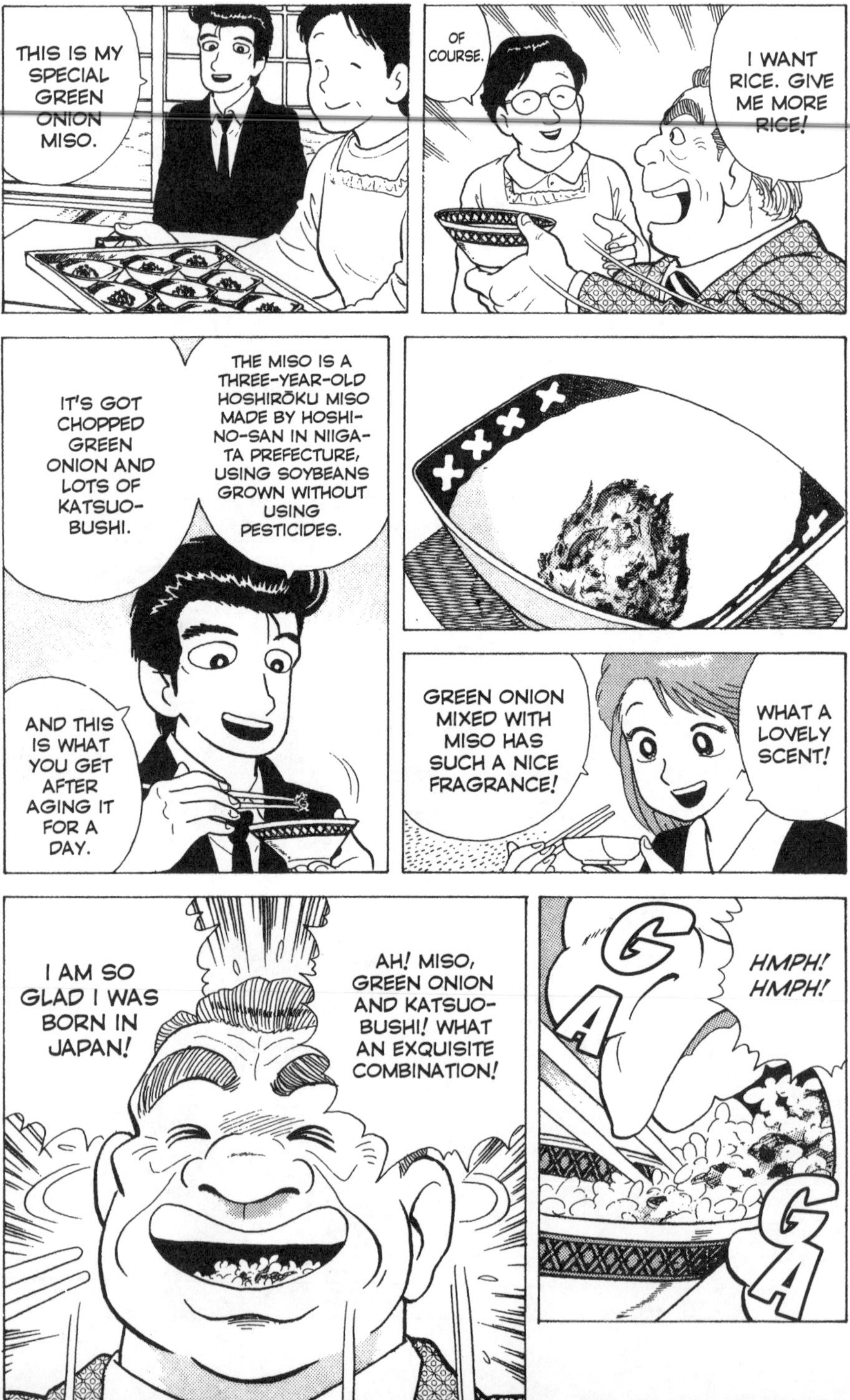
I WANT RICE. GIVE ME MORE RICE!
OF COURSE.
THIS IS MY SPECIAL GREEN ONION MISO.
WHAT A LOVELY SCENT!
GREEN ONION MIXED WITH MISO HAS SUCH A NICE FRAGRANCE!
THE MISO IS A THREE-YEAR-OLD HOSHIRŌKU MISO MADE BY HOSHI-NO-SAN IN NIIGATA PREFECTURE, USING SOYBEANS GROWN WITHOUT USING PESTICIDES.
IT'S GOT CHOPPED GREEN ONION AND LOTS OF KATSUOBUSHI.
AND THIS IS WHAT YOU GET AFTER AGING IT FOR A DAY.
GA
HMPH! HMPH!
GA
AH! MISO, GREEN ONION AND KATSUOBUSHI! WHAT AN EXQUISITE COMBINATION!
I AM SO GLAD I WAS BORN IN JAPAN!

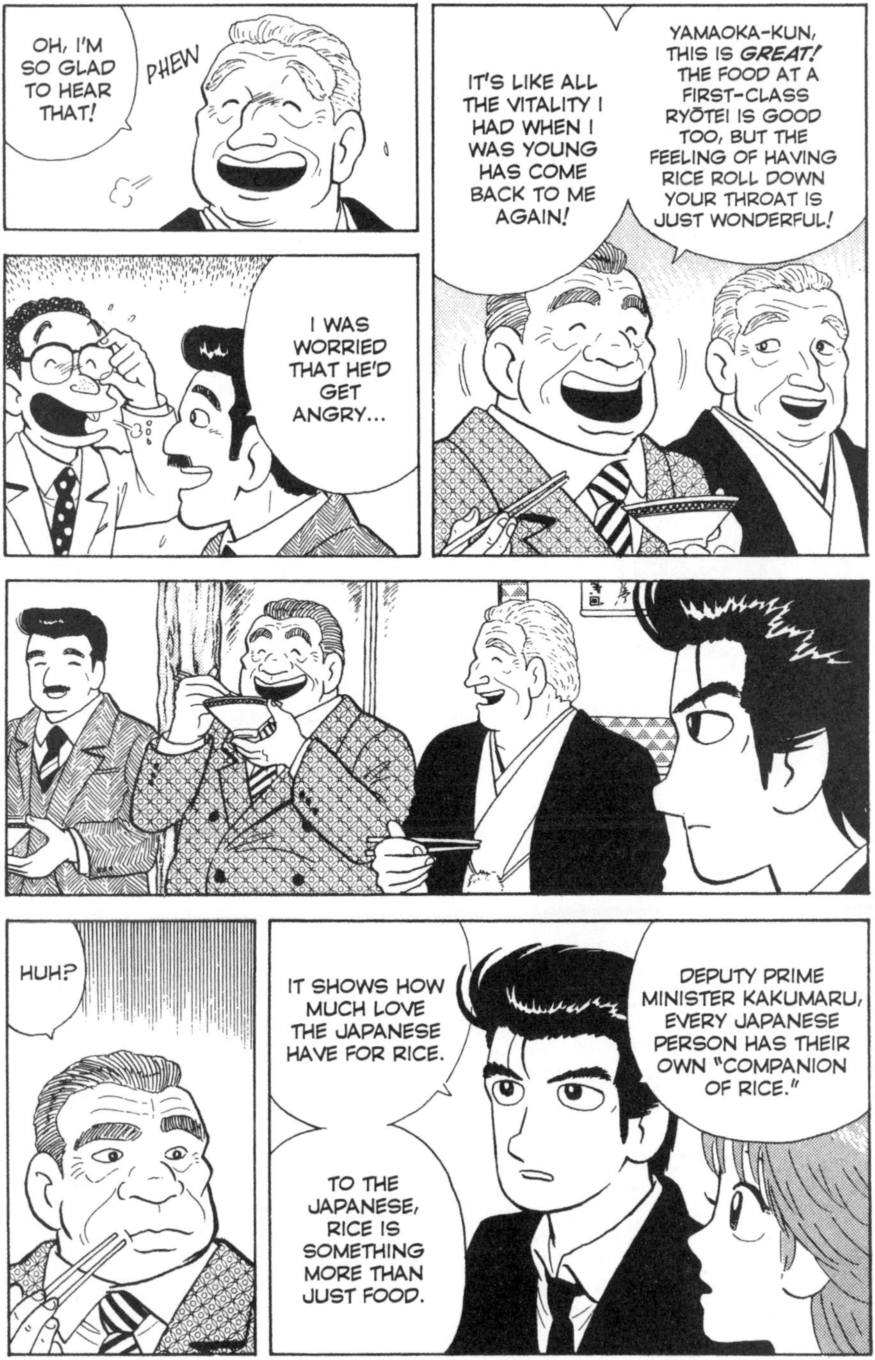
YAMAOKA-KUN, THIS IS ***GREAT!*** THE FOOD AT A FIRST-CLASS RYŌTEI IS GOOD TOO, BUT THE FEELING OF HAVING RICE ROLL DOWN YOUR THROAT IS JUST WONDERFUL!
IT'S LIKE ALL THE VITALITY I HAD WHEN I WAS YOUNG HAS COME BACK TO ME AGAIN!
PHEW
OH, I'M SO GLAD TO HEAR THAT!
I WAS WORRIED THAT HE'D GET ANGRY...
DEPUTY PRIME MINISTER KAKUMARU, EVERY JAPANESE PERSON HAS THEIR OWN "COMPANION OF RICE."
IT SHOWS HOW MUCH LOVE THE JAPANESE HAVE FOR RICE.
TO THE JAPANESE, RICE IS SOMETHING MORE THAN JUST FOOD.
HUH?

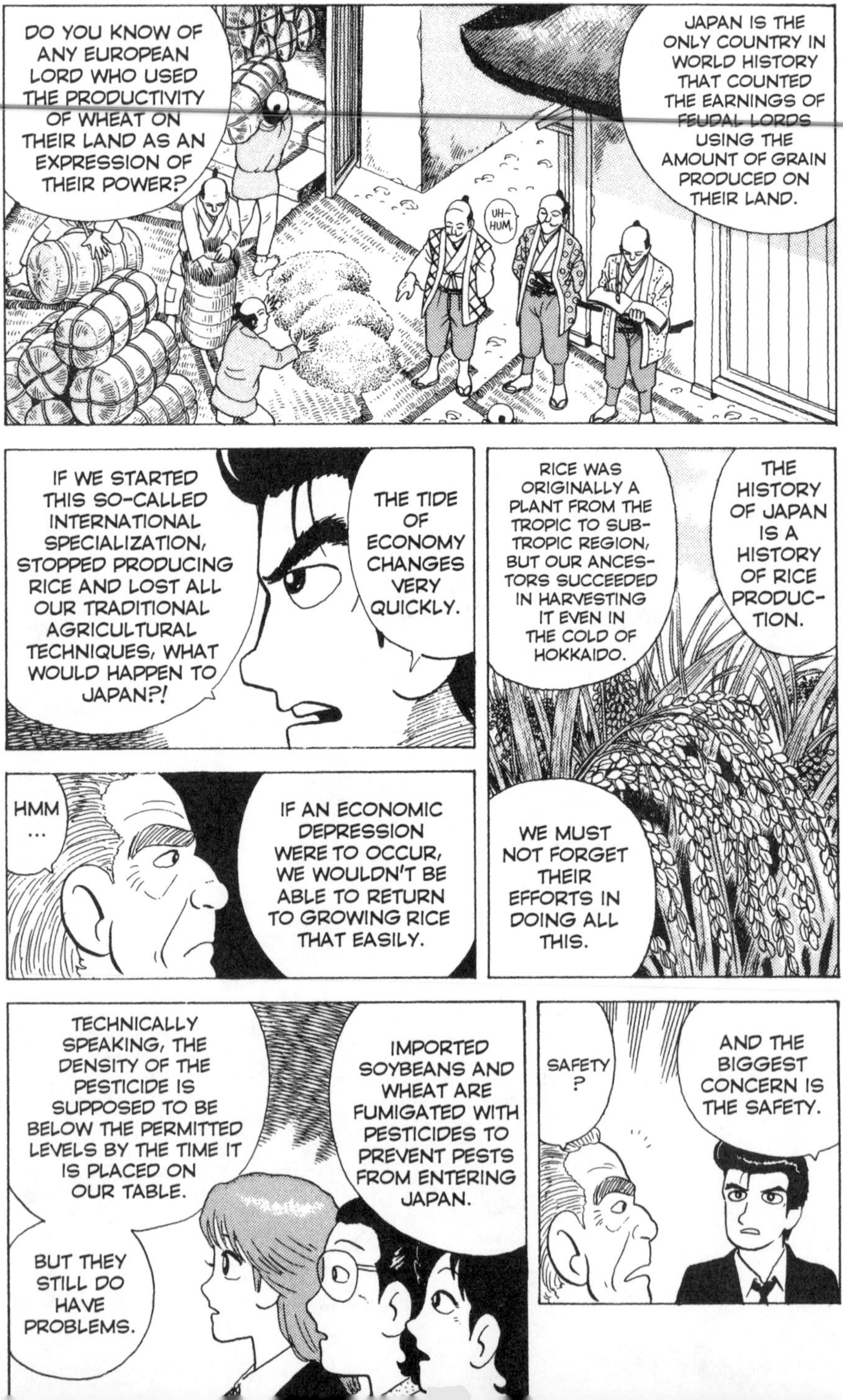
JAPAN IS THE ONLY COUNTRY IN WORLD HISTORY THAT COUNTED THE EARNINGS OF FEUDAL LORDS USING THE AMOUNT OF GRAIN PRODUCED ON THEIR LAND.
UH-HUM.
DO YOU KNOW OF ANY EUROPEAN LORD WHO USED THE PRODUCTIVITY OF WHEAT ON THEIR LAND AS AN EXPRESSION OF THEIR POWER?
THE HISTORY OF JAPAN IS A HISTORY OF RICE PRODUCTION.
RICE WAS ORIGINALLY A PLANT FROM THE TROPIC TO SUB-TROPIC REGION, BUT OUR ANCESTORS SUCCEEDED IN HARVESTING IT EVEN IN THE COLD OF HOKKAIDO.
WE MUST NOT FORGET THEIR EFFORTS IN DOING ALL THIS.
THE TIDE OF ECONOMY CHANGES VERY QUICKLY.
IF WE STARTED THIS SO-CALLED INTERNATIONAL SPECIALIZATION, STOPPED PRODUCING RICE AND LOST ALL OUR TRADITIONAL AGRICULTURAL TECHNIQUES, WHAT WOULD HAPPEN TO JAPAN?!
IF AN ECONOMIC DEPRESSION WERE TO OCCUR, WE WOULDN'T BE ABLE TO RETURN TO GROWING RICE THAT EASILY.
HMM ...
AND THE BIGGEST CONCERN IS THE SAFETY.
SAFETY?
IMPORTED SOYBEANS AND WHEAT ARE FUMIGATED WITH PESTICIDES TO PREVENT PESTS FROM ENTERING JAPAN.
TECHNICALLY SPEAKING, THE DENSITY OF THE PESTICIDE IS SUPPOSED TO BE BELOW THE PERMITTED LEVELS BY THE TIME IT IS PLACED ON OUR TABLE.
BUT THEY STILL DO HAVE PROBLEMS.

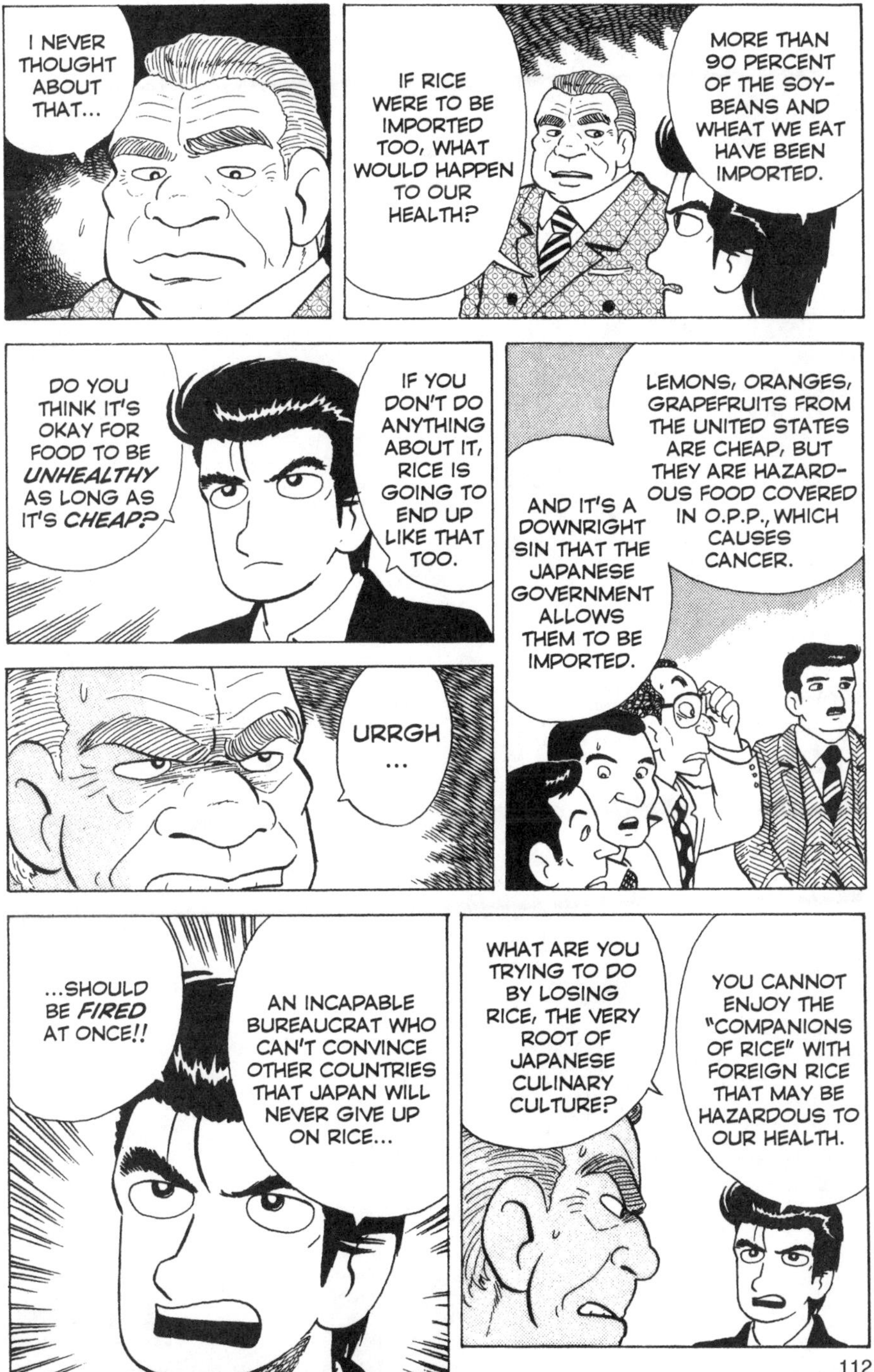
MORE THAN 90 PERCENT OF THE SOYBEANS AND WHEAT WE EAT HAVE BEEN IMPORTED.
IF RICE WERE TO BE IMPORTED TOO, WHAT WOULD HAPPEN TO OUR HEALTH?
I NEVER THOUGHT ABOUT THAT...
LEMONS, ORANGES, GRAPEFRUITS FROM THE UNITED STATES ARE CHEAP, BUT THEY ARE HAZARDOUS FOOD COVERED IN O.P.P., WHICH CAUSES CANCER.
AND IT'S A DOWNRIGHT SIN THAT THE JAPANESE GOVERNMENT ALLOWS THEM TO BE IMPORTED.
IF YOU DON'T DO ANYTHING ABOUT IT, RICE IS GOING TO END UP LIKE THAT TOO.
DO YOU THINK IT'S OKAY FOR FOOD TO BE *UNHEALTHY* AS LONG AS IT'S *CHEAP*?
URRGH ...
YOU CANNOT ENJOY THE "COMPANIONS OF RICE" WITH FOREIGN RICE THAT MAY BE HAZARDOUS TO OUR HEALTH.
WHAT ARE YOU TRYING TO DO BY LOSING RICE, THE VERY ROOT OF JAPANESE CULINARY CULTURE?
AN INCAPABLE BUREAUCRAT WHO CAN'T CONVINCE OTHER COUNTRIES THAT JAPAN WILL NEVER GIVE UP ON RICE...
...SHOULD BE *FIRED* AT ONCE!!

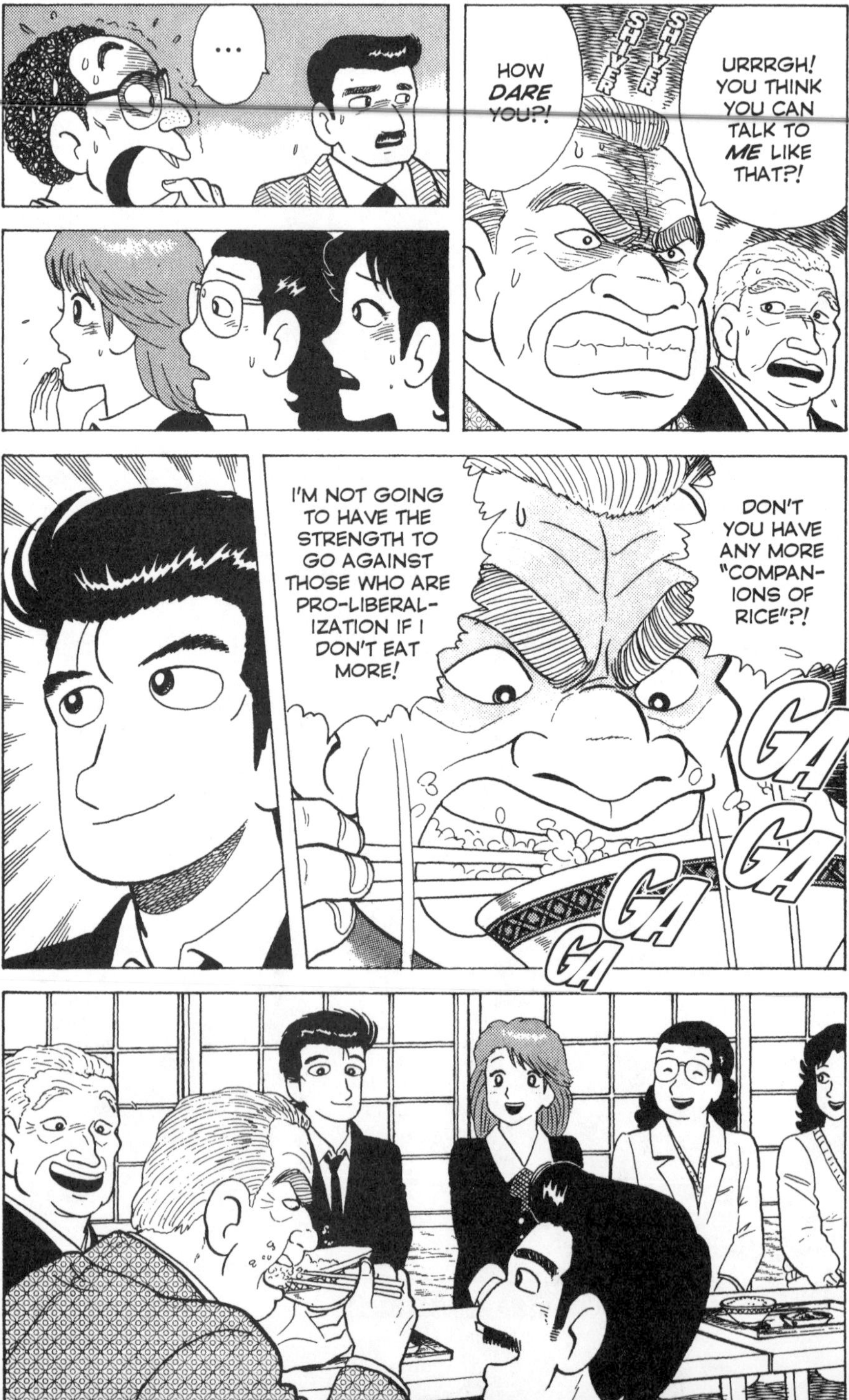
URRRGH! YOU THINK YOU CAN TALK TO *ME* LIKE THAT?!
SHIVER
SHIVER
HOW *DARE* YOU?!
...
DON'T YOU HAVE ANY MORE "COMPANIONS OF RICE"?!
I'M NOT GOING TO HAVE THE STRENGTH TO GO AGAINST THOSE WHO ARE PRO-LIBERALIZATION IF I DON'T EAT MORE!
GA
GA
GA
GA

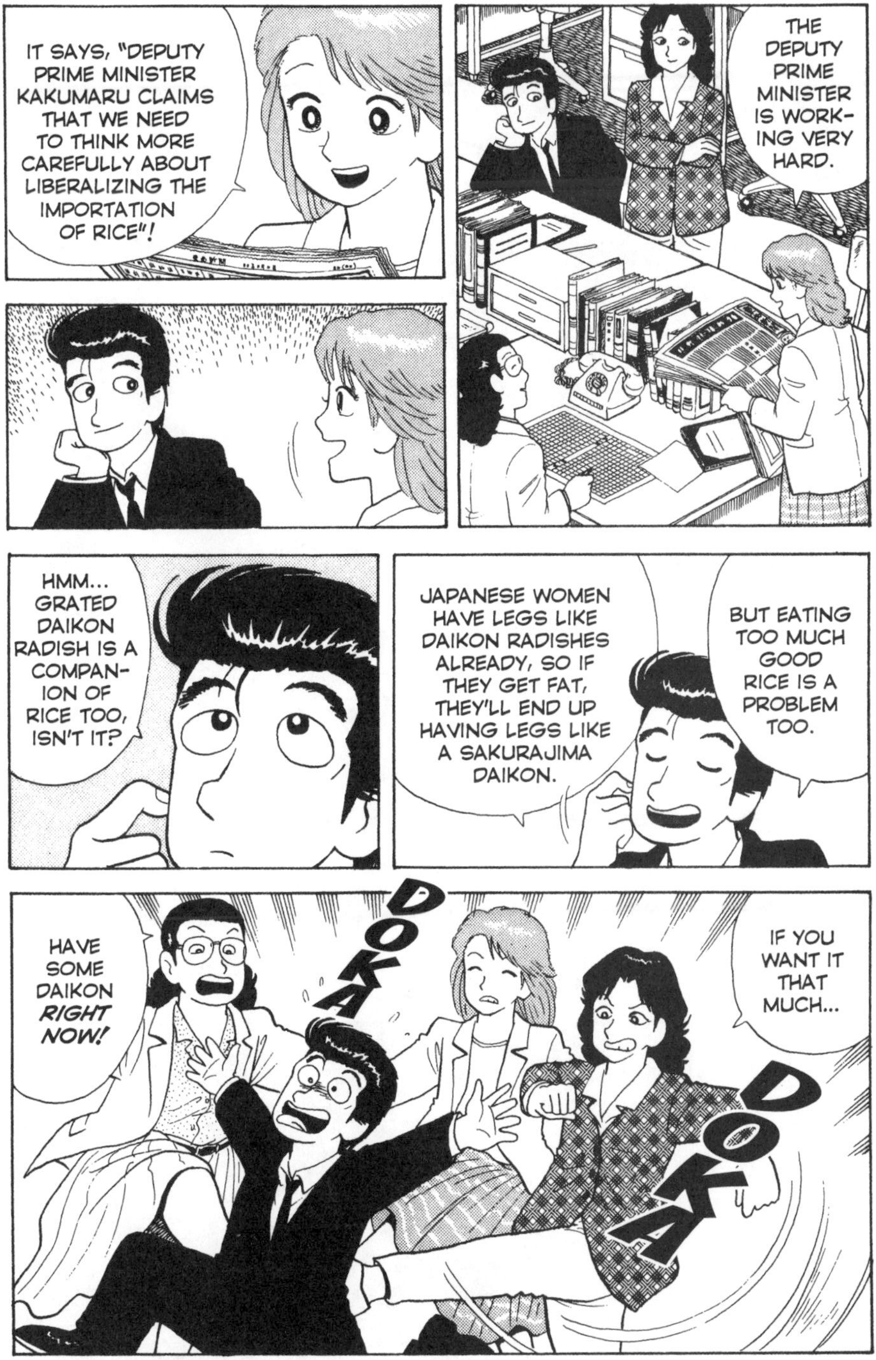
THE DEPUTY PRIME MINISTER IS WORKING VERY HARD.
IT SAYS, "DEPUTY PRIME MINISTER KAKUMARU CLAIMS THAT WE NEED TO THINK MORE CAREFULLY ABOUT LIBERALIZING THE IMPORTATION OF RICE"!
BUT EATING TOO MUCH GOOD RICE IS A PROBLEM TOO.
JAPANESE WOMEN HAVE LEGS LIKE DAIKON RADISHES ALREADY, SO IF THEY GET FAT, THEY'LL END UP HAVING LEGS LIKE A SAKURAJIMA DAIKON.
HMM... GRATED DAIKON RADISH IS A COMPANION OF RICE TOO, ISN'T IT?
IF YOU WANT IT THAT MUCH...
DOKA
DOKA
HAVE SOME DAIKON ***RIGHT NOW!***

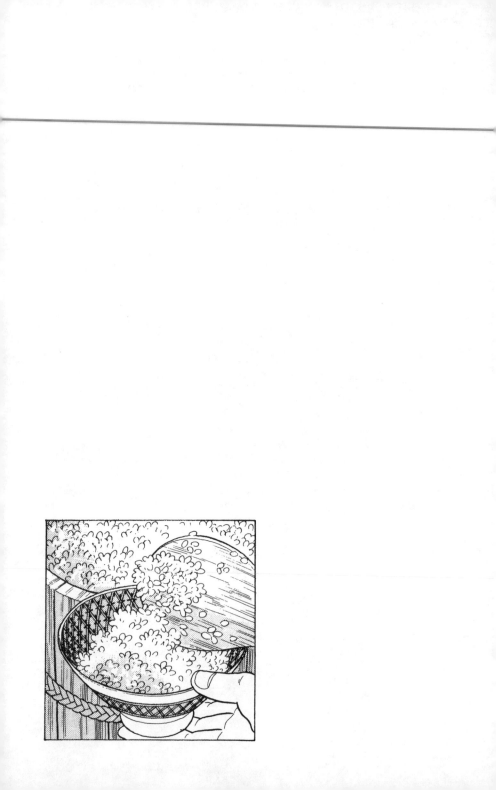

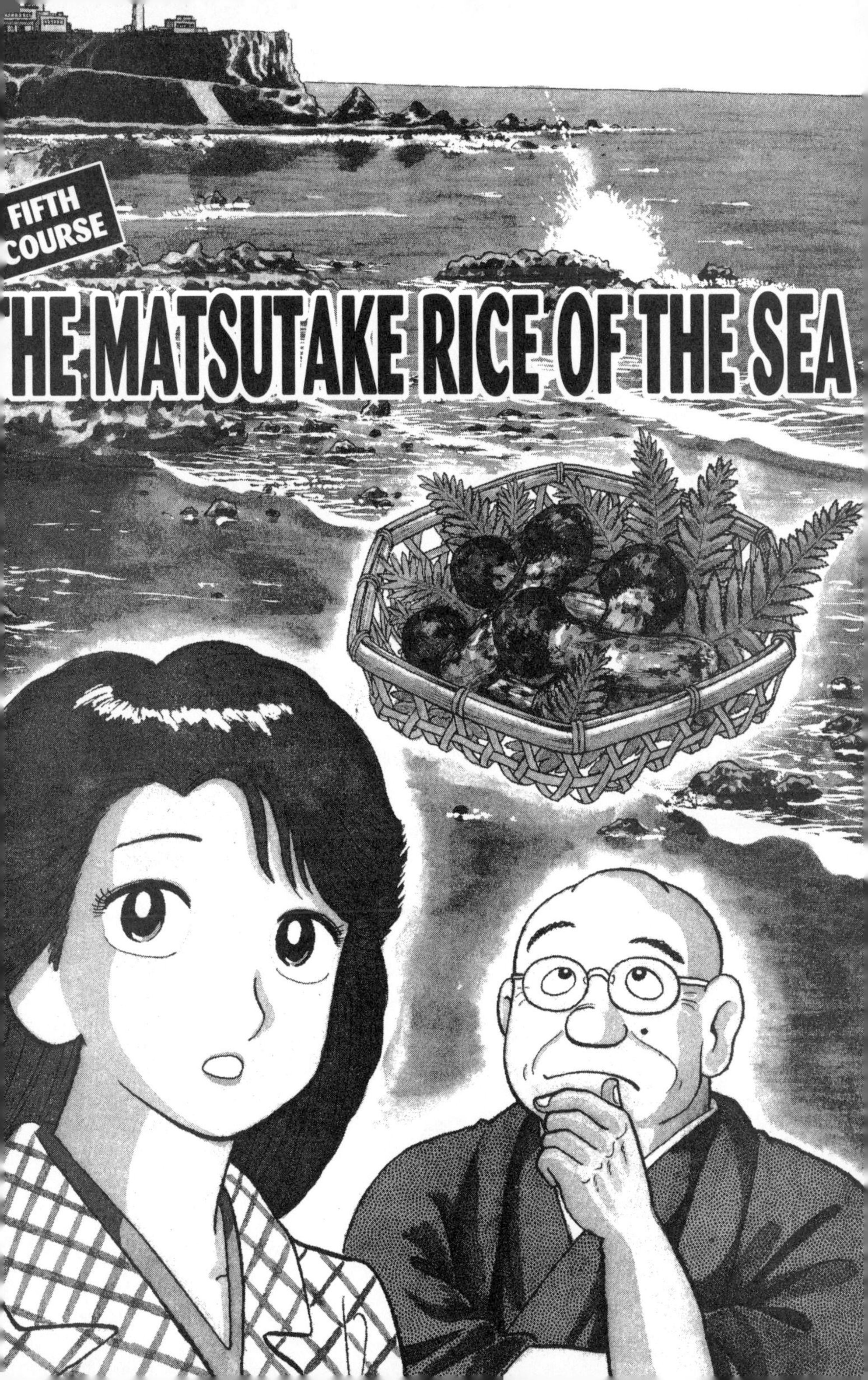
FIFTH COURSE
HE MATSUTAKE RICE OF THE SEA

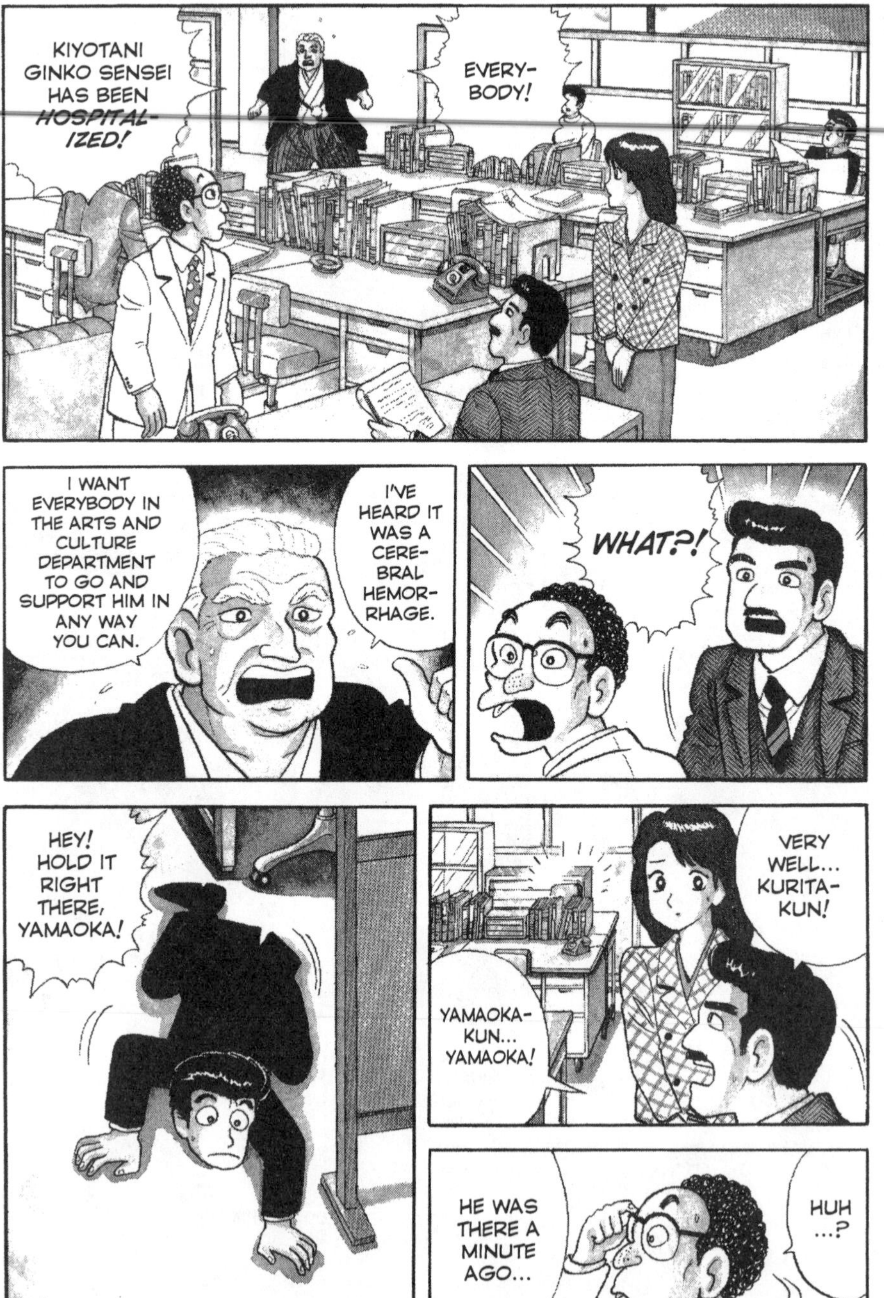
EVERY-BODY!
KIYOTANI GINKO SENSEI HAS BEEN *HOSPITAL-IZED!*
WHAT?!
I'VE HEARD IT WAS A CERE-BRAL HEMOR-RHAGE.
I WANT EVERYBODY IN THE ARTS AND CULTURE DEPARTMENT TO GO AND SUPPORT HIM IN ANY WAY YOU CAN.
VERY WELL... KURITA-KUN!
YAMAOKA-KUN... YAMAOKA!
HUH ...?
HE WAS THERE A MINUTE AGO...
HEY! HOLD IT RIGHT THERE, YAMAOKA!

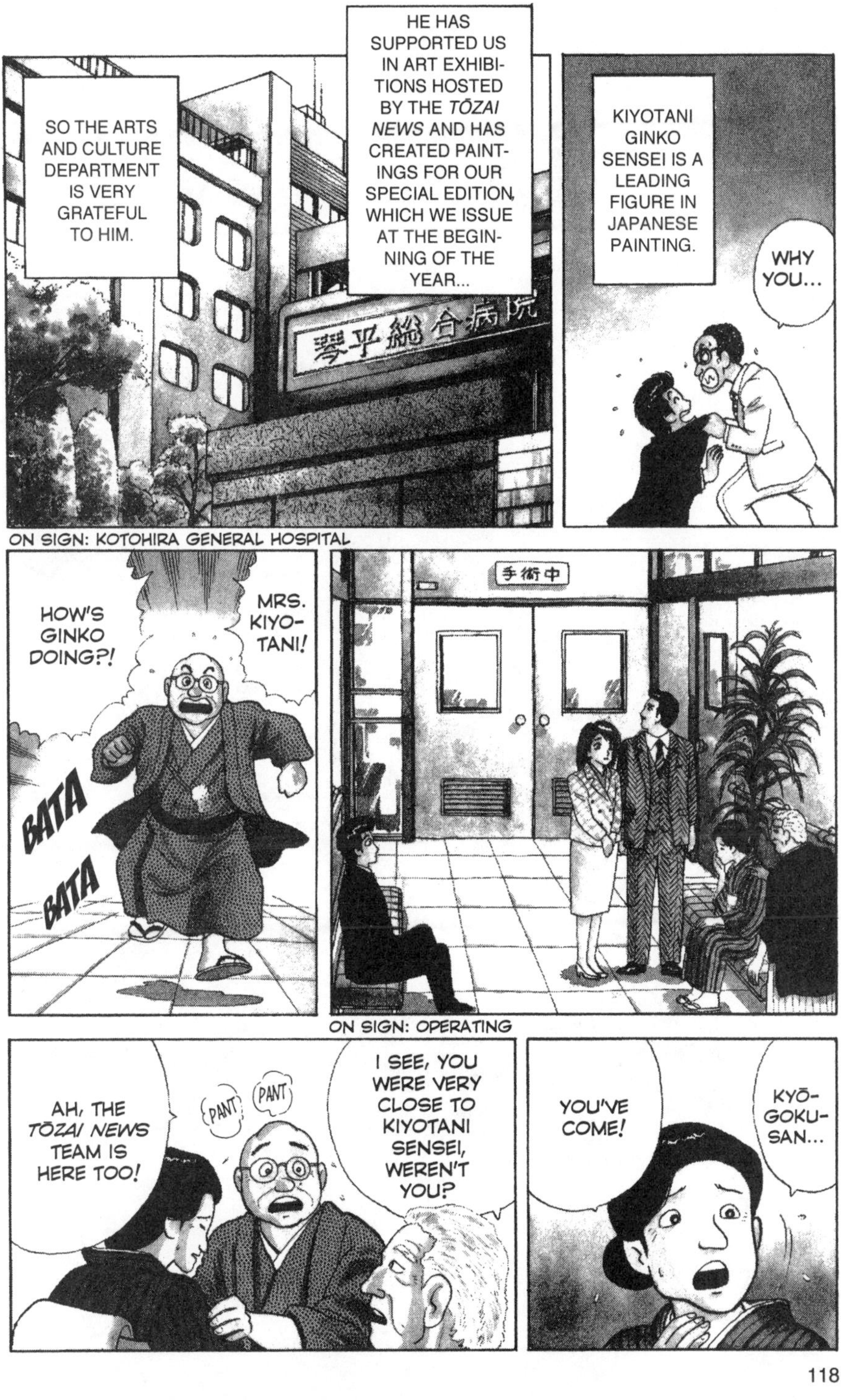
KIYOTANI GINKO SENSEI IS A LEADING FIGURE IN JAPANESE PAINTING.
WHY YOU...
HE HAS SUPPORTED US IN ART EXHIBITIONS HOSTED BY THE *TŌZAI NEWS* AND HAS CREATED PAINTINGS FOR OUR SPECIAL EDITION, WHICH WE ISSUE AT THE BEGINNING OF THE YEAR...
SO THE ARTS AND CULTURE DEPARTMENT IS VERY GRATEFUL TO HIM.
琴平総合病院
ON SIGN: KOTOHIRA GENERAL HOSPITAL
手術中
ON SIGN: OPERATING
MRS. KIYOTANI!
HOW'S GINKO DOING?!
BATA
BATA
KYŌ-GOKU-SAN...
YOU'VE COME!
I SEE, YOU WERE VERY CLOSE TO KIYOTANI SENSEI, WEREN'T YOU?
PANT
PANT
AH, THE *TŌZAI NEWS* TEAM IS HERE TOO!

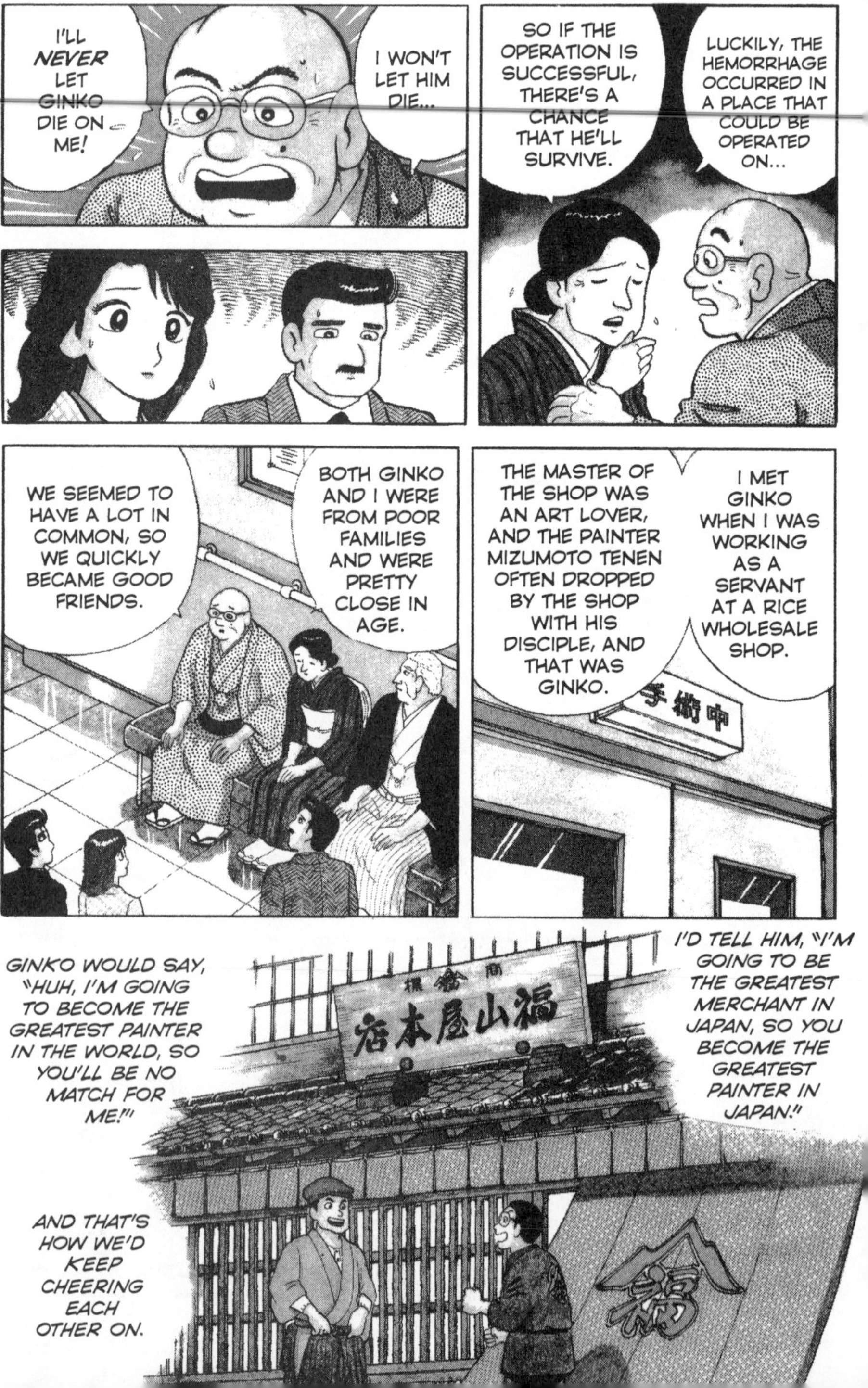
LUCKILY, THE HEMORRHAGE OCCURRED IN A PLACE THAT COULD BE OPERATED ON...
SO IF THE OPERATION IS SUCCESSFUL, THERE'S A CHANCE THAT HE'LL SURVIVE.
I WON'T LET HIM DIE...
I'LL *NEVER* LET GINKO DIE ON ME!
I MET GINKO WHEN I WAS WORKING AS A SERVANT AT A RICE WHOLESALE SHOP.
THE MASTER OF THE SHOP WAS AN ART LOVER, AND THE PAINTER MIZUMOTO TENEN OFTEN DROPPED BY THE SHOP WITH HIS DISCIPLE, AND THAT WAS GINKO.
BOTH GINKO AND I WERE FROM POOR FAMILIES AND WERE PRETTY CLOSE IN AGE.
WE SEEMED TO HAVE A LOT IN COMMON, SO WE QUICKLY BECAME GOOD FRIENDS.
I'D TELL HIM, "I'M GOING TO BE THE GREATEST MERCHANT IN JAPAN, SO YOU BECOME THE GREATEST PAINTER IN JAPAN."
福山屋本店
GINKO WOULD SAY, "HUH, I'M GOING TO BECOME THE GREATEST PAINTER IN THE WORLD, SO YOU'LL BE NO MATCH FOR ME!"
AND THAT'S HOW WE'D KEEP CHEERING EACH OTHER ON.

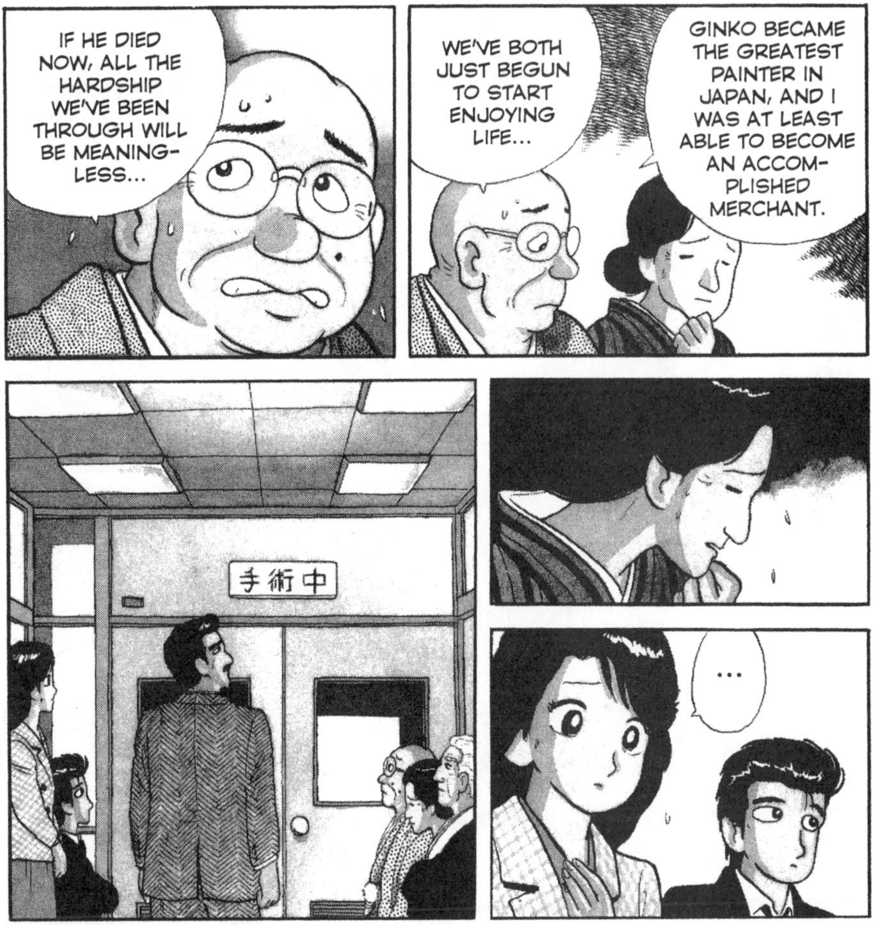
GINKO BECAME THE GREATEST PAINTER IN JAPAN, AND I WAS AT LEAST ABLE TO BECOME AN ACCOMPLISHED MERCHANT.
WE'VE BOTH JUST BEGUN TO START ENJOYING LIFE...
IF HE DIED NOW, ALL THE HARDSHIP WE'VE BEEN THROUGH WILL BE MEANINGLESS...
...
手術中

ON SIGN: OPERATING

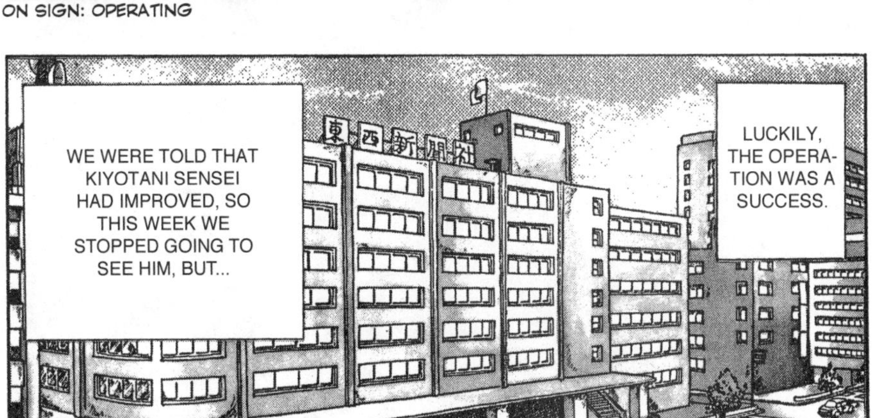
LUCKILY, THE OPERATION WAS A SUCCESS.
WE WERE TOLD THAT KIYOTANI SENSEI HAD IMPROVED, SO THIS WEEK WE STOPPED GOING TO SEE HIM, BUT...
東西新聞社

ON SIGN: TŌZAI NEWS COMPANY

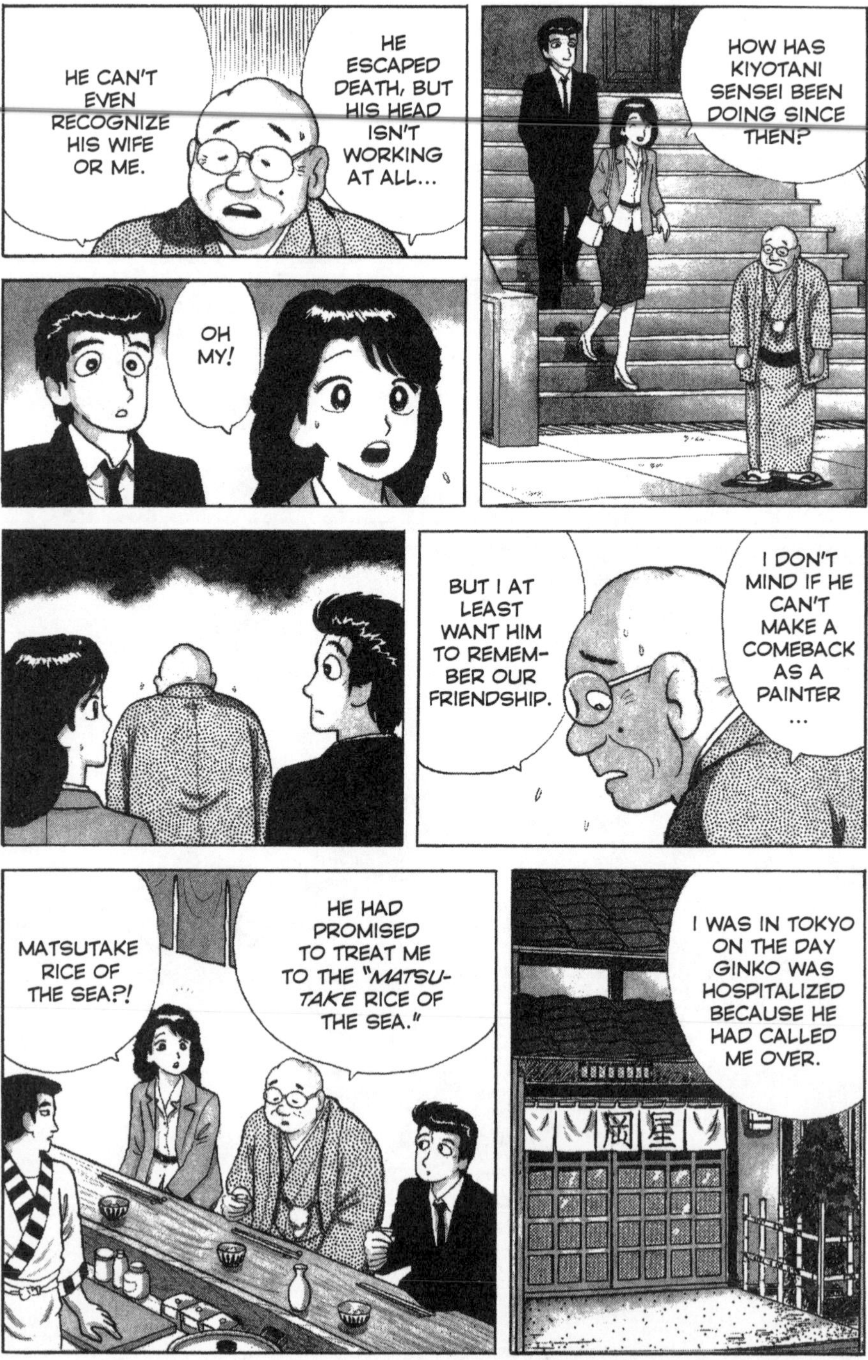
HOW HAS KIYOTANI SENSEI BEEN DOING SINCE THEN?
HE ESCAPED DEATH, BUT HIS HEAD ISN'T WORKING AT ALL...
HE CAN'T EVEN RECOGNIZE HIS WIFE OR ME.
OH MY!
I DON'T MIND IF HE CAN'T MAKE A COMEBACK AS A PAINTER ...
BUT I AT LEAST WANT HIM TO REMEMBER OUR FRIENDSHIP.
I WAS IN TOKYO ON THE DAY GINKO WAS HOSPITALIZED BECAUSE HE HAD CALLED ME OVER.
岡星
HE HAD PROMISED TO TREAT ME TO THE "*MATSUTAKE* RICE OF THE SEA."
MATSUTAKE RICE OF THE SEA?!

ON CURTAIN: OKABOSHI

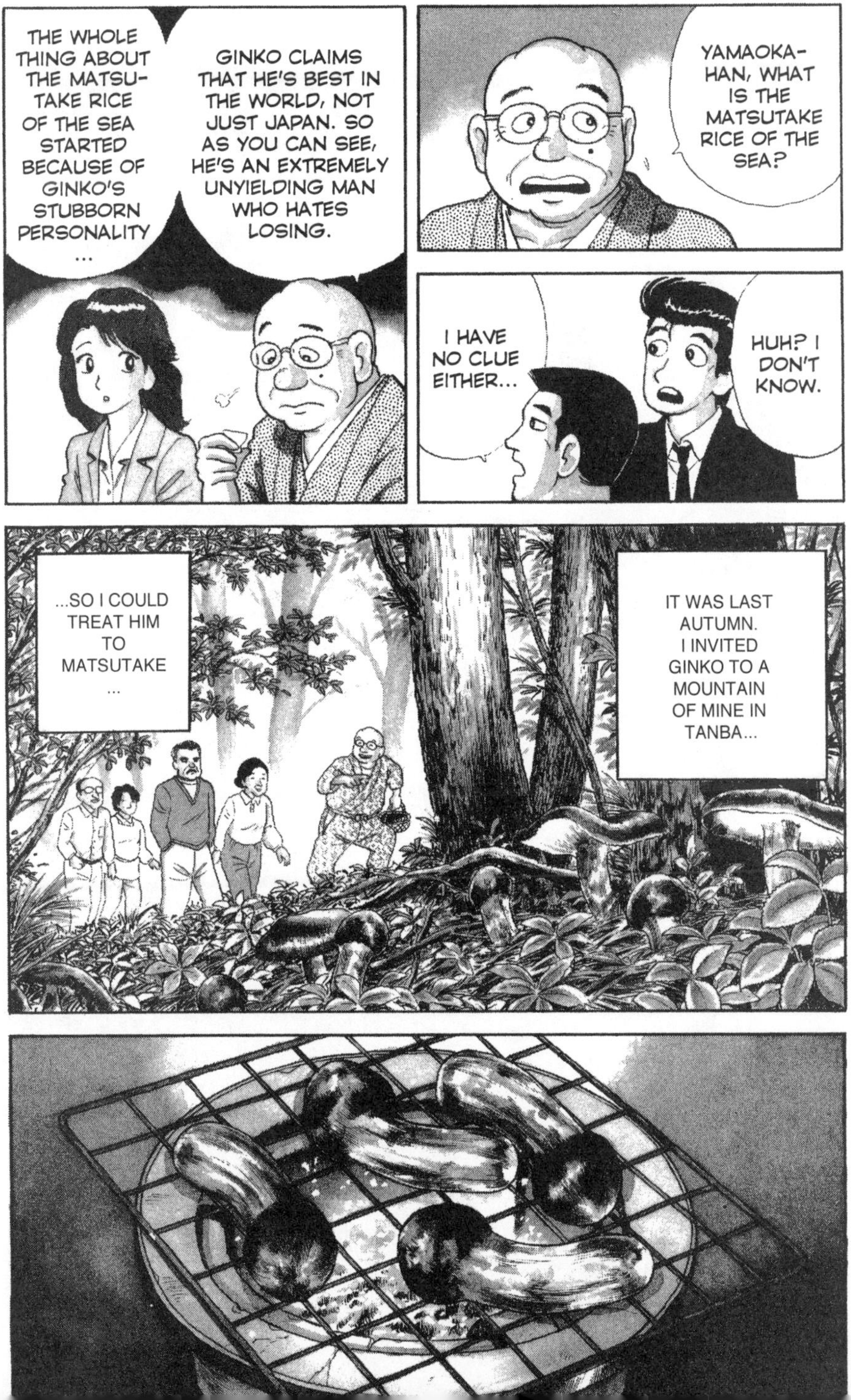
YAMAOKA-HAN, WHAT IS THE MATSUTAKE RICE OF THE SEA?
HUH? I DON'T KNOW.
I HAVE NO CLUE EITHER...
GINKO CLAIMS THAT HE'S BEST IN THE WORLD, NOT JUST JAPAN. SO AS YOU CAN SEE, HE'S AN EXTREMELY UNYIELDING MAN WHO HATES LOSING.
THE WHOLE THING ABOUT THE MATSU-TAKE RICE OF THE SEA STARTED BECAUSE OF GINKO'S STUBBORN PERSONALITY ...
IT WAS LAST AUTUMN. I INVITED GINKO TO A MOUNTAIN OF MINE IN TANBA...
...SO I COULD TREAT HIM TO MATSUTAKE ...

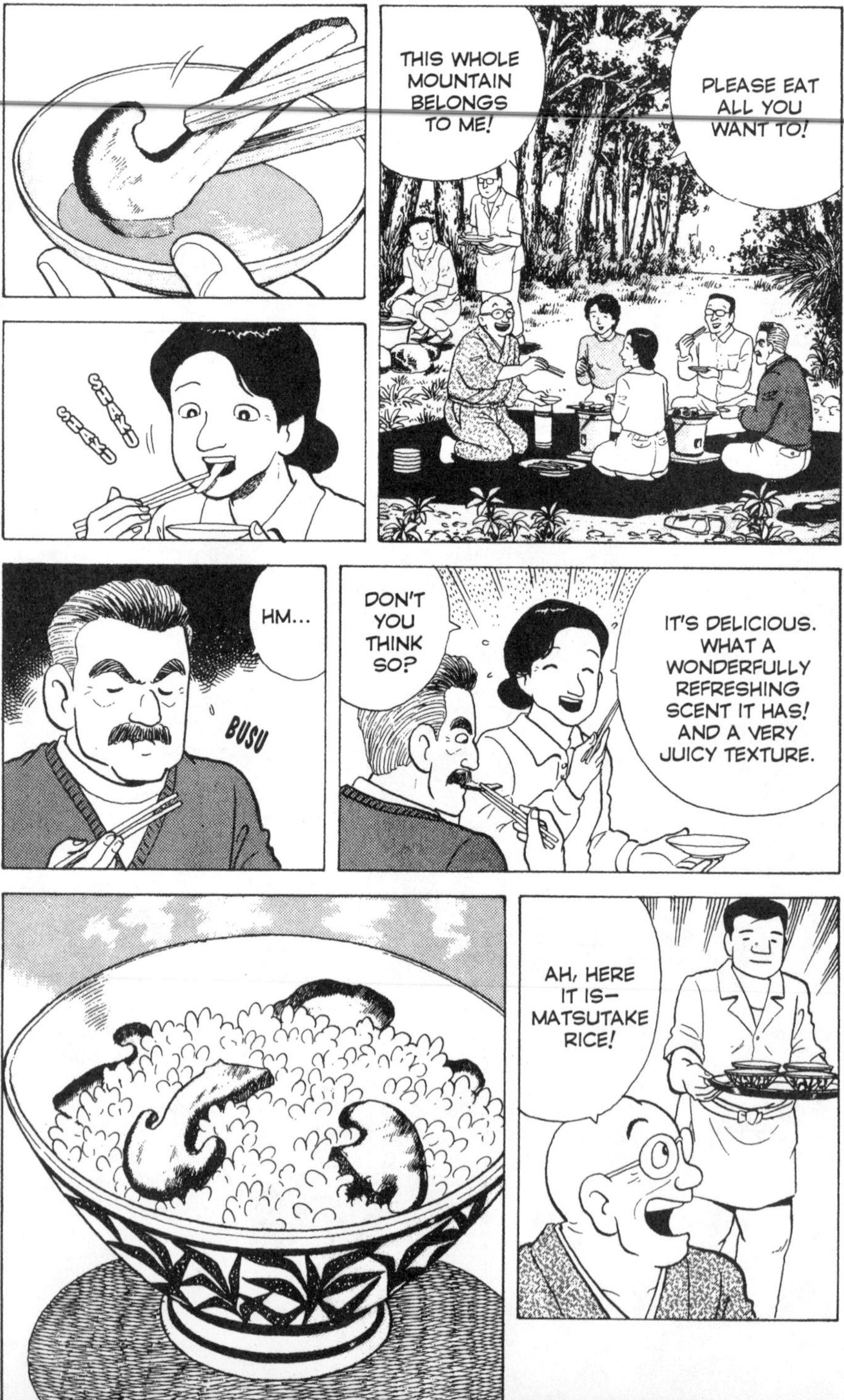
PLEASE EAT ALL YOU WANT TO!
THIS WHOLE MOUNTAIN BELONGS TO ME!
SHAKU
SHAKU
IT'S DELICIOUS. WHAT A WONDERFULLY REFRESHING SCENT IT HAS! AND A VERY JUICY TEXTURE.
DON'T YOU THINK SO?
HM...
BUSU
AH, HERE IT IS— MATSUTAKE RICE!

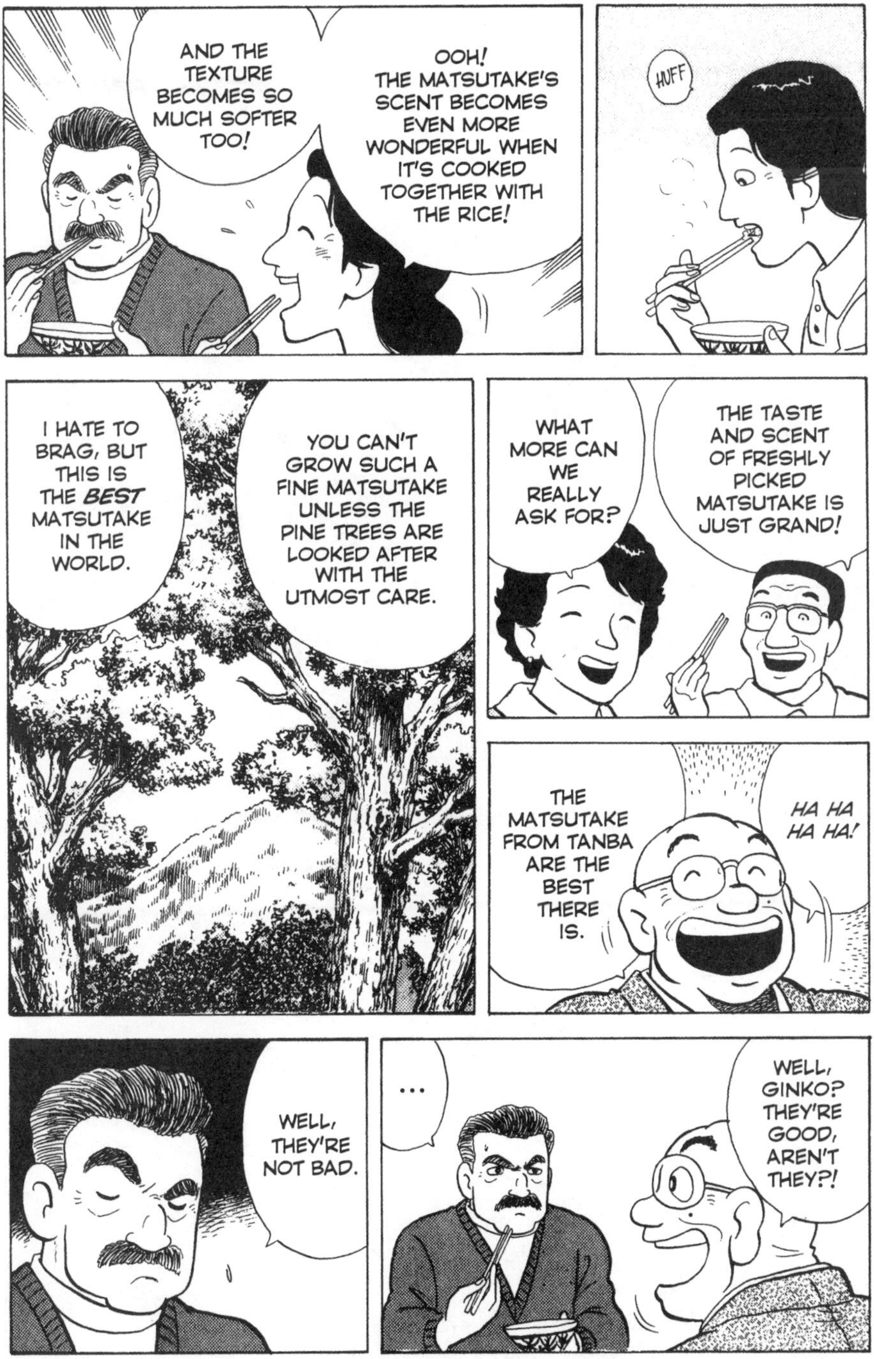
HUFF
OOH! THE MATSUTAKE'S SCENT BECOMES EVEN MORE WONDERFUL WHEN IT'S COOKED TOGETHER WITH THE RICE!
AND THE TEXTURE BECOMES SO MUCH SOFTER TOO!
THE TASTE AND SCENT OF FRESHLY PICKED MATSUTAKE IS JUST GRAND!
WHAT MORE CAN WE REALLY ASK FOR?
HA HA HA HA!
THE MATSUTAKE FROM TANBA ARE THE BEST THERE IS.
YOU CAN'T GROW SUCH A FINE MATSUTAKE UNLESS THE PINE TREES ARE LOOKED AFTER WITH THE UTMOST CARE.
I HATE TO BRAG, BUT THIS IS THE *BEST* MATSUTAKE IN THE WORLD.
WELL, GINKO? THEY'RE GOOD, AREN'T THEY?!
...
WELL, THEY'RE NOT BAD.

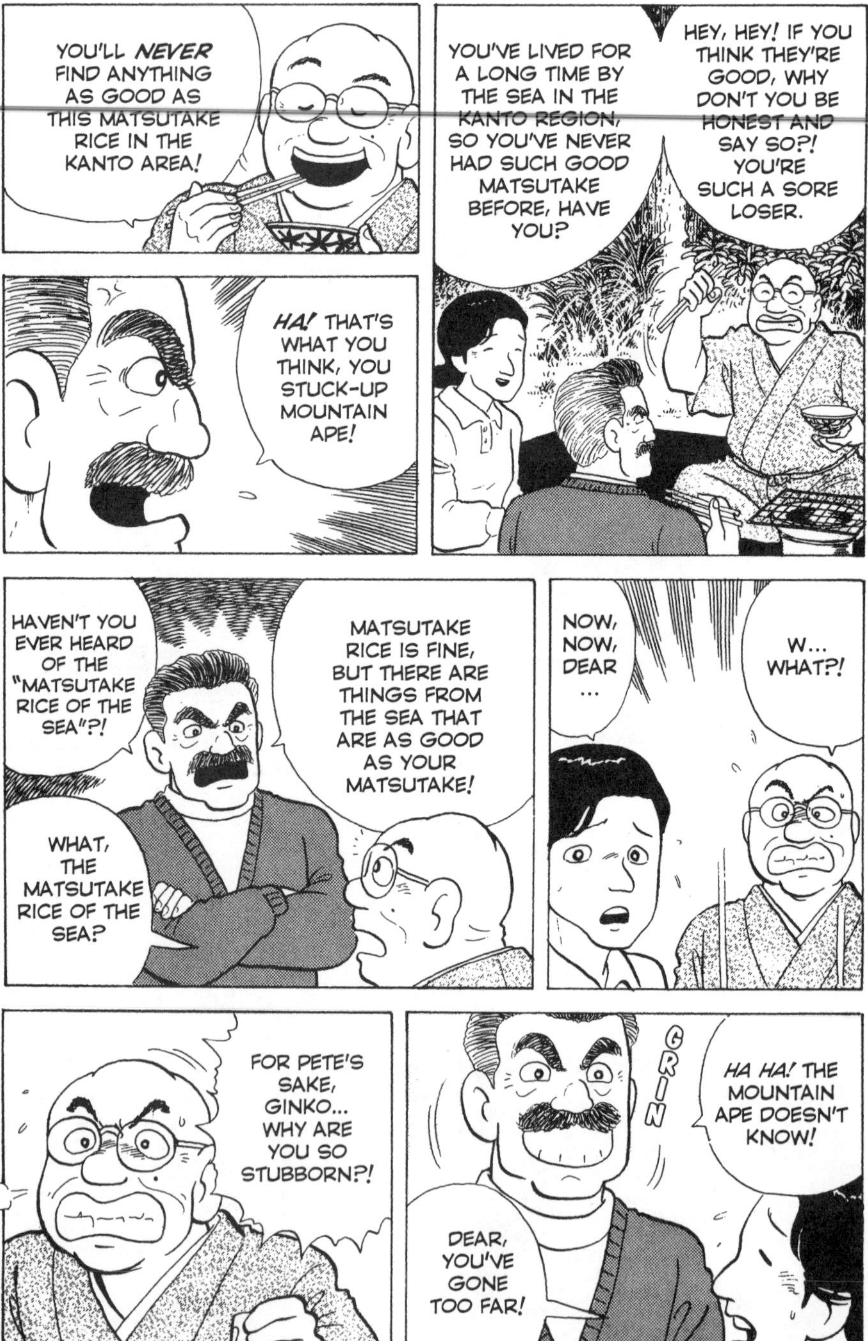
HEY, HEY! IF YOU THINK THEY'RE GOOD, WHY DON'T YOU BE HONEST AND SAY SO?! YOU'RE SUCH A SORE LOSER.
YOU'VE LIVED FOR A LONG TIME BY THE SEA IN THE KANTO REGION, SO YOU'VE NEVER HAD SUCH GOOD MATSUTAKE BEFORE, HAVE YOU?
YOU'LL *NEVER* FIND ANYTHING AS GOOD AS THIS MATSUTAKE RICE IN THE KANTO AREA!
HA! THAT'S WHAT YOU THINK, YOU STUCK-UP MOUNTAIN APE!
W... WHAT?!
NOW, NOW, DEAR ...
MATSUTAKE RICE IS FINE, BUT THERE ARE THINGS FROM THE SEA THAT ARE AS GOOD AS YOUR MATSUTAKE!
HAVEN'T YOU EVER HEARD OF THE "MATSUTAKE RICE OF THE SEA"?!
WHAT, THE MATSUTAKE RICE OF THE SEA?
GRIN
HA HA! THE MOUNTAIN APE DOESN'T KNOW!
DEAR, YOU'VE GONE TOO FAR!
FOR PETE'S SAKE, GINKO... WHY ARE YOU SO STUBBORN?!

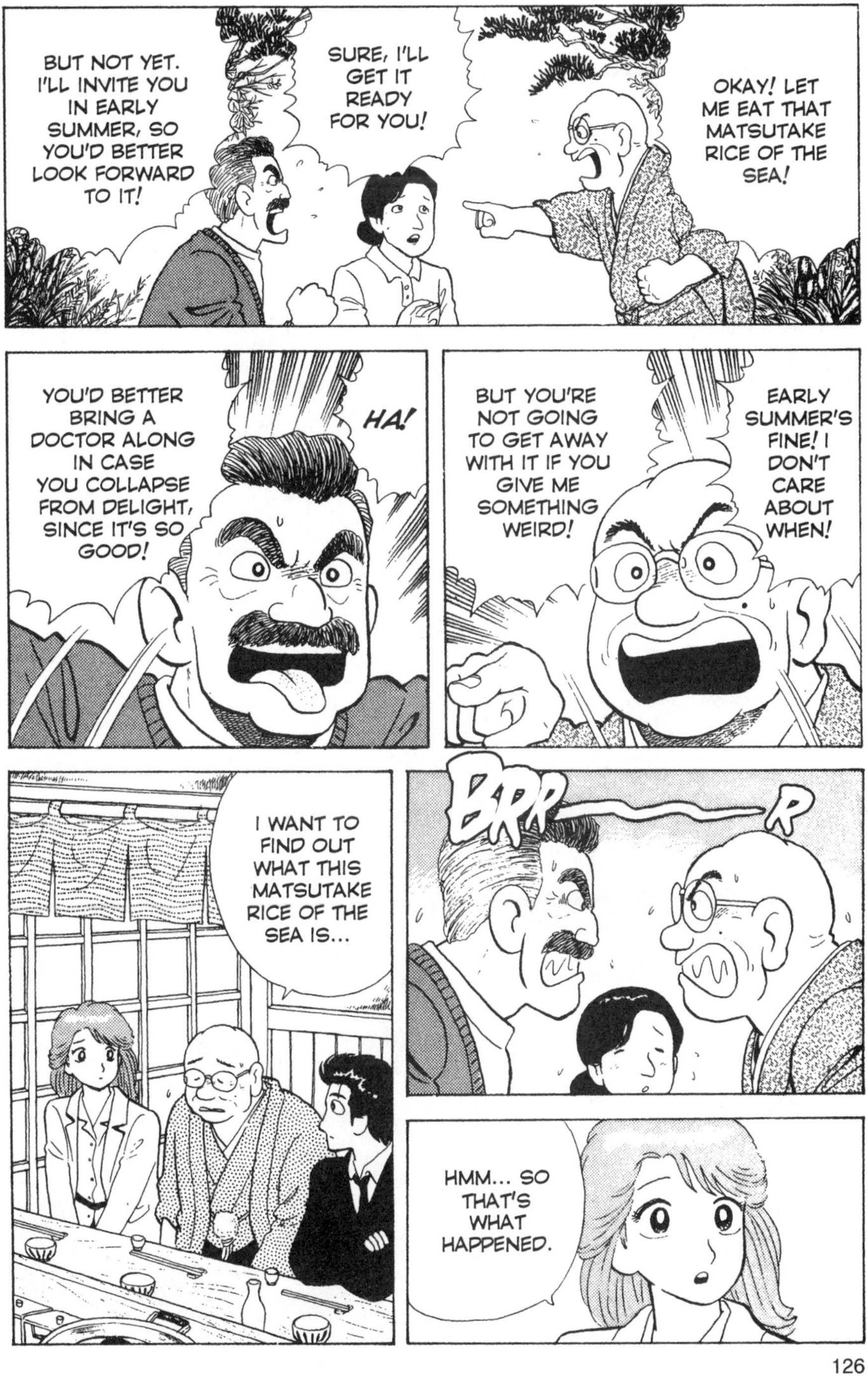
OKAY! LET ME EAT THAT MATSUTAKE RICE OF THE SEA!
SURE, I'LL GET IT READY FOR YOU!
BUT NOT YET. I'LL INVITE YOU IN EARLY SUMMER, SO YOU'D BETTER LOOK FORWARD TO IT!
EARLY SUMMER'S FINE! I DON'T CARE ABOUT WHEN!
BUT YOU'RE NOT GOING TO GET AWAY WITH IT IF YOU GIVE ME SOMETHING WEIRD!
HA!
YOU'D BETTER BRING A DOCTOR ALONG IN CASE YOU COLLAPSE FROM DELIGHT, SINCE IT'S SO GOOD!
BRR—R
HMM... SO THAT'S WHAT HAPPENED.
I WANT TO FIND OUT WHAT THIS MATSUTAKE RICE OF THE SEA IS...

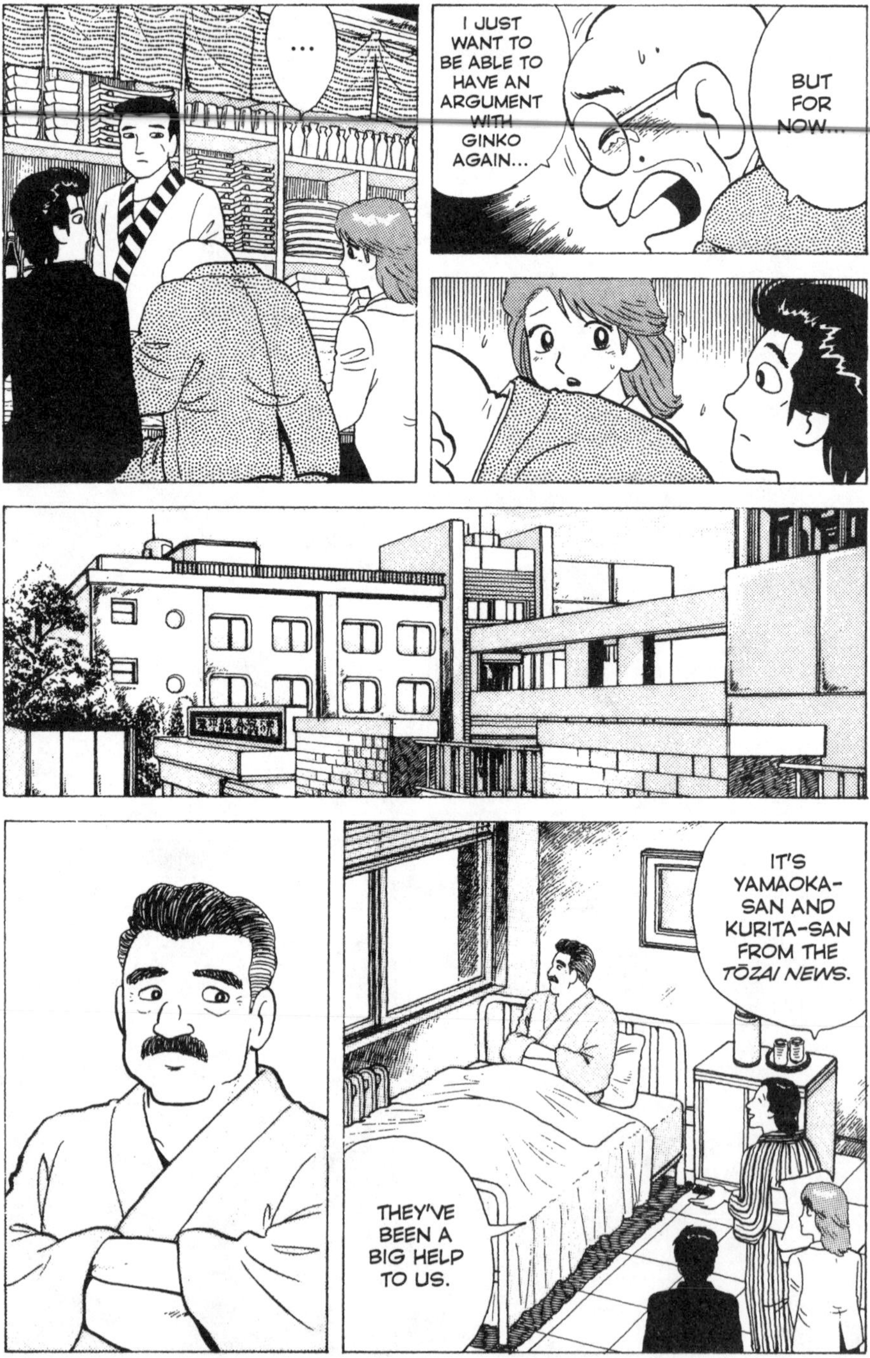
BUT FOR NOW...
I JUST WANT TO BE ABLE TO HAVE AN ARGUMENT WITH GINKO AGAIN...
...
IT'S YAMAOKA-SAN AND KURITA-SAN FROM THE *TŌZAI NEWS*.
THEY'VE BEEN A BIG HELP TO US.

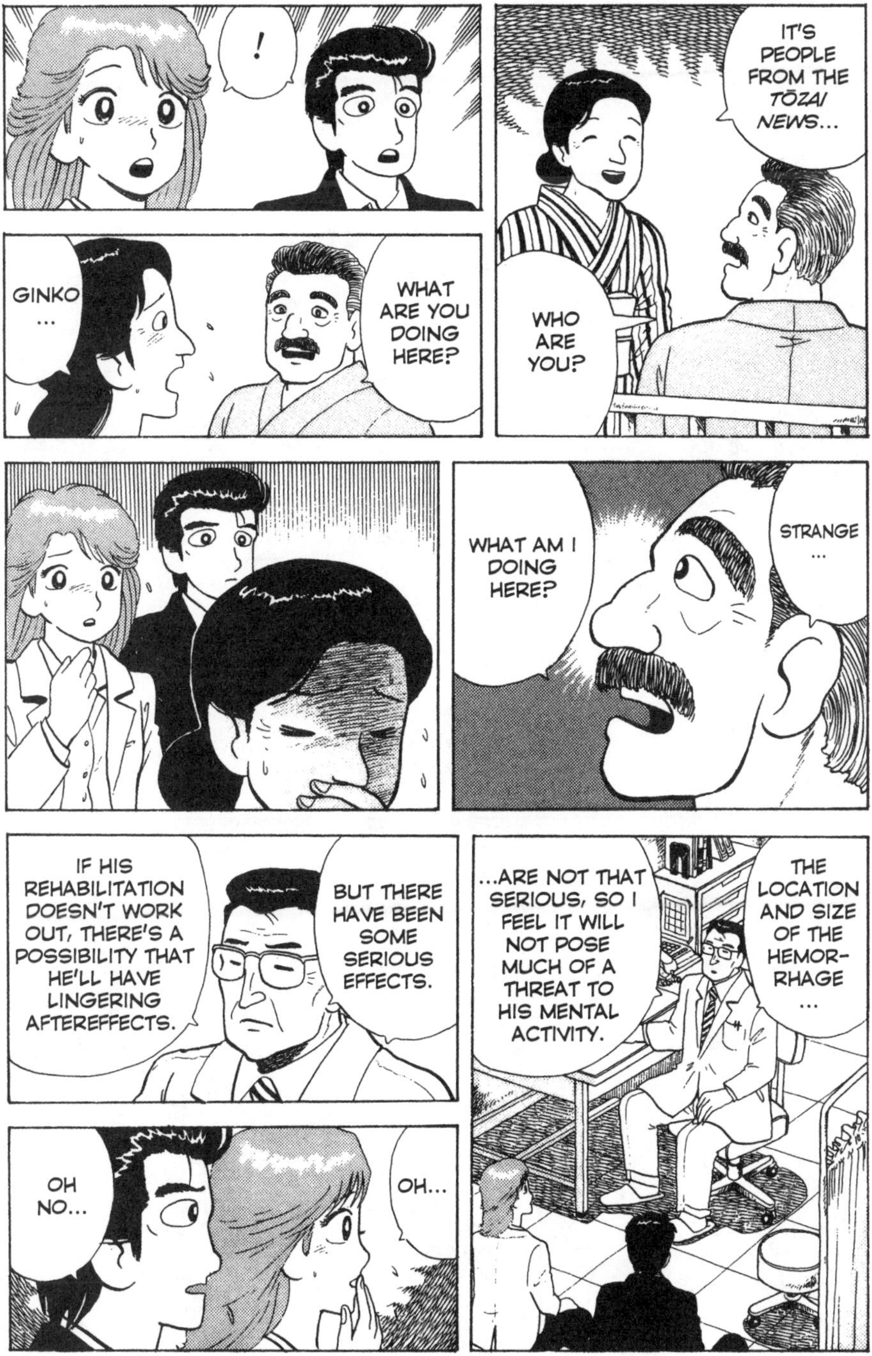
IT'S PEOPLE FROM THE *TŌZAI NEWS*...
WHO ARE YOU?
!
WHAT ARE YOU DOING HERE?
GINKO ...
STRANGE ...
WHAT AM I DOING HERE?
THE LOCATION AND SIZE OF THE HEMOR-RHAGE ...
...ARE NOT THAT SERIOUS, SO I FEEL IT WILL NOT POSE MUCH OF A THREAT TO HIS MENTAL ACTIVITY.
BUT THERE HAVE BEEN SOME SERIOUS EFFECTS.
IF HIS REHABILITATION DOESN'T WORK OUT, THERE'S A POSSIBILITY THAT HE'LL HAVE LINGERING AFTEREFFECTS.
OH...
OH NO...

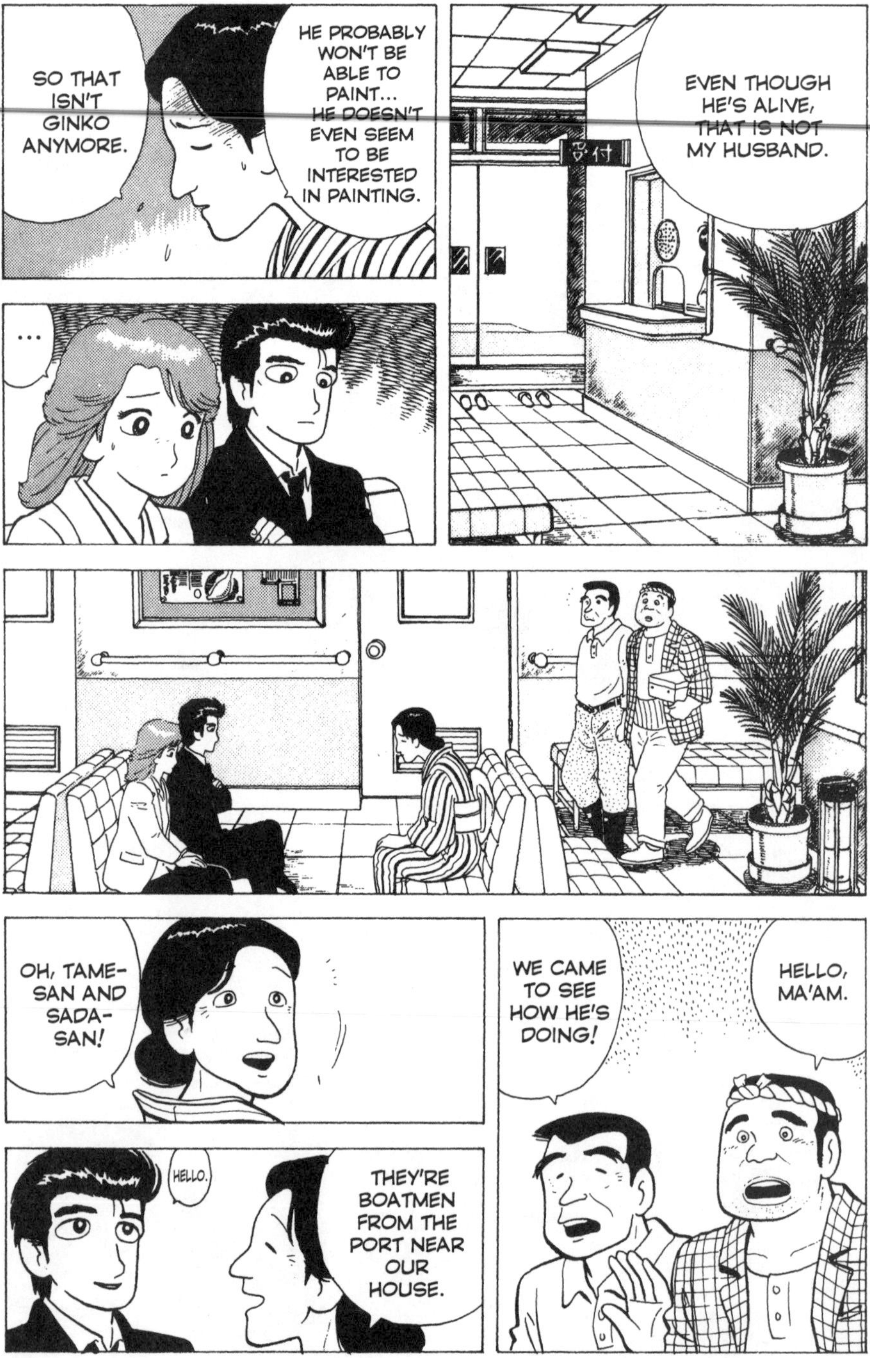
EVEN THOUGH HE'S ALIVE, THAT IS NOT MY HUSBAND.
受付
HE PROBABLY WON'T BE ABLE TO PAINT... HE DOESN'T EVEN SEEM TO BE INTERESTED IN PAINTING.
SO THAT ISN'T GINKO ANYMORE.
...
HELLO, MA'AM.
WE CAME TO SEE HOW HE'S DOING!
OH, TAME-SAN AND SADA-SAN!
THEY'RE BOATMEN FROM THE PORT NEAR OUR HOUSE.
HELLO.

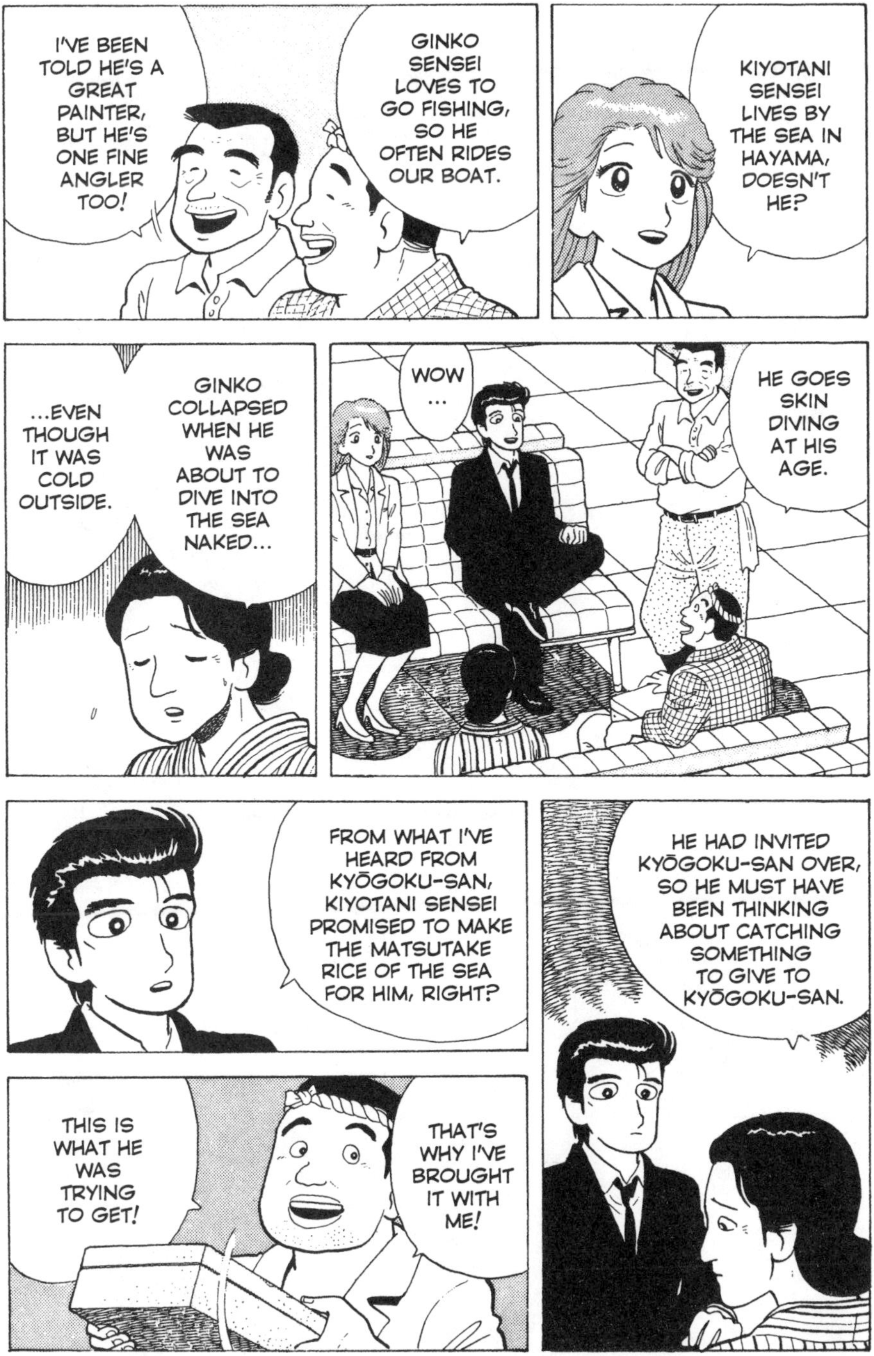
KIYOTANI SENSEI LIVES BY THE SEA IN HAYAMA, DOESN'T HE?
GINKO SENSEI LOVES TO GO FISHING, SO HE OFTEN RIDES OUR BOAT.
I'VE BEEN TOLD HE'S A GREAT PAINTER, BUT HE'S ONE FINE ANGLER TOO!
HE GOES SKIN DIVING AT HIS AGE.
WOW ...
GINKO COLLAPSED WHEN HE WAS ABOUT TO DIVE INTO THE SEA NAKED...
...EVEN THOUGH IT WAS COLD OUTSIDE.
HE HAD INVITED KYŌGOKU-SAN OVER, SO HE MUST HAVE BEEN THINKING ABOUT CATCHING SOMETHING TO GIVE TO KYŌGOKU-SAN.
FROM WHAT I'VE HEARD FROM KYŌGOKU-SAN, KIYOTANI SENSEI PROMISED TO MAKE THE MATSUTAKE RICE OF THE SEA FOR HIM, RIGHT?
THAT'S WHY I'VE BROUGHT IT WITH ME!
THIS IS WHAT HE WAS TRYING TO GET!

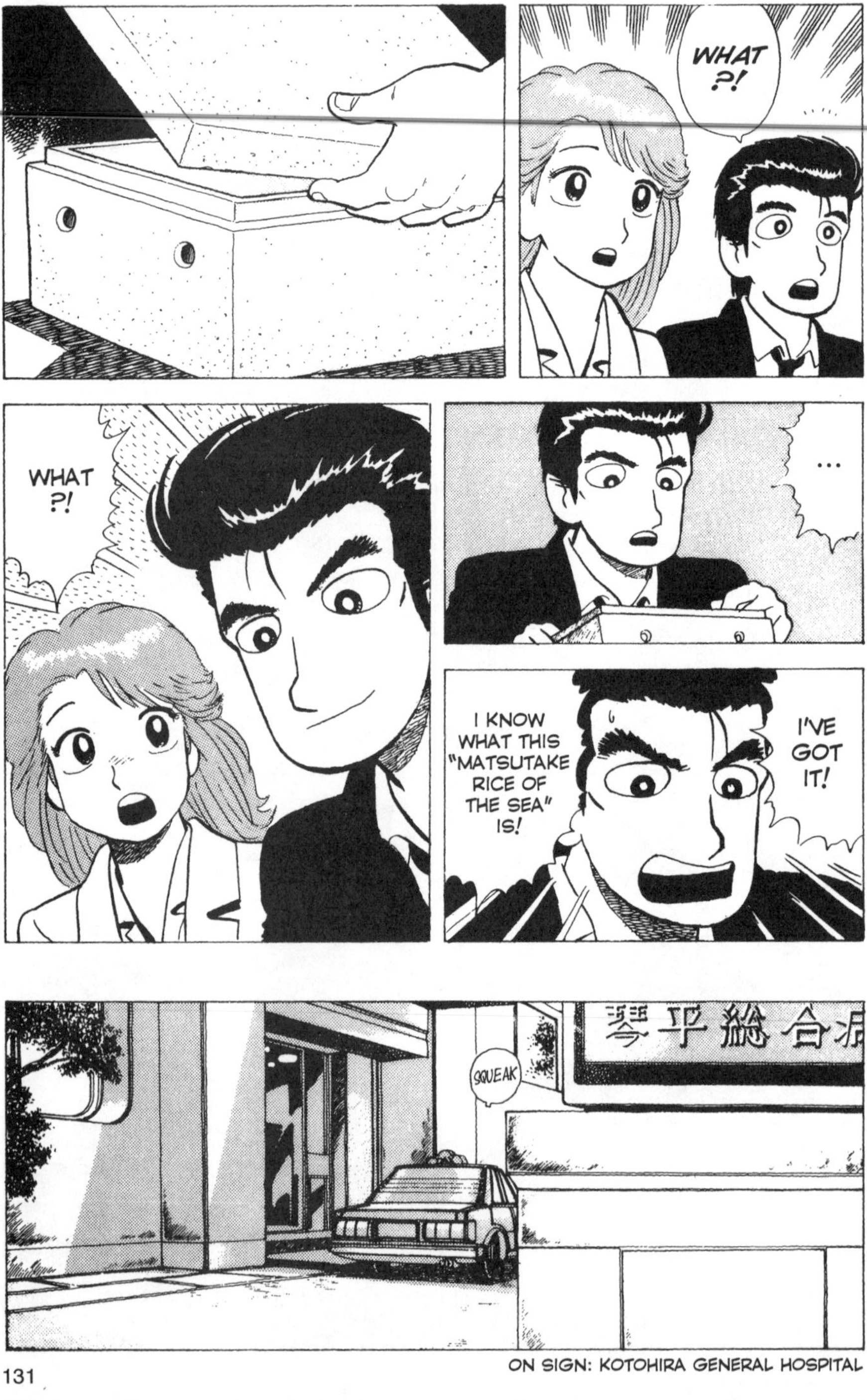
WHAT ?!
...
I'VE GOT IT!
I KNOW WHAT THIS "MATSUTAKE RICE OF THE SEA" IS!
WHAT ?!
琴平総合
SQUEAK

ON SIGN: KOTOHIRA GENERAL HOSPITAL

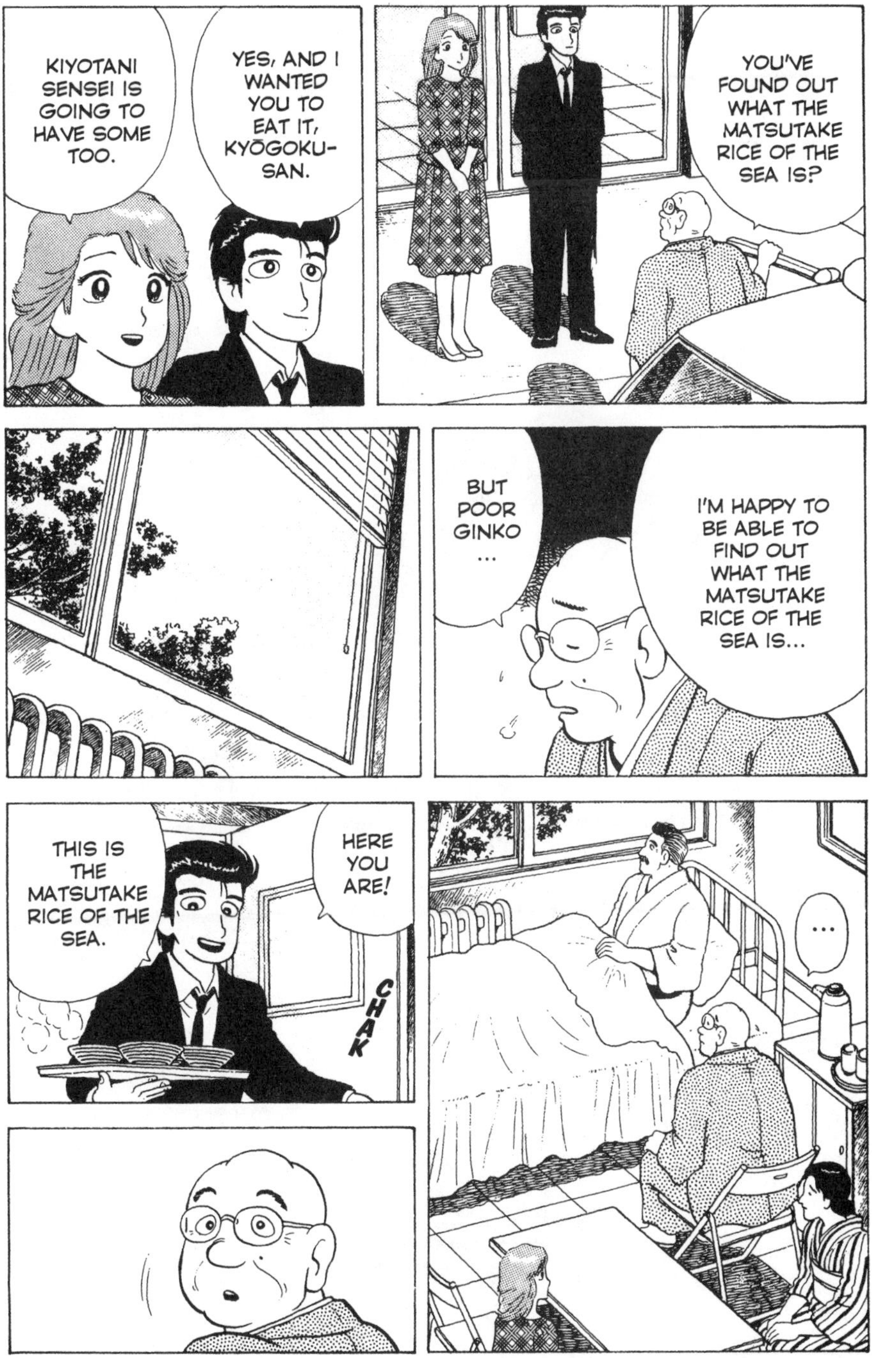
YOU'VE FOUND OUT WHAT THE MATSUTAKE RICE OF THE SEA IS?
KIYOTANI SENSEI IS GOING TO HAVE SOME TOO.
YES, AND I WANTED YOU TO EAT IT, KYŌGOKU-SAN.
I'M HAPPY TO BE ABLE TO FIND OUT WHAT THE MATSUTAKE RICE OF THE SEA IS...
BUT POOR GINKO ...
...
HERE YOU ARE!
THIS IS THE MATSUTAKE RICE OF THE SEA.
CHAK

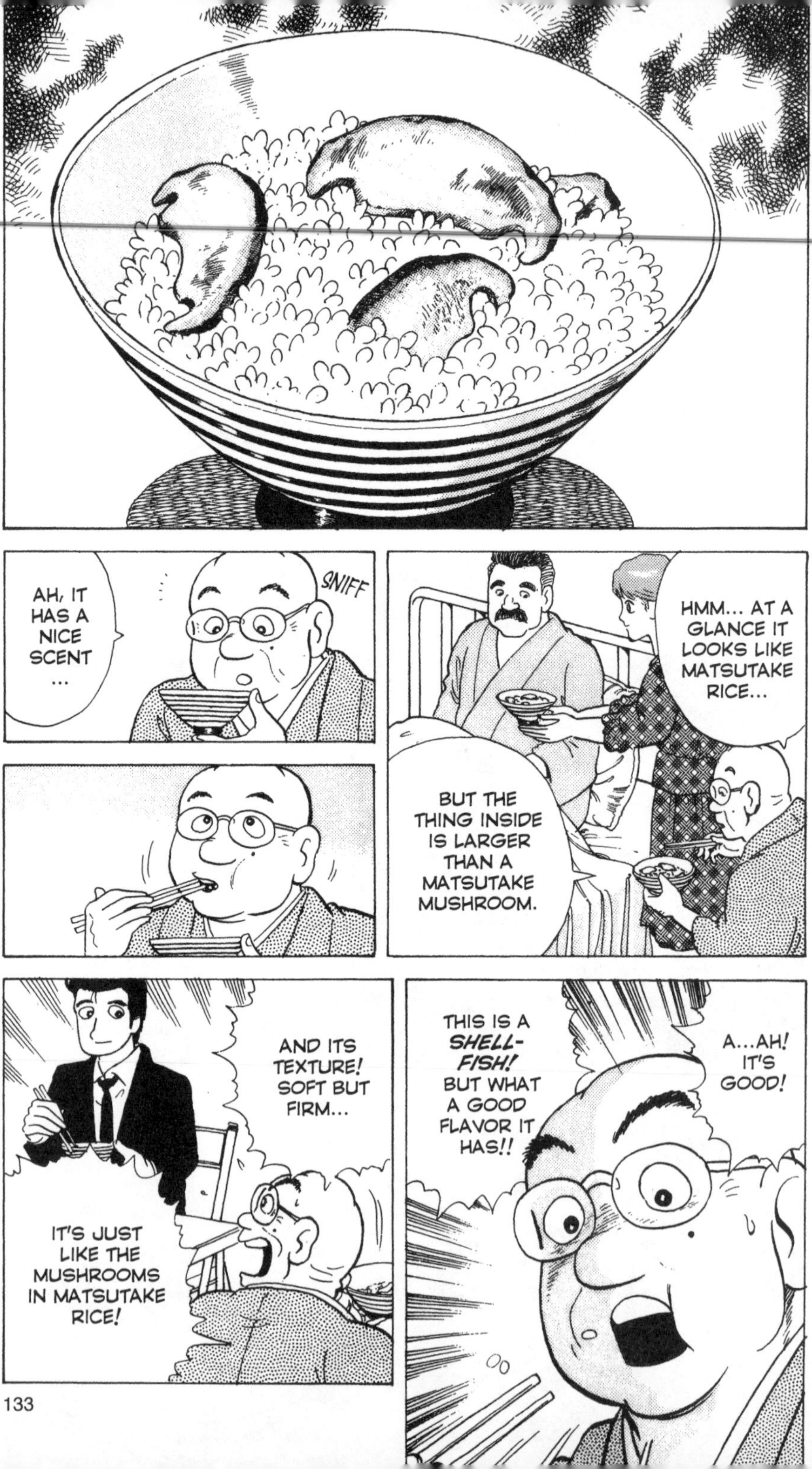
HMM... AT A GLANCE IT LOOKS LIKE MATSUTAKE RICE...
BUT THE THING INSIDE IS LARGER THAN A MATSUTAKE MUSHROOM.
SNIFF
AH, IT HAS A NICE SCENT ...
A...AH! IT'S GOOD!
THIS IS A *SHELL-FISH!* BUT WHAT A GOOD FLAVOR IT HAS!!
AND ITS TEXTURE! SOFT BUT FIRM...
IT'S JUST LIKE THE MUSHROOMS IN MATSUTAKE RICE!

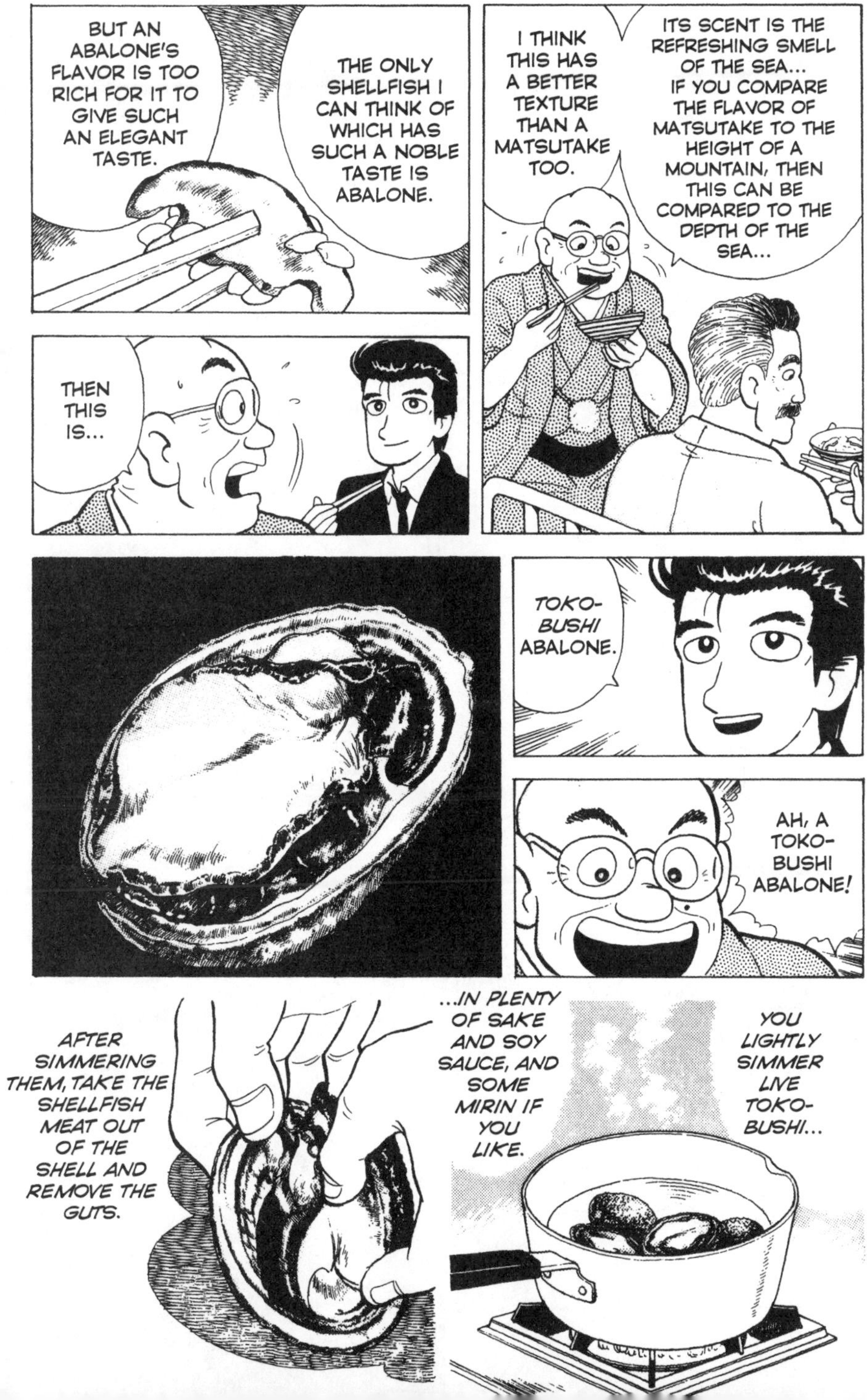
ITS SCENT IS THE REFRESHING SMELL OF THE SEA... IF YOU COMPARE THE FLAVOR OF MATSUTAKE TO THE HEIGHT OF A MOUNTAIN, THEN THIS CAN BE COMPARED TO THE DEPTH OF THE SEA...
I THINK THIS HAS A BETTER TEXTURE THAN A MATSUTAKE TOO.
THE ONLY SHELLFISH I CAN THINK OF WHICH HAS SUCH A NOBLE TASTE IS ABALONE.
BUT AN ABALONE'S FLAVOR IS TOO RICH FOR IT TO GIVE SUCH AN ELEGANT TASTE.
THEN THIS IS...
TOKO-BUSHI ABALONE.
AH, A TOKO-BUSHI ABALONE!
YOU LIGHTLY SIMMER LIVE TOKO-BUSHI...
...IN PLENTY OF SAKE AND SOY SAUCE, AND SOME MIRIN IF YOU LIKE.
AFTER SIMMERING THEM, TAKE THE SHELLFISH MEAT OUT OF THE SHELL AND REMOVE THE GUTS.

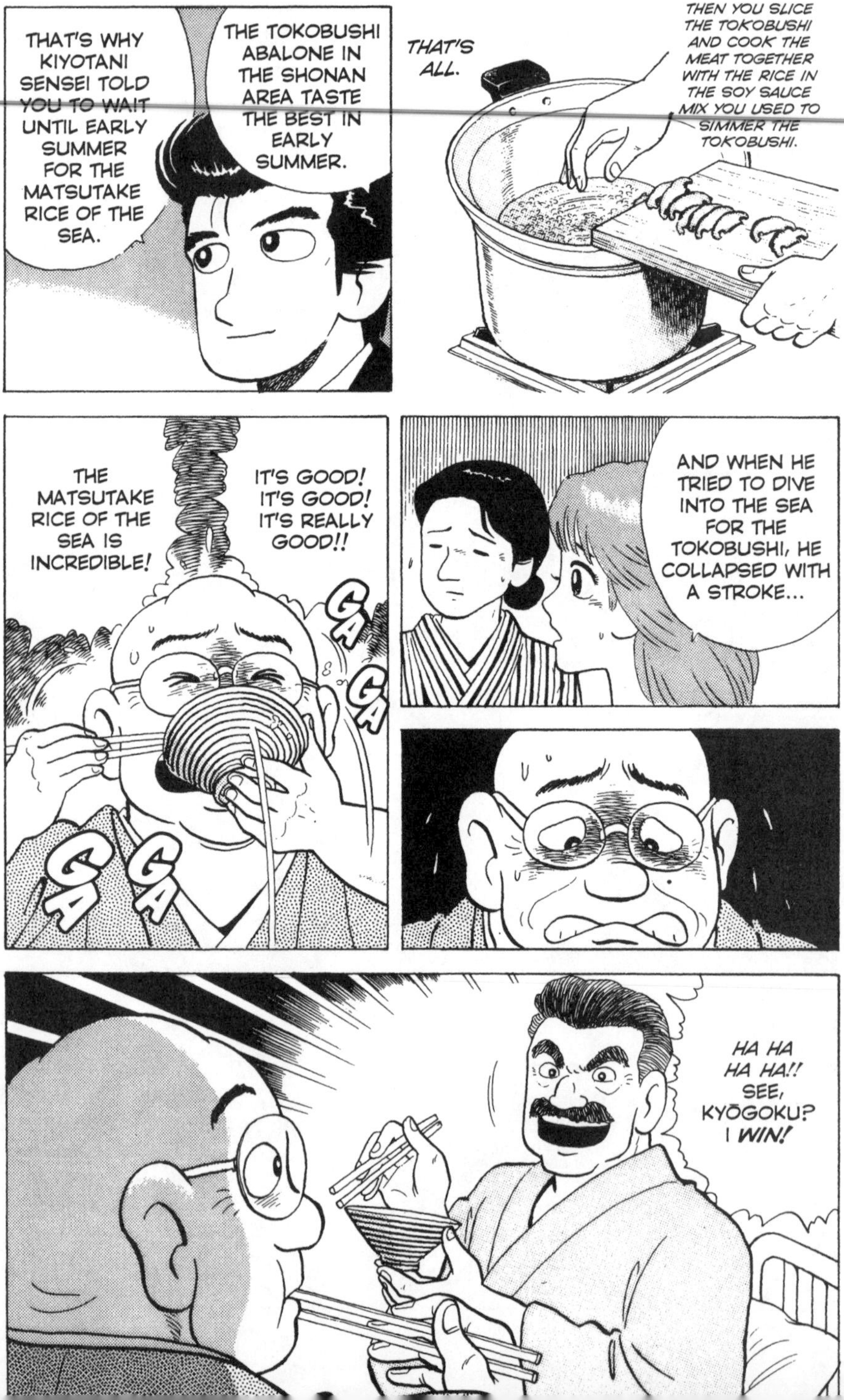
THEN YOU SLICE THE TOKOBUSHI AND COOK THE MEAT TOGETHER WITH THE RICE IN THE SOY SAUCE MIX YOU USED TO SIMMER THE TOKOBUSHI.
THAT'S ALL.
THE TOKOBUSHI ABALONE IN THE SHONAN AREA TASTE THE BEST IN EARLY SUMMER.
THAT'S WHY KIYOTANI SENSEI TOLD YOU TO WAIT UNTIL EARLY SUMMER FOR THE MATSUTAKE RICE OF THE SEA.
AND WHEN HE TRIED TO DIVE INTO THE SEA FOR THE TOKOBUSHI, HE COLLAPSED WITH A STROKE...
IT'S GOOD! IT'S GOOD! IT'S REALLY GOOD!!
THE MATSUTAKE RICE OF THE SEA IS INCREDIBLE!
GA GA
GA GA
HA HA HA HA!! SEE, KYŌGOKU? I *WIN!*

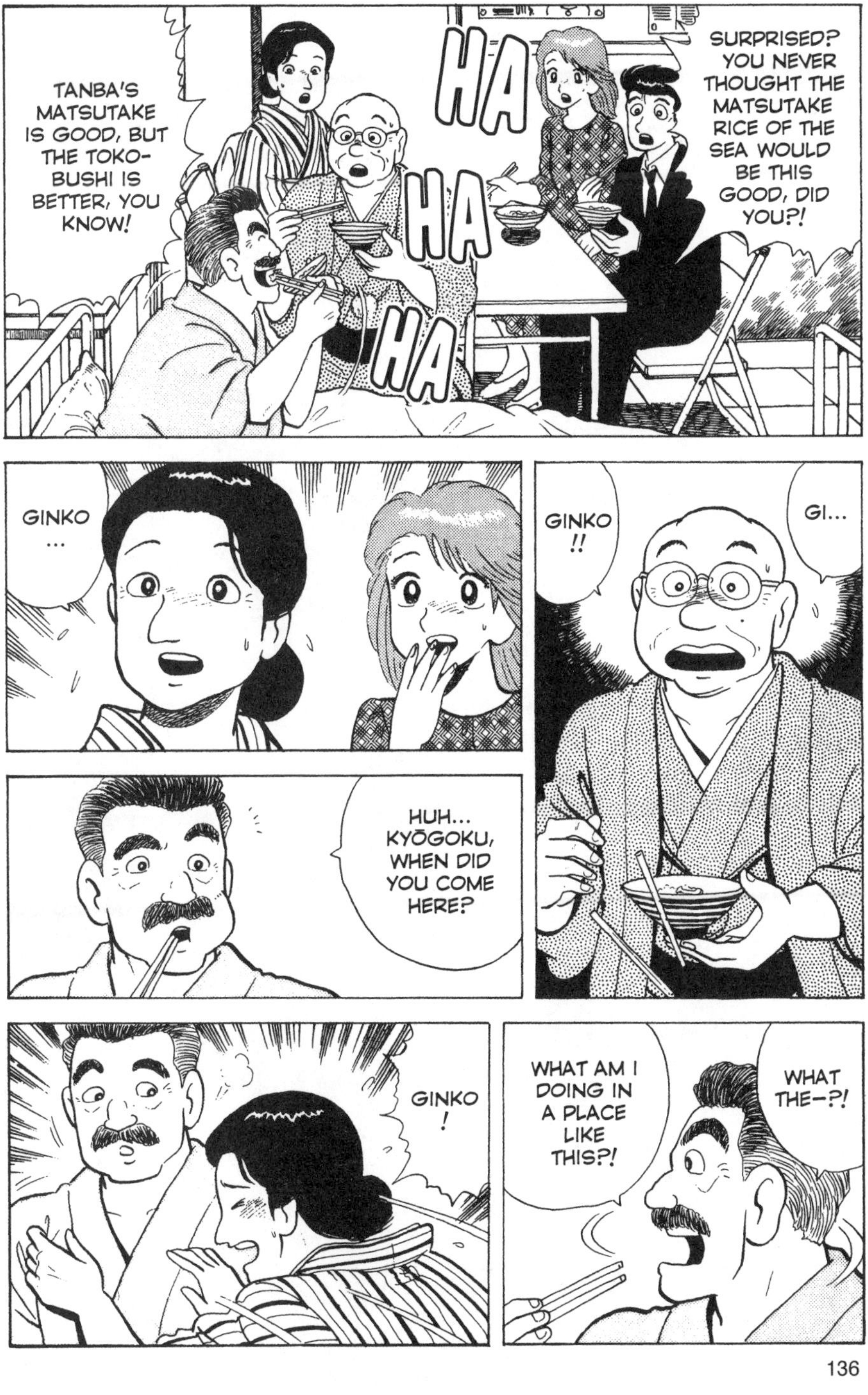
SURPRISED? YOU NEVER THOUGHT THE MATSUTAKE RICE OF THE SEA WOULD BE THIS GOOD, DID YOU?!
HA HA HA
TANBA'S MATSUTAKE IS GOOD, BUT THE TOKO-BUSHI IS BETTER, YOU KNOW!
GI...
GINKO !!
GINKO ...
HUH... KYŌGOKU, WHEN DID YOU COME HERE?
WHAT THE-?!
WHAT AM I DOING IN A PLACE LIKE THIS?!
GINKO !

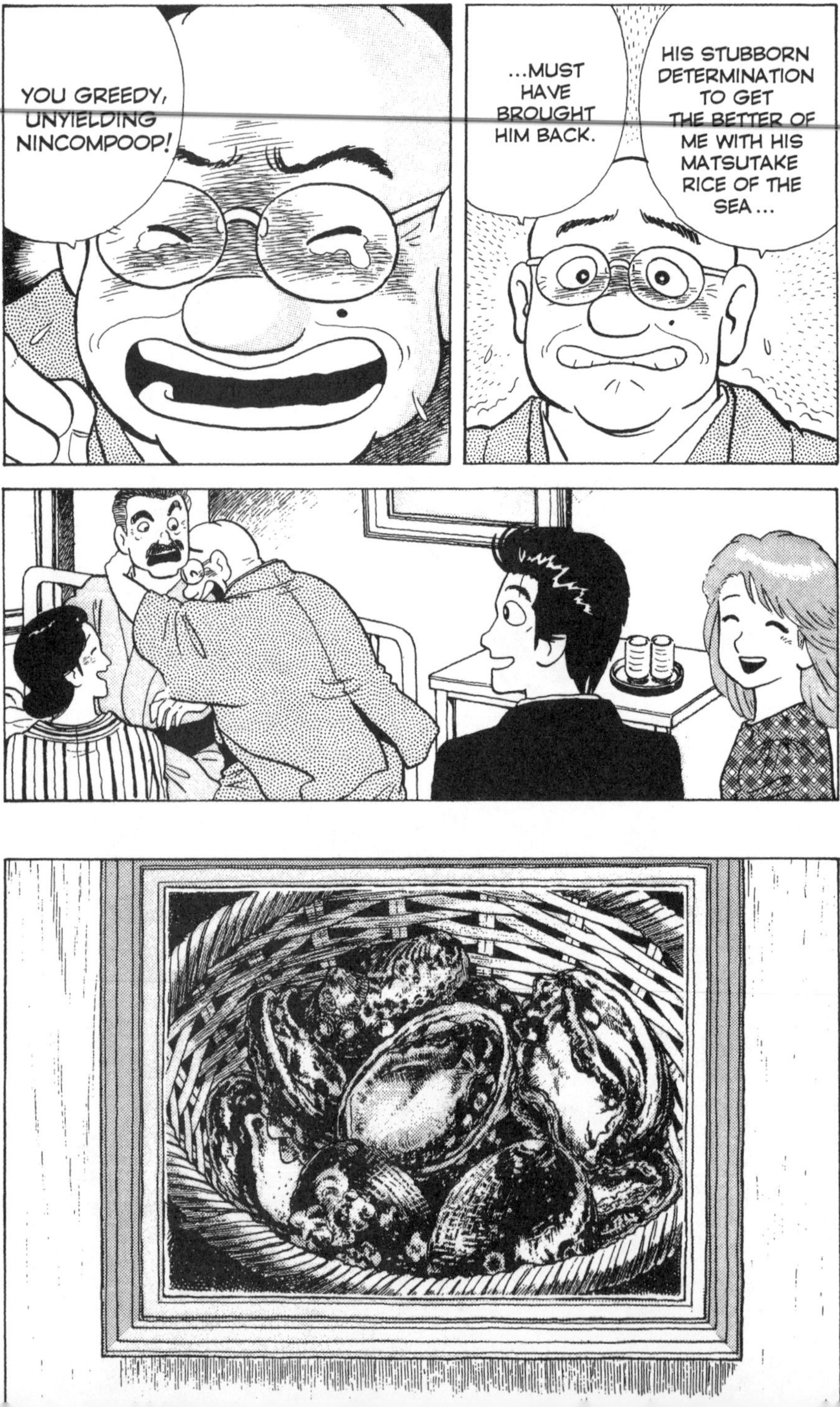
HIS STUBBORN DETERMINATION TO GET THE BETTER OF ME WITH HIS MATSUTAKE RICE OF THE SEA...
...MUST HAVE BROUGHT HIM BACK.
YOU GREEDY, UNYIELDING NINCOMPOOP!

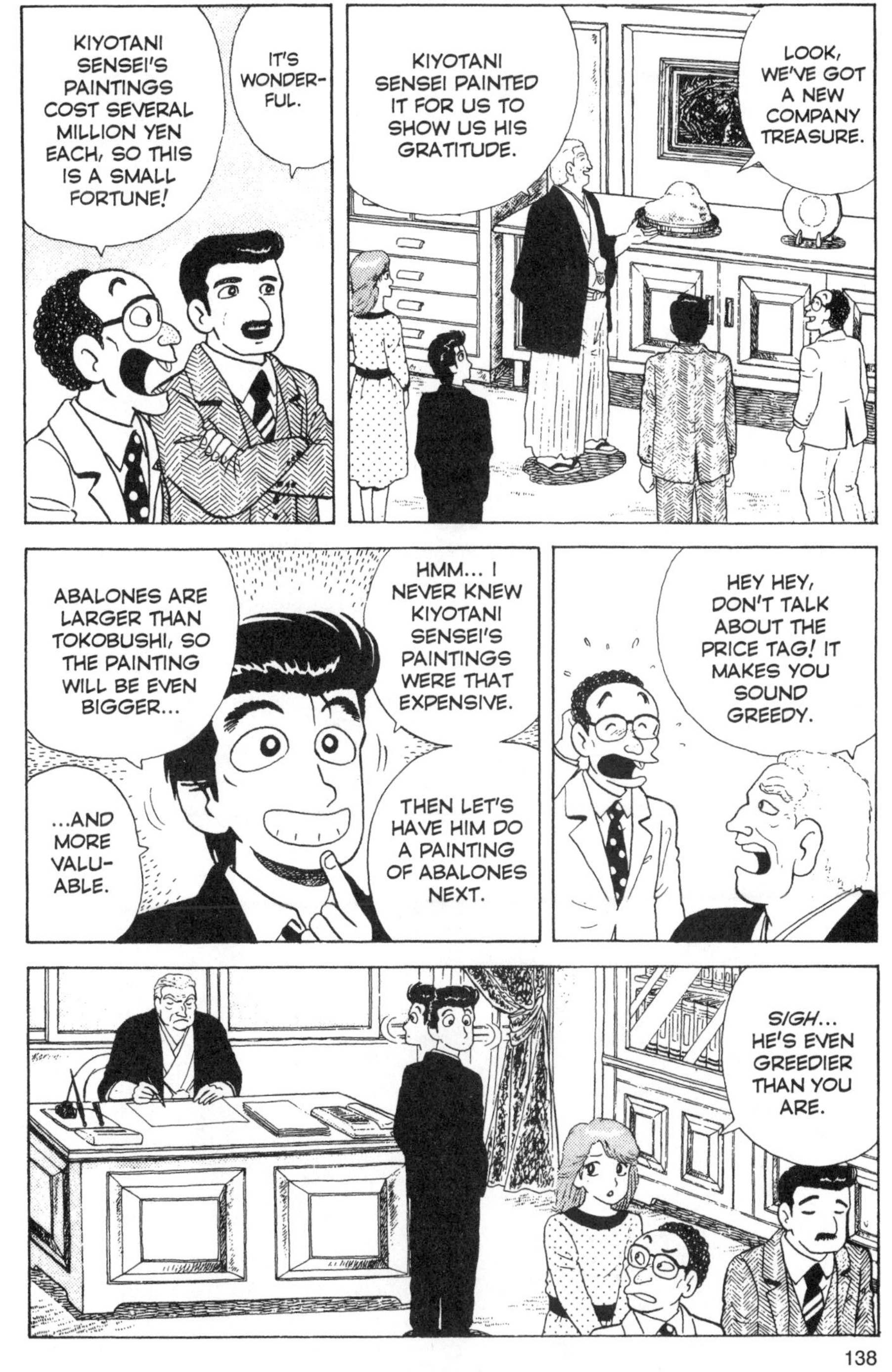
LOOK, WE'VE GOT A NEW COMPANY TREASURE.
KIYOTANI SENSEI PAINTED IT FOR US TO SHOW US HIS GRATITUDE.
IT'S WONDER-FUL.
KIYOTANI SENSEI'S PAINTINGS COST SEVERAL MILLION YEN EACH, SO THIS IS A SMALL FORTUNE!
HEY HEY, DON'T TALK ABOUT THE PRICE TAG! IT MAKES YOU SOUND GREEDY.
HMM... I NEVER KNEW KIYOTANI SENSEI'S PAINTINGS WERE THAT EXPENSIVE.
ABALONES ARE LARGER THAN TOKOBUSHI, SO THE PAINTING WILL BE EVEN BIGGER...
THEN LET'S HAVE HIM DO A PAINTING OF ABALONES NEXT.
...AND MORE VALU-ABLE.
SIGH... HE'S EVEN GREEDIER THAN YOU ARE.

Author commentary

Oishinbo Day-by-Day

Tetsu Kariya

The Most Delicious Way to Eat Rice

The fundamental difference between the eating manners of the Chinese and Japanese.

As I sit in Sydney's Chinatown and watch the Chinese people eat, I've noticed that they usually place the food on top of the rice and then scarf them down together. In Japan, it is considered rude to scarf down rice, and it is something you should not do when eating at a high-end restaurant specializing in *kaiseki ryōri*. But the Chinese dining etiquette seems to be rather different from the Japanese, and a lot of Chinese people eat in the way I described. Whenever a Japanese person eats rice, they hold

the chopsticks diagonally and move the rice into their mouth, but the Chinese spread their elbows out, hold the chopsticks diagonally to their face and scarf. Or rather, they push the rice into their mouth with the rice bowl right in front of them. I think it's a rather dynamic, spirited and admirable way to eat.

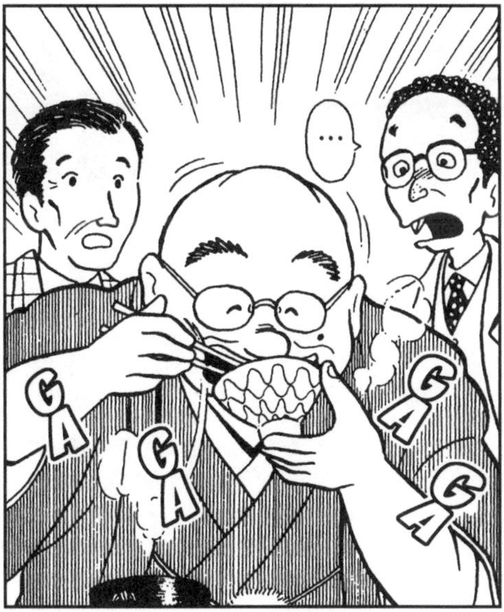
...
GA
GA
GA
GA

Actually, most kinds of food taste better when they are placed on rice rather than eating them on their own. And to be even more precise, they taste better when you put them into your mouth along with the rice. This means, rather than eating elegantly by taking a bite of the accompanying dish and then a bite of the rice, the food tastes much better if you just shovel them into your mouth at the same time.

To taste the full flavor of a donburi dish, scarf it down!

Even Japanese cuisine has a dish with food placed upon the rice that must be scarfed down to taste its full flavor. And that is the *donburi* bowl. For example, if you're eating an *unadon* (eel bowl), it won't taste good if you take a bite of the eel and then eat the rice after a bit. It tastes best when you eat the eel and rice together. But to do that, you inevitably must shovel the rice into your mouth. It's the same whether you eat *katsudon* (pork cutlet on rice), *gyudon* (beef bowl) or *oyakodon* (chicken and egg on rice). For katsudon, you take the fresh deep-fried pork cutlet and shove it into your mouth together with the rice! Now you're not supposed to chew on it that much. If you've got a healthy set of teeth, you just need to chew on it a couple of times. I start getting annoyed when I see people chewing on it forever. I even want to raise my voice and say, "Stop chewing on it

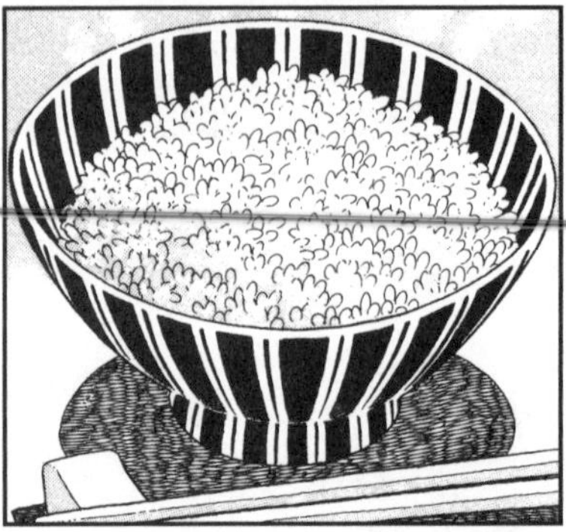

so much! Hurry up and swallow it! If you couldn't chew on it enough with your teeth, use your throat! You're supposed to swallow the stuff quickly!"

The feeling of swallowing pork cutlet covered in the egg and rice together and letting it slide down your throat is so pleasurable that it brings tears to my eyes. You can't really enjoy rice if you eat it a little at a time like a little bird. So I think I can say that Japanese *donburi* lovers (the people who don't like *donburi* dishes probably won't read this, so I'm ignoring them) have proven that the way Chinese people scarf the rice down is the right way to eat rice.

Some foods taste better when they are placed into the mouth together with rice rather than eating them on their own!

I'm amazed at the wonderful common bond I've been able to create just by writing about the way to eat rice. I'm sure I've been able to unravel some of the complicated relationship between Japan and China by doing this.

A way of eating that transcends the culinary cultural differences between China, Japan and Korea!

Well, after all this bragging, I may start getting complaints from Korea. That is because in order to scarf down rice, you must sit straight up, spread your elbows out, hold the bowl in one hand and your chopsticks in the other, and quickly shove the rice into your mouth. But in Korea, it is rude to pick the bowls and plates up off the table. For

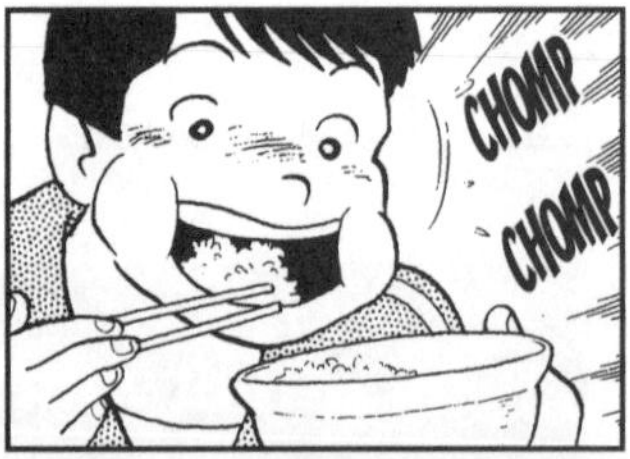
CHOMP
CHOMP

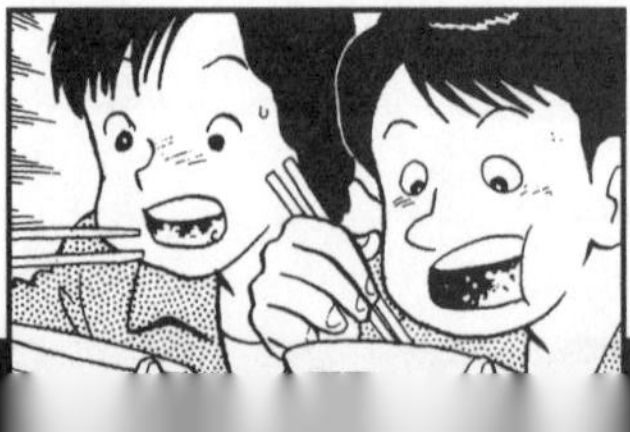

example, even when eating *bibimbap* the bowl must be left on the table, and you must eat it by moving your face close to it and using a spoon. And with *dolsot bibimbap*, it is impossible to pick up the bowl to start with since the bowl itself is piping hot. So it is not surprising for a Korean person to complain that they cannot scarf rice in the Japanese and Chinese manner.

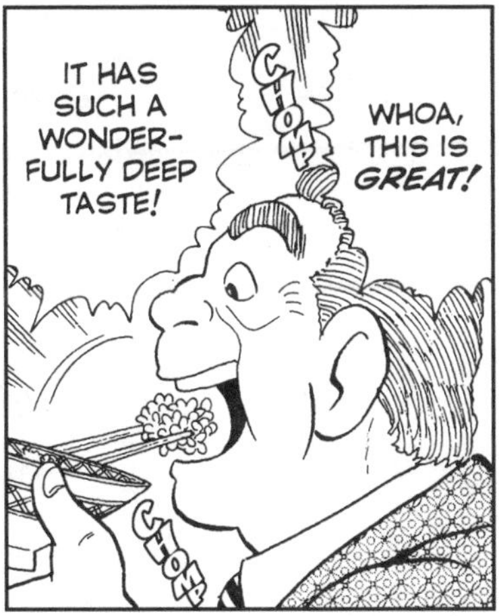
WHOA, THIS IS *GREAT!*
CHOMP
IT HAS SUCH A WONDERFULLY DEEP TASTE!
CHOMP

But a man with great diplomatic sensitivities like myself is not afraid of something like that. The whole point of this is to shovel the food and rice into your mouth in large chunks. So I tested it out myself over a *bibimbap*. Even with the bowl on the table and my body leaning toward it, I was able to shovel in a large chunk about the size of an adult's fist.

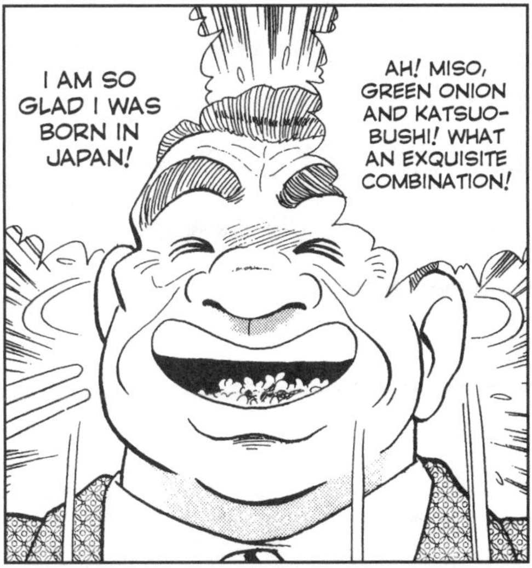
AH! MISO, GREEN ONION AND KATSUOBUSHI! WHAT AN EXQUISITE COMBINATION!
I AM SO GLAD I WAS BORN IN JAPAN!

So there's nothing to worry about. The Korean people can scarf rice into their mouths too. Ah, I'm so glad.

The whole point of this is to shovel the food and rice into your mouth in large chunks.

SIXTH COURSE

NO MIXING

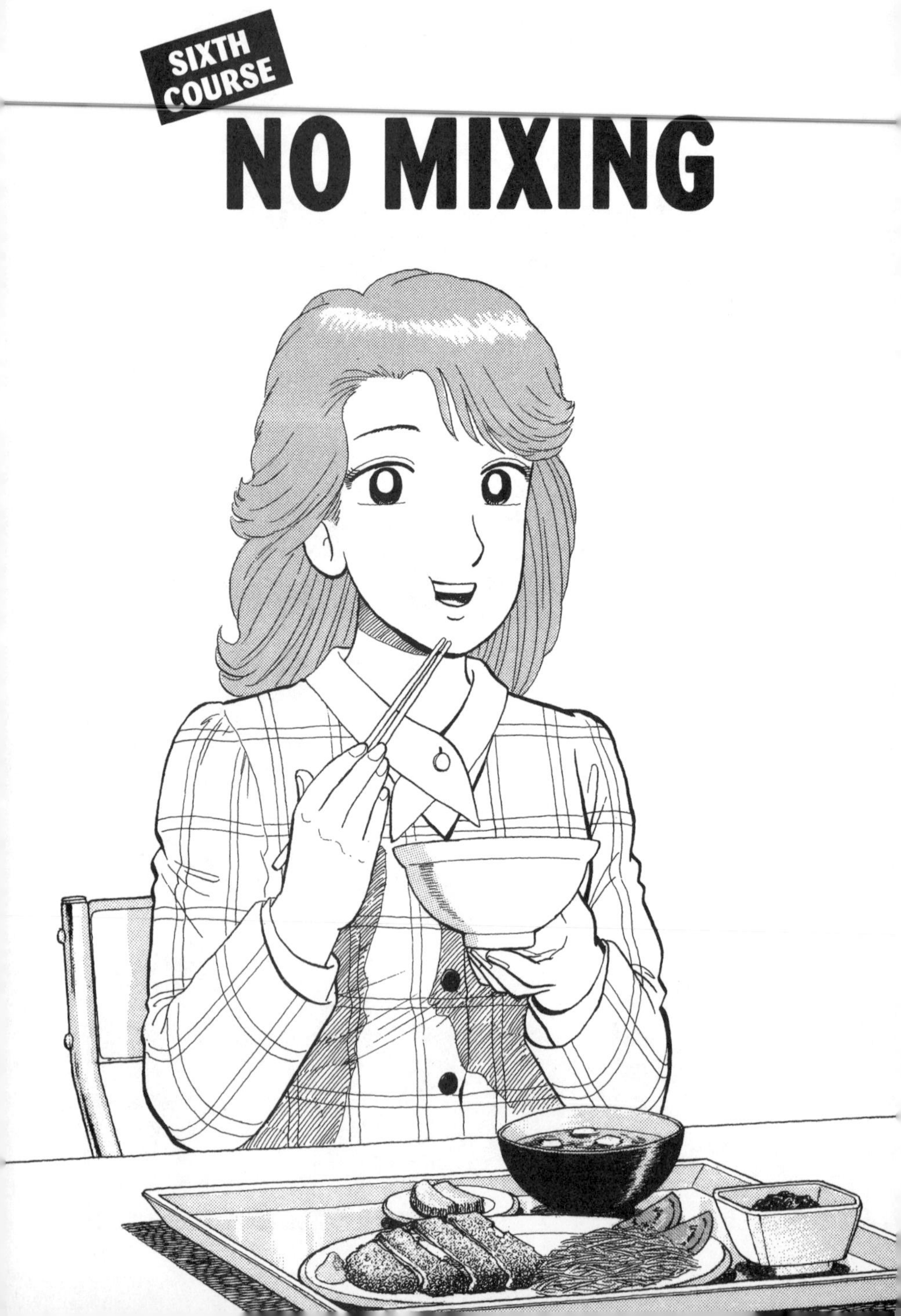

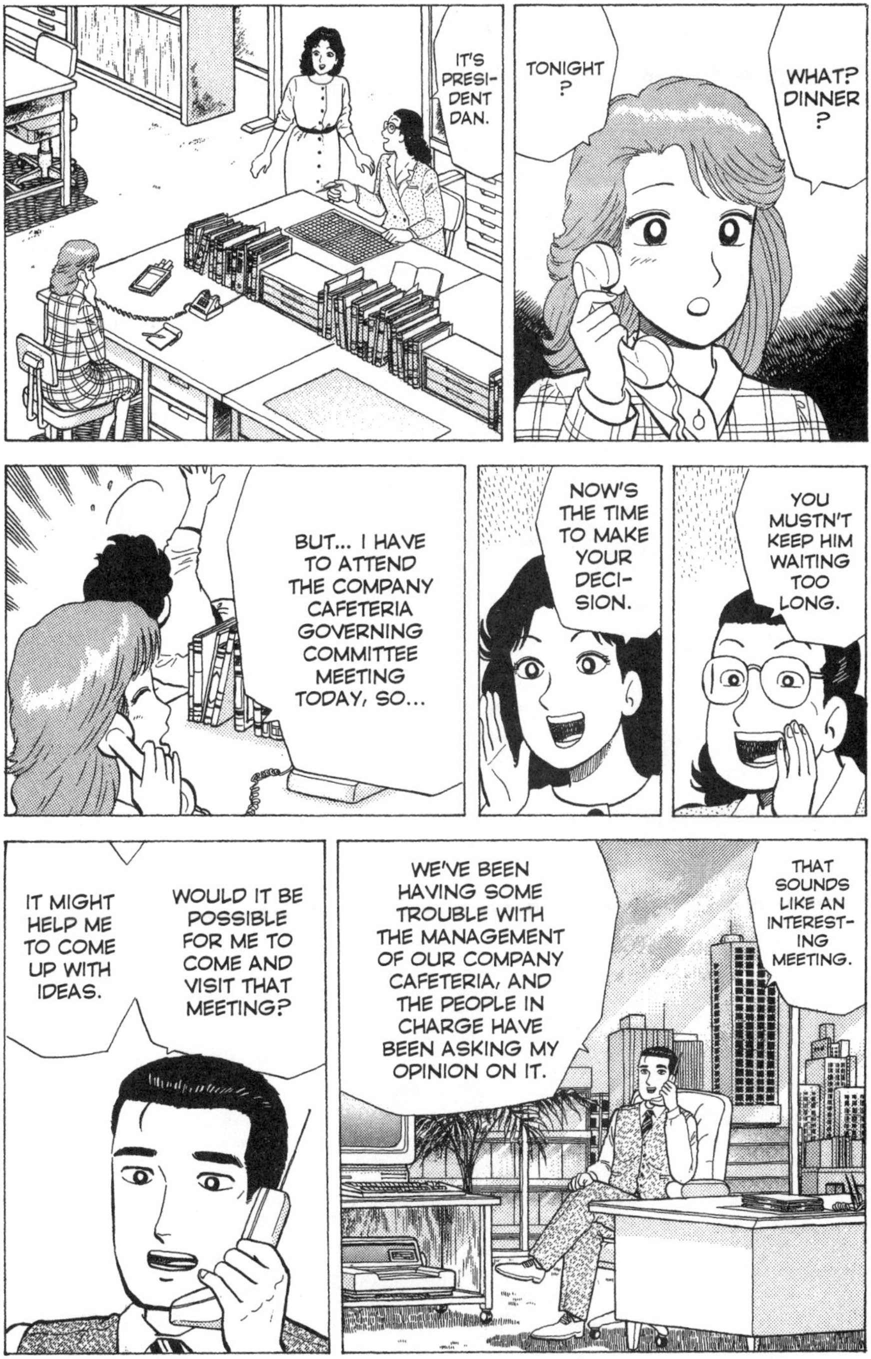
WHAT? DINNER?
TONIGHT?
IT'S PRESIDENT DAN.
YOU MUSTN'T KEEP HIM WAITING TOO LONG.
NOW'S THE TIME TO MAKE YOUR DECISION.
BUT... I HAVE TO ATTEND THE COMPANY CAFETERIA GOVERNING COMMITTEE MEETING TODAY, SO...
THAT SOUNDS LIKE AN INTERESTING MEETING.
WE'VE BEEN HAVING SOME TROUBLE WITH THE MANAGEMENT OF OUR COMPANY CAFETERIA, AND THE PEOPLE IN CHARGE HAVE BEEN ASKING MY OPINION ON IT.
WOULD IT BE POSSIBLE FOR ME TO COME AND VISIT THAT MEETING?
IT MIGHT HELP ME TO COME UP WITH IDEAS.

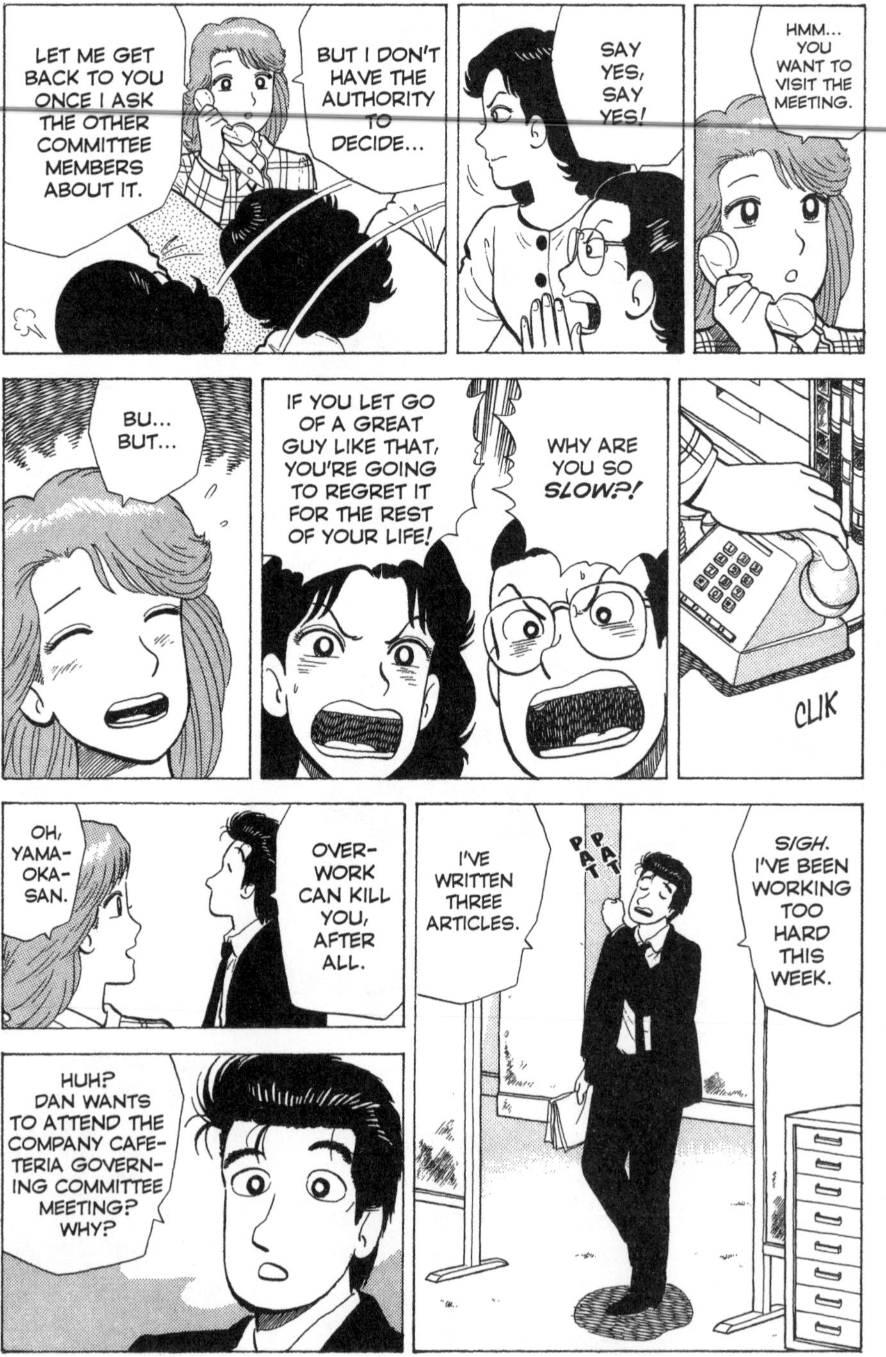
HMM... YOU WANT TO VISIT THE MEETING.
SAY YES, SAY YES!
BUT I DON'T HAVE THE AUTHORITY TO DECIDE...
LET ME GET BACK TO YOU ONCE I ASK THE OTHER COMMITTEE MEMBERS ABOUT IT.
CLIK
WHY ARE YOU SO *SLOW?!*
IF YOU LET GO OF A GREAT GUY LIKE THAT, YOU'RE GOING TO REGRET IT FOR THE REST OF YOUR LIFE!
BU... BUT...
SIGH. I'VE BEEN WORKING TOO HARD THIS WEEK.
PAT PAT
I'VE WRITTEN THREE ARTICLES.
OVER-WORK CAN KILL YOU, AFTER ALL.
OH, YAMA-OKA-SAN.
HUH? DAN WANTS TO ATTEND THE COMPANY CAFE-TERIA GOVERN-ING COMMITTEE MEETING? WHY?

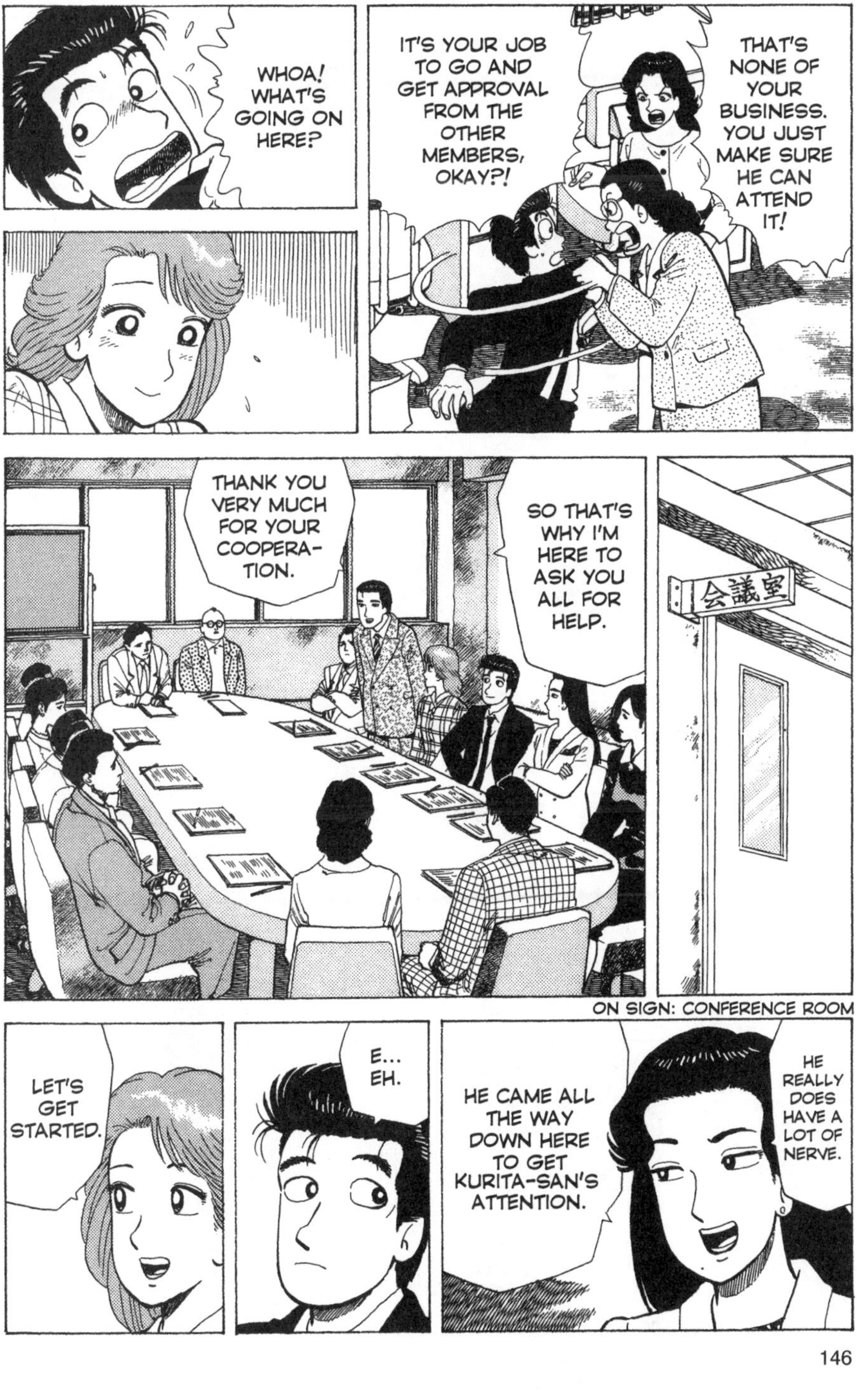
THAT'S NONE OF YOUR BUSINESS. YOU JUST MAKE SURE HE CAN ATTEND IT!
IT'S YOUR JOB TO GO AND GET APPROVAL FROM THE OTHER MEMBERS, OKAY?!
WHOA! WHAT'S GOING ON HERE?
会議室
ON SIGN: CONFERENCE ROOM
SO THAT'S WHY I'M HERE TO ASK YOU ALL FOR HELP.
THANK YOU VERY MUCH FOR YOUR COOPERATION.
HE REALLY DOES HAVE A LOT OF NERVE.
HE CAME ALL THE WAY DOWN HERE TO GET KURITA-SAN'S ATTENTION.
E... EH.
LET'S GET STARTED.

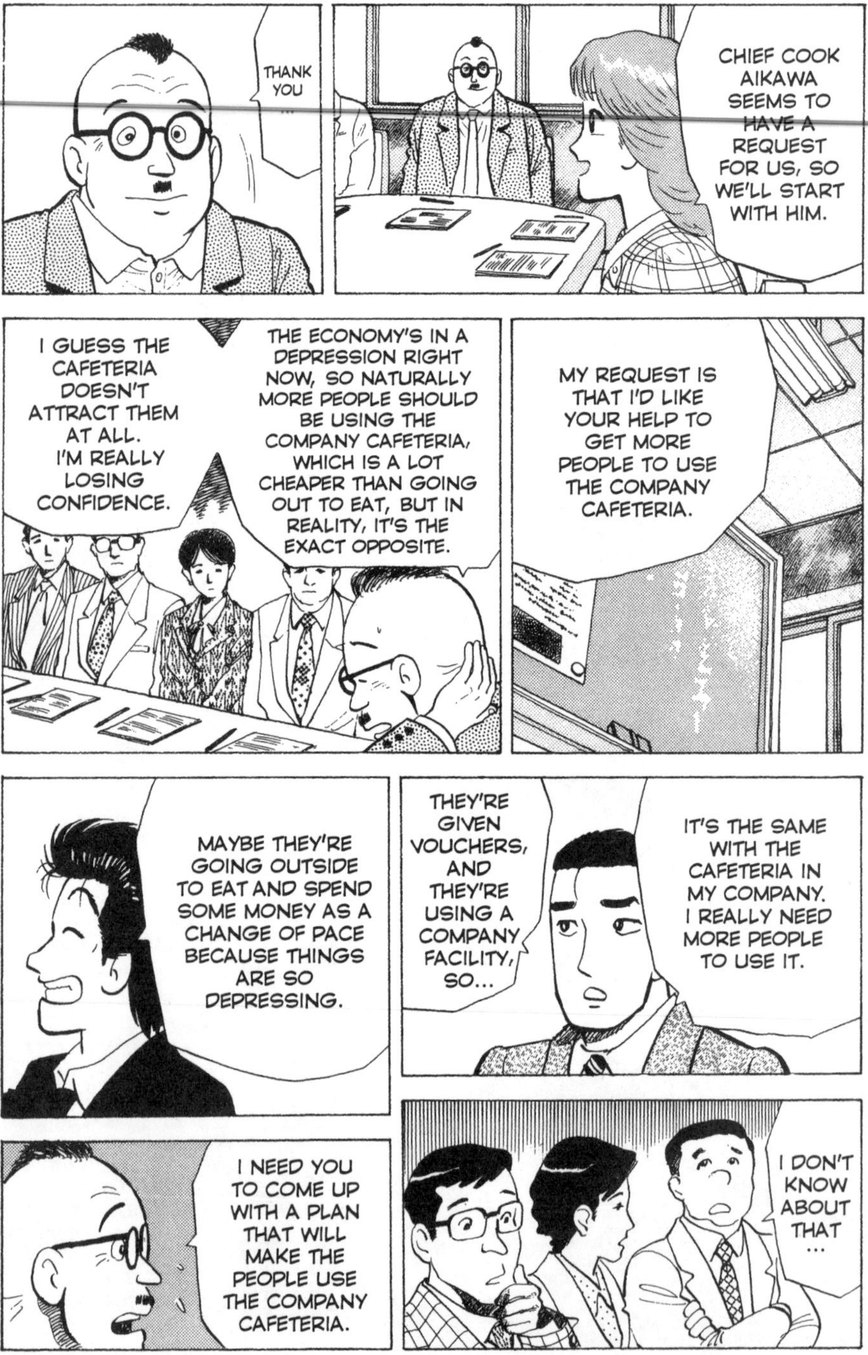
CHIEF COOK AIKAWA SEEMS TO HAVE A REQUEST FOR US, SO WE'LL START WITH HIM.
THANK YOU ...
MY REQUEST IS THAT I'D LIKE YOUR HELP TO GET MORE PEOPLE TO USE THE COMPANY CAFETERIA.
THE ECONOMY'S IN A DEPRESSION RIGHT NOW, SO NATURALLY MORE PEOPLE SHOULD BE USING THE COMPANY CAFETERIA, WHICH IS A LOT CHEAPER THAN GOING OUT TO EAT, BUT IN REALITY, IT'S THE EXACT OPPOSITE.
I GUESS THE CAFETERIA DOESN'T ATTRACT THEM AT ALL. I'M REALLY LOSING CONFIDENCE.
IT'S THE SAME WITH THE CAFETERIA IN MY COMPANY. I REALLY NEED MORE PEOPLE TO USE IT.
THEY'RE GIVEN VOUCHERS, AND THEY'RE USING A COMPANY FACILITY, SO...
MAYBE THEY'RE GOING OUTSIDE TO EAT AND SPEND SOME MONEY AS A CHANGE OF PACE BECAUSE THINGS ARE SO DEPRESSING.
I DON'T KNOW ABOUT THAT ...
I NEED YOU TO COME UP WITH A PLAN THAT WILL MAKE THE PEOPLE USE THE COMPANY CAFETERIA.

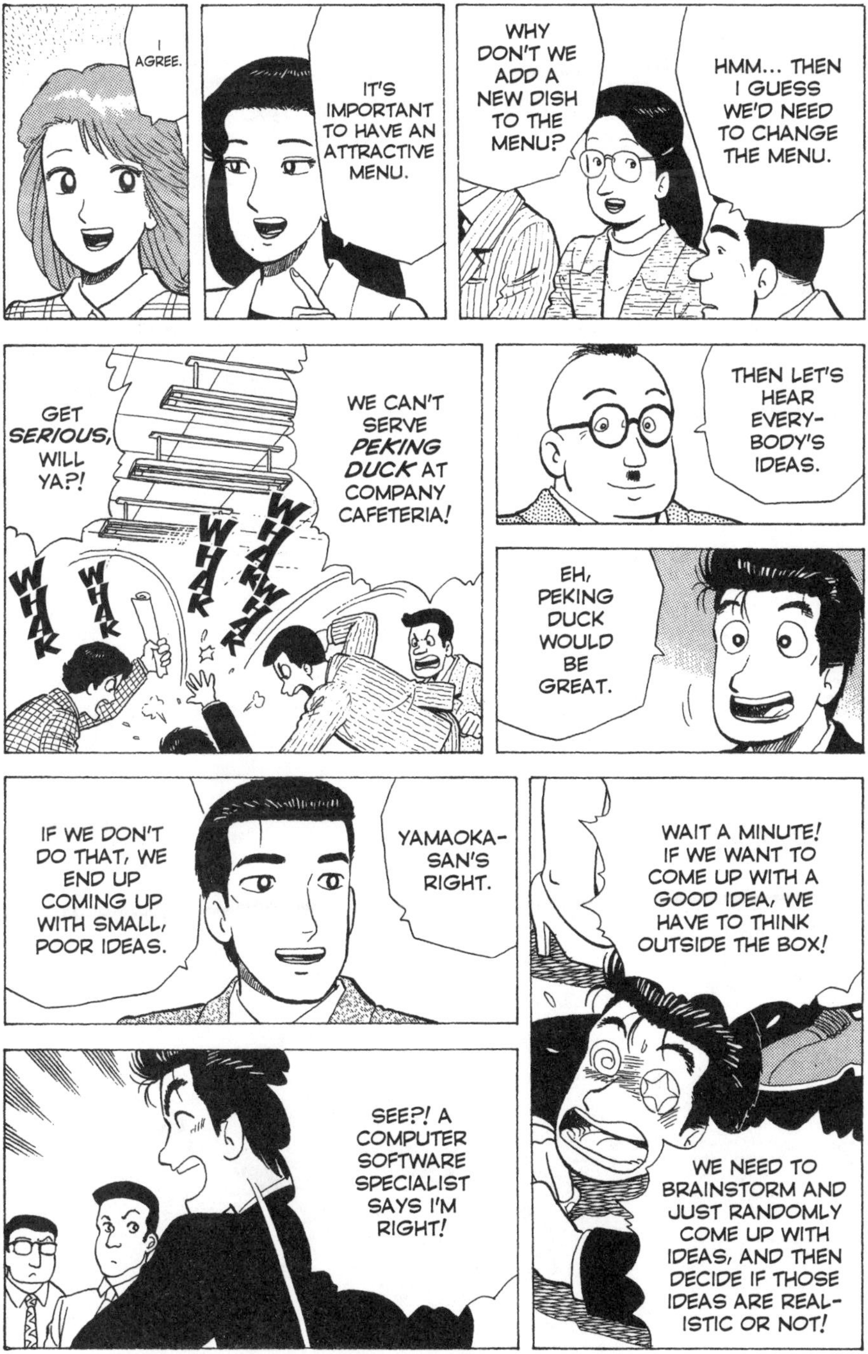
HMM... THEN I GUESS WE'D NEED TO CHANGE THE MENU.
WHY DON'T WE ADD A NEW DISH TO THE MENU?
IT'S IMPORTANT TO HAVE AN ATTRACTIVE MENU.
I AGREE.
THEN LET'S HEAR EVERY-BODY'S IDEAS.
EH, PEKING DUCK WOULD BE GREAT.
WE CAN'T SERVE PEKING DUCK AT COMPANY CAFETERIA!
GET SERIOUS, WILL YA?!
WHAK WHAK
WHAK
WHAK
WHAK WHAK
WAIT A MINUTE! IF WE WANT TO COME UP WITH A GOOD IDEA, WE HAVE TO THINK OUTSIDE THE BOX!
WE NEED TO BRAINSTORM AND JUST RANDOMLY COME UP WITH IDEAS, AND THEN DECIDE IF THOSE IDEAS ARE REAL-ISTIC OR NOT!
YAMAOKA-SAN'S RIGHT.
IF WE DON'T DO THAT, WE END UP COMING UP WITH SMALL, POOR IDEAS.
SEE?! A COMPUTER SOFTWARE SPECIALIST SAYS I'M RIGHT!

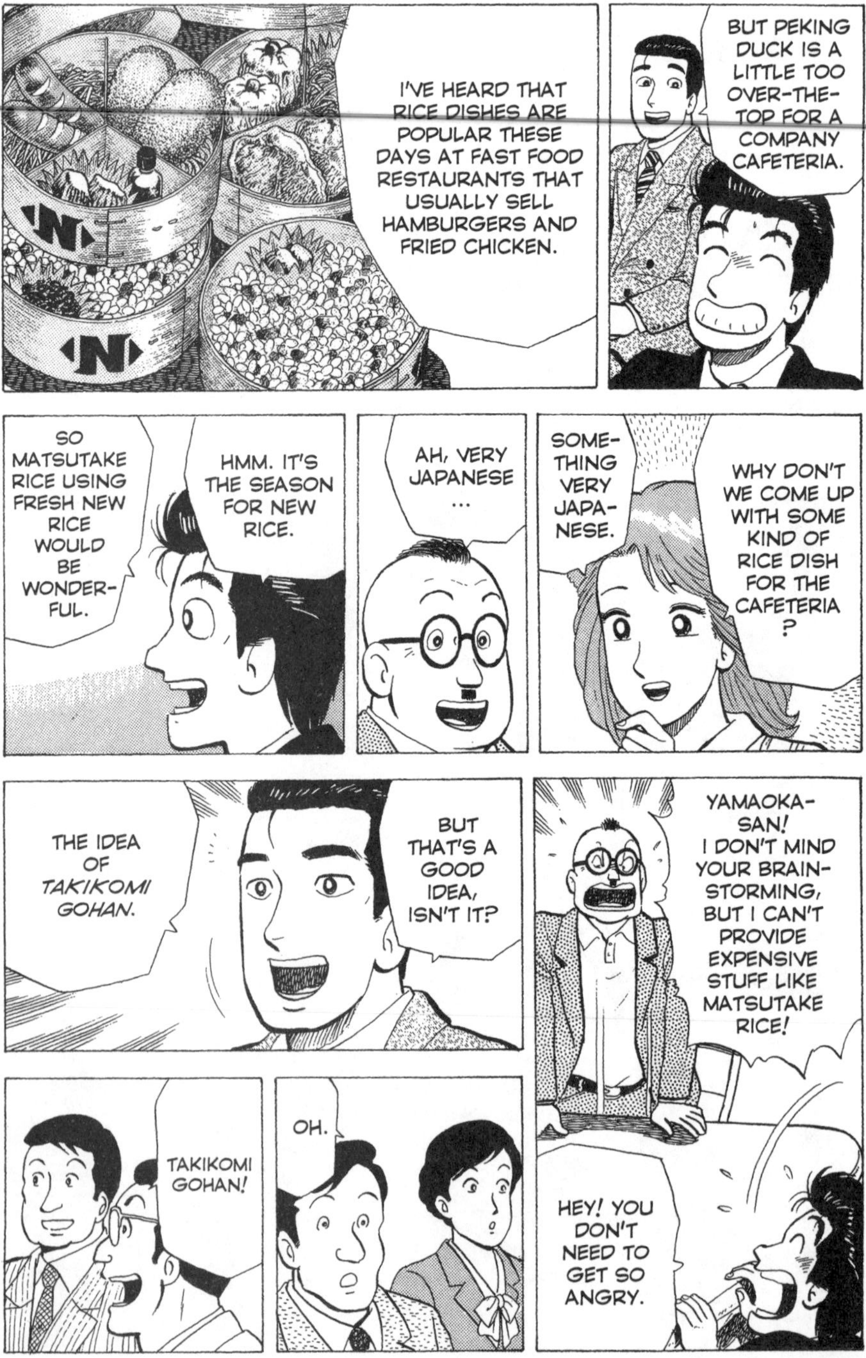
BUT PEKING DUCK IS A LITTLE TOO OVER-THE-TOP FOR A COMPANY CAFETERIA.
I'VE HEARD THAT RICE DISHES ARE POPULAR THESE DAYS AT FAST FOOD RESTAURANTS THAT USUALLY SELL HAMBURGERS AND FRIED CHICKEN.
WHY DON'T WE COME UP WITH SOME KIND OF RICE DISH FOR THE CAFETERIA?
SOME-THING VERY JAPA-NESE.
AH, VERY JAPANESE...
HMM. IT'S THE SEASON FOR NEW RICE.
SO MATSUTAKE RICE USING FRESH NEW RICE WOULD BE WONDER-FUL.
YAMAOKA-SAN! I DON'T MIND YOUR BRAIN-STORMING, BUT I CAN'T PROVIDE EXPENSIVE STUFF LIKE MATSUTAKE RICE!
HEY! YOU DON'T NEED TO GET SO ANGRY.
BUT THAT'S A GOOD IDEA, ISN'T IT?
THE IDEA OF *TAKIKOMI GOHAN*.
OH.
TAKIKOMI GOHAN!

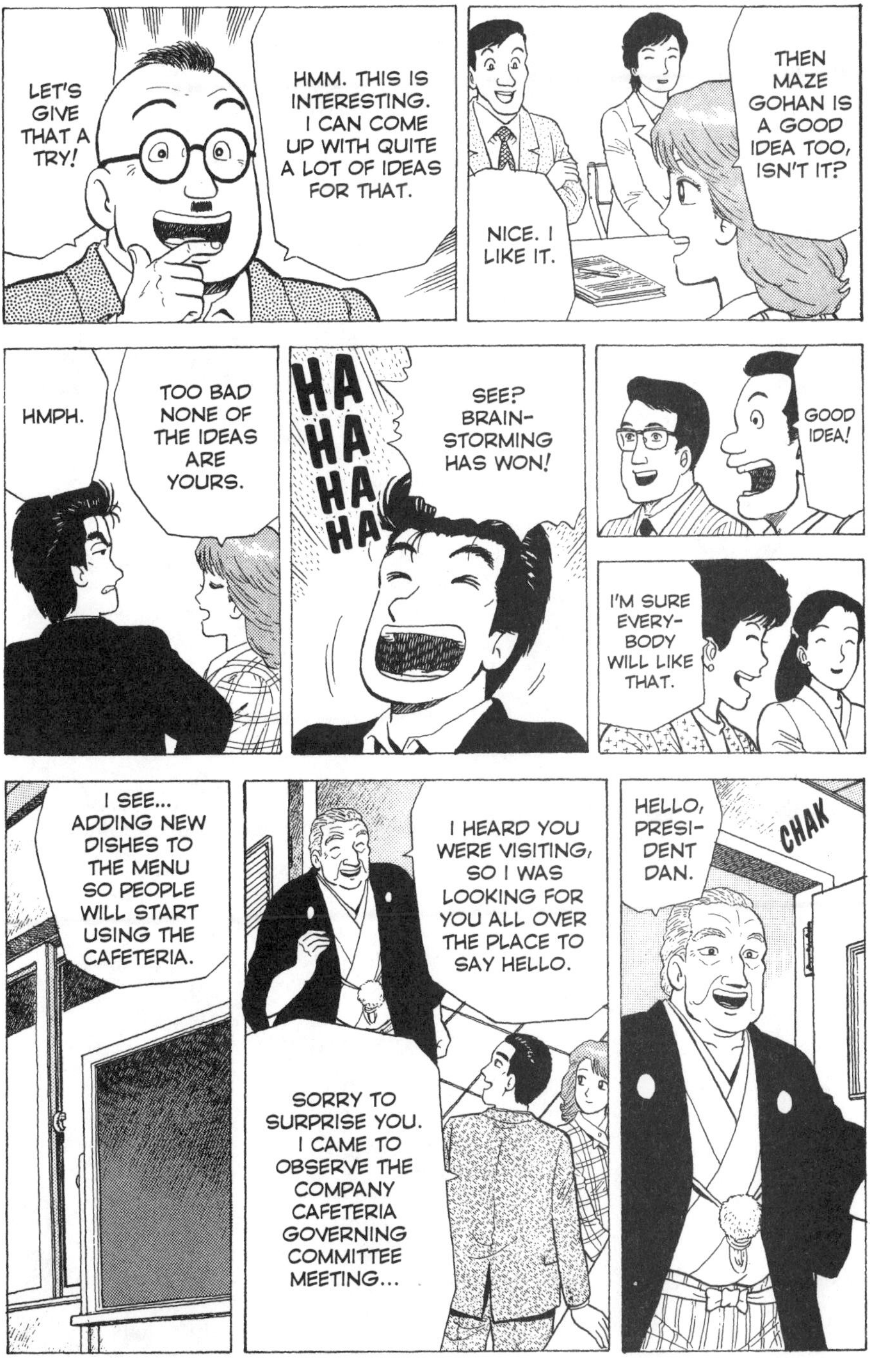
THEN MAZE GOHAN IS A GOOD IDEA TOO, ISN'T IT?
NICE. I LIKE IT.
HMM. THIS IS INTERESTING. I CAN COME UP WITH QUITE A LOT OF IDEAS FOR THAT.
LET'S GIVE THAT A TRY!
GOOD IDEA!
I'M SURE EVERY-BODY WILL LIKE THAT.
SEE? BRAIN-STORMING HAS WON!
HA HA HA HA HA HA HA
TOO BAD NONE OF THE IDEAS ARE YOURS.
HMPH.
CHAK
HELLO, PRESI-DENT DAN.
I HEARD YOU WERE VISITING, SO I WAS LOOKING FOR YOU ALL OVER THE PLACE TO SAY HELLO.
SORRY TO SURPRISE YOU. I CAME TO OBSERVE THE COMPANY CAFETERIA GOVERNING COMMITTEE MEETING...
I SEE... ADDING NEW DISHES TO THE MENU SO PEOPLE WILL START USING THE CAFETERIA.

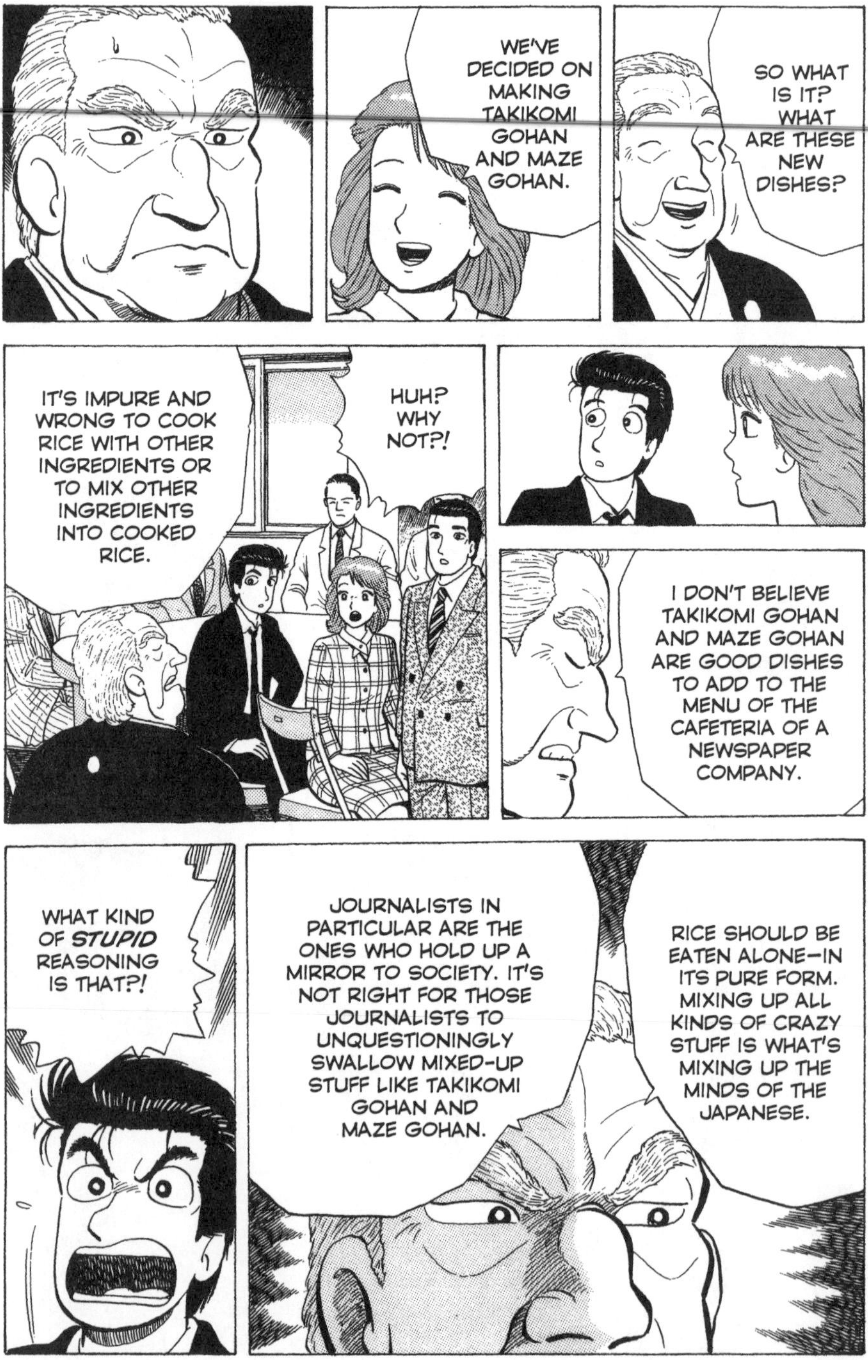
SO WHAT IS IT? WHAT ARE THESE NEW DISHES?
WE'VE DECIDED ON MAKING TAKIKOMI GOHAN AND MAZE GOHAN.
I DON'T BELIEVE TAKIKOMI GOHAN AND MAZE GOHAN ARE GOOD DISHES TO ADD TO THE MENU OF THE CAFETERIA OF A NEWSPAPER COMPANY.
HUH? WHY NOT?!
IT'S IMPURE AND WRONG TO COOK RICE WITH OTHER INGREDIENTS OR TO MIX OTHER INGREDIENTS INTO COOKED RICE.
RICE SHOULD BE EATEN ALONE—IN ITS PURE FORM. MIXING UP ALL KINDS OF CRAZY STUFF IS WHAT'S MIXING UP THE MINDS OF THE JAPANESE.
JOURNALISTS IN PARTICULAR ARE THE ONES WHO HOLD UP A MIRROR TO SOCIETY. IT'S NOT RIGHT FOR THOSE JOURNALISTS TO UNQUESTIONINGLY SWALLOW MIXED-UP STUFF LIKE TAKIKOMI GOHAN AND MAZE GOHAN.
WHAT KIND OF *STUPID* REASONING IS THAT?!

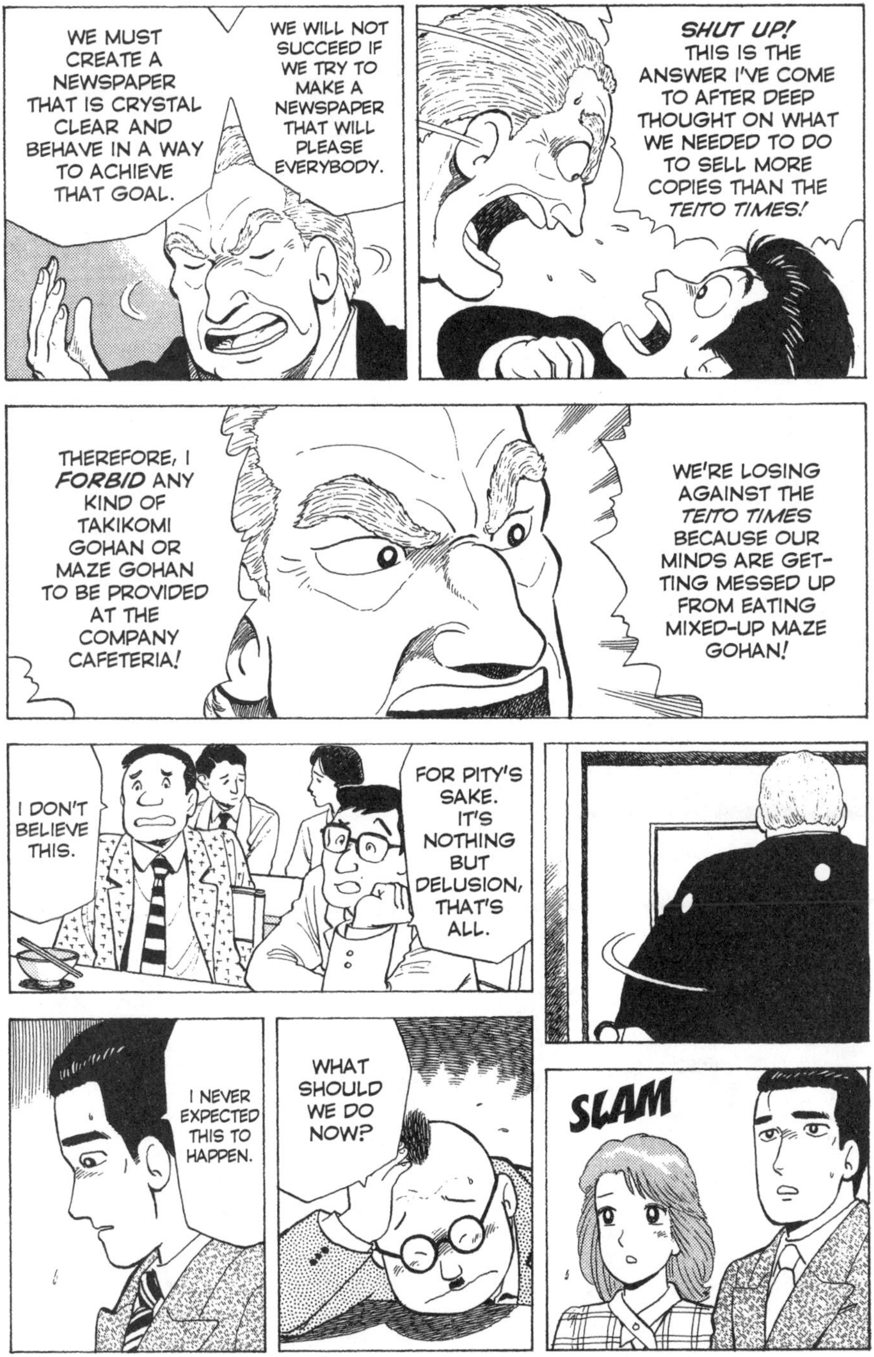
WE MUST CREATE A NEWSPAPER THAT IS CRYSTAL CLEAR AND BEHAVE IN A WAY TO ACHIEVE THAT GOAL.
WE WILL NOT SUCCEED IF WE TRY TO MAKE A NEWSPAPER THAT WILL PLEASE EVERYBODY.
SHUT UP! THIS IS THE ANSWER I'VE COME TO AFTER DEEP THOUGHT ON WHAT WE NEEDED TO DO TO SELL MORE COPIES THAN THE *TEITO TIMES!*
THEREFORE, I *FORBID* ANY KIND OF TAKIKOMI GOHAN OR MAZE GOHAN TO BE PROVIDED AT THE COMPANY CAFETERIA!
WE'RE LOSING AGAINST THE *TEITO TIMES* BECAUSE OUR MINDS ARE GET-TING MESSED UP FROM EATING MIXED-UP MAZE GOHAN!
I DON'T BELIEVE THIS.
FOR PITY'S SAKE. IT'S NOTHING BUT DELUSION, THAT'S ALL.
I NEVER EXPECTED THIS TO HAPPEN.
WHAT SHOULD WE DO NOW?
SLAM

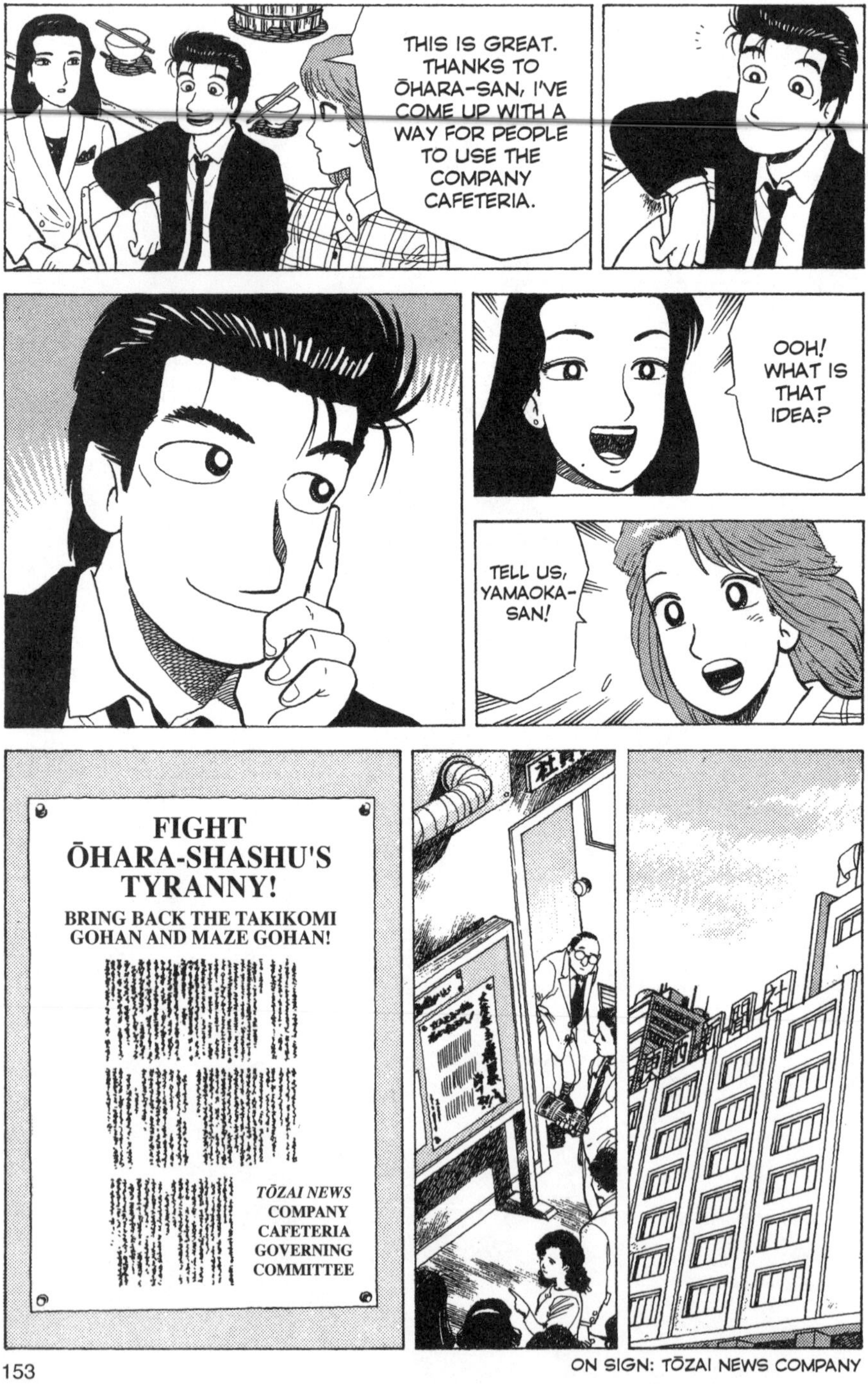
THIS IS GREAT. THANKS TO ŌHARA-SAN, I'VE COME UP WITH A WAY FOR PEOPLE TO USE THE COMPANY CAFETERIA.
OOH! WHAT IS THAT IDEA?
TELL US, YAMAOKA-SAN!
FIGHT ŌHARA-SHASHU'S TYRANNY!
BRING BACK THE TAKIKOMI GOHAN AND MAZE GOHAN!
TŌZAI NEWS COMPANY CAFETERIA GOVERNING COMMITTEE

ON SIGN: TŌZAI NEWS COMPANY

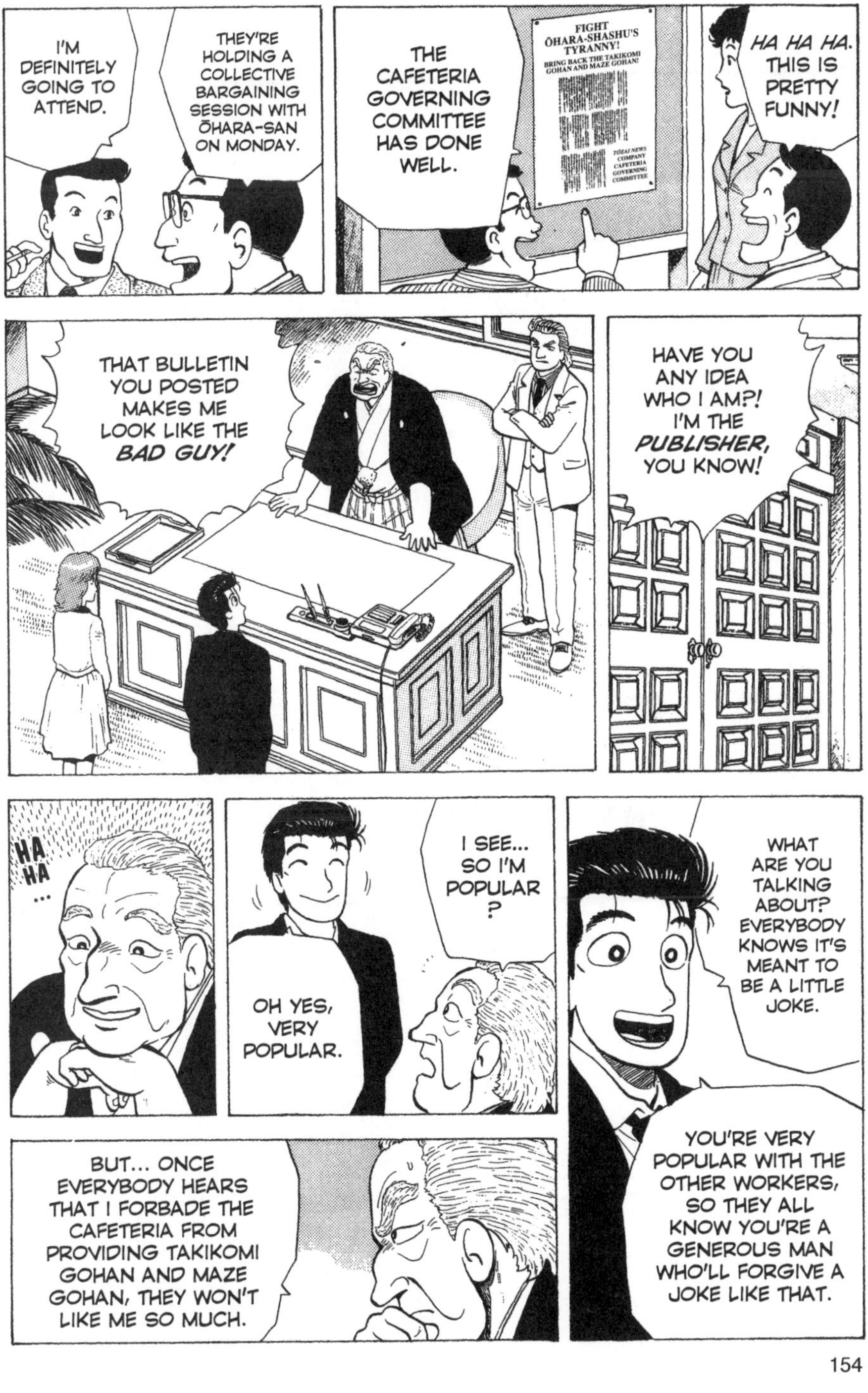
HA HA HA. THIS IS PRETTY FUNNY!
FIGHT ŌHARA-SHASHU'S TYRANNY!
BRING BACK THE TAKIKOMI GOHAN AND MAZE GOHAN!
TŌZAI NEWS COMPANY CAFETERIA GOVERNING COMMITTEE
THE CAFETERIA GOVERNING COMMITTEE HAS DONE WELL.
THEY'RE HOLDING A COLLECTIVE BARGAINING SESSION WITH ŌHARA-SAN ON MONDAY.
I'M DEFINITELY GOING TO ATTEND.
HAVE YOU ANY IDEA WHO I AM?! I'M THE PUBLISHER, YOU KNOW!
THAT BULLETIN YOU POSTED MAKES ME LOOK LIKE THE BAD GUY!
WHAT ARE YOU TALKING ABOUT? EVERYBODY KNOWS IT'S MEANT TO BE A LITTLE JOKE.
YOU'RE VERY POPULAR WITH THE OTHER WORKERS, SO THEY ALL KNOW YOU'RE A GENEROUS MAN WHO'LL FORGIVE A JOKE LIKE THAT.
I SEE... SO I'M POPULAR?
OH YES, VERY POPULAR.
HA HA ...
BUT... ONCE EVERYBODY HEARS THAT I FORBADE THE CAFETERIA FROM PROVIDING TAKIKOMI GOHAN AND MAZE GOHAN, THEY WON'T LIKE ME SO MUCH.

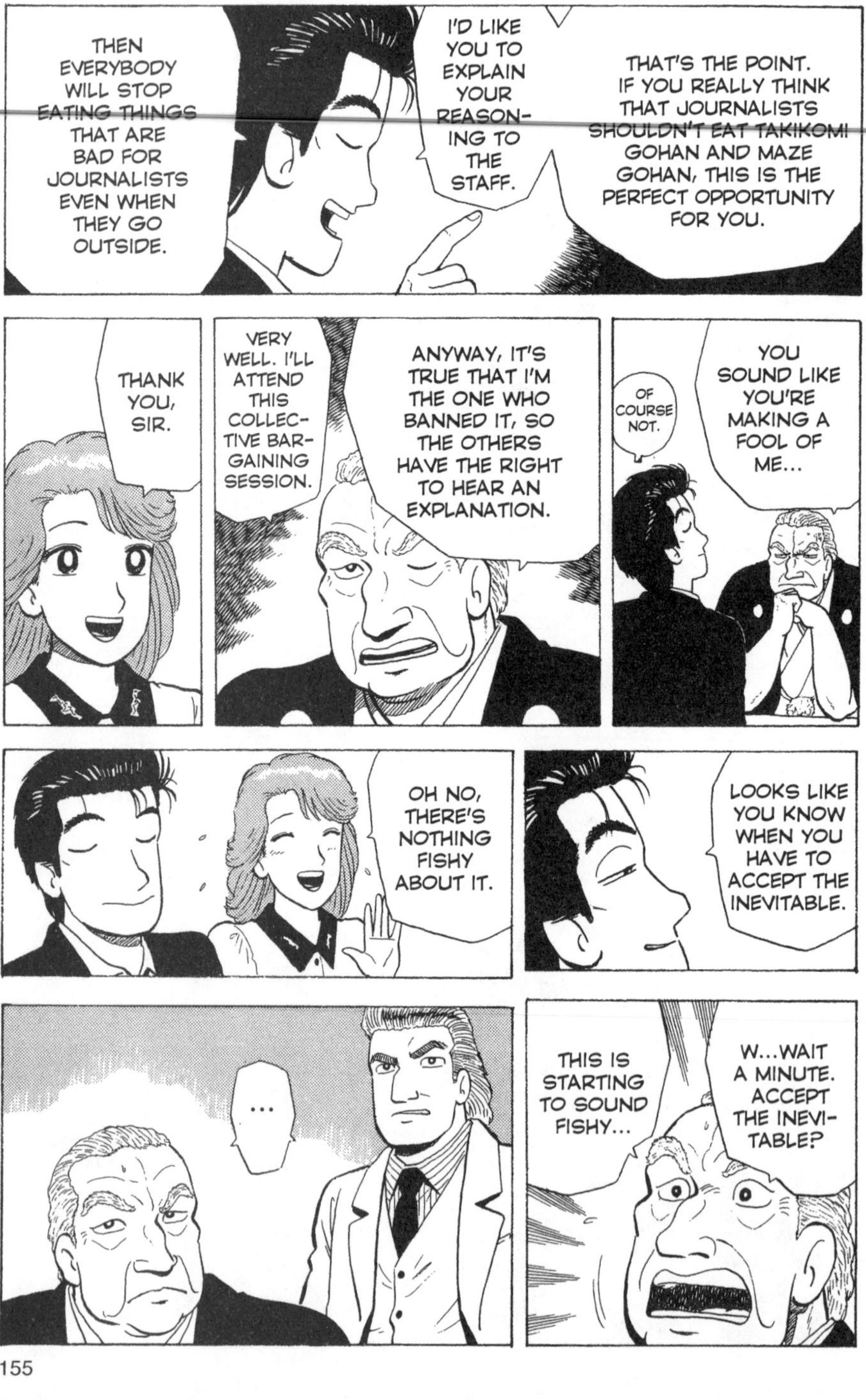
THAT'S THE POINT. IF YOU REALLY THINK THAT JOURNALISTS SHOULDN'T EAT TAKIKOMI GOHAN AND MAZE GOHAN, THIS IS THE PERFECT OPPORTUNITY FOR YOU.
I'D LIKE YOU TO EXPLAIN YOUR REASONING TO THE STAFF.
THEN EVERYBODY WILL STOP EATING THINGS THAT ARE BAD FOR JOURNALISTS EVEN WHEN THEY GO OUTSIDE.
YOU SOUND LIKE YOU'RE MAKING A FOOL OF ME...
OF COURSE NOT.
ANYWAY, IT'S TRUE THAT I'M THE ONE WHO BANNED IT, SO THE OTHERS HAVE THE RIGHT TO HEAR AN EXPLANATION.
VERY WELL. I'LL ATTEND THIS COLLECTIVE BARGAINING SESSION.
THANK YOU, SIR.
LOOKS LIKE YOU KNOW WHEN YOU HAVE TO ACCEPT THE INEVITABLE.
OH NO, THERE'S NOTHING FISHY ABOUT IT.
W...WAIT A MINUTE. ACCEPT THE INEVITABLE?
THIS IS STARTING TO SOUND FISHY...
...

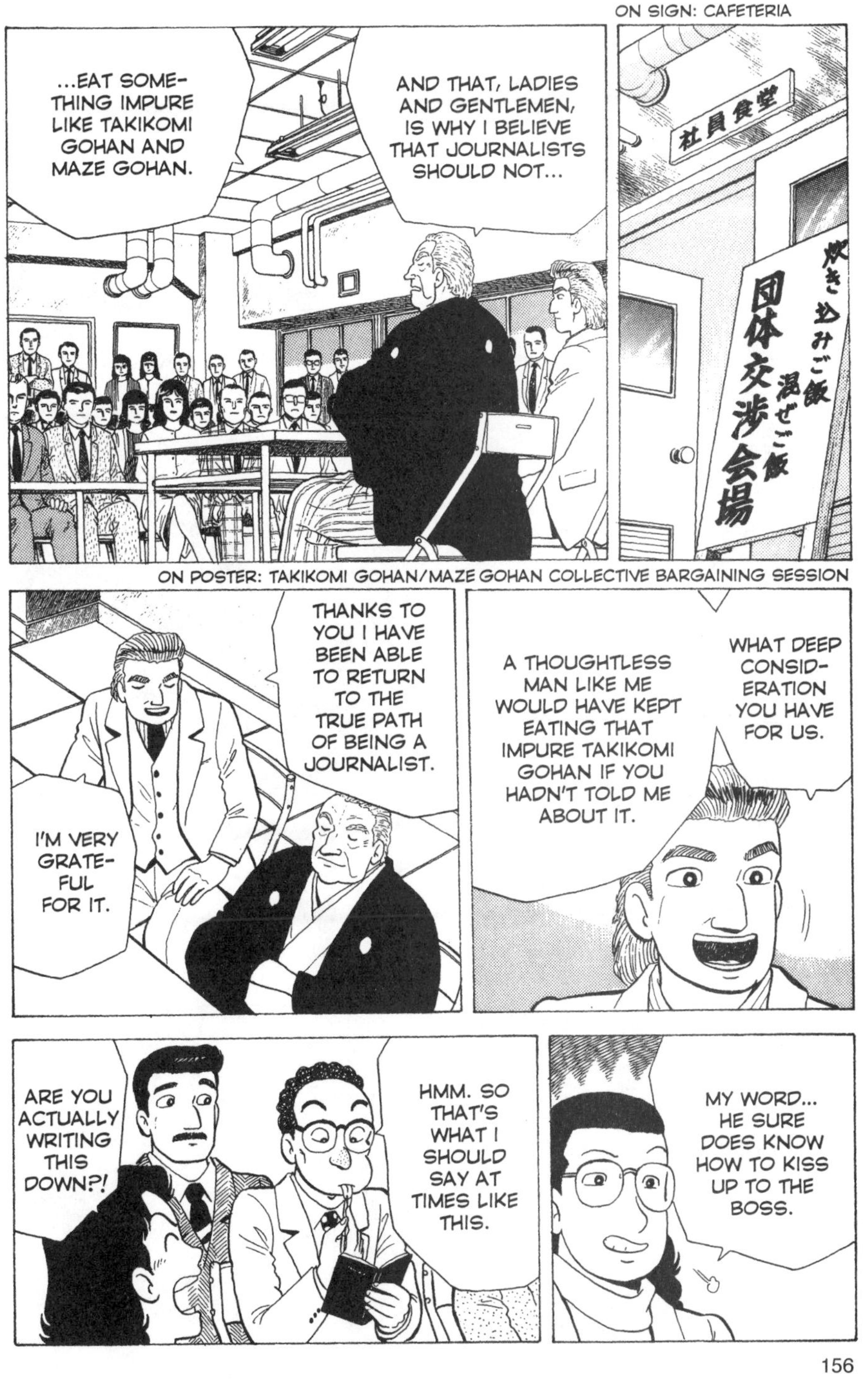
ON SIGN: CAFETERIA
AND THAT, LADIES AND GENTLEMEN, IS WHY I BELIEVE THAT JOURNALISTS SHOULD NOT...
...EAT SOMETHING IMPURE LIKE TAKIKOMI GOHAN AND MAZE GOHAN.
ON POSTER: TAKIKOMI GOHAN/MAZE GOHAN COLLECTIVE BARGAINING SESSION
WHAT DEEP CONSIDERATION YOU HAVE FOR US.
A THOUGHTLESS MAN LIKE ME WOULD HAVE KEPT EATING THAT IMPURE TAKIKOMI GOHAN IF YOU HADN'T TOLD ME ABOUT IT.
THANKS TO YOU I HAVE BEEN ABLE TO RETURN TO THE TRUE PATH OF BEING A JOURNALIST.
I'M VERY GRATEFUL FOR IT.
MY WORD... HE SURE DOES KNOW HOW TO KISS UP TO THE BOSS.
HMM. SO THAT'S WHAT I SHOULD SAY AT TIMES LIKE THIS.
ARE YOU ACTUALLY WRITING THIS DOWN?!

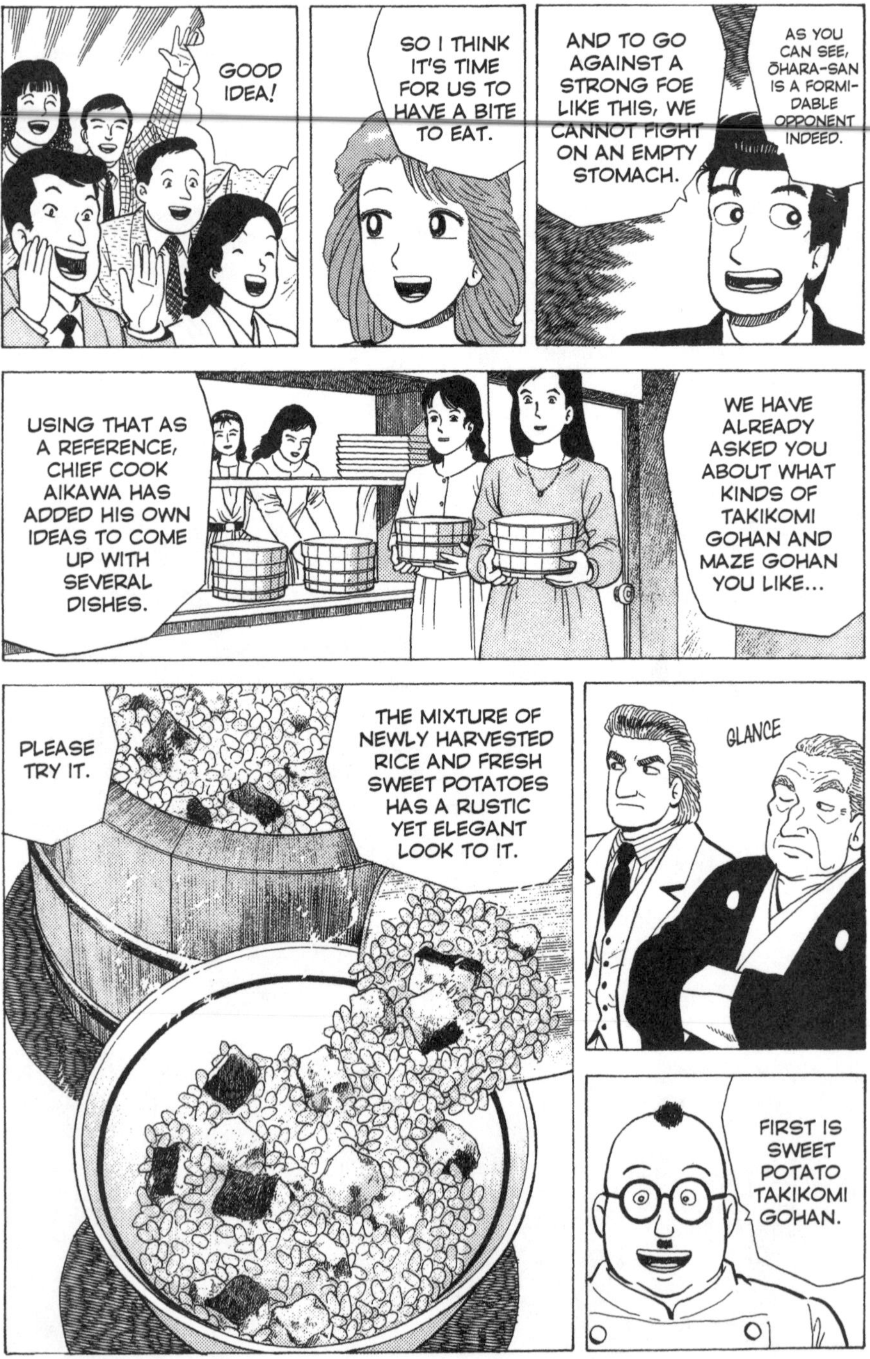
AS YOU CAN SEE, ŌHARA-SAN IS A FORMIDABLE OPPONENT INDEED.
AND TO GO AGAINST A STRONG FOE LIKE THIS, WE CANNOT FIGHT ON AN EMPTY STOMACH.
SO I THINK IT'S TIME FOR US TO HAVE A BITE TO EAT.
GOOD IDEA!
WE HAVE ALREADY ASKED YOU ABOUT WHAT KINDS OF TAKIKOMI GOHAN AND MAZE GOHAN YOU LIKE...
USING THAT AS A REFERENCE, CHIEF COOK AIKAWA HAS ADDED HIS OWN IDEAS TO COME UP WITH SEVERAL DISHES.
GLANCE
FIRST IS SWEET POTATO TAKIKOMI GOHAN.
THE MIXTURE OF NEWLY HARVESTED RICE AND FRESH SWEET POTATOES HAS A RUSTIC YET ELEGANT LOOK TO IT.
PLEASE TRY IT.

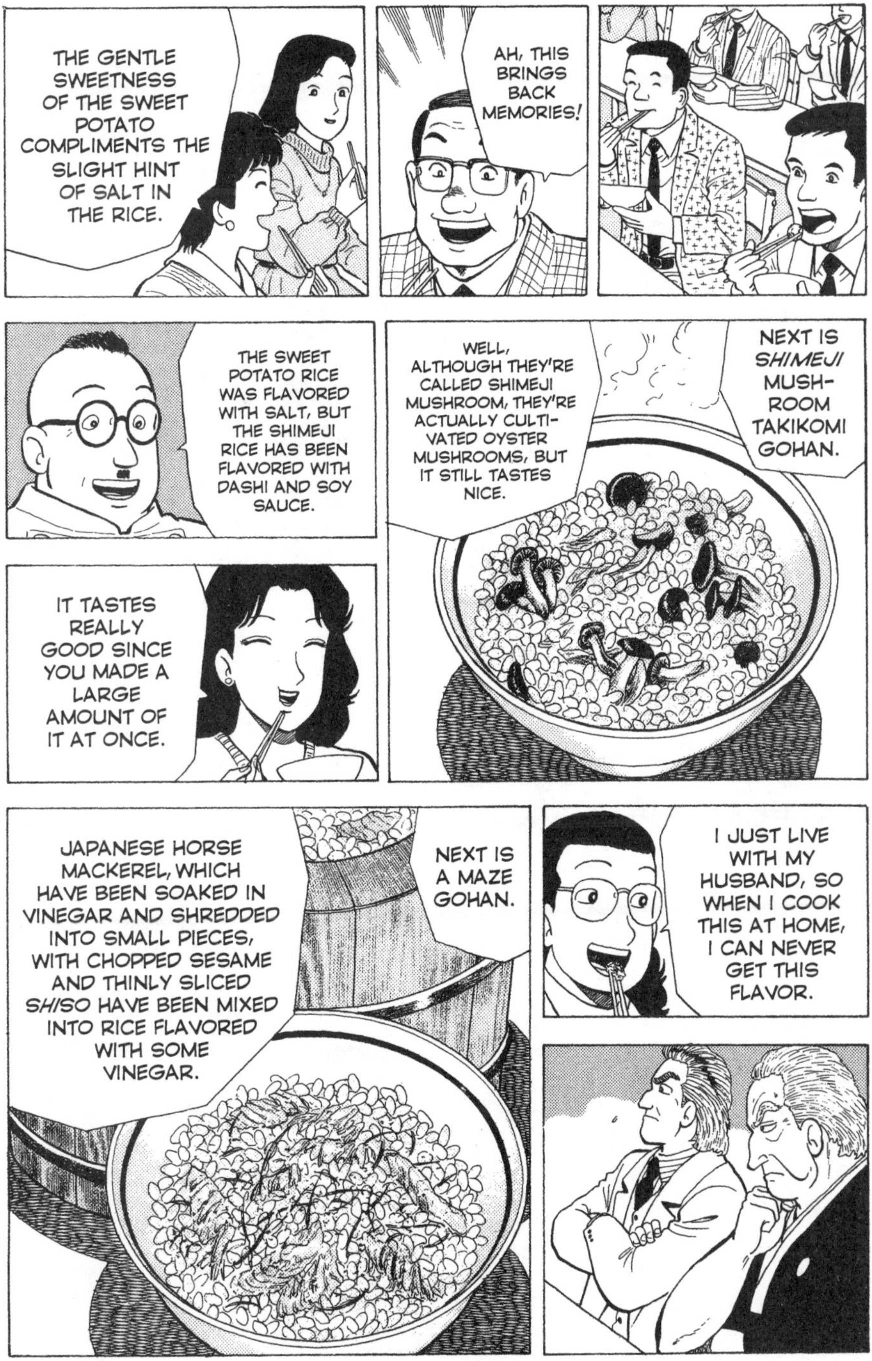
AH, THIS BRINGS BACK MEMORIES!
THE GENTLE SWEETNESS OF THE SWEET POTATO COMPLIMENTS THE SLIGHT HINT OF SALT IN THE RICE.
NEXT IS *SHIMEJI* MUSHROOM TAKIKOMI GOHAN.
WELL, ALTHOUGH THEY'RE CALLED SHIMEJI MUSHROOM, THEY'RE ACTUALLY CULTIVATED OYSTER MUSHROOMS, BUT IT STILL TASTES NICE.
THE SWEET POTATO RICE WAS FLAVORED WITH SALT, BUT THE SHIMEJI RICE HAS BEEN FLAVORED WITH DASHI AND SOY SAUCE.
IT TASTES REALLY GOOD SINCE YOU MADE A LARGE AMOUNT OF IT AT ONCE.
I JUST LIVE WITH MY HUSBAND, SO WHEN I COOK THIS AT HOME, I CAN NEVER GET THIS FLAVOR.
NEXT IS A MAZE GOHAN.
JAPANESE HORSE MACKEREL, WHICH HAVE BEEN SOAKED IN VINEGAR AND SHREDDED INTO SMALL PIECES, WITH CHOPPED SESAME AND THINLY SLICED *SHISO* HAVE BEEN MIXED INTO RICE FLAVORED WITH SOME VINEGAR.

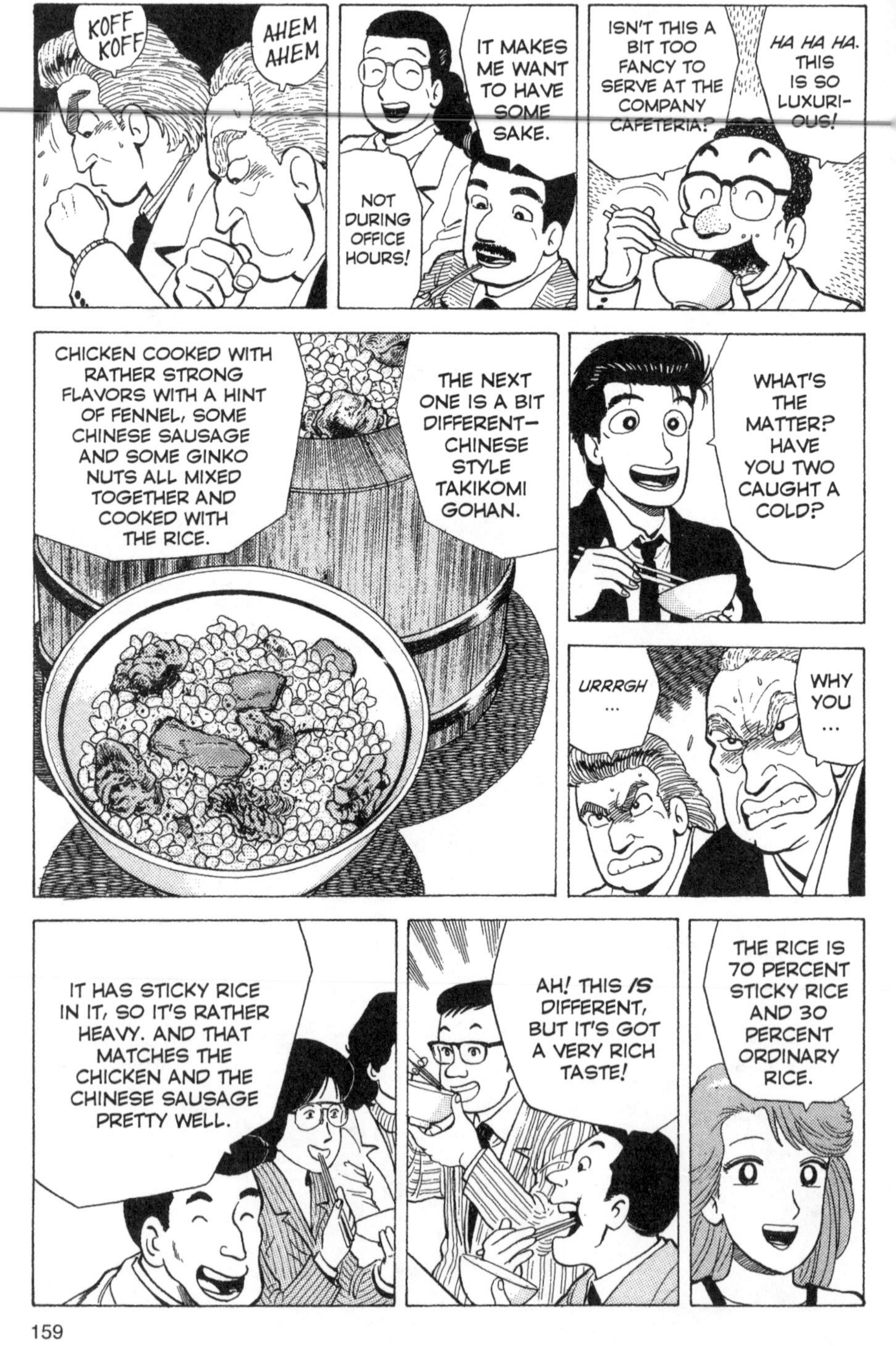
HA HA HA. THIS IS SO LUXURIOUS!
ISN'T THIS A BIT TOO FANCY TO SERVE AT THE COMPANY CAFETERIA?
IT MAKES ME WANT TO HAVE SOME SAKE.
NOT DURING OFFICE HOURS!
AHEM AHEM
KOFF KOFF
WHAT'S THE MATTER? HAVE YOU TWO CAUGHT A COLD?
WHY YOU ...
URRRGH ...
THE NEXT ONE IS A BIT DIFFERENT— CHINESE STYLE TAKIKOMI GOHAN.
CHICKEN COOKED WITH RATHER STRONG FLAVORS WITH A HINT OF FENNEL, SOME CHINESE SAUSAGE AND SOME GINKO NUTS ALL MIXED TOGETHER AND COOKED WITH THE RICE.
THE RICE IS 70 PERCENT STICKY RICE AND 30 PERCENT ORDINARY RICE.
AH! THIS IS DIFFERENT, BUT IT'S GOT A VERY RICH TASTE!
IT HAS STICKY RICE IN IT, SO IT'S RATHER HEAVY. AND THAT MATCHES THE CHICKEN AND THE CHINESE SAUSAGE PRETTY WELL.

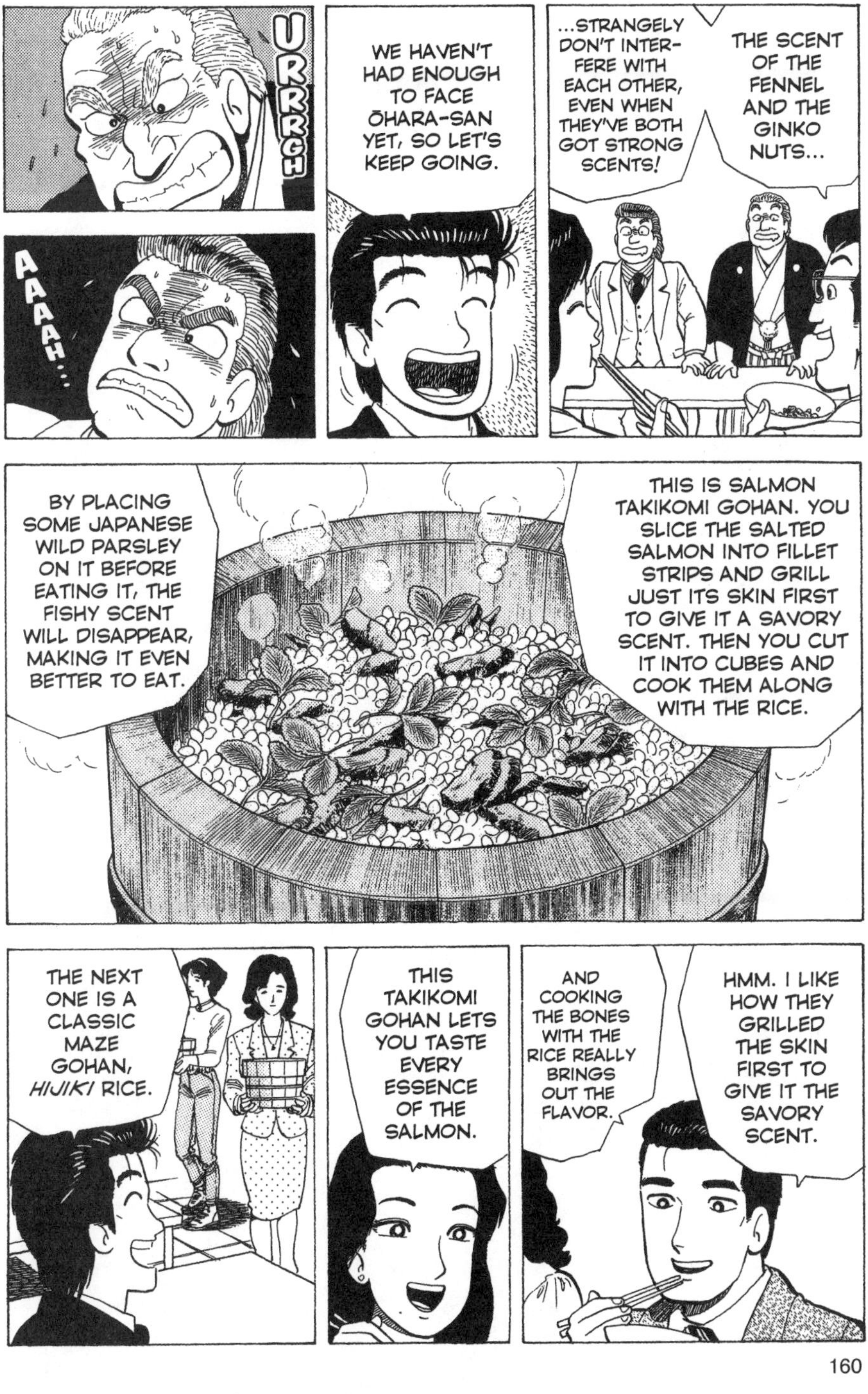
THE SCENT OF THE FENNEL AND THE GINKO NUTS...
...STRANGELY DON'T INTERFERE WITH EACH OTHER, EVEN WHEN THEY'VE BOTH GOT STRONG SCENTS!
WE HAVEN'T HAD ENOUGH TO FACE ŌHARA-SAN YET, SO LET'S KEEP GOING.
URRRGH
AAAAH...
THIS IS SALMON TAKIKOMI GOHAN. YOU SLICE THE SALTED SALMON INTO FILLET STRIPS AND GRILL JUST ITS SKIN FIRST TO GIVE IT A SAVORY SCENT. THEN YOU CUT IT INTO CUBES AND COOK THEM ALONG WITH THE RICE.
BY PLACING SOME JAPANESE WILD PARSLEY ON IT BEFORE EATING IT, THE FISHY SCENT WILL DISAPPEAR, MAKING IT EVEN BETTER TO EAT.
HMM. I LIKE HOW THEY GRILLED THE SKIN FIRST TO GIVE IT THE SAVORY SCENT.
AND COOKING THE BONES WITH THE RICE REALLY BRINGS OUT THE FLAVOR.
THIS TAKIKOMI GOHAN LETS YOU TASTE EVERY ESSENCE OF THE SALMON.
THE NEXT ONE IS A CLASSIC MAZE GOHAN, *HIJIKI* RICE.

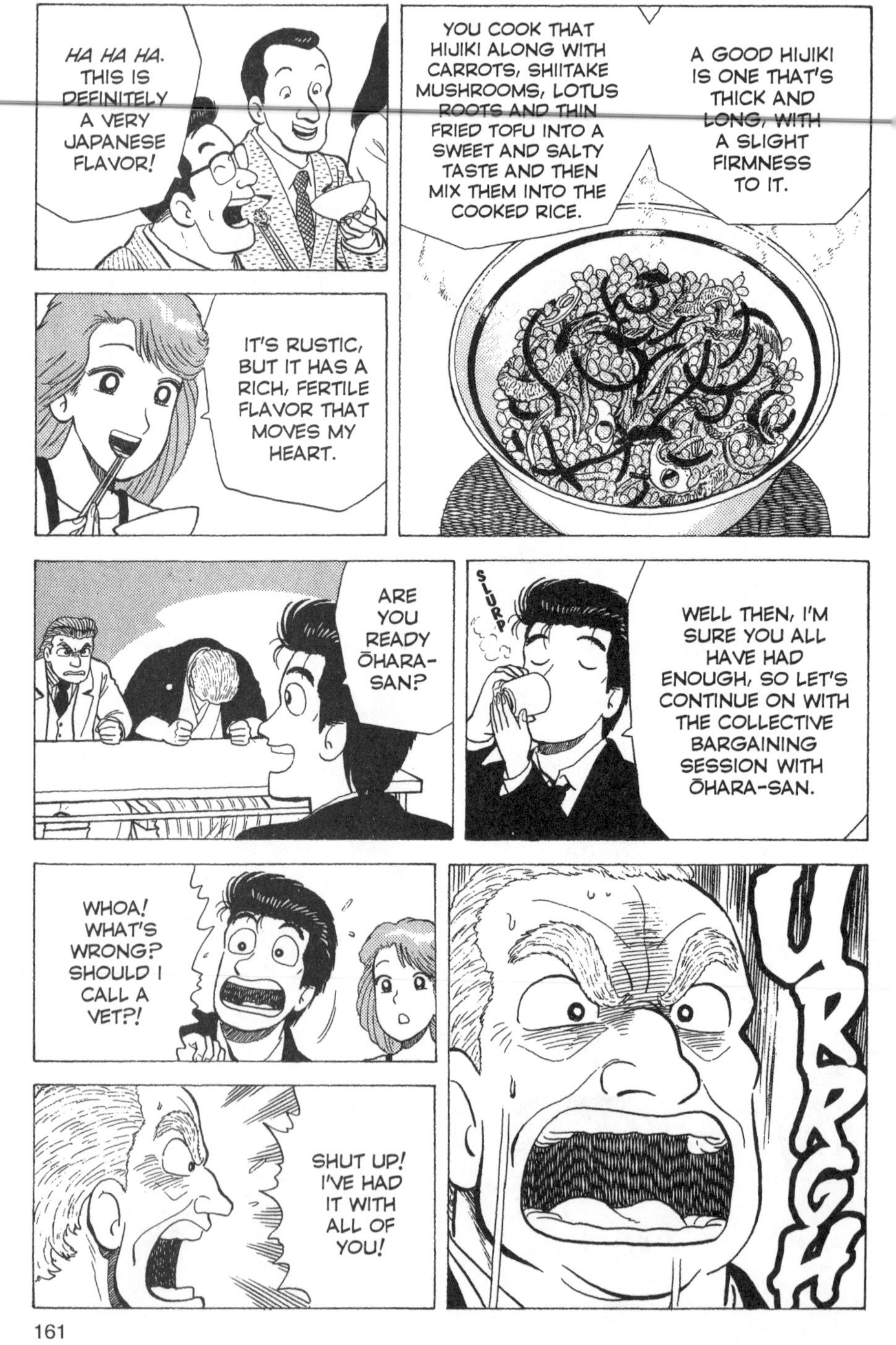
A GOOD HIJIKI IS ONE THAT'S THICK AND LONG, WITH A SLIGHT FIRMNESS TO IT.
YOU COOK THAT HIJIKI ALONG WITH CARROTS, SHIITAKE MUSHROOMS, LOTUS ROOTS AND THIN FRIED TOFU INTO A SWEET AND SALTY TASTE AND THEN MIX THEM INTO THE COOKED RICE.
HA HA HA. THIS IS DEFINITELY A VERY JAPANESE FLAVOR!
IT'S RUSTIC, BUT IT HAS A RICH, FERTILE FLAVOR THAT MOVES MY HEART.
SLURP
WELL THEN, I'M SURE YOU ALL HAVE HAD ENOUGH, SO LET'S CONTINUE ON WITH THE COLLECTIVE BARGAINING SESSION WITH ŌHARA-SAN.
ARE YOU READY ŌHARA-SAN?
URRGH
WHOA! WHAT'S WRONG? SHOULD I CALL A VET?!
SHUT UP! I'VE HAD IT WITH ALL OF YOU!

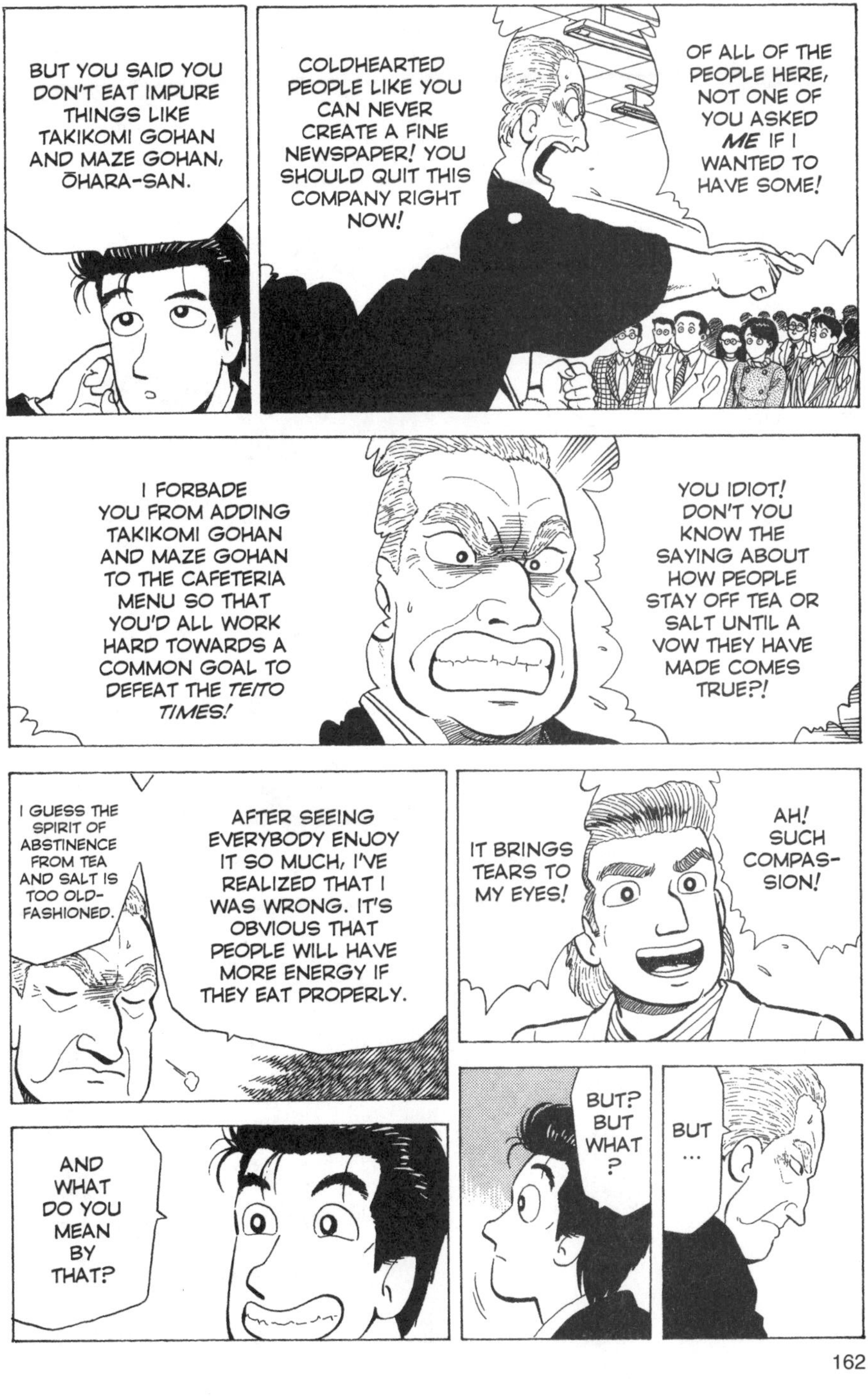
OF ALL OF THE PEOPLE HERE, NOT ONE OF YOU ASKED *ME* IF I WANTED TO HAVE SOME!
COLDHEARTED PEOPLE LIKE YOU CAN NEVER CREATE A FINE NEWSPAPER! YOU SHOULD QUIT THIS COMPANY RIGHT NOW!
BUT YOU SAID YOU DON'T EAT IMPURE THINGS LIKE TAKIKOMI GOHAN AND MAZE GOHAN, ŌHARA-SAN.
YOU IDIOT! DON'T YOU KNOW THE SAYING ABOUT HOW PEOPLE STAY OFF TEA OR SALT UNTIL A VOW THEY HAVE MADE COMES TRUE?!
I FORBADE YOU FROM ADDING TAKIKOMI GOHAN AND MAZE GOHAN TO THE CAFETERIA MENU SO THAT YOU'D ALL WORK HARD TOWARDS A COMMON GOAL TO DEFEAT THE *TEITO TIMES!*
AH! SUCH COMPAS-SION!
IT BRINGS TEARS TO MY EYES!
AFTER SEEING EVERYBODY ENJOY IT SO MUCH, I'VE REALIZED THAT I WAS WRONG. IT'S OBVIOUS THAT PEOPLE WILL HAVE MORE ENERGY IF THEY EAT PROPERLY.
I GUESS THE SPIRIT OF ABSTINENCE FROM TEA AND SALT IS TOO OLD-FASHIONED.
BUT ...
BUT? BUT WHAT?
AND WHAT DO YOU MEAN BY THAT?

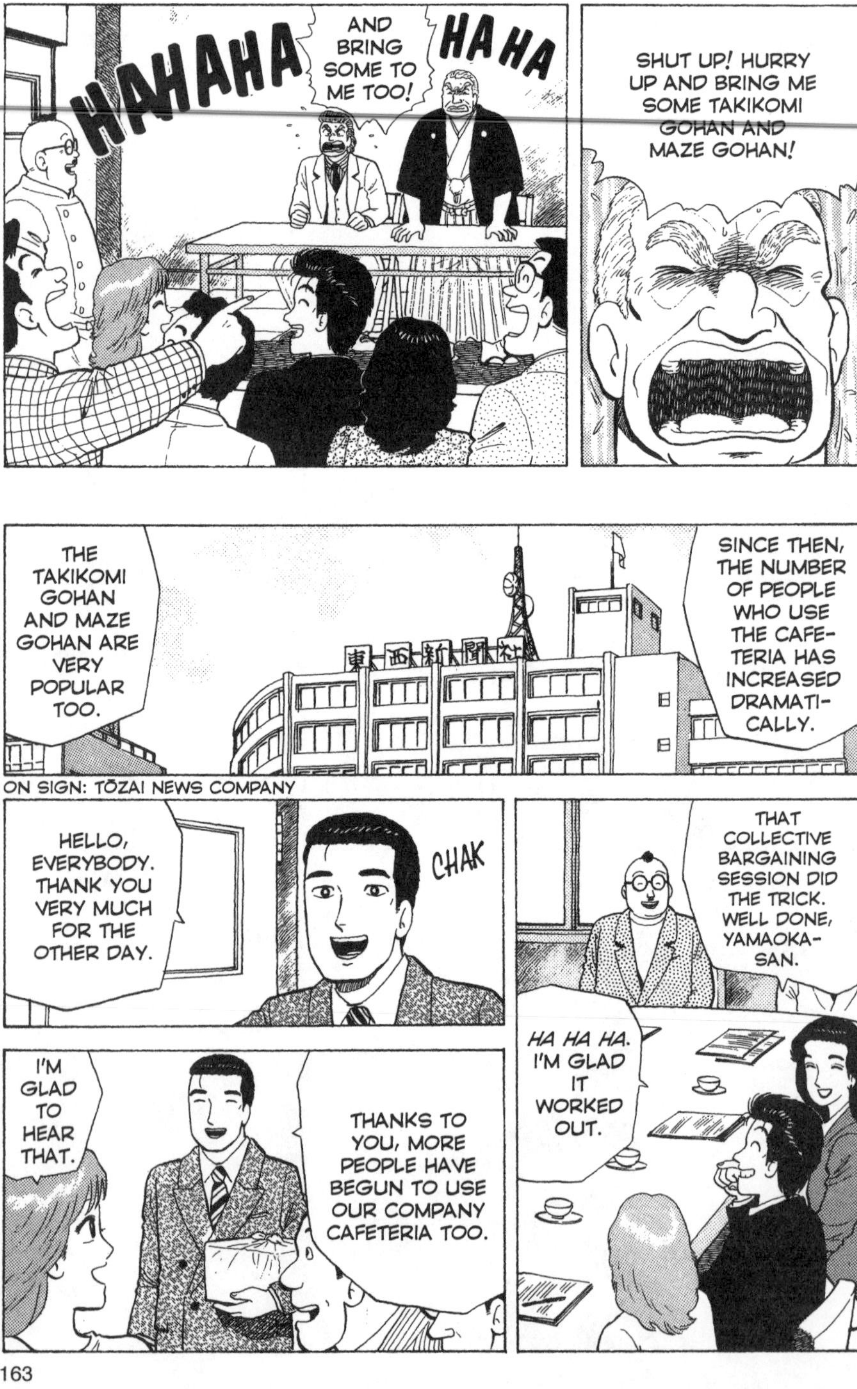
SHUT UP! HURRY UP AND BRING ME SOME TAKIKOMI GOHAN AND MAZE GOHAN!
HAHA
AND BRING SOME TO ME TOO!
HAHAHA
SINCE THEN, THE NUMBER OF PEOPLE WHO USE THE CAFETERIA HAS INCREASED DRAMATICALLY.
東西新聞社
THE TAKIKOMI GOHAN AND MAZE GOHAN ARE VERY POPULAR TOO.
ON SIGN: TŌZAI NEWS COMPANY
THAT COLLECTIVE BARGAINING SESSION DID THE TRICK. WELL DONE, YAMAOKA-SAN.
HA HA HA. I'M GLAD IT WORKED OUT.
CHAK
HELLO, EVERYBODY. THANK YOU VERY MUCH FOR THE OTHER DAY.
THANKS TO YOU, MORE PEOPLE HAVE BEGUN TO USE OUR COMPANY CAFETERIA TOO.
I'M GLAD TO HEAR THAT.

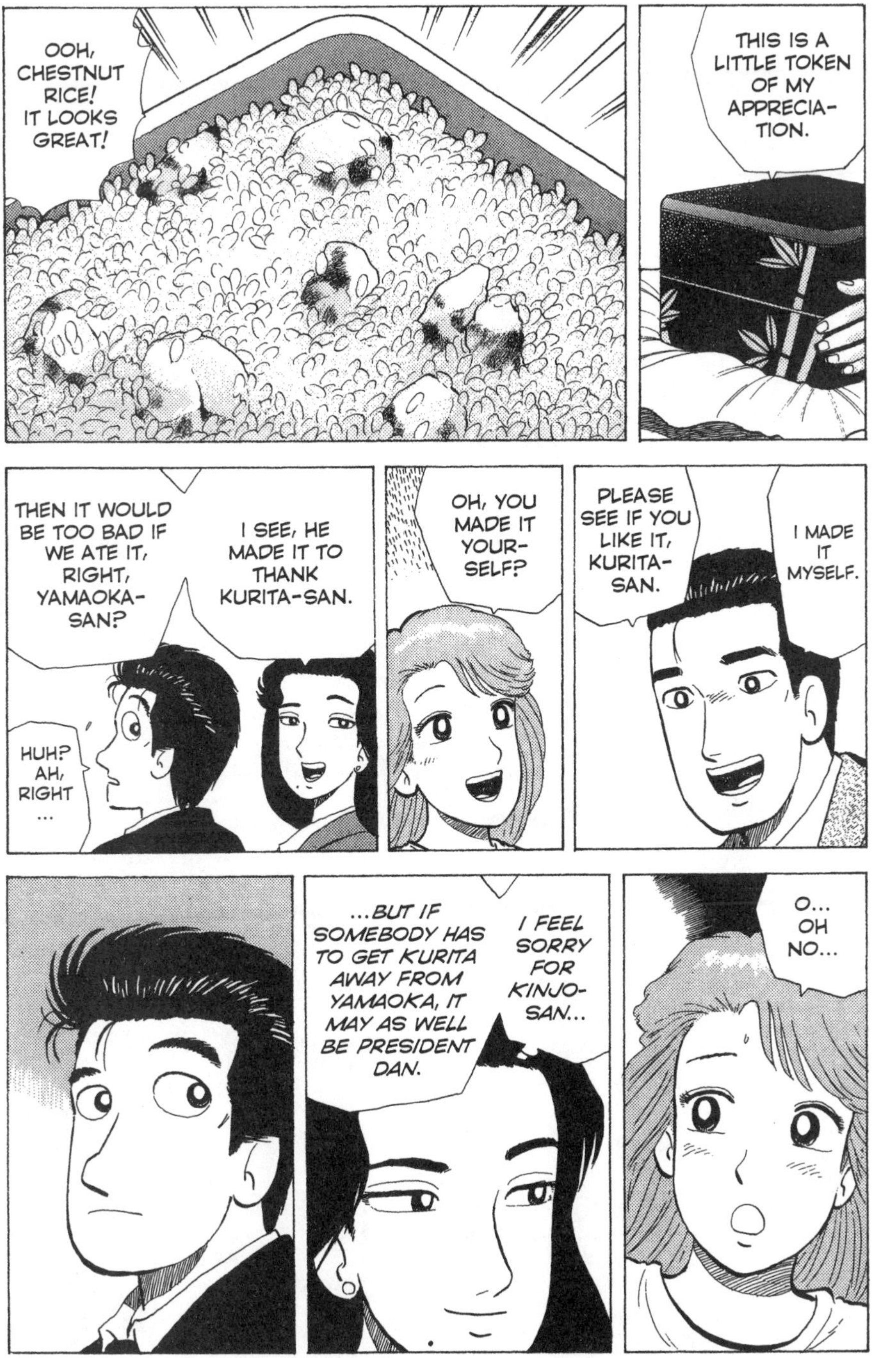
THIS IS A LITTLE TOKEN OF MY APPRECIATION.
OOH, CHESTNUT RICE! IT LOOKS GREAT!
I MADE IT MYSELF.
PLEASE SEE IF YOU LIKE IT, KURITA-SAN.
OH, YOU MADE IT YOURSELF?
I SEE, HE MADE IT TO THANK KURITA-SAN.
THEN IT WOULD BE TOO BAD IF WE ATE IT, RIGHT, YAMAOKA-SAN?
HUH? AH, RIGHT ...
O... OH NO...
I FEEL SORRY FOR KINJO-SAN...
...BUT IF SOMEBODY HAS TO GET KURITA AWAY FROM YAMAOKA, IT MAY AS WELL BE PRESIDENT DAN.

SEVENTH COURSE

THE SEASON FOR OYSTERS

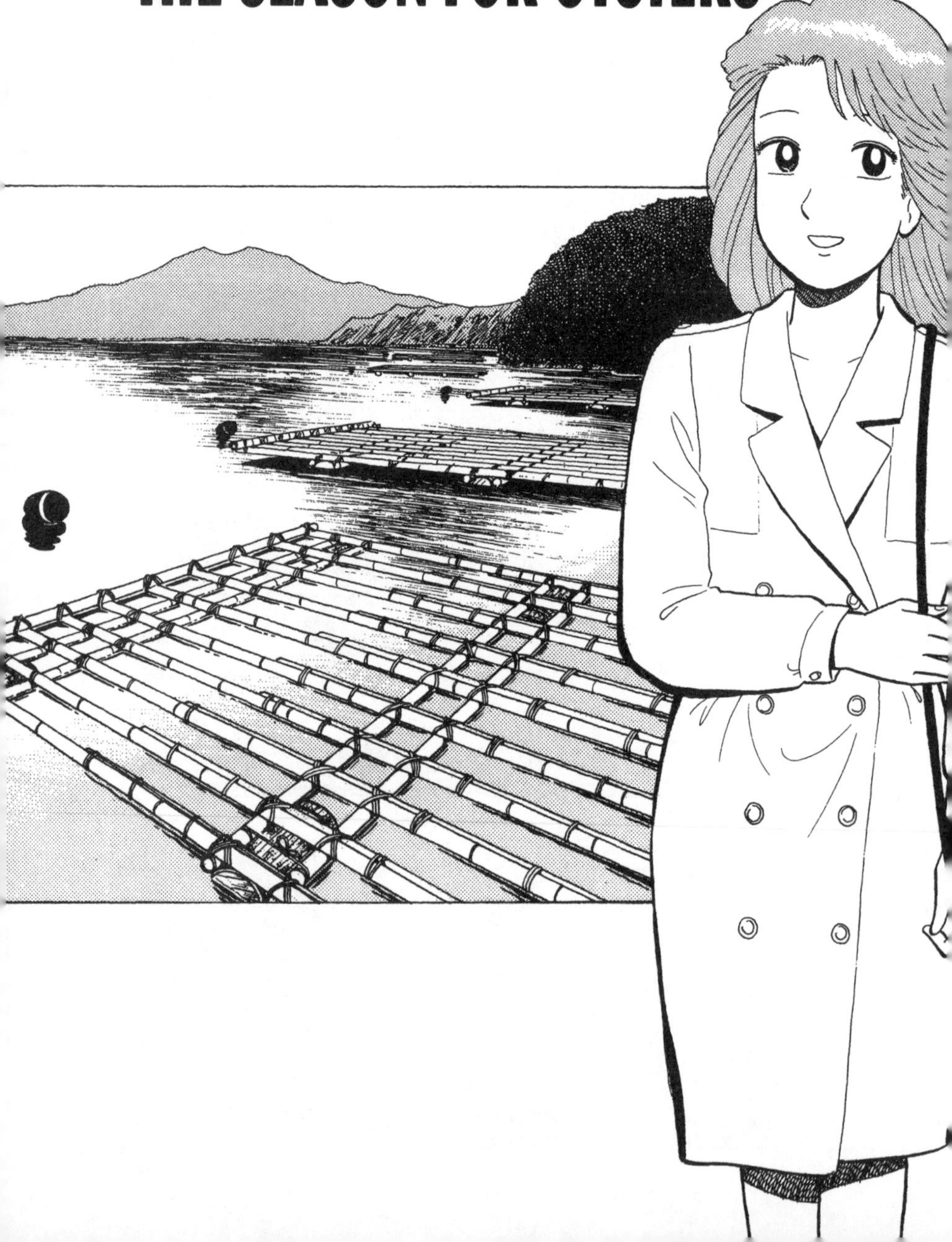

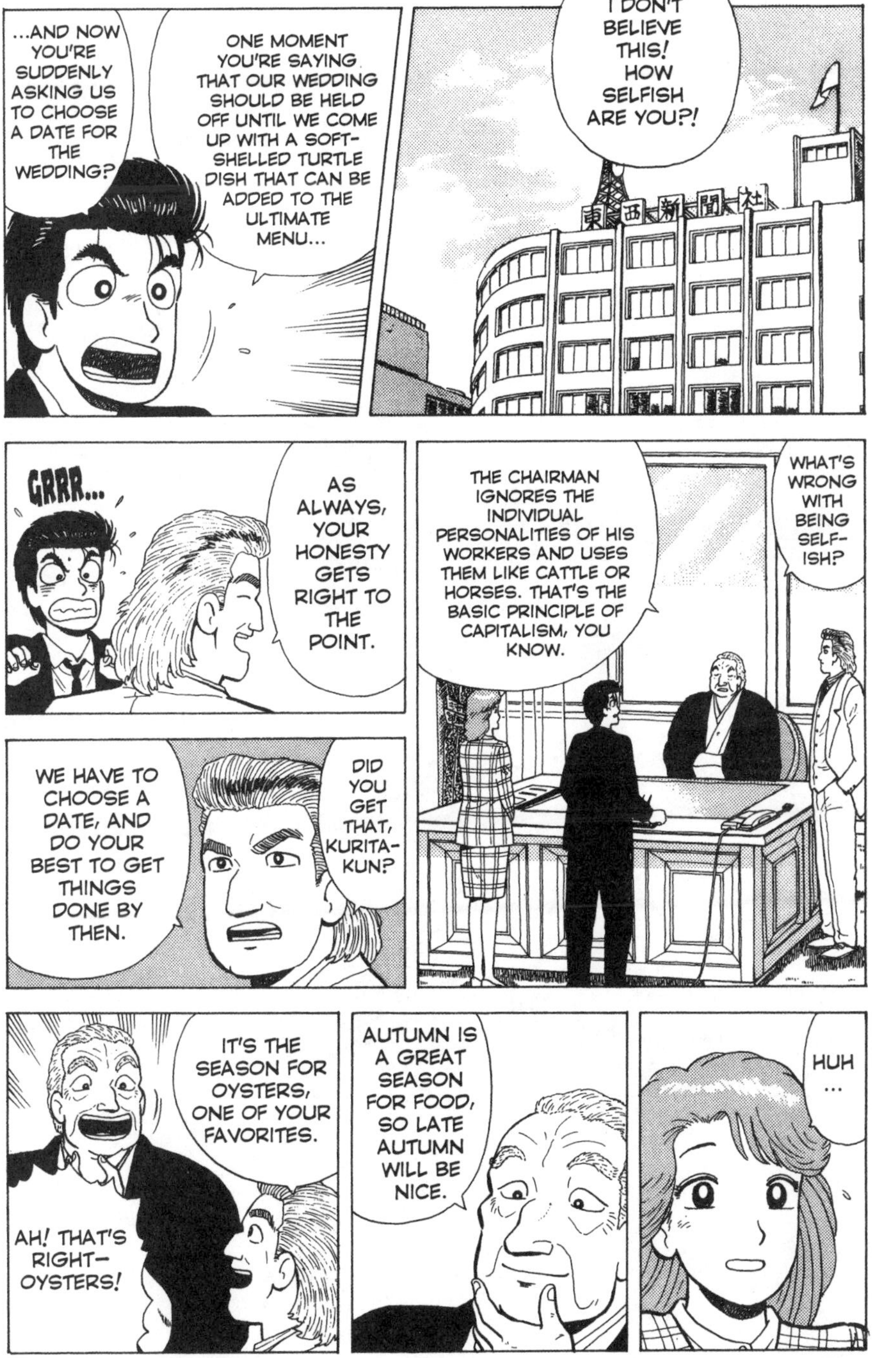
I DON'T BELIEVE THIS! HOW SELFISH ARE YOU?!
東西新聞社
ONE MOMENT YOU'RE SAYING THAT OUR WEDDING SHOULD BE HELD OFF UNTIL WE COME UP WITH A SOFT-SHELLED TURTLE DISH THAT CAN BE ADDED TO THE ULTIMATE MENU...
...AND NOW YOU'RE SUDDENLY ASKING US TO CHOOSE A DATE FOR THE WEDDING?
WHAT'S WRONG WITH BEING SELF-ISH?
THE CHAIRMAN IGNORES THE INDIVIDUAL PERSONALITIES OF HIS WORKERS AND USES THEM LIKE CATTLE OR HORSES. THAT'S THE BASIC PRINCIPLE OF CAPITALISM, YOU KNOW.
AS ALWAYS, YOUR HONESTY GETS RIGHT TO THE POINT.
GRRR...
DID YOU GET THAT, KURITA-KUN?
WE HAVE TO CHOOSE A DATE, AND DO YOUR BEST TO GET THINGS DONE BY THEN.
HUH ...
AUTUMN IS A GREAT SEASON FOR FOOD, SO LATE AUTUMN WILL BE NICE.
IT'S THE SEASON FOR OYSTERS, ONE OF YOUR FAVORITES.
AH! THAT'S RIGHT— OYSTERS!

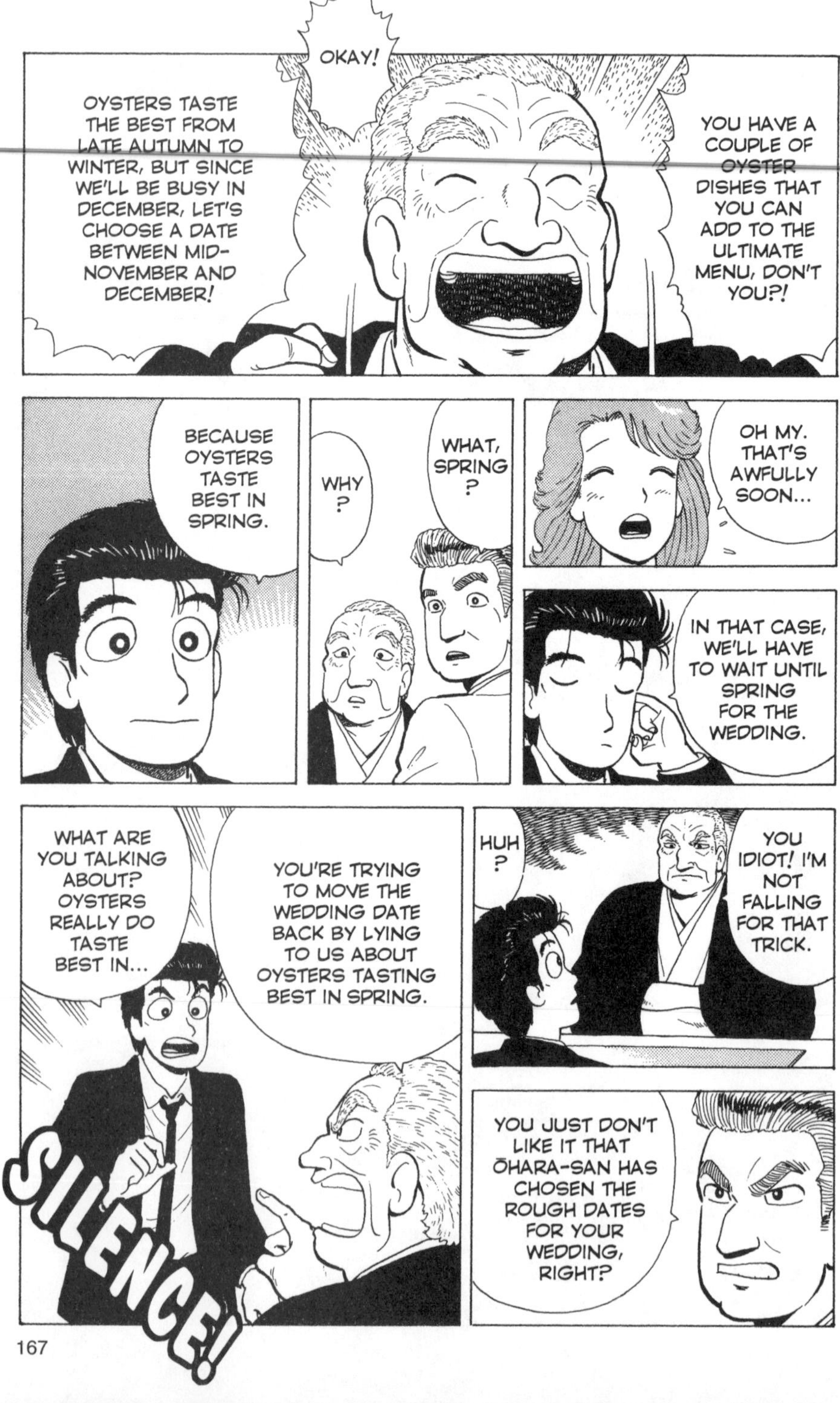
OKAY!
YOU HAVE A COUPLE OF OYSTER DISHES THAT YOU CAN ADD TO THE ULTIMATE MENU, DON'T YOU?!
OYSTERS TASTE THE BEST FROM LATE AUTUMN TO WINTER, BUT SINCE WE'LL BE BUSY IN DECEMBER, LET'S CHOOSE A DATE BETWEEN MID-NOVEMBER AND DECEMBER!
OH MY. THAT'S AWFULLY SOON...
IN THAT CASE, WE'LL HAVE TO WAIT UNTIL SPRING FOR THE WEDDING.
WHAT, SPRING?
WHY?
BECAUSE OYSTERS TASTE BEST IN SPRING.
YOU IDIOT! I'M NOT FALLING FOR THAT TRICK.
HUH?
YOU JUST DON'T LIKE IT THAT ŌHARA-SAN HAS CHOSEN THE ROUGH DATES FOR YOUR WEDDING, RIGHT?
YOU'RE TRYING TO MOVE THE WEDDING DATE BACK BY LYING TO US ABOUT OYSTERS TASTING BEST IN SPRING.
WHAT ARE YOU TALKING ABOUT? OYSTERS REALLY DO TASTE BEST IN...
SILENCE!

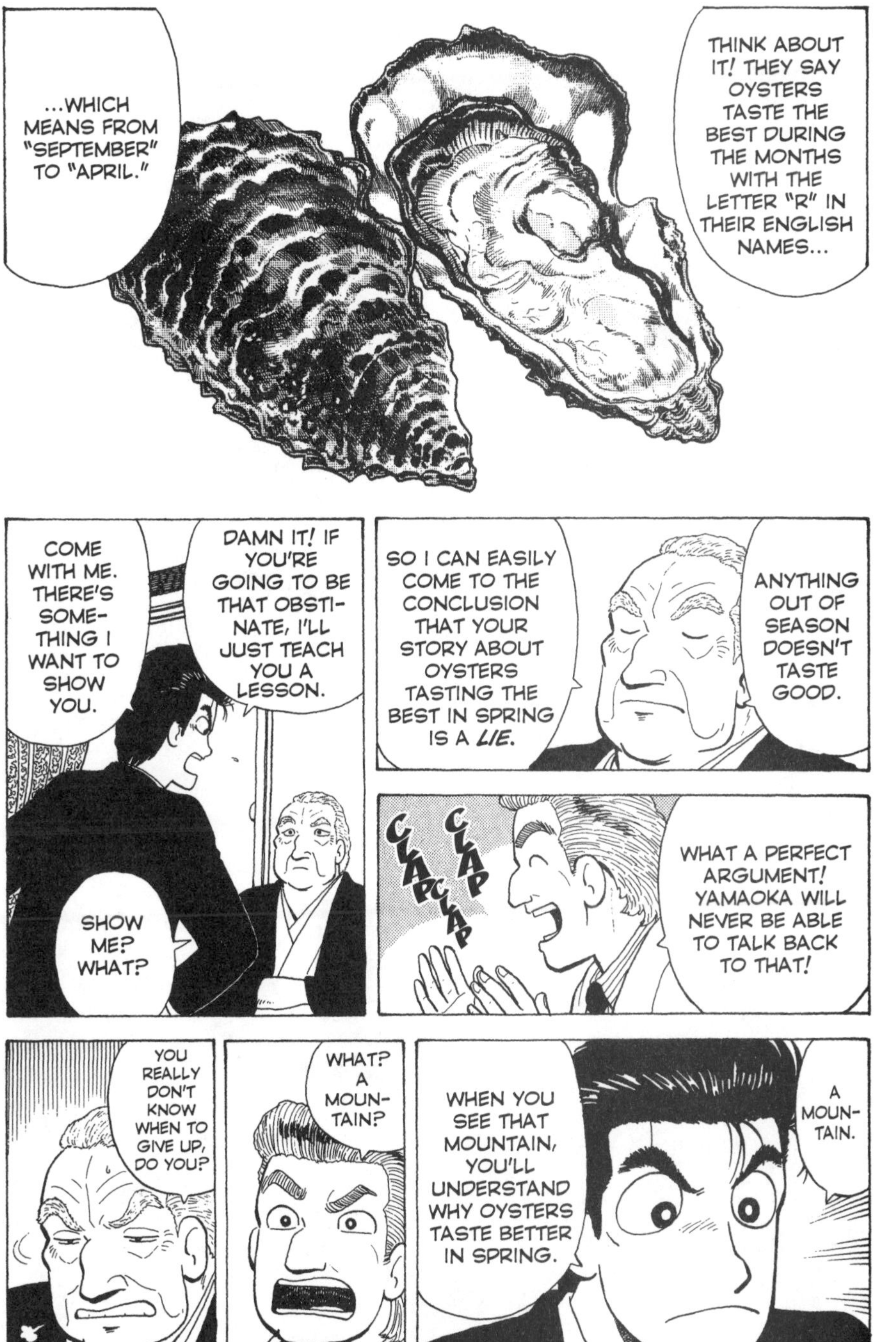
THINK ABOUT IT! THEY SAY OYSTERS TASTE THE BEST DURING THE MONTHS WITH THE LETTER "R" IN THEIR ENGLISH NAMES...
...WHICH MEANS FROM "SEPTEMBER" TO "APRIL."
ANYTHING OUT OF SEASON DOESN'T TASTE GOOD.
SO I CAN EASILY COME TO THE CONCLUSION THAT YOUR STORY ABOUT OYSTERS TASTING THE BEST IN SPRING IS A *LIE*.
WHAT A PERFECT ARGUMENT! YAMAOKA WILL NEVER BE ABLE TO TALK BACK TO THAT!
CLAP CLAP CLAP
DAMN IT! IF YOU'RE GOING TO BE THAT OBSTINATE, I'LL JUST TEACH YOU A LESSON.
COME WITH ME. THERE'S SOMETHING I WANT TO SHOW YOU.
SHOW ME? WHAT?
A MOUNTAIN.
WHEN YOU SEE THAT MOUNTAIN, YOU'LL UNDERSTAND WHY OYSTERS TASTE BETTER IN SPRING.
WHAT? A MOUNTAIN?
YOU REALLY DON'T KNOW WHEN TO GIVE UP, DO YOU?

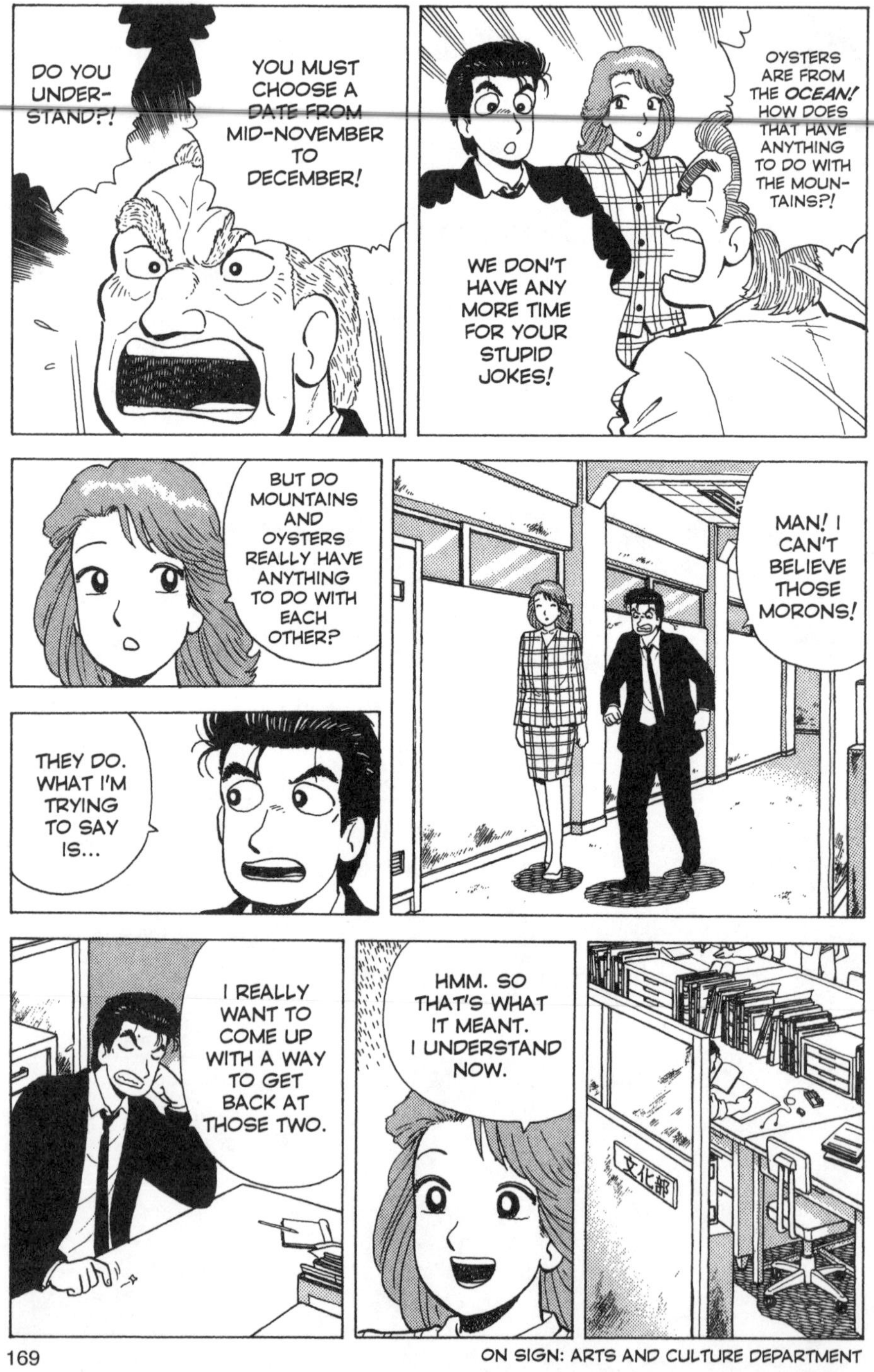
OYSTERS ARE FROM THE *OCEAN!* HOW DOES THAT HAVE ANYTHING TO DO WITH THE MOUNTAINS?!
WE DON'T HAVE ANY MORE TIME FOR YOUR STUPID JOKES!
YOU MUST CHOOSE A DATE FROM MID-NOVEMBER TO DECEMBER!
DO YOU UNDER-STAND?!
MAN! I CAN'T BELIEVE THOSE MORONS!
BUT DO MOUNTAINS AND OYSTERS REALLY HAVE ANYTHING TO DO WITH EACH OTHER?
THEY DO. WHAT I'M TRYING TO SAY IS...
文化部
HMM. SO THAT'S WHAT IT MEANT. I UNDERSTAND NOW.
I REALLY WANT TO COME UP WITH A WAY TO GET BACK AT THOSE TWO.

ON SIGN: ARTS AND CULTURE DEPARTMENT

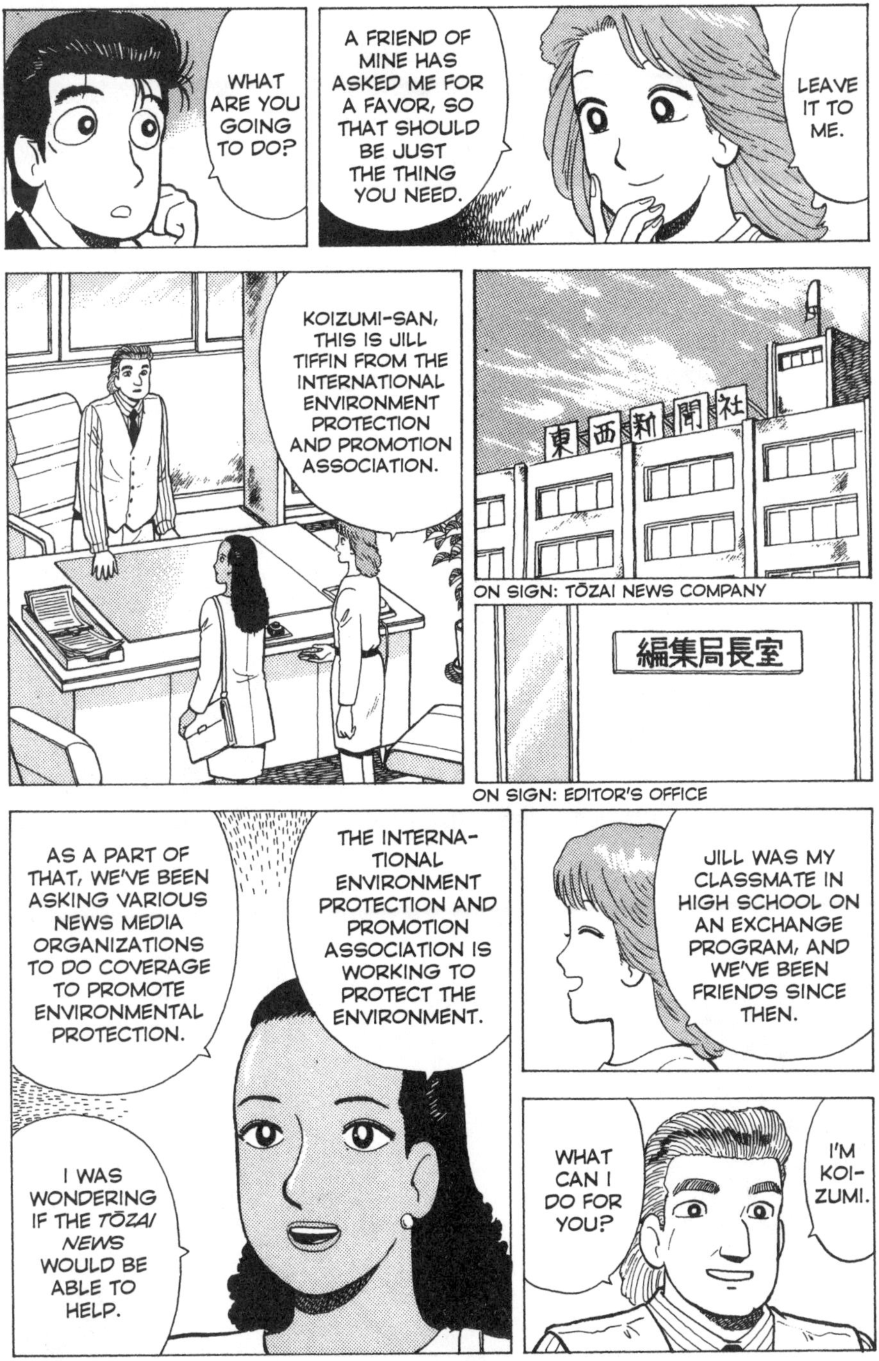
LEAVE IT TO ME.
A FRIEND OF MINE HAS ASKED ME FOR A FAVOR, SO THAT SHOULD BE JUST THE THING YOU NEED.
WHAT ARE YOU GOING TO DO?
東西新聞社
ON SIGN: TŌZAI NEWS COMPANY
編集局長室
ON SIGN: EDITOR'S OFFICE
KOIZUMI-SAN, THIS IS JILL TIFFIN FROM THE INTERNATIONAL ENVIRONMENT PROTECTION AND PROMOTION ASSOCIATION.
JILL WAS MY CLASSMATE IN HIGH SCHOOL ON AN EXCHANGE PROGRAM, AND WE'VE BEEN FRIENDS SINCE THEN.
I'M KOI-ZUMI.
WHAT CAN I DO FOR YOU?
THE INTERNA-TIONAL ENVIRONMENT PROTECTION AND PROMOTION ASSOCIATION IS WORKING TO PROTECT THE ENVIRONMENT.
AS A PART OF THAT, WE'VE BEEN ASKING VARIOUS NEWS MEDIA ORGANIZATIONS TO DO COVERAGE TO PROMOTE ENVIRONMENTAL PROTECTION.
I WAS WONDERING IF THE *TŌZAI NEWS* WOULD BE ABLE TO HELP.

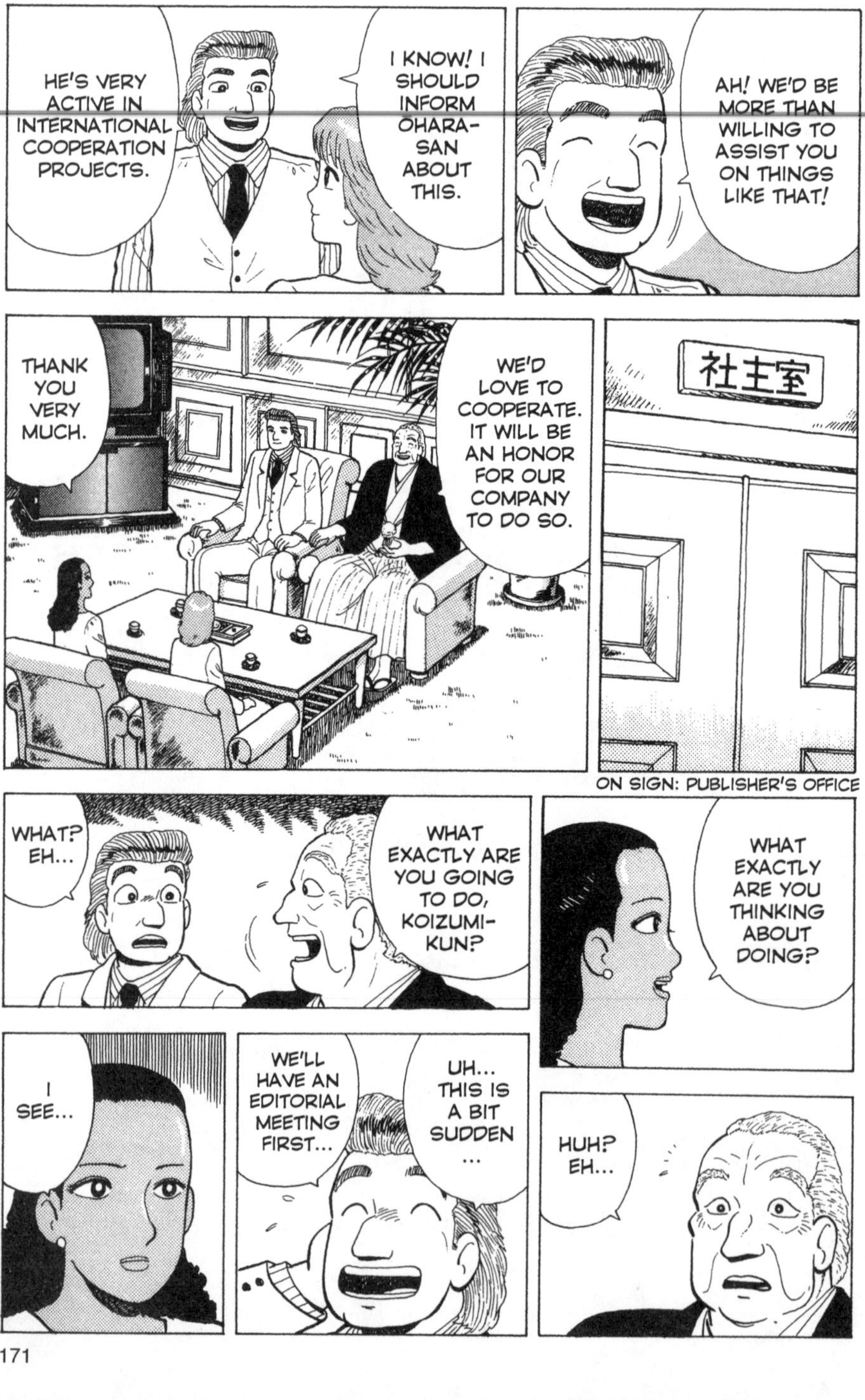
AH! WE'D BE MORE THAN WILLING TO ASSIST YOU ON THINGS LIKE THAT!
I KNOW! I SHOULD INFORM OHARA-SAN ABOUT THIS.
HE'S VERY ACTIVE IN INTERNATIONAL COOPERATION PROJECTS.
社主室
WE'D LOVE TO COOPERATE. IT WILL BE AN HONOR FOR OUR COMPANY TO DO SO.
THANK YOU VERY MUCH.
ON SIGN: PUBLISHER'S OFFICE
WHAT EXACTLY ARE YOU THINKING ABOUT DOING?
WHAT EXACTLY ARE YOU GOING TO DO, KOIZUMI-KUN?
WHAT? EH...
HUH? EH...
UH... THIS IS A BIT SUDDEN ...
WE'LL HAVE AN EDITORIAL MEETING FIRST...
I SEE...

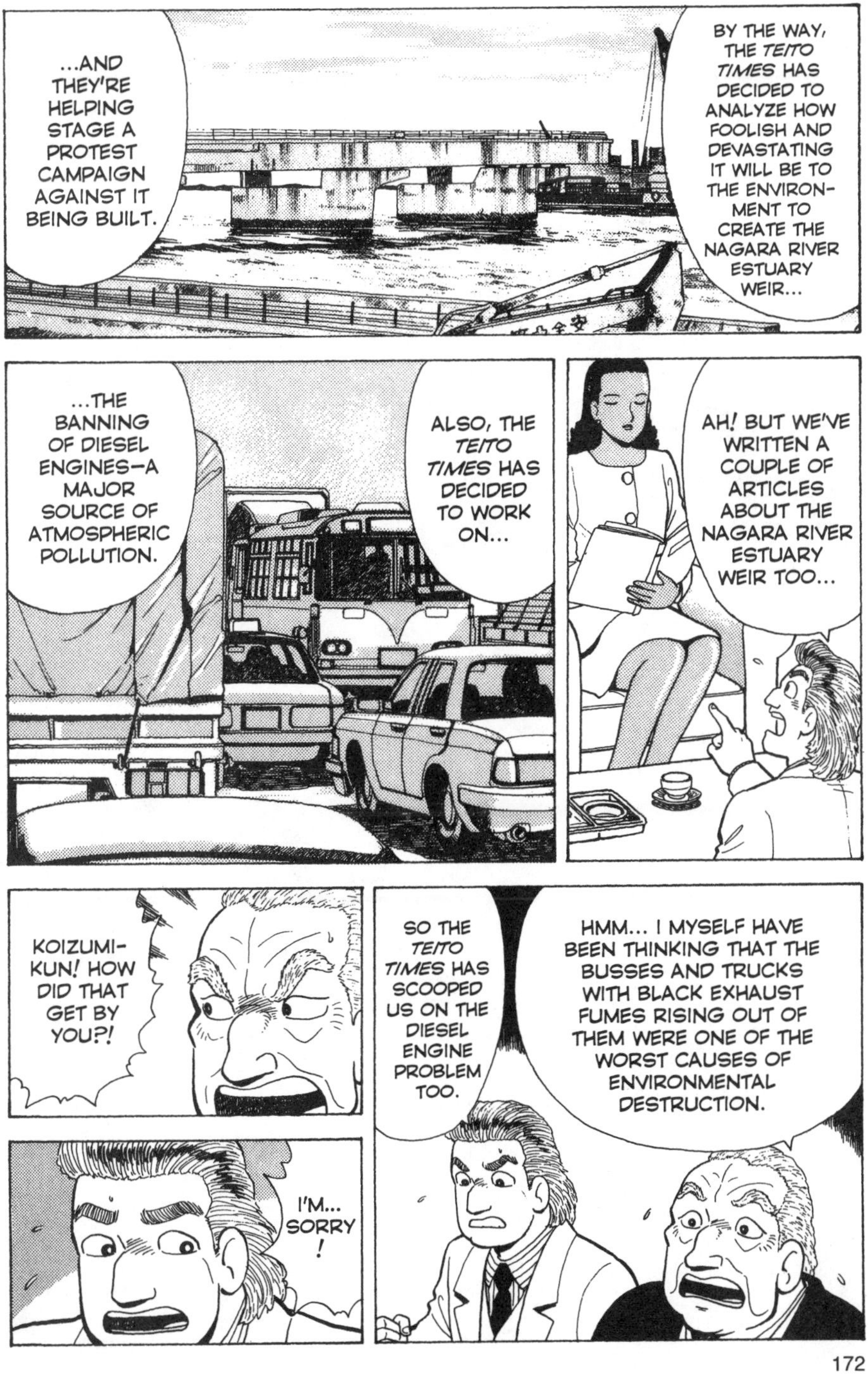
BY THE WAY, THE *TEITO TIMES* HAS DECIDED TO ANALYZE HOW FOOLISH AND DEVASTATING IT WILL BE TO THE ENVIRONMENT TO CREATE THE NAGARA RIVER ESTUARY WEIR...
...AND THEY'RE HELPING STAGE A PROTEST CAMPAIGN AGAINST IT BEING BUILT.
AH! BUT WE'VE WRITTEN A COUPLE OF ARTICLES ABOUT THE NAGARA RIVER ESTUARY WEIR TOO...
ALSO, THE *TEITO TIMES* HAS DECIDED TO WORK ON...
...THE BANNING OF DIESEL ENGINES—A MAJOR SOURCE OF ATMOSPHERIC POLLUTION.
HMM... I MYSELF HAVE BEEN THINKING THAT THE BUSSES AND TRUCKS WITH BLACK EXHAUST FUMES RISING OUT OF THEM WERE ONE OF THE WORST CAUSES OF ENVIRONMENTAL DESTRUCTION.
SO THE *TEITO TIMES* HAS SCOOPED US ON THE DIESEL ENGINE PROBLEM TOO.
KOIZUMI-KUN! HOW DID THAT GET BY YOU?!
I'M... SORRY!

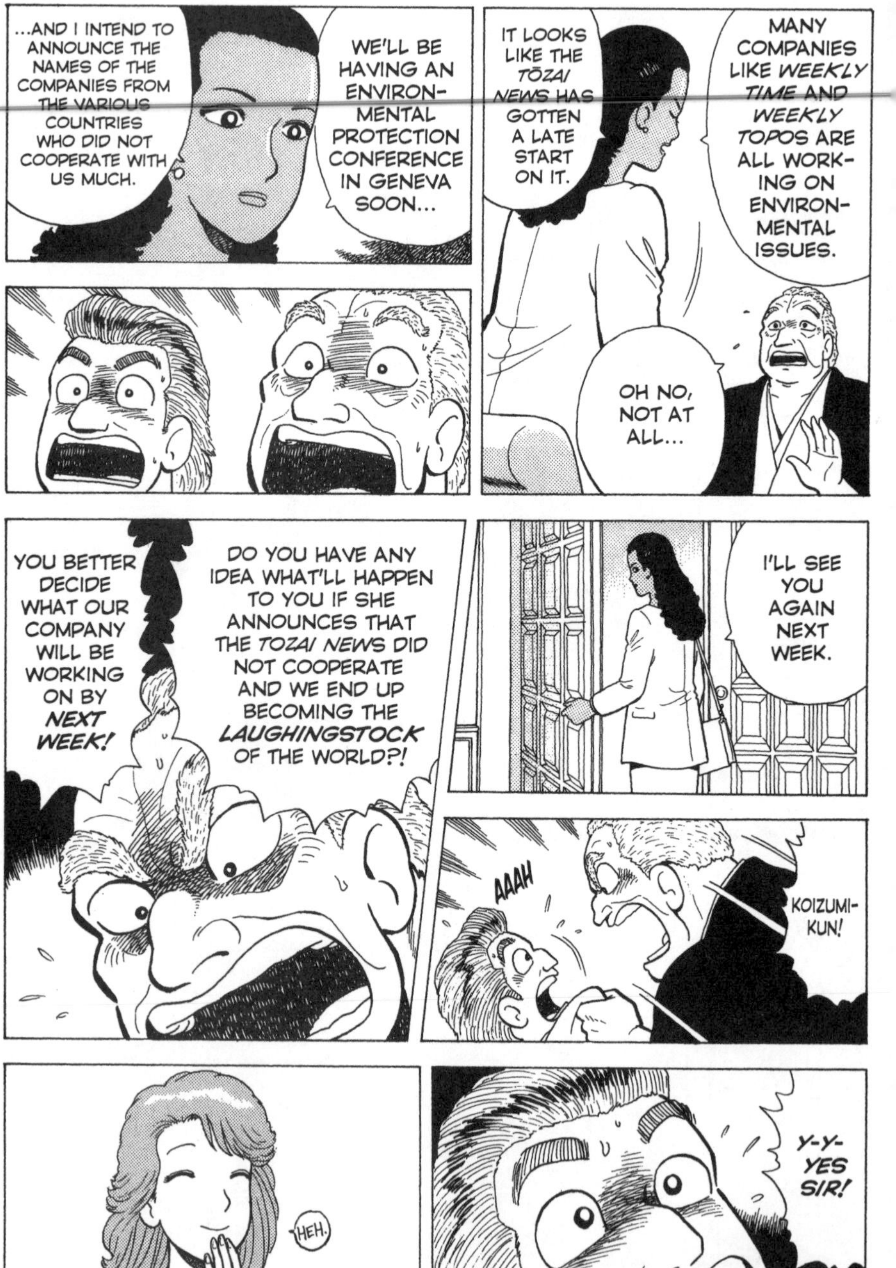
MANY COMPANIES LIKE WEEKLY TIME AND WEEKLY TOPOS ARE ALL WORKING ON ENVIRONMENTAL ISSUES.
IT LOOKS LIKE THE TŌZAI NEWS HAS GOTTEN A LATE START ON IT.
OH NO, NOT AT ALL...
WE'LL BE HAVING AN ENVIRONMENTAL PROTECTION CONFERENCE IN GENEVA SOON...
...AND I INTEND TO ANNOUNCE THE NAMES OF THE COMPANIES FROM THE VARIOUS COUNTRIES WHO DID NOT COOPERATE WITH US MUCH.
I'LL SEE YOU AGAIN NEXT WEEK.
KOIZUMI-KUN!
AAAH
DO YOU HAVE ANY IDEA WHAT'LL HAPPEN TO YOU IF SHE ANNOUNCES THAT THE TOZAI NEWS DID NOT COOPERATE AND WE END UP BECOMING THE LAUGHINGSTOCK OF THE WORLD?!
YOU BETTER DECIDE WHAT OUR COMPANY WILL BE WORKING ON BY NEXT WEEK!
Y-Y-YES SIR!
HEH.

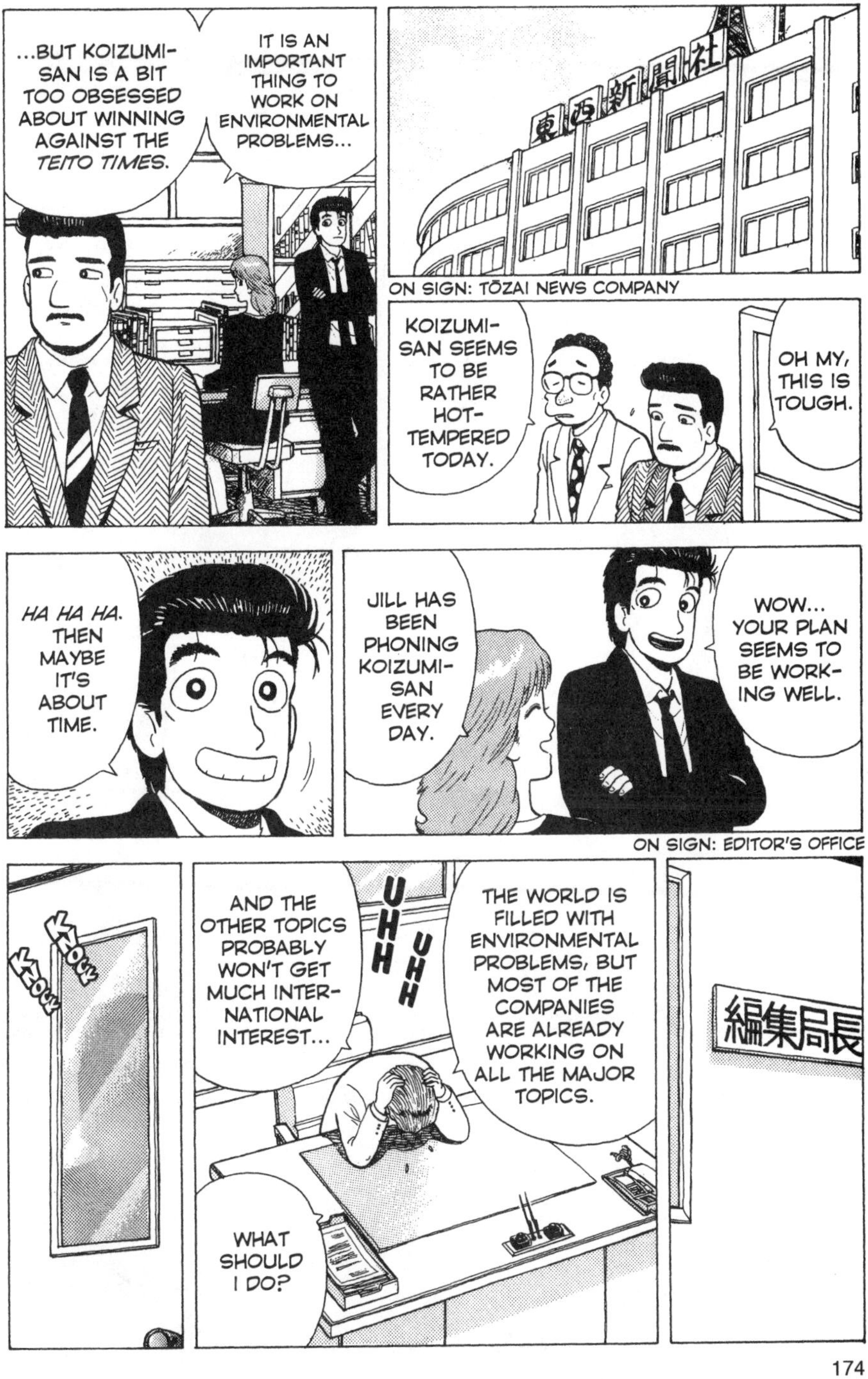
ON SIGN: TŌZAI NEWS COMPANY
東西新聞社
OH MY, THIS IS TOUGH.
KOIZUMI-SAN SEEMS TO BE RATHER HOT-TEMPERED TODAY.
IT IS AN IMPORTANT THING TO WORK ON ENVIRONMENTAL PROBLEMS...
...BUT KOIZUMI-SAN IS A BIT TOO OBSESSED ABOUT WINNING AGAINST THE *TEITO TIMES*.
WOW... YOUR PLAN SEEMS TO BE WORKING WELL.
JILL HAS BEEN PHONING KOIZUMI-SAN EVERY DAY.
HA HA HA. THEN MAYBE IT'S ABOUT TIME.
ON SIGN: EDITOR'S OFFICE
編集局長
THE WORLD IS FILLED WITH ENVIRONMENTAL PROBLEMS, BUT MOST OF THE COMPANIES ARE ALREADY WORKING ON ALL THE MAJOR TOPICS.
UHH UHH
AND THE OTHER TOPICS PROBABLY WON'T GET MUCH INTER-NATIONAL INTEREST...
WHAT SHOULD I DO?
KNOCK KNOCK

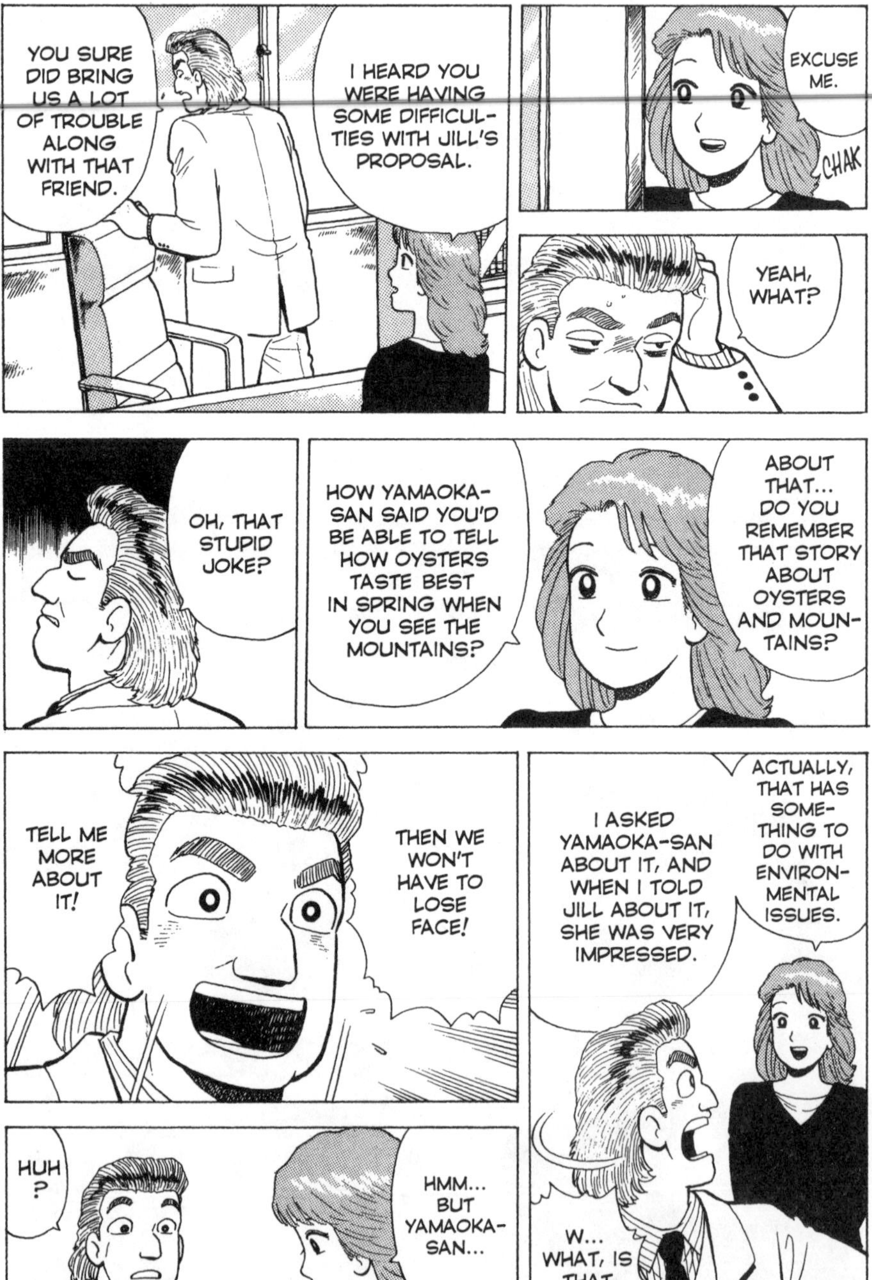
EXCUSE ME.
CHAK
YEAH, WHAT?
I HEARD YOU WERE HAVING SOME DIFFICULTIES WITH JILL'S PROPOSAL.
YOU SURE DID BRING US A LOT OF TROUBLE ALONG WITH THAT FRIEND.
ABOUT THAT... DO YOU REMEMBER THAT STORY ABOUT OYSTERS AND MOUNTAINS?
HOW YAMAOKA-SAN SAID YOU'D BE ABLE TO TELL HOW OYSTERS TASTE BEST IN SPRING WHEN YOU SEE THE MOUNTAINS?
OH, THAT STUPID JOKE?
ACTUALLY, THAT HAS SOMETHING TO DO WITH ENVIRONMENTAL ISSUES.
I ASKED YAMAOKA-SAN ABOUT IT, AND WHEN I TOLD JILL ABOUT IT, SHE WAS VERY IMPRESSED.
W... WHAT, IS THAT *TRUE?!*
THEN WE WON'T HAVE TO LOSE FACE!
TELL ME MORE ABOUT IT!
HMM... BUT YAMAOKA-SAN...
HUH?

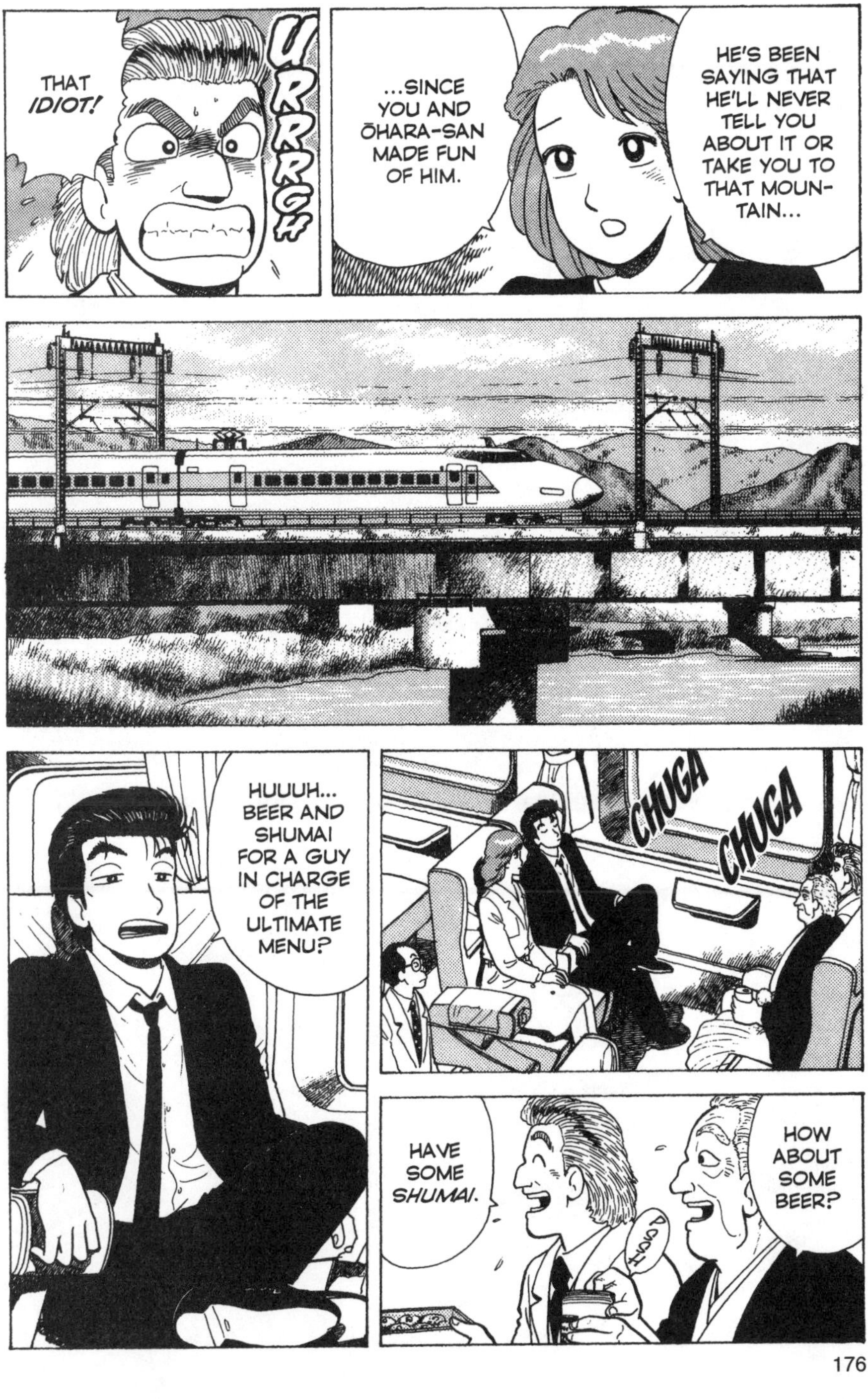

HE'S BEEN SAYING THAT HE'LL NEVER TELL YOU ABOUT IT OR TAKE YOU TO THAT MOUN-TAIN...
...SINCE YOU AND ŌHARA-SAN MADE FUN OF HIM.
URRRGH
THAT *IDIOT!*
CHUGA CHUGA
HOW ABOUT SOME BEER?
HAVE SOME *SHUMAI.*
HUUUH... BEER AND SHUMAI FOR A GUY IN CHARGE OF THE ULTIMATE MENU?

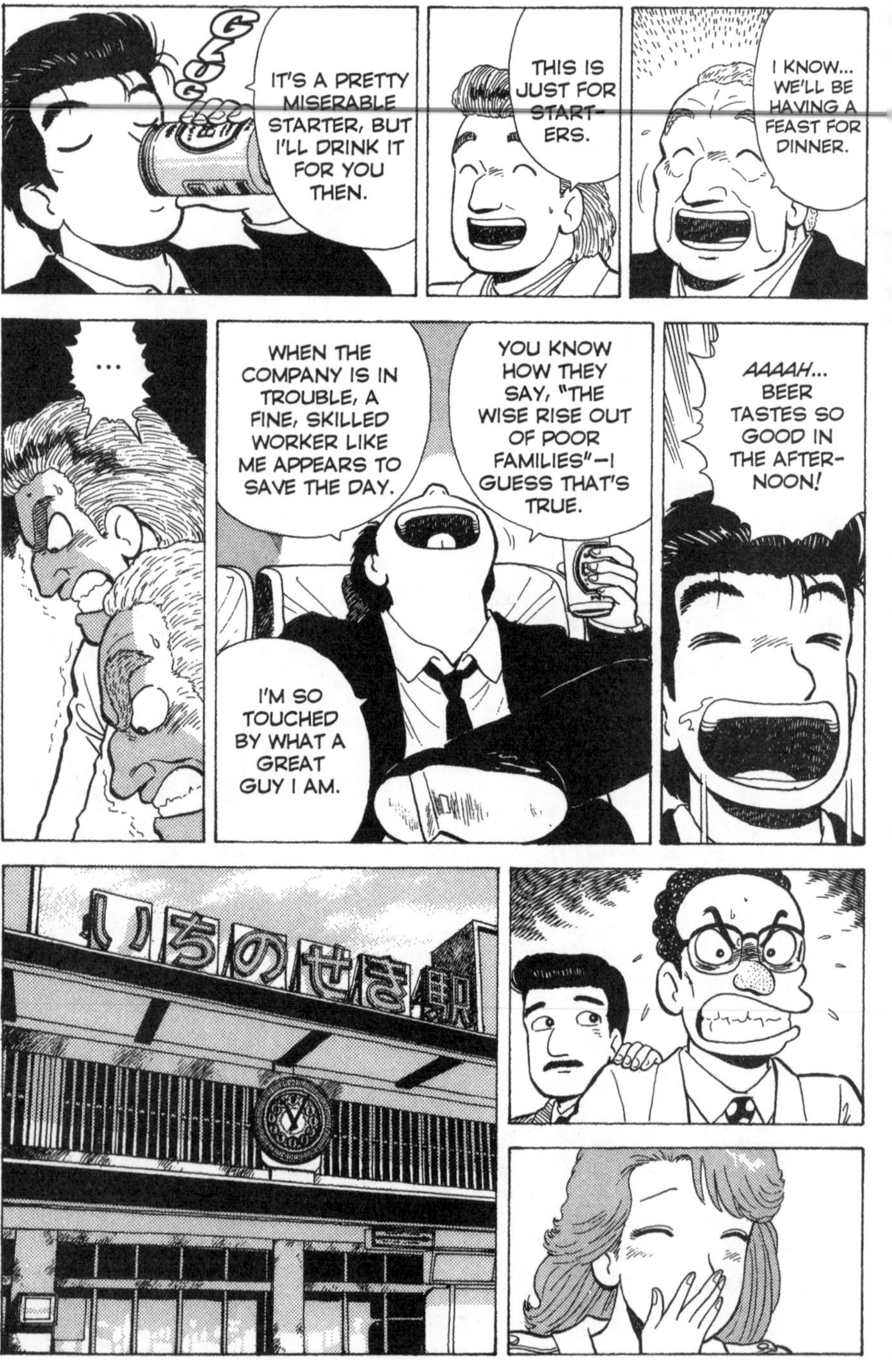
I KNOW... WE'LL BE HAVING A FEAST FOR DINNER.
THIS IS JUST FOR STARTERS.
GLUG
IT'S A PRETTY MISERABLE STARTER, BUT I'LL DRINK IT FOR YOU THEN.
AAAAH... BEER TASTES SO GOOD IN THE AFTERNOON!
YOU KNOW HOW THEY SAY, "THE WISE RISE OUT OF POOR FAMILIES"—I GUESS THAT'S TRUE.
WHEN THE COMPANY IS IN TROUBLE, A FINE, SKILLED WORKER LIKE ME APPEARS TO SAVE THE DAY.
I'M SO TOUCHED BY WHAT A GREAT GUY I AM.
...
いちのせき駅

ON SIGN: ICHINOSEKI STATION

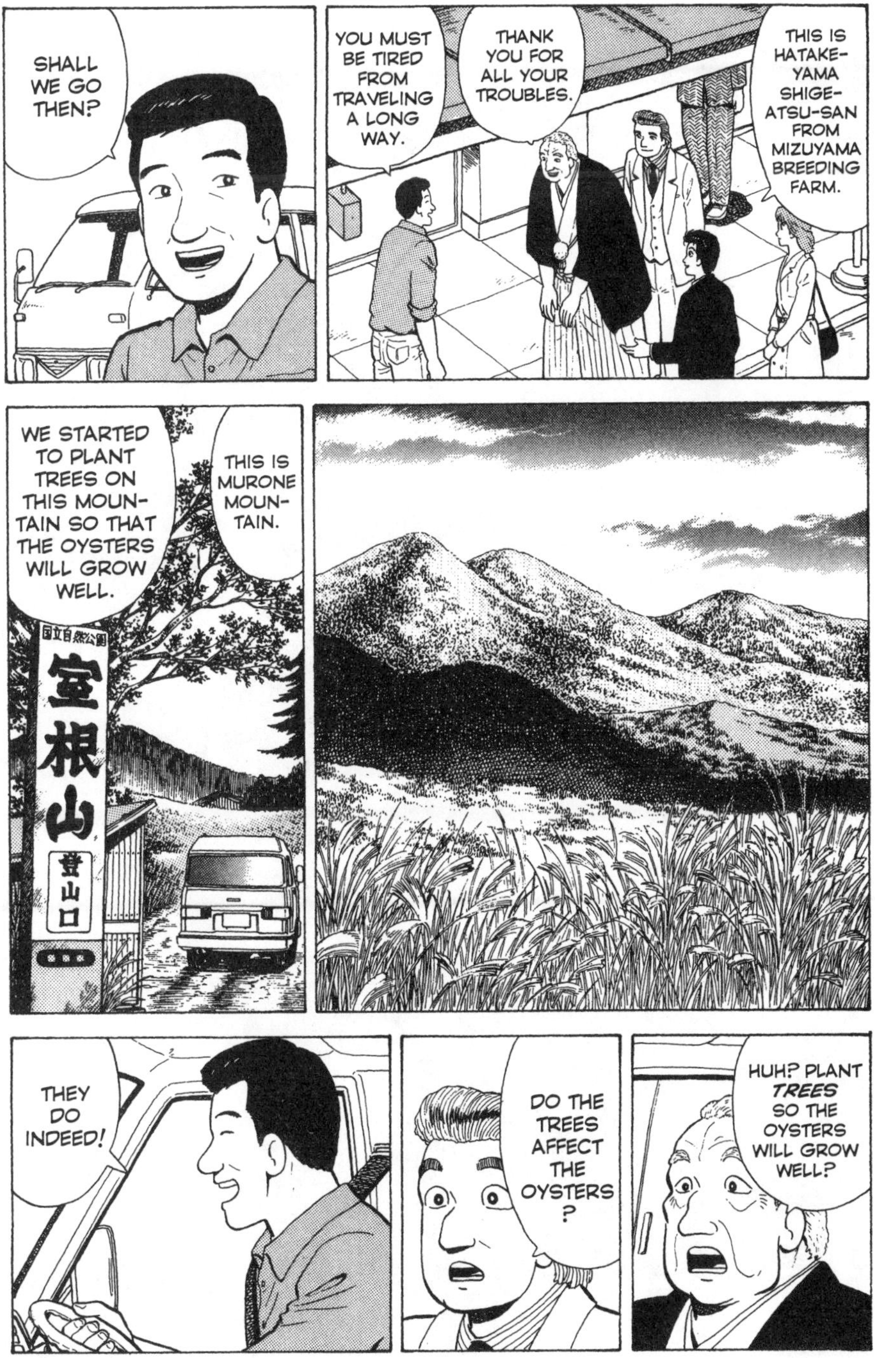
THIS IS HATAKE-YAMA SHIGE-ATSU-SAN FROM MIZUYAMA BREEDING FARM.
THANK YOU FOR ALL YOUR TROUBLES.
YOU MUST BE TIRED FROM TRAVELING A LONG WAY.
SHALL WE GO THEN?
THIS IS MURONE MOUN-TAIN.
WE STARTED TO PLANT TREES ON THIS MOUN-TAIN SO THAT THE OYSTERS WILL GROW WELL.
国立自然公園
室根山
登山口
HUH? PLANT *TREES* SO THE OYSTERS WILL GROW WELL?
DO THE TREES AFFECT THE OYSTERS?
THEY DO INDEED!

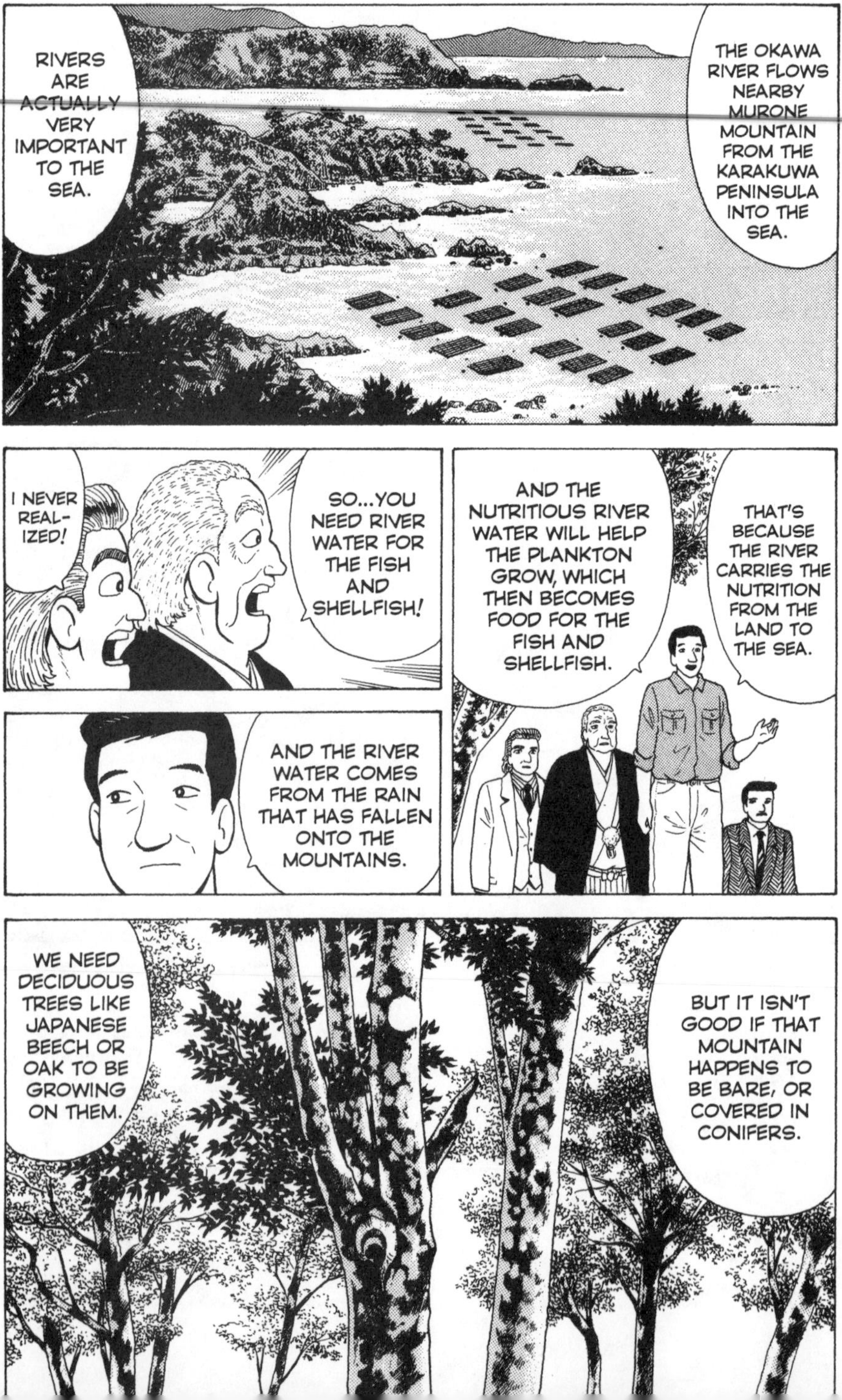
THE OKAWA RIVER FLOWS NEARBY MURONE MOUNTAIN FROM THE KARAKUWA PENINSULA INTO THE SEA.
RIVERS ARE ACTUALLY VERY IMPORTANT TO THE SEA.
THAT'S BECAUSE THE RIVER CARRIES THE NUTRITION FROM THE LAND TO THE SEA.
AND THE NUTRITIOUS RIVER WATER WILL HELP THE PLANKTON GROW, WHICH THEN BECOMES FOOD FOR THE FISH AND SHELLFISH.
SO...YOU NEED RIVER WATER FOR THE FISH AND SHELLFISH!
I NEVER REAL-IZED!
AND THE RIVER WATER COMES FROM THE RAIN THAT HAS FALLEN ONTO THE MOUNTAINS.
BUT IT ISN'T GOOD IF THAT MOUNTAIN HAPPENS TO BE BARE, OR COVERED IN CONIFERS.
WE NEED DECIDUOUS TREES LIKE JAPANESE BEECH OR OAK TO BE GROWING ON THEM.

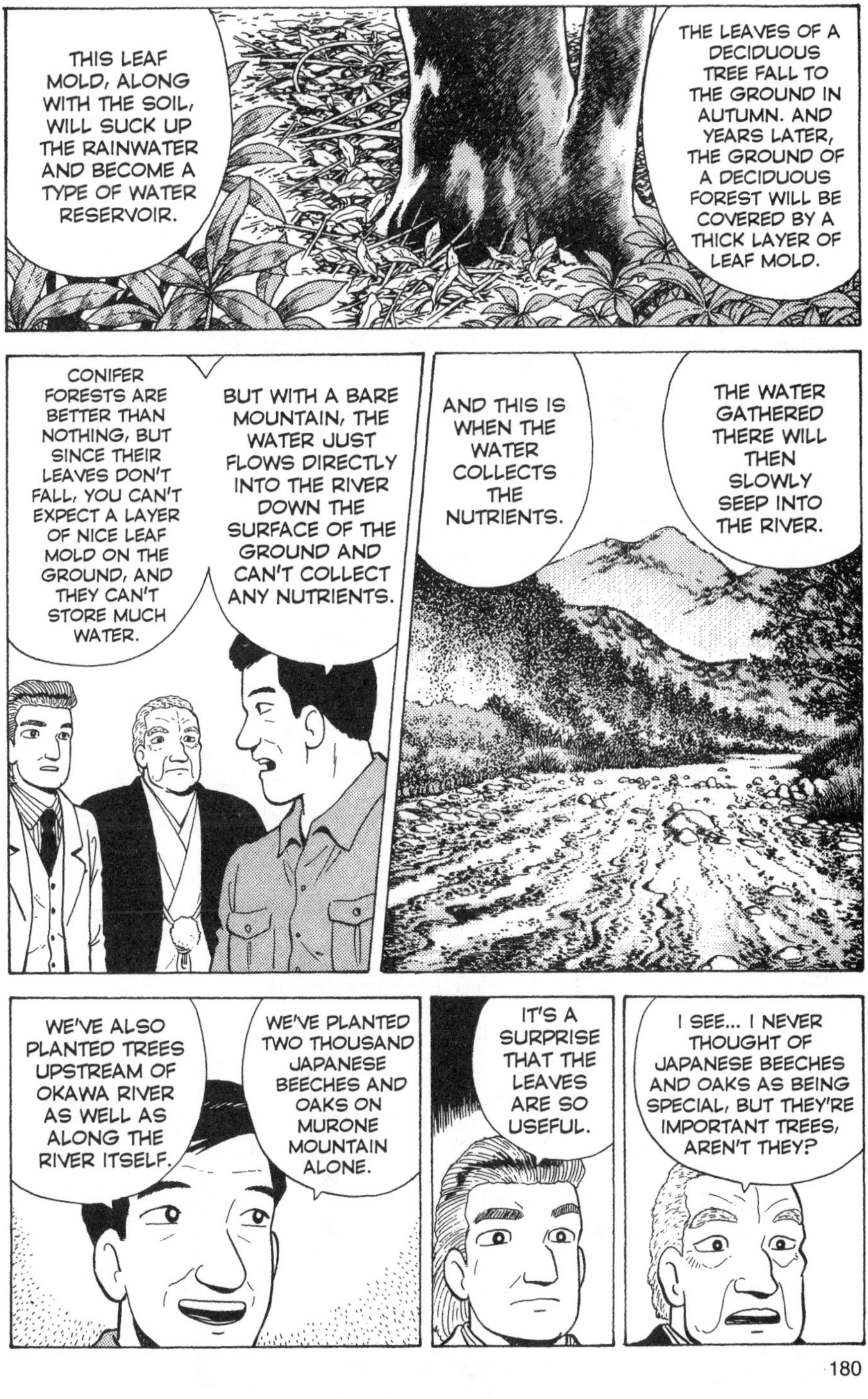
THE LEAVES OF A DECIDUOUS TREE FALL TO THE GROUND IN AUTUMN. AND YEARS LATER, THE GROUND OF A DECIDUOUS FOREST WILL BE COVERED BY A THICK LAYER OF LEAF MOLD.
THIS LEAF MOLD, ALONG WITH THE SOIL, WILL SUCK UP THE RAINWATER AND BECOME A TYPE OF WATER RESERVOIR.
THE WATER GATHERED THERE WILL THEN SLOWLY SEEP INTO THE RIVER.
AND THIS IS WHEN THE WATER COLLECTS THE NUTRIENTS.
BUT WITH A BARE MOUNTAIN, THE WATER JUST FLOWS DIRECTLY INTO THE RIVER DOWN THE SURFACE OF THE GROUND AND CAN'T COLLECT ANY NUTRIENTS.
CONIFER FORESTS ARE BETTER THAN NOTHING, BUT SINCE THEIR LEAVES DON'T FALL, YOU CAN'T EXPECT A LAYER OF NICE LEAF MOLD ON THE GROUND, AND THEY CAN'T STORE MUCH WATER.
I SEE... I NEVER THOUGHT OF JAPANESE BEECHES AND OAKS AS BEING SPECIAL, BUT THEY'RE IMPORTANT TREES, AREN'T THEY?
IT'S A SURPRISE THAT THE LEAVES ARE SO USEFUL.
WE'VE PLANTED TWO THOUSAND JAPANESE BEECHES AND OAKS ON MURONE MOUNTAIN ALONE.
WE'VE ALSO PLANTED TREES UPSTREAM OF OKAWA RIVER AS WELL AS ALONG THE RIVER ITSELF.

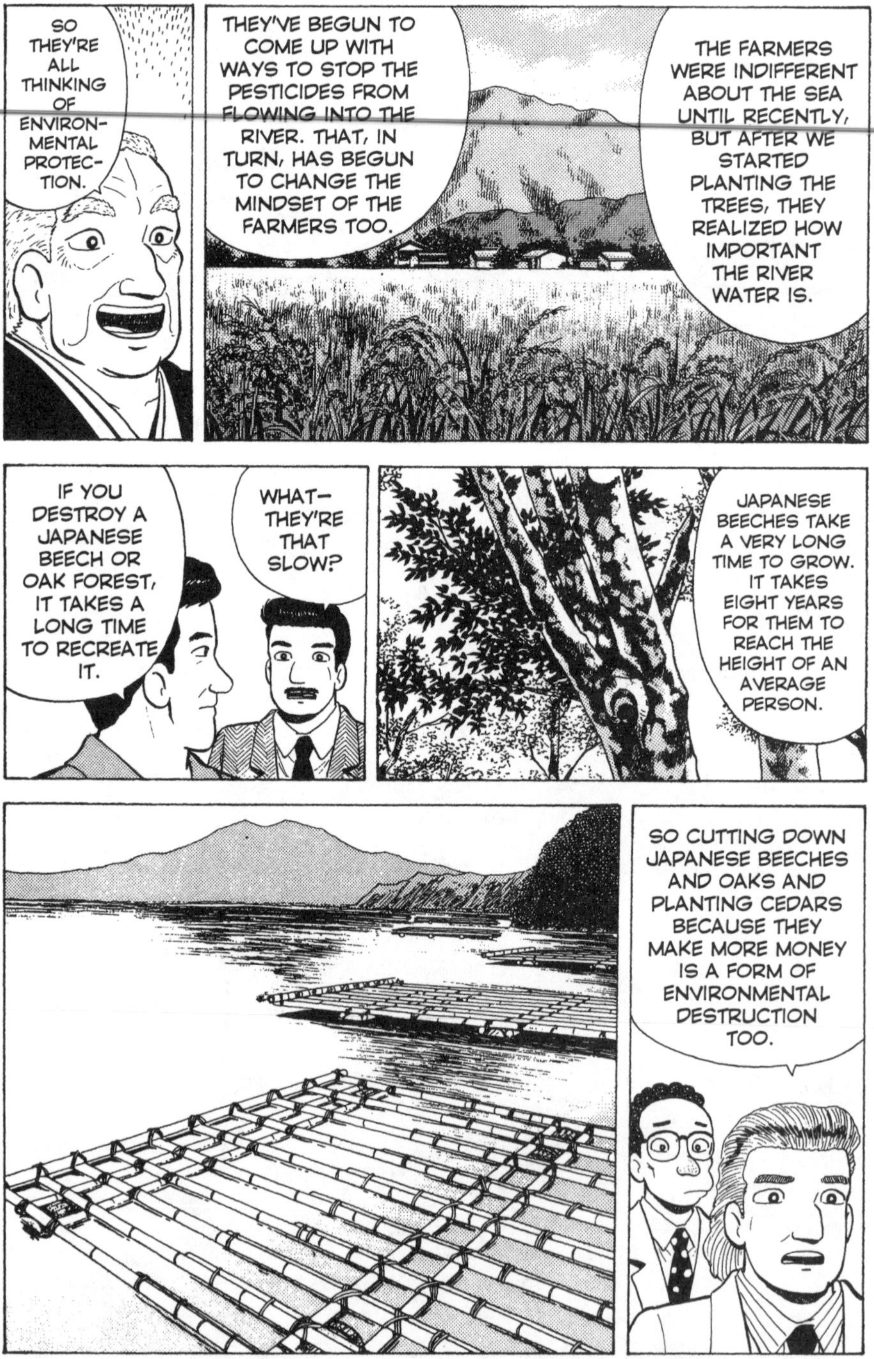
THE FARMERS WERE INDIFFERENT ABOUT THE SEA UNTIL RECENTLY, BUT AFTER WE STARTED PLANTING THE TREES, THEY REALIZED HOW IMPORTANT THE RIVER WATER IS.
THEY'VE BEGUN TO COME UP WITH WAYS TO STOP THE PESTICIDES FROM FLOWING INTO THE RIVER. THAT, IN TURN, HAS BEGUN TO CHANGE THE MINDSET OF THE FARMERS TOO.
SO THEY'RE ALL THINKING OF ENVIRON-MENTAL PROTEC-TION.
JAPANESE BEECHES TAKE A VERY LONG TIME TO GROW. IT TAKES EIGHT YEARS FOR THEM TO REACH THE HEIGHT OF AN AVERAGE PERSON.
WHAT— THEY'RE THAT SLOW?
IF YOU DESTROY A JAPANESE BEECH OR OAK FOREST, IT TAKES A LONG TIME TO RECREATE IT.
SO CUTTING DOWN JAPANESE BEECHES AND OAKS AND PLANTING CEDARS BECAUSE THEY MAKE MORE MONEY IS A FORM OF ENVIRONMENTAL DESTRUCTION TOO.

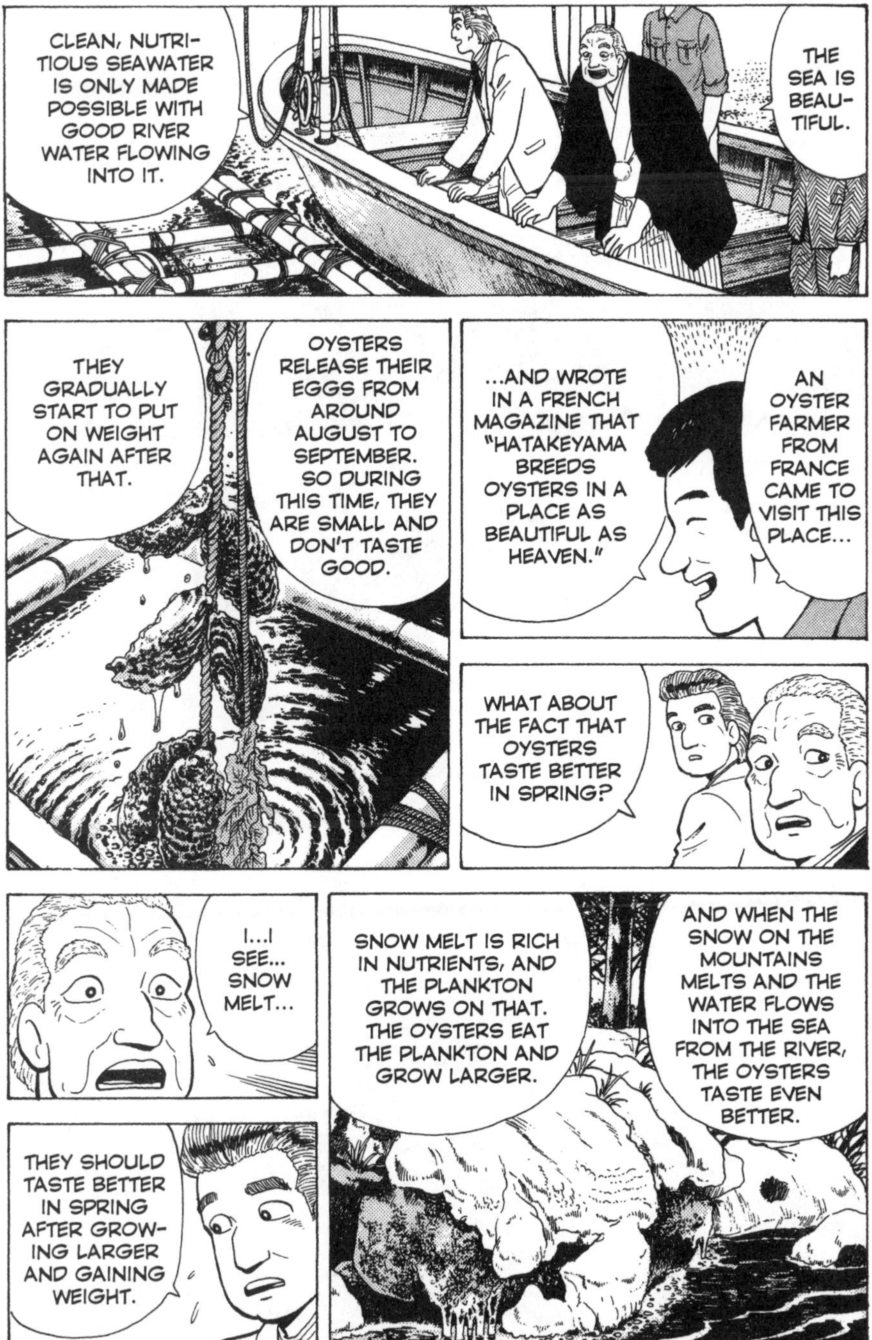
THE SEA IS BEAUTIFUL.
CLEAN, NUTRITIOUS SEAWATER IS ONLY MADE POSSIBLE WITH GOOD RIVER WATER FLOWING INTO IT.
AN OYSTER FARMER FROM FRANCE CAME TO VISIT THIS PLACE...
...AND WROTE IN A FRENCH MAGAZINE THAT "HATAKEYAMA BREEDS OYSTERS IN A PLACE AS BEAUTIFUL AS HEAVEN."
WHAT ABOUT THE FACT THAT OYSTERS TASTE BETTER IN SPRING?
OYSTERS RELEASE THEIR EGGS FROM AROUND AUGUST TO SEPTEMBER. SO DURING THIS TIME, THEY ARE SMALL AND DON'T TASTE GOOD.
THEY GRADUALLY START TO PUT ON WEIGHT AGAIN AFTER THAT.
AND WHEN THE SNOW ON THE MOUNTAINS MELTS AND THE WATER FLOWS INTO THE SEA FROM THE RIVER, THE OYSTERS TASTE EVEN BETTER.
SNOW MELT IS RICH IN NUTRIENTS, AND THE PLANKTON GROWS ON THAT. THE OYSTERS EAT THE PLANKTON AND GROW LARGER.
I...I SEE... SNOW MELT...
THEY SHOULD TASTE BETTER IN SPRING AFTER GROWING LARGER AND GAINING WEIGHT.

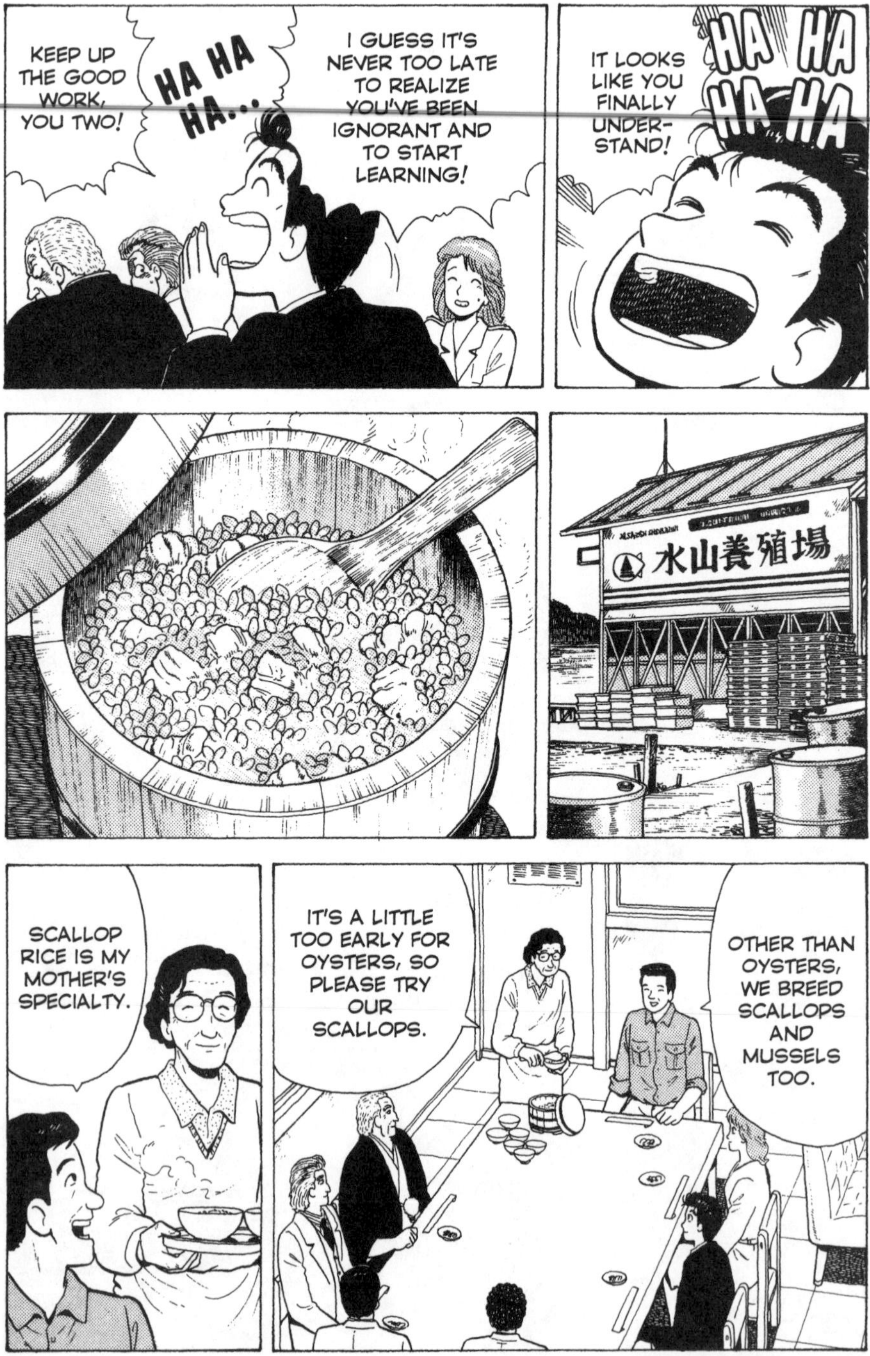
HA HA HA HA
IT LOOKS LIKE YOU FINALLY UNDERSTAND!
I GUESS IT'S NEVER TOO LATE TO REALIZE YOU'VE BEEN IGNORANT AND TO START LEARNING!
HA HA HA...
KEEP UP THE GOOD WORK, YOU TWO!
水山養殖場
OTHER THAN OYSTERS, WE BREED SCALLOPS AND MUSSELS TOO.
IT'S A LITTLE TOO EARLY FOR OYSTERS, SO PLEASE TRY OUR SCALLOPS.
SCALLOP RICE IS MY MOTHER'S SPECIALTY.

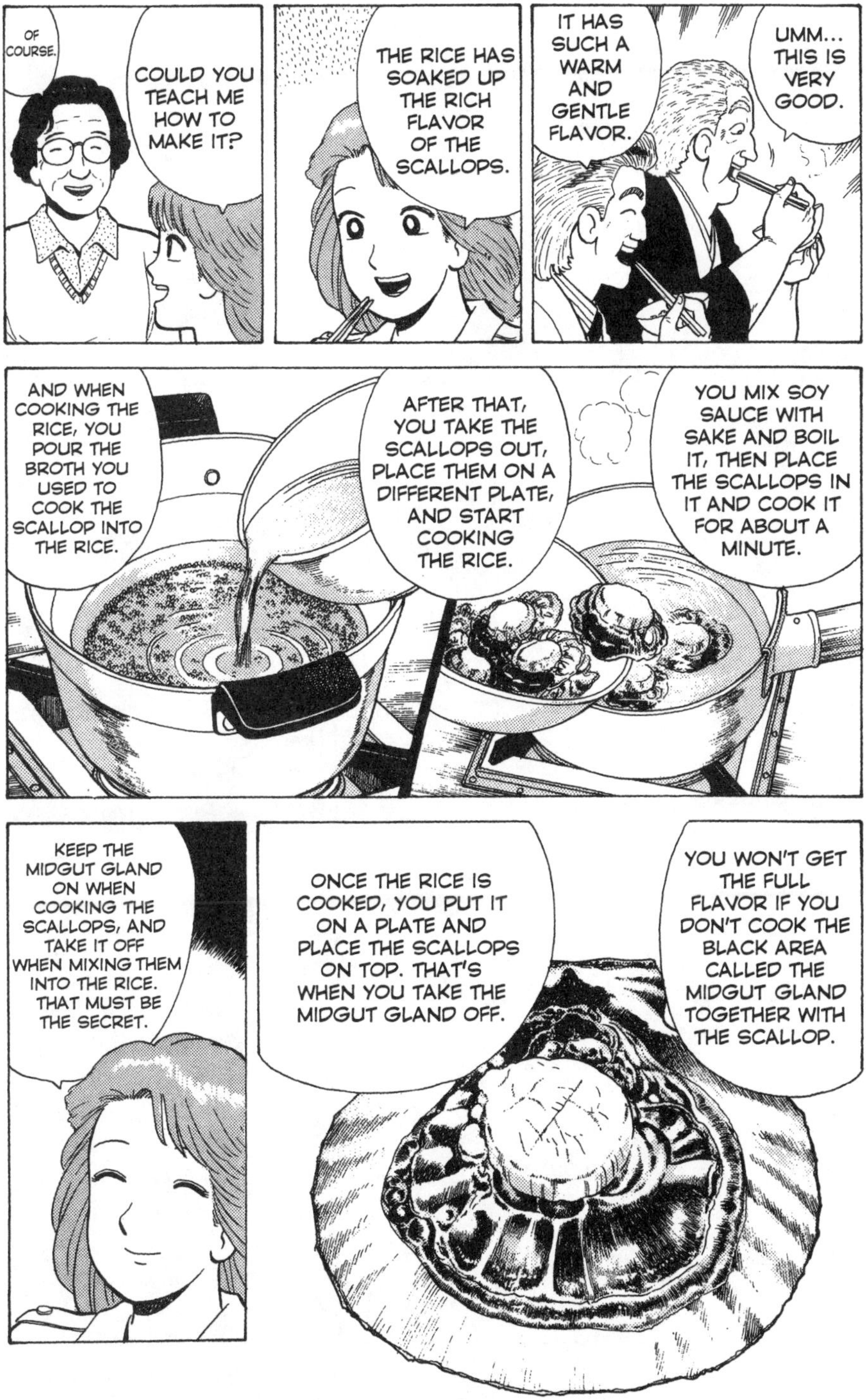
UMM... THIS IS VERY GOOD.
IT HAS SUCH A WARM AND GENTLE FLAVOR.
THE RICE HAS SOAKED UP THE RICH FLAVOR OF THE SCALLOPS.
COULD YOU TEACH ME HOW TO MAKE IT?
OF COURSE.
YOU MIX SOY SAUCE WITH SAKE AND BOIL IT, THEN PLACE THE SCALLOPS IN IT AND COOK IT FOR ABOUT A MINUTE.
AFTER THAT, YOU TAKE THE SCALLOPS OUT, PLACE THEM ON A DIFFERENT PLATE, AND START COOKING THE RICE.
AND WHEN COOKING THE RICE, YOU POUR THE BROTH YOU USED TO COOK THE SCALLOP INTO THE RICE.
YOU WON'T GET THE FULL FLAVOR IF YOU DON'T COOK THE BLACK AREA CALLED THE MIDGUT GLAND TOGETHER WITH THE SCALLOP.
ONCE THE RICE IS COOKED, YOU PUT IT ON A PLATE AND PLACE THE SCALLOPS ON TOP. THAT'S WHEN YOU TAKE THE MIDGUT GLAND OFF.
KEEP THE MIDGUT GLAND ON WHEN COOKING THE SCALLOPS, AND TAKE IT OFF WHEN MIXING THEM INTO THE RICE. THAT MUST BE THE SECRET.

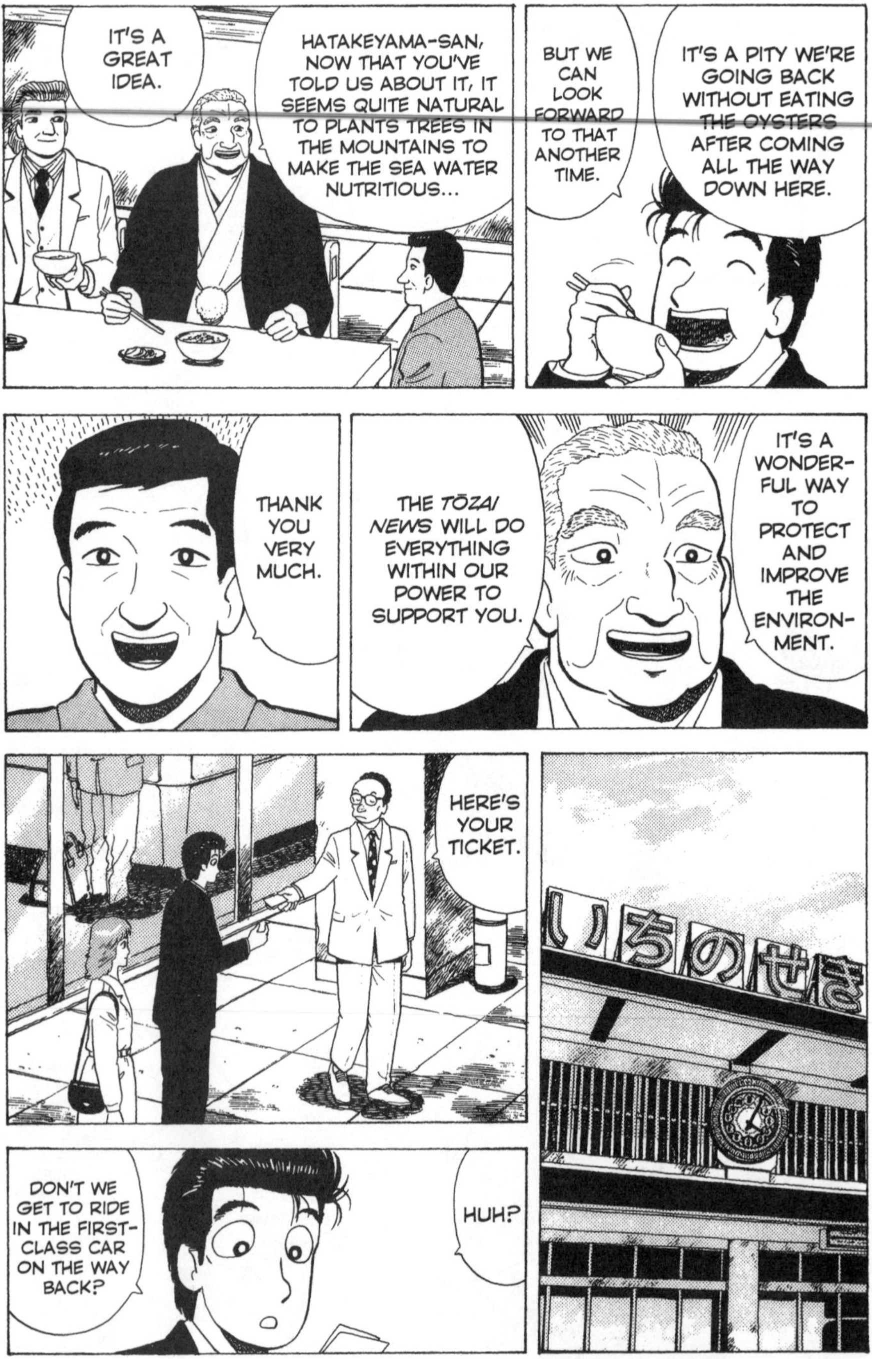
IT'S A PITY WE'RE GOING BACK WITHOUT EATING THE OYSTERS AFTER COMING ALL THE WAY DOWN HERE.
BUT WE CAN LOOK FORWARD TO THAT ANOTHER TIME.
HATAKEYAMA-SAN, NOW THAT YOU'VE TOLD US ABOUT IT, IT SEEMS QUITE NATURAL TO PLANTS TREES IN THE MOUNTAINS TO MAKE THE SEA WATER NUTRITIOUS...
IT'S A GREAT IDEA.
IT'S A WONDER-FUL WAY TO PROTECT AND IMPROVE THE ENVIRON-MENT.
THE *TŌZAI NEWS* WILL DO EVERYTHING WITHIN OUR POWER TO SUPPORT YOU.
THANK YOU VERY MUCH.
いちのせき
HERE'S YOUR TICKET.
HUH?
DON'T WE GET TO RIDE IN THE FIRST-CLASS CAR ON THE WAY BACK?

ON SIGN: ICHINOSEKI

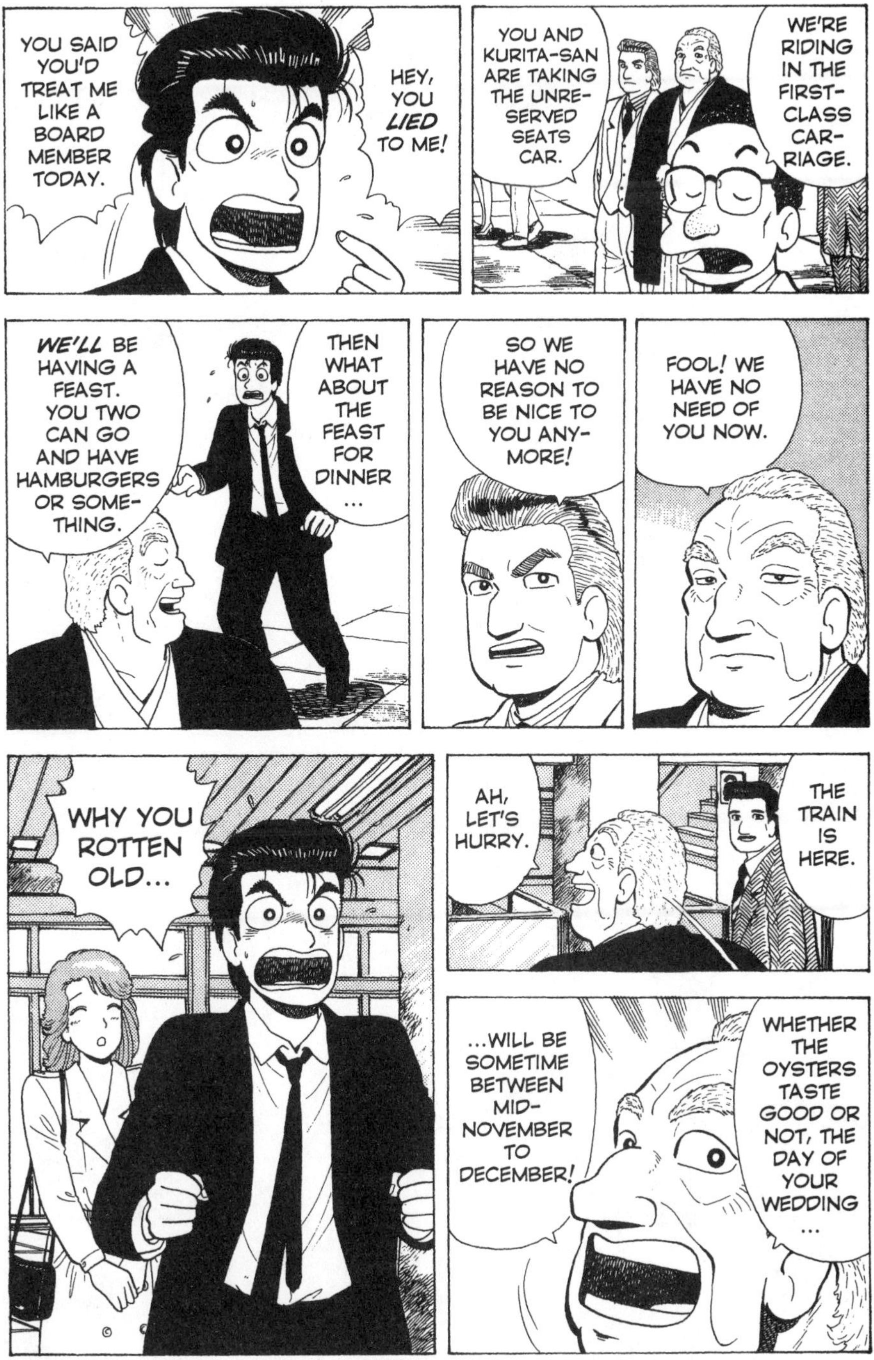
WE'RE RIDING IN THE FIRST-CLASS CAR-RIAGE.
YOU AND KURITA-SAN ARE TAKING THE UNRE-SERVED SEATS CAR.
HEY, YOU *LIED* TO ME!
YOU SAID YOU'D TREAT ME LIKE A BOARD MEMBER TODAY.
FOOL! WE HAVE NO NEED OF YOU NOW.
SO WE HAVE NO REASON TO BE NICE TO YOU ANY-MORE!
THEN WHAT ABOUT THE FEAST FOR DINNER ...
WE'LL BE HAVING A FEAST. YOU TWO CAN GO AND HAVE HAMBURGERS OR SOME-THING.
THE TRAIN IS HERE.
AH, LET'S HURRY.
WHETHER THE OYSTERS TASTE GOOD OR NOT, THE DAY OF YOUR WEDDING ...
...WILL BE SOMETIME BETWEEN MID-NOVEMBER TO DECEMBER!
WHY YOU ROTTEN OLD...

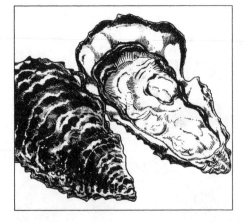

OISHINBO

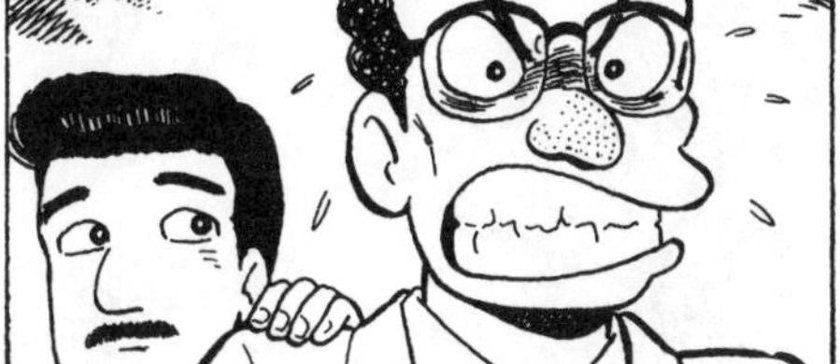

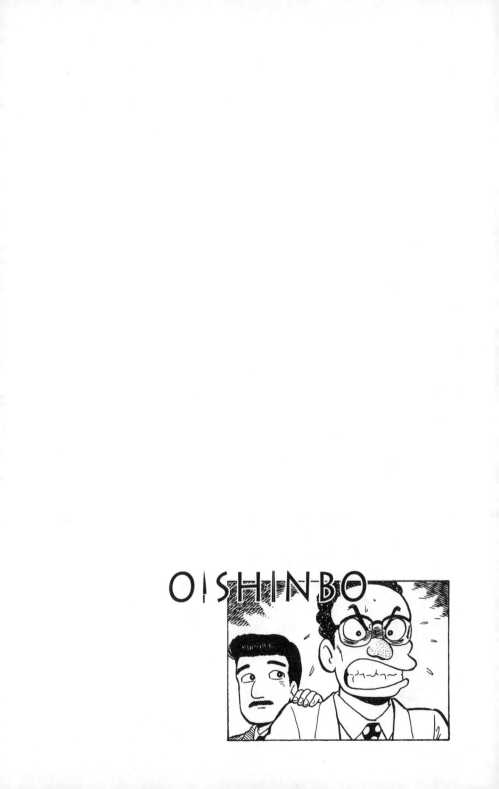

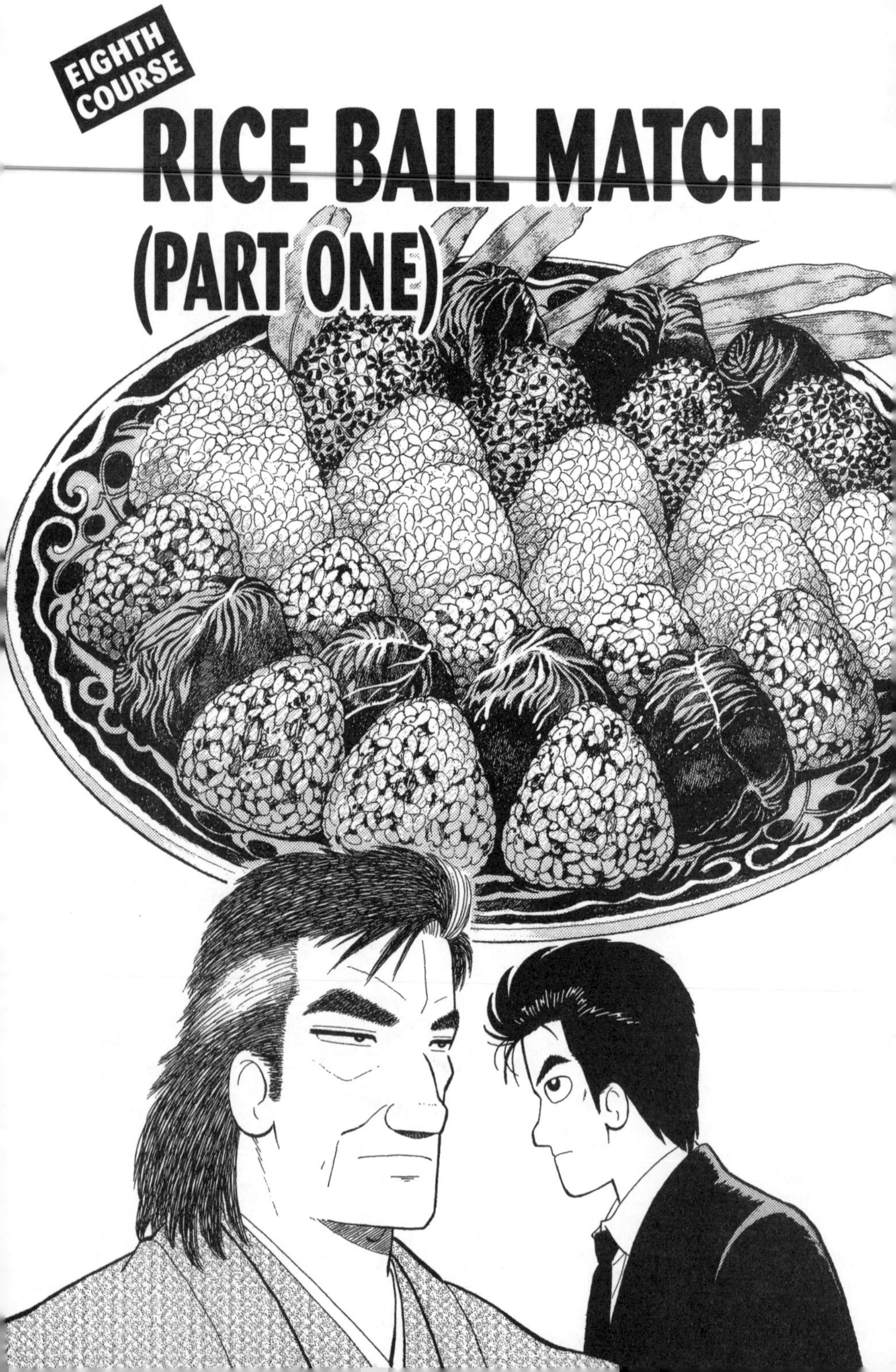
EIGHTH COURSE
RICE BALL MATCH
(PART ONE)

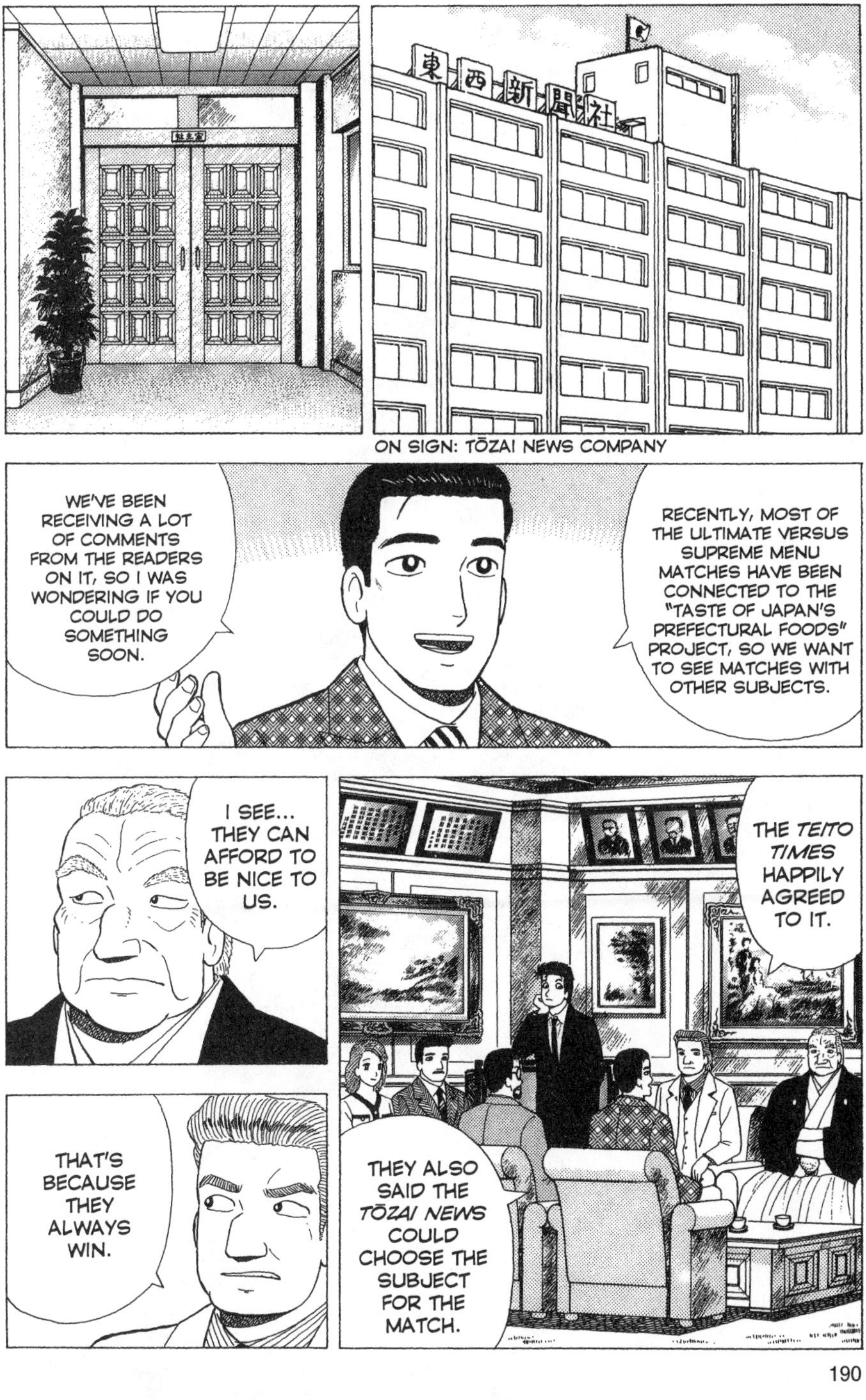
ON SIGN: TŌZAI NEWS COMPANY
RECENTLY, MOST OF THE ULTIMATE VERSUS SUPREME MENU MATCHES HAVE BEEN CONNECTED TO THE "TASTE OF JAPAN'S PREFECTURAL FOODS" PROJECT, SO WE WANT TO SEE MATCHES WITH OTHER SUBJECTS.
WE'VE BEEN RECEIVING A LOT OF COMMENTS FROM THE READERS ON IT, SO I WAS WONDERING IF YOU COULD DO SOMETHING SOON.
THE *TEITO TIMES* HAPPILY AGREED TO IT.
THEY ALSO SAID THE *TŌZAI NEWS* COULD CHOOSE THE SUBJECT FOR THE MATCH.
I SEE... THEY CAN AFFORD TO BE NICE TO US.
THAT'S BECAUSE THEY ALWAYS WIN.

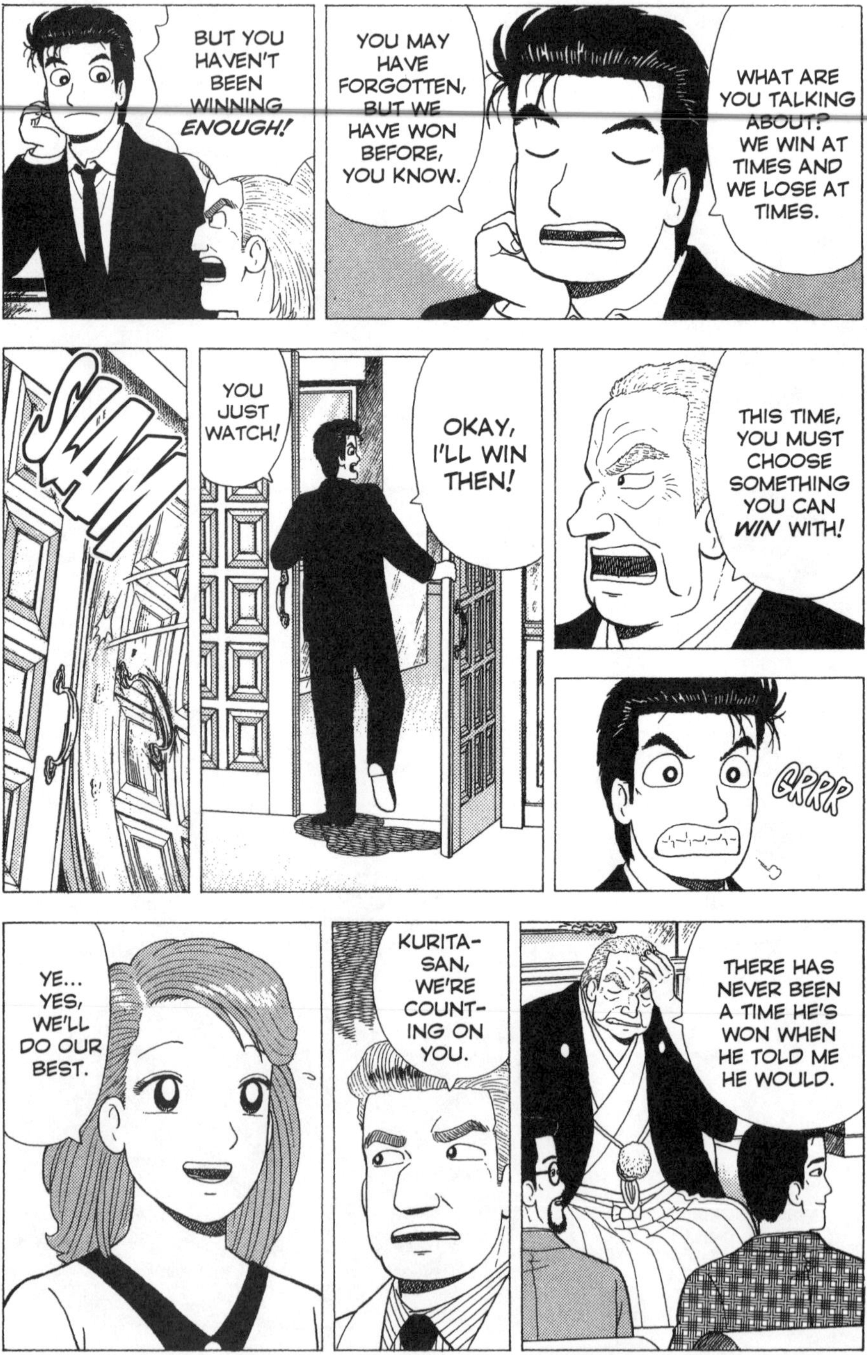
WHAT ARE YOU TALKING ABOUT? WE WIN AT TIMES AND WE LOSE AT TIMES.
YOU MAY HAVE FORGOTTEN, BUT WE HAVE WON BEFORE, YOU KNOW.
BUT YOU HAVEN'T BEEN WINNING *ENOUGH!*
THIS TIME, YOU MUST CHOOSE SOMETHING YOU CAN *WIN* WITH!
GRRR
OKAY, I'LL WIN THEN!
YOU JUST WATCH!
SLAM
THERE HAS NEVER BEEN A TIME HE'S WON WHEN HE TOLD ME HE WOULD.
KURITA-SAN, WE'RE COUNTING ON YOU.
YE... YES, WE'LL DO OUR BEST.

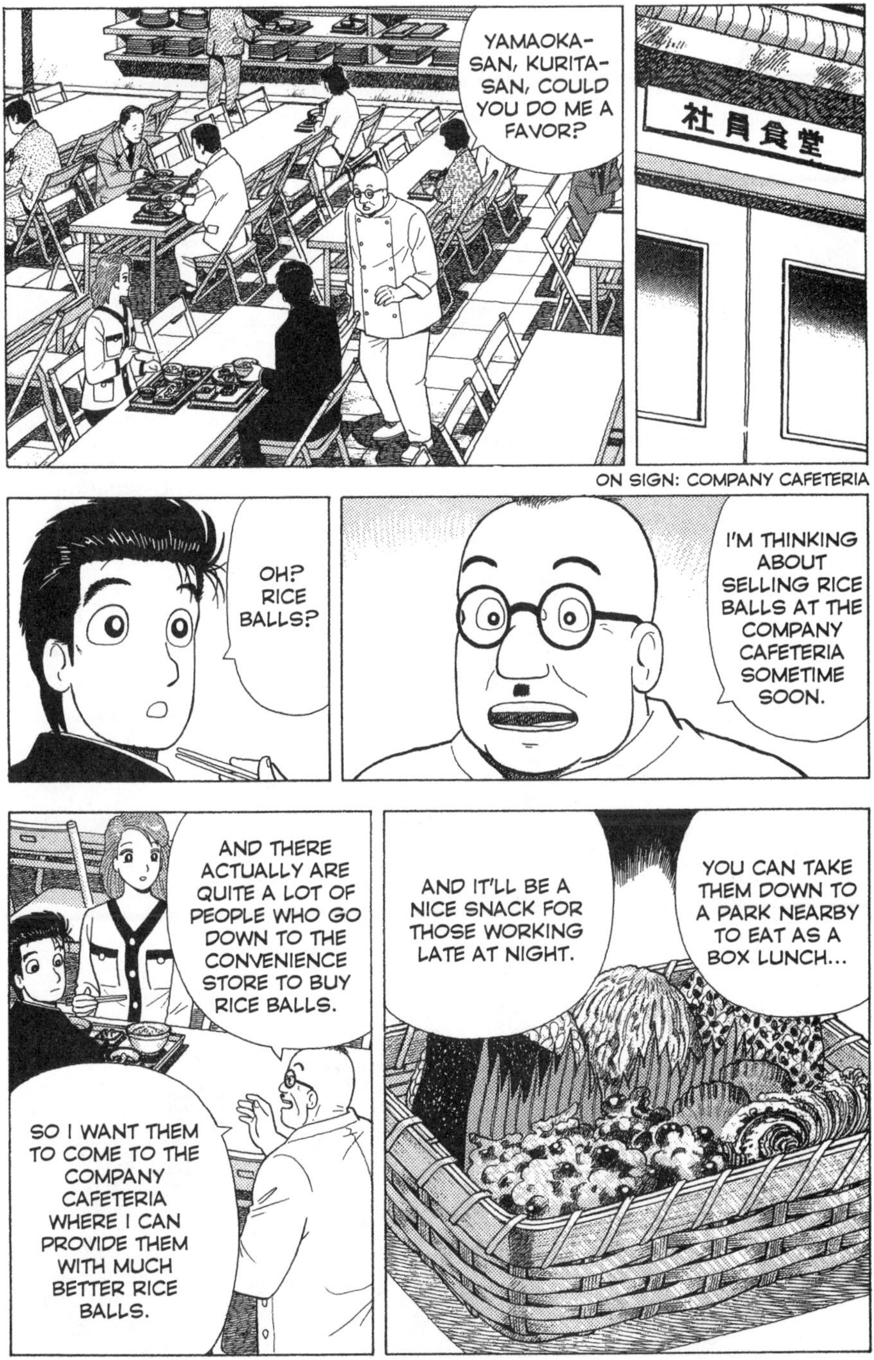
社員食堂
ON SIGN: COMPANY CAFETERIA
YAMAOKA-SAN, KURITA-SAN, COULD YOU DO ME A FAVOR?
I'M THINKING ABOUT SELLING RICE BALLS AT THE COMPANY CAFETERIA SOMETIME SOON.
OH? RICE BALLS?
YOU CAN TAKE THEM DOWN TO A PARK NEARBY TO EAT AS A BOX LUNCH...
AND IT'LL BE A NICE SNACK FOR THOSE WORKING LATE AT NIGHT.
AND THERE ACTUALLY ARE QUITE A LOT OF PEOPLE WHO GO DOWN TO THE CONVENIENCE STORE TO BUY RICE BALLS.
SO I WANT THEM TO COME TO THE COMPANY CAFETERIA WHERE I CAN PROVIDE THEM WITH MUCH BETTER RICE BALLS.

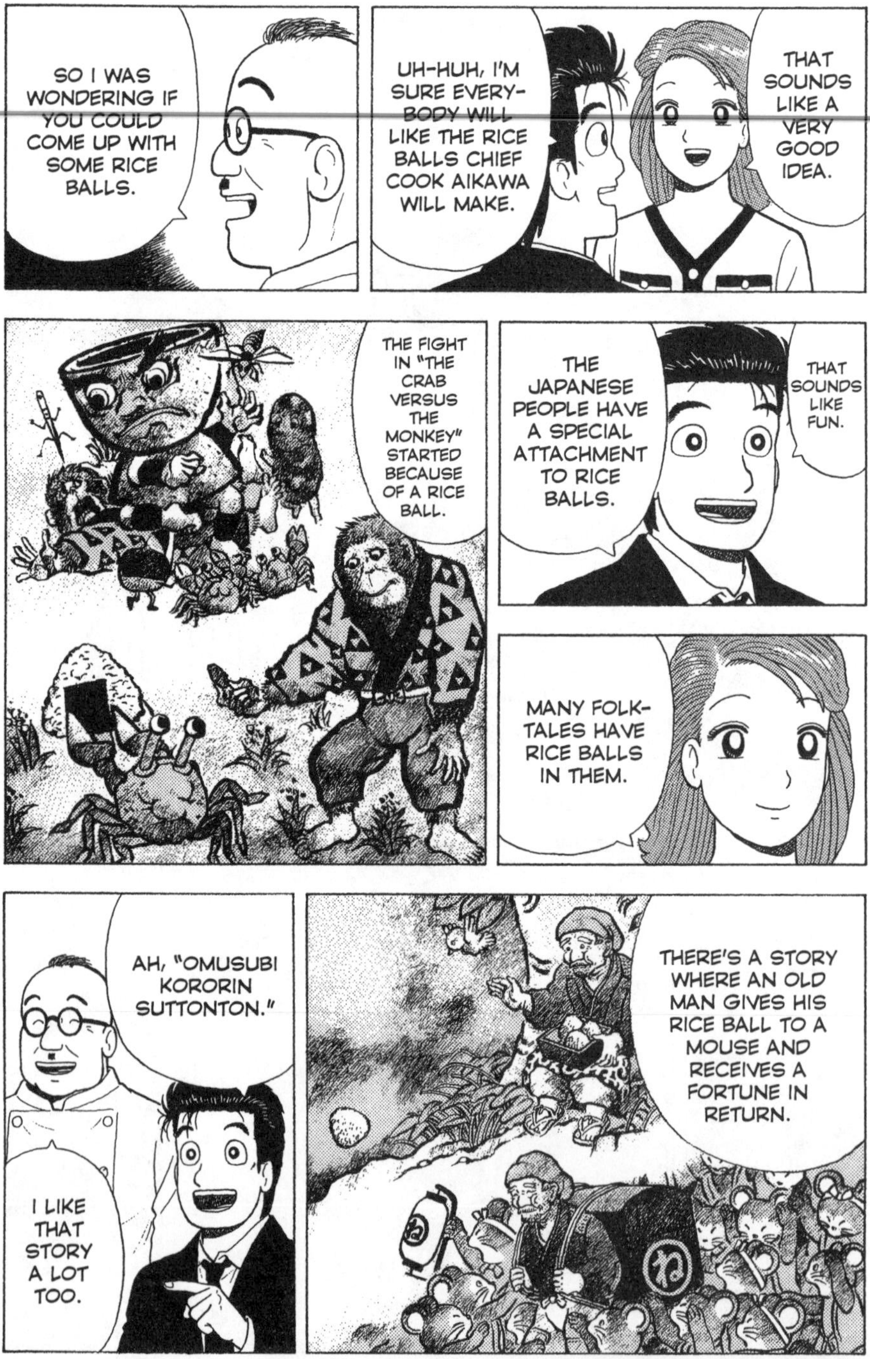
THAT SOUNDS LIKE A VERY GOOD IDEA.
UH-HUH, I'M SURE EVERY-BODY WILL LIKE THE RICE BALLS CHIEF COOK AIKAWA WILL MAKE.
SO I WAS WONDERING IF YOU COULD COME UP WITH SOME RICE BALLS.
THAT SOUNDS LIKE FUN.
THE JAPANESE PEOPLE HAVE A SPECIAL ATTACHMENT TO RICE BALLS.
MANY FOLK-TALES HAVE RICE BALLS IN THEM.
THE FIGHT IN "THE CRAB VERSUS THE MONKEY" STARTED BECAUSE OF A RICE BALL.
THERE'S A STORY WHERE AN OLD MAN GIVES HIS RICE BALL TO A MOUSE AND RECEIVES A FORTUNE IN RETURN.
AH, "OMUSUBI KORORIN SUTTONTON."
I LIKE THAT STORY A LOT TOO.
PICTURE: SHIMIZU KOZO, "THE CRAB VERSUS THE MONKEY" / FAMOUS JAPANESE FOLKTALES FOR THE MOTHER AND CHILD, VOL. 1 (SHOGAKUKAN)

PICTURE: SHIMIZU KOZO, "OMUSUBI KORORIN" / FAMOUS JAPANESE FOLKTALES FOR THE MOTHER AND CHILD, VOL. 1 (SHOGAKUKAN)

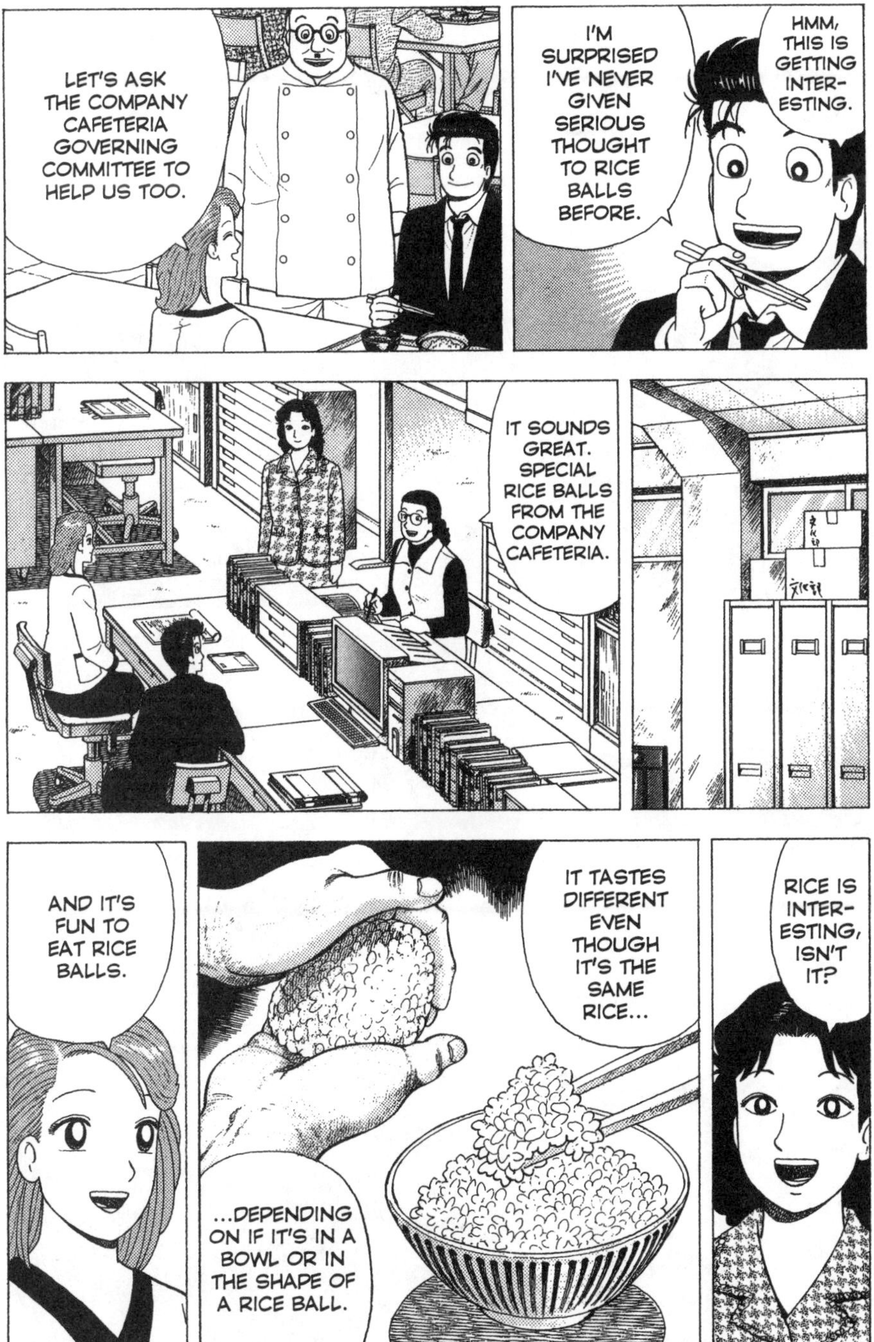
HMM, THIS IS GETTING INTER-ESTING.
I'M SURPRISED I'VE NEVER GIVEN SERIOUS THOUGHT TO RICE BALLS BEFORE.
LET'S ASK THE COMPANY CAFETERIA GOVERNING COMMITTEE TO HELP US TOO.
IT SOUNDS GREAT. SPECIAL RICE BALLS FROM THE COMPANY CAFETERIA.
RICE IS INTER-ESTING, ISN'T IT?
IT TASTES DIFFERENT EVEN THOUGH IT'S THE SAME RICE...
...DEPENDING ON IF IT'S IN A BOWL OR IN THE SHAPE OF A RICE BALL.
AND IT'S FUN TO EAT RICE BALLS.

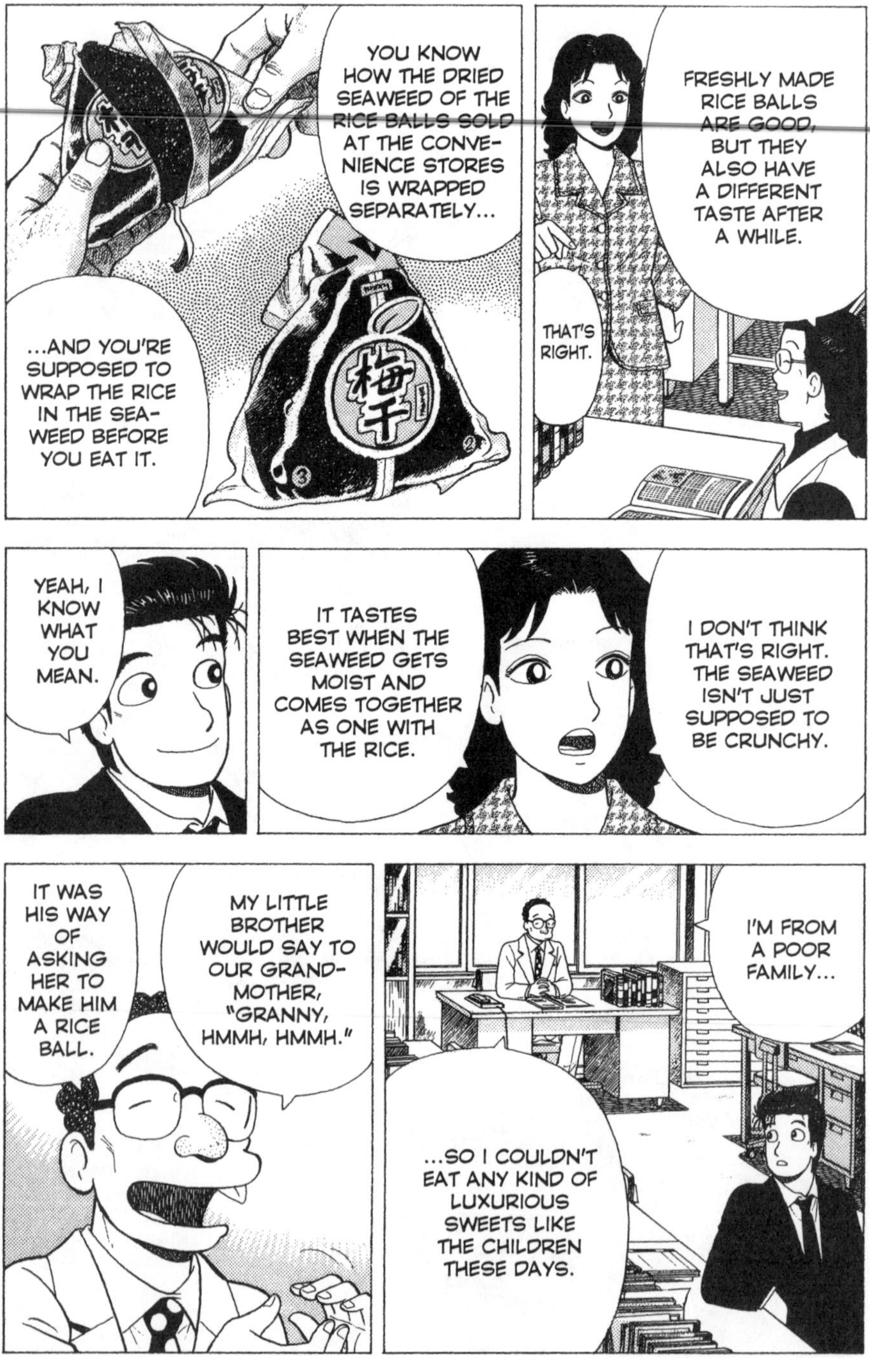
FRESHLY MADE RICE BALLS ARE GOOD, BUT THEY ALSO HAVE A DIFFERENT TASTE AFTER A WHILE.
THAT'S RIGHT.
YOU KNOW HOW THE DRIED SEAWEED OF THE RICE BALLS SOLD AT THE CONVENIENCE STORES IS WRAPPED SEPARATELY...
梅干
...AND YOU'RE SUPPOSED TO WRAP THE RICE IN THE SEAWEED BEFORE YOU EAT IT.
I DON'T THINK THAT'S RIGHT. THE SEAWEED ISN'T JUST SUPPOSED TO BE CRUNCHY.
IT TASTES BEST WHEN THE SEAWEED GETS MOIST AND COMES TOGETHER AS ONE WITH THE RICE.
YEAH, I KNOW WHAT YOU MEAN.
I'M FROM A POOR FAMILY...
...SO I COULDN'T EAT ANY KIND OF LUXURIOUS SWEETS LIKE THE CHILDREN THESE DAYS.
MY LITTLE BROTHER WOULD SAY TO OUR GRANDMOTHER, "GRANNY, HMMH, HMMH."
IT WAS HIS WAY OF ASKING HER TO MAKE HIM A RICE BALL.

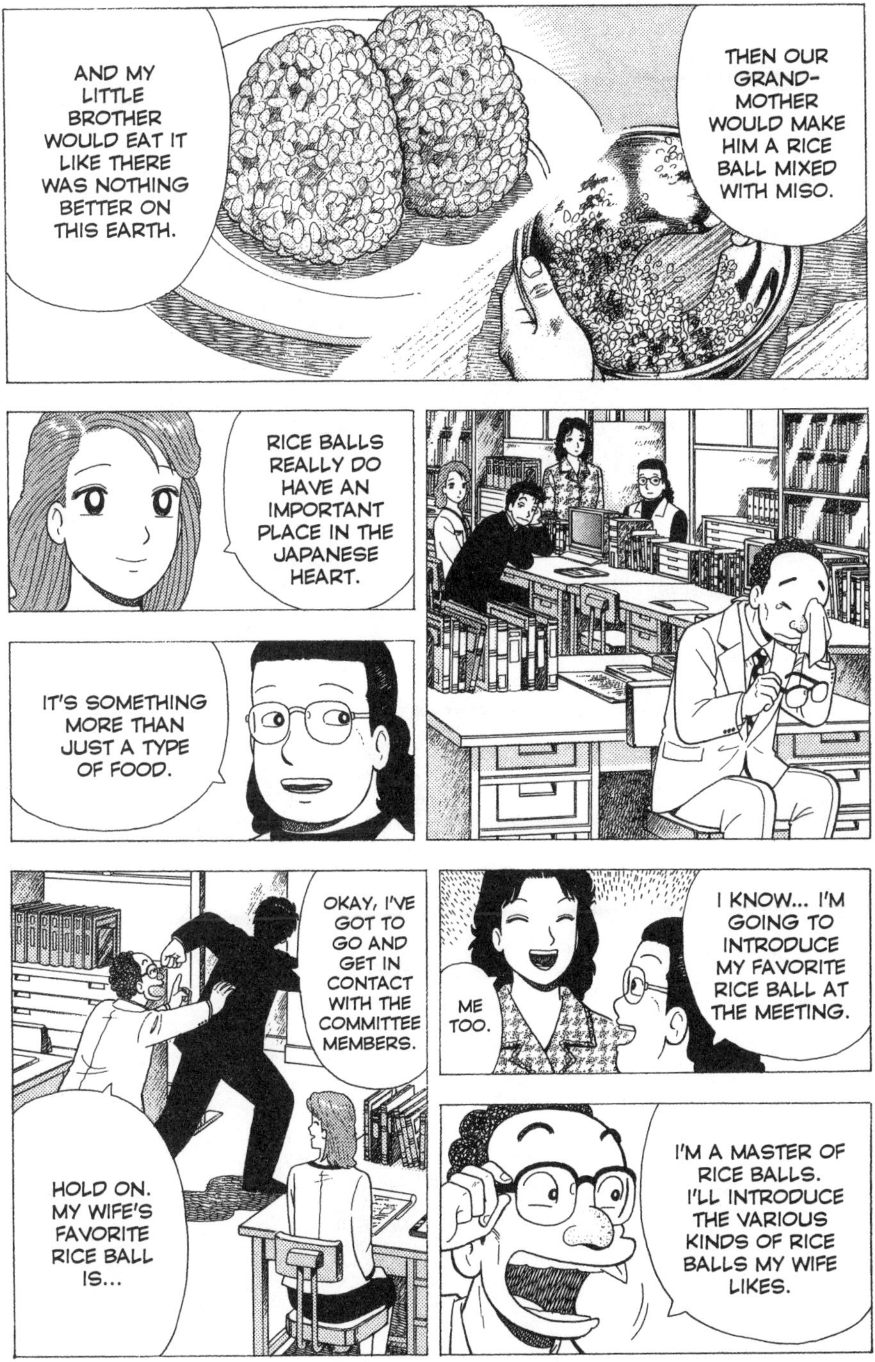
THEN OUR GRAND-MOTHER WOULD MAKE HIM A RICE BALL MIXED WITH MISO.
AND MY LITTLE BROTHER WOULD EAT IT LIKE THERE WAS NOTHING BETTER ON THIS EARTH.
RICE BALLS REALLY DO HAVE AN IMPORTANT PLACE IN THE JAPANESE HEART.
IT'S SOMETHING MORE THAN JUST A TYPE OF FOOD.
I KNOW... I'M GOING TO INTRODUCE MY FAVORITE RICE BALL AT THE MEETING.
ME TOO.
I'M A MASTER OF RICE BALLS. I'LL INTRODUCE THE VARIOUS KINDS OF RICE BALLS MY WIFE LIKES.
OKAY, I'VE GOT TO GO AND GET IN CONTACT WITH THE COMMITTEE MEMBERS.
HOLD ON. MY WIFE'S FAVORITE RICE BALL IS...

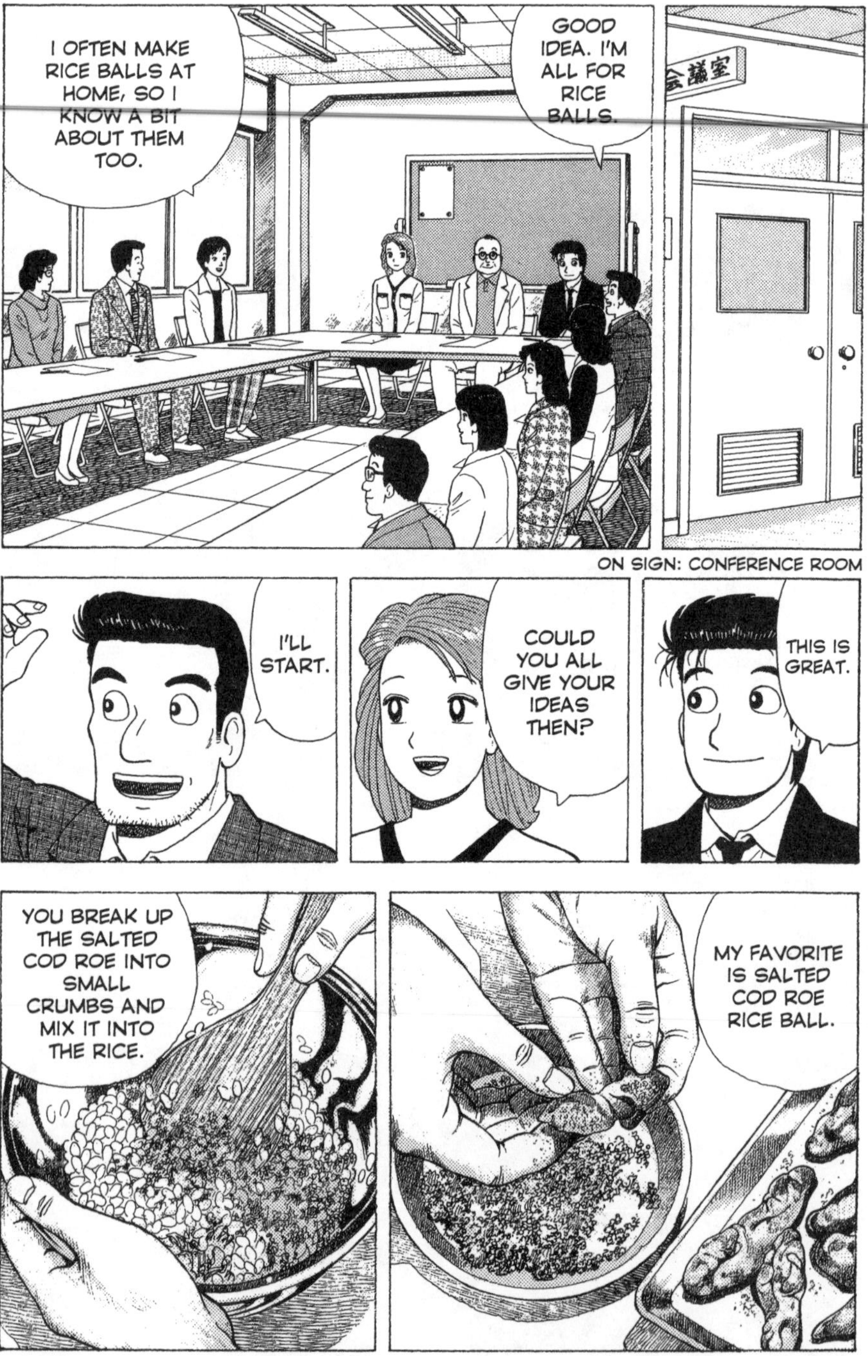
ON SIGN: CONFERENCE ROOM
GOOD IDEA. I'M ALL FOR RICE BALLS.
I OFTEN MAKE RICE BALLS AT HOME, SO I KNOW A BIT ABOUT THEM TOO.
THIS IS GREAT.
COULD YOU ALL GIVE YOUR IDEAS THEN?
I'LL START.
MY FAVORITE IS SALTED COD ROE RICE BALL.
YOU BREAK UP THE SALTED COD ROE INTO SMALL CRUMBS AND MIX IT INTO THE RICE.

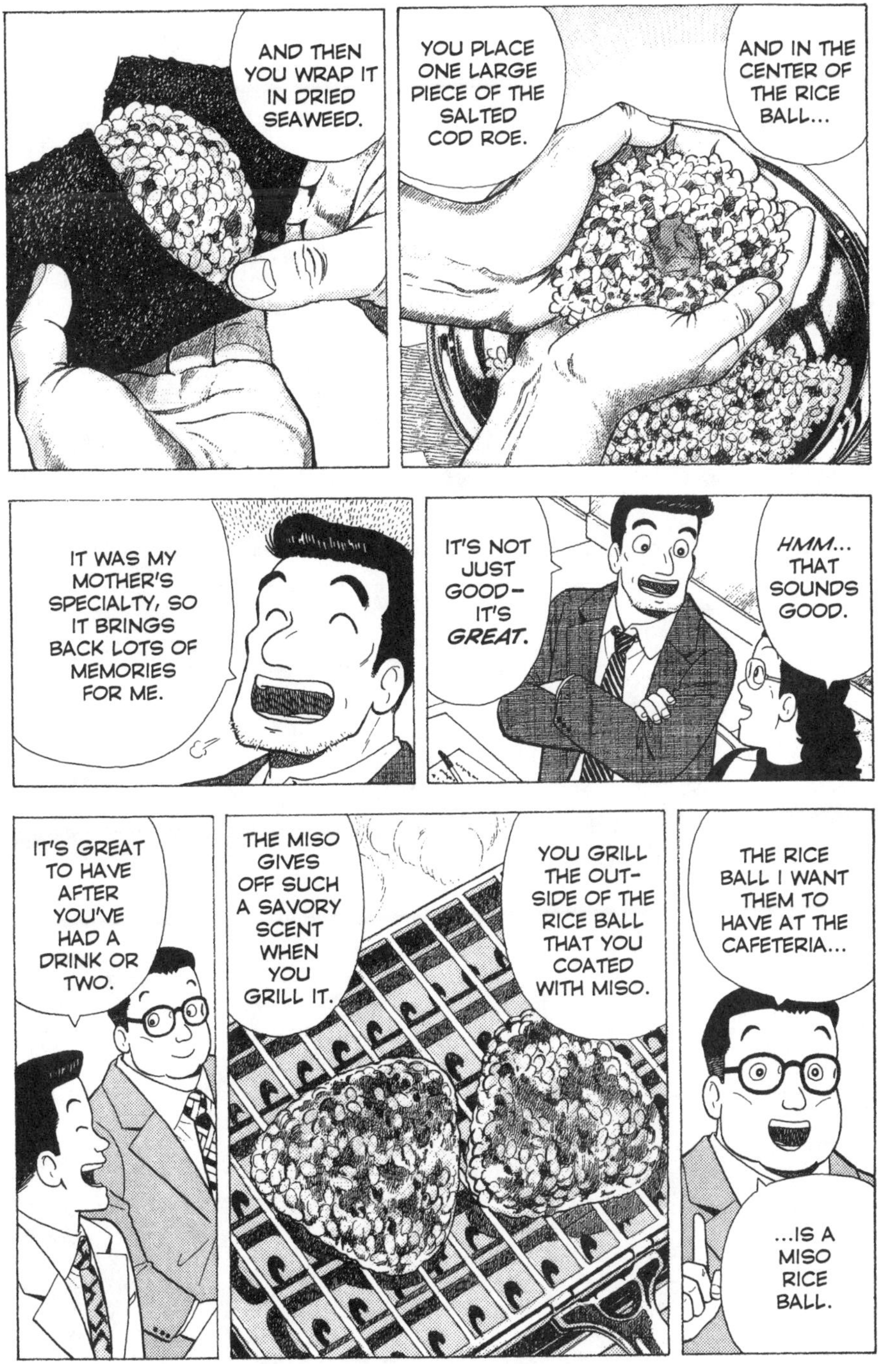
AND IN THE CENTER OF THE RICE BALL...
YOU PLACE ONE LARGE PIECE OF THE SALTED COD ROE.
AND THEN YOU WRAP IT IN DRIED SEAWEED.
HMM... THAT SOUNDS GOOD.
IT'S NOT JUST GOOD—IT'S *GREAT*.
IT WAS MY MOTHER'S SPECIALTY, SO IT BRINGS BACK LOTS OF MEMORIES FOR ME.
THE RICE BALL I WANT THEM TO HAVE AT THE CAFETERIA...
...IS A MISO RICE BALL.
YOU GRILL THE OUT-SIDE OF THE RICE BALL THAT YOU COATED WITH MISO.
THE MISO GIVES OFF SUCH A SAVORY SCENT WHEN YOU GRILL IT.
IT'S GREAT TO HAVE AFTER YOU'VE HAD A DRINK OR TWO.

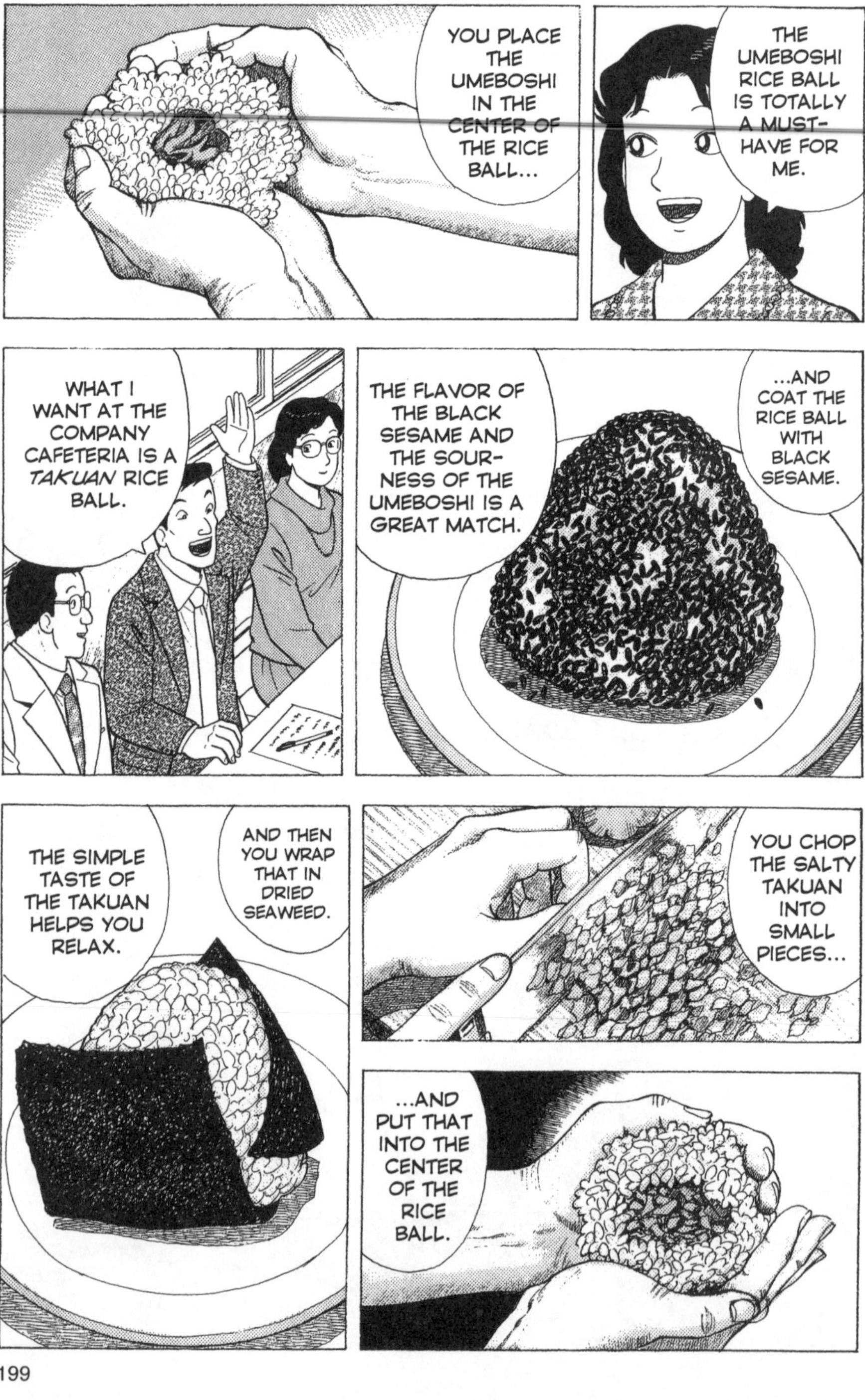
THE UMEBOSHI RICE BALL IS TOTALLY A MUST-HAVE FOR ME.
YOU PLACE THE UMEBOSHI IN THE CENTER OF THE RICE BALL...
...AND COAT THE RICE BALL WITH BLACK SESAME.
THE FLAVOR OF THE BLACK SESAME AND THE SOURNESS OF THE UMEBOSHI IS A GREAT MATCH.
WHAT I WANT AT THE COMPANY CAFETERIA IS A *TAKUAN* RICE BALL.
YOU CHOP THE SALTY TAKUAN INTO SMALL PIECES...
...AND PUT THAT INTO THE CENTER OF THE RICE BALL.
AND THEN YOU WRAP THAT IN DRIED SEAWEED.
THE SIMPLE TASTE OF THE TAKUAN HELPS YOU RELAX.

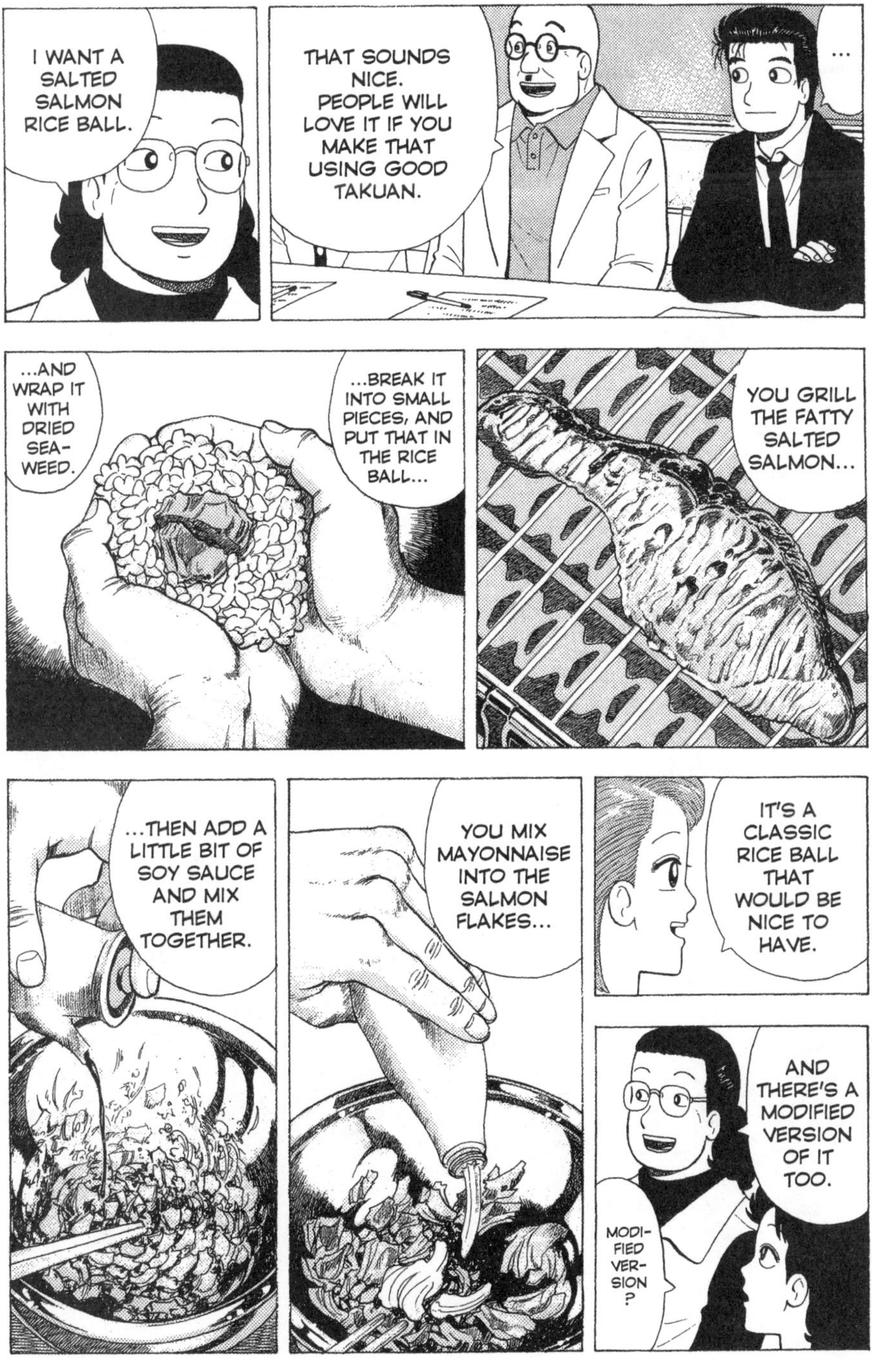
...
THAT SOUNDS NICE. PEOPLE WILL LOVE IT IF YOU MAKE THAT USING GOOD TAKUAN.
I WANT A SALTED SALMON RICE BALL.
YOU GRILL THE FATTY SALTED SALMON...
...BREAK IT INTO SMALL PIECES, AND PUT THAT IN THE RICE BALL...
...AND WRAP IT WITH DRIED SEA-WEED.
IT'S A CLASSIC RICE BALL THAT WOULD BE NICE TO HAVE.
AND THERE'S A MODIFIED VERSION OF IT TOO.
MODI-FIED VER-SION ?
YOU MIX MAYONNAISE INTO THE SALMON FLAKES...
...THEN ADD A LITTLE BIT OF SOY SAUCE AND MIX THEM TOGETHER.

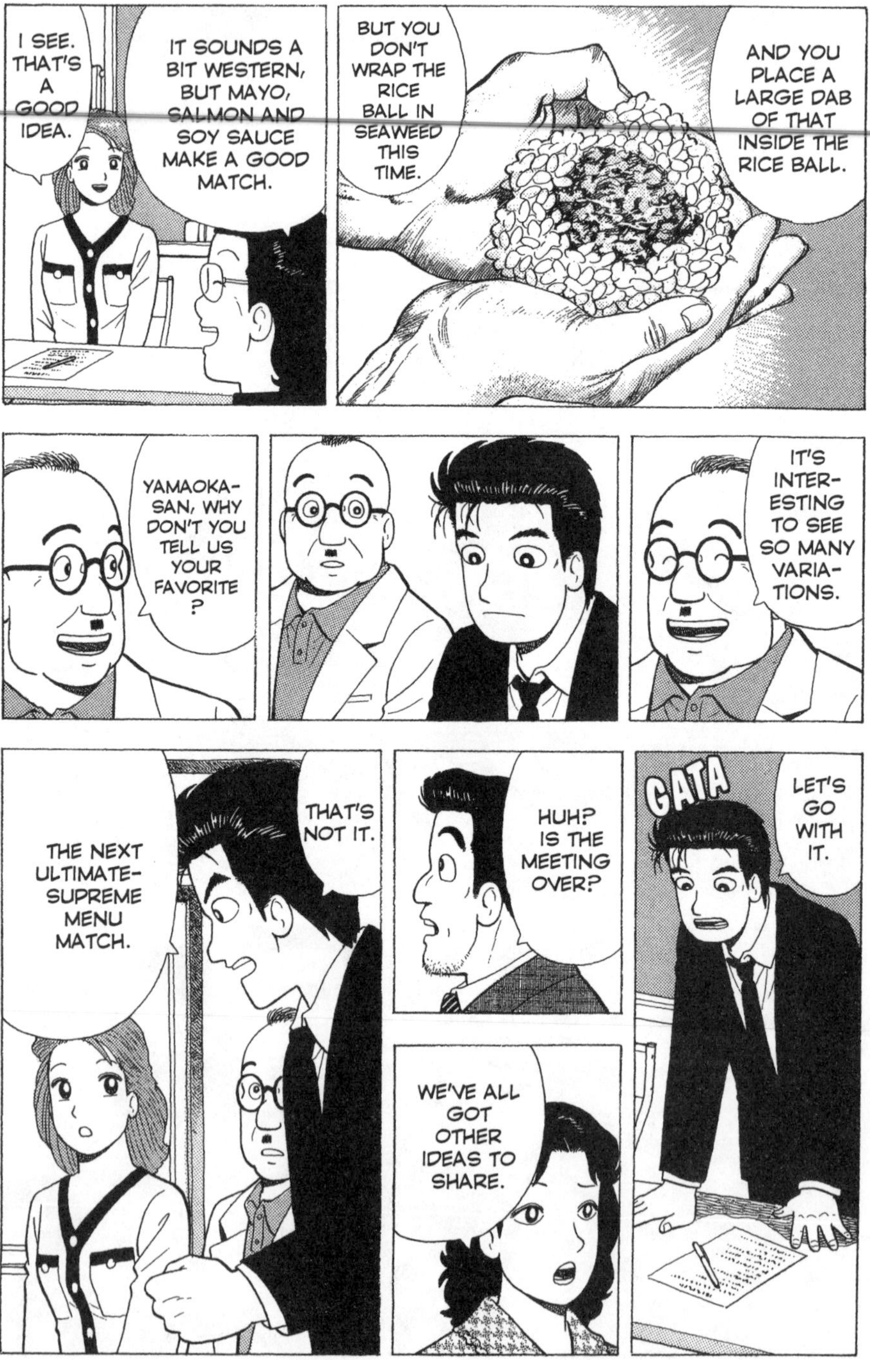
AND YOU PLACE A LARGE DAB OF THAT INSIDE THE RICE BALL.
BUT YOU DON'T WRAP THE RICE BALL IN SEAWEED THIS TIME.
IT SOUNDS A BIT WESTERN, BUT MAYO, SALMON AND SOY SAUCE MAKE A GOOD MATCH.
I SEE. THAT'S A GOOD IDEA.
IT'S INTER-ESTING TO SEE SO MANY VARIA-TIONS.
YAMAOKA-SAN, WHY DON'T YOU TELL US YOUR FAVORITE ?
GATA
LET'S GO WITH IT.
HUH? IS THE MEETING OVER?
WE'VE ALL GOT OTHER IDEAS TO SHARE.
THAT'S NOT IT.
THE NEXT ULTIMATE-SUPREME MENU MATCH.

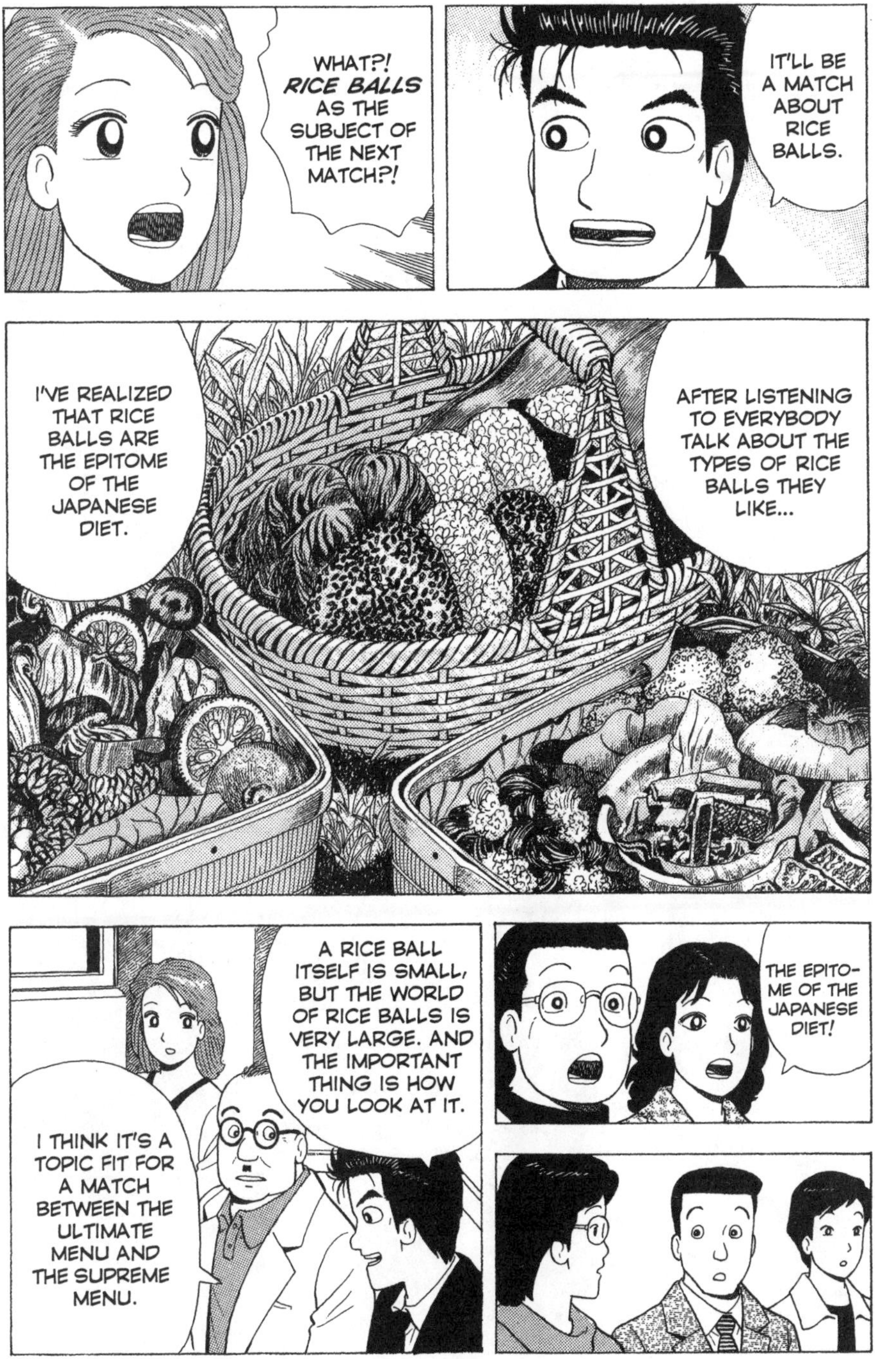
IT'LL BE A MATCH ABOUT RICE BALLS.
WHAT?! *RICE BALLS* AS THE SUBJECT OF THE NEXT MATCH?!
AFTER LISTENING TO EVERYBODY TALK ABOUT THE TYPES OF RICE BALLS THEY LIKE...
I'VE REALIZED THAT RICE BALLS ARE THE EPITOME OF THE JAPANESE DIET.
THE EPITO-ME OF THE JAPANESE DIET!
A RICE BALL ITSELF IS SMALL, BUT THE WORLD OF RICE BALLS IS VERY LARGE. AND THE IMPORTANT THING IS HOW YOU LOOK AT IT.
I THINK IT'S A TOPIC FIT FOR A MATCH BETWEEN THE ULTIMATE MENU AND THE SUPREME MENU.

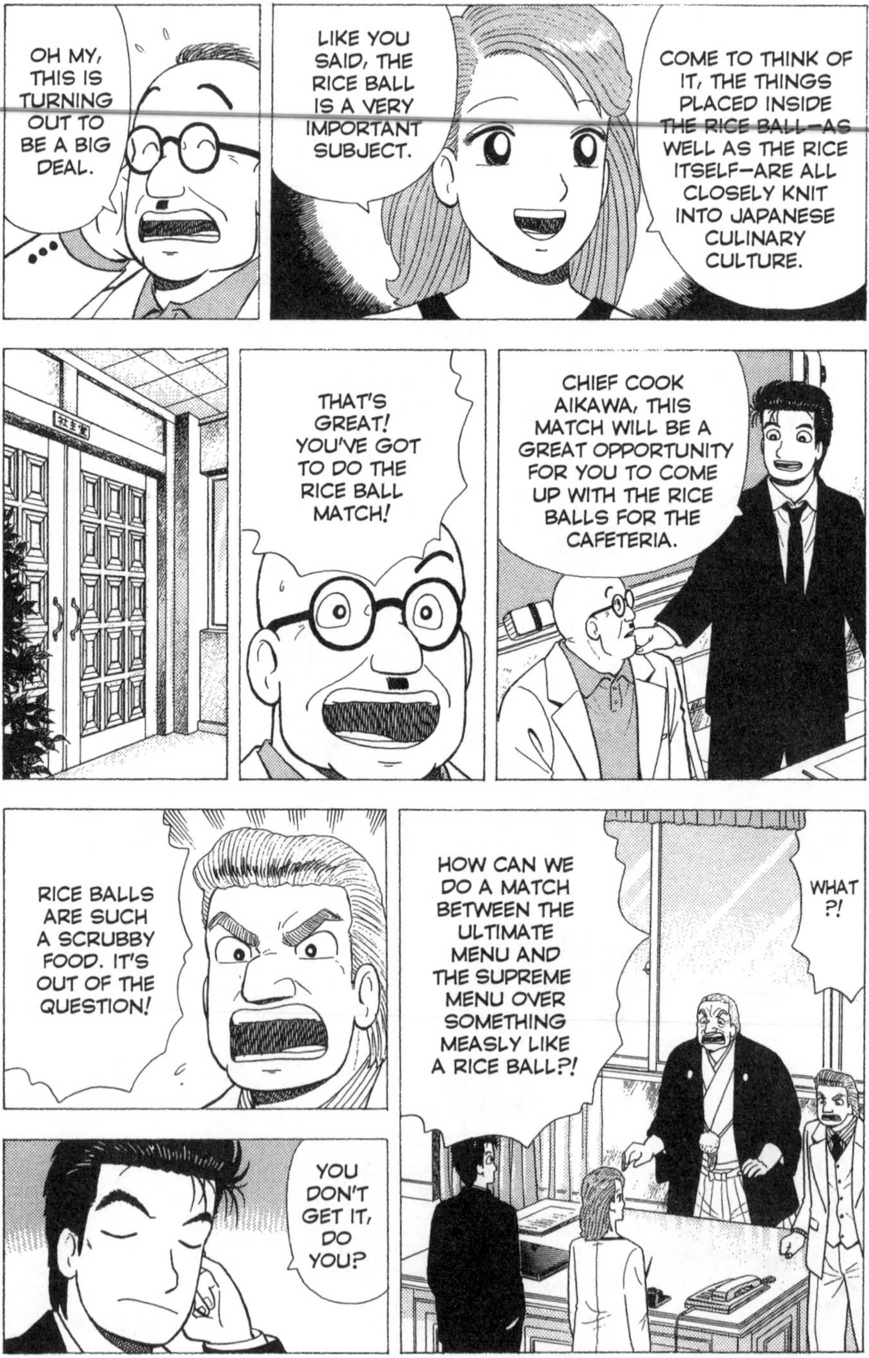
LIKE YOU SAID, THE RICE BALL IS A VERY IMPORTANT SUBJECT.
COME TO THINK OF IT, THE THINGS PLACED INSIDE THE RICE BALL—AS WELL AS THE RICE ITSELF—ARE ALL CLOSELY KNIT INTO JAPANESE CULINARY CULTURE.
OH MY, THIS IS TURNING OUT TO BE A BIG DEAL.
CHIEF COOK AIKAWA, THIS MATCH WILL BE A GREAT OPPORTUNITY FOR YOU TO COME UP WITH THE RICE BALLS FOR THE CAFETERIA.
THAT'S GREAT! YOU'VE GOT TO DO THE RICE BALL MATCH!
WHAT ?!
HOW CAN WE DO A MATCH BETWEEN THE ULTIMATE MENU AND THE SUPREME MENU OVER SOMETHING MEASLY LIKE A RICE BALL?!
RICE BALLS ARE SUCH A SCRUBBY FOOD. IT'S OUT OF THE QUESTION!
YOU DON'T GET IT, DO YOU?

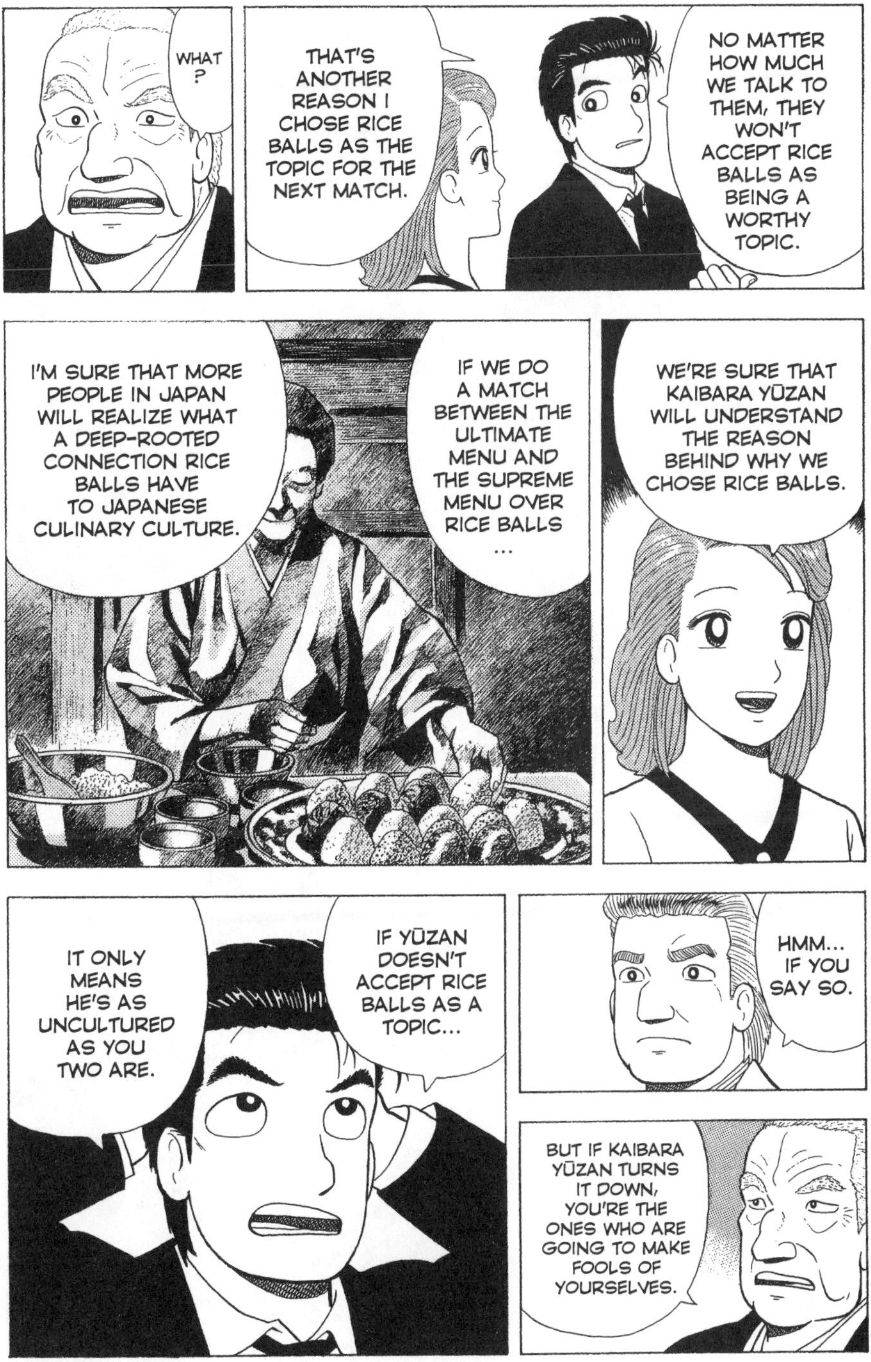
NO MATTER HOW MUCH WE TALK TO THEM, THEY WON'T ACCEPT RICE BALLS AS BEING A WORTHY TOPIC.
THAT'S ANOTHER REASON I CHOSE RICE BALLS AS THE TOPIC FOR THE NEXT MATCH.
WHAT?
WE'RE SURE THAT KAIBARA YŪZAN WILL UNDERSTAND THE REASON BEHIND WHY WE CHOSE RICE BALLS.
IF WE DO A MATCH BETWEEN THE ULTIMATE MENU AND THE SUPREME MENU OVER RICE BALLS ...
I'M SURE THAT MORE PEOPLE IN JAPAN WILL REALIZE WHAT A DEEP-ROOTED CONNECTION RICE BALLS HAVE TO JAPANESE CULINARY CULTURE.
HMM... IF YOU SAY SO.
BUT IF KAIBARA YŪZAN TURNS IT DOWN, YOU'RE THE ONES WHO ARE GOING TO MAKE FOOLS OF YOURSELVES.
IF YŪZAN DOESN'T ACCEPT RICE BALLS AS A TOPIC...
IT ONLY MEANS HE'S AS UNCULTURED AS YOU TWO ARE.

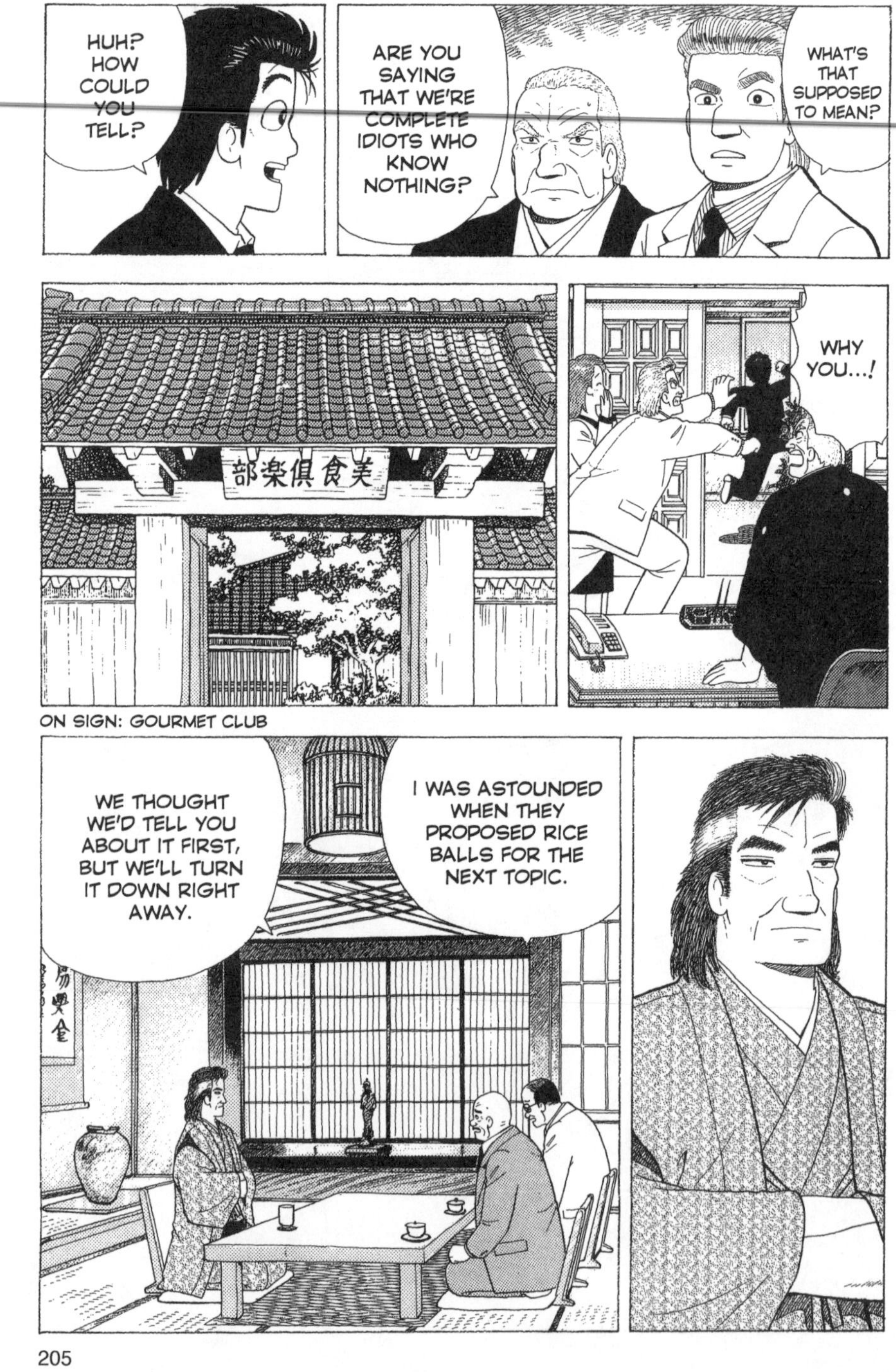
WHAT'S THAT SUPPOSED TO MEAN?
ARE YOU SAYING THAT WE'RE COMPLETE IDIOTS WHO KNOW NOTHING?
HUH? HOW COULD YOU TELL?
WHY YOU...!
美食倶楽部
I WAS ASTOUNDED WHEN THEY PROPOSED RICE BALLS FOR THE NEXT TOPIC.
WE THOUGHT WE'D TELL YOU ABOUT IT FIRST, BUT WE'LL TURN IT DOWN RIGHT AWAY.

ON SIGN: GOURMET CLUB

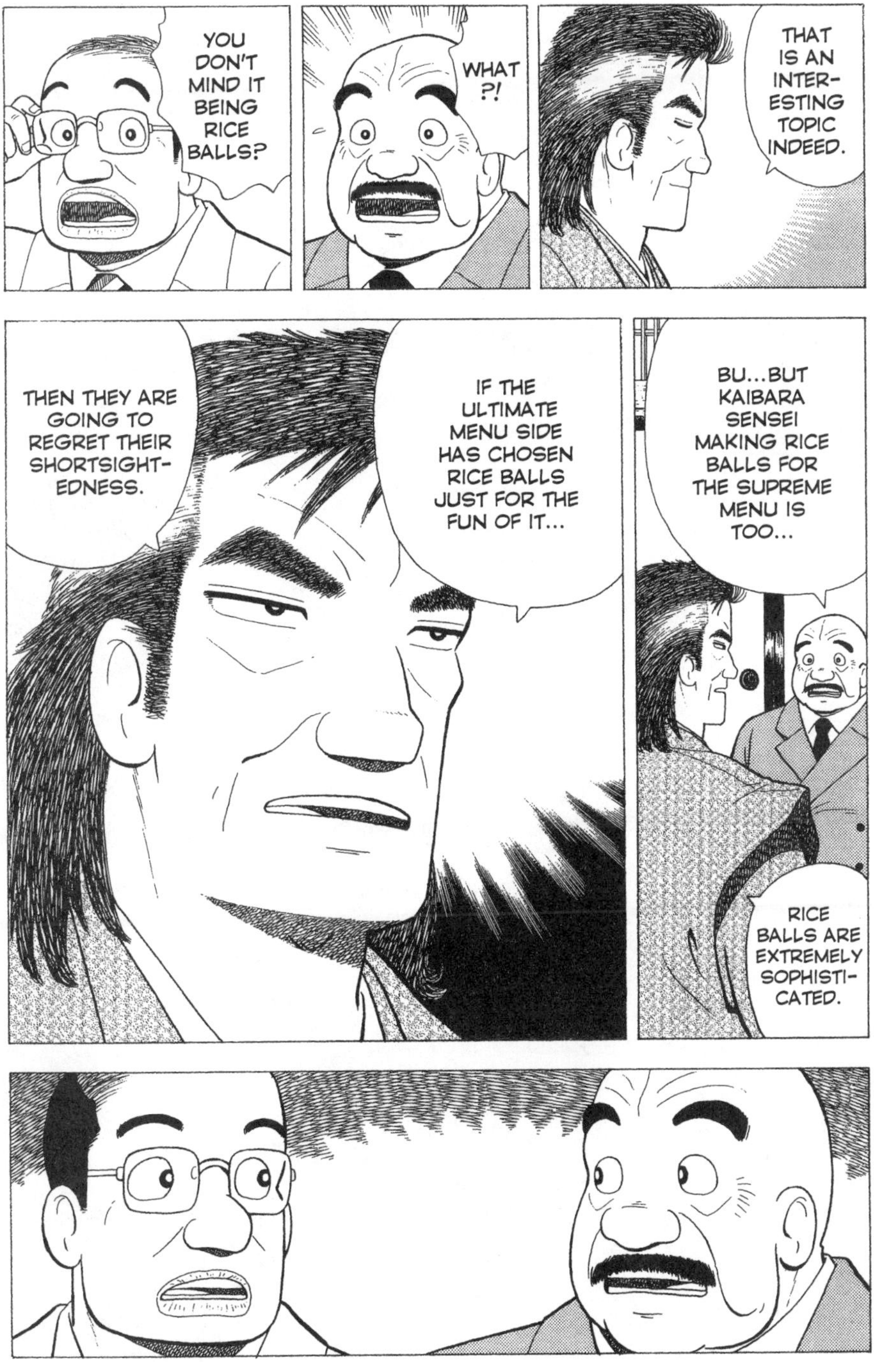
THAT IS AN INTERESTING TOPIC INDEED.
WHAT?!
YOU DON'T MIND IT BEING RICE BALLS?
BU...BUT KAIBARA SENSEI MAKING RICE BALLS FOR THE SUPREME MENU IS TOO...
RICE BALLS ARE EXTREMELY SOPHISTICATED.
IF THE ULTIMATE MENU SIDE HAS CHOSEN RICE BALLS JUST FOR THE FUN OF IT...
THEN THEY ARE GOING TO REGRET THEIR SHORTSIGHTEDNESS.

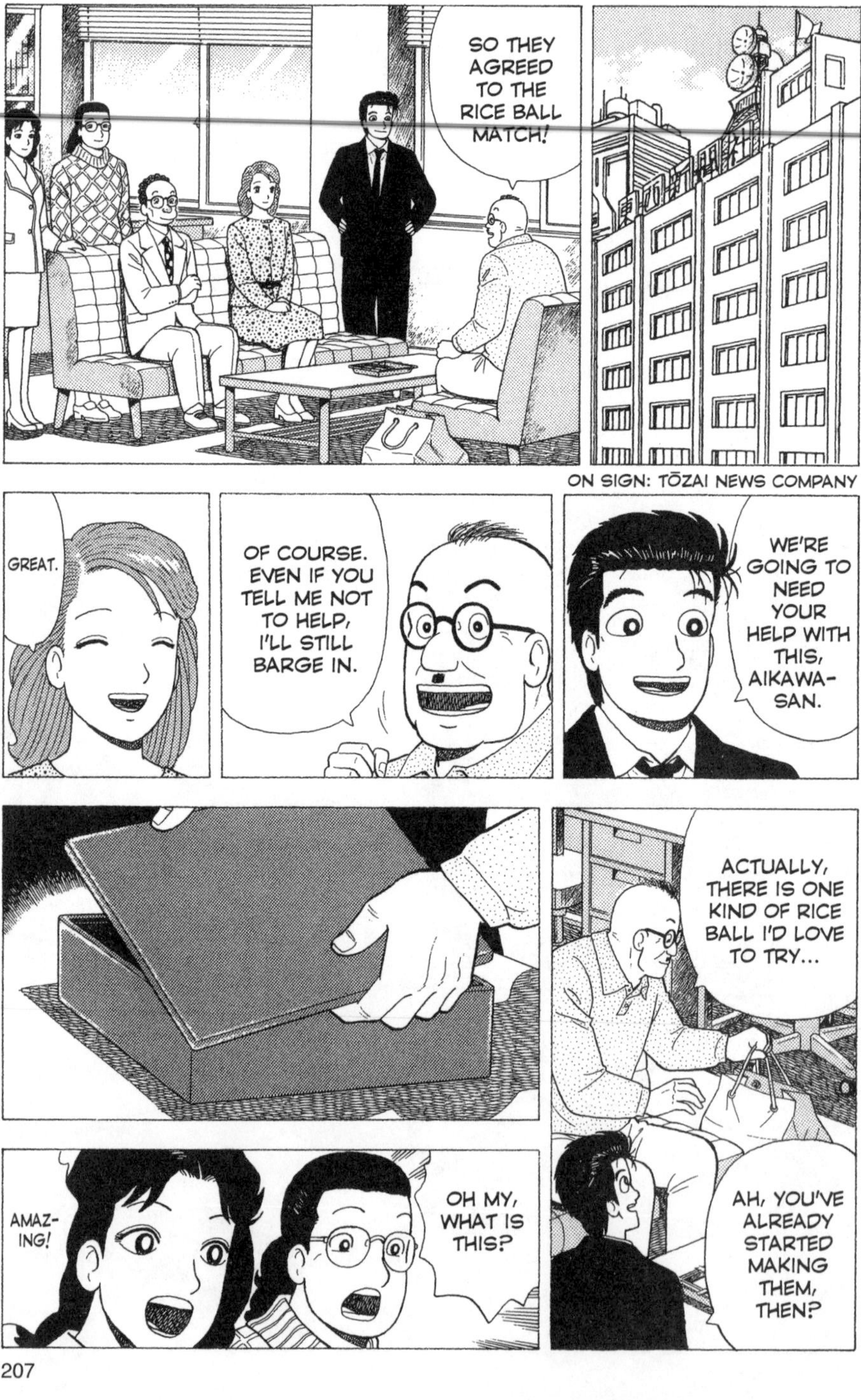
ON SIGN: TŌZAI NEWS COMPANY
SO THEY AGREED TO THE RICE BALL MATCH!
WE'RE GOING TO NEED YOUR HELP WITH THIS, AIKAWA-SAN.
OF COURSE. EVEN IF YOU TELL ME NOT TO HELP, I'LL STILL BARGE IN.
GREAT.
ACTUALLY, THERE IS ONE KIND OF RICE BALL I'D LOVE TO TRY...
AH, YOU'VE ALREADY STARTED MAKING THEM, THEN?
OH MY, WHAT IS THIS?
AMAZ-ING!

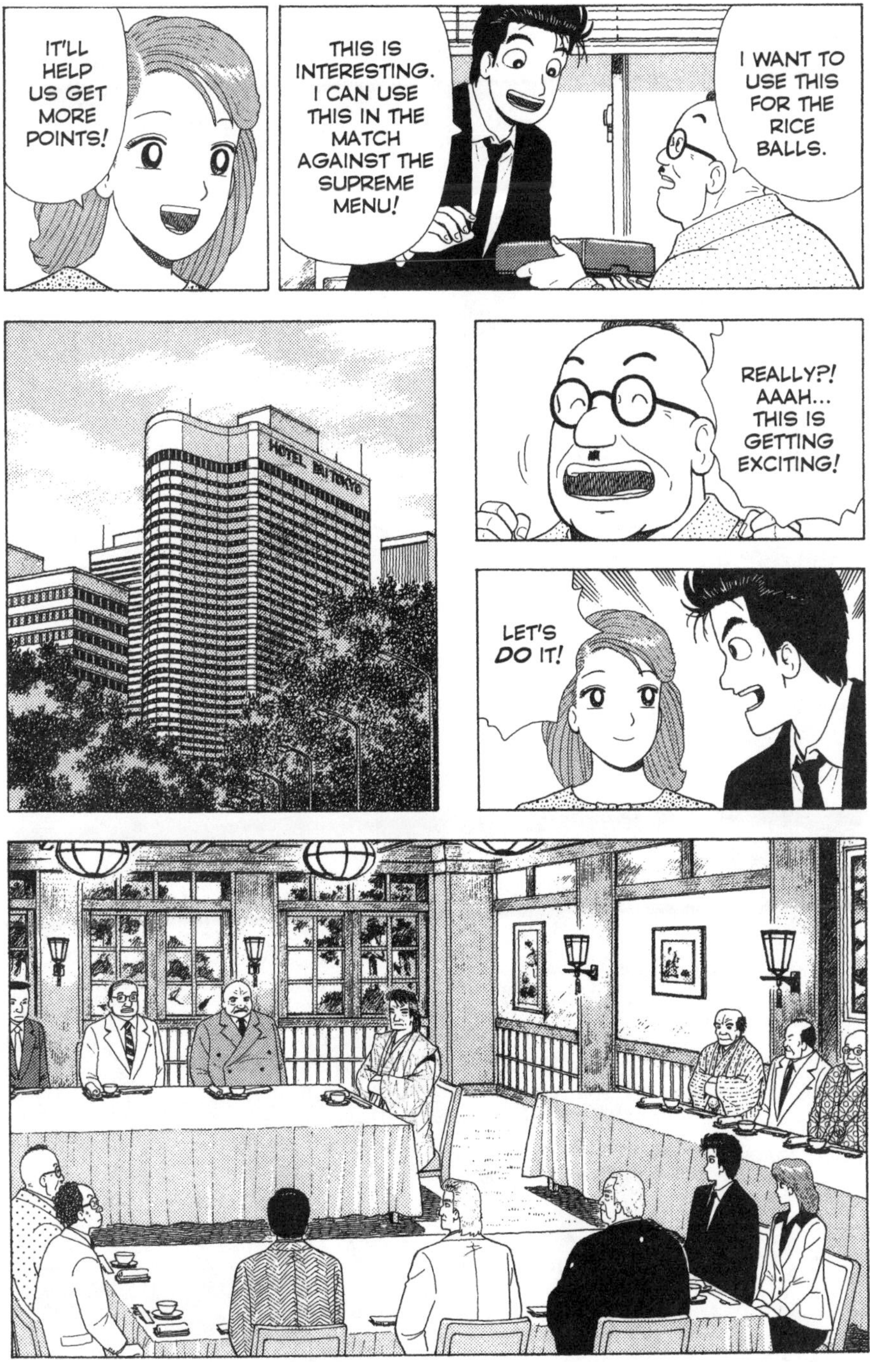
I WANT TO USE THIS FOR THE RICE BALLS.
THIS IS INTERESTING. I CAN USE THIS IN THE MATCH AGAINST THE SUPREME MENU!
IT'LL HELP US GET MORE POINTS!
REALLY?! AAAH... THIS IS GETTING EXCITING!
LET'S DO IT!

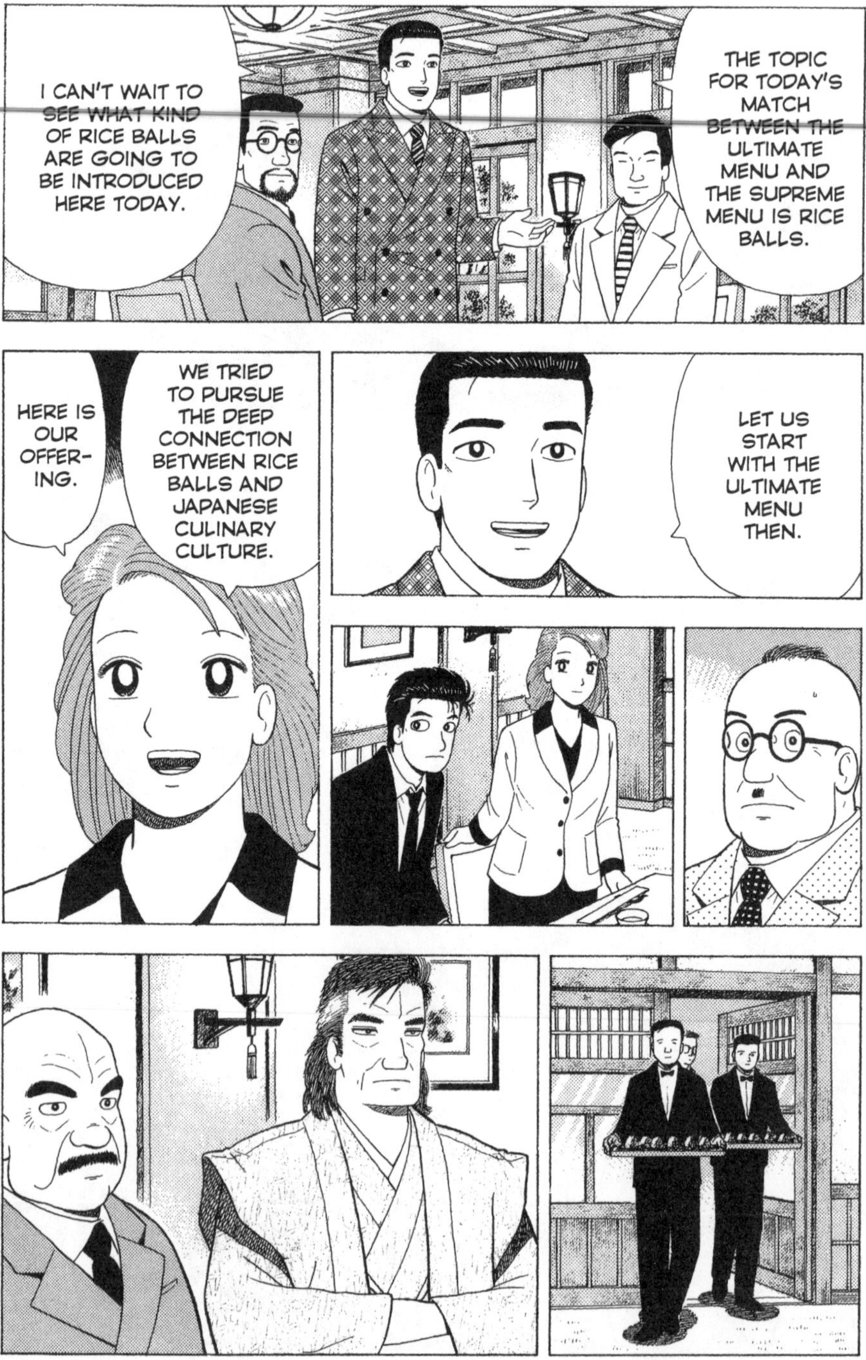
THE TOPIC FOR TODAY'S MATCH BETWEEN THE ULTIMATE MENU AND THE SUPREME MENU IS RICE BALLS.
I CAN'T WAIT TO SEE WHAT KIND OF RICE BALLS ARE GOING TO BE INTRODUCED HERE TODAY.
LET US START WITH THE ULTIMATE MENU THEN.
WE TRIED TO PURSUE THE DEEP CONNECTION BETWEEN RICE BALLS AND JAPANESE CULINARY CULTURE.
HERE IS OUR OFFERING.

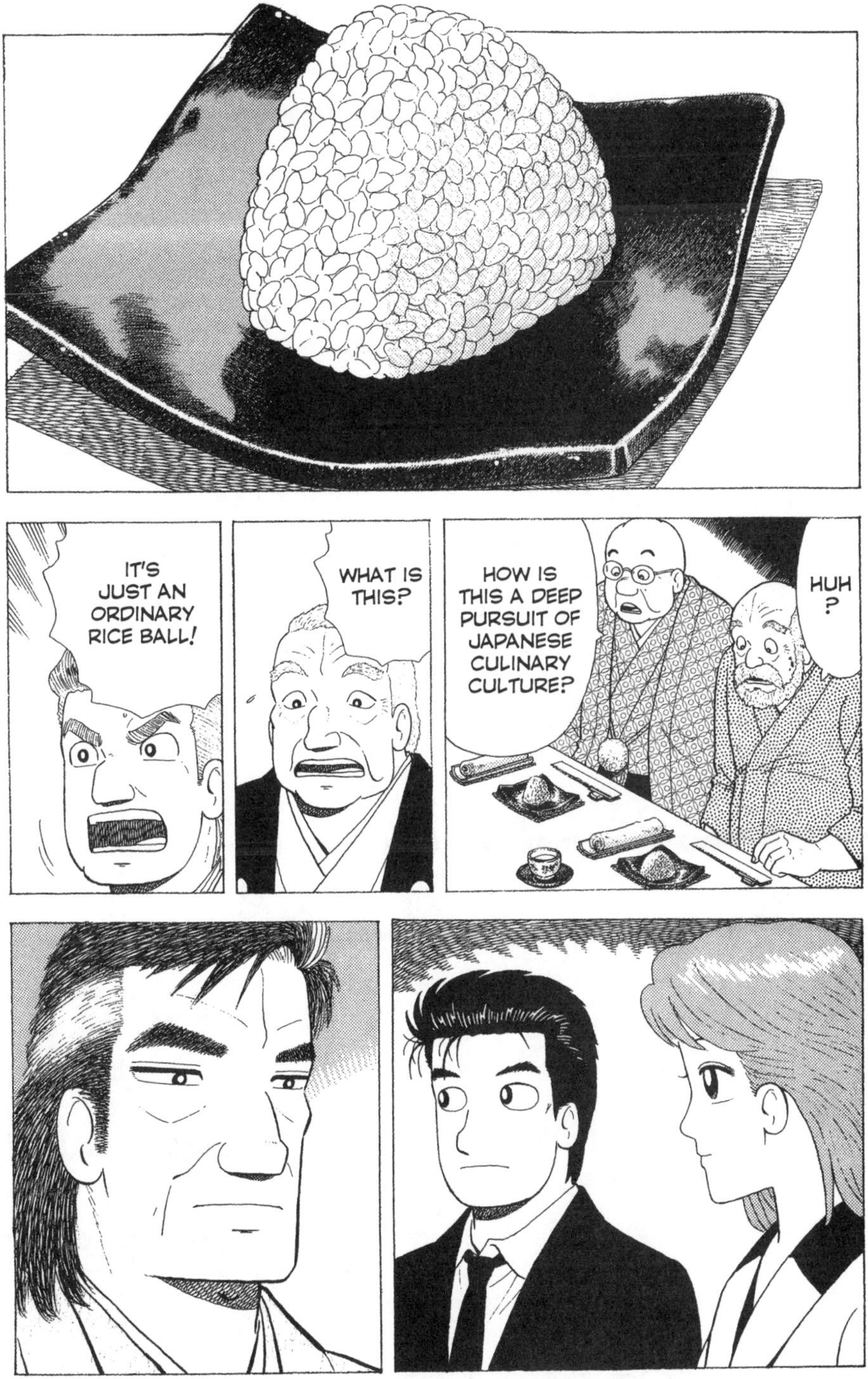
HUH ?
HOW IS THIS A DEEP PURSUIT OF JAPANESE CULINARY CULTURE?
WHAT IS THIS?
IT'S JUST AN ORDINARY RICE BALL!

EIGHTH COURSE
RICE BALL MATCH (PART TWO)

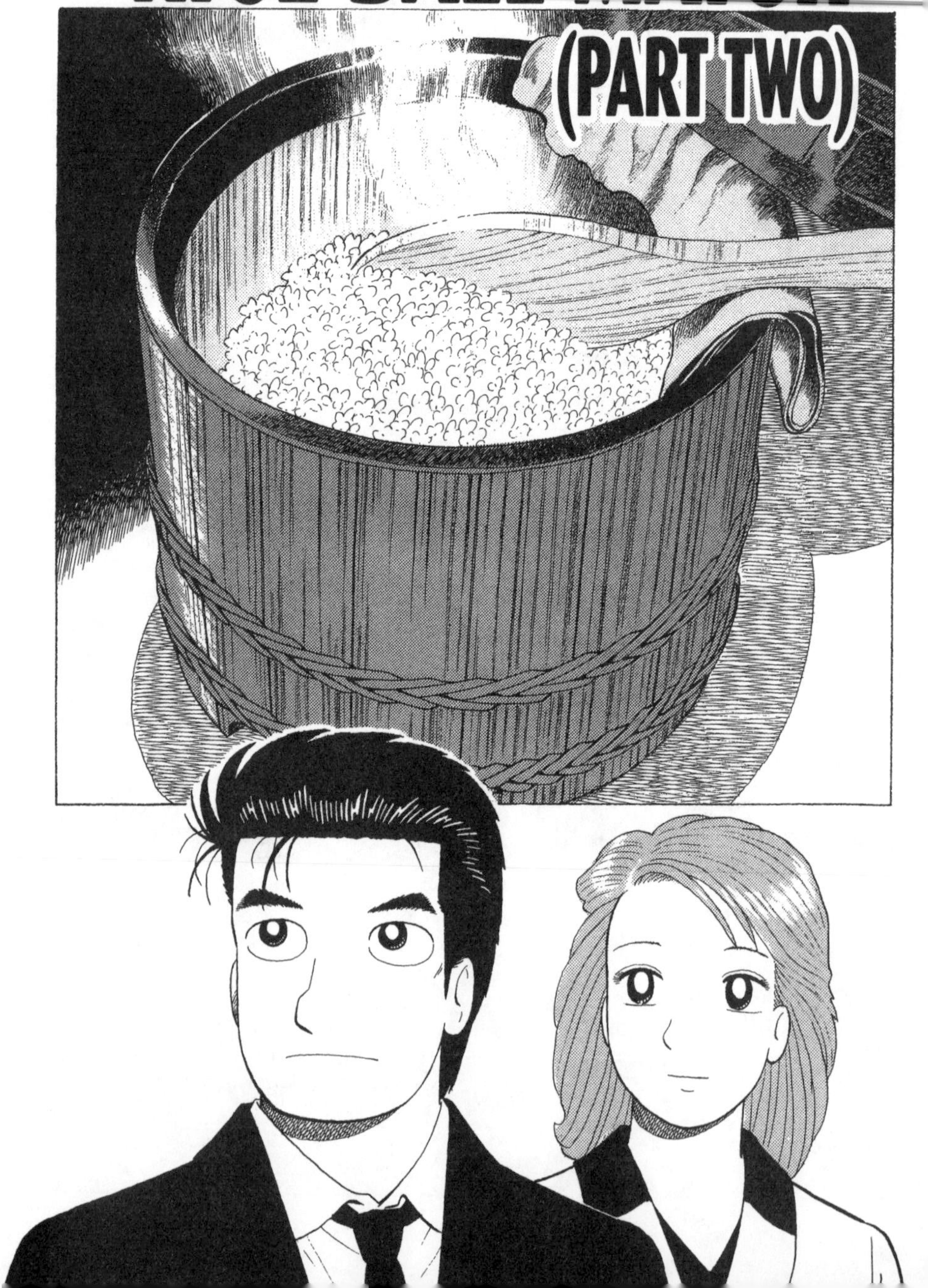

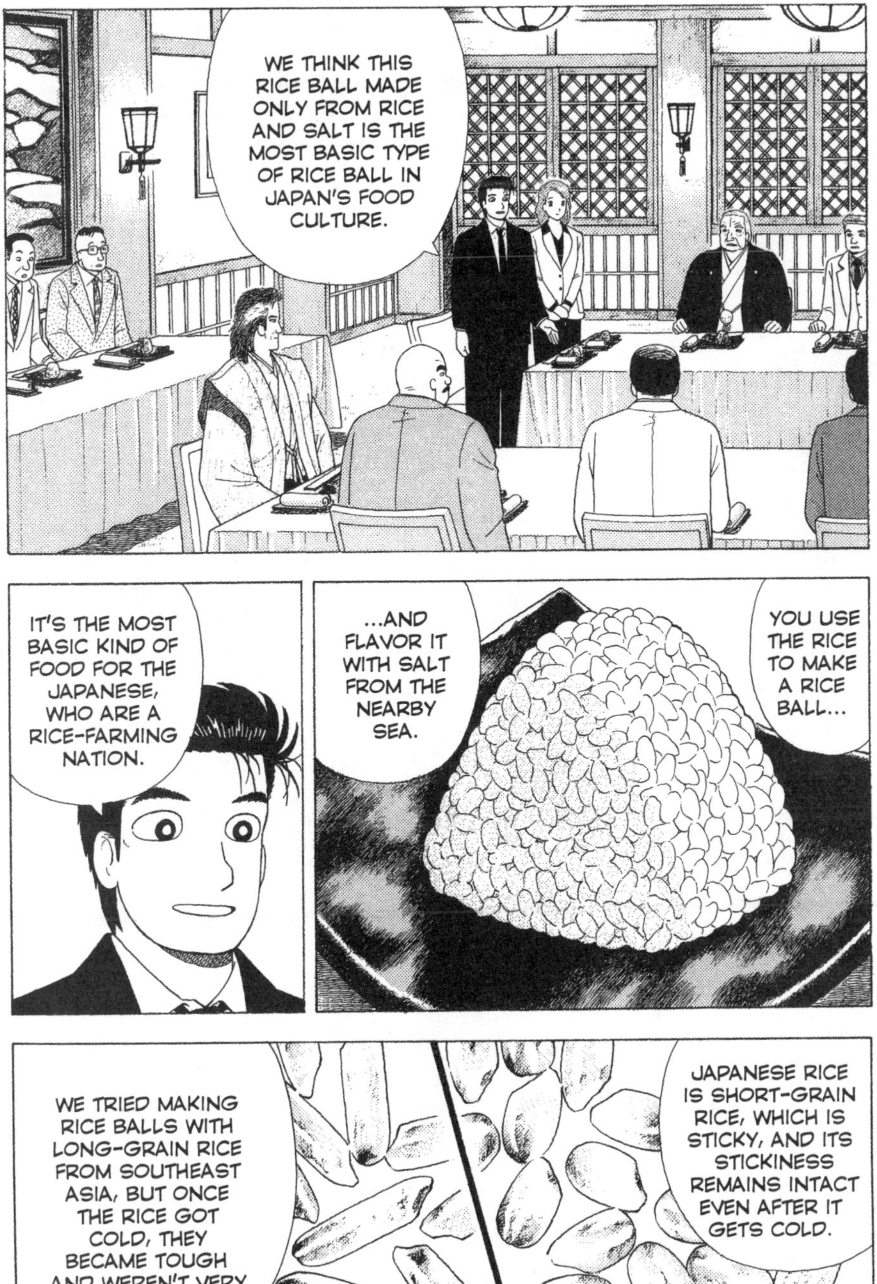
WE THINK THIS RICE BALL MADE ONLY FROM RICE AND SALT IS THE MOST BASIC TYPE OF RICE BALL IN JAPAN'S FOOD CULTURE.
YOU USE THE RICE TO MAKE A RICE BALL...
...AND FLAVOR IT WITH SALT FROM THE NEARBY SEA.
IT'S THE MOST BASIC KIND OF FOOD FOR THE JAPANESE, WHO ARE A RICE-FARMING NATION.
JAPANESE RICE IS SHORT-GRAIN RICE, WHICH IS STICKY, AND ITS STICKINESS REMAINS INTACT EVEN AFTER IT GETS COLD.
WE TRIED MAKING RICE BALLS WITH LONG-GRAIN RICE FROM SOUTHEAST ASIA, BUT ONCE THE RICE GOT COLD, THEY BECAME TOUGH AND WEREN'T VERY GOOD TO EAT.

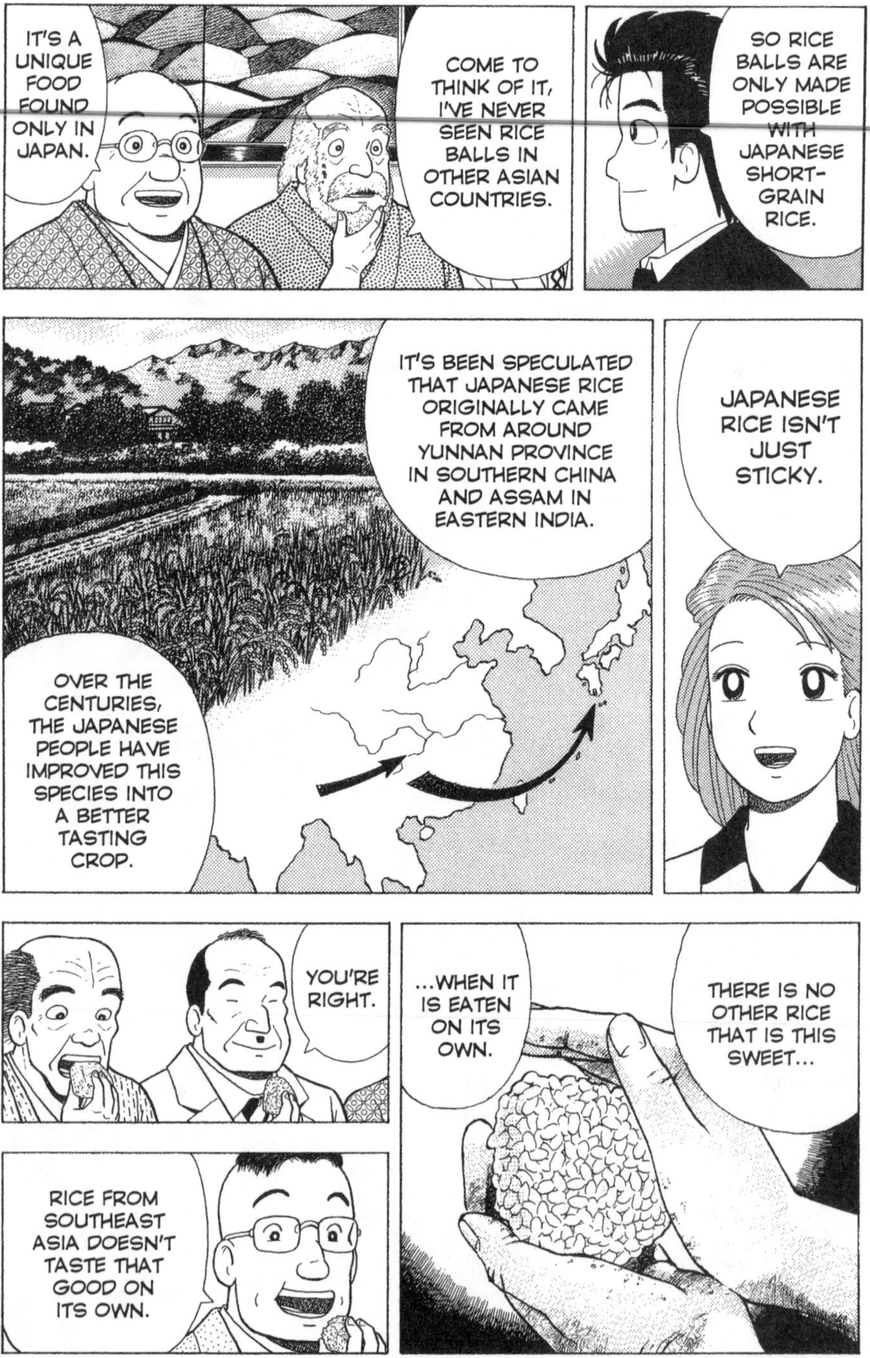
SO RICE BALLS ARE ONLY MADE POSSIBLE WITH JAPANESE SHORT-GRAIN RICE.
COME TO THINK OF IT, I'VE NEVER SEEN RICE BALLS IN OTHER ASIAN COUNTRIES.
IT'S A UNIQUE FOOD FOUND ONLY IN JAPAN.
JAPANESE RICE ISN'T JUST STICKY.
IT'S BEEN SPECULATED THAT JAPANESE RICE ORIGINALLY CAME FROM AROUND YUNNAN PROVINCE IN SOUTHERN CHINA AND ASSAM IN EASTERN INDIA.
OVER THE CENTURIES, THE JAPANESE PEOPLE HAVE IMPROVED THIS SPECIES INTO A BETTER TASTING CROP.
THERE IS NO OTHER RICE THAT IS THIS SWEET...
...WHEN IT IS EATEN ON ITS OWN.
YOU'RE RIGHT.
RICE FROM SOUTHEAST ASIA DOESN'T TASTE THAT GOOD ON ITS OWN.

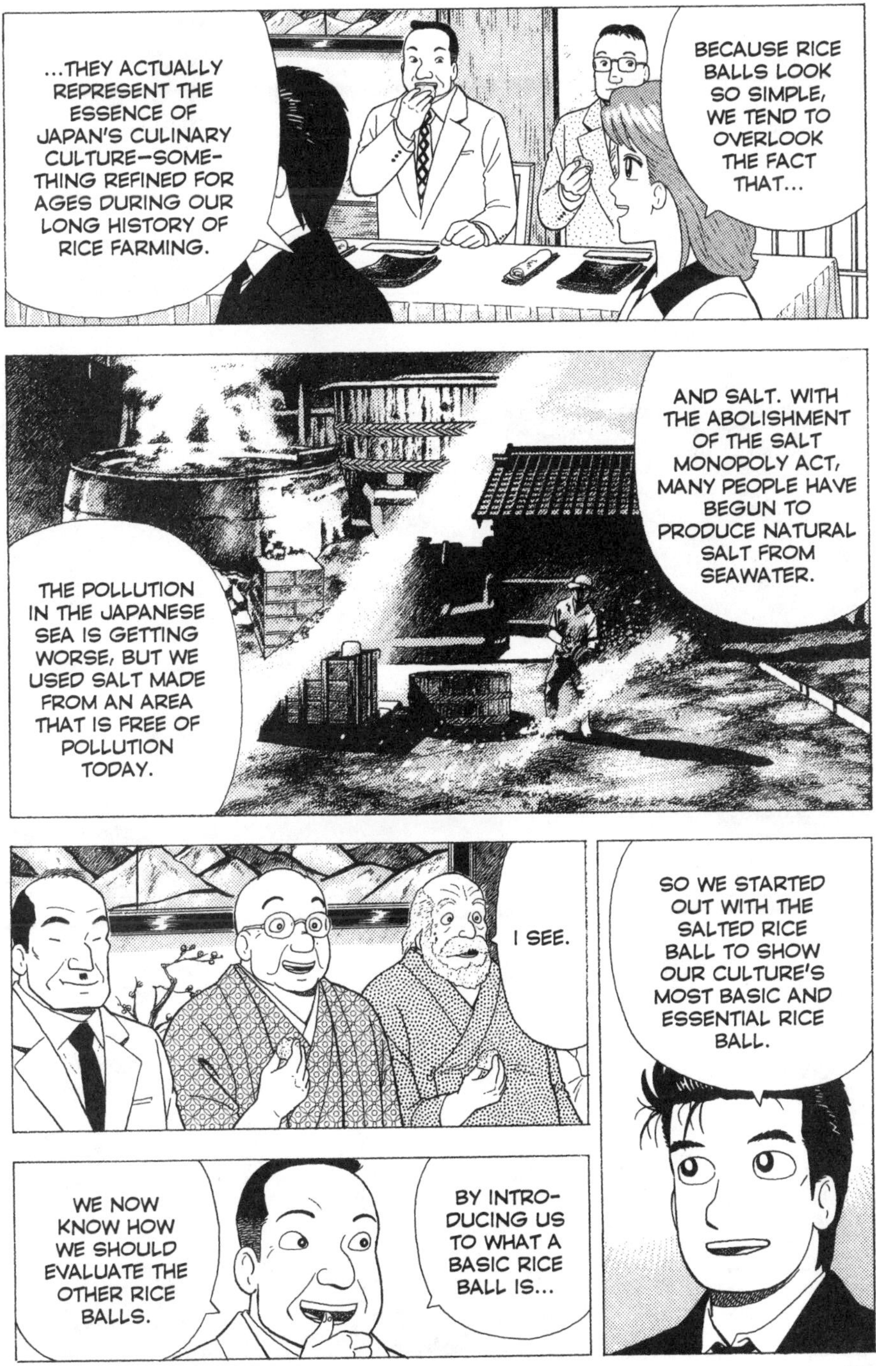
BECAUSE RICE BALLS LOOK SO SIMPLE, WE TEND TO OVERLOOK THE FACT THAT...
...THEY ACTUALLY REPRESENT THE ESSENCE OF JAPAN'S CULINARY CULTURE—SOME-THING REFINED FOR AGES DURING OUR LONG HISTORY OF RICE FARMING.
AND SALT. WITH THE ABOLISHMENT OF THE SALT MONOPOLY ACT, MANY PEOPLE HAVE BEGUN TO PRODUCE NATURAL SALT FROM SEAWATER.
THE POLLUTION IN THE JAPANESE SEA IS GETTING WORSE, BUT WE USED SALT MADE FROM AN AREA THAT IS FREE OF POLLUTION TODAY.
SO WE STARTED OUT WITH THE SALTED RICE BALL TO SHOW OUR CULTURE'S MOST BASIC AND ESSENTIAL RICE BALL.
I SEE.
BY INTRO-DUCING US TO WHAT A BASIC RICE BALL IS...
WE NOW KNOW HOW WE SHOULD EVALUATE THE OTHER RICE BALLS.

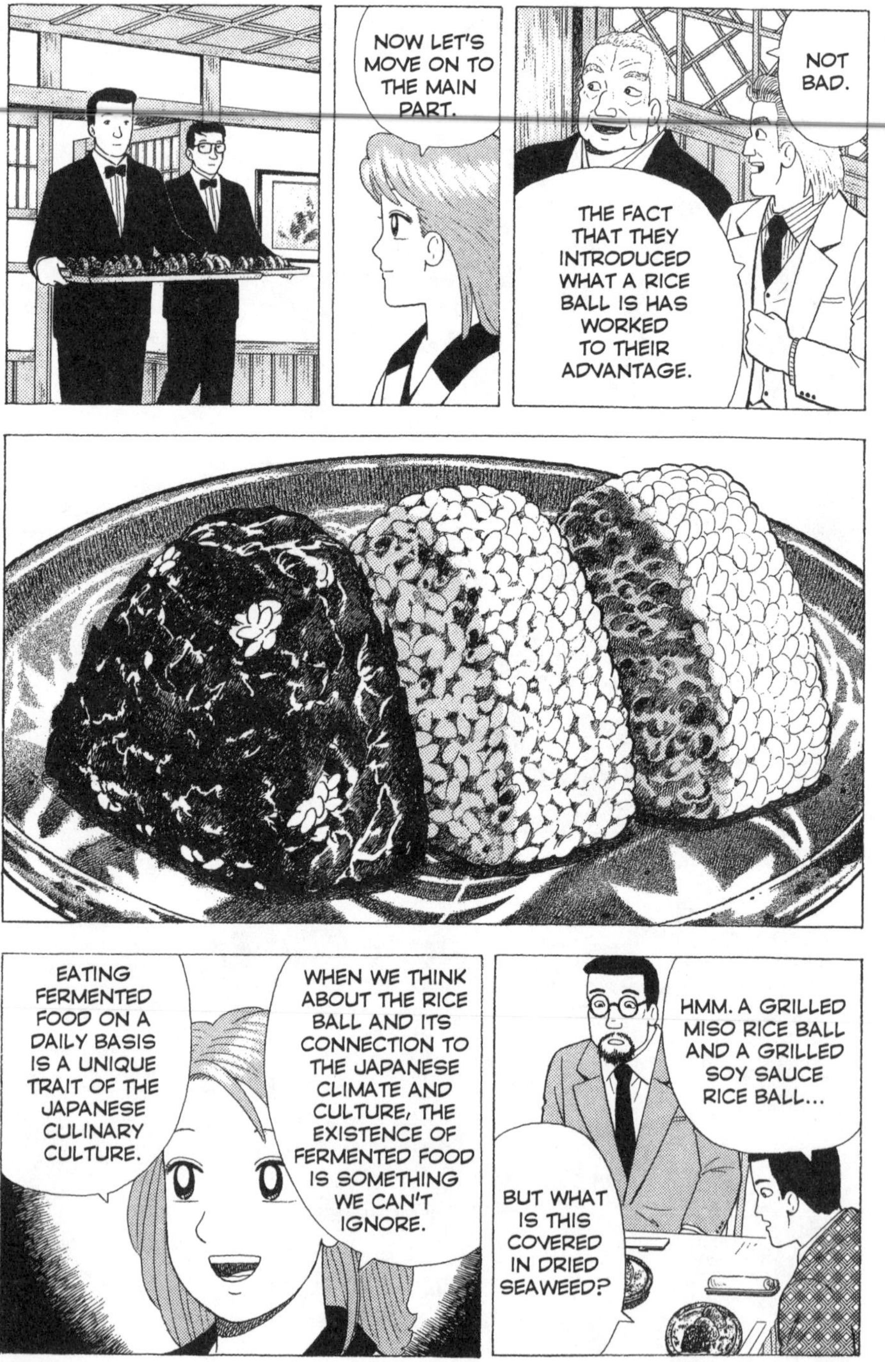
NOT BAD.
THE FACT THAT THEY INTRODUCED WHAT A RICE BALL IS HAS WORKED TO THEIR ADVANTAGE.
NOW LET'S MOVE ON TO THE MAIN PART.
HMM. A GRILLED MISO RICE BALL AND A GRILLED SOY SAUCE RICE BALL...
BUT WHAT IS THIS COVERED IN DRIED SEAWEED?
WHEN WE THINK ABOUT THE RICE BALL AND ITS CONNECTION TO THE JAPANESE CLIMATE AND CULTURE, THE EXISTENCE OF FERMENTED FOOD IS SOMETHING WE CAN'T IGNORE.
EATING FERMENTED FOOD ON A DAILY BASIS IS A UNIQUE TRAIT OF THE JAPANESE CULINARY CULTURE.

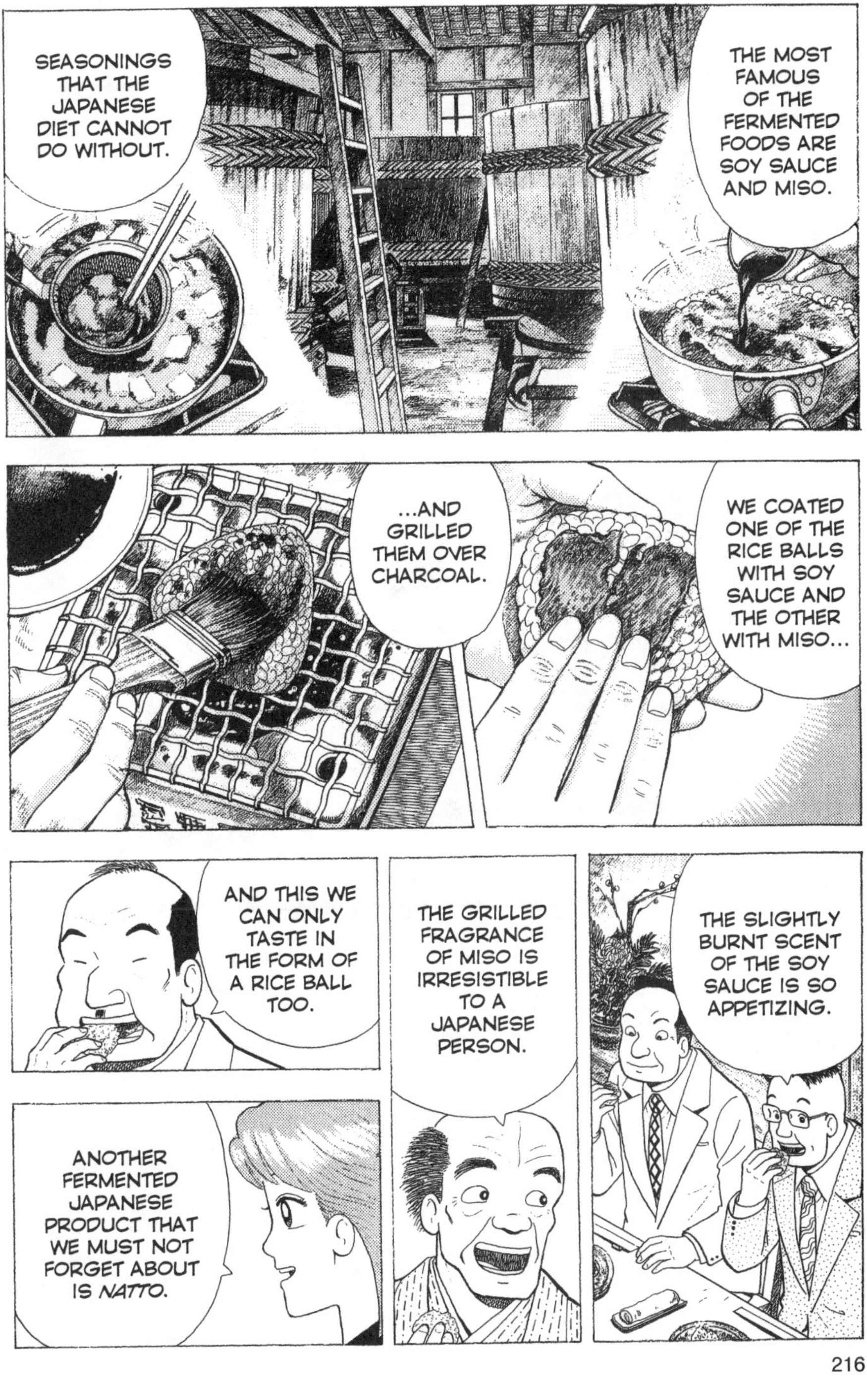
THE MOST FAMOUS OF THE FERMENTED FOODS ARE SOY SAUCE AND MISO.
SEASONINGS THAT THE JAPANESE DIET CANNOT DO WITHOUT.
WE COATED ONE OF THE RICE BALLS WITH SOY SAUCE AND THE OTHER WITH MISO...
...AND GRILLED THEM OVER CHARCOAL.
THE SLIGHTLY BURNT SCENT OF THE SOY SAUCE IS SO APPETIZING.
THE GRILLED FRAGRANCE OF MISO IS IRRESISTIBLE TO A JAPANESE PERSON.
AND THIS WE CAN ONLY TASTE IN THE FORM OF A RICE BALL TOO.
ANOTHER FERMENTED JAPANESE PRODUCT THAT WE MUST NOT FORGET ABOUT IS *NATTO*.

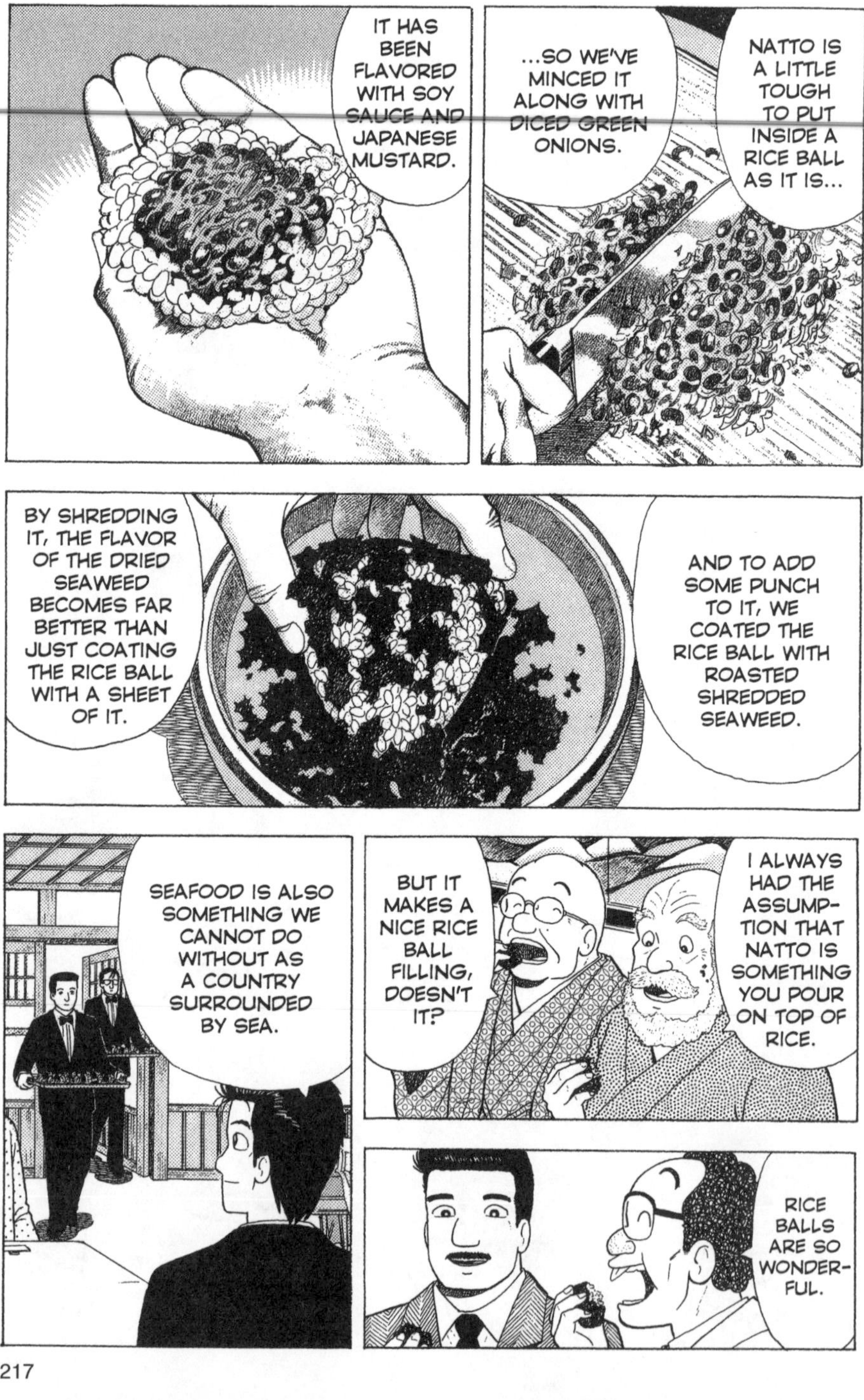
NATTO IS A LITTLE TOUGH TO PUT INSIDE A RICE BALL AS IT IS...
...SO WE'VE MINCED IT ALONG WITH DICED GREEN ONIONS.
IT HAS BEEN FLAVORED WITH SOY SAUCE AND JAPANESE MUSTARD.
AND TO ADD SOME PUNCH TO IT, WE COATED THE RICE BALL WITH ROASTED SHREDDED SEAWEED.
BY SHREDDING IT, THE FLAVOR OF THE DRIED SEAWEED BECOMES FAR BETTER THAN JUST COATING THE RICE BALL WITH A SHEET OF IT.
I ALWAYS HAD THE ASSUMP-TION THAT NATTO IS SOMETHING YOU POUR ON TOP OF RICE.
BUT IT MAKES A NICE RICE BALL FILLING, DOESN'T IT?
RICE BALLS ARE SO WONDER-FUL.
SEAFOOD IS ALSO SOMETHING WE CANNOT DO WITHOUT AS A COUNTRY SURROUNDED BY SEA.

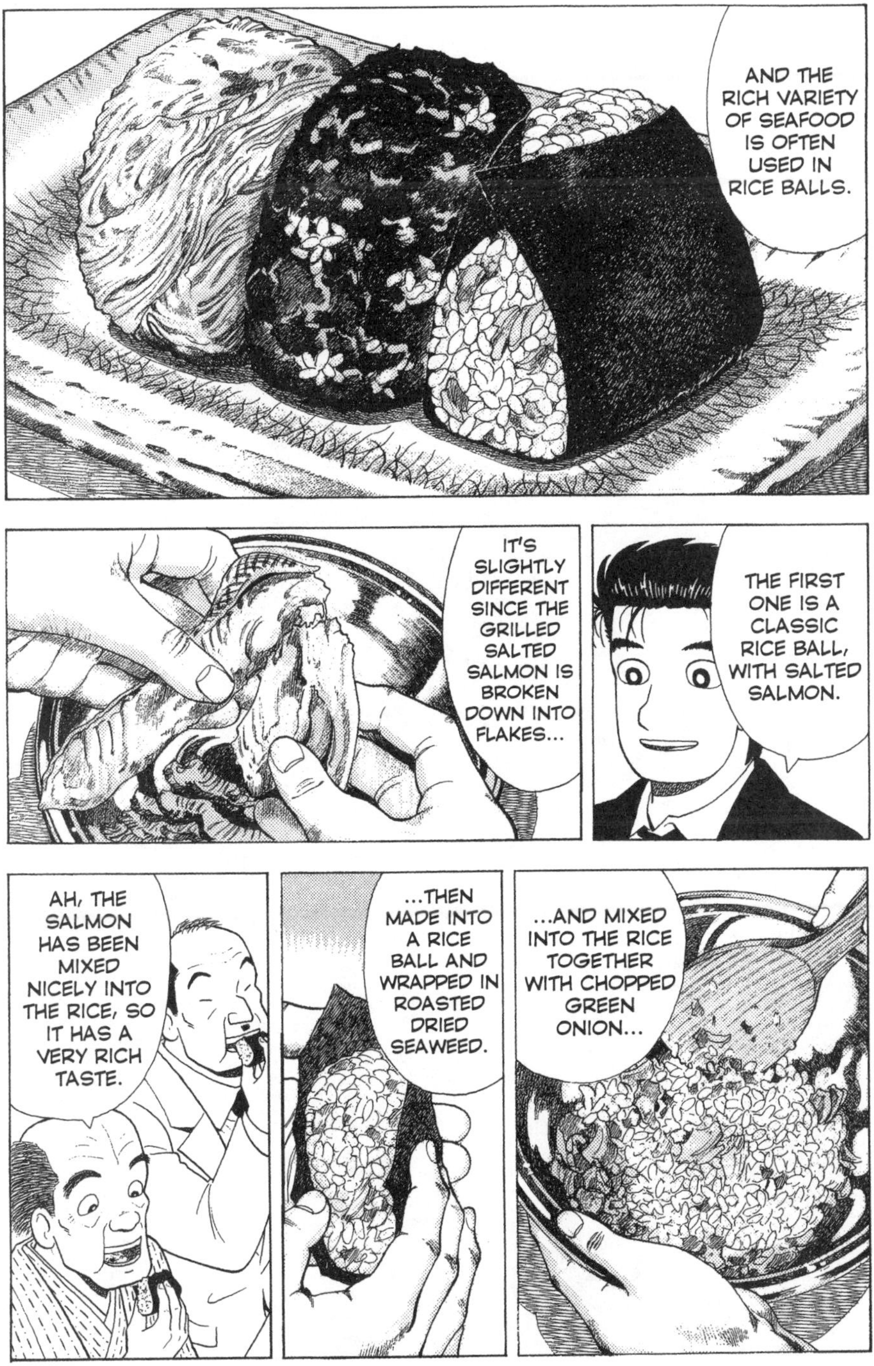
AND THE RICH VARIETY OF SEAFOOD IS OFTEN USED IN RICE BALLS.
THE FIRST ONE IS A CLASSIC RICE BALL, WITH SALTED SALMON.
IT'S SLIGHTLY DIFFERENT SINCE THE GRILLED SALTED SALMON IS BROKEN DOWN INTO FLAKES...
...AND MIXED INTO THE RICE TOGETHER WITH CHOPPED GREEN ONION...
...THEN MADE INTO A RICE BALL AND WRAPPED IN ROASTED DRIED SEAWEED.
AH, THE SALMON HAS BEEN MIXED NICELY INTO THE RICE, SO IT HAS A VERY RICH TASTE.

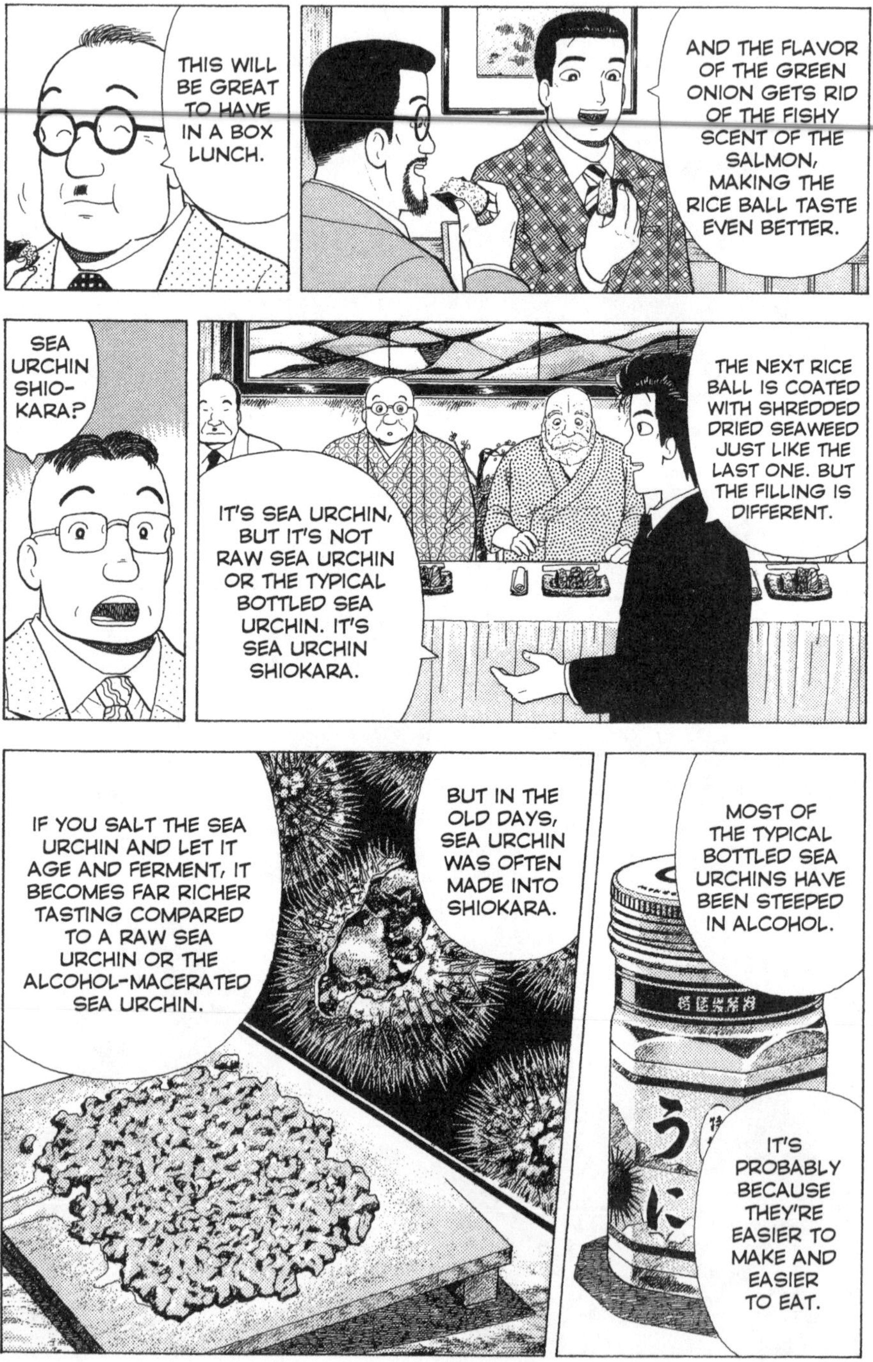
AND THE FLAVOR OF THE GREEN ONION GETS RID OF THE FISHY SCENT OF THE SALMON, MAKING THE RICE BALL TASTE EVEN BETTER.
THIS WILL BE GREAT TO HAVE IN A BOX LUNCH.
THE NEXT RICE BALL IS COATED WITH SHREDDED DRIED SEAWEED JUST LIKE THE LAST ONE. BUT THE FILLING IS DIFFERENT.
IT'S SEA URCHIN, BUT IT'S NOT RAW SEA URCHIN OR THE TYPICAL BOTTLED SEA URCHIN. IT'S SEA URCHIN SHIOKARA.
SEA URCHIN SHIO-KARA?
MOST OF THE TYPICAL BOTTLED SEA URCHINS HAVE BEEN STEEPED IN ALCOHOL.
うに
IT'S PROBABLY BECAUSE THEY'RE EASIER TO MAKE AND EASIER TO EAT.
BUT IN THE OLD DAYS, SEA URCHIN WAS OFTEN MADE INTO SHIOKARA.
IF YOU SALT THE SEA URCHIN AND LET IT AGE AND FERMENT, IT BECOMES FAR RICHER TASTING COMPARED TO A RAW SEA URCHIN OR THE ALCOHOL-MACERATED SEA URCHIN.

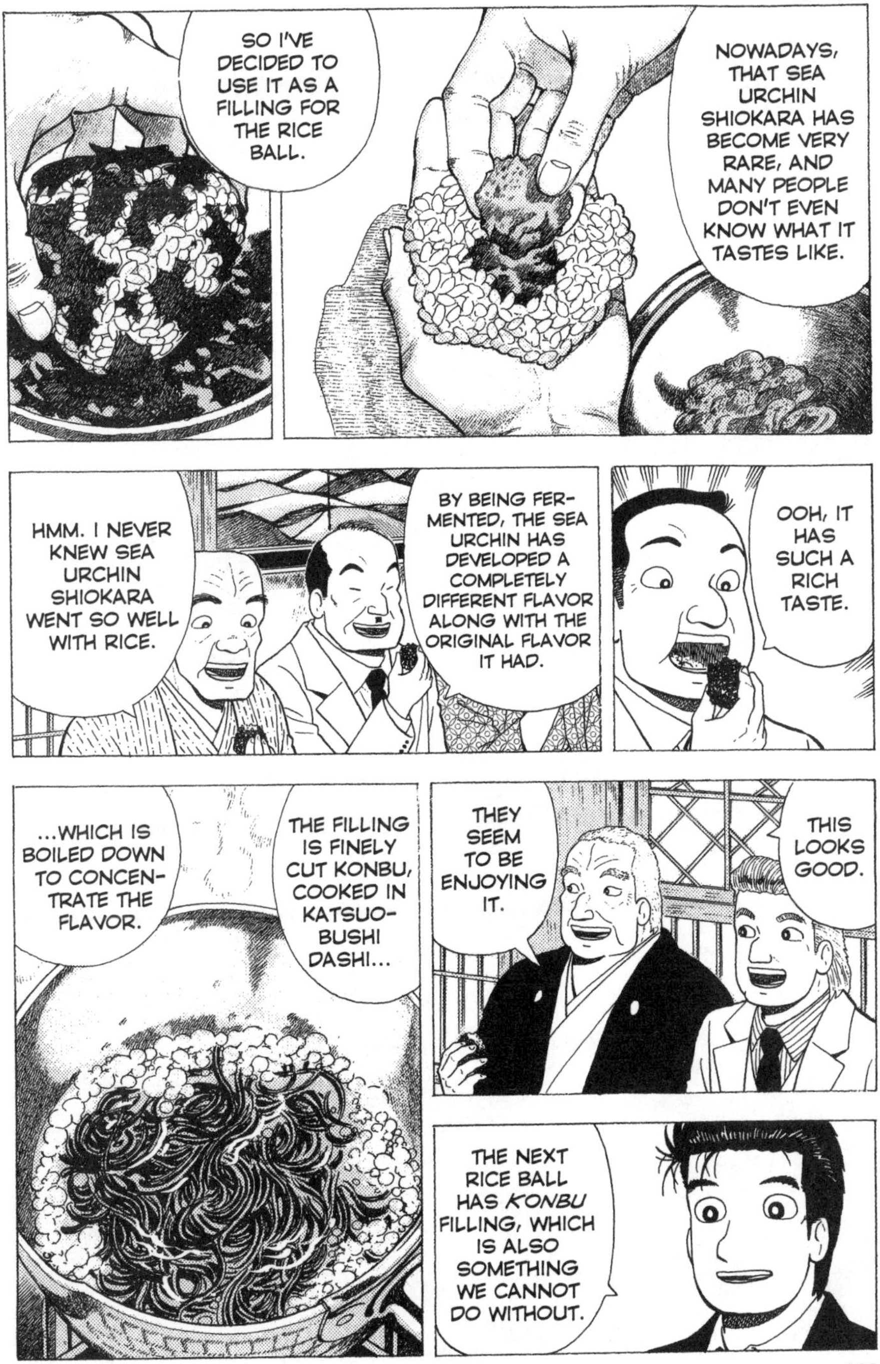
NOWADAYS, THAT SEA URCHIN SHIOKARA HAS BECOME VERY RARE, AND MANY PEOPLE DON'T EVEN KNOW WHAT IT TASTES LIKE.
SO I'VE DECIDED TO USE IT AS A FILLING FOR THE RICE BALL.
OOH, IT HAS SUCH A RICH TASTE.
BY BEING FER-MENTED, THE SEA URCHIN HAS DEVELOPED A COMPLETELY DIFFERENT FLAVOR ALONG WITH THE ORIGINAL FLAVOR IT HAD.
HMM. I NEVER KNEW SEA URCHIN SHIOKARA WENT SO WELL WITH RICE.
THIS LOOKS GOOD.
THEY SEEM TO BE ENJOYING IT.
THE NEXT RICE BALL HAS *KONBU* FILLING, WHICH IS ALSO SOMETHING WE CANNOT DO WITHOUT.
THE FILLING IS FINELY CUT KONBU, COOKED IN KATSUO-BUSHI DASHI...
...WHICH IS BOILED DOWN TO CONCEN-TRATE THE FLAVOR.

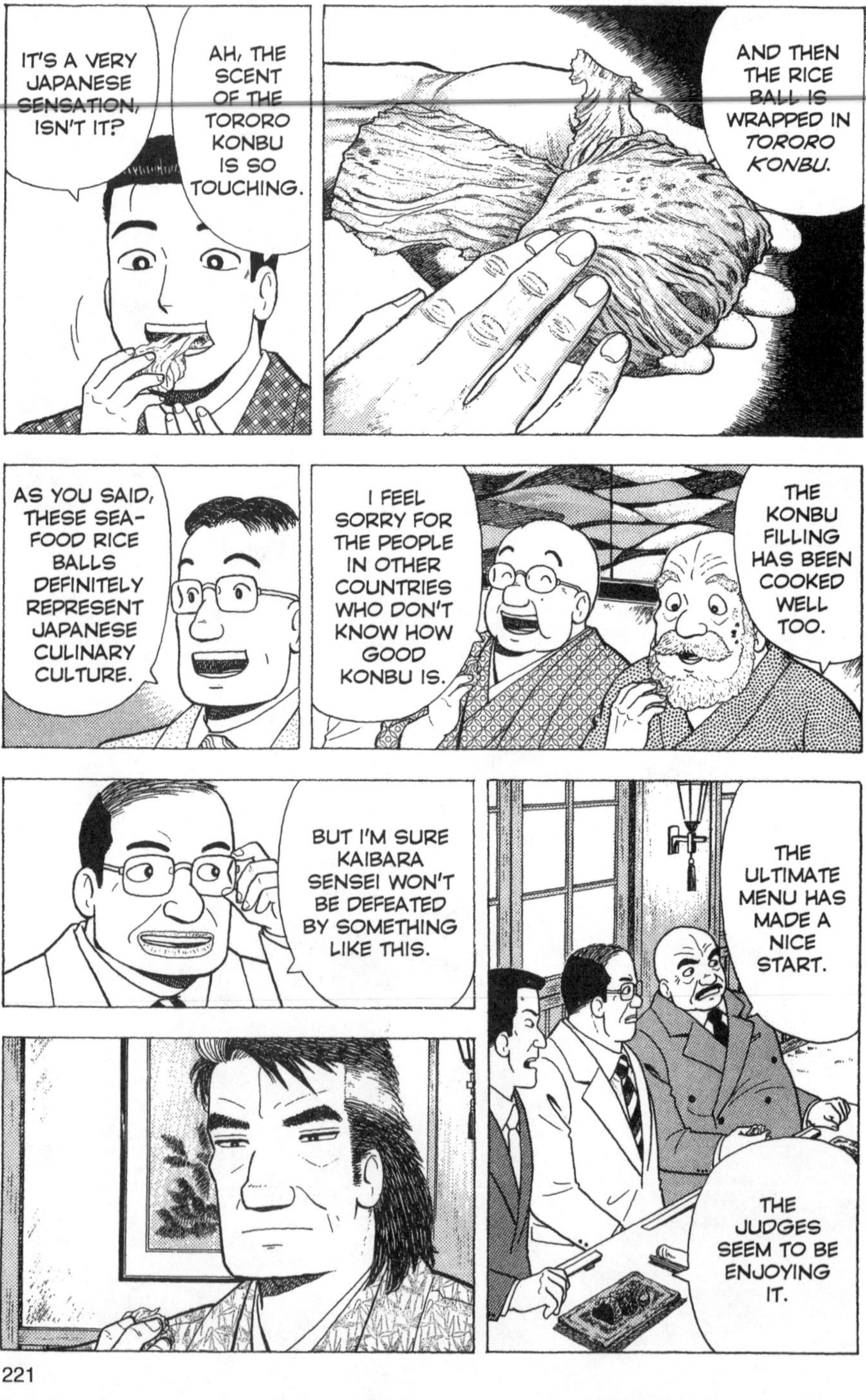
AND THEN THE RICE BALL IS WRAPPED IN *TORORO KONBU*.
AH, THE SCENT OF THE TORORO KONBU IS SO TOUCHING.
IT'S A VERY JAPANESE SENSATION, ISN'T IT?
THE KONBU FILLING HAS BEEN COOKED WELL TOO.
I FEEL SORRY FOR THE PEOPLE IN OTHER COUNTRIES WHO DON'T KNOW HOW GOOD KONBU IS.
AS YOU SAID, THESE SEA-FOOD RICE BALLS DEFINITELY REPRESENT JAPANESE CULINARY CULTURE.
THE ULTIMATE MENU HAS MADE A NICE START.
THE JUDGES SEEM TO BE ENJOYING IT.
BUT I'M SURE KAIBARA SENSEI WON'T BE DEFEATED BY SOMETHING LIKE THIS.

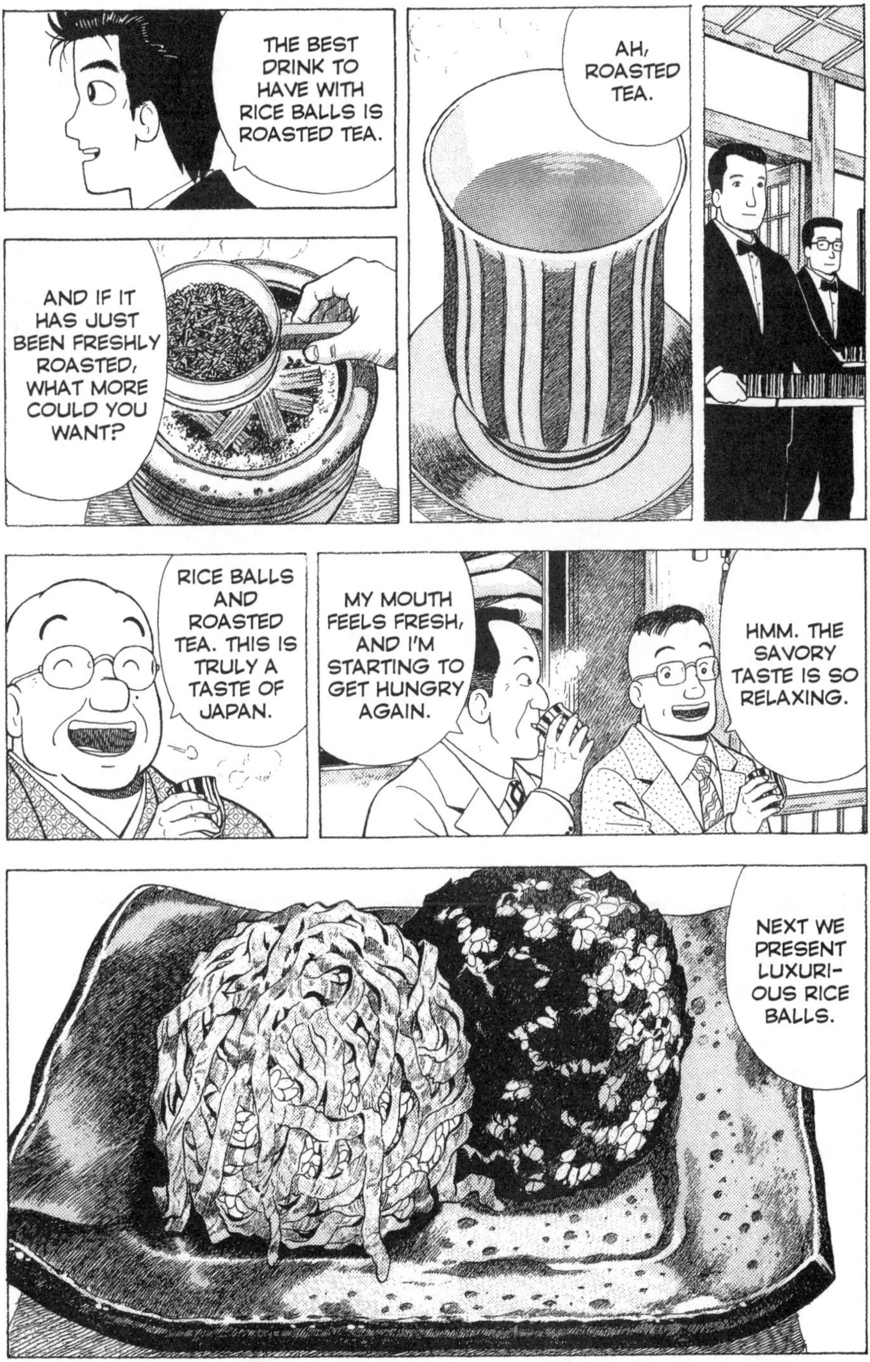
AH, ROASTED TEA.
THE BEST DRINK TO HAVE WITH RICE BALLS IS ROASTED TEA.
AND IF IT HAS JUST BEEN FRESHLY ROASTED, WHAT MORE COULD YOU WANT?
HMM. THE SAVORY TASTE IS SO RELAXING.
MY MOUTH FEELS FRESH, AND I'M STARTING TO GET HUNGRY AGAIN.
RICE BALLS AND ROASTED TEA. THIS IS TRULY A TASTE OF JAPAN.
NEXT WE PRESENT LUXURIOUS RICE BALLS.

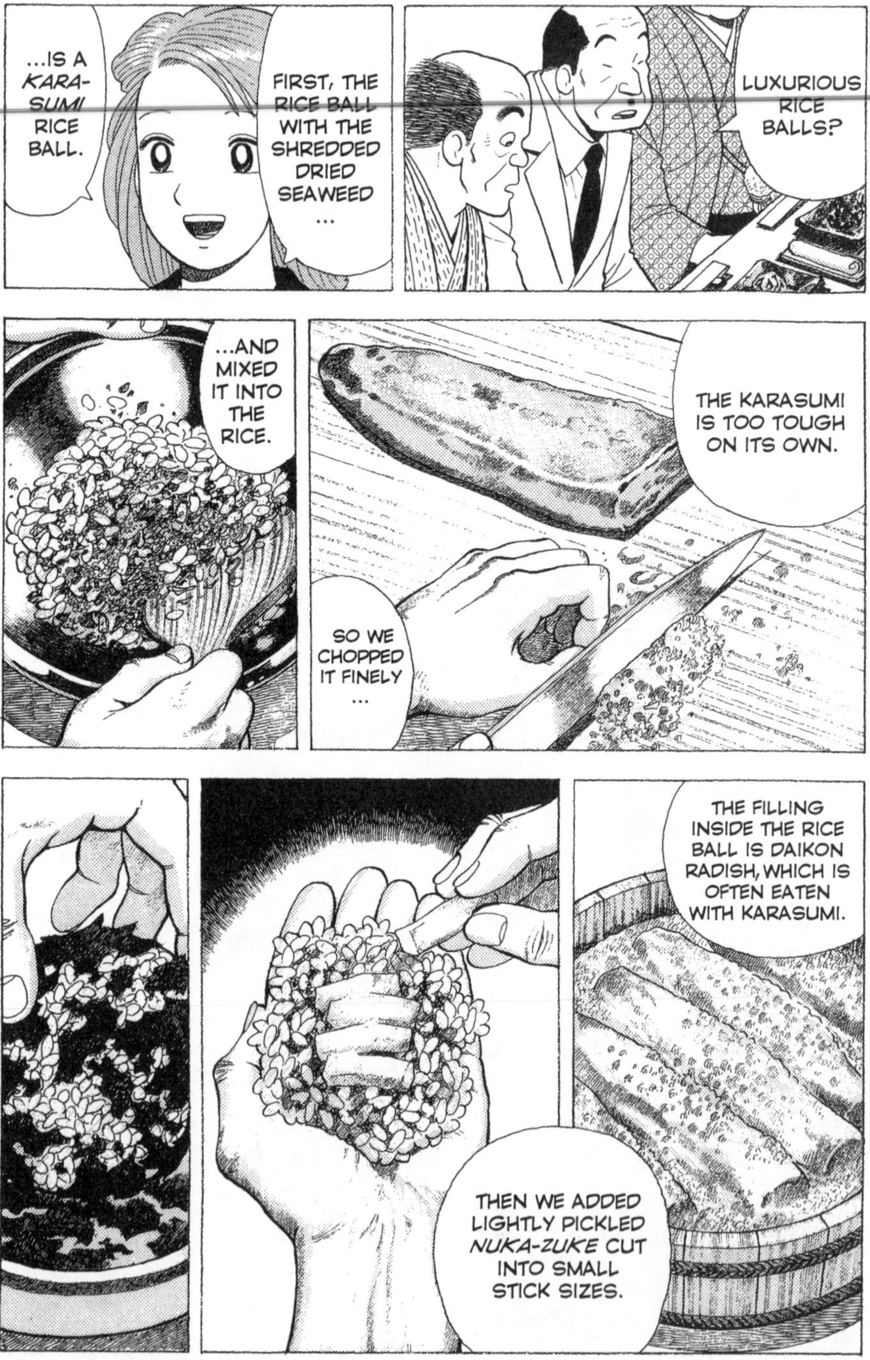
LUXURIOUS RICE BALLS?
FIRST, THE RICE BALL WITH THE SHREDDED DRIED SEAWEED ...
...IS A *KARA-SUMI* RICE BALL.
THE KARASUMI IS TOO TOUGH ON ITS OWN.
SO WE CHOPPED IT FINELY ...
...AND MIXED IT INTO THE RICE.
THE FILLING INSIDE THE RICE BALL IS DAIKON RADISH, WHICH IS OFTEN EATEN WITH KARASUMI.
THEN WE ADDED LIGHTLY PICKLED *NUKA-ZUKE* CUT INTO SMALL STICK SIZES.

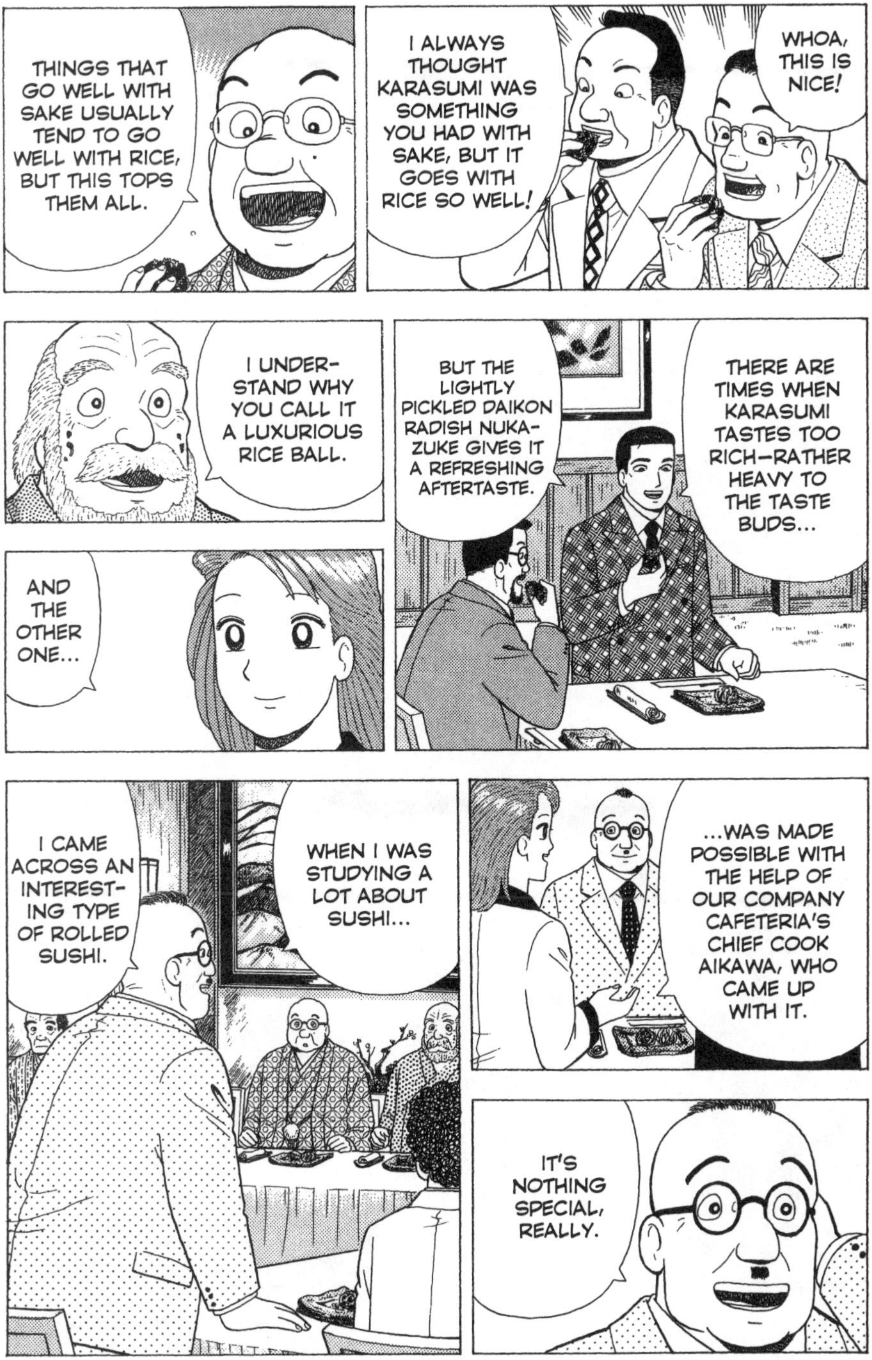
WHOA, THIS IS NICE!
I ALWAYS THOUGHT KARASUMI WAS SOMETHING YOU HAD WITH SAKE, BUT IT GOES WITH RICE SO WELL!
THINGS THAT GO WELL WITH SAKE USUALLY TEND TO GO WELL WITH RICE, BUT THIS TOPS THEM ALL.
THERE ARE TIMES WHEN KARASUMI TASTES TOO RICH—RATHER HEAVY TO THE TASTE BUDS...
BUT THE LIGHTLY PICKLED DAIKON RADISH NUKA-ZUKE GIVES IT A REFRESHING AFTERTASTE.
I UNDER-STAND WHY YOU CALL IT A LUXURIOUS RICE BALL.
AND THE OTHER ONE...
...WAS MADE POSSIBLE WITH THE HELP OF OUR COMPANY CAFETERIA'S CHIEF COOK AIKAWA, WHO CAME UP WITH IT.
IT'S NOTHING SPECIAL, REALLY.
WHEN I WAS STUDYING A LOT ABOUT SUSHI...
I CAME ACROSS AN INTEREST-ING TYPE OF ROLLED SUSHI.

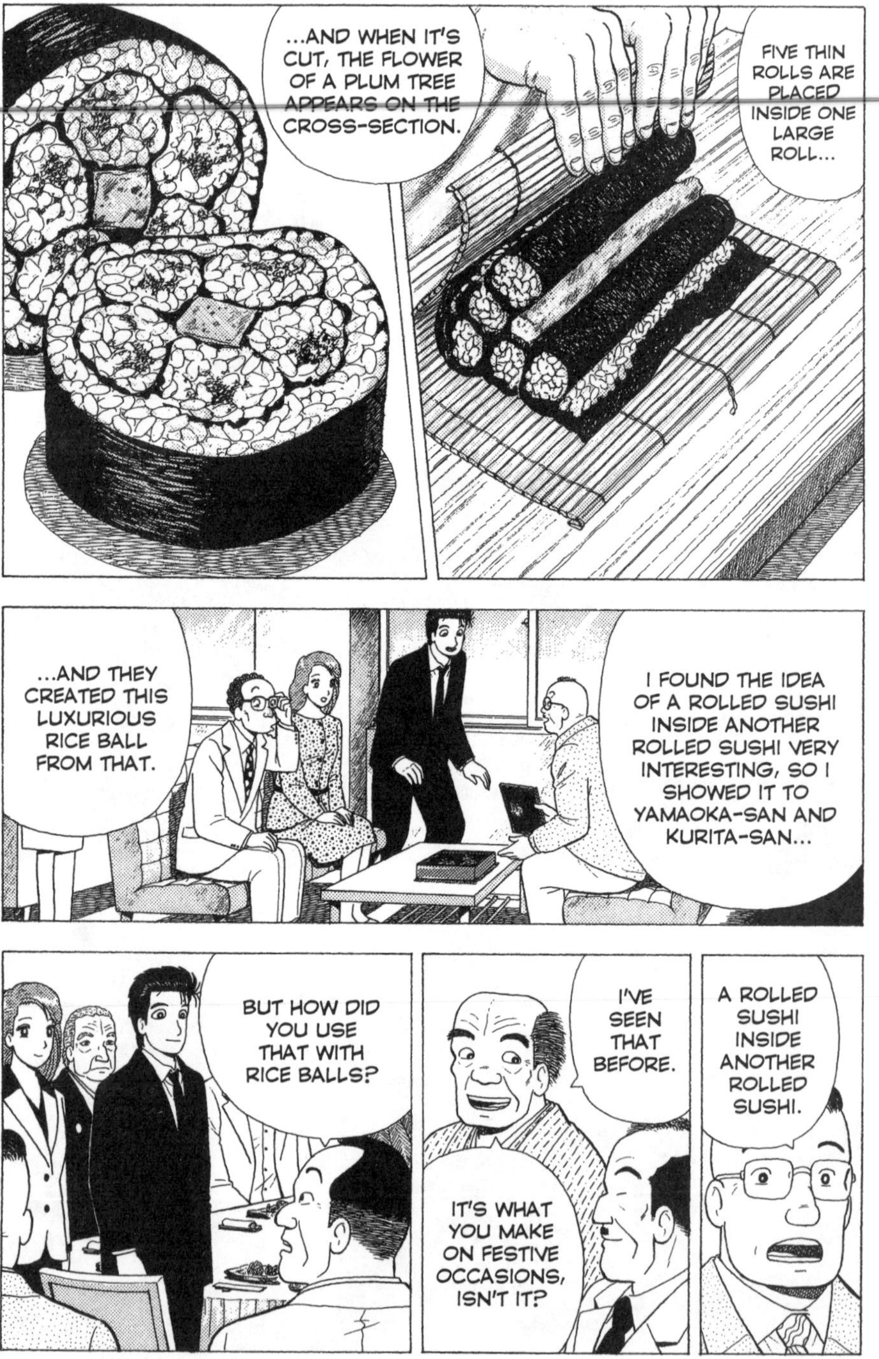
FIVE THIN ROLLS ARE PLACED INSIDE ONE LARGE ROLL...
...AND WHEN IT'S CUT, THE FLOWER OF A PLUM TREE APPEARS ON THE CROSS-SECTION.
I FOUND THE IDEA OF A ROLLED SUSHI INSIDE ANOTHER ROLLED SUSHI VERY INTERESTING, SO I SHOWED IT TO YAMAOKA-SAN AND KURITA-SAN...
...AND THEY CREATED THIS LUXURIOUS RICE BALL FROM THAT.
A ROLLED SUSHI INSIDE ANOTHER ROLLED SUSHI.
I'VE SEEN THAT BEFORE.
IT'S WHAT YOU MAKE ON FESTIVE OCCASIONS, ISN'T IT?
BUT HOW DID YOU USE THAT WITH RICE BALLS?

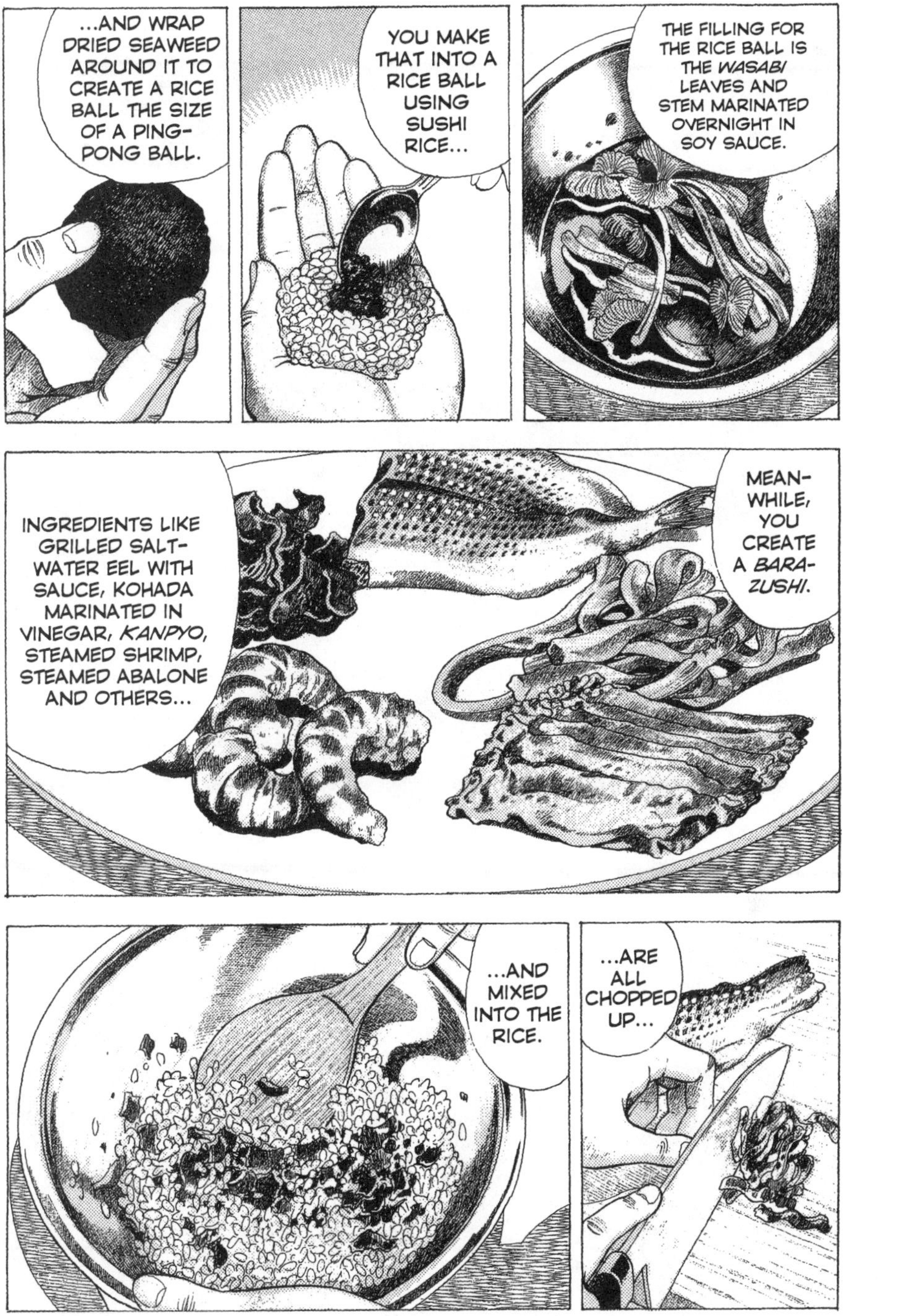
THE FILLING FOR THE RICE BALL IS THE *WASABI* LEAVES AND STEM MARINATED OVERNIGHT IN SOY SAUCE.
YOU MAKE THAT INTO A RICE BALL USING SUSHI RICE...
...AND WRAP DRIED SEAWEED AROUND IT TO CREATE A RICE BALL THE SIZE OF A PING-PONG BALL.
MEAN-WHILE, YOU CREATE A *BARA-ZUSHI*.
INGREDIENTS LIKE GRILLED SALT-WATER EEL WITH SAUCE, KOHADA MARINATED IN VINEGAR, *KANPYO*, STEAMED SHRIMP, STEAMED ABALONE AND OTHERS...
...ARE ALL CHOPPED UP...
...AND MIXED INTO THE RICE.

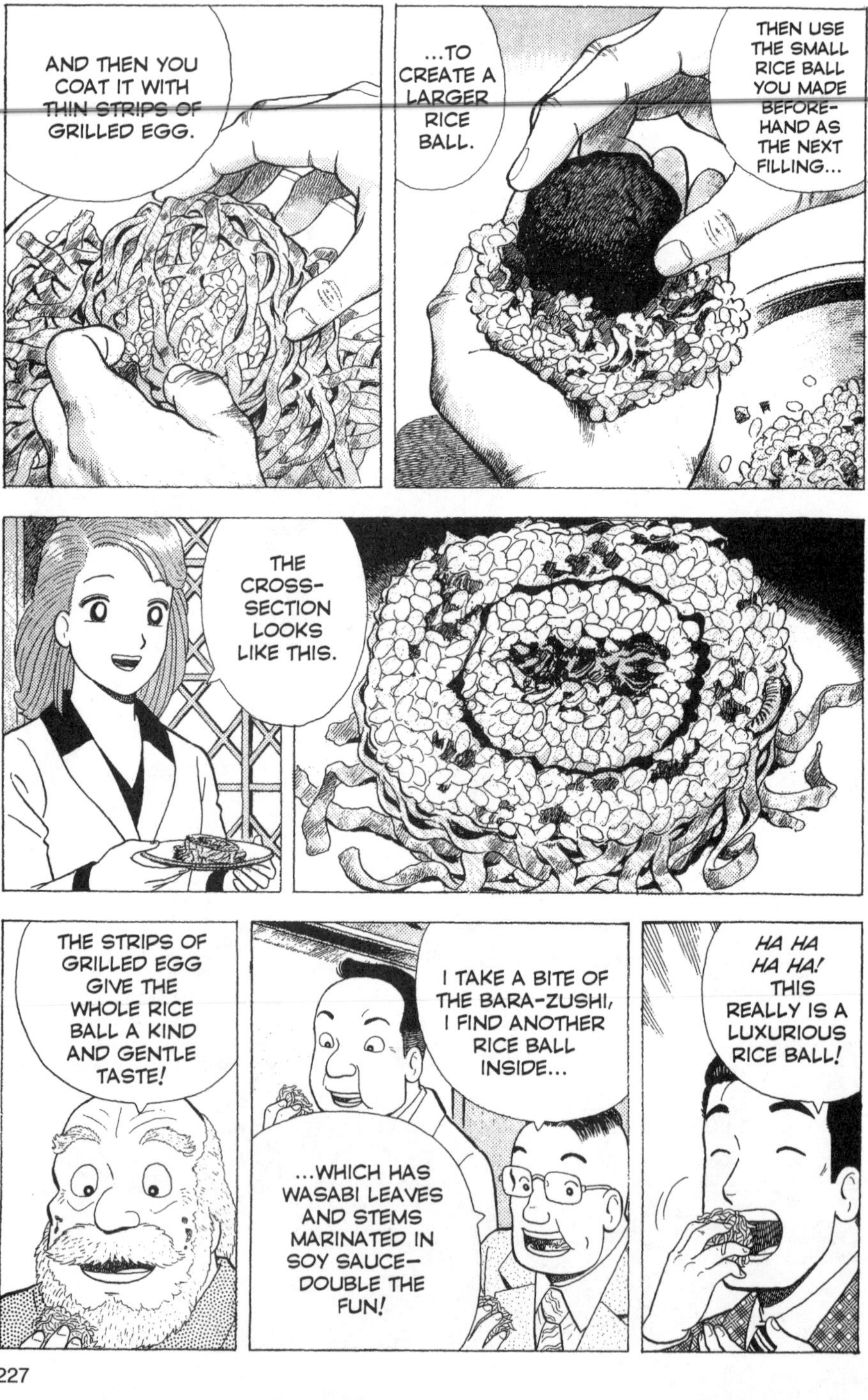
THEN USE THE SMALL RICE BALL YOU MADE BEFORE-HAND AS THE NEXT FILLING...
...TO CREATE A LARGER RICE BALL.
AND THEN YOU COAT IT WITH THIN STRIPS OF GRILLED EGG.
THE CROSS-SECTION LOOKS LIKE THIS.
HA HA HA HA! THIS REALLY IS A LUXURIOUS RICE BALL!
I TAKE A BITE OF THE BARA-ZUSHI, I FIND ANOTHER RICE BALL INSIDE...
...WHICH HAS WASABI LEAVES AND STEMS MARINATED IN SOY SAUCE—DOUBLE THE FUN!
THE STRIPS OF GRILLED EGG GIVE THE WHOLE RICE BALL A KIND AND GENTLE TASTE!

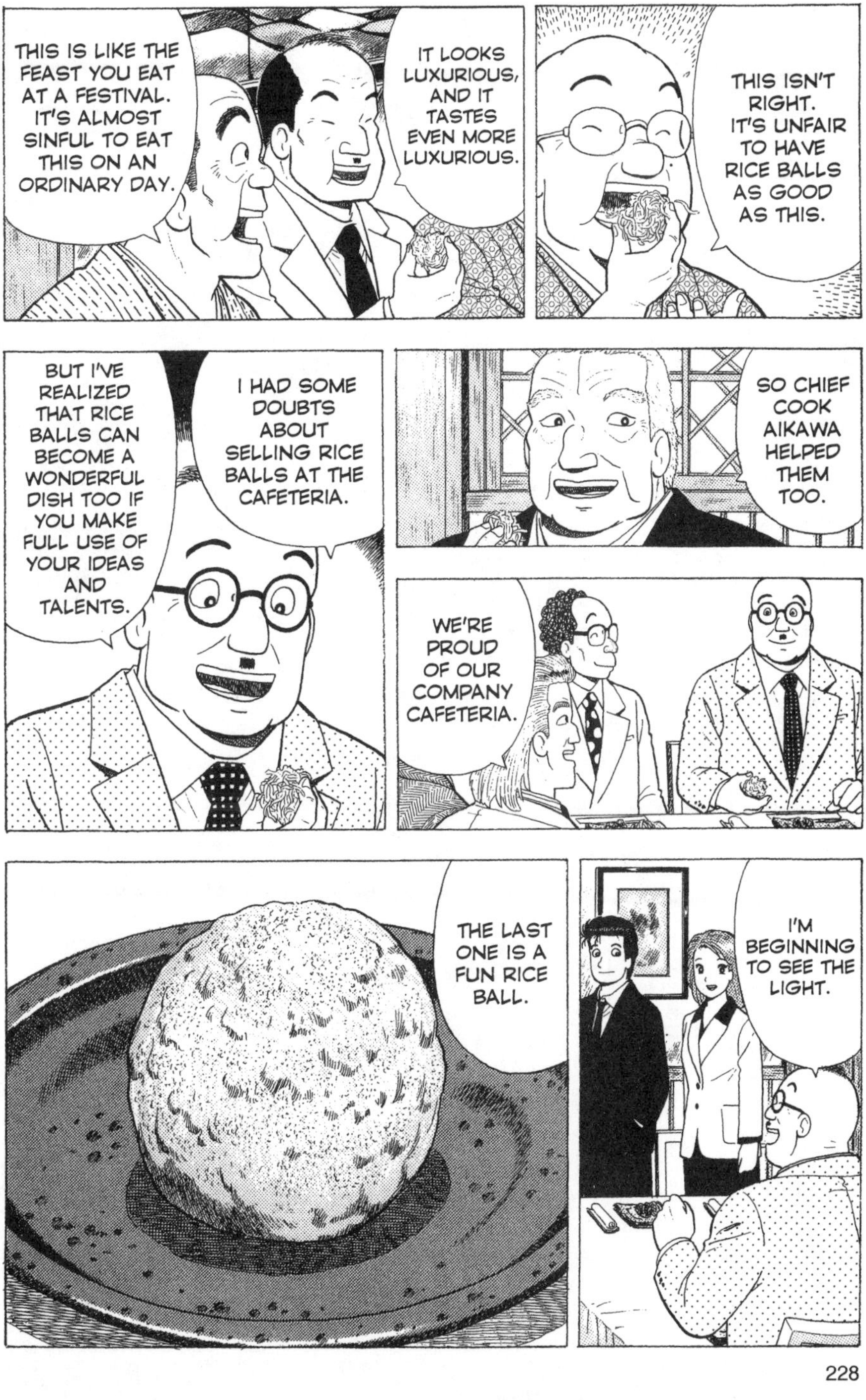
THIS ISN'T RIGHT. IT'S UNFAIR TO HAVE RICE BALLS AS GOOD AS THIS.
IT LOOKS LUXURIOUS, AND IT TASTES EVEN MORE LUXURIOUS.
THIS IS LIKE THE FEAST YOU EAT AT A FESTIVAL. IT'S ALMOST SINFUL TO EAT THIS ON AN ORDINARY DAY.
SO CHIEF COOK AIKAWA HELPED THEM TOO.
WE'RE PROUD OF OUR COMPANY CAFETERIA.
I HAD SOME DOUBTS ABOUT SELLING RICE BALLS AT THE CAFETERIA.
BUT I'VE REALIZED THAT RICE BALLS CAN BECOME A WONDERFUL DISH TOO IF YOU MAKE FULL USE OF YOUR IDEAS AND TALENTS.
I'M BEGINNING TO SEE THE LIGHT.
THE LAST ONE IS A FUN RICE BALL.

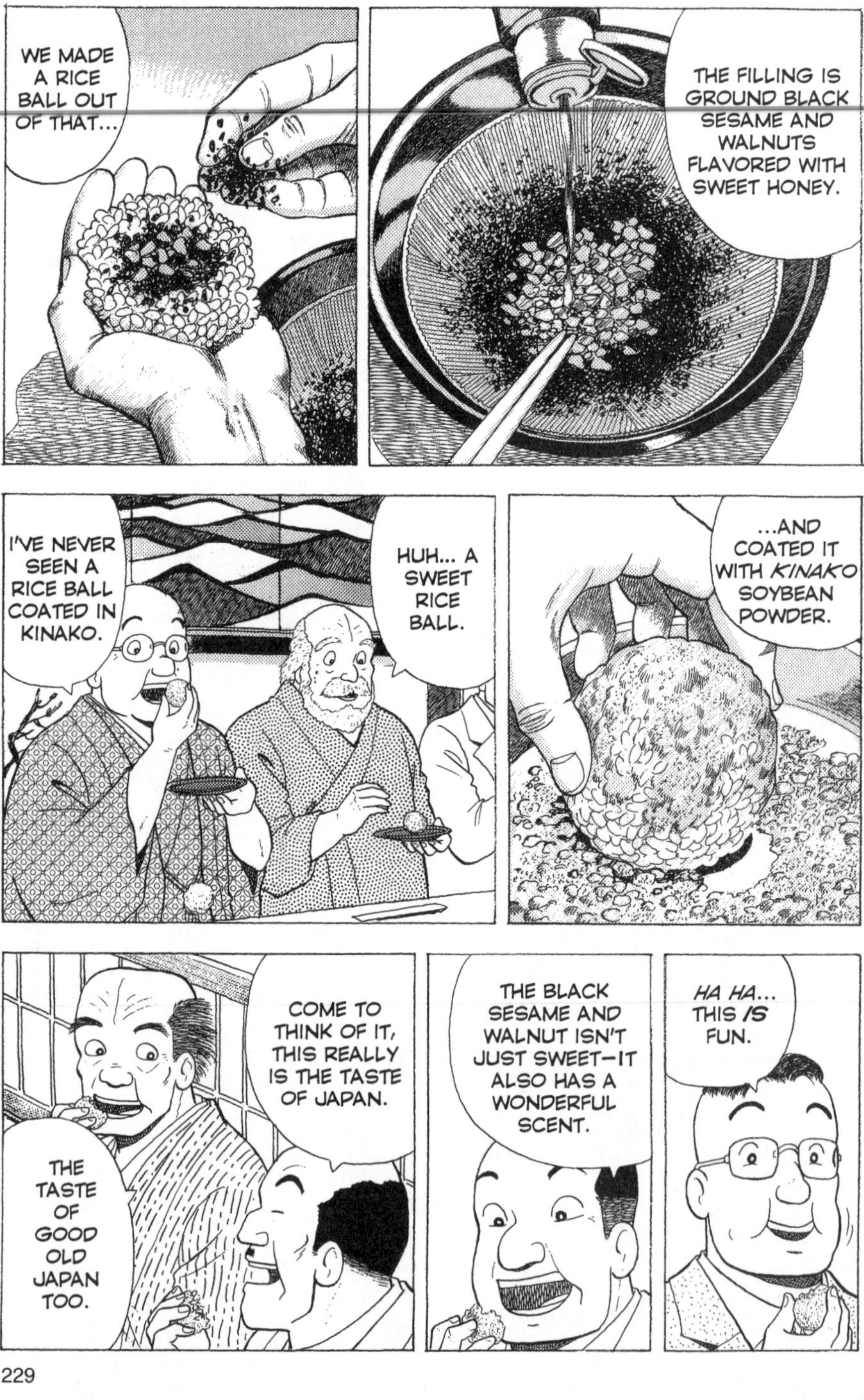
THE FILLING IS GROUND BLACK SESAME AND WALNUTS FLAVORED WITH SWEET HONEY.
WE MADE A RICE BALL OUT OF THAT...
...AND COATED IT WITH *KINAKO* SOYBEAN POWDER.
HUH... A SWEET RICE BALL.
I'VE NEVER SEEN A RICE BALL COATED IN KINAKO.
HA HA... THIS *IS* FUN.
THE BLACK SESAME AND WALNUT ISN'T JUST SWEET—IT ALSO HAS A WONDERFUL SCENT.
COME TO THINK OF IT, THIS REALLY IS THE TASTE OF JAPAN.
THE TASTE OF GOOD OLD JAPAN TOO.

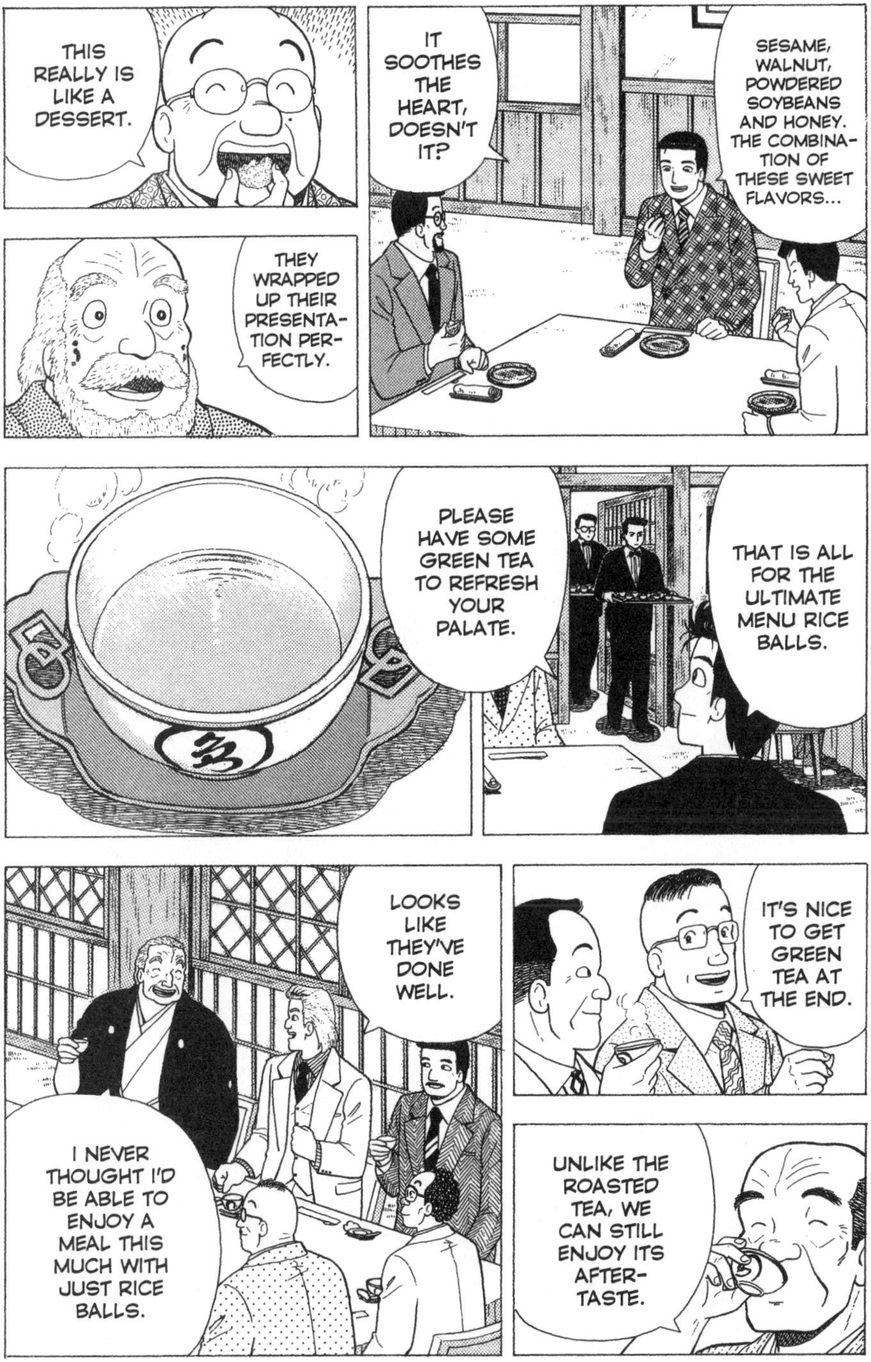
SESAME, WALNUT, POWDERED SOYBEANS AND HONEY. THE COMBINATION OF THESE SWEET FLAVORS...
IT SOOTHES THE HEART, DOESN'T IT?
THIS REALLY IS LIKE A DESSERT.
THEY WRAPPED UP THEIR PRESENTATION PERFECTLY.
THAT IS ALL FOR THE ULTIMATE MENU RICE BALLS.
PLEASE HAVE SOME GREEN TEA TO REFRESH YOUR PALATE.
IT'S NICE TO GET GREEN TEA AT THE END.
UNLIKE THE ROASTED TEA, WE CAN STILL ENJOY ITS AFTERTASTE.
LOOKS LIKE THEY'VE DONE WELL.
I NEVER THOUGHT I'D BE ABLE TO ENJOY A MEAL THIS MUCH WITH JUST RICE BALLS.

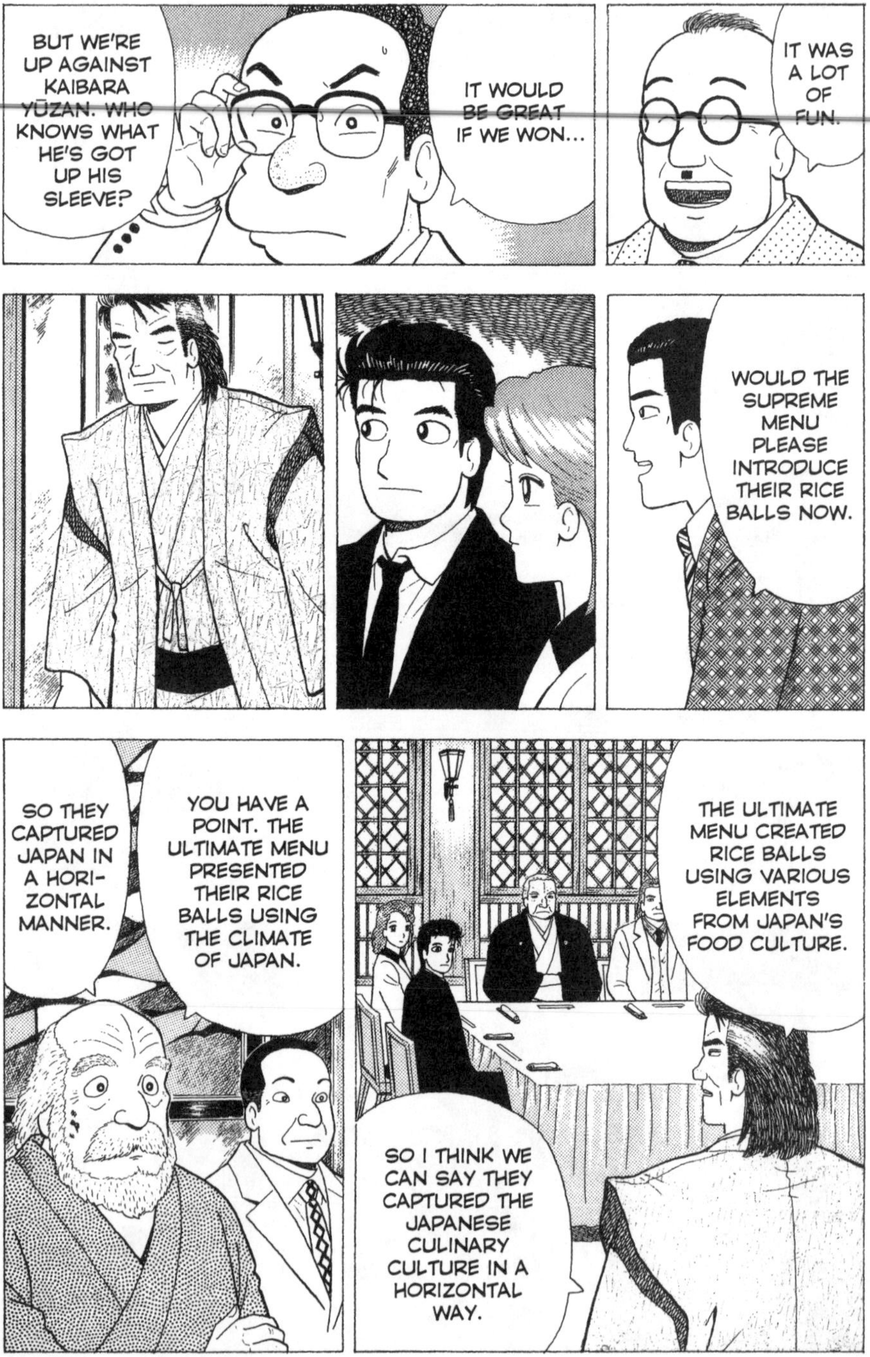
IT WAS A LOT OF FUN.
IT WOULD BE GREAT IF WE WON...
BUT WE'RE UP AGAINST KAIBARA YŪZAN. WHO KNOWS WHAT HE'S GOT UP HIS SLEEVE?
WOULD THE SUPREME MENU PLEASE INTRODUCE THEIR RICE BALLS NOW.
THE ULTIMATE MENU CREATED RICE BALLS USING VARIOUS ELEMENTS FROM JAPAN'S FOOD CULTURE.
SO I THINK WE CAN SAY THEY CAPTURED THE JAPANESE CULINARY CULTURE IN A HORIZONTAL WAY.
YOU HAVE A POINT. THE ULTIMATE MENU PRESENTED THEIR RICE BALLS USING THE CLIMATE OF JAPAN.
SO THEY CAPTURED JAPAN IN A HORI-ZONTAL MANNER.

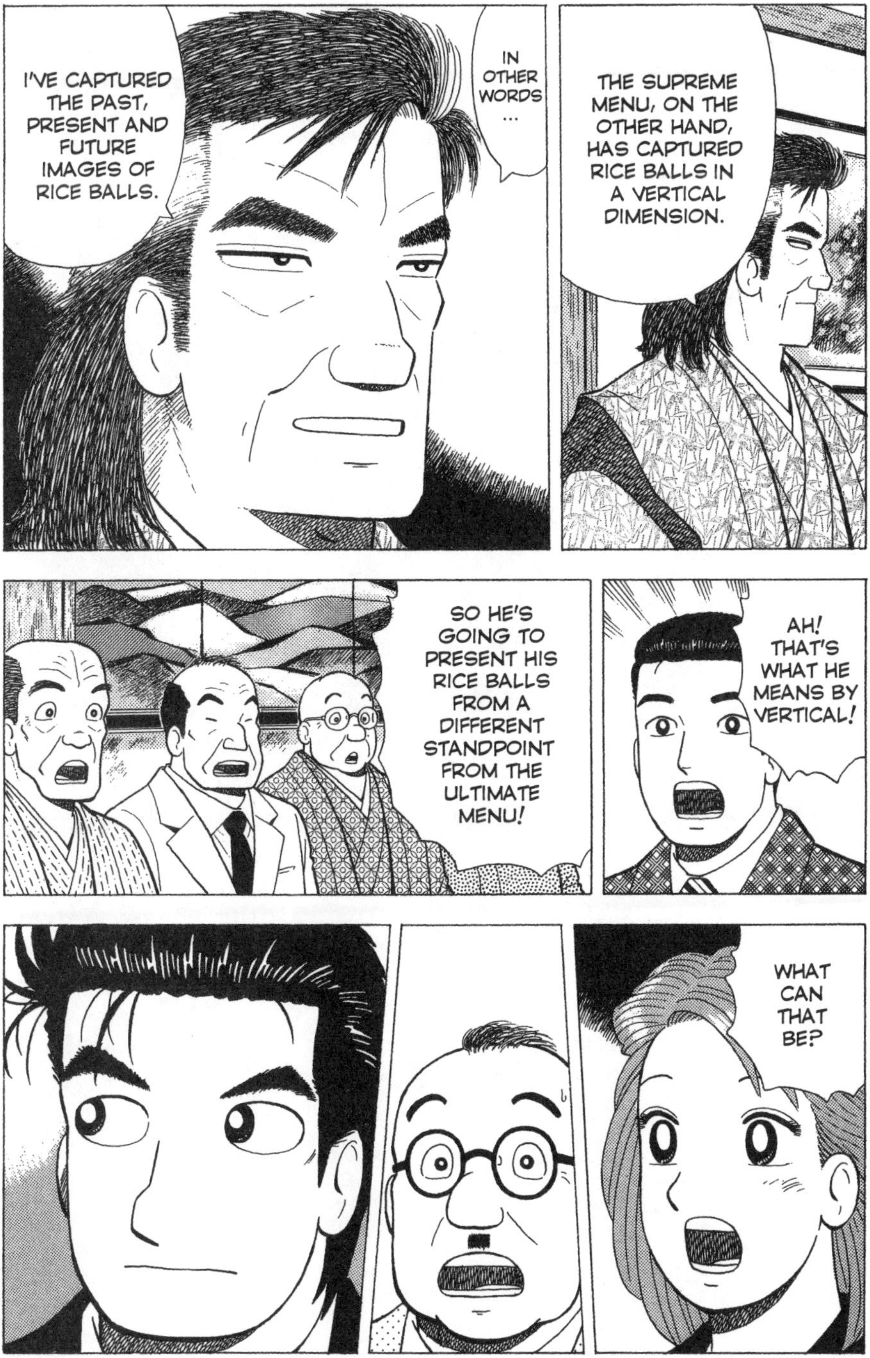
THE SUPREME MENU, ON THE OTHER HAND, HAS CAPTURED RICE BALLS IN A VERTICAL DIMENSION.
IN OTHER WORDS ...
I'VE CAPTURED THE PAST, PRESENT AND FUTURE IMAGES OF RICE BALLS.
AH! THAT'S WHAT HE MEANS BY VERTICAL!
SO HE'S GOING TO PRESENT HIS RICE BALLS FROM A DIFFERENT STANDPOINT FROM THE ULTIMATE MENU!
WHAT CAN THAT BE?

EIGHTH COURSE

RICE BALL MATCH (PART THREE)

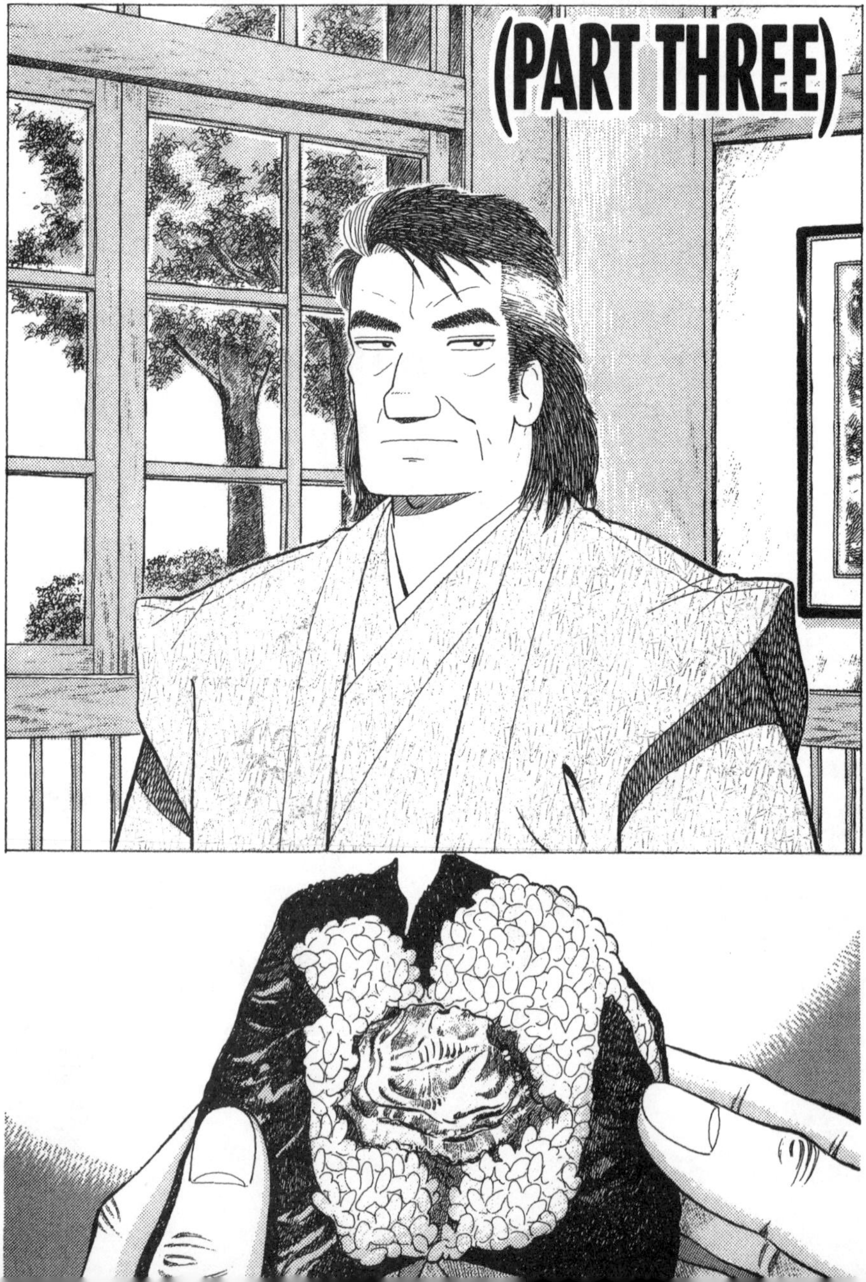

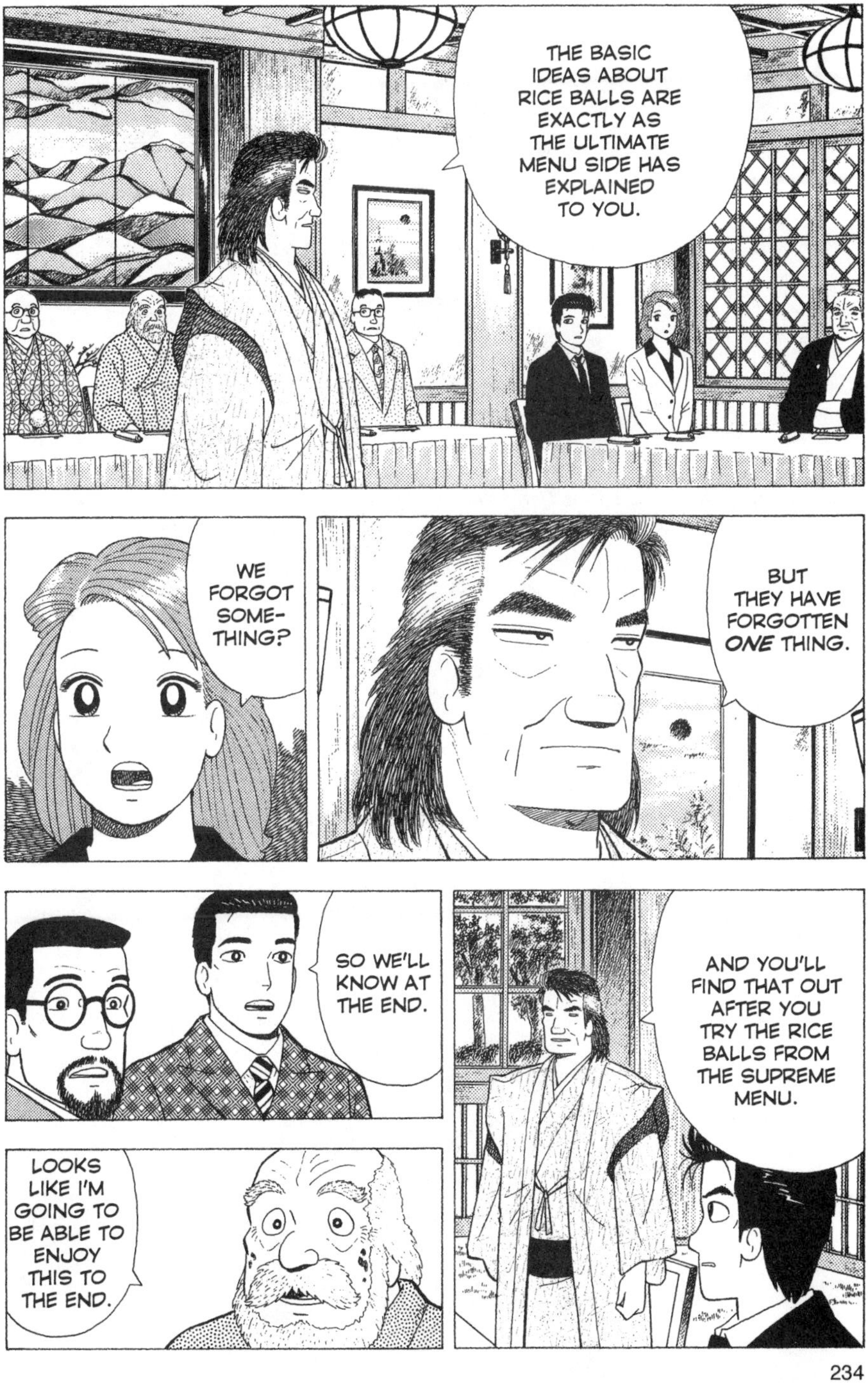
THE BASIC IDEAS ABOUT RICE BALLS ARE EXACTLY AS THE ULTIMATE MENU SIDE HAS EXPLAINED TO YOU.
BUT THEY HAVE FORGOTTEN *ONE* THING.
WE FORGOT SOME-THING?
AND YOU'LL FIND THAT OUT AFTER YOU TRY THE RICE BALLS FROM THE SUPREME MENU.
SO WE'LL KNOW AT THE END.
LOOKS LIKE I'M GOING TO BE ABLE TO ENJOY THIS TO THE END.

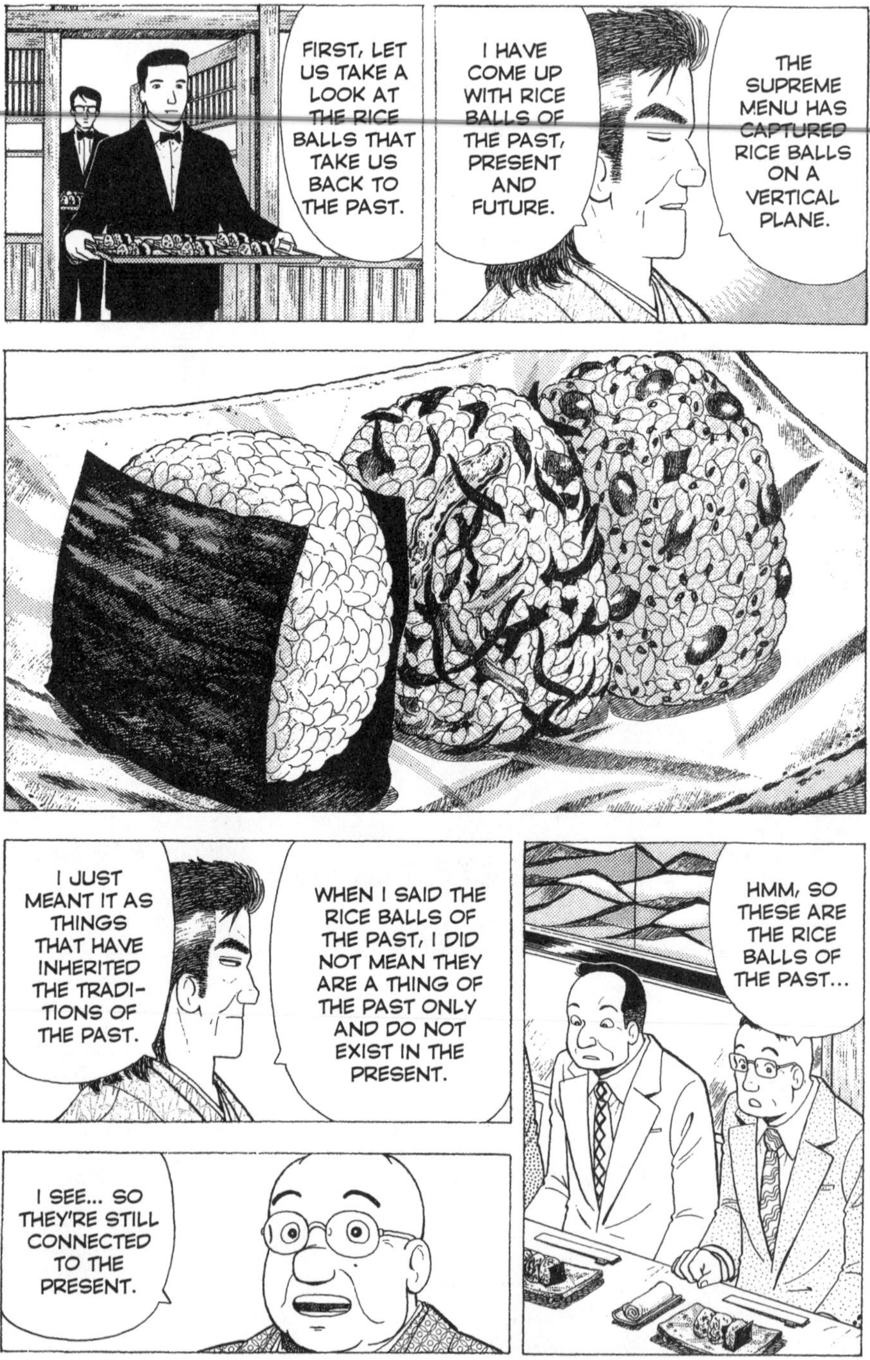
THE SUPREME MENU HAS CAPTURED RICE BALLS ON A VERTICAL PLANE.
I HAVE COME UP WITH RICE BALLS OF THE PAST, PRESENT AND FUTURE.
FIRST, LET US TAKE A LOOK AT THE RICE BALLS THAT TAKE US BACK TO THE PAST.
HMM, SO THESE ARE THE RICE BALLS OF THE PAST...
WHEN I SAID THE RICE BALLS OF THE PAST, I DID NOT MEAN THEY ARE A THING OF THE PAST ONLY AND DO NOT EXIST IN THE PRESENT.
I JUST MEANT IT AS THINGS THAT HAVE INHERITED THE TRADITIONS OF THE PAST.
I SEE... SO THEY'RE STILL CONNECTED TO THE PRESENT.

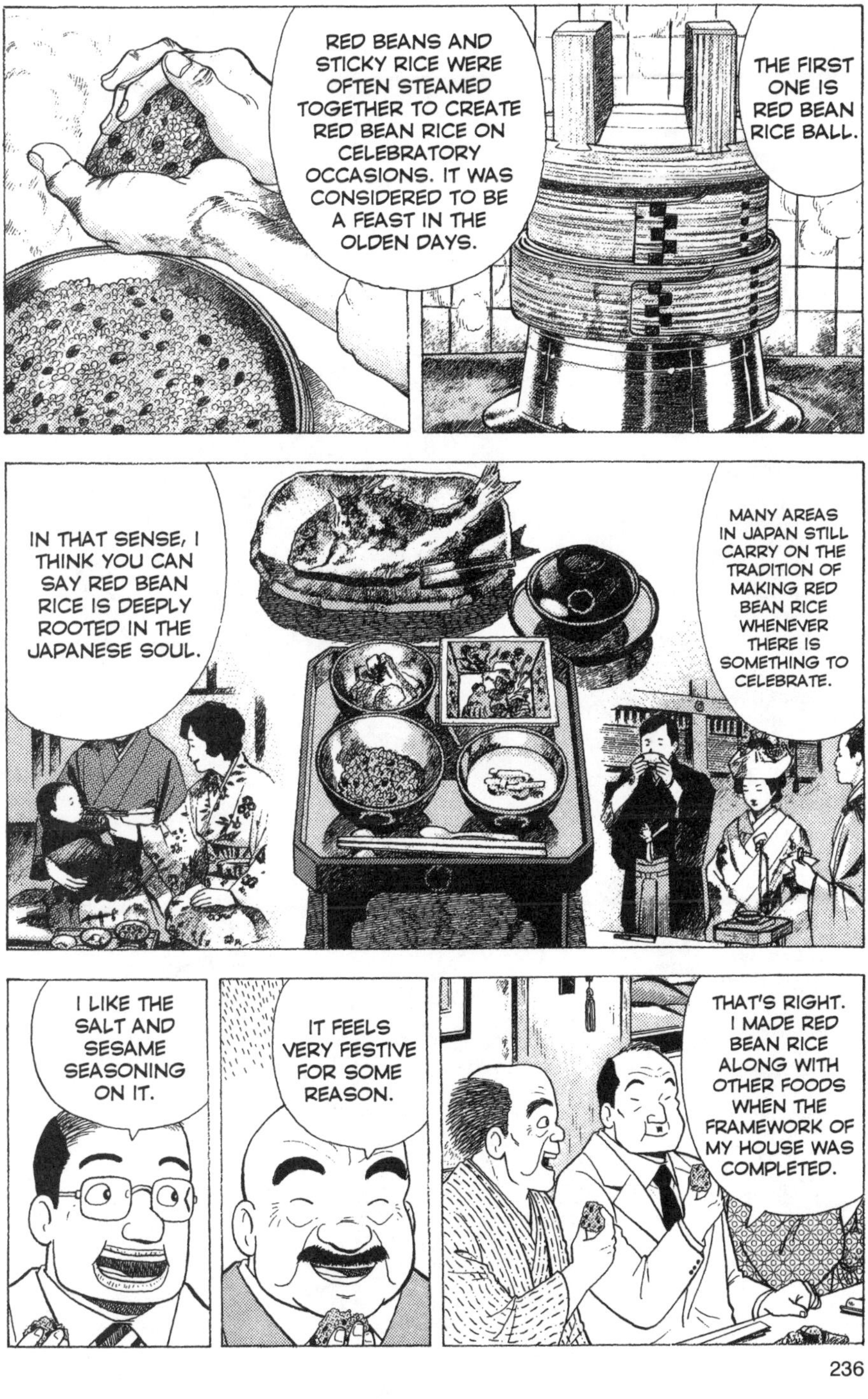
THE FIRST ONE IS RED BEAN RICE BALL.
RED BEANS AND STICKY RICE WERE OFTEN STEAMED TOGETHER TO CREATE RED BEAN RICE ON CELEBRATORY OCCASIONS. IT WAS CONSIDERED TO BE A FEAST IN THE OLDEN DAYS.
MANY AREAS IN JAPAN STILL CARRY ON THE TRADITION OF MAKING RED BEAN RICE WHENEVER THERE IS SOMETHING TO CELEBRATE.
IN THAT SENSE, I THINK YOU CAN SAY RED BEAN RICE IS DEEPLY ROOTED IN THE JAPANESE SOUL.
THAT'S RIGHT. I MADE RED BEAN RICE ALONG WITH OTHER FOODS WHEN THE FRAMEWORK OF MY HOUSE WAS COMPLETED.
IT FEELS VERY FESTIVE FOR SOME REASON.
I LIKE THE SALT AND SESAME SEASONING ON IT.

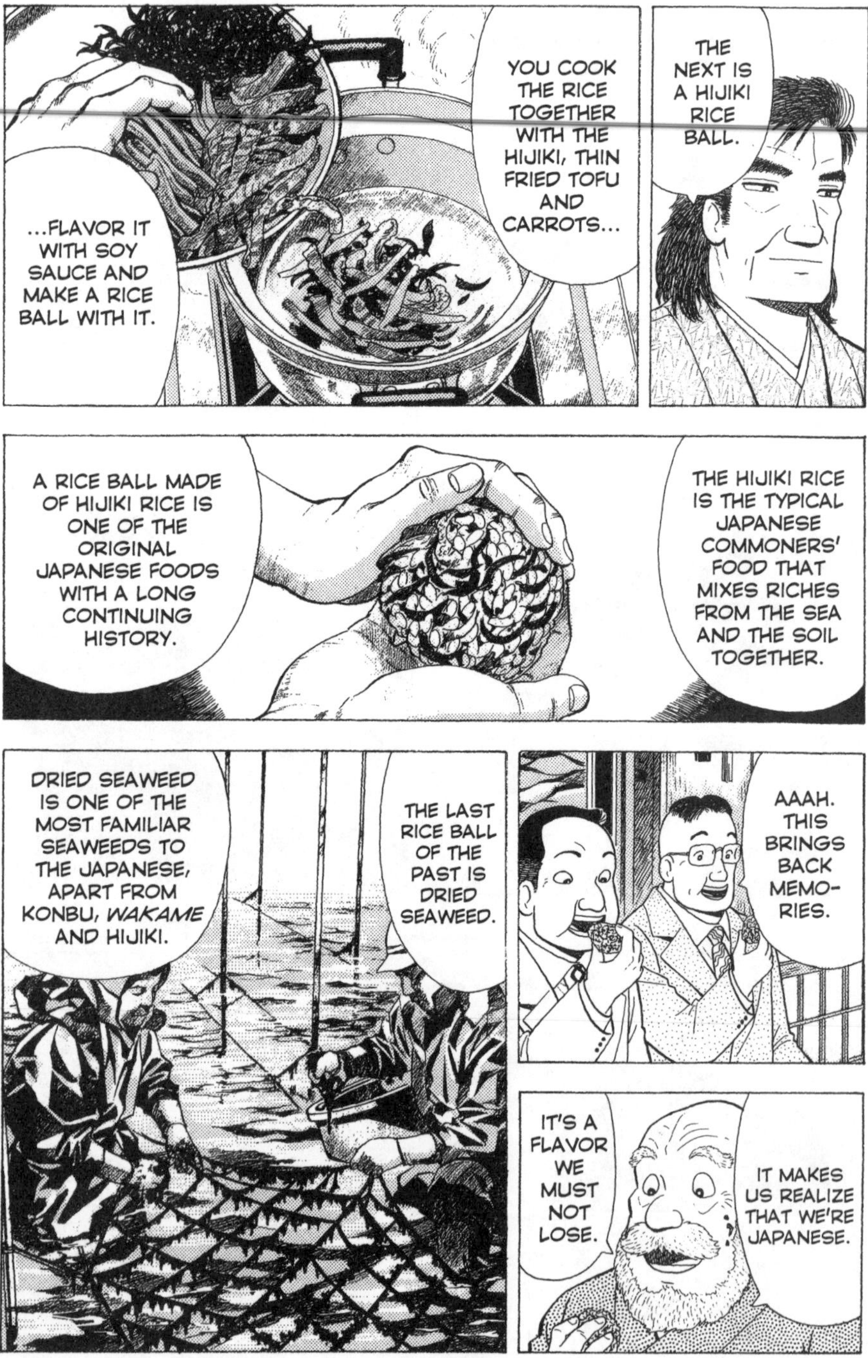
THE NEXT IS A HIJIKI RICE BALL.
YOU COOK THE RICE TOGETHER WITH THE HIJIKI, THIN FRIED TOFU AND CARROTS...
...FLAVOR IT WITH SOY SAUCE AND MAKE A RICE BALL WITH IT.
THE HIJIKI RICE IS THE TYPICAL JAPANESE COMMONERS' FOOD THAT MIXES RICHES FROM THE SEA AND THE SOIL TOGETHER.
A RICE BALL MADE OF HIJIKI RICE IS ONE OF THE ORIGINAL JAPANESE FOODS WITH A LONG CONTINUING HISTORY.
AAAH. THIS BRINGS BACK MEMO-RIES.
IT MAKES US REALIZE THAT WE'RE JAPANESE.
IT'S A FLAVOR WE MUST NOT LOSE.
THE LAST RICE BALL OF THE PAST IS DRIED SEAWEED.
DRIED SEAWEED IS ONE OF THE MOST FAMILIAR SEAWEEDS TO THE JAPANESE, APART FROM KONBU, *WAKAME* AND HIJIKI.

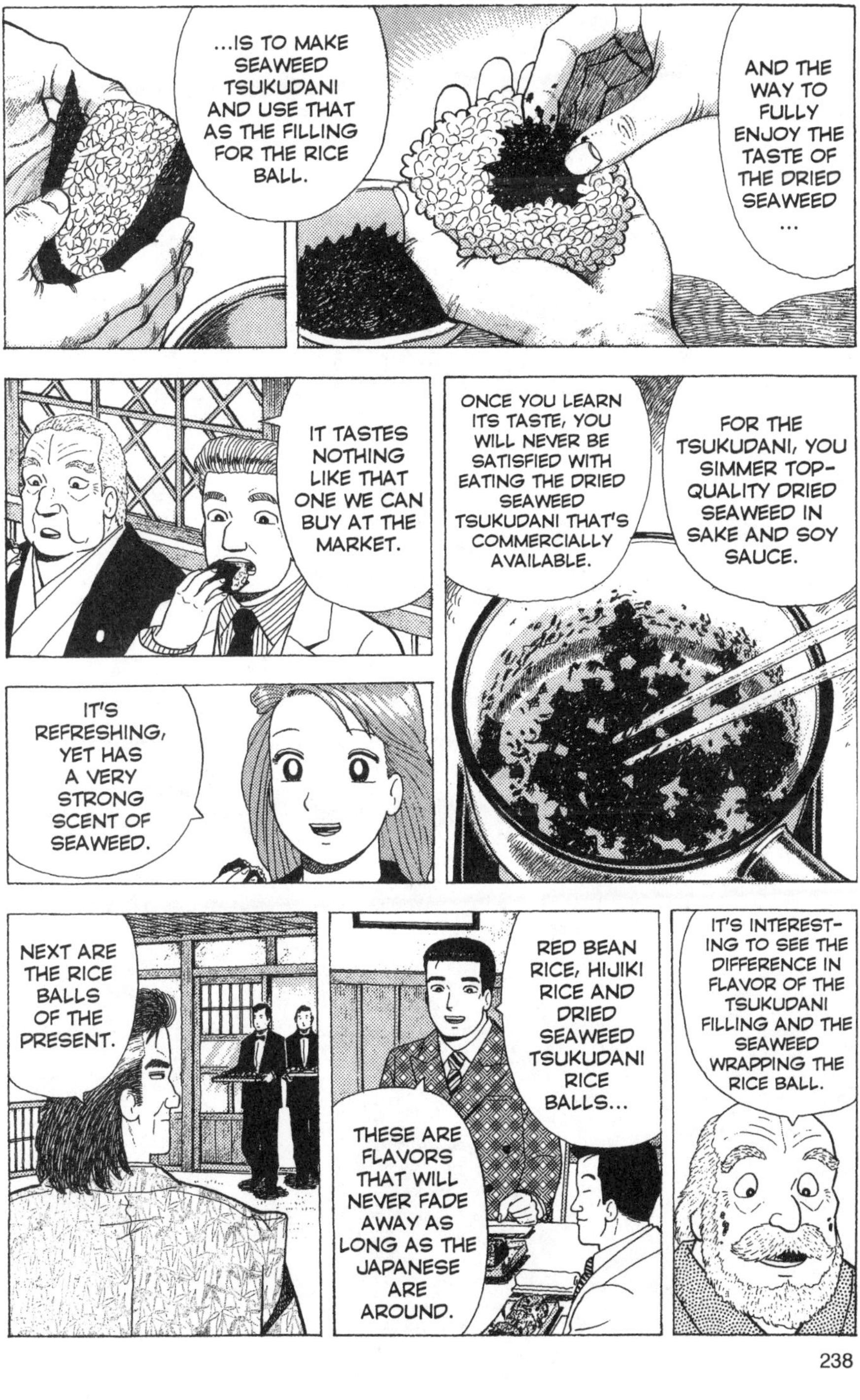
AND THE WAY TO FULLY ENJOY THE TASTE OF THE DRIED SEAWEED ...
...IS TO MAKE SEAWEED TSUKUDANI AND USE THAT AS THE FILLING FOR THE RICE BALL.
FOR THE TSUKUDANI, YOU SIMMER TOP-QUALITY DRIED SEAWEED IN SAKE AND SOY SAUCE.
ONCE YOU LEARN ITS TASTE, YOU WILL NEVER BE SATISFIED WITH EATING THE DRIED SEAWEED TSUKUDANI THAT'S COMMERCIALLY AVAILABLE.
IT TASTES NOTHING LIKE THAT ONE WE CAN BUY AT THE MARKET.
IT'S REFRESHING, YET HAS A VERY STRONG SCENT OF SEAWEED.
IT'S INTERESTING TO SEE THE DIFFERENCE IN FLAVOR OF THE TSUKUDANI FILLING AND THE SEAWEED WRAPPING THE RICE BALL.
RED BEAN RICE, HIJIKI RICE AND DRIED SEAWEED TSUKUDANI RICE BALLS...
THESE ARE FLAVORS THAT WILL NEVER FADE AWAY AS LONG AS THE JAPANESE ARE AROUND.
NEXT ARE THE RICE BALLS OF THE PRESENT.

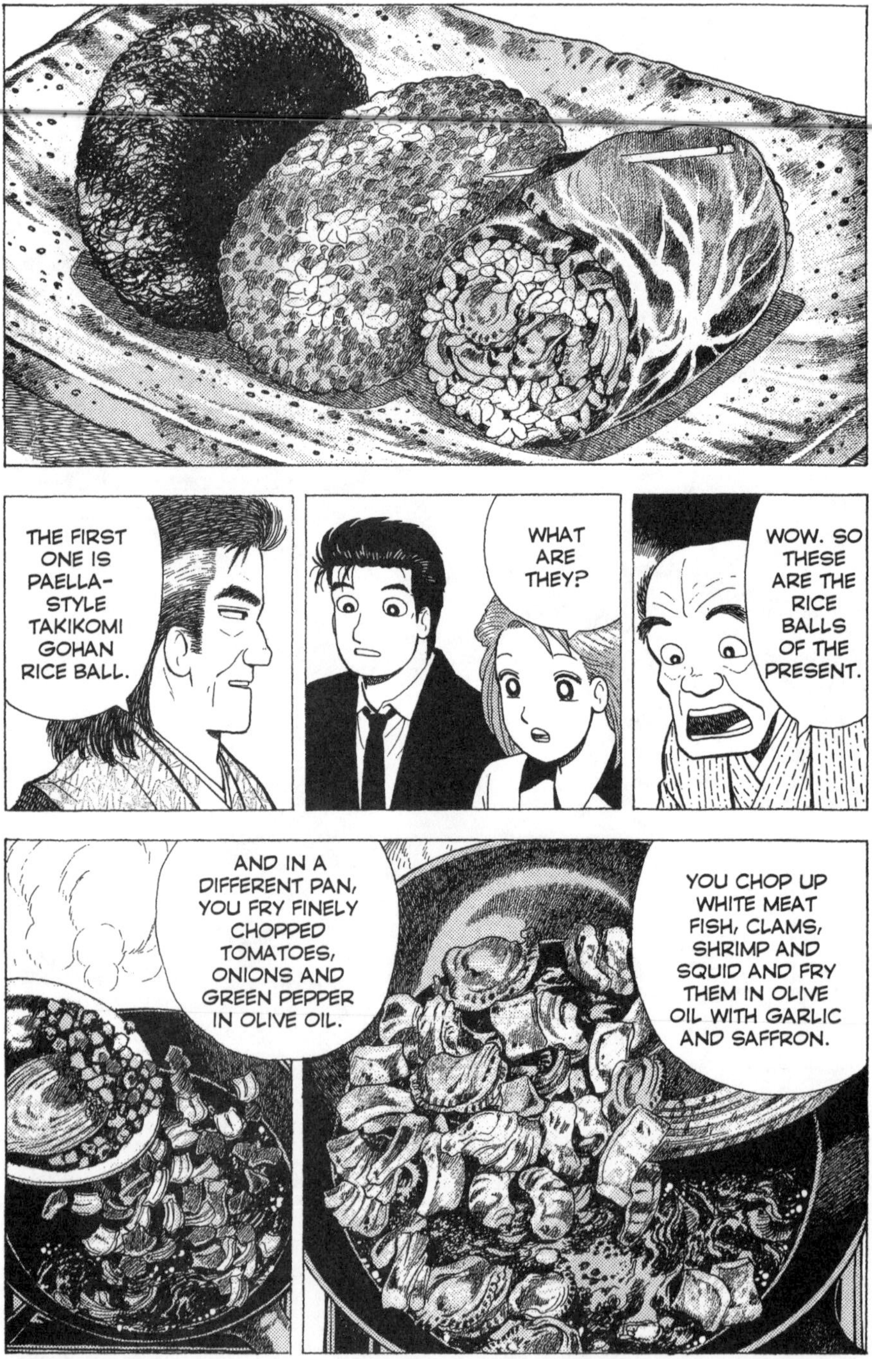
WOW. SO THESE ARE THE RICE BALLS OF THE PRESENT.
WHAT ARE THEY?
THE FIRST ONE IS PAELLA-STYLE TAKIKOMI GOHAN RICE BALL.
YOU CHOP UP WHITE MEAT FISH, CLAMS, SHRIMP AND SQUID AND FRY THEM IN OLIVE OIL WITH GARLIC AND SAFFRON.
AND IN A DIFFERENT PAN, YOU FRY FINELY CHOPPED TOMATOES, ONIONS AND GREEN PEPPER IN OLIVE OIL.

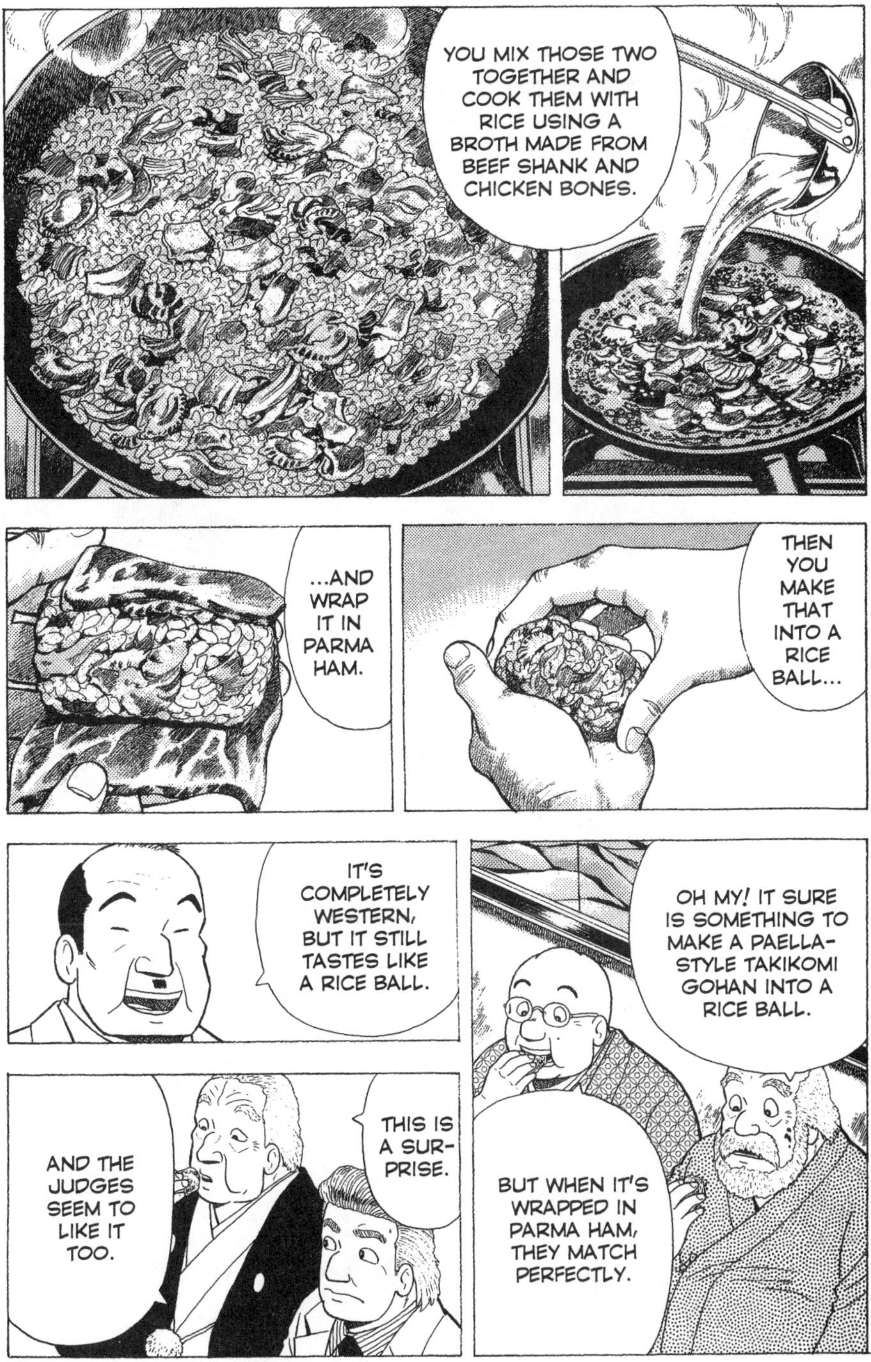
YOU MIX THOSE TWO TOGETHER AND COOK THEM WITH RICE USING A BROTH MADE FROM BEEF SHANK AND CHICKEN BONES.
THEN YOU MAKE THAT INTO A RICE BALL...
...AND WRAP IT IN PARMA HAM.
OH MY! IT SURE IS SOMETHING TO MAKE A PAELLA-STYLE TAKIKOMI GOHAN INTO A RICE BALL.
BUT WHEN IT'S WRAPPED IN PARMA HAM, THEY MATCH PERFECTLY.
IT'S COMPLETELY WESTERN, BUT IT STILL TASTES LIKE A RICE BALL.
THIS IS A SUR-PRISE.
AND THE JUDGES SEEM TO LIKE IT TOO.

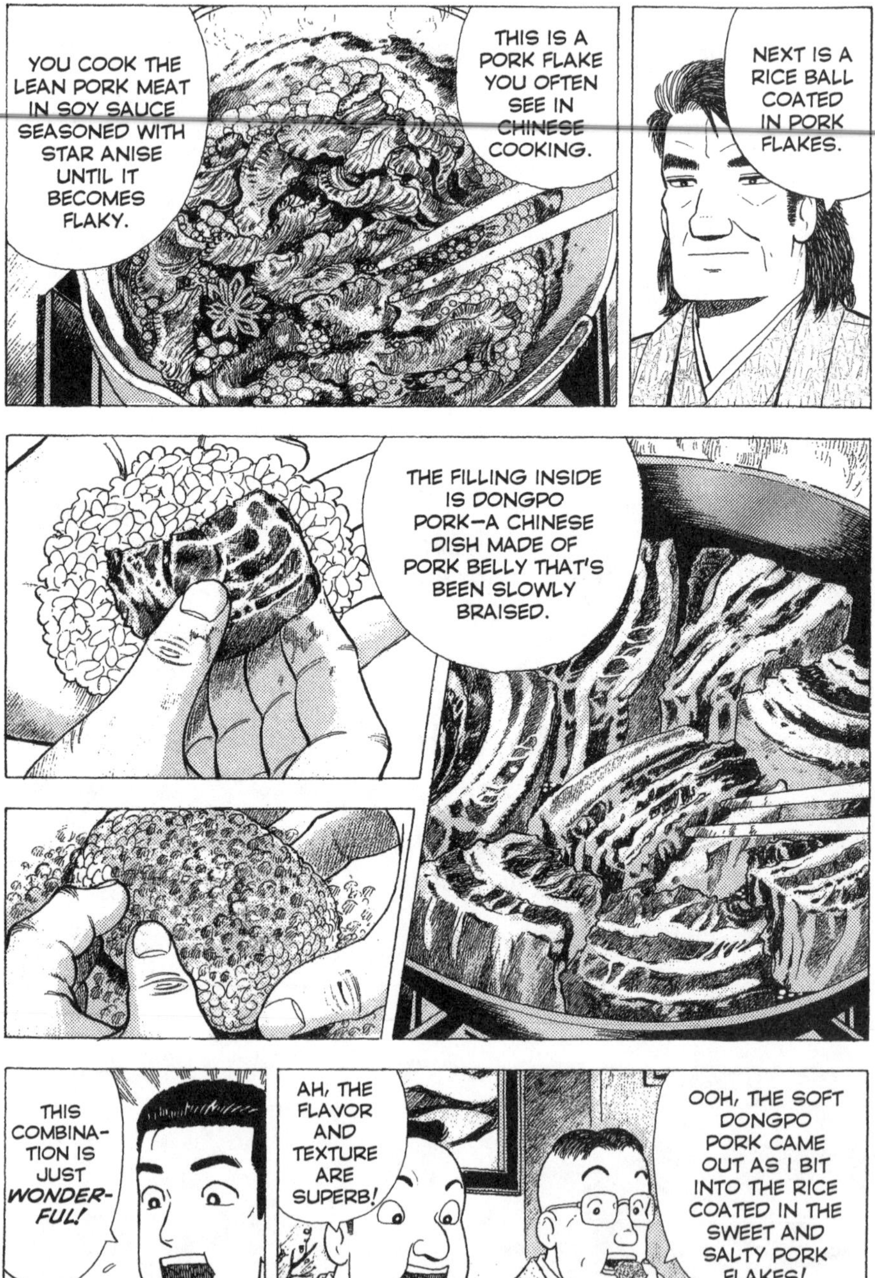
NEXT IS A RICE BALL COATED IN PORK FLAKES.
THIS IS A PORK FLAKE YOU OFTEN SEE IN CHINESE COOKING.
YOU COOK THE LEAN PORK MEAT IN SOY SAUCE SEASONED WITH STAR ANISE UNTIL IT BECOMES FLAKY.
THE FILLING INSIDE IS DONGPO PORK—A CHINESE DISH MADE OF PORK BELLY THAT'S BEEN SLOWLY BRAISED.
OOH, THE SOFT DONGPO PORK CAME OUT AS I BIT INTO THE RICE COATED IN THE SWEET AND SALTY PORK FLAKES!
AH, THE FLAVOR AND TEXTURE ARE SUPERB!
THIS COMBINATION IS JUST *WONDERFUL!*

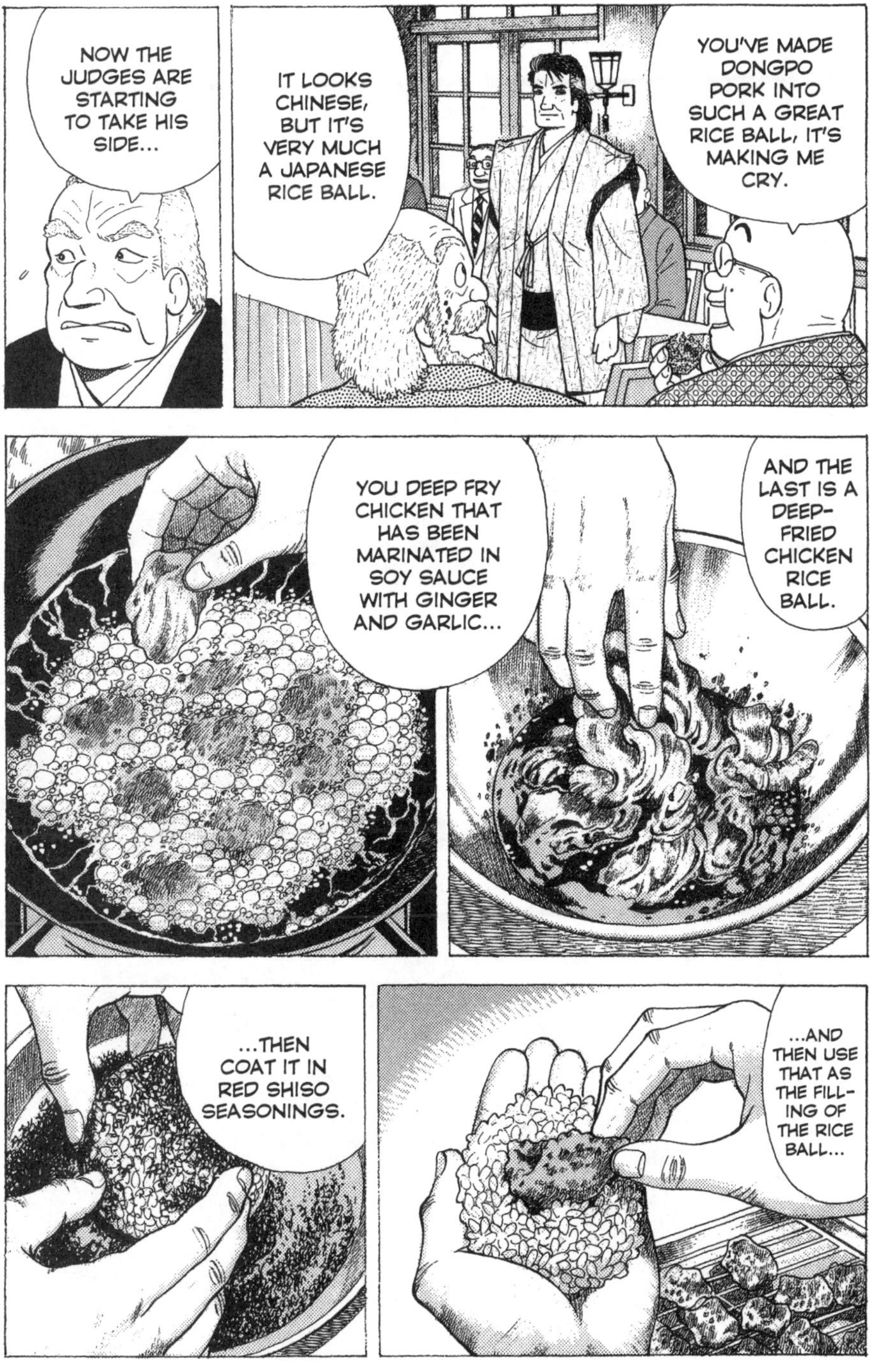
YOU'VE MADE DONGPO PORK INTO SUCH A GREAT RICE BALL, IT'S MAKING ME CRY.
IT LOOKS CHINESE, BUT IT'S VERY MUCH A JAPANESE RICE BALL.
NOW THE JUDGES ARE STARTING TO TAKE HIS SIDE...
AND THE LAST IS A DEEP-FRIED CHICKEN RICE BALL.
YOU DEEP FRY CHICKEN THAT HAS BEEN MARINATED IN SOY SAUCE WITH GINGER AND GARLIC...
...AND THEN USE THAT AS THE FILL-ING OF THE RICE BALL...
...THEN COAT IT IN RED SHISO SEASONINGS.

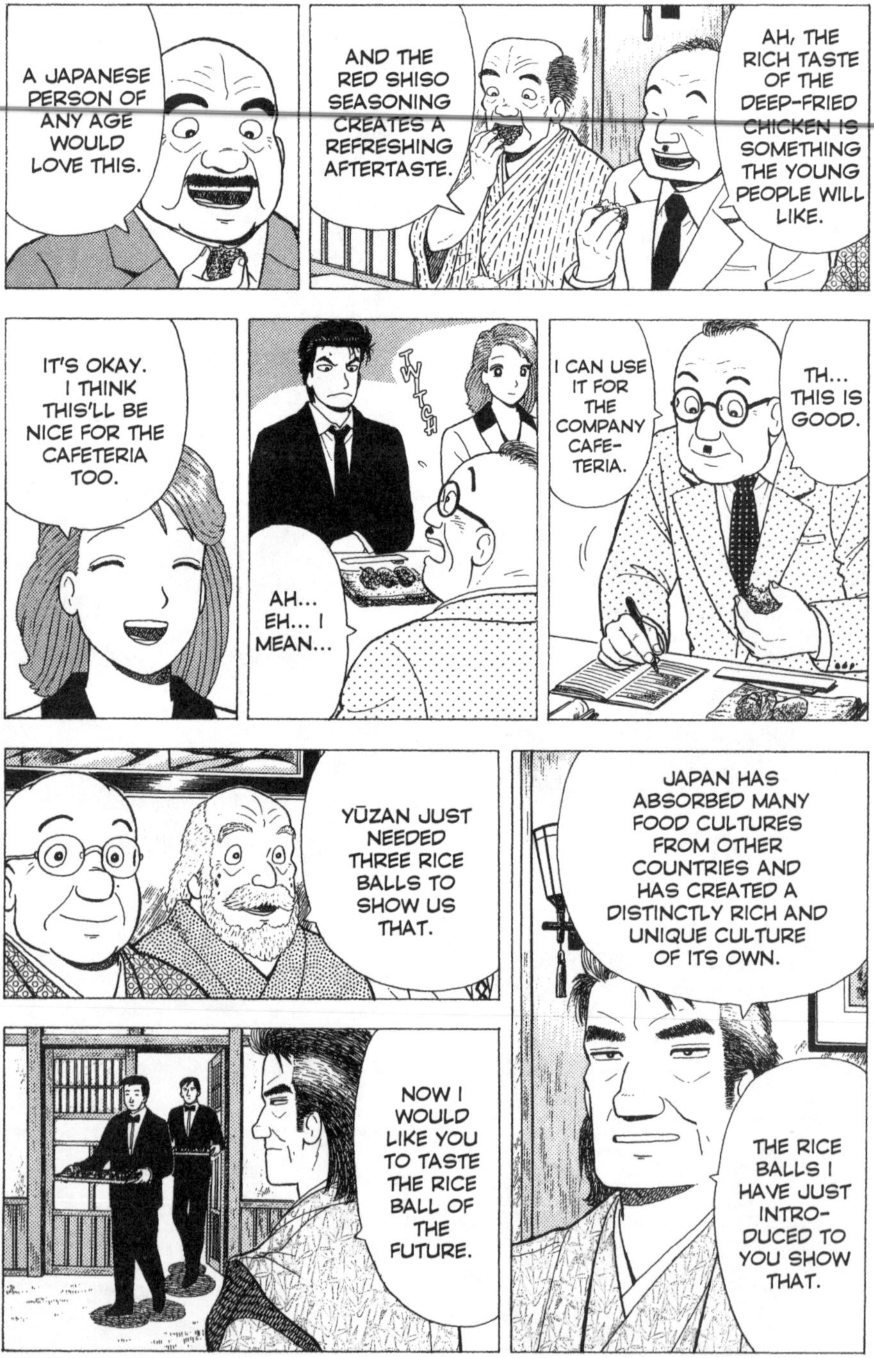
AH, THE RICH TASTE OF THE DEEP-FRIED CHICKEN IS SOMETHING THE YOUNG PEOPLE WILL LIKE.
AND THE RED SHISO SEASONING CREATES A REFRESHING AFTERTASTE.
A JAPANESE PERSON OF ANY AGE WOULD LOVE THIS.
TH... THIS IS GOOD.
I CAN USE IT FOR THE COMPANY CAFE-TERIA.
TWITCH
AH... EH... I MEAN...
IT'S OKAY. I THINK THIS'LL BE NICE FOR THE CAFETERIA TOO.
JAPAN HAS ABSORBED MANY FOOD CULTURES FROM OTHER COUNTRIES AND HAS CREATED A DISTINCTLY RICH AND UNIQUE CULTURE OF ITS OWN.
THE RICE BALLS I HAVE JUST INTRO-DUCED TO YOU SHOW THAT.
YŪZAN JUST NEEDED THREE RICE BALLS TO SHOW US THAT.
NOW I WOULD LIKE YOU TO TASTE THE RICE BALL OF THE FUTURE.

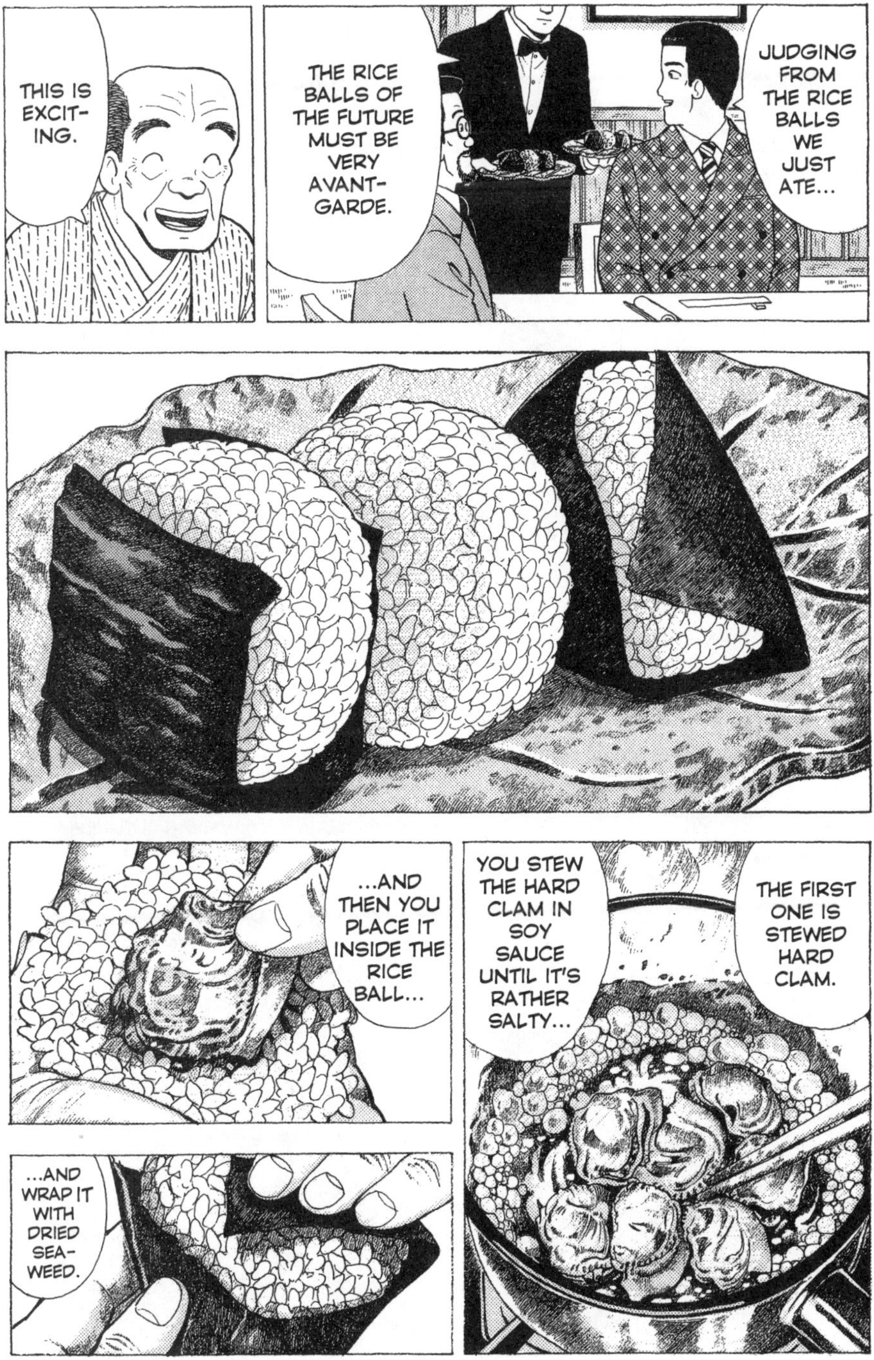
JUDGING FROM THE RICE BALLS WE JUST ATE...
THE RICE BALLS OF THE FUTURE MUST BE VERY AVANT-GARDE.
THIS IS EXCITING.
THE FIRST ONE IS STEWED HARD CLAM.
YOU STEW THE HARD CLAM IN SOY SAUCE UNTIL IT'S RATHER SALTY...
...AND THEN YOU PLACE IT INSIDE THE RICE BALL...
...AND WRAP IT WITH DRIED SEAWEED.

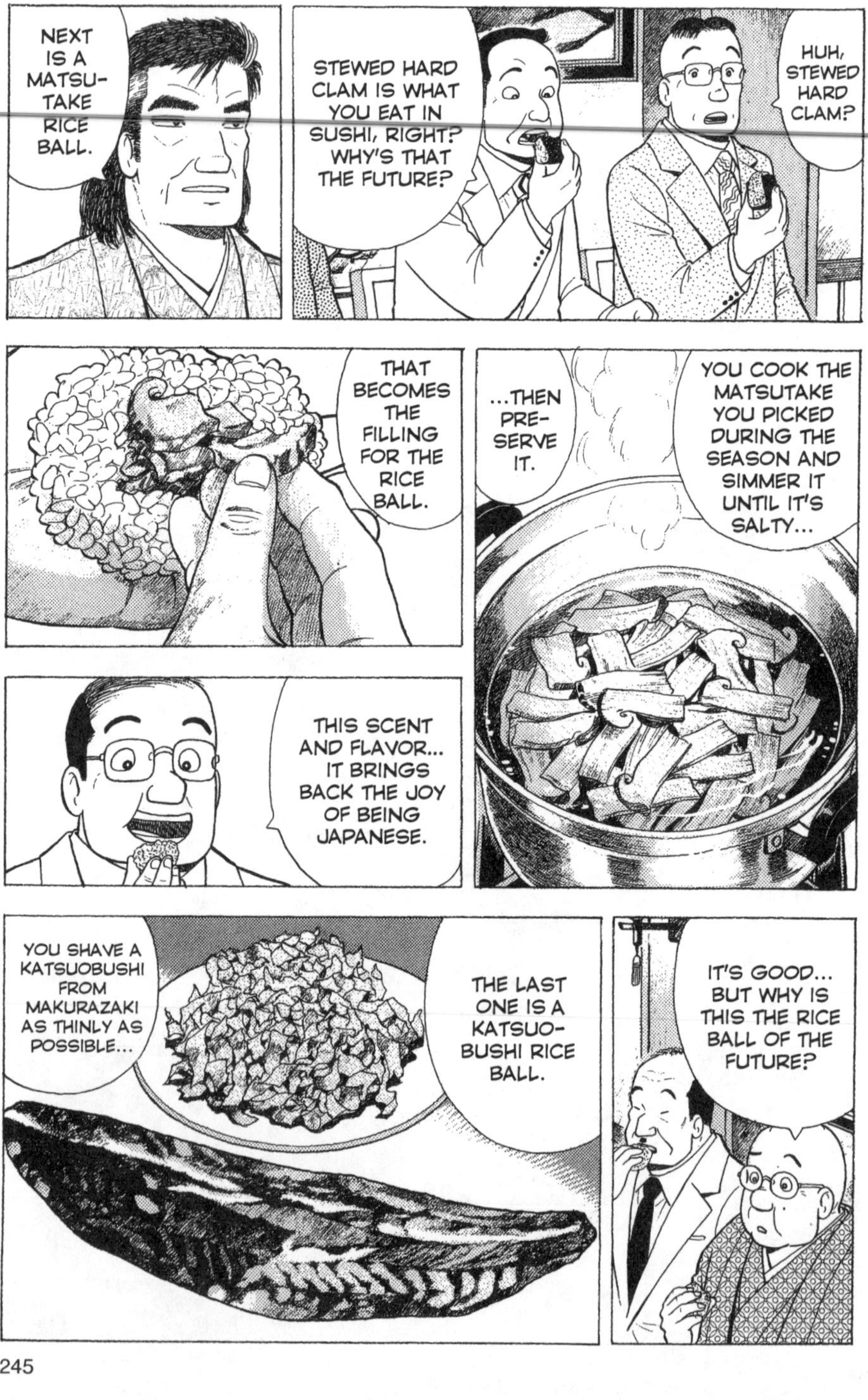
HUH, STEWED HARD CLAM?
STEWED HARD CLAM IS WHAT YOU EAT IN SUSHI, RIGHT? WHY'S THAT THE FUTURE?
NEXT IS A MATSU-TAKE RICE BALL.
YOU COOK THE MATSUTAKE YOU PICKED DURING THE SEASON AND SIMMER IT UNTIL IT'S SALTY...
...THEN PRE-SERVE IT.
THAT BECOMES THE FILLING FOR THE RICE BALL.
THIS SCENT AND FLAVOR... IT BRINGS BACK THE JOY OF BEING JAPANESE.
IT'S GOOD... BUT WHY IS THIS THE RICE BALL OF THE FUTURE?
THE LAST ONE IS A KATSUO-BUSHI RICE BALL.
YOU SHAVE A KATSUOBUSHI FROM MAKURAZAKI AS THINLY AS POSSIBLE...

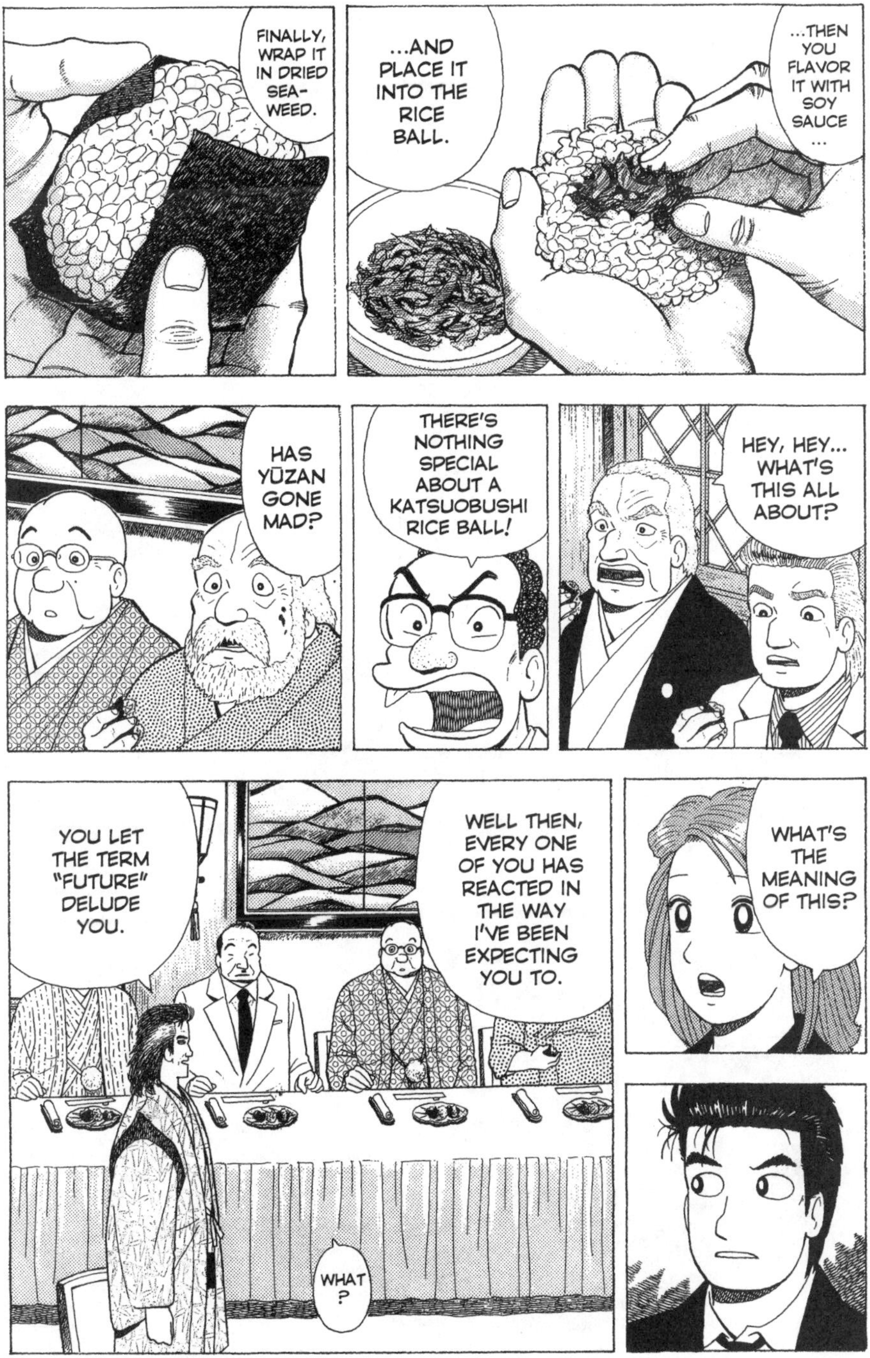
...THEN YOU FLAVOR IT WITH SOY SAUCE ...
...AND PLACE IT INTO THE RICE BALL.
FINALLY, WRAP IT IN DRIED SEA-WEED.
HEY, HEY... WHAT'S THIS ALL ABOUT?
THERE'S NOTHING SPECIAL ABOUT A KATSUOBUSHI RICE BALL!
HAS YŪZAN GONE MAD?
WHAT'S THE MEANING OF THIS?
WELL THEN, EVERY ONE OF YOU HAS REACTED IN THE WAY I'VE BEEN EXPECTING YOU TO.
YOU LET THE TERM "FUTURE" DELUDE YOU.
WHAT ?

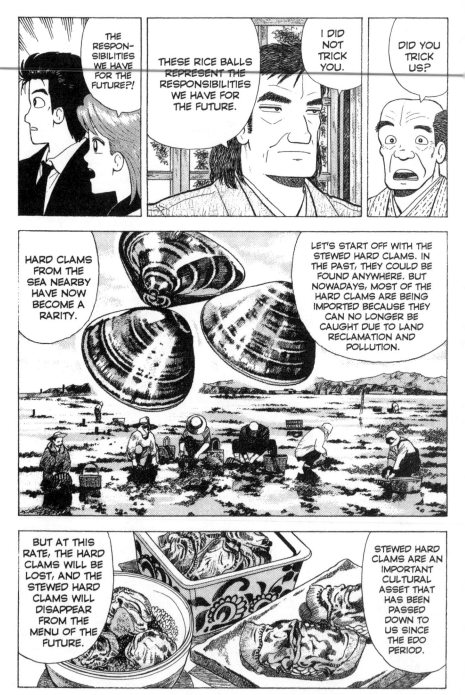

DID YOU TRICK US?
I DID NOT TRICK YOU.
THESE RICE BALLS REPRESENT THE RESPONSIBILITIES WE HAVE FOR THE FUTURE.
THE RESPON-SIBILITIES WE HAVE FOR THE FUTURE?!
LET'S START OFF WITH THE STEWED HARD CLAMS. IN THE PAST, THEY COULD BE FOUND ANYWHERE. BUT NOWADAYS, MOST OF THE HARD CLAMS ARE BEING IMPORTED BECAUSE THEY CAN NO LONGER BE CAUGHT DUE TO LAND RECLAMATION AND POLLUTION.
HARD CLAMS FROM THE SEA NEARBY HAVE NOW BECOME A RARITY.
STEWED HARD CLAMS ARE AN IMPORTANT CULTURAL ASSET THAT HAS BEEN PASSED DOWN TO US SINCE THE EDO PERIOD.
BUT AT THIS RATE, THE HARD CLAMS WILL BE LOST, AND THE STEWED HARD CLAMS WILL DISAPPEAR FROM THE MENU OF THE FUTURE.

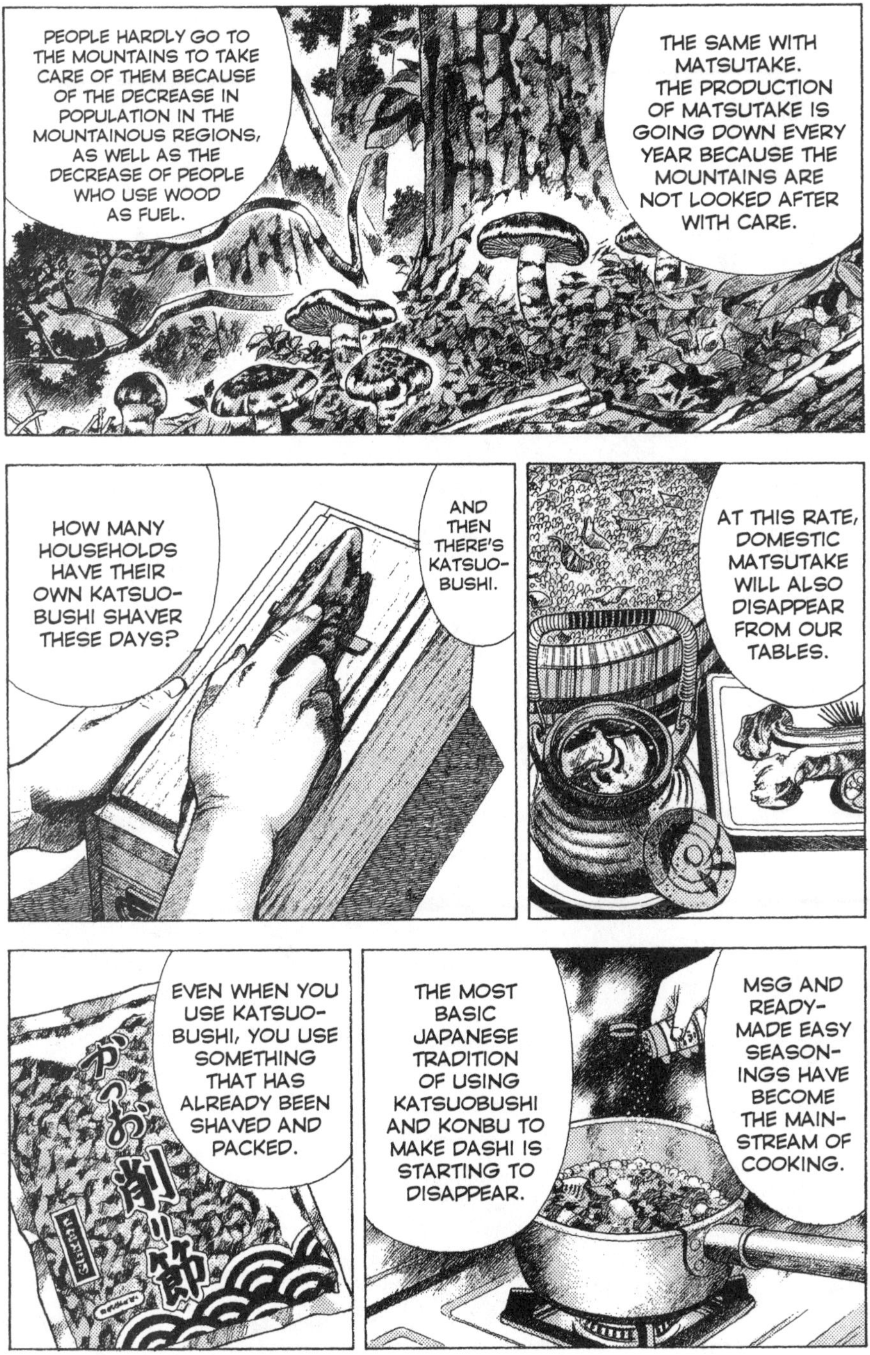
THE SAME WITH MATSUTAKE. THE PRODUCTION OF MATSUTAKE IS GOING DOWN EVERY YEAR BECAUSE THE MOUNTAINS ARE NOT LOOKED AFTER WITH CARE.
PEOPLE HARDLY GO TO THE MOUNTAINS TO TAKE CARE OF THEM BECAUSE OF THE DECREASE IN POPULATION IN THE MOUNTAINOUS REGIONS, AS WELL AS THE DECREASE OF PEOPLE WHO USE WOOD AS FUEL.
AT THIS RATE, DOMESTIC MATSUTAKE WILL ALSO DISAPPEAR FROM OUR TABLES.
AND THEN THERE'S KATSUO-BUSHI.
HOW MANY HOUSEHOLDS HAVE THEIR OWN KATSUO-BUSHI SHAVER THESE DAYS?
MSG AND READY-MADE EASY SEASON-INGS HAVE BECOME THE MAIN-STREAM OF COOKING.
THE MOST BASIC JAPANESE TRADITION OF USING KATSUOBUSHI AND KONBU TO MAKE DASHI IS STARTING TO DISAPPEAR.
EVEN WHEN YOU USE KATSUO-BUSHI, YOU USE SOMETHING THAT HAS ALREADY BEEN SHAVED AND PACKED.
かつお削り節

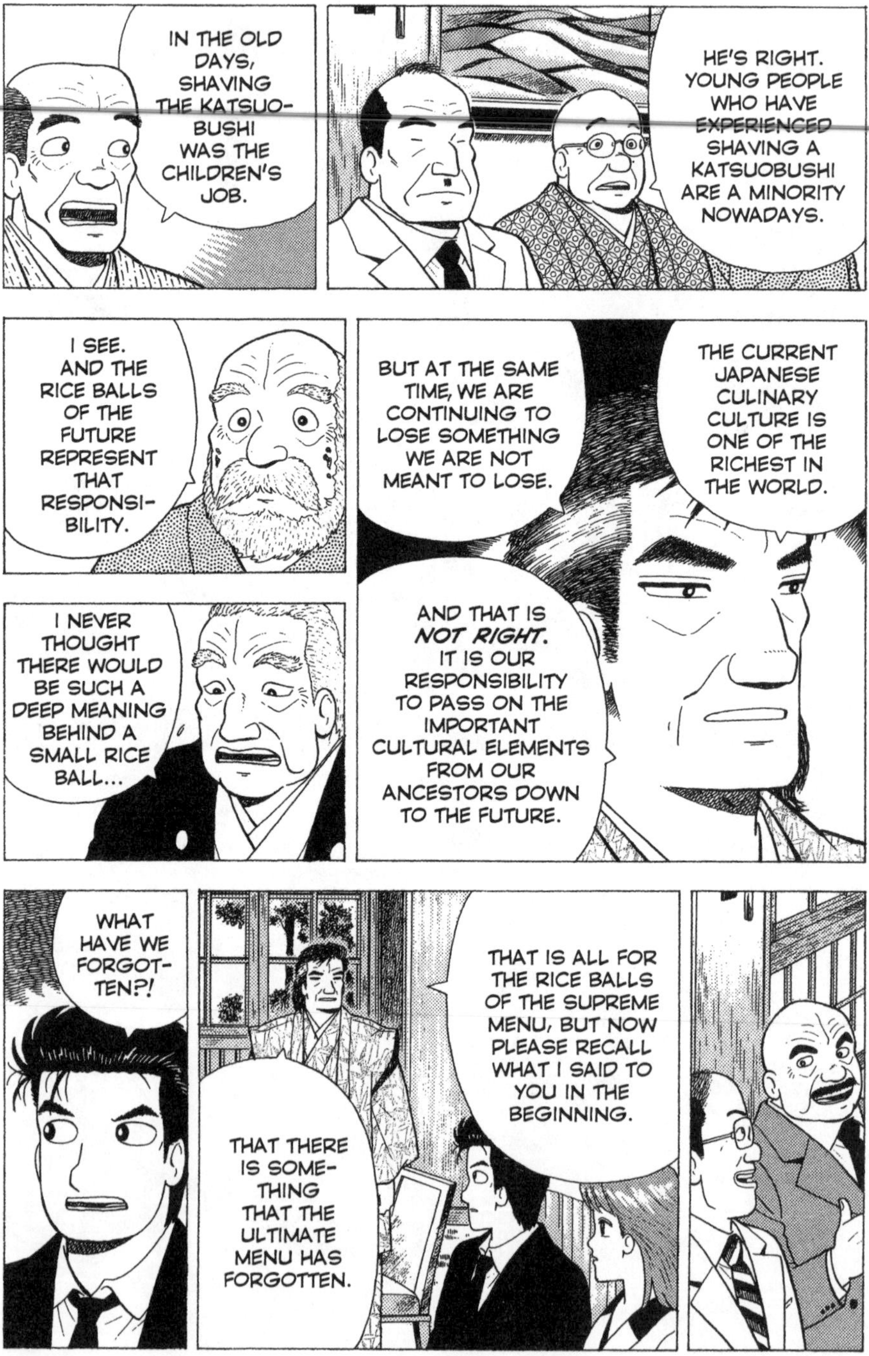
HE'S RIGHT. YOUNG PEOPLE WHO HAVE EXPERIENCED SHAVING A KATSUOBUSHI ARE A MINORITY NOWADAYS.
IN THE OLD DAYS, SHAVING THE KATSUO-BUSHI WAS THE CHILDREN'S JOB.
THE CURRENT JAPANESE CULINARY CULTURE IS ONE OF THE RICHEST IN THE WORLD.
BUT AT THE SAME TIME, WE ARE CONTINUING TO LOSE SOMETHING WE ARE NOT MEANT TO LOSE.
AND THAT IS *NOT RIGHT*. IT IS OUR RESPONSIBILITY TO PASS ON THE IMPORTANT CULTURAL ELEMENTS FROM OUR ANCESTORS DOWN TO THE FUTURE.
I SEE. AND THE RICE BALLS OF THE FUTURE REPRESENT THAT RESPONSI-BILITY.
I NEVER THOUGHT THERE WOULD BE SUCH A DEEP MEANING BEHIND A SMALL RICE BALL...
THAT IS ALL FOR THE RICE BALLS OF THE SUPREME MENU, BUT NOW PLEASE RECALL WHAT I SAID TO YOU IN THE BEGINNING.
THAT THERE IS SOME-THING THAT THE ULTIMATE MENU HAS FORGOTTEN.
WHAT HAVE WE FORGOT-TEN?!

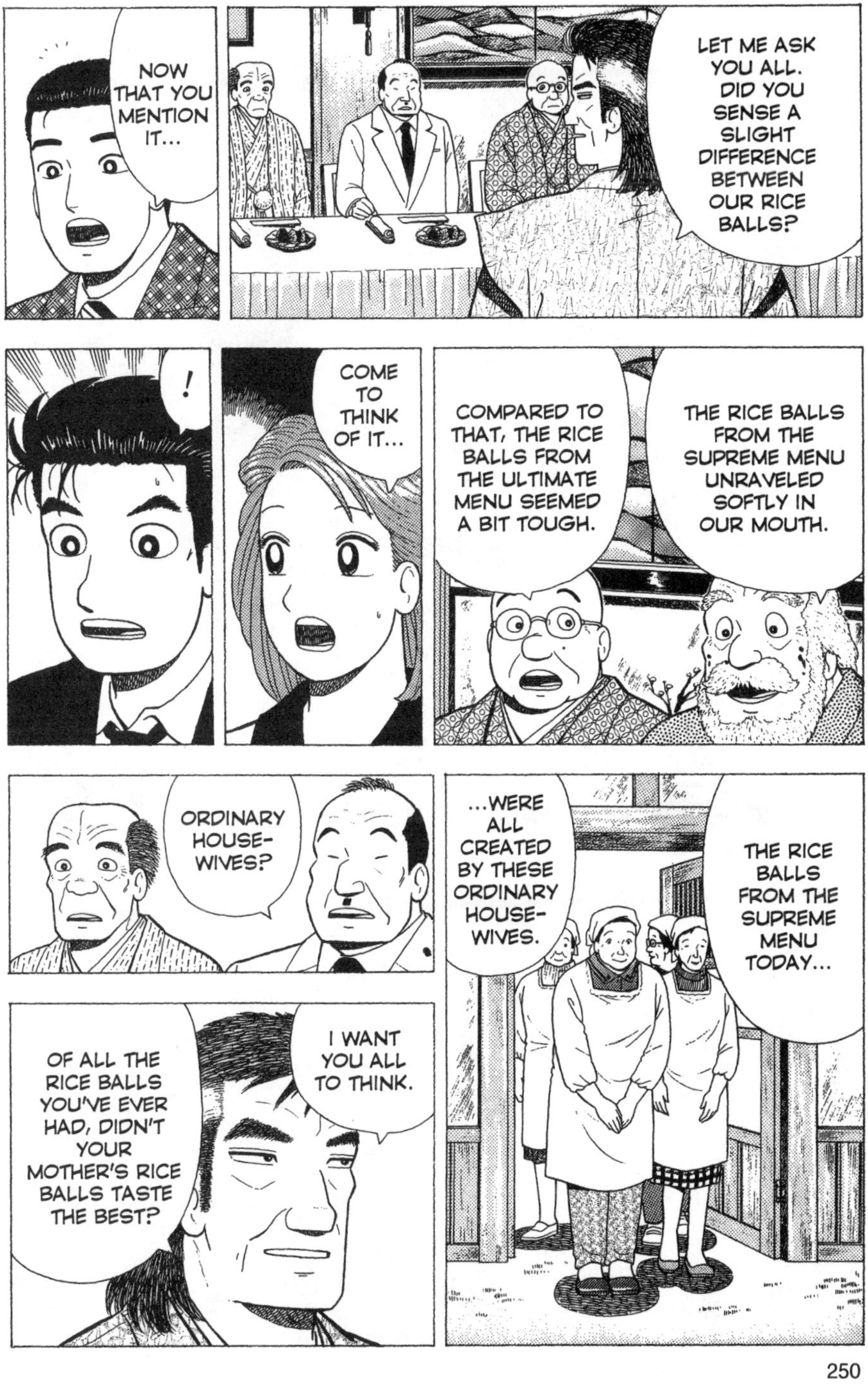
LET ME ASK YOU ALL. DID YOU SENSE A SLIGHT DIFFERENCE BETWEEN OUR RICE BALLS?
NOW THAT YOU MENTION IT...
THE RICE BALLS FROM THE SUPREME MENU UNRAVELED SOFTLY IN OUR MOUTH.
COMPARED TO THAT, THE RICE BALLS FROM THE ULTIMATE MENU SEEMED A BIT TOUGH.
COME TO THINK OF IT...
!
THE RICE BALLS FROM THE SUPREME MENU TODAY...
...WERE ALL CREATED BY THESE ORDINARY HOUSE-WIVES.
ORDINARY HOUSE-WIVES?
I WANT YOU ALL TO THINK.
OF ALL THE RICE BALLS YOU'VE EVER HAD, DIDN'T YOUR MOTHER'S RICE BALLS TASTE THE BEST?

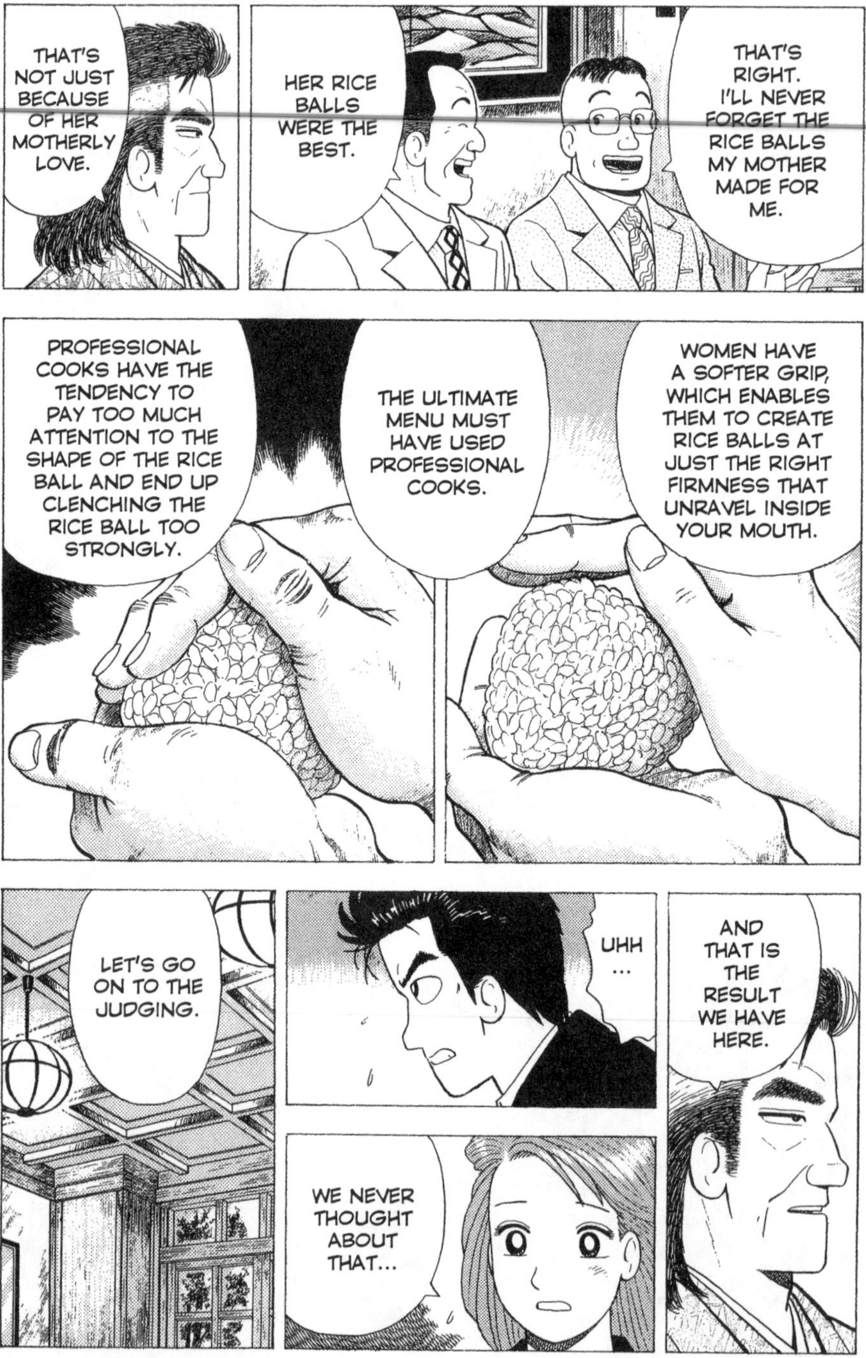
THAT'S RIGHT. I'LL NEVER FORGET THE RICE BALLS MY MOTHER MADE FOR ME.
HER RICE BALLS WERE THE BEST.
THAT'S NOT JUST BECAUSE OF HER MOTHERLY LOVE.
WOMEN HAVE A SOFTER GRIP, WHICH ENABLES THEM TO CREATE RICE BALLS AT JUST THE RIGHT FIRMNESS THAT UNRAVEL INSIDE YOUR MOUTH.
THE ULTIMATE MENU MUST HAVE USED PROFESSIONAL COOKS.
PROFESSIONAL COOKS HAVE THE TENDENCY TO PAY TOO MUCH ATTENTION TO THE SHAPE OF THE RICE BALL AND END UP CLENCHING THE RICE BALL TOO STRONGLY.
AND THAT IS THE RESULT WE HAVE HERE.
UHH ...
WE NEVER THOUGHT ABOUT THAT...
LET'S GO ON TO THE JUDGING.

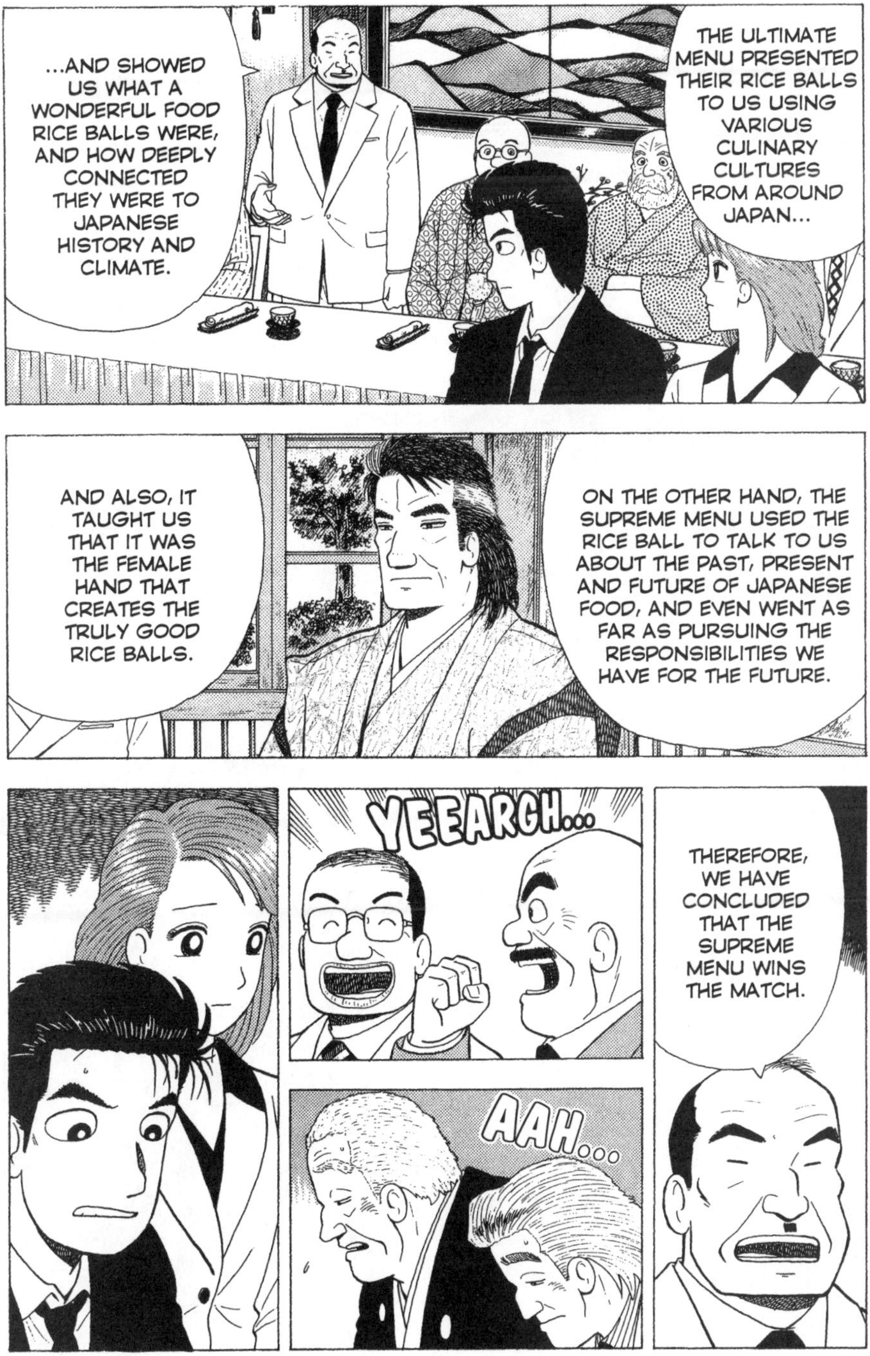
THE ULTIMATE MENU PRESENTED THEIR RICE BALLS TO US USING VARIOUS CULINARY CULTURES FROM AROUND JAPAN...
...AND SHOWED US WHAT A WONDERFUL FOOD RICE BALLS WERE, AND HOW DEEPLY CONNECTED THEY WERE TO JAPANESE HISTORY AND CLIMATE.
ON THE OTHER HAND, THE SUPREME MENU USED THE RICE BALL TO TALK TO US ABOUT THE PAST, PRESENT AND FUTURE OF JAPANESE FOOD, AND EVEN WENT AS FAR AS PURSUING THE RESPONSIBILITIES WE HAVE FOR THE FUTURE.
AND ALSO, IT TAUGHT US THAT IT WAS THE FEMALE HAND THAT CREATES THE TRULY GOOD RICE BALLS.
THEREFORE, WE HAVE CONCLUDED THAT THE SUPREME MENU WINS THE MATCH.
YEEARGH...
AAH...

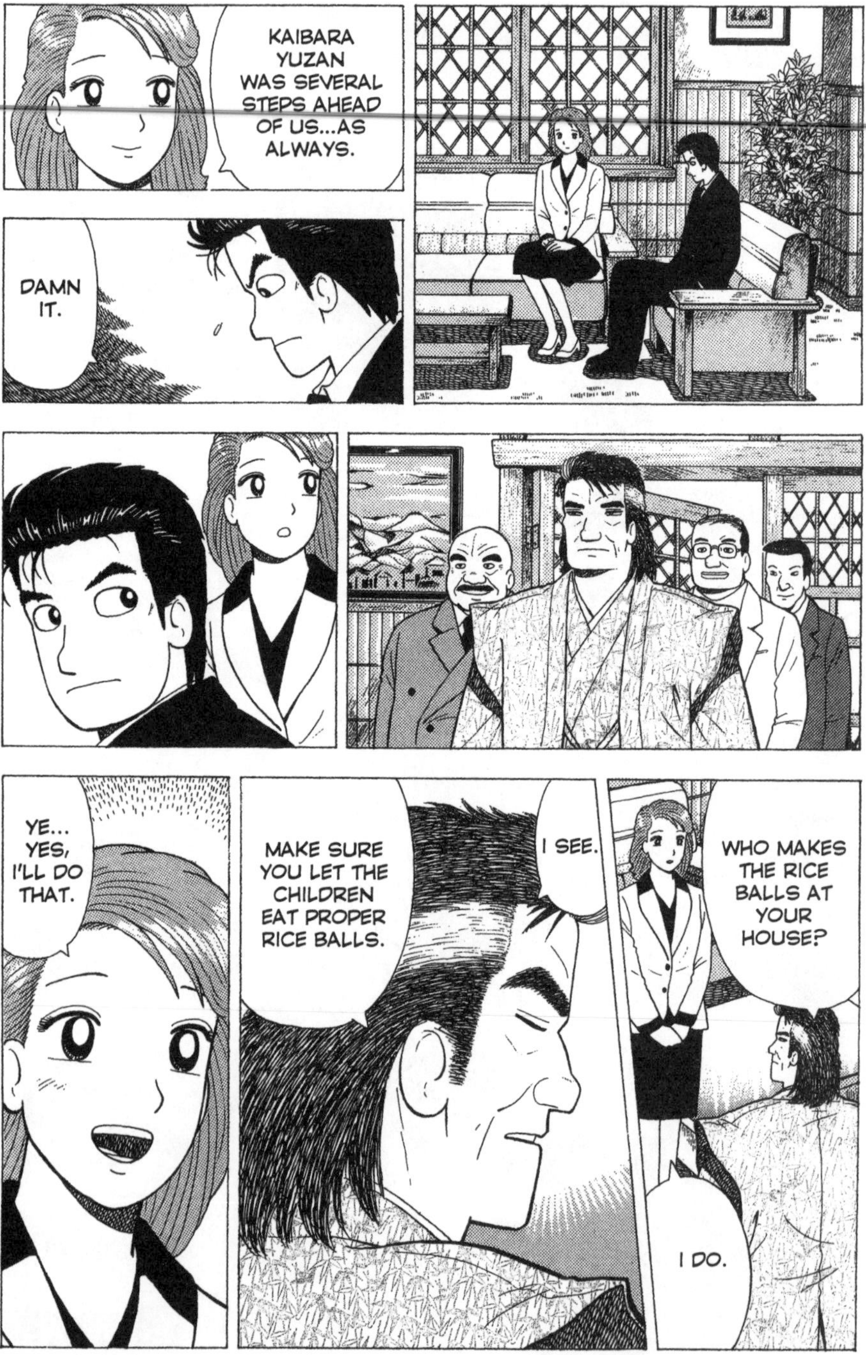
KAIBARA YUZAN WAS SEVERAL STEPS AHEAD OF US...AS ALWAYS.
DAMN IT.
WHO MAKES THE RICE BALLS AT YOUR HOUSE?
I DO.
I SEE.
MAKE SURE YOU LET THE CHILDREN EAT PROPER RICE BALLS.
YE... YES, I'LL DO THAT.

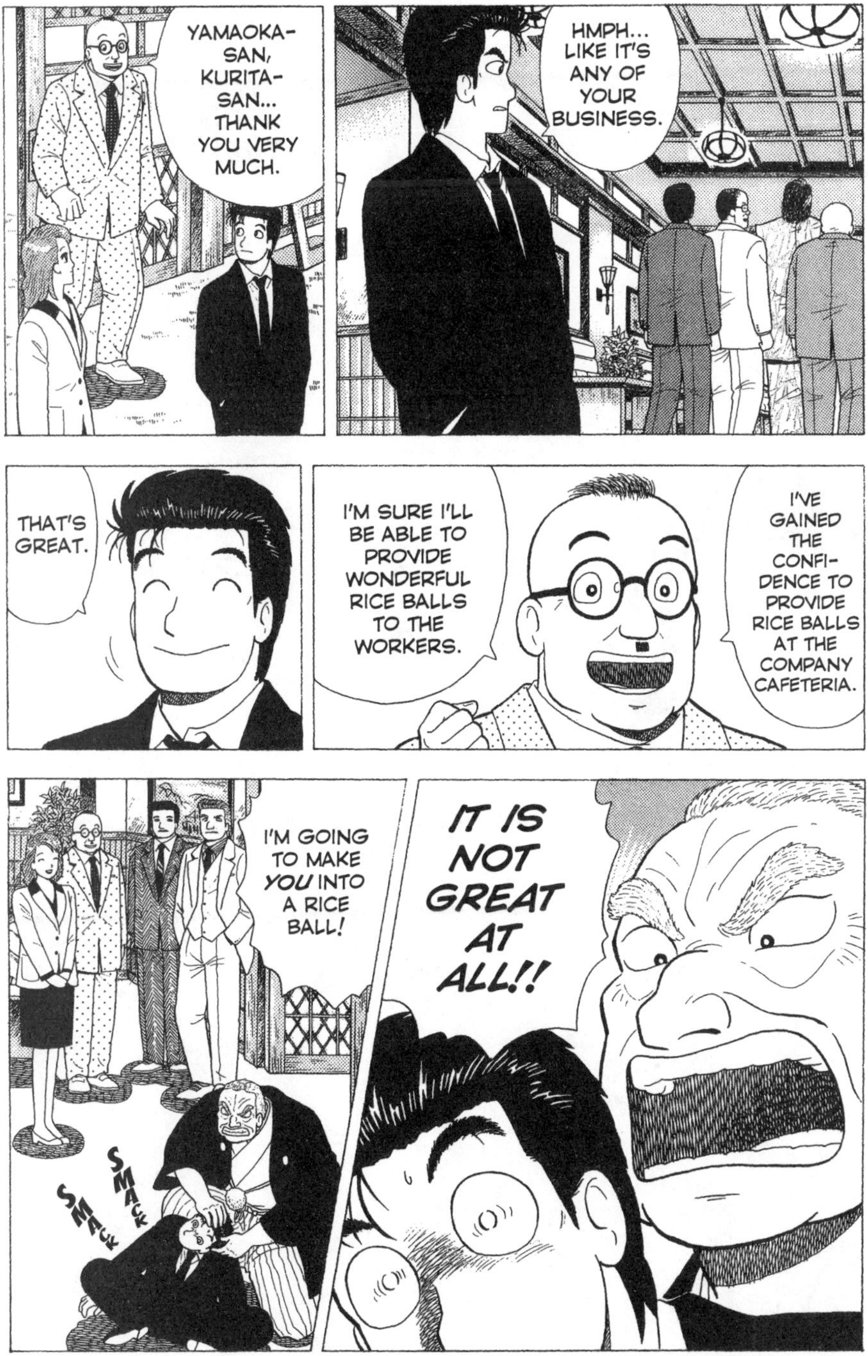
HMPH... LIKE IT'S ANY OF YOUR BUSINESS.
YAMAOKA-SAN, KURITA-SAN... THANK YOU VERY MUCH.
I'VE GAINED THE CONFIDENCE TO PROVIDE RICE BALLS AT THE COMPANY CAFETERIA.
I'M SURE I'LL BE ABLE TO PROVIDE WONDERFUL RICE BALLS TO THE WORKERS.
THAT'S GREAT.
IT IS NOT GREAT AT ALL!!
I'M GOING TO MAKE *YOU* INTO A RICE BALL!
SMACK
SMACK

END *OISHINBO: RICE*

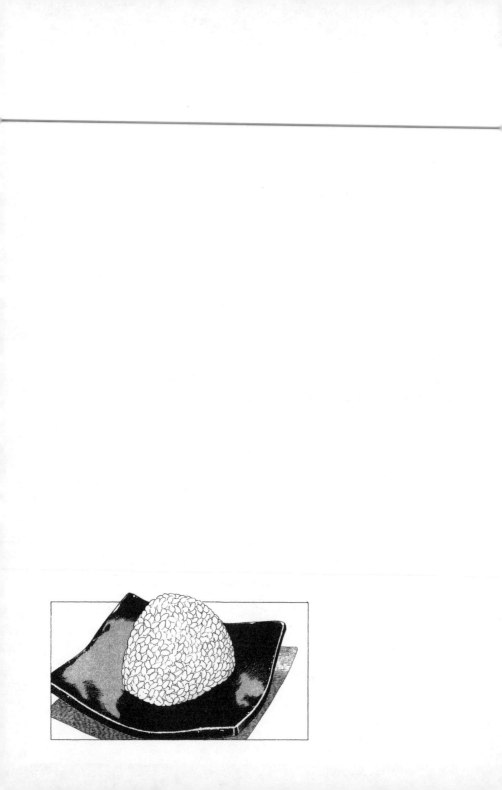

First Course

Page 8, panel 1
This is a pivotal early episode in the series, where Yamaoka and his colleagues meet Kyōgoku Mantarō for the first time and charm him by serving him food from his own home region. Thereafter, Kyōgoku becomes a constant champion of how certain flavors bring back memories of childhood and how the purity of domestic food is at the very heart of Japanese identity.

Page 8, panel 4
Ryōtei is the term used for extremely fine Japanese restaurants (which are also usually quite costly).

Page 12, panel 1
Junsai (*Brasenia schreberi*), known as "watershield" in English, is an edible water lily with a green shoot covered in a slimy, gelatin-like skin. Japan is one of the few countries where people eat this plant.

Page 12, panel 7
Sweetfish is the English name for *ayu* (*Plecoglossus altivelis*), which lives only in the rivers, lakes and coastal waters of Japan and East Asia. The name "sweetfish" is due to the sweetness of its meat.

Page 18, panel 5
Tokobushi abalone (*Sulculus diversicolor aquatilis*) is a shellfish called "round abalone" or "Japanese abalone" in English-speaking markets. It is related to but not the same as the more popular *awabi*.

Page 20, panel 2
This episode also contains the first appearance in the series of Okaboshi and his restaurant. From this point on, Okaboshi becomes a powerful ally in Yamaoka's quest for the Ultimate Menu, and his restaurant serves as Yamaoka's unofficial headquarters.

Page 23, panel 6

Sasanishiki is a special type of rice developed by Japanese agricultural specialists in Miyagi Prefecture in the 1960s. The Shonai Plain is an area in the northwest corner of Yamagata Prefecture known for rice production. The town of Amarume is a part of Shonai City. Kyōgoku is demonstrating how extremely sensitive his palate is by being able to identify the species of rice and the specific area it was grown in.

Page 24, panel 4

Dashi is a stock that's one of the cornerstones of Japanese cuisine. Though there are many kinds of dashi, there are three basic types: dashi made from *katsuobushi* (shaved dried bonito), dashi made from *konbu* (dried kelp), and dashi made from both katsuobushi and konbu.

Katsuobushi is dried bonito, or skipjack tuna (*Katsuwonus pelamis*). Chunks of the fish are smoked and dried into hard blocks, which keep for several months. In the past people would shave off flakes of the fish by hand with a tool that resembles an inverted carpenter's plane, but these days katsuobushi flakes are sold by the bag. Along with konbu, katsuobushi is the other main ingredient used in making dashi.

Katsuobushi can be divided into several types. When the bonito is just sliced into three fillets, then the katsuobushi is called *kamebushi*, and when those three fillets are divided into the back meat and stomach meat, it is called *honbushi*. Honbushi can be then divided into two parts: the katsuobushi using the back meat is *obushi* and the katsuobushi using the stomach meat is *mebushi*.

Page 26, panel 4

At this point in the series, the readers don't know Yamaoka's backstory or the fact that Kaibara Yūzan is his father.

Second Course, Part 1

Page 31, panel 4
Hama-nabe translated literally is "beach hot pot," and is a type of seafood and miso stew. The concept is that seafood is caught fresh and immediately cooked right there on the beach.

Second Course, Part 2

Page 68, panel 2
In judo matches, a win is declared when one player scores a full point, the literal meaning of *ippon*. This can be done by either throwing the opponent on their back, pinning them on the ground for 25 seconds, or making the opponent submit through a choke hold or an arm lock. Partial points can also be scored using other techniques.

Third Course

Page 71
This is the story mentioned in the first chapter of *Oishinbo A la Carte: Vegetables*. To show her gratitude for helping out Kinue, Mrs. Arakawa gives Yamaoka several bottles of her homemade grape juice.

Page 72, panel 5
This story (which appears rather quaint now) was published during the genesis of Internet activity in Japan. NIFTY was one of the very first service providers in Japan, and it is now the largest ISP in Japan.

Page 76, panel 1
Arakawa's father died when he was very young, and he was brought up by his mother in a single-parent household.

Page 79, panel 6
In the Japanese version, Arakawa's mother speaks with a strong Iwate accent.

Page 81, panel 1

Sake is made from rice, so there is an old saying in Japan: "If you can't (or don't) drink sake, have some rice."

Page 83, panel 8

Boiled rice paste was used for glue in Japan from ancient times. Rice that has been overcooked is looked upon as something akin to library paste.

Fourth Course

Page 93

Meshi no tomo, literally "a rice companion," is any food item eaten together with rice. It can be any kind of condiment, side dish or additive; anything you eat on, in or next to rice as part of the meal.

Page 94, panel 1

Liberalizing the importation of American rice into Japan has been a political hot-button issue since the early 1990s. The U.S. government has pressured Japan to import American rice (along with beef and other agricultural products) to offset the trade deficit. But along with the social, economic and environmental issues, some Japanese emphasize the emotional image of rice consumption as the heart of Japanese culture.

Page 97, panel 4

Research whaling is another hot-button political issue. Bowing to world pressure, Japan agreed to stop commercial whaling in 1985. But the country soon instituted a "research whaling" program, ostensibly to provide data as a basis for the resumption of sustainable commercial whaling. Pro-whaling interests claim that research whaling is an unfair limitation imposed to appease foreign interest, and Japan should be free to resume commercial whaling as it pleases. Anti-whaling groups claim that research whaling is a fraud meant to circumvent the whaling ban, and that meat from whales caught for so-called research goes directly into the marketplace.

Page 101, panel 4

A *dokaben* is a large-sized bento box. Unlike fancier bento, the food inside is typically more about quantity than about elaborate preparation.

Page 101, panel 7
The salmon mentioned here is *shiojake*, a very salty grilled piece of salmon. Its heavy flavor means that one small piece is enough to spice up a large quantity of rice.

Page 102, panel 1
Donburi is the term for a large rice bowl. By extension, it's also used to refer to cooking where food is place on top of rice and served in a *donburi* bowl.

Page 102, panel 3
Mezashi is a dried salted fish, usually made from a small fish in the sardine family.

Furuzuke (old/aged pickle) denotes something that has been pickled for a long period of time, resulting in a strongly salty taste.

Page 102, panel 4
Furikake is a dry Japanese condiment that is sprinkled on top of rice. It can be made up of any number of ingredients including katsuobushi, *umeboshi*, *shiso* and dried fish.

Page 102, panel 5
Umezu, sometimes translated as "plum vinegar," is the juice that accumulates in the jar when making umeboshi. It can be used for flavoring dishes in the way Westerners use regular vinegar.

Page 102, panel 6
Shiokara is a dish made by fermenting finely chopped seafood (usually squid) in a mixture consisting of salt, rice malt and the creature's own internal organs.

Kinzanji-miso, a specialty of Wakayama Prefecture, is a unique miso made by fermenting vegetables such as eggplant and lotus root along with soybeans, barley, wheat and salt. Unlike other types of miso, this is not used as a seasoning and is eaten on its own as a condiment or side dish to go with sake or rice.

Page 103, panel 1
Tsukudani is a condiment for rice made of seafood, meat or seaweed that has been simmered in soy sauce and *mirin*.

Page 108, panel 4
Ume-okaka is umeboshi mixed with katsuobushi. *Okaka* is another name for katsuobushi.

Page 111, panel 1
In feudal Japan, a *koku* was a unit of rice (approximately 330 pounds). The koku was used as a unit of monetary exchange. The value of land was assessed by how many koku it could produce, and by extension the koku value of land was a measure of the landowner's wealth.

Page 114, panel 4
Sakurajima daikon are the largest daikon radishes in the world. They have an average size of 15 pounds, but some grow to be as large as 60 pounds.

Sixth Course

Page 144, panel 2
Dan is the young president of Daikensha, the company that produces *Weekly Time*. He quickly starts courting Yūko and becomes a rival to Yamaoka.

Page 149, panel 7
In this and the following chapters, *takikomi gohan* and *maze gohan* are the focus of the story. Takikomi gohan and maze gohan are two methods of cooking rice mixed with other ingredients, and they cover a wide range of similar dishes. Roughly speaking, takikomi gohan is a dish where the ingredients are cooked together with the rice, while maze gohan is a dish where the ingredients are mixed into the rice after it is cooked.

Page 158, panel 4
Real *shimeji* mushrooms are very hard to cultivate and hence are difficult to come by. *Hiratake* (oyster mushrooms) are sold in the market under the name "shimeji" as a substitute for the real thing.

Page 160, panel 8

Hijiki is a black seaweed that is frequently used as a condiment on rice.

Seventh Course

Page 166, panel 2

In a prior episode of the series, Yamaoka and Yūko get engaged. Their superiors at the newspaper decide that their wedding banquet would be an opportunity to display the Ultimate Menu as it stands. Yamaoka clearly sees the banquet as an unnecessary hassle.

Eighth Course, Part 1

Page 193, panel 5

Sarukani Gasen is a famous Japanese folktale. It starts when the monkey tricks the crab into trading its rice ball for a seed.

Page 193, panel 6

Omusubi Kororin is a folktale that begins when an old man's rice ball tumbles down a mountain trail, falling into a mouse hole. When the old man allows the mouse to keep it, he receives a fortune in return.

Page 199, panel 4

Takuan is pickled daikon radish. Along with umeboshi, it is the most popular Japanese side dish for rice.

Eighth Course, Part 2

Page 214, panel 2

The Japanese Government Monopoly in Salt Act was created in 1905, creating a government monopoly over the manufacture (and hence the content and quality) of salt. This law was repealed in 1997, allowing independent salt manufacturers to start production.

Page 216, panel 7
Natto is fermented soybeans, a popular breakfast item in eastern Japan. Its pungent smell, strong taste and sticky consistency make it a food that people either love or detest.

Page 221, panel 1
Tororo konbu is a processed form of konbu that has been pickled in vinegar, shaved into flakes and then dried.

Page 223, panel 2
Karasumi is salt-cured, sun-dried mullet roe. A specialty of Nagasaki, it is similar to the Italian *bottarga*, Greek *avgotaraho* or Turkish *tarama*. A highly priced delicacy, it is considered one of the "three rarest flavors of Japan" (along with pickled sea urchin and *konowata*).

Page 226, panel 4
Bara-zushi is a mixture of vegetables and seafood on a bed of rice. It is similar to *chirashi-zushi*.

Kohada, a regional name for *Konoshiro (Konosirus punctatus)*, is a gizzard shad. In the Edo period, it was an extremely abundant and inexpensive fish, at one point cheaper than rice.

Page 229, panel 3
Kinako is a powder made from roasted soybeans and used as a seasoning or ingredient of traditional Japanese sweets.

Eighth Course, Part 3

Page 236, panel 1
Sekihan (literally "red rice") is sticky rice steamed with red *azuki* beans, which give it a reddish color. It is served on special occasions in the same way that champagne is used in America and Europe.

In the next volume of *Oishinbo*, Yamaoka and his team take a break from the Ultimate vs. Supreme Menu contest to explore the world of *izakaya*—Japanese bars and drinking establishments. Izakaya have a repertoire of foods and snacks all their own, with dishes designed especially for alcohol and socializing. When challenged to create a completely original izakaya dish, Yamaoka is at a total

OISHINBO

A la Carte

The Joy of Rice

VIZ Signature Edition

Story by Tetsu Kariya
Art by Akira Hanasaki

Translation/Tetsuichiro Miyaki
Touch-up & Lettering/Kelle Han
Cover & Graphic Design/Hidemi Dunn
Editors/Leyla Aker, Jonathan Tarbox

Recipe Credits:
Food Photography/Hideo Sawai (Assistant: Kunihiro Yokoi, Ayako Nakano)
Food Styling/Yuko Tanaka – Le Treat (Assistant: Yoshiko Watanabe)
Recipe Composition/Yoko Yasui – The Tracks

Printed in Canada

Published by VIZ Media, LLC
P.O. Box 77010
San Francisco, CA 94107

10 9 8 7 6 5
First printing, November 2009
Fifth printing, November 2020

www.viz.com

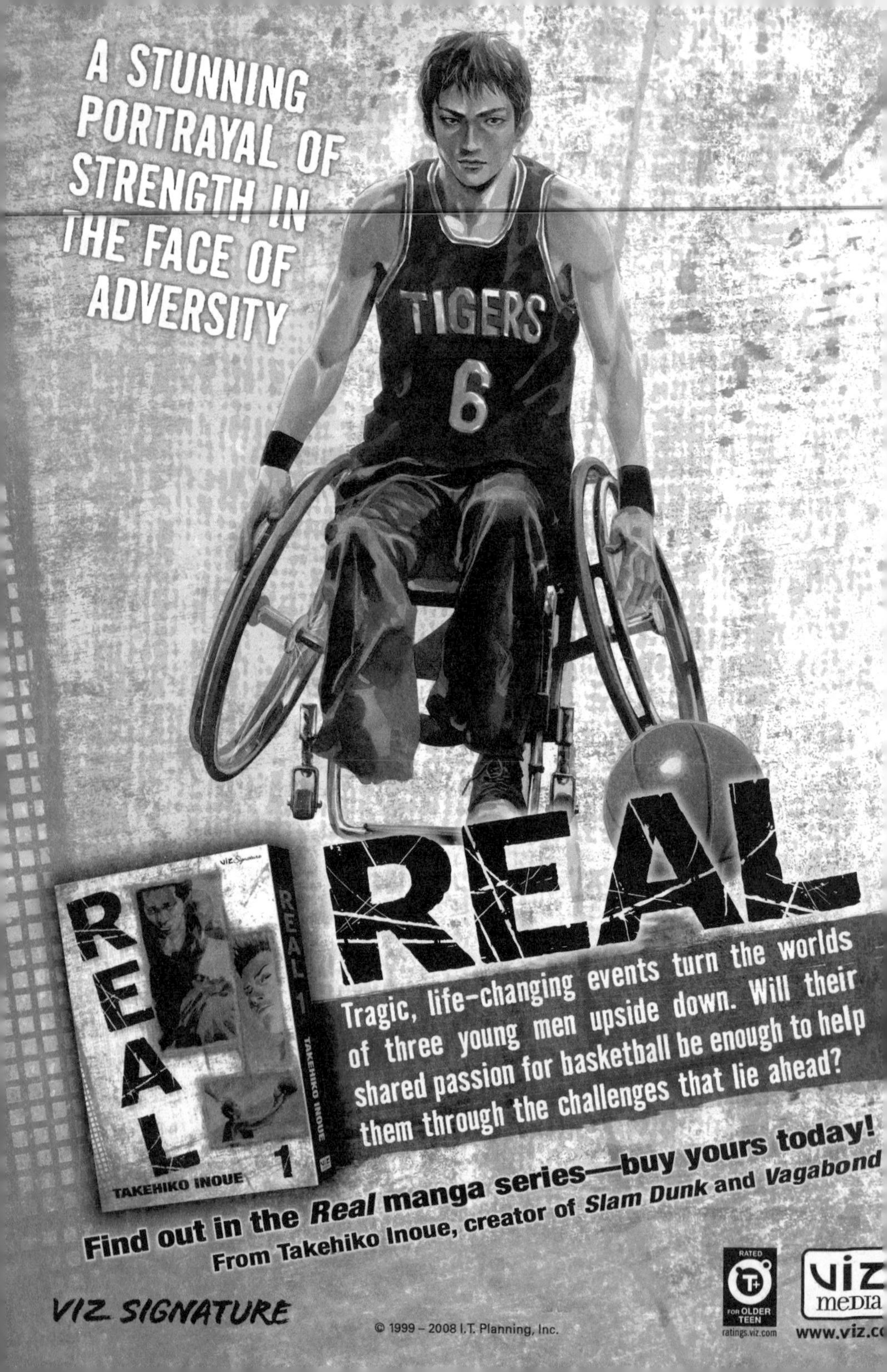
A STUNNING PORTRAYAL OF STRENGTH IN THE FACE OF ADVERSITY
TIGERS
6
REAL
TAKEHIKO INOUE
REAL 1
TAKEHIKO INOUE
REAL
Tragic, life-changing events turn the worlds of three young men upside down. Will their shared passion for basketball be enough to help them through the challenges that lie ahead?
Find out in the *Real* manga series—buy yours today!
From Takehiko Inoue, creator of *Slam Dunk* and *Vagabond*
VIZ SIGNATURE
© 1999 – 2008 I.T. Planning, Inc.
RATED
T+
FOR OLDER TEEN
ratings.viz.com
VIZ media
www.viz.c

Hey! You're Reading in the Wrong Direction!

This is the *end* of this graphic novel!

To properly enjoy this VIZ graphic novel, please turn it around and begin reading from *right to left.* Unlike English, Japanese is read right to left, so Japanese comics are read in reverse order from the way English comics are typically read.

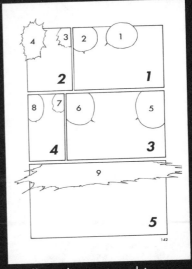

Follow the action this way

This book has been printed in the original Japanese format in order to preserve the orientation of the original artwork. Have fun with it!